1 MONTH OF
FREE
READING

at
www.ForgottenBooks.com

By purchasing this book you are
eligible for one month membership to
ForgottenBooks.com, giving you
unlimited access to our entire
collection of over 700,000 titles via
our web site and mobile apps.

To claim your free month visit:
www.forgottenbooks.com/free436714

ISBN 978-0-331-04008-1
PIBN 10436714

THE

Herald and Genealogist.

EDITED BY

JOHN GOUGH NICHOLS, F.S.A.

HON. MEMBER OF THE SOCIETIES OF ANTIQUARIES OF SCOTLAND AND
NEWCASTLE-UPON-TYNE, AND OF THE NEW ENGLAND
HISTORIC-GENEALOGICAL SOCIETY.

VOLUME THE THIRD.

LONDON:

J. G. NICHOLS AND R. C. NICHOLS,

PRINTERS TO THE SOCIETY OF ANTIQUARIES,

25, PARLIAMENT STREET, WESTMINSTER.

1866.

ADVERTISEMENT.

In the present Volume we flatter ourselves to have maintained the standard of THE HERALD AND GENEALOGIST in the importance, originality, and interest of its contents.

In our researches into the antiquities of Armory we have endeavoured to penetrate to the fountain head, as well in two articles devoted to that subject as in that on the effigies in the Temple church; intending to pursue the inquiry as further opportunities may occur. Many minor articles throughout our pages bear upon the same subject.

The history of one of our grades of hereditary rank has been for the first time investigated in the articles on the Institution and early history of the dignity of Baronet, which are also to be continued.

Upon Family History several very important articles have appeared, especially those on the Lees, the Temples, and the Carys Viscounts Falkland. The last, which is replete with original documentary evidence, will be succeeded in the next volume by a correspondent compilation on the house of Carey Lords Hunsdon.

The annals of the conventual house of the English Ladies of Pontoise will be regarded with particular interest in connection with the numerous families of ancient Catholic descent from which its members were derived, as shown in the illustrative pedigrees.

Upon the many valuable works of our fellow-labourers that we have had occasion to notice, we may well congratulate those

who partake our interest in the studies of Heraldry and Genealogy, bearing witness as they do to the increasing popularity of
these studies, and to the just appreciation which is now entertained
of the important assistance they afford to the labours of the
biographer and the historian; whilst the honest and scientific
spirit which has at length been applied to the investigation of
these subjects, affords the best encouragement that they will
henceforth be pursued with an assurance of progress, based upon
sound premises and supported by judicious deductions.

ERRATA.

Page 67, note, *for* 1825 *read* 1865.

Page 96, lin. antepenult. *for* Hanley *read* Hoby.

Page 178, line 13, *read* bend sinister; line 23, *for* head *read* hand.

Page 205, line 14 of notes, *for* seventeen *read* five, and *for* 1612 *read* 1611.

Page 214, line 12, *for* lower *read* bowed.

Page 352, line 12, *for* 1612 *read* 1611.

Page 397, see corrections to the pedigree of Grenville in p. 535.

Page 429, line 15, *for* his *read* her.

Page 475, line 28, *for* Gordon *read* Gorham.

Page 512, last line, the family of Tichborne is not extinct, as will appear in the next volume.

Page 542, last line of text, *for* p. 514 *read* p. 520.

Page 553, line 25, *read* the 9th March.

Other Errata will be found in pp. 145, 146.

THE ORIGIN AND DEVELOPMENT OF COAT ARMOUR.

" Not know the figures of Heraldry ? of what could your father be thinking?''

Rob Roy, vol. i. chapter x.

IN taking up this subject *ab initio*, it is our object to divest it entirely of theory and conjecture, and to proceed, if we can, wholly upon evidence presented to our eyes, or upon well ascertained historical facts. It was the pleasure of those who treated of Armory in former days to envelope it with a factitious mystery, to give it interpretations wholly allegorical and fanciful, and to connect it with a visionary antiquity. In their view it was identical with the symbolism of other times, and had actually existed from the earliest ages of the world. The ensigns of the Jewish tribes, the shields of the heroes of Homer and Æschylus, the devices of the Greek cities as displayed on their coins, and those of the Roman standards, were all enlisted into the ranks of heraldry, and put forth as so many proofs of the antiquity of Coat-Armour.

This error was committed by some of the very earliest commentators on Armory, and amplified more or less by all their fanciful successors. It has been resumed with fresh· zeal from time to time by other theorists. Upon the work of one of these, the *Historical Discourse of the Original and Growth of Heraldry*, by Thomas Philipot, M.A. 1672, the following censure was passed by Dallaway:—

" A Treatise in the last century, very replete with erudition, deduces the introduction of Heraldry from the ancient mythology, and considers the hieroglyphics and emblems of Greece and Rome, impressed on the reverses of their medals, as the indubitable prototypes of modern armories; but with the usual success of misapplied learning." (*Researches into the origin and progress of the Science of Heraldry in England*, p. 3.)

But Dallaway himself falls into the like mistake when he is inclined to regard the devices upon the coins of the Anglo-Saxon kings as incipient coat-armour. He had found that at a very early period, as early at least as the time of Matthew Paris, a series of armorial coats had been invented for the old race of English sovereigns, and that they continued to be employed *historically* in mediæval times, as indeed they have in our own days,—very extensively, in the new Houses of Parliament. Dallaway, being unable clearly to fix an epoch for the origin of Armory, failed to discriminate between this posthumous, or fictitious, and actual Coat-Armour, though in regard to "the Danes" at least he had a correct impression (p. 8) that it was "the device of the illuminator" in the manuscript chronicles where it occurred.

Much more recently, and in the midst of what we must take leave to style more practical researches, a gentleman has expended great ingenuity in *A Plea for the Antiquity of Heraldry, with an attempt to expound its Theory and elucidate its History*,—an essay put forth by WILLIAM SMITH ELLIS, Esq., of the Middle Temple, in 1853 (8vo. pp. 23), as an exposition of the views he had adopted in some memoirs inserted in the *Sussex Archæological Collections*. This writer endeavours to maintain the ancient argument that hereditary family arms have been prevalent in all ages and countries. He deduces such distinctions from the devices painted on the bodies and shields of savages, from "the parti-coloured shields" of the ancient Germans, mentioned by Tacitus,[1] which he thinks may have descended in the Teutonic tribes like the plaids of the Highland clans;[2] he suggests that

---

[1] After admitting that "Historical testimonies to the early existence of modern heraldry are scanty," Mr. Ellis proceeds, "The earliest and undoubtedly the most important, is the passage from Tacitus (De Mor. Ger. vi.) Scuta tantum *lectissimis coloribus distinguunt:* thus indicating the use by the Germans of *parti-coloured* shields." So far as we understand these words, they mean that the Germans painted their shields with the choicest or brightest colours, but whether in any manner resembling "modern heraldry" there seems to be no word in the passage that at all intimates.

[2] We have seen it affirmed that these plaids or tartans are really of no antiquity. We do not find the subject mentioned in Mr. Seton's *Scottish Heraldry*, though at p. 259 he enumerates the different sprigs or leaves of trees or shrubs worn as badges in the Highland bonnets.

many Welsh coats, partaking as some of them do of the nature of legendary pictures,—as a wolf issuing from a cave, a cradle under a tree, with a child guarded by a goat, &c., are probably of Romano-British origin; and he even proceeds to prove the existence of arms at the Norman Conquest, by what he calls a *reductio ad absurdum*, having first satisfied himself that "armorial bearings were in use for centuries among our Saxon ancestors." For this he cites, in particular, the well-known White-horse of Kent; and points out the remarkable absence of the horse from Norman heraldry, though found plentifully in that of Germany. Finally, he naturally is inclined to fraternise with the barbaric symbols of the Transatlantic Continent, where the native tribes of Indians distinguish themselves under the appellations of the Bear, the Turtle, the Eagle, &c., and, in consistence with his previous argument, he accepts the assertion of Mr. Taylor, an American author, that " this is *Indian heraldry.*"

Mr. Ellis shows, it is true, many remarkable instances of correspondency in the bearings of cognate families, in the earliest era of Armory; it does not, however, follow, as he has concluded, that they must have been inherited from a common ancestor, who lived two or three generations earlier, at a time when we have no tangible evidence of the existence of Coat-Armour at all.[1] We agree with Mr. Ellis that a spirit of clanship led to the adoption of a general resemblance of colours and charges; and that, therefore, the origin of many coats may be attributed to the influence of consanguinity, though not wholly to the exclusion, as Mr. Ellis is disposed to contend, of what has been termed the feudal origin of Coat-Armour, where mesne tenants imitated the bearings of their chief.

It is now generally admitted by the most judicious investigators of the subject, that the present system of Armory in Europe is of indigenous origin, and was the product of the feudal age of chivalry; that it was invented for use rather than show; and that its signification, generally speaking, was practical rather than poetical.

[1] The most abundant class of armorial monuments is presented by Seals: and a careful study of those of the twelfth century will generally show when persons of the foremost rank still sealed without armorial bearings, and when they first used them.

It was in reality a symbolic language, written in colours and devices instead of letters, and having in many cases some phonetic association, echoing to the names of persons or places, and thereby assisting the memory of those who read it. This quality, called by our own heralds *canting*, and described by the French under the term *armes parlantes*,—figures which were endowed with silent speech, has in every age been recognised as bearing a considerable share in Armory, but has sometimes been hastily and inconsiderately condemned as a foolish accessory, and very untruly treated as if of comparatively modern date.[1] Those who have adopted such notions have betrayed at once their ignorance of the antiquities of the art, and their want of consideration and comprehension of its original purpose. When armorial symbols are viewed in their proper light as a pictorial language, a language addressed in great measure to those who were unlettered men, it becomes a merit and a recommendation that such symbols should be phonetic, and should establish their hold on the attention and the memory by their allusions and associations. How largely this quality exists in the earliest Coat-Armour has been ably shown in the writings of Mr. Planché, the present Rouge Croix pursuivant; particularly in his very original and suggestive work *The Pursuivant of Arms*, first published (in 1852), whilst he was still

---

[1] A few years before Mr. Planché, Mr. M. A. Lower undertook to discourse on *The Curiosities of Heraldry*; and, although he treated the subject, to our mind, altogether in too humorous and jocular a tone, we must do him the justice to remark that, in regard to this leading characteristic of ancient Armory, he very judiciously rebuked the perverse opinions of some earlier writers. In his chapter on Allusive Armory, he remarks, "Dallaway, Porny, and other modern writers condemn this species of bearings as of recent origin, and unworthy of a place amongst the classical devices of antient heraldry. Porny places them in the category of Assumptive Arms,—'such as are taken up by the caprice or fancy of upstarts, though of never so mean an extraction.' This notion, with whomsoever it originated, is decidedly erroneous, for such charges are found, not only in the arms of distinguished nobles and knights in the very earliest days of hereditary Armory, but occur also in those of several of the states of Europe"—of which Mr. Lower proceeds to give ample proof and numerous examples. And he very truly adds, "There can be no doubt but that, from the mutations our language [and the French also] has experienced within the last six centuries, many of the allusions contained in coats of arms are greatly obscured, whilst others are totally lost." (*The Curiosities of Heraldry*, 8vo. 1845, pp. 120, 126.) It has been in elucidating many of these obscure allusions that Mr. Planché has since been peculiarly happy.

an amateur herald.   Armorial insignia were there, almost for the
first time, or at least for the first time so thoroughly and entirely,
investigated with a purely inductive spirit, and discussed in a
common-sense way, as any other objects of antiquarian attention
might be.

In this country, essays on Heraldry had been very numerous,
but greatly devoid of originality.   They had been usually mere
repetitions, the pouring forth from one vessel into another, as if
there was nothing new to be learned; and this was the more
remarkable, because no art was ever so much burdened and
deformed with extraneous and adventitious overgrowth.   Mr.
Planché boldly declared himself to be one that was

Nullius addictus jurare in verba magistri.

He set the good example of casting away the fictions and imagi-
nations of the old writers, and of rejecting their maxims and
dicta, wherever they were unsupported by documentary proof, or
not deduced from plain and obvious premises.

" I start (he says) with the declaration that, as I have implicitly
believed nobody, I desire not that any one should blindly credit me :
but form his own conclusions from the evidence I may succeed in producing; rating mere speculations (for he will find some of my own) at
their lowest value."

It will be in the like spirit that we shall pursue the investigations to be made in the course of the papers which we now
commence.

We consider it fruitless to inquire whether any other devices,
in any other part of the world, have at any time *resembled* our
system of Armory.   It is sufficient to know that the latter was
not derived from them, nor had any connection with them
whatever.

The first points to be defined are merely,—1. When did
Armory originate?   2. For what reason?   3. In what manner?

1. As to the date of its origin, it appears to be now unanimously
conceded by all judicious and unprejudiced inquirers, that it was
in the latter portion of the twelfth century that Coat-Armour was
first adopted, and that it was scarcely prevalent, if at all, before
the year 1180.

2. The reason or cause of the adoption of armorial distinctions was, in the first place, the same which has prevailed at all periods in all armies with regard to standards or ensigns, *i.e.* that soldiers should recognise their proper leaders; but, in the second place, the adoption of individual insignia evidently arose from the concealment of the person and features occasioned by the use of defensive armour, which made other external and visible means of recognition desirable.

3. The manner in which Armory was devised, developed, and differenced, was various, and has to be discovered and ascertained in each instance. As already mentioned, it frequently bore allusion to names. This was certainly one of its first origins. It was then imparted to other names by connections of consanguinity or feudal dependence. It was continually differenced by cadets, in order to distinguish their personal coats from those of their chief and the elder members of their house.

Some of the simplest coats are those which bear what are called the Ordinaries,—the Chief, the Pale, the Bend, the Fess, and the Chevron ; the Cross and the Saltire ; the five former of which may all be regarded as having originally been bars placed in various directions to strengthen the shield, and the two latter as crossed bars. When these additions were tinctured differently to the field or surface of the shield, some of the simplest coats were at once formed.

But there are other coats still more simple than these, which are wholly uncharged, and either of one tincture throughout, or merely parted by division into two colours.

BANNERS OR COATS WITHOUT CHARGES.

Such ensigns, it is obvious, may fairly claim an antiquity higher than Armory itself. They give room for that fancied connection with the painted shields of the Germans, or of the Britons, to which we have already referred; and may even in some cases have been really derived from an *hereditary* preference for a particular colour. However, we shall be justified in treating them as part of our subject, as they were perpetuated in conjunction with the more customary armorial devices, and in some cases even are so still.

The famous Oriflamme or Auriflamme of France, which always appeared at the head of the French armies, from the 12th to the 15th century, was a square banner of flame-coloured silk, thus described by Guilaume Guiart:—

> Oriflamme est une banniere
> Aucune soi plus foit que guimple,
> De cendal roujeant et simple
> Sans portraiture d'autre affaire.

"The oriflamme is a banner made of a silk stronger than guimp, it is of flaring cendal, and that simply, without any figure upon it."

Its home during peace was the abbey of St. Denis ;[1] and it was entrusted by the sanction of that community to the Kings of France, who were graciously pleased to rank themselves as vassals of the abbey in their capacity of Counts of the Vexin.

At a later period, the Oriflamme was sometimes powdered with golden flakes of fire, as it is represented in the *Indice Armorial* of Louvain Geliot, folio 1635, and there thus described :

"L'Oriflambe estoit faite de sendal, c'est à dire de tafetas ou tissu de soys rouge, aucunefois semée de flames d'or, d'ou ellè prenoit le nom d' Oriflambe."

We read of a *White banner* that was carried in the army of the Kings of England when they went in war against Scotland. The manor of Shorne[2] in Kent was held in capite by the service of carrying it, in conjunction with other tenants of the King.

---

[1] With the Oriflamme may be compared *the Dragon* ordered for the church of St. Peter at Westminster by King Henry the Third in 1244 : it was to be in the form of a standard (*vexillum*), made of some red samite that sparkled throughout with gold, its tongue as if a burning fire, and continually moving, and its eyes of sapphires or other suitable stones. See the original order for this printed in the *Excerpta Historica*, 1831, p. 404. That this Dragon was sometimes sent forth to battle may be presumed, from it being stated with regard to the battle of Lewes in 1262, that a Dragon was then borne before King Henry the Third : and of a much earlier battle—that between Edmund Ironside and Canute—it is stated, "Regius locus erat inter Draconem et Standardum." (See further on this point in *Retrospective Review*, New Series, 1827, i. 94.)

[2] It is thus mentioned in the Inquis. post mortem of Sir Roger de Northwode, who died 34 Edw. III. (having been summoned to parliament in the previous year,) and in that of Sir Arnold Savage, 12 Hen. IV. "Schorne maner' extent' tent' de domino Rege in capite per servicium portandi cum aliis tenentibus domini Regis *vexillum album* versus Scotiam in guerra Regis."

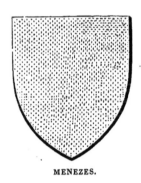

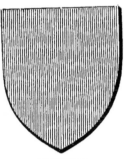

MENEZES.   NARBONNE.

A shield of pure Gold was borne by the family of Menezes in
Portugal,[1] and a simple shield of Gules by the Viscounts of Narbonne.[2]   In the Salles des Croisades at Versailles such a shield,
de gueules plein, is placed for Aymery, first of the name, Vicomte
de Narbonne, who died in the Holy Land, about the year 1105;
again, for Raymond Pelet, dit *le Croisé;* and a third time for
Amanjeu II. sire d'Albret, both crusaders under the command of
the Count of Toulouse in 1096.[3]

The house of Albret or la Brette became Kings of Navarre.

The same entirely red banner appeared at the siege of Carlaverock in 1301, borne by a cadet of that family named Amaneus
de la Brette, as he is styled in records of the time,[4]—or, by the
poet of the expedition, Eurmenions—

> Mais Eurmenions de la Brette
> La baniere eus toute rougette.

By the English chronicler Peter Langtoft he is called " Sir
Emery the Brette."   His father had borne the same name (in
Latin, Amaneus); as did one who is supposed to have been
his son ; for, at the siege of Calais in 1346, there was a Sir
Amayen la Brette, serving King Edward the Third ; and he
had then on his red shield the golden lion of England passant
in chief, a distinction evidently derived from the long services

[1] Anselme, Hist. Genealogique de France, vol. i. p. 638.

[2] Ibid. vii. 759.

[3] Galeries Historiques du Palais de Versailles, 8vo. 1840, tome vi. pp. 112, 210,
deuxième partie, p. 9.

[4] Rymer, Fœdera, New Edit. i. 708, 922.

which this family, originally frôm Gascoigne, had rendered to the kings of this country.[1]

The barons of Gournay in Normandy bore an uncharged shield of Sable.[2] The town of Gournay placed upon this shield a knight fully armed, ermine, and in chief a fleur-de-lis or; which arms are said to have been conferred upon the town after its capture by Philip Augustus, on which occasion he knighted Arthur Duke of Britany, the unfortunate nephew of our King John. There was therefore histo-

GOURNAY.

rical allusion, both in the Knight (bearing the ermine of Britany) and in the golden fleur-de-lis of the monarch who conferred this distinction.

The ducal house of Britany bore a shield of simple Ermine; down to the time of the marriage of its heiress in 1499 to Louis XII. On the coats of those members of this house who were Earls of Rich-mond in England this usually appears as a canton: as in the very interesting banner of John de Dreux, the Earl in the reign of Edward the First, who bore the Checquy coat of Dreux, surrounded by a bordure of England, and a canton of Bretagne.

BRETAGNE.

> Baniere avoit cointe et paree
> De or et de azur eschequeree
> Au rouge ourle o jaunes lupars,
> D'ermine estoit la quarte pars.

The bordure of England is described as "a red orle with yellow leopards."

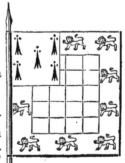

—a very remarkable example of the com-posite heraldry of the close of the thirteenth century: the Earl being a nephew of King Edward the First through his mother, that

<hr />

[1] See the memoir of Sir Eurmenions de la Brette in Sir Harris Nicolas's edition of *The Siege of Carlaverock*, p. 178.

[2] See *The Record of the House of Gournay*, 4to. 1848, p. 19.

is to say, the youngest son of John duke of Bretagne and the princess Beatrice of England.

A division of the shield into two colours PER PALE still constitutes the entire coat of the ancient family of Waldegrave, Per pale argent and gules. The name of Styrlee is said to have borne Per pale or and sable.[1]

A banner parted by pale indented argent and gules was borne by the great Simon de Montfort, Earl of Leicester, as he was represented in one of the windows of the cathedral of Chartres; whilst on his

[1] Glover's Ordinary.   In Burke's *General Armory*, the coat of Sturley is Paly of six or and sable.

shield he carried a lion rampant with a double tail.[1]   The English roll of the reign of Henry III. agrees as to both these bearings:

Le Conte De Leister, goules ung leon rampand d'argent, le cowe fourchée.   Et le Banner party endentée d'argent et de goules.

In some early rolls of arms[2] this Party coat is termed *Le vielle escu de Leicester;* whilst other authorities[3] state it to have been the banner of the Honour of Hinckley in Leicestershire, by the tenure of which the Earls of that county were Stewards of England.   It appears,[4] however, to have been really a personal coat of the Montfort family, and at a time before their connection with Leicestershire; for we find it stated[5] that "Simon Montfort, brother to the Erle of Evreux, and father to Simon Erle of Leicester that maryed the kinges daughter, bare these armes: so did Almaric of Evreux, Erle of Gloucester." And the latter statement is confirmed by a seal of Earl Almaric (who died 1226) existing among the Harleian charters (45 C. 28).

The same coat was also borne by Newsells or Nucelles: Party indented or and sable by Sir Henry Borle, and the like gules and argent by Posyngworth.[6]

On the seal[7] of John Holand, Earl of Huntingdon, as Admiral of England, in the reign of Henry V., the stern of his ship has a banner party per pale dancette.   This (remarks Sir Harris Nicolas,[8]) "was evidently intended for the ancient coat of Holand, namely, Per pale dancette or and gules."   Such a coat is attributed in the ordinaries to Holand of Lincolnshire.

---

[1] Willemin, *Monumens Francais Inedits :* copied in the title-page of the *Rolls of Arms of Henry III. and Edward III.* edited by Sir Harris Nicolas, 1829, and by Planché, *Pursuivant of Arms,* p. 39, from which work we now extract it.

[2] Named by Nicolas, *Rolls,* &c. p. xlii.   In the Roll of Arms at the Society of Antiquaries, No. 17, the coat is inscribed *Cike de Leycr.,* a word that has foiled interpretation.

[3] A volume of records in the Duchy of Lancaster office is mentioned in the *History of Leicestershire,* i. 671, in which the arms of the Duchy are accompanied by the banners of the various lordships which centred in that dignity, and among them is this for the Honour of Hinckley.   Also in the Harleian MS. 6163.   The coat of Grandmesnil, the ancient Barons of Hinckley, is said to have been Gules, a pale or.

[4] Brooke, *Catalogue of Nobility;* and charter in the Harleian collection, 45 C 28.

[5] In the fine copy of Glover's Ordinary, Cotton MS. Tiberius, D. x. p. 677.

[6] Glover, ubi supra.

[7] Engraved in the Gentleman's Magazine, 1797, vol. lxvii. p. 549.

[8] Retrospective Review, New Series, i. 107.

The partition of the shield was blasoned in France by terms which we have not adopted in England. Besides *Parti* for parted by pale, they used *Coupé* for parted by fess, *Tranché* for parted by bend, and *Taillé* for parted by bend sinister. There are several French coats that are parted in these various ways.

The banner of the Templars was merely Coupé, or parted by fess, sable and argent. It has been remarked as a peculiarity that it was oblong in form: but such was really the customary shape of banners in the thirteenth century, when the Templars were in their vigour. The name of *Bauseant* was given to it, which is thus explained in a passage describing the Knights, written by a contemporary, the cardinal Jacques de Vitré, bishop of Acre:

Lions they are in war, gentle lambs in the convent; fierce soldiers in the field, hermits and monks in the Church: to the enemies of Christ fierce and inexorable, but to Christians kind and gracious. They have a standard biparted of White and Black, that they call *Bauceant*, because to the friends of Christ they are white (*candidi*) and kind, but to his enemies black and terrible. (Jacques de Vitré, *Historia Iherosolimitana*, cap. lxv. in *Gesta Dei apud Francos*.)

This idea was quite Oriental, black and white being constantly used by the Arabs metaphorically. Their customary salutation is, *May your day be white!* But the ensign of the Knights Templars, by which they were personally distinguished, was their well-known red cross: and in a roll of arms of the thirteenth century, which has been recently edited for the *Archæologia* of the Society of Antiquaries, by W. S. Walford, esq. from the Harl. MS. 6589, both these devices are combined for

Le auntient de Temple, d'argent vn chief sable vn crois gulez passant.

—the word *auntient* being varied in Leland's copy of that roll to *baucent*—which is the same word as *bauseant* above.[1]

[1] In another work of de Vitré, his *Historia Orientalis*, lib. iii. cap. 10, (edited by Martene,) it appears as *Baucant*—" Vexillum bicolorum, quod dicitur *Baucant*, ipsos in bello præcedit." *Bausan* was a term more frequently applied to a horse. " *Bauçant* fut un cheval ferrant et gris, moitie Arabe, moitie Maure." Raynouard, *Lexique Roman*, i. 20, (from the Roman de Gerard de Rousillon) ; where also we find this citation as to the standard of the Templars—

Preiro baneira . . . . lo Bausa.

Cat. dels apost. de Roma, fol. 151.

i. e. they took for banner the Bausa.

We do not find any English coat formed Party PER FESS of two colours; but such division occurs, Party per fess or and azure, for Sturre, a noble family of Hungary.

A shield parted by fess indented was borne by Landas, a noble family of Flanders, and is among those of the crusaders displayed at Versailles, in the description of which it is thus blasoned: Emmanché de dix pièces d'argent et de gueules.[1]

A division of the shield into two colours PER CHEVRON is the bearing of the ancient family of Aston, of Aston in Cheshire, who enjoyed the rank of Baronet from 1628 to 1815. Their shield was Per chevron sable and argent. The Astons barons of Forfar in Scotland varied this to Argent, a fess sable and in chief three lozenges of the last.

The QUARTERLY coat of or and gules, without charge, was considered to be that of the ancient Earls of Essex of the name of Mandeville, and was borne during many later generations by their descendants the family of Say. It was also, with the simple difference of a mullet in the first quarter, the arms of the long line of the Veres, Earls of Oxford, and in their case was probably derived from the same origin. It was borne with other differences by the baronial houses of Clavering and Eure, and by a groupe of families, the relationship of which, in connection with this bearing, will form an interesting subject of armorial study on some future opportunity.

Guy de Rochford, le Poitevin, bore Quarterly argent and gules, temp. Hen. III., and Foulke FitzWaren Quarterly argent and gules indented.

Among the Crusaders at Versailles there are several simple Quarterly coats. That of Quarterly or and gules is erected for Senlis seigneur de Chantilly, for Hervé de Boisberthelot, for Bertrand de Thésan (1249), and for A. de Valon (1250). Quarterly or and azure was borne by Gauthier de Beyviers in Bresse (1120); Quarterly argent and gules by Jean seigneur of Dol in Bretagne; Quarterly argent and sable by the seigneur of Ganges in Languedoc.

To revert to England, and to still existing families. The Stanhopes bear Quarterly ermine and gules; the Leightons of

[1] Galeries Historiques, &c. VI. ii. 220.

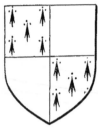 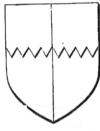 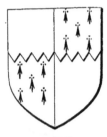

STANHOPE.   LEIGHTON.   SANDFORD.

Shropshire Quarterly per fess indented or and gules; and the Sandfords of the same county Quarterly per fess indented azure and ermine.

The shield of VAIRE, or and gules, was adopted by Ferrers Earl of Derby, at a very early period of armory, evidently because it resembled his name in its sound—

Le Comte de Ferrers, verree de or et de goules.   *Roll Hen. III.*

It was derived from Ferrers to Gresley, by which family it is still borne tinctured ermine and gules.   This was a coat assumed in token of feudality, for the manor of Drakelow was held under the Earl by Gresley, in the year 1200, by the yearly service of a bow, quiver, and twelve arrows.

FERRERS.   GRESLEY.   MEYNELL.

The more ordinary Vaire, argent and azure, was borne by the Beauchamps of Somersetshire, and was displayed on the banner of John de Beauchamp at Carlaverock.

The Meynells of Staffordshire and Derbyshire also still bear Vaire, argent and sable.   This they took as heirs of De la Warde; which is found in the Roll temp. Edw. II. among les Armes abatues de Grand' Seignors,

Sire Roberd de la Warde, verre de argent e de sable.

And the old rolls contain several other names that bore simple Vaire, without further charge.   In the cuts in the opposite page the shield of Ferrers exhibits Vaire as it was drawn in early times; those of Gresley and Meynell present the modern appearance of Vaire.

In the English roll of Arms of the reign of Henry the Third, various coats will be found that have no charges, but are simply composed of two colours, either Barry, or Paly, or Undée, or Bendy. One is called Roelée, argent and azure; this being a technical description of the *gurges*, or whirlpool, of Rauf de Gorges: and there is one Gyronny of the same tinctures, for Warin de Bassingborne. Mr. Seton, in his *Scottish Heraldry*, remarks that Gyronny is a favourite arrangement in Scotland, as in the frequently occurring escucheon of the Campbells, where the tinctures are usually or and sable. It is also borne by the surnames of Matthew and Matthison (sable and gules), and by certain branches of the family of Spence (argent and azure). In Spain it is of common occurrence, being there borne by several distinguished families, including the house of Giron, from which the Dukes of Ossuna are descended. Indeed its name seems to be derived from Spain, where the word signifies a gusset, or triangular piece of cloth.

We have thus found a greater number of coats of arms than would at first be imagined, that were considered complete in their parti-coloured guise, though without charges. And there can be no doubt that we see in these uncharged coats the earliest features of the art of Armory. The next step was the employment of the bars, or crossed bars, by which the shield was sometimes strengthened, and of its central boss, which was modified into the Cross Flory,[1] to form those simple figures which are termed the Ordinaries. To these we shall next pay attention on resuming our investigation.

---

[1] Also into the Escarboncle; but we do not add this in the text, because the latter is really a subsequent fabrication, belonging to the fictitious armory which later heralds have fastened upon their predecessors.

PLAYFORD AND THE FELTONS. A paper read at a Meeting of the Suffolk
Institute of Archæology, etc., at Playford Hall, on October 24th, 1860.
By the Hon. and Ven. Lord ARTHUR HERVEY, President of the Institute.
8vo. pp. 52.

This copious memoir is a separate impression from the Transactions of
the Suffolk Institute of Archæology. It includes many important historical
papers : and terminates with three tabular pedigrees, 1. that of the Feltons ;
2. the royal descent from the Kings of England and France of the Lady
Elizabeth Howard (ob. 1681), the wife of Sir Thomas Felton, Bart.; and
3. Bigod or Felbrigge,—Sir Simon le Bigod, in 28 Edw. I., having assumed
the latter name from the family of his paternal grandmother ; and again
Sir George le Bigod, his great-nephew, having again assumed it. The
heiress of Felbrigge was married to Thomas Sampson, esq. who died in
1439 ; and Margaret, sister and heiress to Sir Thomas Sampson, who died
in 1513, was married to Robert Felton, esq. The Feltons were descended
in the male line from the Bertrams barons of Mitford in Northumberland : Roger Bertram, who died in 1242, having left an elder son
Roger, ancestor of the subsequent Bertrams, and a younger son Payne,
who assumed the name of Felton from his residence in the same county.
A branch of the Feltons became lords of Playford in 1513 ; and the heiress
was married to John first Earl of Bristol in 1695. Sir Thomas Felton,
Seneschal of Acquitaine, and a Knight of the Garter in the reign of
Edward the Third, was a younger brother of Hamon de Felton, of Litcham
in Norfolk, Knight of that Shire in 1377. His garter-plate remains at
Windsor, and a fac-simile printed in coloured lithography illustrates this
memoir. He bore, Gules, two lions passant ermine, crowned or. On his
helmet, a golden coronet, with a panache of red feathers, quilled gold.
The father of these brothers, Sir John de Felton, who was Governor of Alnwick, and their grandfather Sir Robert, Governor of Scarborough, had
both been summoned to Parliament temp. Edw. II., as was their cousin Sir
William de Felton, Governor of Bamborough ; but in none of these cases
does an hereditary barony appear to have originated. Appendix B. (contributed by Richard Almack, esq. F.S.A.) contains a discussion on the
parentage of John Felton, the assassin of the first Villiers Duke of Buckingham : his genealogy is not ascertained, but is supposed to have been
derived from the Feltons of Pentlow near Sudbury, who bore the Felton
coat differenced by a crescent. Nicholas Felton, successively Bishop of
Bristol and Ely, who died in 1626, one of the translators of the Bible, was
the third son of Mr. John Felton, an alderman of Great Yarmouth.

VIRTUTE VERBIS NON

C.N.Eunn del.

Baker & Norton

JOHN ROSS COULTHART,

OF

COULTHART, COLLYN AND

ASHTON-UNDER-LYNE.

A GENEALOGICAL AND HERALDIC ACCOUNT OF THE COULTHARTS OF COULT-
HART AND COLLYN, CHIEFS OF THE NAME: from their first settlement in
Scotland in the reign of Conarus, to the Year of Our Lord 1854; to
which are added, the Pedigrees of seven other considerable Families,
that, through Heiresses, became incorporated with the House of Coult-
hart. By GEORGE PARKER KNOWLES, Genealogist and Heraldic Artist.
Derived from the Family Muniments. London: printed for private cir-
culation only, by Harrison and Sons, MDCCCLV. Royal 8vo. pp. 24.
COULTHART, OF COULTHART, COLLYN, AND ASHTON-UNDER-LYNE. [A
broadside Pedigree] derived from the Family Muniments, and brought
down to A.D. 1853 by ALEXANDER CHEYNE, Esq. B.A. of Ashton-under-
Lyne, Barrister-at-Law, and GEORGE PARKER KNOWLES, of Manchester,
Genealogist and Heraldic Artist.
A GENEALOGICAL AND HERALDIC ACCOUNT OF THE ROSSES OF DALTON, in
the County of Dumfries, from their first Settlement in Scotland, in the
Twelfth Century; to the year of our Lord 1854. (By the Same, and
printed at the same time.) Royal 8vo. pp. 8.
Notes and Memoranda to the Coulthart and Ross Pedigrees. Royal 8vo.
pp. 11. [Accompanied by a Declaration of Mr. George Parker Knowles,
dated 3 Feb. 1864.]   (Of all, 75 copies printed.)

These genealogical records are dedicated to John Ross Coulthart, esq. of
Croft House, Ashton-under-Lyne, co. Lancaster, and to George Ross, esq.
of Newport, co. Salop; and they were printed at the expense of the former,
the representative of the Coultharts of Coulthart and Collyn. In a brief
Preface we are informed that the more laborious part of the work, in tran-
scribing and translating the documents from which the pedigrees are composed, had been accomplished by Alexander Cheyne, esq. of Ashton-under-
Lyne, barrister-at-law, shortly before his death on the 26th August, 1853:
their arrangement was completed by the gentleman whose name and designation appears in the title-page.

"Few families (remarks Mr. Knowles) can justly claim so ancient and
honourable a descent as the Coultharts of Coulthart and Collyn, and fewer
still can establish their lineage by such unerring documentary evidence.
Deriving an uninterrupted male succession from the era of Julius Agricola,
the genealogy is clearly traceable by means of monkish chronicles, historical achievements, marriage alliances, royal charters, baronial leases,
sepulchral inscriptions, sasine precepts, judicial decreets, and fragmentary
pedigrees, to the present lineal representative, who has furnished me with
such an extensive collection of ancestral muniments, partly arranged by
domestic annalists and antiquaries, that I am enabled to compile from the
family archives the following brief record of the COULTHARTS OF COULTHART
AND COLLYN, chiefs of the name, and also to annex thereto heraldic and
genealogical accounts of the ROSSES of Renfrew, the MACKNYGHTES of
Macknyghte, the GLENDONYNS of Glendonyn, the CARMICHAELS of Carspherne, the FORBESES of Pitscottie, the MACKENZIES of Craighall, and the

Gordons of Sorbie; who have all, through heiresses, become incorporated with the house of Coulthart, as successive generations meandered down the stream of time."

It has been thought sufficient in the southern half of Britain to trace a genealogy up to one of those Norman knights who "came in with the Conqueror," and are named on the Roll of Battle Abbey: but the extraordinary antiquity of the Coultharts mounts for more than thirty generations higher than that, up to "Coulthartus, a Roman lieutenant, who fought under Julius Agricola, at the foot of the Grampian mountains;" and who, "versed in all the wisdom and learning of the Romans, appears to have lived at Leucaphibia, as a Caledonian chieftain, and to have died there, beloved and lamented, in the 12th year of the reign of King Conarus." The genealogy is carried on by the names of Julius, Ackaline, Doraldus, Moraldus, Thorwaldus, and a great variety of others, but Coulthartus occurs again in it at intervals. Coulthartus II. in the fifth generation from the first, "surpassed most men of his time in the manly exercises of running, riding, shooting arrows, throwing the dart, and wielding the battle-axe;" and his son and successor Diorthaca was "the first of the family that embraced the Christian religion." In the 14th generation we come to Coulthartus III. whose mother was a daughter of Lothus king of the Picts; in the 19th to Coulthartus IV. who was chiefly remarkable for his benefactions to the abbey of Candida Casa, or Whithorn, built in his time; in the 26th to Coulthartus V. who was equally liberal in erecting and repairing churches in Galloway; and in the 32d to Coulthartus VI. who having stood aloof from the usurper Macbeth, joyfully assisted in the restoration of Malcolm Kianmore. Immediately after his death, his two sons Alfred and Theodore went on a pilgrimage to the holy sepulchre of St. Peter at Rome; and the former, on his return, "had a confirmation charter from King Malcolm of the barony of Coulthart, on condition that three horses should always be furnished to the sovereigns of Scotland when required in time of war: *for which reason three colts, courant, have ever since been borne by the family of Coulthart as an armorial ensign.*"

We need scarcely say, after all that has been stated on that point in former numbers of this periodical, that we consider this epoch too early for the origin of armorial bearings: and in the present case the anachronism is the more obvious, since it is placed two generations before the surname of Coulthart itself was established: for Alfred used none, nor his son Godofredus: and we are told that it was his grandson, Sir Radulphus de Coulthart, who first used the territorial designation as a surname. He was also the first Crusader of his family.

Still later by three generations we meet with an addition to the armorial legend. When Sir Roger de Coulthart had highly distinguished himself in a tournament held at Haddington in 1240, King Alexander II. "personally invested him with the knightly girdle, and heraldically added to the three black colts courant on his silver shield a fess sable, which armorial ensigns have ever since, without alteration, been borne by the chiefs of the family." The wife of Sir Roger was Isabella Stewart, a daughter of Walter the Steward of Scotland.

The earliest seal bearing the arms now known to exist is attached to a charter granted by a later Sir Roger de Coulthart, in 1443, to his brother-in-law Robert de Agnew of the lands of Fellmore in Galloway. This seal is said to be "still remarkably perfect." The legend is unusual in form and position, mentioning only the surname and not the personal name of its owner. The supporters form a rebus of the name —a *colt*, attired as a war-horse, and a *hart*, gorged with a coronet.

The father of this Roger, Sir Gilbert, died in 1391 at Dantzick, in the service of Prussia against the Turks; and for some generations after, the fate of each successive head of the family is remarkable. Sir Roger fell at the siege of Roxburgh castle in 1460; Sir Roger, his son, was killed at Sauchyburn in 1488: Sir Richard, the next laird, was slain at Flodden in 1513; and Cuthbert, his successor, at Solway Moss in 1542. One of the sons of the Sir Roger that died in 1488 was Henry, who settled in Craven in Yorkshire, and was ancestor of the late H. W. Coulthurst, D.D. Vicar of Halifax. In the next century occurs another remarkable cadet, one "Roger, a major in the army of King Charles II. [or I.?] who, to avoid persecution when Oliver Cromwell was proclaimed Lord Protector, flew beyond seas, and never afterwards returned from exile." If there are any Coultharts in America, they may claim descent from this Major.

We arrive at more peaceful times; and Richard Coulthart, esq. the chief who was born in 1659 and died in 1717, was an eminent agriculturist and author of *The Economy of Agriculture*, long a favourite text-book of the farmers of Scotland. His wife was the heiress of Gordon of Sorbie, whose pedigree we shall have to mention.

He was great-grandfather of the last chief of the house, who was also devoted to the science of agriculture, residing in Cumberland, where his tomb is placed in his parish churchyard of Bolton-le-Gate, and is similar to those of the Coulthart family at Kells and Kirkpatrick-Fleming. It bears the following inscription to his memory, written by the Bishop of Manchester:—

"Gulielmus Coulthart de Coulthart et Collyn Arm. Gentis nominisque sue facile primarius. Nat. die Martis xxi° MDCCLXXIV. Denat. die Octob. vii° MDCCCXLVII."

Not long after the decease of this gentleman his widow caused the west window of Bolton-le-Gate church to be filled with stained glass by Mr. Willement, of London; a commission executed with such success, that it is

WEST WINDOW OF BOLTON-LE-GATE CHURCH, CUMBERLAND.

considered superior to any of the same size in Cumberland. Its design is
shown in the annexed engraving, the upper openings being occupied by angels,
and the three principal lights by whole-length figures of the prophets
Zacharias, Amos, and Jeremias. Beneath these, in square compartments,
are armorial achievements. The first, being Coulthart impaling Ross, is
accompanied with this inscription:—"Ad gloriam Dei et in memoriam
Helenæ Gulielmi Coulthart ux. ob. xv. Apr. MDCCCLX." The second
panel has the quartered arms, crest, supporters, and motto of the chief of
the family, with this inscription:—"Gulielmus Coulthart ob. vii. Oct.
MDCCCXLVII." In the third panel a shield of arms with this inscription:—"Ad gloriam Dei et in memoriam Margaritæ Gul. Coulthart fil,
Jacobi Macguffie ux. ob. xix. Mart. MDCCCLVI."

There is an account of the family of Macguffie of Crossmichael, co. Kirk-cudbright, in Burke's *Landed Gentry*. Their ARMS are, Argent, a fess between three boar's heads couped sable. The lady above mentioned left the numerous progeny of six sons and five daughters.

John Ross Coulthart, esq. the present chief of the name, (from whom, as already mentioned, we receive these genealogies,) is a magistrate for Lancashire, a barrister of Lincoln's Inn, a banker at Ashton-under-Lyne, where he served the office of mayor from Nov. 1855 to Nov. 1857, a Fellow of the Society of Antiquaries of Scotland, and a Member of the Royal Society of Literature.

The other families whose genealogies are traced in these pages, are—

2. Ross, *of Renfrew:* one of whose coheirs, the daughter of Sir John the Ross, knighted in 1412, was married to Sir Roger de Coulthart. ARMS. Argent, a chevron checky of three tracks sable and or between three water-bougets of the second. *Crest.* A dexter arm in armour proper, garnished or, holding a water-bouget sable.

3. MACKNYGHTE, *of Macknyghte,* in the Regality of Galloway : the heiress of which was married to Sir John the Ross of Renfrew on the 4th July, 1408. ARMS. Sable, an escocheon checky argent and or, between three lion's heads erased of the second. *Crest.* A demi-lion rampant argent.

4. GLENDONYN, *of Glendonyn,* in the shire of Ayr: whose heiress was married in 1386 to Donald de Macknyghte. ARMS. Quarterly argent and sable, a cross parted per cross engrailed and counterchanged. *Crest.* Two arms dexter and sinister, erect and embowed in armour proper, grasping a cross-crosslet fitchée or.

5. CARMICHAEL, *of Carspherne,* in the stewartry of Kirkcudbright : whose heiress was married in 1447 to Sir Roger de Coulthart. ARMS. Argent, on a bend cotised potentée sable a tilting-spear of the first. *Crest.* A dexter hand and arm in armour, brandishing a tilting-spear proper.

6. FORBES, *of Pitscottie,* co. Ayr: whose heiress was married in 1575 to John Coulthart, of Coulthart and Largmore. ARMS. Ermine, a chevron checky argent and sable between three bear's heads couped of the last, muzzled gules, within a bordure nebulée of the third. *Crest.* Out of a coronet or, a dexter arm in armour, holding a scimitar proper.

7. MACKENZIE, *of Craighall,* in the district of Kyle: whose heiress was married in 1624 to William Coulthart, of Coulthart. ARMS. Quarterly: 1 and 4. Azure, a stag's head caboshed or; 2 and 3. Argent, three human legs, united in the centre at the upper part of the thigh, and triangularly flexed, armed and spurred proper: an escocheon surtout, Ermine, a stag's head caboshed sable, within a bordure argent. *Crest.* A demi-savage, wreathed about the head and loins with laurel, holding in the dexter hand on his shoulder a club, all proper.

8. GORDON, *of Sorbie,* co. Wigton: whose heiress was married in 1698 to Richard Coulthart, of Coulthart. ARMS. Ermine, on a fess between three boar's heads erased erect sable a spear argent. *Crest.* Out of a mural crown, a boar's head, as in the arms.

ROSS, OF RENFREW.

GLENDONYN, OF GLENDONYN.

MACKNYGHTE, OF MACKNYGHTE.

CARMICHAEL, OF CARSPHERNE.

FORBES, OF PITSCOTTIE.

GORDON, OF SORBIE.

MACKENZIE, OF CRAIGHALL.

ROSS, OF KEIR, CLOSEBURN,
ST. MUNGO, AND DALTON.

The second Memoir of which the title is prefixed contains the genealogy of Ross, *of Dalton*, co. Dumfries. This is a younger branch of Ross, *of Halkhead*, co. Renfrew, which became Barons of parliament in 1490, or thereabouts, and continued to sustain that dignity until 1754. They derive their descent from the same Yorkshire house from whence we have still the English barony of Ros or de Roos; and bear the same charges of water-bougets; whilst the crest of a hawk's head is allusive to their seat already named. The junior line whose pedigree is here deduced were long of Rosshill, co. Ayr, where Patrick Ross had royal licence to erect a castle in 1556. Mr. Coulthart's mother was Helen the second daughter of John Ross, esq. of Keir, Closeburn, St. Mungo, and Dalton, all co. Dumfries, by Margaret, daughter of Alexander Glendinning, esq. of the Isle of Dalton, in the same county. ARMS. Gules, three water-bougets argent. *Crest.* A hawk's head couped proper.

The third fasciculus, which has been only recently printed, contains additional notes and memoranda to both the Coulthart and Ross pedigrees; translations of charters; some biographical memoirs; a copy of the Seize Quartiers of John Ross Coulthart, esq. (as compiled by Mr. Bridger, of Witley, for his collection of *Seize Quartiers*); and the Royal Descent of the same gentleman from William the Conqueror, on one hand by twenty-five descents, through the Hays,—Lady Elizabeth Hay, eldest daughter of George sixth Earl of Erroll, having married Cuthbert de Coulthart, who died in 1542; and on the other, by twenty-seven descents, through the families of Ross and Edmonstone, Sir William Edmonstone of Culloden and Duntreath, who died in 1460, having been the fourth husband of Mary Countess of Angus, one of the daughters of King Robert III. Her grandson Sir Archibald Edmonstone, of Duntreath, was one of those who surrounded his arms with the double tressure in commemoration of his royal descent.

Mr. Coulthart quarters with his own arms those of the seven families commemorated in the first Memoir, thus marshalled: 1. Coulthart; 2. Ross; 3. Macknyghte; 4. Glendonyn; 5. Carmichael; 6. Forbes; 7. Mackenzie; and 8. Gordon,—as shown at the foot of the stained-glass window.

1864.

A COLLECTION OF PEDIGREES OF THE FAMILY OF TRAVERS: or Abstracts of certain Documents collected towards a History of that Family, by S. SMITH TRAVERS, Esq. Arranged by Henry J. SIDES of the Bodleian Library. Oxford: printed by J. H. and J. Parker. 1864. 4to. Title, leaf of introduction, three folding pedigrees, and 44 very closely printed pages. (A private work, 55 copies.)

In modern times the name of Travers has been well known in the City of London for prosperous and honourable commercial transactions, and for no small share of political influence. In the ranks of surgical skill also it has taken a foremost place for more than one generation: whilst, in the department of political and legal science, a gentleman who from his maternal descent has derived Travers for his baptismal name has attained a great reputation at once with his professional and academic friends and with the general public.

It is to one of this London family that we are indebted for the genealogical "Collection" which we now notice: and all the parties to whom we have alluded are to be found in the tabular pedigrees with which it is commenced.

We would not quarrel, as Sir Harris Nicolas was disposed to do with Mr. Nicholas Carlisle, with any one for gathering into one focus all that can be collected respecting a particular name, and arranging such collections in one or more volumes, under the several counties, or as may be most convenient. The error that laid Mr. Carlisle open to Sir Harris Nicolas's animadversion, and somewhat unfair ridicule, was that of entitling his book *Collections for a History of the Family of Carlisle* (1822, 4to.); and the editors of the volume before us fall into the same inadvertence when they say on their title-page, "the Family of Travers," instead of *the families*,—for it is not pretended that all the families of the name have sprung from one stock.

Mr. Lower, in his *Patronymica Britannica*, derives the name of Travers from the "Fr. *traverse*, a cross path or foot-road leading from one village to another:" and again, of Maltravers, "It may be of local origin, and allusive to some *bad passage*, or traject." It might apply, we imagine, to a passage, or ferry, across a river.

At p. 22 of the Collection before us we find it stated, that "from Trevières, a town in the department of Calvados, midway between Dives and Valognes, came the ancestors of Ralph Travers, who in the reign of Richard I. married Petronilla Tresgoz, the inheritrix, from her maternal grandfather, Walter de Valognes, of half the lordship of Berney, co. Norfolk;" and that, at the present day, the surname of Travers is common in that district, for at Valognes was born, on 31st Jan. 1802, Julian Gilles Travers, a celebrated French professor, poet, and archæologist, the still surviving author and editor of many valuable works.

Again, as the name was often spelt Travis, or Traves, may not some of the families that have borne it have come from the imperial city of Treves, or even from another Treves, a town on the Loire?

It may sometimes have had a personal instead of a local origin: for we find that Trévier was a maritime term, applied to one who looked after the sails of a ship,—"le maître des voiles, qui a soin de l'envergure, et qui les visite à chaque quart, pour voir si elles sont en bon etat. *Velis præpositus.* Trévier, ou Maître voilier." (*Dictionnaire Universel.*)

At various periods foreigners of the name may have come to England.

In p. 21 is a notice of Peregrine Trevis, a merchant in Mincing Lane, who was a Jew by birth and a native of Venice, and obtained a patent of naturalisation in 1762.

As a personal name, Travers is found in England as early as the Domesday survey. At Egrafel in Hampshire (which was in the hundred of Bowcombe, but its modern name has not been identified,) William son of Stur held half a hide, and Travers held it of William.

There are few parts of England, if any, in which some of the name cannot be traced, and Mr. Smith Travers, with very persevering research, has amassed a large mass of documents respecting them: which he has arranged under the several counties,—as was done by Captain Archer in his volume on the Archers which we recently described; and occasionally there occur in a single county two or more families of the name between whom no relationship can be traced. There appear in Burke's *General Armory* some ten different coats of arms for the name; but that which belonged to the most

ancient and distinguished house was *Sable, a chevron between three boar's heads couped argent,* borne by Travers of Horton in the county of Chester: from which Mr. Smith Travers derives his own linear descent, the name at the head of the first tabular pedigree being that of Hamon or Hamlet Travers, of Horton-hall, who is enrolled on the list of Cheshire gentry in 1522-3, and of whom various other memorials are extant. He is supposed to have descended from the still more antient race that resided at Mount Travers, Nateby, &c. in the county of Lancaster.

For these two ancient houses Mr. Travers has collected further materials, which he reserves at present for a more extended work: his principal object being to solicit assistance from any genealogist who can render it, particularly to verify the descent of the Cheshire family from that of Lancashire, or to attach any others of the outlying branches to the parent stem.

The pedigrees that are now printed are illustrated by many important and curious records, especially wills. In Lancashire, particularly, there are several ancient families of Travers besides the chief house at Nateby.

One of them at Blackley is traced to the first half of the sixteenth century. John Bradford the martyr wrote during his imprisonment many long letters to his friend "good Father Travers, minister of Blackley," which are given at length in Foxe's Actes and Monuments. From that time to the present Blackley Chapel has been constantly under the care of members of this family, either as trustees or ministers.

There was a Peter Travers (p. 13) who, after having received his education at Westminster and Cambridge, was Rector of Bury and Hodsall in Lancashire, and became Bishop of Sodor and Man in 1643, but of his parentage nothing is known.

Christopher Travers of Doncaster (p. 38) is supposed to have been that retainer of the Earl of Northumberland who makes a short entry upon the stage in the Second Part of Shakespeare's *Henry the Fourth*. He made his will in London in 1466, and desired to be buried in the cathedral church of St. Paul.

Under Devonshire is presented the pedigree of a family seated for five generations at Pille in the parish of Bishop's Tawton, from the reign of Edward IV. to that of Elizabeth. John, the second son in the last generation, has been fixed upon for identification with a brother-in-law of the poet Spenser (Craik's *Spenser and his Poetry*, iii. 250); but in the pages before us it is remarked that this John Travers, baptised at Coleridge in 1567, would have been but thirteen years old in 1580, when the Poet's brother-in-law is said to have repaired to Ireland; and a still more serious objection to the identity is offered by the same register recording the burial in 1573 of the child born in 1567.

John Travers was an alderman of London, and three times sheriff, early in the thirteenth century, in 1215, 1223, and 1224. The last of those years was remarkable for the first arrival of the Franciscan friars in this country; and they were lodged for some time in Cornhill, at the house of John Travers, who was then chamberlain as well as sheriff.

Another London family of the name, which flourished for several generations, descended from Richard Travers, citizen and merchant-taylor, who was born at Maidstone circ. 1480-5, and died in 1540. It was partly upon his estate that the Royal Exchange was erected by Sir Thomas Gresham. He was father-in-law of Sir Thomas Blanck, Lord Mayor in 1582, and his great-grand-daughter was the wife of Sir John Dethick, another Lord Mayor. His posterity is traced to the end of the following century.

Walter Travers of Nottingham, goldsmith, whose will, made in 1757, is presented to us, is supposed to have been one of the sons of Richard Travers, merchant-taylor, of London. He was the father of Walter Travers, B.D. a celebrated Puritan divine, who became Provost of Trinity College, Dublin, in 1594; and also of John Travers, Rector of Faringdon, co. Devon, who married Alice Hooker sister to the still more celebrated Master of the Temple. The latter had four sons, all beneficed clergymen, and the pedigree of this branch of Travers is amply exemplified for five generations.

Walter Travers for a time was lecturer at the Temple ; and when Hooker
and Travers preached there, there were, says Fuller, almost as many writers
as hearers : for not only students, but even the gravest Benchers—such as
Sir Edward Coke and Sir James Altham, might be observed taking notes.
" The worst was, these two preachers, though joyned in affinity, (their
nearest kindred being married together,) acted with different principles,
and clashed one against the other. So that what Mr. Hooker delivered in
the forenoon, Mr. Travers confuted in the afternoon. At the building of
Solomon's Temple (1 Kings vi. 7) neither hammer, nor axe, nor tool of
iron was heard therein : whereas, alas ! in this Temple much knocking was
heard, but (which was the worst) the nailes and pins which one master
builder drave in, were driven out by the other." Hooker allowed the
Church of Rome, though not a pure and perfect, yet to be a true church ;
but Travers maintained that the Church of Rome was no true church at
all ; so that such as live therein, holding justification in part by works,
cannot be said by the Scripture to be saved. For these extreme opinions
Travers was silenced by archbishop Whitgift ; and it was this which led to
his acceptance of the invitation of archbishop Loftus, his ancient colleague
at Cambridge, to become provost of Trinity College, Dublin. He remained
there only three years and a half, and spent the remainder of his life in
London, making his will in 1634. The history of this family of learned
divines is very fully related, and their wills are singularly curious. The personal biography of Walter Travers was previously well known, but his
parentage, and his relationship to the Devonshire divines, has been discovered by Mr. Sides.

   Altogether, it will be perceived from the slight sketch we have now given
of this Collection, that it contains a very large and copious amount of
original materials for the history of all the English families of the name of
Travers : and we sincerely hope that the perseverance of the collector, and
his able and intelligent coadjutor, will be rewarded in obtaining such additional information as may re-unite, on reliable evidence, some of the scattered
branches to the parent tree.

1860.

THE JEWELL REGISTER, containing a List of the Descendants of Thomas
    Jewell of Braintree, near Boston, Mass. Hartford : Press of Case,
    Lockwood, and Company. 1860. 8vo. pp. 104.

   This is one of those pedigrees in the form of a catalogue or register
which have of late years been diligently compiled in considerable numbers
by our consins of New England. The introductory advertisement is
signed by Pliny Jewell of Hartford, Connecticut, and the Rev. Joel Jewell
of French's Mills, Philadelphia. The ancestor named in the title-page
" was probably born in England, not far from the year 1600." The
editors add, " We have been unable positively to connect him with any,

European family; but various circumstances coincide to render it most likely that he was from the same original stock as Bishop John Jewell, who was born in the north of Devonshire in 1522, and died in 1571. The name has been written Jule, Joyell, Jewel, and then Jewell. The first authentic account of Thomas is in the early part of 1639, but little more than 18 years after the landing of the Pilgrims at Plymouth, and shows that he had then a wife and one child, probably a daughter." He received at that date a grant of twelve acres, as "Thomas Jewell of the Mount, miller," the spot having been first settled in 1625 as Mount Wollaston (so named from Captain Wollaston); and it was incorporated as "Braintree" in 1640. Probate of the miller's will (which is given) was granted to his widow Grisell in 1654.

His descendants are in this Register arranged in eight generations. "Our lists (say the Editors,) contain over eighteen hundred [persons], and there may be as many more [of the name] that we cannot trace to one progenitor. George Jewell was at Saco, Maine, in 1637, and Samuel at Boston in 1655; they *may* have been brethren or kinsmen of Thomas. Nathaniel of Boston (1694) and George sen. of Elizabethtown, New Jersey, were brothers, and probably related to the above. We find some in Maine; some in New Hampshire (which descend from Mark); some along the Hudson River; in Philadelphia; in New Jersey, and at the South and West, that have Abraham, Isaac, Jacob, Harmon, and Robert to their fathers; and some who are the children of Richard, which came from Devonshire, England, in 1774."

Thus we see that New England may fairly boast of the abundance of her Jewels. With regard to the presumed descent from the family of Bishop Jewell, it would have been more satisfactory had the Editors explained what the "various circumstances" are which in their view coincide to render it probable that Thomas Jewell was of the same stock as that eminent man. They have prefixed an engraving of the Bishop's arms from the Wiltshire Visitation of 1565, but have not given its blason. With this therefore we will now present them:—

Or, on a chevron azure between three gillyflowers gules, slipt vert, a maiden head proper, wearing a chaplet of the third; on a chief sable a hawk's lure, double-stringed, between two falcons argent. Crest, on a wreath, a cubit arm vested azure, cuffed argent, holding in the hand proper a gilly-flower gules, slipt vert.

"This patent gyven to John Jule of Bowden in the Contey of Dewonshire," by Benolte Clarencieux, 22 Hen. VIII. (1530), as stated in MS. Coll. Arm. 2 G. 4, f. 33 b., also on record as the arms of Bishop Jewell in Harvy's Visitation of Wiltshire, G. 8, fol. 3.

The maiden-head points not improbably to John Jule having been a Mercer, being the head of the Blessed Virgin borne as the arms of that company: it was a singular accident that it should figure in the coat of the first *Protestant* Bishop of Salisbury.

John Jule named *both* his sons John, and two of his daughters Joan. Westcote, in his *View of Devonshire*, 1630, (edit. 1845, p. 536,) has inserted the pedigree of Jewell from the Visitation of Devon, 1563, but omitting the elder John in the enumeration of his father's children. We shall there-fore take the opportunity of printing this genealogy *verbatim* from the MS. in the Heralds' office :—

"John Jule of Bowden in the countie of Devon, gent. maryed Alys doughter to Rychard Bellamye,[1] and by her had yssue John his eldeste sonne, John bysshoppe of Sarum, second sonne, Jone maryed to John Dunne[2] of Holdysworthie, Jackett maryed to John Rede of Bery in erber, Xp'ian maryed to Anthonye Wethye of Bery in erber, Jone the yonger maryed to John Wethie, Cescellie maryed to Henrye Downe of Barnestable.

"John Jule of Est Downe[3] in the saide countie, gent', eldeste sonne and heire to John, maryed Agnes doughter and sole heire to Rychard Cuttclyffe of Northcott in the countie of Devon, gent. and by her hath yssue Jone, Margaret,[4] Alys,[5] Agnes,[6] and Cescellie.[7] Jone maryed to Thomas Hamont[8] of Arlington, and hath yssne Rebecca." (MS. Coll. Arm. D. 7, fol. 8.)

The male line does not appear to have been perpetuated. Burke in his *General Armory* gives the same coat without the maiden-head for Jewell of Scotland : and also this simple coat,—Azure, three gilly-flowers argent, for Jewell of Salisbury. The *gilly-flowers* were a canting allusion to the name, originally written Jule; and which was derived, as Mr. Lower points out in his *Patronymica Britannica*, from the baptismal name *Jules*, the French of Julius. Jewell, we find, is not an uncommon name in Eng-land as well as America.

---

[1] The editors of Westcote have quoted from the will of John Bellamy, incumbent of Highampton and Countisbury, dated 5 Dec. 1543, these items : " I gyve and bequethe to John Jueli the yonger now Scholar at Oxford, at such tyme that he dothe proceede master of artes, lxvj s. vilj d. Item, I gyve and bequethe to Jacquet Juell xx s. Item, I gyve and bequethe to every other child of John Juell of Bowdon ys children one sheepe." John Bellamy was probably uncle and godfather of the Bishop.

[2] Downe, alias Dunne. (Westcote).

[3] *i.e.* the eldest son. He is styled " of Northcot in the parish of East Down" by Westcote; but (as already mentioned) his relationship to the foregoing is not specified.

[4] Margaret married to Richard Ley of Northcot. (Westcote.)

[5] Alice married to Thomas Fursdon of Raddon court in the parish of Thorver-ton. (Ibid.)

[6] Agnes, married to George Peard of Barnstaple. (Ibid.)

[7] Cecily, married to Bradford in Wales. (Ibid.)　　　　[8] Hamond.

1709.

A Manuscript copy of Verses addressed :

To The Honourable S^r ROB^t MARSHAM BAR^t. on the HAPPY BIRTH of a SON.

(In the hands of Mr. J. C. Hotten of Piccadilly.)

They consist of seventy-three lines, in the usual inflated style of such compositions at the beginning of the last century. Apostrophising the infant, the Poet offers these heroics :—

> If thy serener Life's more halcyon Fate
> Shall plant Thee at the peaceful Helme of State,
> Copy thy *Marsham Sire.*   When *Albion* calls
> The Delphick Heads to her St Stephen's Walls,
> Whether to give New Gallick Tyrants Laws, &c. &c.

Again,—

> Or if by rougher Glory Thou'rt called forth
> T'exert the Virtues of thy *Cloud'sly* Birth,
> Set out a Heroe round the Watry World,
> By thy Bold Arm the British Thunder hurld,
> In either Post thy Birthright's equal Due,
> May the pleasd World thy dazling Luster view :
> Thus whilst this Double-portiond Glory reigns
> The Inborn Worth from such Parental Veins,
> May both the *Shovel* and the *Marsham* shine
> Both in One equal Transmigration joyn,
> And on that Darling Head descending, All
> Like th' old Elijah's Spirited Mantle fall.

The concluding lines of the piece allude to the monument of Sir Cloudesly Shovell in Westminster Abbey, then recently erected at the expense of Queen Anne, with its inappropriate effigy,[1] from the chisel of Francis Bird ; where, as described in Pope's mocking line, the Admiral's peruke

> Eternal buckle takes in Parian stone.

Sir Robert Marsham, the fifth Baronet, of Cuxton in Kent, was married to Elizabeth, daughter and coheir of Sir Cloudesly Shovell,[2] Rear-Admiral

---

[1] " The hardy admiral is represented on his tomb (as described by Addison) by the figure of a beau, dressed in a long periwig, and reposing himself upon velvet cushions under a canopy of state." See also Walpole's censure in Cunningham's *Handbook to London.*

[2] Sir Cloudesly Shovell (modern books incorrectly present his name as Cloudesley Shovel) was born of humble parentage near Clay, in Norfolk. He married the widow of his patron, Admiral Sir John Narborough, Knt. who was Elizabeth, daughter of John Hill, esq. a commissioner of the Navy. It is stated in Chalmers's *Biographical Dictionary,* that " Sir Cloudesly Shovell left two daughters, co-heiresses, the eldest

of Great Britain; and his eldest son, Shovell Marsham, was born on the 15th Oct. 1709. This, therefore, is the age of the composition before us. There is no intimation whatever of its author: but we may plausibly imagine that it was the chaplain of the household.

Shovell Marsham did not live to fulfil the flattering anticipations of the Poet. He died in his infancy; and the second son, Robert, born in 1712, became the second Lord Romney in 1724, his father having been advanced to the peerage in 1716.

But the document is of most curiosity in its decorative features. It is written on four leaves of cardboard, measuring 14½ inches by 10½. The margins are stamped from book-binders' tools in gold, heightened with colours, their ornaments consisting of the usual scroll-patterns, inclosing figures of angels, urns, birds, flowers, &c. In the title-page is a shield of arms, surmounted with mantling, stamped in like manner, the bearings being, Argent, a lion passant gules between two bendlets azure, the hand of Ulster in canton, and on an escocheon of pretence, Gules, a chevron ermine between two crescents in chief argent and a fleur de lis in base or, for Shovell. Crest, on a helmet and wreath, a lion's head erased gules.

Sir Cloudesly Shovell's coat was granted Jan. 6, 1691-2, in commemoration of his victories over the Turks and French, and it is one of the simplest and best conceived of the historical class. The crest was, Out of a naval coronet or, a demi-lion gules holding a sail argent charged with an anchor or. We are allowed the annexed cut from Seton's *Scottish Heraldry.*

Sir Cloudesly Shovell's armorial insignia are still conspicuous on the ceiling of the Town-hall at Rochester, which is a remarkable specimen of the plaster-work of the time. It is "curiously enriched with trophies of war, fruits, and flowers, with the arms of the City, and those of Sir Cloudesly Shovell, at whose expense it was done in 1695. The whole is executed in a masterly manner." (*History of Rochester,* 8vo. 1817, p. 241.) In the same room is a whole-length portrait of Sir Cloudesly Shovell, who was a further benefactor to the city in rebuilding the public clock-house in 1706. He represented Rochester in Parliament from 1695 to 1701, and from 1705 to his death.

of whom married Lord Rodney, and the other Sir Narborough D'Aeth, Bart.;" but that statement is not correct. Elizabeth Narborough, the *half*-sister of Lady Marsham, was married to Thomas D'Aeth, esq. who was created a Baronet in 1716; and she became in 1707 the heiress of her brother Sir John Narborough, Bart. (so created 1688,) who and his only brother James were both lost on the rocks of Scilly with their step-father Sir Cloudesly Shovell. Her son Sir Narborough D'Aeth was the second Baronet (1745), and his son Sir Narborough was the third (1773) and last, dying unmarried in 1808. See the *Extinct Baronetages* by Courthope and Burke.

CARY: VISCOUNTS FALKLAND.

THE history of the Cary family remains yet to be written, but there can be little doubt that in able hands it would prove a most valuable as well as interesting contribution to the literature of our country. I shall not attempt in these pages to do more than mention some of its leading features, and these mainly for the special purpose of illustrating the subjoined Pedigrees. I shall, however, be very glad if the materials here collected prove of service to some genealogist, whose leisure exceeds my own, and whose interest is not less.

The family is said to have received its name from the manor of Cary or Kari, lying in the parish of St. Giles in the Heath, near Launceston; but, if such be the case, a migration into Somerset must have taken place at an early period, as in the year 1198 one Adam de Karry is mentioned as Lord of Castle Cary in that county. Perhaps the real root of the name (which is very probably allied to Carew, and perhaps to Carr and Ker,) is to be found in the Celtic Caer, and it would thus be equivalent to the more common patronymic Chester. On this point it is well to observe, that, in Sir B. Burke's genealogy of the Carews of Haccombe, co. Devon, an ancestor who died in 1173 is described as William of the Castle Kerrin, co. Caermarthen. The similarity between Castle-Kerrin and Castle-Cary is at least remarkable, and in both cases I am inclined to think that the double name is made up of a Celtic and Roman equivalent. At any rate, whether or no the two families sprung from the same source, it is certain that they became afterwards allied by marriage, and the punning allusion to what was implied in the slight change of *Care I* into *Care you* will be remembered by every reader of Prince's Worthies.

As the chief object of the following pages is to trace the descent of a particular branch of the Cary family, it has not been thought necessary to go further back than to the ancestor, in the date of whose death we find a convenient starting-point. Sir William Cary, who heads the Pedigree, espoused the cause of the House of Lancaster, and fought in its behalf at the battle of Tewkes-

bury. He is by some accounts said to have been slain in the
fight, but by others to have been taken prisoner and beheaded
immediately afterwards.   He was twice married; by his first wife
he became ancestor to the Carys, formerly of Cockington, and
now of Torr Abbey, co. Devon (one of whom was Treasurer and
afterwards Lord Deputy of Ireland in the reign of James I.), and
also of the Carys of Clovelly in the same county (the last of whom
was Edward Cary, Sub-dean of Exeter and Rector of Silverton,
who died about the year 1693).   Sir William Cary's second wife
was Alice, daughter of Sir Baldwin Fulford, knight, Sheriff of
Devon 38 Hen. VI. and Vice-Admiral of England.   By her he
had a son Thomas Cary, who is described in the Visitation pedigrees as of Chilton Foliot, co. Wilts.   I have not been able to
substantiate this statement; but it will be observed that in the
will of his son, Sir John Cary of Plashey, a reference is made to
ancestral property in Wiltshire.   There is some little doubt as to
the number of his children.   In the Visitation pedigrees six are
assigned to him; viz. Sir John of Plashey, William father of Lord
Hunsdon, a *second* William, Mary wife of Sir John Delaval, and
Margaret and Anne both unmarried.   It is possible that the
second William is identical with " Edward Cary de London,"
who was buried at Aldenham in 1567. (See Extracts from Parish
and other Registers, hereafter.)

The eldest son of Thomas Cary was John Cary, commonly
called Sir John Cary of Plashey, co. Essex, whose will I shall
give *in extenso*.   On the 21st July, 1536, he obtained from the
Crown a grant of the dissolved Priory of Thremhall, co. Essex,
being at that time married to Joyce, widow of William Walsingham (and by him mother of Sir Francis, the statesman), and
daughter of Sir Edmund Denny. (Patent Rolls.)   He was
knighted on the 22 Feb. 1546-7, two days after the coronation
of Edward VI., and was buried at Hunsdon 8 Sept. 1551.
Whether Plashey was ever leased by him from the Crown seems
very doubtful; it is more probable that his connection with that
place was simply occasioned by residence.

His two children were, 1, Sir Wymond Cary, of Snettisham,
co. Norfolk (knighted 30 May, 1604,) who died without issue
13 April, 1612; and 2, Sir Edward Cary, of Aldenham and

Great Berkhamstead, co. Herts. Sir Edward enjoyed several offices of trust. He was a Groom of the Privy Chamber, Keeper of Marylebone Park, Master of the Jewel-house, &c., and in 1596 was knighted by Queen Elizabeth. His property must at one time have been very extensive; for, in addition to that which he inherited from his father, and held in right of his wife, he obtained from the Crown a lease of Berkhamstead Castle in 1560, and, when the estates of Sir John Neville were confiscated, the Queen granted to him the manor of Hunslet, near Leeds. This was subsequently (10 Jac. I.) settled upon his second son Sir Philip Cary, who parted with it to the Fenton family. In 1588 he purchased the manor of Aldenham, which continued to be the chief residence of himself and his descendants until it was sold by Lucius, Viscount Falkland, in 1642. Sir Edward Cary died at his house in Great St. Bartholomew's, London, 18 July, 1618, and was buried at Aldenham on the 6th August following. By his wife Katharine, daughter of Sir Henry Knyvett, and widow of Henry, 2nd Baron Paget of Beaudesert, he had a numerous family.

The eldest son, Henry, was born at Aldenham, and educated at Exeter College, Oxford. He was created a Knight of the Bath in 1616, and made Comptroller of the Royal Household, and a Privy Councillor. On 10th of November he was elevated to the Peerage as Viscount Falkland of Fife in the kingdom of Scotland, and in 1622 was made Lord Deputy of Ireland. About the year 1610 he married Elizabeth, daughter and heiress of Chief Baron Tanfield; but his domestic life was from various causes an unhappy one. He seems to have been greatly deficient in ordinary prudence, and in spite of his ample fortune to have suffered continually from the pressure of monetary difficulties. In 1618 he sold the office of Master of the Jewel-house to Sir H. Mildmay, and he is also said to have prevailed upon his wife to mortgage the remainder of her jointure, by which act she so offended her father, that he disinherited both her and her husband, and settled his property on their eldest son Lucius.[1]

[1] For this fact and several particulars relating to Lady Falkland and her children, I am indebted to a recently published work, entitled "The Lady Falkland: her Life, from a MS. in the Imperial Archives at Lille." London: Dolman. 1861.

Another source of trouble was the change in his wife's religion, and her consequent separation from him and from her family. She, too, seems to have been involved in debt, and after she had become a Roman Catholic to have been a pensioner upon her husband's bounty, which was neither large nor punctually paid. Their children are all mentioned in the subjoined pedigrees, but in the Appendix to the Life of Lady Falkland, just cited, another son is recorded whose name is unknown, but who was called " Father Placid" after his entry into the Benedictine order. It is, however, not impossible that this son was Patrick Cary, who, as we shall see, assumed for a brief space the monastic habit· Lord Falkland died at Theobalds Park, aged 37, and was buried at Aldenham 25 Sept. 1633. He was succeeded by his eldest son Lucius, who was born at Burford about the year 1610.

The brief but brilliant part which this great nobleman played belongs rather to the pen of the biographer than to that of the genealogist. It will be sufficient to mention that he was sometime M.P. for Newport and a Secretary of State to Charles I. He was with the King at Edgehill and at the siege of Gloucester, and fell fighting in the first rank of Lord Byron's regiment at the battle of Newbury, 20 Sept. 1643. He was buried in the church of Great Tew, co. Oxford, but no monument marks his last resting-place; and the manor of Great Tew, which came to him from his maternal grandfather, has long passed away from the Cary family. Lady Falkland survived her husband, and died in 1647, leaving behind her a just reputation for virtue and piety.[1]

The successor to the title was Lucius, eldest son of the great Viscount, whose existence has been altogether ignored by the Peerage writers. He died at Montpelier, in France, in 1649, at the early age of 17; and was succeeded by his brother Henry, as fourth Viscount Falkland, who seems to have inherited some of the talents of his father and grandfather. Like the former, he identified himself closely with the royal cause, and was impri-

[1] See a curious little tract, entitled " The Vertuous, Holy, Christian Life and Death of the late Lady Lettice, Viscountess Falkland." London. R. Royston. 1653. Written in a letter to her mother, the Lady Morison, at Great Tew, in Oxon, 15 April, 1647.

soned during the usurpation on the charge of having taken part in Sir George Booth's rising. After the Restoration he repre-sented Arundel in Parliament, and was Lord Lieutenant of Ox-fordshire till his death in 1663.

His only son Sir Anthony Cary was his successor in the title and estates. He was clever enough to preserve his influence un-impaired in the difficult times of the Revolution, and, after having been Paymaster of the Forces under King James, became a Privy Councillor and a Commissioner of Admiralty under King William. His reputation, however, was injured by a charge of something like peculation, upon which he was committed to the Tower. He died, perhaps in consequence, soon afterwards; and, having no surviving issue, the title passed to his second-cousin Lucius Henry Cary, who succeeded in 1694 as sixth Viscount Falkland.

His place in the Pedigree will be found in direct descent from Patrick Cary, the youngest son of the first Peer. This Patrick Cary was born in Ireland during the viceroyalty of his father, and was brought up by his mother as a Roman Catholic. On this account his fortunes seem to have greatly suffered, and it is very difficult to follow him throughout his chequered career. He was probably educated abroad, and at any rate we find him in 1650 at Brussels writing to Sir Edw. Hyde in great distress. (Claren-don's State Papers, ii. 535.) After this he entered a monastery at Douay; but, the life not suiting his constitution, quitted it within the year. He then came to England in the hope of ob-taining a pension from his relatives there. It seems probable that he resided at this time with his sister Victoria, wife of Sir William Uvedale, in Hampshire, for he dates a small volume of " Trivial Poems " (edited by Sir Walter Scott in 1819) from Warnford in that county, 20 Aug. 1651, and states that they were written in obedience to the commands of Mr. Tomkins. This lady was, I suspect, a daughter of Sir Will. Uvedale by his *first* wife, Anne, daughter of Sir Edmund Cary, third son of Henry, Lord Huns-don. We may also conjecture that it was while staying in this neighbourhood he became acquainted with Sir William's niece, Susan Uvedale, whom he must have married at least as early as 1652. I have not been able to ascertain the date of his death, but it must have occurred before September 1685. (See Will of John Cary of Stanwell, p. 29.)

The lives of his children are involved in the same obscurity which surrounds his own career, and all the printed Peerages are equally silent about them and himself. Perhaps "Mrs. Faith Cary," who was buried at Wykeham, co. Hants, in 1652, was an infant daughter; and there is some reason to believe that the son, John Cary, whose birth and baptism took place at Great Tew, died young and without issue.

The only son of whom we know anything is Edward Cary,[1] who was resident in the parish of St. James Westminster in 1687; inherited property under the will of his cousin John Cary of Stanwell; and died in Westminster in 1692. He married his cousin Anne daughter and coheir of Charles Lord Lucas, and had an only son Lucius Henry, who succeeded to the title upon the death of Anthony 5th Viscount. All the Peerages which I have been able to consult make this Lucius Henry a *son* of Anthony; and Debrett, with a certain sort of consistency, omits in his account of the arms of the present peer all notice of the Lucas quartering.

It is not necessary to trace the further descent of the title, which has been in almost regular succession since the death of the 6th Viscount in 1730. Some few particulars, which are not to be found in the printed Peerages, are given in the subjoined Pedigrees. I can scarcely hope that they are free from error, though I may take this opportunity of recording that I have had the advantage, in their compilation, of the valuable assistance of G. E. Adams, esq. Rouge Dragon, Colonel J. L. Chester, Robert Dymond, esq. of Exeter, Rev. W. M. H. Church, and the incumbents of the parishes of Great Tew, Plashey, and Hunsdon.

C. J. ROBINSON.

Great Berkhamstead.

---

[1] He was probably identical with Edward Cary, of Ch. Ch. Oxford, whose matriculation entry is thus expressed :—

"1673. Jun. 27. Edwardus Cary, a.n. 17. Patric. C. Dubliniens. Hib. Gen." He would thus have been born about the year 1656.

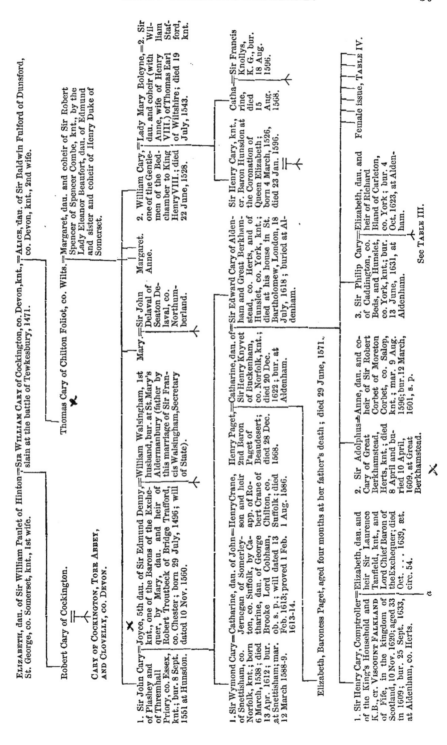

ELIZABETH, dau. of Sir William Paulet of Hinton = SIR WILLIAM CARY of Cockington, co. Devon, knt. = ALICE, dau. of Sir Baldwin Fulford of Dunsford, St. George, co. Somerset, knt., 1st wife. | slain at the battle of Tewkesbury, 1471. | co. Devon, knt., 2nd wife.

Thomas Cary of Chilton Foliot, co. Wilts. = Margaret, dau. and coheir of Sir Robert Spencer of Spencer Combe, knt., by the Lady Eleanor Beaufort, dau. of Edmund and sister and coheir of Henry Duke of Somerset.

Robert Cary of Cockington.

CARY OF COCKINGTON, TORR ABBEY, AND CLOVELLY, CO. DEVON.

2. William Cary, one of the Gentlemen of the Bedchamber to King Henry VIII.; died 22 June, 1528. = Lady Mary Boleyne, = 2. Sir William Stafford, knt. — dau. and coheir (with Anne, wife of Henry VIII.) of Thomas Earl of Wiltshire; died 19 July, 1543.

Margaret. Anne.

Mary = Sir John Delaval of Seaton Delaval, co. Northumberland.

Sir Henry Cary, knt., cr. Baron Hunsdon at the Coronation of Queen Elizabeth; born 4 March, 1526, died 23 Jan. 1596. = Catharine = Sir Francis Knollys, K.G., bur. 18 Aug. 1596. — rine, died 15 Aug. 1568.

1. Sir John Cary of Plashey and Thremhall Priory, co. Essex, knt.; bur. 8 Sept. 1561 at Hunsdon. = Joyce, 5th dau. of Sir Edmund Denny knt., one of the Barons of the Exchequer, by Mary, dau. and heir of Robert Troutbeck of Bridge Trafford, co. Chester; born 29 July, 1496; will dated 10 Nov. 1560. = William Walsingham, 1st husband, bur. at St. Mary's Aldermanbury (father by this marriage of Sir Francis Walsingham, Secretary of State).

Sir Edward Cary of Aldenham and Great Berkhamstead, co. Herts., and of Hunslet, co. York, knt.; died at his house in St. Bartholomew, London, 18 July, 1618; buried at Aldenham. = Catharine, dau. of Sir Henry Knyvet of Buckenham, co. Norfolk, knt.; died 28 Dec. 1622; bur. at Aldenham.

1. Sir Wymond Cary, of Snettisham, co. Norfolk, knt.; born 6 March, 1538; died 13 Apr. 1612; bur. at Snettisham; mar. 12 March 1588-9. = Catharine, dau. of John Jernegan of Somerleyton, co. Suffolk, dau. of George Brooke Lord Cobham, ob. s. p.; will dated 13 Feb. 1613; proved 1 Feb. 1613-14. = Henry Crane, son and heir app. of Robert Crane of Chilton, co. Suffolk; died 1 Aug. 1586.

Henry Paget, 2nd Baron Paget of Beaudesert; died 28 Dec. 1568.

Elizabeth, Baroness Paget, aged four months at her father's death; died 29 June, 1571.

1. Sir Henry Cary, Comptroller of the King's Household and K.B., cr. VISCOUNT FALKLAND of Fife, in the kingdom of Scotland, 10 Nov. 1620; aged 33 in 1609; bur. 25 Sept. 1633, at Aldenham, co. Herts. = Elizabeth, dau. and heir Sir Laurence Tanfield, knt., and Lord Chief Baron of the Exchequer; died Oct. . . . 1639, æt. circ. 54.

2. Sir Adolphus Cary of Great Berkhamstead, Herts, knt.; died 8 April and buried 10 April, 1609, at Great Berkhamstead. = Anne, dau. and coheir of Sir Robert Corbet of Moreton Corbet, co. Salop, knt.; mar. 9 Aug. 1596; bur. 12 March, 1601, s. p.

3. Sir Philip Cary of Caddington, co. Beds, and Hunslet, co. York, knt.; bur. 13 June, 1631, at Aldenham. = Elizabeth, dau. and heir of Richard Bland of Carleton, co. York; bur. 4 Oct. 1623, at Aldenham.

Female issue, TABLE IV.

See TABLE III.

TABLE I.—*continued.*

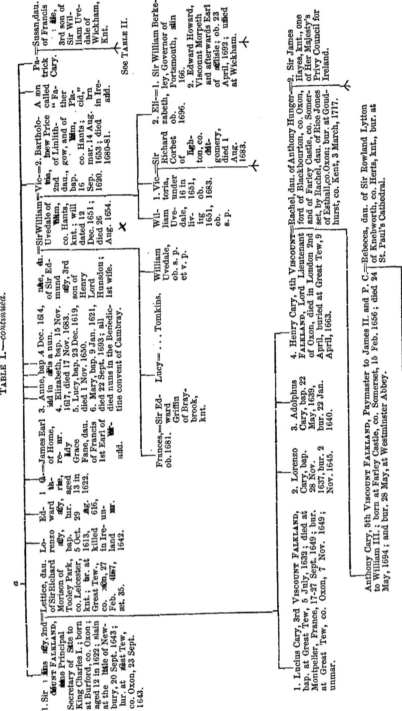

TABLE II.

Hon. PATRICK CARY, sometime a monk at Douay;=SUSAN, dau. of Francis Uvedale, 3rd son of Sir William Uvedale of Wickham, born in Ireland circa 1622 ; living in 1651. | co. Hants, knt.

John Cary, born at Great Tew, 30 Oct., bap. 2 Nov. 1654.

Edward Cary, of St. James's=Anne, dau. and coheir of Charles=2. Lord Archibald Hamilton (son of Anne Duchess of Ha-
Westminster, succeeded to Cal- | Lord Lucas of Shenfield by Pene- | milton by Lord William Douglas), Governor of Jamaica, &c.;
dicote under the will of John | lope, dau. of Francis Leke, Earl of | remar. and had issue; bap. 17 Feb. 1673; died 5 April, 1754,
Cary of Stanwell; adm. granted | Scarsdale ; will dat. 30 April, 1708, | aged 87; bur. at Taplow.
24 Nov. 1692. | prov. 15 Feb. 1710. (See TABLE IV.)

Frances, mar.=John Villiers Viscount
Feb. 1705-6, | Grandison, cr. Earl Gran-
died 17 Jan. | dison of Limerick, in Ire-
1768, bur. at | land, 11 Sept. 1721; died
Yonghal. | 14 May, 1766, aged 85, and
| bur. at Yonghal.

2. Laura, dau. of Lt.-Genl. Arthur=Lucius Henry Cary, 6th VISCOUNT=1. Dorothy, dau. of Francis
Dillon, Governor of Toulon, and | FALKLAND, born 27 Aug. and bap. | Molineux of St. Gregory
sister of Charles and Henry Vis- | 7 Sep. 1687, at St. James's West- | by St. Paul's par. London,
counts Dillon ; died 12 July, 1741, | minster; died 31 Dec. 1730; bur. in | woollen draper, by Mary,
at St. Germain-en-laye. | church of St. Sulpice, Paris. | dau. of Charles Tancred of
| Whixley, co. York; mar.
| 5 Oct. 1704, bur. 2 July,
| 1722.

Other issue.

James Fitzgerald
Lord Villiers,
eldest son of
John Earl
Grandison ; died
before his father,
12 Dec. 1732,
bur. 24 Dec. at
Hertford.

Lt.-Genl. Comte de Rothe, Colonel in the=Lucy Cary, died 7 Feb. 1804,
service of the King of France. | in Somerset Street, London.

Henry How-=2. Sarah, dau. and=Lucius Charles=1. Jane, dau. and
ard,10th Earl | heir of Thomas | Cary, 7th Vis- | heir of Richard
of Suffolk, | Inwen of South- | COUNT FALK- | Butler of London,
died at And- | wark, co. Surrey, | LAND, died 27 | conveyancer,
ley End, co. | M.P. ; mr. Vis- | Feb. 1785. | mar. Viscount
Essex, 22 | count Falk- | | Falkland 6 April,
April, 1745, | land, 10 | | 1734, died in
æt. 39, | Oct. 1752; died 27 | | France, Dec.
et s. p. s. | May, 1776; bur. | | 1751.
| at Ward, co. |
| Essex. |

George Cary,=Isabella,
of Leven | dau. and
Grove and | heir of Ar-
Scouters- | thur In-
kelfe, co. | gram of
York, a Ge- | Barraby,
neral in the | co. York,
Army, died | died 12
11 April, | April,
1792. | 1799.

Leeke
Cary,
died
at
Cadiz,
20
Mar.,
1729-30.

Henry
John
Cary,
bap.
21
Jan.
1716-7.

Frances,
bap. 12
Jan.,
bur.
14 Jan.
1718-9.

Doro-
thy,
bur. 9
Feb.
1719-20.

Lucius Ferdinand=Anne,
der-in- | dau.
chief of | of
Her Majesty's | Knel
Forces in Tobago, | Leith.
died 20 Aug.,
1780; grandfather
of the present
(10th) VISCOUNT
FALKLAND.

2. Jane,
born
1736.

6. Char-=Anthony
lotte. | Chap-
| man.

3. Mary = John Law,
Elizabeth, | D.D.,
born 1738; | deacon of
died 1 Oct. | Rochester
1783, aged | and Rec-
44; buried | tor of
at Brox- | Westmill,
bourne. | co. Herts,
| died 5 Feb.
| 1827, aged
| 88.

4. Frances.
5. Mary.

Arthur
Cary.
Isabella.
Mary, | died
| young.

Eliza=Jeffrey Am-=1. Jane,
beth, | herst, cr. | only
mr. | Baron Am- | dau.
26 | herst of | of Tho-
Dec. | Montreal, | mas Da-
1767, | co. Kent, | son, of
died | a Field Mar- | Ep-
22 | shal and | soms, co.
May, | Comman- | York,
1830; | der-in- | died 12
2nd | Chief, died | April,
wife. | 3 Aug. 1797. | 1799.

Catha-=Sir John Rus-
rine, | sell of Check-
mar. | ers, co. Bucks
25 Oct. | and Chippen-
1775, | ham, co. Cam-
died 26 | bridge, Bart.;
Dec. | born 31 Oct.
1780, | 1741, died 7
aged 34. | Aug. 1785.

Sir John Russell, Bart., | Sir George Russell, Bart.,
died 1802 unmar. | died 25 April, 1804, s. p.

TABLE III.

SIR PHILIP CARY.═ELIZABETH, dau. of Richard Bland.

Muriel, ett an., bap. 3 May, 1610, bur. 9 Dec., 1611.

2. Elizabeth, dau. of Sir Richard Wilbraham, Bart. 3. Anne, widow of Richard Moreton, Esq. 4. Magdalen, dau. of Sir John Corbet, Bart.

2. Eliza-beth, bap. 1 Sep. 1611; 1st wife.

Sir Humphrey═Brigges of Haughton, co. Salop, Knt. and Bart., died 1691.

Edward, died young.

Other issue.

Anne, died young.

James Bertie, of Westminster, 2nd son of James, 1st Earl of Abingdon, born 18 March, 1673, died . . . 1734.

William, Governor of the Ar-nee . . . his; suc-ceeded in 1666 as 6th Baron Willoughby of Parham; died at Bar-ham; bur. at Knaith, co.

Moreton, died young.

Elizabeth, dau. and coheir of Henry Flennes alias Clinton, mar. 9 Oct., 1666.

Other issue.

3. Anne, bap. 20 Jun p 1615, bur. 12 Jan, 1671, at Alden-ham.

Elizabeth, sole eventual heir of this branch of the Cary family, car-ried Stanwell to the Berties; born 29 April, 1673; mar. 5 Jan. 1691-2; died 26 Sept. and bur. 2 Oct. 1715, at Stanwell as aforesaid.

4. Phi-lip, bap. 7 Oct. 1623, bur. 6 July, 1624.

Willoughby Bertie, 3rd Earl of Abingdon.

Other issue.

3. Ed-Cary, born ante 1592, bur. 10 Feb. 1639-40, s. p.

George Willoughby, 7th Baron Willoughby of Parham; born at Belvoir Castle, co. Lincoln, 18 March, 1638; died 1674, and bur. at Knaith.

1. and heir of Sir Montagne, Knt., and wi-dow of Sir Ed-ward Baesh of Stansted, Knt., (see IV.) bur. 29 Dec. 1657.

John Cary═of Stan-well, co. Mid-

Catha-rine,* dau. of Mer of the Buck-hounds, bap. 23 Dec. 1612.

John Willoughby, 8th Baron Willoughby, born 16 July, 1669; bur. . . . 1677, at Stanwell, s. p.

2. Adol-phus Cary, bap. 5 Jan. 1613-4, bur. 9 May, 1625.

* The name of this lady has not been discovered, but we find that by a deed dated 1 Aug. 1673, she gave 100l. to be distri-buted among six poor widows at Windsor. (Ashmole's Berks, iii. 105).

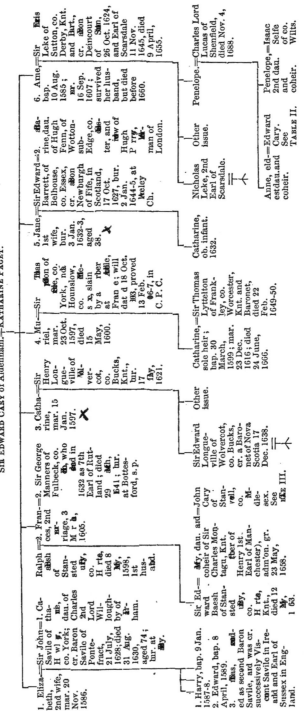

TABLE IV.

FEMALE ISSUE OF
Sir Edward Cary of Aldenham.=Katharine Paget.

EXTRACTS FROM PARISH AND OTHER REGISTERS.

ALDENHAM, HERTS.

Marriages.

1597. Jan. 15. Mr. Henry Longvile, esq. and Mrs. Katherine Carye.

1605. Mar. 3. Sir George Manners, kn^t and Mrs. Frances Bashe, vidua.

Baptisms.

1599. Mar. 30. Katherine, the da. of Mr Thom. Crumpton, esq.

1604. Apr. 29. Edward ye son of the right worshipfull Sir Henrie Longvile, knight.

1610. May 3. Miriall, ye dau. of ye right worshipfull Sir Philip Carye, knight.

1620. Sep. 16. Vittoria, ye dau' of Mr. Carye.

1621. Jan. 9. Marye, ye da. of ye r^t ho^{ble} Henry Lord Carye, Viscount Falkland.

1637. Nov. 28. Lorenzo, son of the right honourable Lucius, Lord Falkland, and of the Lady Lettice his wife.

1639. May 22. Adolphus, son of Lucius, Lord Viscount Falkland, and the Lady Lettice his wife.

Burials.

1567. June 23. Edward Cary de London.

1599. May 16[1]. Mrs. Mirriall, wife of the right wor. Mr. Thomas Crumpton, esq.

1601. March 12. Anne the wife of the r^t wor. Mr. Adolphus Carey, esq.

1616. Aug. 26. Edward ye son of ye right worsh^{ll} Sir Henrie Carie, knight.

1618. Aug. 6. Sir Edward Carye, knight.

1622. Dec. 22. The right ho^{ble} Lady Katherine Paget.

1623. Oct. 4. The Ladye Elizabeth, ye wife of the right wor^{ll} Sir Philippe Carye, knight.

1624. July 8. Philippe, ye so. of the right wor^{ll} Sir Philippe Carey, knight.

1625. May 9. Adolphus, ye so. of the right worshipfull Sir Philippe Carye, knight.

---

[1] It will be observed that the M. I. at Aldenham (Clutterbuck's Herts.) states May 16, 1600, to have been the date.

1631. June 16. The right wor[ll] Sir Philippe Cary.

1633. Sep. 25. The right hon[ble] Henry, Lord Cary, Viscount Falkland.

1639. Feb. 10. Mr. Edward Carey, gent.

1640. Jan. 22. Mr. Adolphus, son to the r[t] hon. L[d] Visc[t] Falkland.

1671. Jan[y] 12. Anne, the wife of the right ho[ble] the Lord Weloby of Param, buryed in the valte of the Lord Cary, Viscount Falkland.

AVELEY, ESSEX.

Burial.

1643-4. Jan. 2. Edward Barrett, Lord Newburgh, vir sanctissimus.

GREAT BERKHAMSTEAD, HERTS.

Marriages.

1586. Nov. 20. Jhon Savell, esq[r] and M[rs] Eliz[th] Carye.

1596. Aug. 9. M[r] Adulphus Carey and M[rs] Anne Corbett.

1597. Oct. 23. Thomas Crumpton, gent. and Meriall Carie.

1607. Sep. 16. Francys Leake, knyght, and Mrs. Anne Carey.

Baptisms.

1585. Aug. 10. Anne, dau. of y[e] r[t] worshippful Edwarde Carye, esq.

1587-8. Jan. 9. Harrye, son of y[e] r[t] wors. Jhon Saville, esq.

1589. April 8. Edwarde, son of y[e] r[t] wors. Jhon Saville, esq.

1609. Aug. 15. Francis, son of S[r] Fra. Leake, knt.

1611. Sept. 1. Elizabeth, dau. of r[t] wo[r]pf. Sir Philip Carye, knt.

1613. Oct. 5. Lorenzo, y[e] sonne of Sir Henry Carye, knighte.

1614. Dec. 4. Anne, dau. of S[r] Henry Carye, knighte.

Burials.

1609. Apr. 10. Sir Adolphus Carye, knighte, a most loving benefactour to y[e] poore of this towne.

1610. Oct. 29. Ursula, y[e] dau. of y[e] Ladye Scroope.

1611. Dec. 9. Mrs. Meryall Carye, d[r] of Sr Philip Carye, knt.

BURFORD.

The Registers of this parish do not commence before 1612.

THE BENEDICTINE CONVENT AT CAMBRAY.

Receptions.

1638. Aug. 31. Hon. Lucy Cary, æt. 19, in religion Magdalena, and her sister Mary, æt. 17, daughters of the r[t] hon. Harry Cary, Viscount Falkland, sometime Viceroy of Ireland.

1638. Oct. 29. Elizabeth Cary, in religion Augustina, æt. 21, dau. of Visc^t Falkland.

1639. Mar. 8. Anne Cary, æt. 24, in religion Clementina, dau. of Viscount Falkland.

Obituary of the Nuns.

1650. Nov. 1. Lucy Magdalen Cary, dau. of Lord Viscount Falkland, sometime Viceroy of Ireland, died.

1683 Nov. 17. Elizabeth Cary, died.

1693. Sept. 22. Mary Cary, died.

CHARLTON, KENT.

1752. Oct. 10. The rt. hon. Lucius Charles, Lord Viscount Falkland, and the rt. hon. Sarah Countess of Suffolk, married at Morden College.

CHISWICK, MIDDLESEX.

1704. Oct. 5. Rt. Hon. Lucius Henry Lord Falkland, of St. James, Westm^r, singleman, and Mad. Dorothee Molyneux, of St. Gregory's, London, singlewoman, married by Licence.

HUNSDON, HERTFORDSHIRE.

Burial.

Anno D'ni 1551. Sr John Cary, knight, was buried the viijth of September, 1551, predict'.

GREAT ST. BARTHOLOMEW'S, LONDON.

Marriage.

1616. Dec. 23. Thomas Littleton de Franckley, co. Worc. esq. and Katherine, dau. of Thomas Crompton, knt.

Baptisms.

1617. Nov. 15. Elisabeth, dau. of Sir Henry Carey.

1619. Dec. 23. Lucie, the dau. of Sir Henry Carey, Viscount Falkland, Controller of the King's Majesty's household and one of his Privy Council, and of Elizabeth his wife.

Burials.

1616-7. Feb. 1. John Pearcivall, servant to Sir Henry Cary.

1618-9. Feb. 22. William, servant to Sir Henry Carey, knt.

St. Benet's, Paul's Wharf.

Marriages.

1653. Aug. 14. Bartholomew Price and Victoria Huvedall (*sic*).

1659. Dec. 13. Patrick Carey [1] and Dorothy . . . . . .

St. Giles, Cripplegate.

Marriage.

1588-9. March 12. Wymond Carey, gent., and Katherine Crane, gent., by Licence.

Gray's Inn Admissions.

1590. Aug. 2. Henry Carey, son and heir of Edward Carey, of Barcomstead, co. Herts, esq.

1590. Aug. 9. Adolph Carey, 2nd son of do.

  ,,   ,,   Philip Carey, 3rd son of do.

St. Olave's, Silver Street.

Baptisms.

1612. Dec. 23. John, son of Sir Philip Carey.

1613-4. Jan. 5. Rudolphus (*sic*), son of same.

1615. June 10. Ann, daughter of Sir Philip Carew (*sic*).

1618. Aug. 10. Edward, son of Sir Philip Carey and Elizabeth his wife.

1623. Oct. 23. Philip, son of Sir Philip Carey and Elizabeth.

1629. Oct. 4. Mary, daughter of Edmund Carey and Mary.

Burials.

1617. June 14. A chrisom of Sir Philip Carew's (*sic*).

1634. Dec. 23. Edward Carey.

1636. July 8. Edmond Carey.

St. Pancras.

Burial.

1762. Apr. 6. The hon[ble] Mrs. Cary. see p. 146

St. Peter le Poor.

Baptism.

1683. July 24. Harriott Cary, dau. of Anthony Lord Viscount Falkland and dame Rebekah his wife.

Burial.

1683. Oct. 21. Harriette, dau. of the right honnerable the Lord Falkland.

[1] This Patrick Carey married apparently Dorothy Ling, and died in 1669, leaving issue. From his will which is at C. P. C. (Coke 82), we gather that he was an Irishman, but resident in the parish of St Andrew's, Holborn, London. He does not seem to have been connected with Lord Falkland's family.

St. Paul's Cathedral.

The Register of St. Paul's is of modern date, but there can be no doubt from the following passage in the will of Francis Raynsford (dat. 22 Apr. 1712), that the widow of Anthony, 5th Viscount Falkland, was buried in the Cathedral,—" to be buried in St. Paul's Cathedral near my very good friend Rebecca, Lady Vicountess Falkland, to whom my wife was executrix."

Stanwell, Middlesex.

Baptisms.

1716-17. Jan. 21. Henry John, son of the r^t hon. Lucius Henry, Ld Visc^t Falkland.

1718-19. Jan. 12. Frances, daughter   do.   do.   do.

Burials.

1657. Dec. 24. Dame Mary, wife of John Cary, esq.

1673. Sep. 1. The Lady Katherine, wife of the hon. John Cary, esq.

1718-19. Jan. 14. Frances, dau. of r^t hon. Lucius Henry Lord Falkland.

1719-20. Feb. 9. Dorothy Cary, dau. of Lucius Henry Lord Falkland.

1722. July 2. Lady Dorothy, wife of the hon. Lord Falkland.

Great Tew, co. Oxon.

Baptisms.

1632. July 5. Lucius, the son of the Honble Sir Lucius Cary, knight.

1654. John Cary, son of the hon^{ble} Patricke Cary, Esq., was born at Great Tew, October the 30th, and was baptized there November the 2nd.

1656. Anthony Cary, the son and heir of the right hon^{ble} Harry Lord Viscount of Falkland, Lord of the Manor of Great Tew, was born at Farley Castle the 15th of February, and baptized the 26th of the same month.

Burials.

1643. Sep. 23. The Right hon^{ble} Sr Lucius Cary, Knyght, Lord Viscount of Falkland, and Lord of the Manor of Great Tew.

1643. Nov. 2. Mr. Lorenzo Cary, son to the right hon^{ble} Lettice Viscountess of Falkland.

1646-7. Feb. 27. The right hon^{ble} Lettice, Viscountess of Falkland.

1649. The right hon^{ble} Lucius Cary, Lord Viscount Falkland, departed this life at Montpellier, in France, in the county of Languedoc, the $\frac{17}{27}$ day of September, Dr. John Maplett, his tutor, and Mr. George Neale, his servant, both them with him when he died.

(Signed)   John Maplett.

George Neale.

The said Lucius, Lord Viscount of Falkland, was buried at Great Tew, in the county of Oxon, the 7th day of November, 1649, being Lord of the manor there.

1663. The right hon^{ble} Harry Lord Viscount of Falkland, lord of the manor of Great Tew, departed this life at London on April 2, was buried at Great Tew April 9, 1663. Lord Lieutenant of this county.

WESTMINSTER ABBEY.

Burial.

1694. May 28. The Ld Falkland.

St. James's, Westminster.

Baptisms.

1687. Sep. 7. Lucius Henry Cary, son of Edward and Ann, born 27 August.

[handwritten] Wolverton, in Bucks, see p. 146

Wykeham, Hampshire.

Burials.

1652. Dec. 3. Sr W. Uvedale miles sepult. fuit tertio die Decemb.

„   Aug. 7. Mrs. Faith Carey sepulta fuit septimo die Augusti.

[handwritten] see also p. 146

Inquisition taken by the Escheator of the County of Devon in 4 Edw. IV.
on the Attainder of Sir William Cary.[1]

Inquisitio capta apud Plumpton Comitis in com. Devon. duodecimo die Octobris anno Edw. IV. quinto, coram Joh'e Fortescue, Esceatore ejusdem d'ni Regis in com. predicto, virtute officii sui, per sacramentum

---

[1] From an old copy in the possession of Robert Dymond, esq. of Exeter. The following draft of a letter on its back, from a young man in miserable plight to his mother, begging for a remittance of money, is so curious as to claim preservation.

Ry3th rev'end and worshypfull' moder, as lowly as a chyld' cane or may vn to hys moder y recomēd' me vn to yo^u, byshechyng yo^u of yor blessyng', desyryng' hartely to hyr' of yor wellfar'. yf ytt lyke yoⁿ to hyr' of my wellfar', att ye makyng of y^s byll y was nott yn good bodly helth thākynd' ſo God off all: furdermor' p^ayng yo^u of yor god' moderhed' for to helpe me nowe att my ned' for to send me sū mony for to pay my fesysione, for yn god' feyth y have sped all' that I had & all' y^t my fader left for to fynd me tyll he came agayne vn to ye fesyc'on all yet he wyll' have mor' or he wyll nott make no lēger hed' to me. y wode fayne speke to my broder for sū mony, save y darnott tell hym y^t y wes syke, & for exchevyng' of . . . ytt, y ly nott w^t hyme, for y ly in tone. allso [y] pray of yo^u to send me a payr of schetes, for y grett ned' for ye good wyfe ther as y ly doth lend' me non.

Jur' &c. Qui dicunt super sacramentum suum quod Willielmus Cary
miles alias dictus Will's Caree miles, qui auctoritate cujusdam actus
parliamenti editi vicesimo primo die Januarij anno quarto regni d'ni
Regis nunc in parliamento tunc apud Westm' existent' vicesimo nono
die Aprilis anno tercio regni Regis predicti inchoato et per diversa
adjornamenta usque dictum vicesimum primum diem Januarii continent' (sic), de alta proditione attinctus est, et fuit seisitus in dominico
suo ut de feodo de maneriis de Northlow, Holewey, Halghewelle,
Hygheheamton juxta Shepewasshe, Cary Lutterford, et de Wrey alias
dict' Wreycombe, cum eorum pertinentiis, in com' predicto, Necnon de
duobus messuagiis et xl acris terræ cum pertinentiis in Shepewasshe in
com' predicto Ac de xl solidatis annui redditus exeunt' de uno mesuagio et
centum acris terræ cum pertin' in Monkeoakhampton in com' predicto Ac
de uno mesuagio et xl acris terræ cum pertin' in Chageford in com' predicto Ac de duobus mesuagiis et xx acris terræ cum pertin' in Beworthy
in eodem com' Ac de uno mesuagio et quinque acris terræ cum pertin' in
Domeslonde in eodem com' Ac de uno mesuagio et iiij^{or} acris terræ cum
pertin' in Wygdon in com' predicto. Et sic inde seisitus vicesimo die Julii
anno regni d'ni Regis nunc quarto de eisdem maneriis, terris, tenemen-
tis et redditibus cum eorum pertin' feoffavit Will'm Paulet militem,
Joh'em Cheyne, Joh'em Byknelle, Joh'em Chilston, et Joh'em More,
habend' et tenend' eis et heredibus suis imperpetuum ad usum et proficuum predicti Will'i Cary et heredum suorum. Virtute cujus feoffamenti iidem Will's Paulet, &c. fuerunt inde seisiti in dominico suo ut de
feodo ad usum et proficuum dicti W. C. et hered. suorum, et statum
suum predictum continuaverunt ad usum et proficuum ejusdem W. C.
et hered. suorum a tempore feoffamenti usque ad primum diem Octobris
dicto anno quarto et eodem die et continue possederunt ad tempus
captionis hujusmodi Inquisitionis. Dicunt ulterius Juratores predicti
quod Christina quæ fuit uxor Philippi Cary patris predicti W. C. tenuit
dicto prius die Octobris in dotem de hereditate predicti Willielmi Cary
ex dotacione Philippi predicti unum mesuagium CCC acris terræ C
acris bosci quadraginta acris prati et C acris bruer' cum pertin' in
Cockington com' predicto reversione inde post mortem dictæ Christinæ
prefato Will'o Cary et hered' suis dicto primo die Octobris spectante.
Et ulterius dicunt Juratores predicti quod dictus Will'us Cary fuit
seisitus in dominico suo ut de feodo vicesimo die Julij dicto anno quarte
de quinque mesuagiis, CCC acris terræ, xl acris prati, et CC acris pas-
turæ in Chilston in com' predicto. Et sic inde seisitus inde feoffavit
predictos Will'um Paulet (&c. ut prius) quod ipsi sic inde feoffati de

exitibus &c. solverent seu solvi facient Joh'i More jun. x li. et xxvj li.
Will'o Assheford in quibus idem W. C. sibi indebitatus fuit. Et dicunt
quod ijdem feoffati ante captionem hujus Inquisitionis solverant prefato
J. M. xvij li. (sic) parcell' dict' x li. et prefato W. A. x li. in partem
solutionis dict' xxvj li. de exitibus &c. Et ulterius dicunt quod Bald-
wynus Fulford miles fuit seisitus in dominico suo ut de feodo de Ma-
nerio de Asshebury in com' predicto ante dictum primum diem Octobris,
et sic inde seisitus idem manerium ante eundem primum diem Octobris
per quandam cartam Juratoribus predictis ostentam tradidit et dimisit
prefato Will'o Cary et Aliciæ ux' ejus et hered' de corpore dictæ Aliciæ
legitime procreatis ; virtute quarum traditionis et dimissionis ipsi W. et
A. fuere inde seisiti, Videlicet ipse W. in dominico suo ut de libero
tenemento, et ipsa A. in dominico suo ut de feodo talliato, et eorum
statum inde predictum continuaverunt &c. usque [diem] captionis
hujus Inquisitionis. Quod quidem manerium de A. valet per annum
ultra reprisas x marcas. Et dicunt quod predicta maneria &c. unde
dictus W. C. feoffavit W. P. &c. una cum dictis quinque acris &c. &c.
in Chilston valent per annum &c. lxvj li. Et quod prefata mesuagium &c.
in Cokyngton valent per annum xl marcas. Et ulterius dicunt quod
Will'us Paulet miles omnia exitus &c. excepto predicto mesuag' &c.
in Cockynton percepit et habuit a tempore feoffamenti &c. usque diem
captionis hujus Inquisitionis. Et dicunt quod omnia predicta Maneria
&c. ad prefatum dominum Regem pertinere et devenire debent ratione
actus predicti. In cujus rei &c.

WILLS AND ADMINISTRATION ACTS.

Sir John Cary of Plashey, co. Essex, knight. In the name of
God Amen, the xx[th] day of August in the yere of o'r Lorde God a
thousande fyve hundreth fyftye and two and in the vj[th] yere of the
reigne of o'r Sou'aigne Lorde Kynge Edwarde the vj[th], I *John Cary*
of Hounesdon, in the countye of Hertford, knyght, having my wytte
and perfyte remembrance, make my testament and last will in this
maner: First I gyve my soule to Almyghtye God, willyng my body
to be buryed in the Church of Hounesdon. It' I will that Joyce my
wyfe shall have durying all her naturall lyfe the late dissolved Priorye
of Thremhall,[1] in the countye of Essex, with all his membres and app'-
ten'nces in what townes or countyes soever they lye, accordyng to the

---

[1] Bacon's Liber Regis, 1786. Archdeaconry of Colchester. Priory of Tremhale
was returned at 60*l*. 18*s*. 7½*d*. per annum.

Kings Maiestyes lettres patents to me and her thereof made, and all my mesuage and lands in Wryttyll in the sayd countye of Essex called Benet Ots, and all the lands whiche I have in the countyes of Som'set, Wilts, and Dorset, or ellswhere within the realme of England, towards the bryngeng up and fyndyng of Wymonde Cary and Edwarde Cary my ij sones duryng there nonages; excepte all those lands and ten'ts whyche I have in the towne of Pole, co. Dorset, called Whytslands, all that mesuage and lands bothe freholde and copyholde called Bonks lyeng in Byrchangre in Essex whyche I late purchased of Thom's Bennysshe, all that copyholde lande lyeng in the parysshe of Stansted Mountfichet in Essex whiche I late purchased of Henry Grave, and excepte that crofte of land lyeng in Takeley in the same countye whiche I late purchased of Nicholas Clerke. Nev'theless I will that the sayd Joyce my wife shall have all the sayd mesuage and lands before excepted called Bonks, and all the sayd lands before excepted whiche I p'chased of Henry Grave, and the sayd crofte of land before excepted whiche I bought of Nicholas Clerke, unto suche time as the sayd Wymonde Cary my son shall be of the full age of xxj yers if she shal so longe lyve, and whan the sayd Wymonde shal be of the full age of xxj yers then I will that he shal entre upon and have to hym and to his heires for ever all the sayd mesuage and lands before mencioned called Bonks, and all the sayd lands before mencioned whiche I p'chased of Henry Grave, and the sayd crofte of lande before mencioned whiche I purchased of Nich's Clerke. And in lyke maner I will that the sayd Joyce shall have all the sayd landes and ten'ts before excepted called Whytslands unto suche tyme as the sayd Edwarde Cary my son shall be of the full age of xxj yers yf she so longe lyve, and whan the sayde Edwarde shalbe of the full age of xxj yers, then I will that he shall entre upon and have to hym and his heires for ever all the sayd lands and ten'ts before mencioned called Whytslands. And aft' the decesse of the sayd Joyce I will that all the sayd late dissolv'd p'orye with all his membres and app'tennences shall holly remayne to the sayd Wymonde Cary my son and to his heires male for ever accordyng to the Kings Maiestyes lettres patents therof made, together with all my sayd lands and ten'ts lyeng in the countyes of Som'set, Wilts, and Dorset, whiche descended to me by enheritance aft' the dethe of Thom's Cary my father. And in lyke wyse I will that aft' the decesse of the sayd Joyce all the sayd mesuage and lands before mencioned called Benet Ots shall holly remayne to the sayde Edwarde my younger son and to his heirs for ever. And as concerning my chattels or moveable goods I will that my sayd wyfe shall have to her and to her assignees my lease of Halyfeld Hall and the resydue of my yers therin, and also my lesse of the parsonage of Stansted Abbot and all the resydue of my yers therin to her and to her assignees in lyke maner. It' I will that after the decesse of my sayd wyfe my newe basyn and ewer of sylver and my great cheyne of golde, and myn olde sygnet of golde with the swan whiche was my father's, shall remayne to the sayd Wymonde Cary my elder son. And also I will that aft' the decesse of my sayd wyfe my newe sygnet of golde with the swan shall remayn to the sayd Edwarde Cary my younger son. And all the resydue of my moveable goods not gyvyn and bequethed herebefore by this my last will, I do gyve and bequethe to my sayd wyfe to bryng up my ij sones, and to pay my detts if any be. And also I ordeyn and make the said Joyce my wyfe my sole executrice to se this my wyll fulfylled and p'formed; in all poynts accordyng to the trust that I putte to her. In witness wherof to this my testam'nt and last will I have putte my seale and sygne the day and yere first above wryten, in the p'sence of Thomas Sydney,[1] Esquyer, and Edmonde Stowell and others. (Extracted from the Registry of the Commissary Court of the Bishop of London for the parts of Essex and Herts, Chelmsford.)

Extracted from the Registry of the Prerogative Court of Canterbury, Doctors' Commons, London:

(Loftes 3.) *Dame Joyce Cary*, late of Thremhall, co. Essex, widow, and late wife of Sir John Carye, knt. deca. Dat. 10 Nov. 1560, prov. 30 Jan. 1560–1.

To be buried in parish church of Aldermanbury, in London, beside my late husband Walsingham. To each of my sons, sons in law, and to everye of my daughters a gowne of black clothe. To Francis Walsingham[2] my sonne a bason and a ewer of sylver which was hys father's and a bole of sylver g'lt without a cover, a goblet of silver gyllt with a cover or seller, and a tester of velvet with gold knottes, &c. To Wymonde Carye my sonne the newe bason and ewer of silver, &c. To Edwarde Carye my sonne a boole of sylver gyllt wi'out a cover, &c. To my daughters Wentworth,[3] Sydney,[4] and

[1] Probably Thomas Sidney, 2nd son of Nicholas Sidney, and great-uncle of Sir Philip Sidney (who married Frances Walsingham, granddaughter of William Walsingham, by Joyce Denny, afterwards wife of Sir John Cary).

[2] Sir Francis Walsingham, Secretary of State to Queen Elizabeth.

[3] Elizabeth Walsingham, married secondly Peter Wentworth, Esq.

[4] Barbara Walsingham, married Henry Sidney, Esq.

Tamworth,[1] to either of them a bracelet of gold; to my daughter Wentworth my gowne of satin; to my dau. Sydney my gowne of damaske; to my dau. Tamworthe my gowne of velvitt. Item, to my dau. Myldmaye[2] two candlesticks of silver; to Martha Myldmaye a salte of silver gilt whiche her father gave to me. Item, to Joyce Gates 6*l*. 13*s*. 4*d*. in reddye money to be delyvered to her by myne executours at her full age of xviii years, or els at the daye of her mariage, if she be married before her said age. My reddye money to be divided equally among my said sonnes Francis, Wymond, and Edward. Executours: My sonnes Sir Walter Mildmaye, knight, and Francis Walsingham, and my nephew Edmonde Danyell.

Signed.   JOYCE CARY.

Witnesses: Margaret Willington, widdow; Elizabeth Andrews, widdow; per me Thomam Sydney. Proved 30 Jan., 1560, by said Francis Walsingham and Edmond Danyell.

(Dorset 33.) *Sir Adolphe Carye, kt.* Dat. March 16, 1604-5, prov. April 14, 1609.

To my brother Sir Harry Cary, knt. those parsonages in Wales which are to descend upon me after the decease of my father as being in law the next heir unto me if I die without issue. To my sister Longfield (Longueville), my jewel of the fashion of a phœnix now in the custody of Mr. Pitt. To my sister Jane and Anne each 40*l*. in diamond rings. To John Darknoll my servant 60*l*. To Richard Speed 40*l*. To Angell Turner 20*l*. To Charles 10*l*. To the poor of Berkhamstead and Aldenham each 10*l*. To my brother Philip Carye my lease of parsonage of Clee, Lincolnshire, and my lease of Cardington, in co. Herts and Beds, with residue of all property, and appoint him sole ex'or. (He proved as Philip Carye, Knight.)

(To be Continued.)

[1] Christiana Walsingham, married first to John Tamworth, and secondly to William Doddington.

[2] Mary Walsingham, married Sir Walter Mildmay, K.G. and P.C. to Queen Elizabeth.

ERRATA.—In p. 35, line 23, *read* 10th Nov. 1620. In p. 37, line 31, *for* Mr. *read* Mrs. Tomkins. In p. 38, line 2, *for* p. 29, *read* p. 133 (hereafter). In the note, *for* a. n. 17, *read* an. 17. P. 40, Sir William Uvedale died in 1652, and was buried on the 3rd Dec. (see p. 49). The date 1654 in the pedigree belongs to the death of his contemporary Sir William Uvedale of Wickham, Hants. In p. 47, note, *for* "was an Irishman," *read* had debts and lands in Ireland, but was, &c. Page 48. The register of marriages at St. Paul's commences in 1697, that of burials not until 1760.

THE ENGLISH LADIES OF PONTOISE.

The town of Pontoise, situate about fifteen English miles west of Paris, takes its name from having grown up around the first bridge erected over the Oise (*Pons ad Isaram*), above the confluence of that river with the Seine.

A convent of English Benedictine Nuns fixed their residence in this town in the year 1658. The community was a filiation from the house of the same order at Ghent, as the latter had been from the abbey at Brussels. This offset had been first established in 1652 at Boulogne, whither six of the convent of Ghent were sent, one of whom appears to have been a lay sister.[1] The following account of their removal to Pontoise, is from a volume entitled "Récherches historiques, archéologiques, et biographiques sur la ville de Pontoise. Par M^r l'Abbé TROU. Pontoise, 1841," 8vo.

Louis XIV. délivra des lettres patentes pour autoriser Christine Forster, fille du Chevalier Richard Forster, Trésorier Général de la Reine Henriette Marie, Mère de Charles II. supérièure des Bénédictines Anglaises de Boulogne sur Mer, à venir s'établir à Pontoise. Touché de compassion, l'Abbé commendataire de St. Martin de Pontoise, Milord Montaigu,[2] leur compatriote, les avait determinées à faire

[1] "Notices of the English Colleges and Convents established on the Continent after the Dissolution of Religious Houses in England. By the late Hon. EDWARD PETRE. Edited by the Rev. F. C. HUSENBETH. Norwich, 1849." 4to.

[2] This was Walter Montagu, second son of Henry first Earl of Manchester, and brother to Lord Kimbolton, of Roundhead celebrity. Having become a convert to the Church of Rome, he entered a French monastery, and was promoted by Anne of Austria to be head of the Benedictine abbey of Nanteuil in the diocese of Meaux, and afterwards removed to that of Pontoise in the diocese of Rouen. He subsequently became Lord Almoner to Henrietta Maria the Queen Mother of England: who confided her youngest son Henry Duke of Gloucester to reside with him at Pontoise about the beginning of November, 1654, but the prince was shortly after summoned to Cologne by the King his brother, who sent the Marquis of Ormonde for him. The abbé Montagu died Feb. 5, 1677, and was buried in the Hospital of the Incurables at Paris. The abbé Trou adds, "Gautier de Montagu rétablit le culte de St. Gautier:" i.e. in his own abbey church of St. Martin at Pontoise, from whence the shrine of that saint has since been removed to the church of Nôtre Dame in the same town. See further of Walter Montagu in Collins's Peerage, Wood's Athenæ Oxonienses, Cooper's Athenæ

choix de notre ville pour leur demeure, se proposant de les aider. L'Archévêque de Rouen approuva leur établissement par un acte du 20 Mai, 1658.

Le Chevalier Forster fit les premiers frais de leur établissement.[1] Milord Charles Carington, père d'une des réligieuses, fut assassiné dans une maison de la Coutellerie par un de ses valets. On l'inhuma à S. Maclou.[2] Le frère du Comte de Bristol, Jean Digby,[3] qui avait

Cantabrigienses, and Granger's Biograph. History of England. There is a portrait of him, whole-length, in the title-page of one of his books, by Marshall.

When Henrietta Maria the Queen-Mother returned to France in 1661-2, taking with her the princess Henrietta her daughter, then affianced to the Duke of Orleans, "M. de Montagu, her grand almoner, abbot of St. Martin at Pontoise, earnestly besought her to do him the honour, before she proceeded to Paris, to alight at his abbatial residence, which he had superbly fitted up and prepared for the purpose. She acquiesced in his request, alighted, and stopped in his house, and found all things in excellent order. While she was surveying the rich pictures, the jewellery, the porcelain, and other embellishments, there was the sound of drums, trumpets, kettledrums, and presently appeared the King, the Queen, and Monsieur, who came to salute the Queen, and to express their joy at her happy arrival. The King and the Queen his consort conversed till night with the Queen of England ; and Monsieur fancied himself in paradise on seeing the Lady Henriette, whom he tenderly loved, and whom he regarded as his future wife, &c. &c. Gladly would he have passed the night thus ; but it grew late, and he was obliged to break off the conversation, and return with the King to the castle of St. Germain. Meanwhile M. de Montagu had prepared a supper of the most delicate viands and the most delicious wines that he could procure for the Queen and all her attendants." See further in the *Memoirs of Father Cyprien des Gamaches*, one of the Capuchins attached to the household of Queen Henrietta Maria, as translated and appended as a make-weight to *The Court and Times of Charles the First*, 2 vols. 8vo. 1848, at vol. ii. p. 42 ; also (less literally translated) in Miss Agnes Strickland's *Lives of the Queens of England*, edit. 1851, vol. v. p. 450.

[1] Sir Richard Forster of Stokesley in Yorkshire, Knt. was created a Baronet by patent dated at St. Germain's Sept. 18, 1649. He died at Paris Jan. 17, 1661, leaving issue Sir Richard his successor ; with whose son, a third Sir Richard, the title became extinct before 1714. See pedigrees of Forster in Graves's *History of Cleveland*, p. 225, and in Ord's *History of Cleveland*, p. 397.

[2] See the particulars in a subsequent page.

[3] Misprinted *d'Ingley* by the Abbé Trou. "John Digby, born in London in 1618, was entered in Magdalen College, Oxford, anno 1634 ; sided with the King in the beginning of the civil war, and, being esteemed a valiant and good man, was made general of horse in the army of Ralph Lord Hopton, and fought bravely in many encounters. When the King's cause declined, he retired into France, and some time followed the court of Charles II. ; but, getting nothing there, he lived very obscurely, and in 1654 came to England, where continuing for a time among the afflicted Royalists, he at length retired to Pontoise, entered himself among the religious there, became a secular priest, said mass daily to the English nuns, and died there after the Restoration, unmarried." (Wood, Athen. Oxon. vol. iii. p. 341.) The records of the

quitté le parti des armes pour entrer dans le sacerdoce, s'interessa aux Benedictines. Elles reçurent près de 300,000 fr., elles enfermèrent un grand terrain de murs, et batirent un couvent dans un bout de cette prop'rieté au S. Ouest de la ville, près la porte St. Martin. Ce couvent fut appellé le Monastère de la Grace de Dieu, et on le considéra comme dependance du Monastère de ce nom dans le comté de Leicester.[1] L'Eglise fut dediée sous le nom de la Conception de la Ste Vierge.

On y voyoit le tombeau de la Pr^sse Honoré (morte en Languedoc 16 janvier, 1698), fille de Guillaume Burke, pair d'Irlande, et épouse de Jacques FitzJames, Duc de Berwick.[2] Le Prince Henry Fitz-James, Lord Perth, Lord Milford [Melfort], Richard Hamilton, Grand Maître de la Garderobe du Roi, Porter Vice-Chambellan du Roi, Milord Waldegrave, Baron et Pair d'Angleterre, furent presents à son enterrement, aussi bien que Dominique Macguirre, Archévêque d'Armagh, Primat d'Irlande.

Les religieuses se signalèrent par leurs œuvres de dévouement, et d'une immense charité envers les soldats du régiment de Hamilton qui séjourna plus d'un an à Pontoise.

The first Abbess was the Lady CATHARINE WIGMORE, daughter of William Wigmore, esq. of Luchton, in Herefordshire, by Anne daughter of Sir John Throckmorton. Her sister Christina was also a nun at Pontoise, and died in 1699, aged 62; and her brother William was one of the Society of Jesus. The Lady Abbess died, whilst the community was still at Boulogne, on the 28th Oct. 1656, aged 67, having been professed 31 years. Her body was afterwards brought to Pontoise, and buried in the

---

convent show that he was ordained in 1660, and, after being a great benefactor, died March 15, 1663 ; when, according to his own orders, he was buried in the church of the English Benedictine nuns, with these words only :

Hic jacet umbra et pulvis nihil.

He had been grievously wounded at the siege of Portsmouth, and, during his long illness, resolved to devote himself to the Divine Service, which he did so fervently, that he was universally respected and admired. At the time he died, he was acting as Ecclesiastical Superior to the Benedictines, in place of the Abbot Montagu, who was obliged to go to England on business.

[1] This statement seems to be unfounded. Though the house had the name of Grace Dieu, it was not dependent on any other. Gracedieu abbey in Leicestershire was a nunnery of the Cistercian Order.—Dugdale, *Monasticon Anglicanum*, (London, 1718,) p. 108.

[2] See the ceremony of her funeral hereafter, p. 64.

choir of the nuns, near the high altar on the Gospel side, on the 10th July 1671, with this inscription :—

Cette pierre enchasse la plus éminente en vertu Mme CATH^ne WIG-MORE, fille de Mon^r Guillaume Wigmore de Luchton dans le Comté de Hereford au pays de Galles. Elle fut envoyée Supérieure en la Mission de Gand à Bouloigne en Picardie, et là choisie la 1ere Abbesse. Son humilité dans sa prélature était très remarquable, aussi était son affabilité et mansuétude : son zèle et ferveur n'était pas moins ardent et rempli de pouvoir. Elle apprenait aux autres par son exemple en silence, et obtenait de Dieu davantage par oraison et recollection que par aucun autre moyen. Elle mourut à Bouloigne l'an MDCLVI. le LXVII. de son âge, le XXXI. de sa profession. Elle fut enterrée en grande estime de sainteté non seulement de ses religieuses, mais aussi de l'Evêque, de son clergé, et de toute la ville : et pour la consolation de ses filles ses ossements furent transportés en notre Eglise le xe de juillet de l'an MDCLXXI. *Requiescat in Pace.*

The second Abbess was the Lady ANNE FORSTER, daughter of Sir Richard Forster, of Stokesley, co. York, Knt. and Bart., by Joan Middleton, of Leighton, in Lancashire. She was professed at Ghent under the name of Anne Christina, Jan. 13, 1641; was afterwards sent to Boulogne; and moved with the rest of the community to Pontoise, where she became Abbess on the 27th of May, 1657. She died at Paris, Dec. 16, 1661, aged 44; when her body, having been embalmed, was buried in the church of the Feuillantines of the Faubourg St. Jacques: her heart, placed in lead, was brought to her sorrowing daughters, and in 1671 her body also was removed to Pontoise. These particulars are more fully related as follows in a MS. formed by her successor the Lady Anne Neville.

Le Chevalier Forster, fondateur du Monastère de Pontoise, eut beaucoup à souffrir pendant les troubles de la Réligion, et fut obligé de se retirer à la campagne, où on ne le laissa pas longtemps en repos. Pour le trouver, il revint à la Cour, et se mit au service de la Reine, qui éprouva en quantité de rencontres sa fidélité, sa prudence, et son zèle. La Reine, ayant parfaitement reconnu son mérite et son integrité, le fit son Trésorier Général, et lui confia tous ses biens. Il s'acquitta de cet emploi avec une fidélité très grande; et si Sa Majesté reconnût ses services, il employa tout cela aussi bien que tout le revenu de ses terres

à faire bâtir des Monastères, et en tirer d'autres de la dernière neces-
sité ; à elever de pauvres gentilshommes Anglais dans les études ; à
marier de pauvres filles, et à faire des aumônes à ceux qui avaient eté
chassés de l'Angleterre pour la Foi Catholique. . . . . Enfin etant trés
dangereusement malade, il fit son Testament, par lequel il légua beaucoup au Monastère (dont sa fille était alors Abbesse) ; mais ces biens
étant en de puissantes mains, nous n'en avons reçus que très peu. Il a
été enterré dans l'Eglise de St. Martin sur Viosne-lès-Pontoise, et enterré devant l'autel de St. Gautier, proche du lieu où a été enterré le
même saint.[1]

La maison qui M. le Chevalier Forster cèda à la communauté lui
avait coûté 30,000 livres, avec la ferme et métairie qui y appartenaient.
Cette maison s'appellait de Maudestour, et avait été autrefois l'Hotel
des anciens seigneurs de Maudestour. . . . . On commença la même
année (1659) le bâtiment neuf, où est à present (1672) la chapelle, le
chœur, et quelques céllules. L'Abbesse Forster étant très malade,
on la fit voyager à Paris avec la permission de Mons[gr] l'Archevêque.
Mais son mal s'augmentant, elle y mourut sur le midi, le 16me jour de
Dec[re] 1661. Son cœur fut enfermé dans un cœur de plomb, et envoyé
à Pontoise ; son corps fut embaumé et mis en dèpôt en l'Eglise des
Feuillantines du Faubourg St. Jacques à Paris, d'où Mme Anne de
Neville 4e Abbesse le fit apporter à Pontoise et enterrer dans le chœur
des Réligieuses, avec l'inscription suivante :

" Ici repose la très illustre Abbesse Madame Christine Forster, fille
du Chevalier Forster d'Ethersod (Ederston) en Northumberland, Baron
de Storsly (Stokesly) en Yorkshire, Trésorier de la Reine Mère d'Angleterre. La charité et liberalité de ce digne Père envers sa fille, et, pour
l'amour d'elle, envers cette communauté, lui donne avec justice le titre
de Fondateur de ce Monastère. Elle fut envoyée de Gand en Flandres
pour notre etablissement à Bouloigne en Picardie, fut 2me Abbesse, et
commença notre Monastère à Pontoise. Sa vie était un miroir très
admirable de toutes sortes de vertus. Elle excellait en grâce et en
nature. Sa prudence ensemble ses comportements et entretiens at-
trayants avoient beaucoup de pouvoir et faisaient de grands effèts sur
tous, mais spécialement ses Réligieuses, qu'elle gouvernoit avec autant
de douceur que d'autorité. Elle mourut à Paris l'an MDC.LXI. le XVI
de Dec[re], le XLIV. de son âge, le XX. de sa profession, et le V. de sa prélature. Elle fut là embaumée, et son cœur généreux fut alors porté à

---

[1] This proves St. Gautier's tomb has been moved. It is now in the church of
Nôtre Dame at Pontoise.

son Monastère pour la consolation de ses filles, et placé dans la muraille
du chœur, audessous de son portrait. En l'année MDC.LXXI. son corps
fut transporté et enterré avec solemnité dans la même chapelle à Pontoise. *Requiescat in Pace.*

The third Abbess was the Lady EUGENIA THOROLD, daughter
of Edmund Thorold, esq., of Hough, near Grantham, in Lincolnshire, by Anne, sister to Sir Robert Thorold, Bart. of Heath.[1] She
was professed at Ghent, Dec. 27, 1639; made Abbess of Pontoise
March 7, 1662; and died Dec. 21, 1667, aged 44, when she was
buried in the church of the monastery, near the high altar, on the
Gospel side,—where a few years after the remains of her predecessors were placed by her side. Her epitaph was as follows:

Cy gist illustre Dame Religieuse Madame EUGENIE THOROLD de
Hough, 3me Abbesse de ce Monastère, premièrement etabli à Boulogne, et depuis érigé à Pontoise, une de ses premières Religieuses qui
sont venues de Gand. Entre toutes ses vertus elle excella en silence,
paix, et douceur—admirable dans sa conversation, ce qui l'a rendue non-
seulement agréable à Dieu, mais encore très aimable à ses Religieuses.
Elle est heureusement décédée le XXI. Dec^re l'an MDC.LXVII. âgée de XLIV.
ans, de profession XXVIII. et de sa prélature VI. *Requiescat in Pace.*

The fourth Abbess was the Lady ANNE NEVILLE, daughter
of Henry Lord Abergavenny and Lady Mary Sackville, daughter
of Thomas first Earl of Dorset. She was professed at Ghent, the
2d July, 1634, and whilst there was first mistress of the school,
then mistress of novices, and afterwards prioress, in all which
offices she had under her care the young lady of the Thorold
family whose history has been just detailed, and who, having
always retained a grateful affection for her former mistress, and
entire confidence in her, at length persuaded her to come to
Pontoise; where, at the Lady Eugenia's decease, she became her
successor. Lady Neville died 15 December, 1689, aged 84.[2]

---

[1] See the account of Lincolnshire Families temp. Charles II. in vol. ii. p. 125.

[2] Lady Abergavenny, the mother of this Abbess, though daughter of the Protestant
Lord Treasurer, was secretly a favourer of the ancient faith. A young lady, whose edu-
cation she had undertaken, the orphan daughter of Henry Blanchard, esq. of Prior's
Court, Berks, retired after Lady Abergavenny's death to the English convent at
Brussels, where she was professed as Dame Alexia, and some years after she became
the fourth Abbess of that community.—(*Pontoise MSS.*)

The ceremony of her Benediction was appointed by the Archbishop of Rouen to be performed at St. Martin's-sur-Viosne, of which Lord Walter Montagu was then Abbot; and it was conferred by the Most Rev. Dr. Edmund O'Reilly, Archbishop of Armagh (who had been obliged to flee from Ireland during the violent persecutions), on the 12th February, 1668. Abbot Montagu after the ceremony gave a noble entertainment to the new Abbess and the four or five Religious who accompanied her, to the Abbess of Maubuisson, Princess Louisa Hollandina (granddaughter of James I.), who, with her niece the Princess Mary, had come purposely to honour Lady Neville on this solemn occasion, and to three or four other English present. In the afternoon Lady Neville returned to her dear community, and was visited by the Princess Louisa on her return to Maubuisson, who assured her of her affection, and ever after continued a kind benefactress to the Nuns, who were, almost from the first, in straitened circumstances, their numbers being too great for their temporalities, and the times making it very difficult to obtain moneys due to them.—(*Pontoise MSS.*)

Catherine Dayrell, described as a niece of Lord Castlemaine,[1] and cousin of Lady Abbess Neville, died whilst at school at the Pontoise convent. This happened shortly after Dame Anne Neville was made Abbess.

The fifth Abbess was Dame ELIZABETH DABRIDGCOURT, daughter of Sir Thomas Dabridgcourt, Bart., and of Anne, daughter of Launcelot Saunders, of Sutton Court, Esq. She died 17 August, 1715, having attained the age of 71, of her profession 55, and of her abbacy 20.

The sixth Abbess was Dame ANNE XAVERIA GIFFORD, daughter of Sir Henry Gifford, Bart., of Burstall, in Leicestershire, and of Joan, daughter of Benjamin Vaughan, Esq., of Ruadon, in Gloucestershire. She was professed in 1676, and

---

[1] Rather of Lady Castlemaine. Roger Palmer, Earl of Castlemaine, (who married Barbara Duchess of Cleveland, the mistress of Charles II.) was a son of Sir James Palmer, younger son of Sir Thomas Palmer, the first Baronet of Wingham, Kent. It does not appear that Catharine Dayrell was so near a relation to him as niece; see the Pedigree hereafter, No. I. There may probably have been some speaking of him as Uncle *à la mode de Bretagne*. He gave the house of Pontoise 480 *livres* (see p. 65), and again 55 *livres*, when he went ambassador to the Pope in 1686. Of that embassy there is a contemporary History, by Mr. Michael Wright, with interesting plates, described in Moule's *Bibliotheca Heraldica*, p. 242, and in Granger's *Biogr. History of England.*

made Abbess in 1710, Lady Elizabeth Dabridgcourt having resigned on account of her great infirmities. She died on the 11th February of the ensuing year, having been Abbess only 11 months. She was 57 years of age, and had been professed 35.[1]

Her sister, Dame Maura Gifford, died 28 August, 1691, aged 34, professed 17.

The seventh Abbess was Dame ELIZABETH JOSEPH WIDDRINGTON, daughter of Lord Widdrington, of Blanckney, in Lincolnshire, and of Elizabeth (who both embraced the Catholic religion,) daughter of Sir Peregrine Bertie, of Evedon, in Lincolnshire. She died 9 November, 1730, aged 71; professed 51; Abbess 20.

The eighth Abbess was Dame MARINA HUNLOKE, daughter of Sir Henry Hunloke, of Wingerworth, co. Derby, and Catharine, only daughter and heir of Francis Tyrwhitt, esq., of Kettleby, co. Lincoln.

The ninth Abbess was Dame ANNA CATHERINE HAGGERSTON.

The tenth Abbess was MARY ANNE CLAVERING, daughter of Ralph Clavering, esq., of Callaly, and of Mary, daughter of Richard Stapleton, esq. of Ponteland and Carleton, Yorkshire; professed 1751, retired to Dunkirk convent in 1784, and died at Hammersmith 8 November, 1795, aged 65. Anne Widdrington was her paternal grandmother, and thus she was great-niece to the seventh Abbess.

On the 4th March, 1665, Charles Carrington, Lord Carrington of Wotton, father of one of the nuns, was murdered at Pontoise by one of his own servants.[2] He was buried in the church of St.

---

[1] "Dans le *Mercure Galant* Avril 1710, pp. 75, 76, on voit que Lord Midleton avait une fille mariée à Sir John Gifford, oncle d'Anne Xavière Gifford abbesse des Dames Benedictines Angloises de Pontoise, mort à St. Germain en Laye en 1708." F. Michel, *Ecossais en France.*

[2] The following account of Lord Carrington's murder was heard by Thomas Dineley esq. when he visited Pontoise in 1675, and is preserved in his MS. journal now in the possession of Sir Thomas Edward Winnington, Bart. Describing the churches of Pontoise, he remarks,—"S. Macloue is the fairest of all, with a square steeple of free stone; in this the first monument and inscription I cast mine eye upon was y[t] of an English gentleman, who was assazined by his servant, a French fellow, his *valet de chambre*, who made his escape after it for some time, and the master of the house being a magistrate of the town, and his whole family, where this gentleman lodged, were secured and a guard sett upon them, by order of the other magistrates, untill the

Maclou, opposite the second pillar on entering at the right-hand side, with this inscription :

D. O. M.

Siste Viator! Terrâ hic non suâ sepultus jacet CAROLUS CARRINGTON de Wootton in comitatu Warwicensi, ex antiquâ et nobili familiâ Carringtonum natus, qui Primogenitorum in fide Romanâ constantiam difficillimis temporibus cum insigni pietate servans Carolo I°. Regi bellis civilibus Angliam vastantibus, tam per se quam per fratres, consanguineos, et amicos perutilem navavit operam. Optimo principe per nefas immane sublato, quâ liberius Deo et conscientiâ frueretur, in Belgium migrans Leodii multa pietatis et misericordiæ exempla edidit, donec Carolo II°. divinâ ope, trium Regnorum gaudio, in solium Patris restituto, ipse quoque, reversus in Patriam, communis lætitiæ partem cepit. Denique quietem in Gallia quærens, Pontisara post multa religionis, devotionis, et munificentiæ in omnes, sed maximè in gentiles suas Ordinis S^{ti} Benedicti Moniales ibi habilitas opera, ad meliorem et permanentem vitam migravit anno ætatis 65, Domini 1665, Martii 4. *Requiescat in Pace.* Amen.

malefactor was found out : which cost ye master of the afores^d house over 200 *Louis d'or*, or French golden pistols, in scouts. At length ye murderer was took in a cabaret and gameing-house not farr from this town, and for this notorious fact of having stabb'd his master in several places as he lay in his bed and stole away his moneys, he rec'd sentence to be broken on the wheele, which accordingly was done. It is said that ye Lord Montague in memory of this bloody accident (happening to Mr. Charles Carington of the ancient family of ye Caringtons of Wotton in the county of Warwyck) erected this Monument of marble against one of the pillars of this church, and hath also founded three masses and the offices for the dead yearly on that day." (But these pious duties were really performed by Lord Carrington's son and successor, as the epitaph states.)

Some biographical notices of Lord Carrington, who was so created on the 4th November, 19 Car. I. 1644, will be found in Dugdale's *Baronage,* ii. 470, and in his *History of Warwickshire* (edit. Thomas,) p. 810. There is a pedigree of the family under Ashby Folvile in Nichols's *History of Leicestershire,* vol. iii. p. 29.

On the death without issue in 1758 of the last male descendant of the Carringtons, William Smith *alias* Carrington, the family estates devolved in equal moieties on his two nieces,—Constantia, the widow of John Wright of Kelvedon hall, Essex, but then the wife of Mr. Peter Holford, and Catherine a nun in the English Benedictine convent at Cambray. Mrs. Holford, by her second husband, left a daughter Catherine Maria, who married Sir Edward Smythe, the fifth Baronet, of Acton Burnell, co. Salop, and Eske, co. Durham, the grandfather of the present Sir Frederick Smythe. (Statement in *Notes and Queries,* 1861, II. xii. 401, by J. F. Wright, esq. of Kelvedon hall, Brentwood, Essex, great-great-grandson of Constantia above-mentioned by her first husband.)

Parenti omni obsequio prosequendo Carolus Carrington primogenitus titulorum hæres et virtutum monumentum mœrens posuit, et anniversarium trium missarum et aliarum precum officium 4 Martii persolvendum perpetuo fundavit contractu, per Fredin notarium publicum facto, 13 Junii, anno 1670.

Dame Francisca Carrington was daughter of the above by his wife Elizabeth, daughter of Sir John Caryll, of Harting in Sussex. She was professed at Ghent 9th April, 1646, and sent to the new foundation at Boulogne in 1653, and removed with the rest to Pontoise—but returned to Ghent after her father's death, and died there 2nd January, 1701.

In 1698 the wife[1] of James Duke of Berwick, natural son of King James the Second, was interred at Pontoise, and the following record of the ceremony has been preserved:—

ACTE DE L'ENTERREMENT DE Mme LA DUCHESSE DE BERWICK.

(From the Pontoise Necrology.)

L'an de grâce 1698, ce jour d'hui 25e de fevrier, a été inhumée dans la Chapelle de l'Eglise de l'Abbaye des Dames Benedictines Anglaises, très-haute, très-puissante, et tres-vertueuse Princesse Honorée Burgh, Duchesse de Berwick, décédée à Perenas en Languedoc le 16 janvier de cette dite année, munie des sacremens de Penitence, de l'Eucharistie, et de l'Extrême Onction; et transférée dans cette dite Abbaye, où elle avait choisi en mourant sa sépulture, le 24 du dit mois de fevrier (âgée de 22 ans 10 mois) par Messire Vincent François Des Marets prêtre, licencié en droit Canon, Grand-Vicaire et Official de Pontoise et du Vexin-le-Français, et Supérieur de ladite Abbaye: en présence de Monseigneur l'Archévêque d'Armagh, Primat d'Irlande; de très-haut, très-puissant, et très-excellent Prince, Milord duc d'Albemarle, Chevalier de l'Ordre de la Jarretière, et chef d'escadre des armées navales de sa Majesté très-Chrétienne; de Milord Perth, Comte et Pair d'Ecosse, Chevalier de l'Ordre de la Jarretière, Gouverneur de son Altesse Royale Monseig^r le Prince de Galles; de Milord Melfort, Comte et Pair d'Ecosse, Chevalier de l'Ordre de la Jarretière; de Milord Galmoy, Comte et Pair d'Irlande; de Milord Waldegrave, Baron et Pair d'Angleterre; de Milord Montleinster, Baron et Pair d'Irlande; de Milord Forth, fils du Milord Melfort; de Milord de Brittas, Baron

---

[1] Honora, third daughter of William Burke, Earl of Clanricard, and widow of Colonel Patrick Sarsfield, called Earl of Lucan, the first wife of the Duke of Berwick : see Sandford, *Geneal. Hist. of England*, edit. 1707, p. 683.

et Pair d'Irlande ; et d'un grand nombre de Seigneurs et Dames de la Cour d'Angleterre. En foi de quoi ont signé ledit Sieur Des Marets, le Sieur Lawrence Breers, Père Confesseur de ladite Abbaye, et le Sieur Louis Du Val, prêtre, bachelier de Sorbonne et Curé de Notre Dame de cette ville de Pontoise.

Extracts from Receipts of Pontoise.[1]

A nameless Friend . . livres	120
Queen Mother and Madame (her dau'r) a legacy . . .	300
Lord Castlemaine . . .	480
2 Mr. Carylls	490
Dutchess of Cleveland . .	540
Cardinal of Boulogne . . .	2,100
Sir Geo. Southcot . . .	300
Mr. Nichs. Timperley, a legacy .	600
Lady Goring, Sir John Gage, and Mr. Roper	513
Lady Powis	500
Lord Cardigan	760
Lady Guildford	200
Lady Hamilton	100
2 Mr. Fermors	252
1685 and 1686, Princess Louisa of Maubuisson	250
15 April, '85, A nameless Friend, to desire our prayers, and proved to be ye glorious King J. R. .	2,000
Sir Rowland Bellasis . . .	55

Lord Castlemaine, then Ambassador from J. R. to the Pope, for masse and prayers . . .	55
Lady Petre	260
Lady Waldegrave the widow .	77
A token to ye com^ty from Mrs. Susan Warner, when she entered to be Religious (at Dunkirk), wch was noe less a concurring kyndness from her worthy Father, Revd. Father Clare (Sir John Warner), and ye consent and goodwill of his other Dau'r Dame Agnes Warner	
428 livres 12 sous.	
Lady Gage, at her death . livres	120
The auncient Mrs. Plowden .	100
Mr. Tunstall	390
Mrs. Blount	600
2 legacies from my cousins Stanley	120
(In some old books only 12 livres are reckoned to make a pound.)	

On a fly-leaf of the same book is the following copy of a mortuary circular transmitted by the community of Maubuisson on the death of their abbess the Princess Louisa (already mentioned), one of the daughters of Frederick Elector Palatine and the Princess Elizabeth of Great Britain, and elder sister of the Princess Sophia, the designated heiress of the English crown.

Nous vous demandons très-instamment, Mesdames, le secours de vos saintes prières pour Mme la Princesse Electorale Louise Marie Palatine de Bavière, notre très-digne et très-chère Abbesse, qui est décédée le IIeme fevrier 1709, munie des Saints Sacremens de l'Eglise, âgée de

[1] In Lady Abbess Neville's writing.

86 ans, de profession religieuse 50, dont elle a été Abbesse 45, et a gouverné ce monastère avec tant de piété, de zèle, de bonté, et d'édification, que dans l'accablement de douleur où nous sommes, nous vous demandons aussi vos prières, Mesdames, pour la consolation et les besoins de cette communauté.

The English nuns left Pontoise in the year 1784: having then grown so impoverished that it became necessary to break up the establishment. The Archbishop of Rouen having given them permission to retire to any other convents, the Abbess, with six of her sisters, retired to the community of their order at Dunkirk, where they were afterwards joined by others of their former companions, and where they remained in peace and happiness until the fatal year 1793, when their church was seized for the meetings of the Jacobin Club of that city. They were then driven from their convent (on the 13th Oct.) at a few hours' notice, and fled to Gravelines; whence, in April 1795, they repaired to England,[1] and before the end of the same year they took possession of the convent at Hammersmith near London. They were then under the government of the Lady Abbess Mary Magdalen Prujean, who died in 1814; and was succeeded by Mary Placida Messenger, who died in 1828; and her successor (living in 1865), is the Abbess Mary Placida Selby.[2]

Very recently, these Benedictine ladies have moved to Teignmouth in Devonshire; and their house at Hammersmith (now threatened by a projected railway or building,) is at present occupied by a small community of sisters of " The Sacred Blood."

---

[1] See fuller details of their sufferings and adventures in Mr. Petre's work before quoted, from which these particulars are derived.

[2] It is to Lady Abbess Selby that we owe most of this information, she having both written with her own hand, and permitted Dame Mary Thais English to make extracts from the Conventual Records and Necrologies for us.

This article will be continued with a list of the Religious Ladies, extracted from the Necrology of the House and other sources, accompanied by some genealogical tables showing their parentage and family connections.

HISTORICAL AND HERALDIC CARDS.[1]

Playing Cards are no longer the engrossing objects of time and attention which they once were in this country, and still are in some others. Since the last century there has been a great change in our manners, and in the distribution of our time. The dinner-hour has become continually later, leaving little or no room for cards after that important ceremonial. The secondary entertainment that was called "Tea and Cards" has given way to the Soirée Dansante and its substantial supper; and, as parents naturally ingraft their own manners on the rising generation, so, in "juvenile parties" and the festivities of the Christmas holidays, the once merry Round Game has been generally banished for the hired showman, the Magician of the North or South, or other more ambitious if not more scientific entertainments,— succeeded in most cases by music and dancing, not by cards.

So, also, in the senior ranks of the existing community, the amusement of card-playing has been greatly relinquished. It is no longer the common pastime, but only the peculiar taste of a few. Many clerics of the last century, and particularly those who enjoyed the social circles of a market-town or a cathedral-close, spent half their time on whist. They were instant in season and out of season, before dinner and after. In great measure such occupation is now considered not merely frivolous,

---

[1] The principal English writers on Playing Cards have been the Hon. Daines Barrington, the Rev. John Bowle, and Mr. Gough, in the *Archæologia*, vol. VIII.; Mr. Pettigrew, in the *Journal of the Archæological Association*, vol. IX.; Singer, Chatto, and Taylor. The works of the three last, which we shall have occasion to quote in the following pages, are:—

Researches on the History of Playing Cards. By SAMUEL WELLER SINGER. 1816. 4to.

Facts and Speculations on the Origin and History of Playing Cards. By WILLIAM ANDREW CHATTO. 1848. 8vo.

The History of Playing Cards, with Anecdotes of their use in Conjuring, Fortune-Telling, and Card-Sharping. Edited by the late Rev. ED. S. TAYLOR, B.A. and others. 1825. 12mo. A very interesting volume just published by Mr. J. C. Hotten, embellished by many curious and well-executed wood engravings, many of which were originally published in "Les Cartes à Jouer et la Cartomancie. Par P. BOITEAU D'AMBLY."

but altogether unbecoming to the cloth.   Like other indulgences, the abuse or excess of which leads to vice and crime, card-playing has become associated in common repute, more or less, with gambling, and total abstinence has been very generally prescribed in lieu of temperance and moderation.

Cards are in fact the resource of the idle, and of those who want to kill time.   The Nineteenth Century is far more busy than the Eighteenth, and on the whole is better employed. Even those who have abundance of leisure can now find other intellectual occupations besides the once favourite cribbage or the eternal whist.   The spoiled children of Fortune have no longer the excuse they once had for spending

A youth of folly, an old age of cards.

All those who have not worn out their eye-sight have now the never-failing newspaper, or magazine, in all shapes, and touching on all topics.   If there are still many who never open a book, the daily paper places before them a constant supply of multifarious mental food and entertainment.   In the last century those who took no pleasure in books were often disposed to make cards their only reading.[1]

When this was the state of things, it was an obvious device, in order to find an entrance to the minds of such limited readers, to attempt to make the cards themselves the vehicles of advice or instruction.

Indeed, the idea is by no means new.   It was broached, with great approbation, by Dr. Thomas Murner, a Franciscan friar, and professor at Cracow, at the beginning of the sixteenth century.[2]   This learned man undertook to teach the art of reasoning by a pack of fifty-two cards : his performance was

---

[1] As cards served first for books, so they next answered the purpose of stationery. An old playing-card was a ready means of conveying a *billet*, or message.   Many a challenge of the duellists of former days has been so transmitted, and many an invitation to more agreeable meetings.   Hence it became customary to use (plain) cards rather than note-paper on all such occasions : and it is only of late years that cards of invitation to dinner or evening parties have been succeeded in fashionable life by engraved forms printed on note-paper.

[2] At a still earlier period the Italian game called *La Menchiata*, which was played with the Tarot cards, was invented by Michael Angelo at Sienna, to teach children Arithmetic.   Archæologia, vol. viii. 172.

printed at Cracow in 1507, and at Strasburg in 1509,[1] under the title of *Chartiludium Logicæ*, and was re-published at Paris in 1629 by M. des Balesdens, an advocate of the parliament.

During the youth of Louis XIV. and it is said for his special instruction, the plan was further pursued by Desmaretz, a well-known academician, in conjunction with the engraver Della Bella. On the 9th April, 1644, letters patent were issued to " Jean Desmaretz, Conseiller, Secretaire, et Controlleur-General de l'extraordinaire des Guerres," granting him the privilege and monopoly of procuring to be executed, in wood or copper-plate, engraving or etching, the figures of the Games of Cards of the History of the Kings and Queens, of Illustrious Men and Women, Fables, Geography, Ethics (*morale*), Politics, Logic, Physic, and generally of all other games of any art, science, history, or fable, which he had invented, or should thereafter invent ; forbidding their sale by any one else, under a penalty of 3000 livres and confiscation of the articles.

Specimens of these cards are still preserved by the curious. The first of the series was the *Jeu de Fables*, 1644, a pack of the usual number, relating to the heathen deities and their meta-morphoses.[2] The next, a *Jeu de l'Histoire de France*, did not adhere to the ordinary arrangement of playing-cards, or corre-spond to the usual suits. Instead of fifty-two cards, it had sixty-five ; presenting the French kings arranged in six divisions— the good, the simple-minded, the cruel, the faithless, the luckless, and those who were neither good nor bad.[3] The last of the series represents Louis XIV. as a child, in a carriage drawn by his mother.

In another, the *Jeu de Cartes des Reines renommées*,[3] all the celebrated Queens of the world were classed in like manner according to their characters, but their number was confined to fifty-two, and divided into four suits, which were distinguished by the colours of gold, silver, green, and columbine.

---

[1] Singer, p. 216, gives the title of the latter edition. The former is mentioned by Mr. Taylor at p. 188.

[2] Described by Taylor, p. 191 : and a specimen the Ace of Clubs,—the subject Arion on his dolphin, engraved as Plate XXXV.

[3] A specimen, representing the *fayneants* (five on one card), is Plate XXXVI. of the same volume.   [4] Described ibid. p. 192.

Something of this kind had already been engrafted on the ordinary playing-cards, of which the figured or court-cards were usually known by these names—the Kings as David, Alexander, Cæsar, and Charlemagne; the Queens as Judith, Rachel, Argine, and Pallas; the Valets as Lahire, Hector, Lancelot, and Hogier.[1] The four Kings were supposed to represent the four ancient monarchies of the Jews, Greeks, Romans, and Franks ; the Queens, Wisdom, Birth, Beauty, and Fortitude. In some packs, Esther, as an impersonation of Piety, was substituted for Rachel. In a French pack of the time of Henri IV. the Kings were named Solomon, Auguste, Clovis, and Constantine; the Queens, Elizabeth, Dido, Clotilda, Pantilisée; the Valets, Valet de Court (a hat under his arm), Valet de Chasse (with a dog in a leash), Valet d'Eté (carrying a flower), Valet de Noblesse (with a hawk and riding rod). The like personifications have been frequently repeated in subsequent times. In a pack published in Paris in the Revolutionary days, the figures of Molière, La Fontaine, Voltaire, and Rousseau were substituted for the four Kings; for the Queens, Prudence, Justice, Temperance, and Fortitude; for the Valets, four Republican citizens, or rather soldiers. After the same fashion, an American represented the Kings by Washington, John Adams, Franklin, and La Fayette; the Queens, by Venus, Fortune, Ceres, and Minerva; and the Knaves by four Indian chiefs. See Mr. Pettigrew's Essay in the *Journal of the Archæological Association*, ix. 124.

The *Jeu de Cartes de la Geographie*, designed by Desmaretz, is described as equally beautiful and interesting, a native of each country being represented in his national costume. Another pack of Geographical cards was published by M. Duval in 1677; and one in London, about 1680, of which there is a copy in the British Museum.[2]

A second English pack[3] of the same period was devoted to a geographical description of *The fifty-two Counties of England and*

[1] These names have been retained on French cards even to modern times, except Lancelot, which was usually displaced to make room for the manufacturer's name.

[2] These are also described in Mr. Taylor's work, pp. 193, 194.

[3] Described by Chatto, p. 150, and the same account quoted by Taylor, p. 196. See also Archæological Journal, vol. vii. p. 306.

Wales; the number of which happened to coincide with that of a pack of cards: and they were declared to be "as plaine and ready for the playing of all our English games as any of the common cards."

There were also published in England, in the reign of Charles the Second, several pictorial cards of an Historical, or perhaps we should rather say Political, character; for they related chiefly to the passing events of the day. A pack containing the history of the Spanish Invasion (published about the year 1679) is said to have been exhibited to the Society of Antiquaries by Sir Joseph Banks in 1773. It is probably the same that is now in the British Museum, where it is publicly exhibited in the show-case No. xiii. in the Royal Library. It is quite perfect.

One satirising the Rump Parliament and the great men of the Commonwealth is fully described by Mr. Pettigrew in the *Journal of the Archæological Association*, vol. ix. pp. 121-154, and 308-329, with eight fac-simile engravings.

One advertised in the *Mercurius Domesticus* of Dec. 19, 1679, was to form "An History of all the Popish Plots that have been in England;" but no existing copy of it has been discovered, unless (which is not improbable) it was afterwards confined to the plots of Oates and Bedloe in 1678, and the murder of Sir Edmund Berry Godfrey,—a pack being preserved representing those occurrences. This is fully described, with eight fac-simile engravings, in the *Gentleman's Magazine* for Sept. 1849; and a perfect copy is in the Print Room at the British Museum.

Another pack commemorated the Rye-house plot, but only four cards of it have been discovered.[1]

In the reign of James the Second one was published representing the most memorable scenes of Monmouth's Rebellion and other recent political events. As this pack has not hitherto been described,[2] we avail ourselves of the opportunity to place upon record the following account of the few cards that we have seen of it. They are only fourteen in number:—

CLUBS.—IV. Argyle Landing in Ila with 5 Hundred Men.

VIII. Severall of yᵉ King's Forces in search after Ferguson.

---

[1] Described by Chatto, p. 155; Taylor, p. 169.

[2] It is briefly mentioned by Taylor, p. 408, and in Notes and Queries, I. ii. 463.

IX. One Pitts is to be Whipt through every town in Dorsetshire for Seaven Years togeather.[1]

Knave. Ferguson Preeching to the Rebells yᵉ Day before yᵉ Defeat on Iosh. 22 v. 22.

Queen. The Defeat of the Rebells 2000 Slayn & their Canon taken.

Spades.—I. Argyle receiving a wound on his Head. (He is wading through a stream, and exclaiming " unfortunate Argyle.")

IV. Severall Officers by Command of yᵉ King going into yᵉ West.

V. 7 Rebells kill'd in a fight at Bridport & 32 taken Prisoners.

VI. The late D: of M: Lᵈ Grey & a German carried to yᵉ Tower. (In two boats on the Thames, London Bridge and St. Mary Overies in the distance.)

VII. The late D. of M. beheaded on Tower Hill 15 july 1685.

VIII. Rebells Marching out of Lime.

Knave. 5 Mon's taking an Oath not to discover who is yᵉ Right. (*Five men* standing together and holding a testament in their hands.)

Queen. The late D of Mˢ. Standard. (It bears only this motto— FEAR NOTHING BUT GOD.)

King. Devils in yᵉ Ayre Bewitch[......] Army. (This card is torn.)

We will add references to some other English historical packs, as in so doing we are giving information that has not hitherto been collected.

6. There is some intimation of a pack relating to the Warming-pan Plot and the Revolution of 1688. (*Taylor*, p. 169.)

7. One of the reign of Anne, commemorating the victories of Marlborough, &c. is in the British Museum (7913 a. 1.) It is a perfect pack of fifty-two.

8. One relating to the South Sea Bubble was exhibited to the Archæological Association by Mr. Palin. Each card has four lines of poetry, and all these verses except those on the Three of Diamonds are printed in *Notes and Queries*, I. v. 217.

9. The Mississippi scheme was in like manner recorded in Holland.

10. A pack satirising contemporary vices and follies, circ.

---

[1] The sentence is represented as in execution at a fair or market. This was " Thomas Pitts, gent." subsequently author of " The New Martyrology, or The Bloody Assize," 1693. His real name was John Tatchin, who had been a busy political writer in promotion of the rebellion. See Roberts's Life of the Duke of Monmouth, 1844, ii. 211, 339 ; and Granger's Biogr. Hist. of England.

1730, is in the British Museum library (7913 a.) having been purchased in 1854, and is partly described by Taylor, p. 170.

11. Another was formed of designs in illustration of English proverbs: see *Notes and Queries*, I. ii. 463.

The same Duval already named invented another pack of cards, called *Le Jeu des Princes de l'Empire*, in which the suits, in lieu of the ordinary pips or symbols,[1] were distinguished by the Imperial Crown, the Ducal Coronet, the Electoral Bonnet, and the Chapeau of the Free Towns.

The combination of instruction in Blason together with Geography and History is said to have originated with M. Claude Oronce[2] Finé *dit* de Brianville, an abbé of Poitiers, to whose publisher, Benoist Coral a bookseller at Lyons, Desmaretz transferred his privilege so far as related to *Cartes de Blason*, by a memorandum dated May 13, 1659: and the first edition of his work was published in that year. [3]

These heraldic cards are divided into the four established suits of *cœurs*, *trefles*, *piques*, and *carreaux*, which are accompanied respectively by the armories of the kingdoms, provinces, and great dignitaries of France, Italy, the North, and Spain. The only changes in designation from ordinary cards are that the

---

[1] Our present symbols, Hearts, Diamonds, Spades, and Clubs, are derived from the French *piquet* cards, of *Cœurs*, *Carreaux*, *Piques*, and *Trefles*, substituted at the beginning of the sixteenth century for the more numerous pack of *Tarot* cards, of which the suits were Cups, Pennies, Clubs, and Swords. It is remarkable that in England we retained the *names* of the two latter, instead of translating the French terms into *pikes* and *trefoils*,—that is to say, we retained the English term in *Clubs*, and a corruption of the Italian or Spanish name of the *spade* or *espadas* in Spades. The Dutch now call the Trefoil *Klaver* (Angl. *clover*); and the Spade *Scop*, *i. e.* a scoop or shovel.

[2] Not Ozonce, as in Taylor, p. 197, nor Brainville as misprinted by Chatto.

[3] According to Guigard (*Bibliothèque Héraldique de la France*, 1861, p. 9,) the second edition was published in 1660, the third in 1665, another in 1672; the fourth (so called) in 1676 ; the fifth in 1781; the eighth at Amsterdam, without date. Mr. Hudson Gurney possessed the third edition (see Mr. Pettigrew's notice of it in *Journal of the Archæological Association*, vol. ix. p. 125). Of the edition of 1676 there is a copy in the British Museum (9930 a). It has no plates. We do not find mentioned by Guigard another edition (or a similar work) which was published at Lyons under Menestrier's own name :

"Jeu des Cartes de Blason, contenant les Armes des Princes des Principales parties de l'Europe, par le Père C. F. MENESTRIER. Lyons, Anauley, 1592." 12mo.

knaves and aces are altered into Princes and Chevaliers,—*pour éviter tout equivoque.* According to an anecdote related by Menestrier in his *Bibliothèque Curieuse et Instructive* (12mo. 1704, ii. 186) this was not done until after offence had been taken with the first edition, and its plates seized by the magistrates (of Lyons?) because certain Princes were arranged under the titles of *Valets* and *As.* This story, as told by Menestrier, is retailed by Singer and his successors, but no English writer has been able to examine a copy of the first edition to test its veracity.

In the edition of 1672 (also printed at Lyons) of which Mr. Taylor has seen a copy by the favour of A. W. Morant, esq., it is recommended in the preface that the games to be played should be those of *Hère, Malcontant,* or *Coucou,* as being the easiest, and not likely to divert the required attention from the Blason, Geography, and History. The players were to range themselves around a table covered with a map of Europe, and after the cards were dealt and exchanged to every one's satisfaction, the lowest was to pay according to the laws of *Hère.* He who was first then described the blason of the card he held, forfeiting one counter if he made an error, either to the player who corrected him, or to the bank if there was one. The next highest then followed suit, and so on with the rest. The first round being completed, the players were to proceed to the second, and describe the Geography of each card; and, in the third, the History in like manner.

There were several editions of this game,[1] and an Italian translation was made, at the procurance (says Menestrier,) of Antoine Bulifon, a bookseller who removed from Lyons to Naples. A gentleman of the latter city, Signor Don Annibale Acquaviva, established a society of young gentlemen, who met weekly to exercise themselves in the game, and, after the fashion of the learned academies then in estimation, took the distinctive name of the *Armeristi.* Their first meeting was on the 19th of September 1677.[2] As it was further thought proper that they

---

[1] One of the book (without plates) is in the British Museum (9930 a). It is called the *Quatrième edition,* and dedicated *à sa Altesse Royale de Savoye.*

[2] This is stated in Lettera di Alessandro Partenio intorno alla Societa degli Armeristi, e nel giuoco detto Lo Splendor della Nobilta Napoletana. Ascritta ne'

should have an *imprese*, or device, of their own, five were proposed, from which one was selected that represented a table
spread with the map of Europe, upon which were laid some
cards of the Game of Blason, with these words, PULCHRA SUB
IMAGINE LUDI ; " intending thereby to shew not only that they
gained instruction by the means of sport; but also that all the
grandeurs of the world and all the powers of the earth, represented by their blasons, are only the sport of Fortune."[1]

In the Italian version the suit of Spades is entitled *Germania*,
but remains the same as Brianville called " le Nort," and the
King of Great Britain is in both packs *the Prince* of this division.
The trey of the same suit displays the arms of the Seventeen Provinces of the Low Countries, and Mr. Taylor's volume furnishes us
the annexed fac-simile.

The blason of the coats is as follows :

Les Pays bas.

Flanders. Or, a lion rampant sable, armed and langued gules, the
shield held by a lion sejant, his head covered in an antient tilting

cinque Seggi. This letter is dated at Naples on the second of the same month, and a
copy is appended to Bulifon's book, which bears the following title : " Giuoco d'Arme
dei Sovrani, et de gli Stati d'Europa, per apprender l'Arme, la Geografia, e la Storia
loro curiosa. Di C. ORONCE FINE, detto di BRIANVILLE. Tradotto del Francesa in
Italiano, et accresciuto di molte notizie necessarie per la perfetta cognizion della
Storia : da BERNARDO GIUSTINIANI, Veneto. In Napoli, cIɔ. Iɔ c. LXXXI. Presso
Antonio Bulifon, All' Insegna della Sirena. *Con lic. et Privil.* 12mo. pp. xxxii.
285. (From a copy now in the hands of Mr. J. C. Hotten.)

In the British Museum (608 a 3) is a copy of a later edition printed at Naples 1692,
and containing the cards printed on paper. It is prefaced by a dedication from the
printer, Giacomo Raillard, to D. Paolo Mattia Doria of Genoa, dated Napoli, 1 Feb.
1692. The arms of the Pope (on the King of Fiori) are Campo di Oro con tre pentoce
in mezo, o uero Pignate nere, due sopra, et una sotto in triangolo. Lo scudo coronato
della Tiara, et ornato della due chiaui della Santa Sede. These three black pots
were the arms of Pope Innocent XII. (*Pignattelli*) 1691-1700.

A still later edition printed at Naples in 1725 by Paolo Petrini is supplemented with
a geographical discourse by Michele Angelo Petrini. The arms of the Pope in this
are, *Sbarra con vna Serpe in Campo d'Oro, sopra una rosa in Campo d'argento,
sotto 4 Sbarre a trauerso rosse in Campo d'argento.* The first-mentioned *Sbarra* is
a fess, the *campo d'argento* a chief ; the lower half of the shield is engraved as if it
were (in English blason) Gules, three bendlets agent. These were the arms of Pope
Benedict XIII. (*Ursini*), 1724-1730.

The arms of the Pope were evidently changed for every reign, but no other alteration appears to have been made for the several editions.

[1] Menestrier, *ut prius.*

ED. COPPIN   BISSON COTTARD

helm, crowned, and crested with a lion's head sable between a pair of wings or.

Brabant.   Sable, a lion rampant or.

Limbourg.   Argent, a lion rampant gules.

Luxembourg.   Barry of ten argent and azure, over all a lion rampant gules, armed, langued, and crowned or.

Gueldres.   Azure, a lion rampant crowned or, contourné to an impalement of *Juliers*, Or, a lion rampant sable crowned.

Aras (Artois).   Semé of *France*, a label of three pendents gules, each charged with three towers or (i. e. *Castille*). This label however is not correctly shewn in the engraving.

Hainaut.   Quarterly of *Flanders* and *Holland*.

Namur.   *Flanders*, surmounted by a bendlet gules.

Hollande.   Or, a lion rampant gules.

Zelande.   Per fess, in base wavy argent and azure, in chief or, a lion naissant gules.

Zutphen.   Or, a lion rampant argent.

Anuers.   Gules, three towers in triangle, joined by walls, argent, masoned sable, in the dexter and sinister chief a head apaumé proper,

one in bend, the other in bar (*Angl.* bend sinister), the whole surmounted by a chief of *the Empire*.

Malines. Or, three pales gules, over all an escocheon of *the Empire*.

Vtrecht. Tranché gules and argent.

Groningue. Or, a double-headed eagle displayed sable (for *the
Empire*), charged on the breast with an escucheon gules, bearing a fess
argent (for Austria). But *Groningen* should be further distinguished
by a chief azure charged with three estoiles argent.

Frize. Azure, semé of *tratti* or billets couché or, two lions passant
in pale of the same.

Oueressel. The shield of *Holland*, debrized by a fess wavy azure.

A pack of these cards is in the library of the British Museum
(C. 31 a). It wants only the King of Hearts and the eight of
Trefoils or Clubs. The armories are coloured. It is of the
period of Pope Innocent XI. 1676-1689, as shown by his arms
(Odeschalchi), which are thus blasoned:—

Porte d'argent à six coupes couuertes de gueules, posées trois deux
et un, entre trois filetes de même mis en face, surmontés d'un lion
leopardé aussi de gueules, un chef cousu d'or chargé d'un aigle esployée
de sable.

But the case in which this pack is preserved is still more
remarkable than the cards themselves. It is of ebony inlaid with
ivory and woods, and fitted with clasps and hinges of chased
steel. On the sides the inlaid materials represent these arms:—

Two lion's jambs couped and crossed in saltire between an
estoile of eight rays in chief and a fleur de lis in base. These
are borne on a shield which is placed within these four letters:

S
T   M
B

We have not ascertained the name to which the arms on the
case belonged. The family of Rasponi of Rome bore Azure,
two lion's jambs crossed in saltire or; and Raspi of Venice had
also lion's jambs in saltire, with a lion's head in chief and an
eagle's leg in base. The letters, however, do not point to a name
commencing with that initial.

In 1682 the idea was adapted to the nobility of Venice by
Casimir Freschot, a Benedictine. His production bears this title:

Li Pregi della Nobilta Veneta abbozzati in un Giuoco d'Arme di tutte le Famiglie. He acknowleges in his preface that he had followed the plan of Brianville. For the four Kings he took the four dignities of the Pope, the Emperor, a King, and the Doge. For the Queens, the armories of Princesses and Provinces. For the Princes, the foreign nobility aggregated to that of Venice; for the Chevaliers, the Generals of the armies of the Republic. The signs he adopted instead of Hearts, Spades, Diamonds, and Clubs, were four flowers, Violets, Roses, Lilies, and Tulips, on which he placed letters for the coat cards, and cyphers for the numbers. A copy of his book, including the plates (printed on paper), is in the Royal Library at the British Museum (269 c. 31).

It appears also from an advertisement of some Amsterdam booksellers so late as 1728, that the Heraldic as well as the Geographical and Historical games were copied in Dutch, but we have no particulars.[1]

In England the plan of Brianville had been imitated very soon after his first publication. A pack, described by Chatto, displayed the following armorial atchievements—the term Knave being converted into Prince, and designated by the initial P.

King of Clubs—the Pope.
Queen   .   .   . King of Naples.
Prince   .   .   . Duke of Savoy.
Ace   .   .   .   . Republics of Venice, Genoa, and Lucca.

King of Spades—King of France.
Queen   .   .   . Sons of France, the Dauphin, Duke of Anjou, and Duke of Orleans.
Prince   .   .   . Princes of the Blood, the Dukes of Bourbon, Barry, Vendome, and Alencon.
Ace   .   .   .   . Ecclesiasticks Dukes and Peirs, Reims, Langres, Laon.

King of Diamonds—King of Spain.
Queen .   .   .   .   . King of Portugal.
Prince.   .   .   .   . Castille and Leon.
Ace   .   .   .   .   . Arragon.

[1] Taylor, p. 205.

King of Hearts—King of England.
Queen . . . The Emperour.
Prince . . . Bohemia and Hungary.
Ace . . . . . Poland.

The date of these cards is closely determined by the arms of the Pope being those of Clement IX. (Quarterly or and azure, four lozenges counterchanged, Rospigliosi,) who was elected 20 June 1667 and died 9 Dec. 1669. The card representing them, together with those of the Emperor, Castille and Leon, and the three French Ecclesiastical Dukes, are engraved in fac-simile in Chatto's work.

In *The Observator*, No. 239, for Feb. 12, 1686-7, are advertised " Cards, containing the Arms of the King, and all the Lords Spiritual and Temporal of England. Printed for John Nicholson, and sold by E. Evets, at the Green Dragon in St. Paul's Church-yard."

Mr. Singer (at p. 218 of his *History of Playing Cards*) has misprinted the word " King " as *Kings*, conveying the idea of something more historical than a series of contemporary armories: but a copy of the title-page of this pack (from a copper-plate) happens to be preserved in the curious collections of Bagford at the British Museum,[1] and it is satisfactory in identifying the production in question. We give a literal copy:—

1688.

(*Royal Arms.*)

CARDS

containing the ARMS *of the*

KING

And all the LORDS

Spirituall & Temporall

OF ENGLAND.

This may be printed

Norfolke and Marshall.

---

[1] Harl. MS. 5947, fol. 4. The date 1688, placed in small figures at top, was probably inserted for a second edition.

It is supposed that these Cards, which thus appeared with the *Imprimatur* of the Earl Marshal, were edited by Gregory King, then Somerset Herald; as " A Pack of Cards containing the Arms of the English Nobility. Lond. 1684," is attributed to him in Watt's *Bibliotheca Britannica*. No copy of them has been seen by any recent writer on the subject, but Chatto[1] believed the pack to be the same which is thus briefly described by Menestrier.[2]

The four pips of Hearts, Diamonds, Spades, and Clubs were all printed in black with their numbers in cypher by their side, and the Kings, Queens, and Princes were designated by the letters K., Q., and P. (as in the preceding). For the four Kings were adopted the four kingdoms of which the King of England bore the armories: England for the King of Hearts;[3] Ireland for the King of Diamonds; France for the King of Spades; and Scotland for the King of Clubs. Upon the Queen of Hearts were given the arms of the Duke of York, afterwards James II.; on the Queen of Diamonds those of Prince Rupert; on the Queen of Spades, those of the Archbishops of Canterbury and York; and on the Queen of Clubs those of the Dukes of Norfolk, Somerset, and Buckingham. The aces were for Barons, as well as the twos, threes, and fours. The fives for Bishops, four together. The sixes, for Viscounts. The sevens, eights, nines, and tens for Earls.

A pack of cards of Scotish Heraldry, lately in the possession of Mrs. Lee Warner, and now of her son-in-law Capt. W. E. G. L. Bulwer, of Quebec, East Dereham, was described by the Rev. G. H.

---

[1] Origin and History of Playing Cards, 1848, p. 152.

[2] *Bibliothèque Curieuse et Instructive*, ut prius. Should any of our readers be prepared to enable us to describe them more particularly, we shall esteem their doing so a particular favour.

[3] The association of the heart with loving affection makes the suit of Hearts naturally the favourite when used in a borrowed or metaphorical way. In one instance we find it applied politically to the unfortunate Charles I. In the Royal collection of Newspapers and Pamphlets at the British Museum, vol. 7, art. 11, is a political piece, entitled " *The Bloody Game at Cards*, As it was played betwixt the King of Hearts and the rest of His Suite against the residue of the packe of cards: wherein is discovered where faire play was plaied, and where was fowl. (*Woodcut of a King of Hearts.*) Shuffled at London, Cut at Westminster, Dealt at Yorke, and Plaid in the open field, by the Citty-clubs, the country Spade-men, Rich-Diamond men, and Loyall Hearted men." 4to. pp. 8. It is dated in MS. Feb. 10, 1642(-3).

Dashwood, F.S.A. in the fifth volume of the *Norfolk Archæology*. It contains the armories of the Nobility of Scotland as they stood in the year 1691. The King of Hearts is accompanied by the arms of Scotland, and the other three Kings by those of England, France, and Ireland. The four Queen cards bear the arms of as many dukes; and the Princes those of the marquesses of Douglas, Graham, and Athol, together with the shields of three earls on the Prince of Diamonds. The other earls, sixty-five in number, occupy the tens, nines, eights, sevens, and sixes; and eighteen viscounts and fifty-three barons are distributed among the smaller cards.[1] The wrapper displays, in two compartments, the official seal of Sir Alexander Araskin, of Cambo, Knight and Baronet, Lyon King of Arms, and the arms of the city of Edinburgh, with this title:—

PHYLARCHARUM SCOTORUM GENTILICIA INSIGNIA ILLUS-TRIUM A GUALTERO SCOT AURIFICE CHARTIS LUSORIIS EX-PRESSA. SCULPSIT EDINBURGI. ANNO DOM. CIƆ.IƆC.XCI.[2]

Four of these cards are represented in the annexed fac-simile engravings (first published in the *Norfolk Archæology*).

THE QUEEN OF CLUBS displays the atchievements of the Duke of Lennox and the Duchess of Buccleuch placed under one coronet, as if they had been man and wife. This, however, can only have been intended by the artist to refer to their enjoying the same dignity in the peerage. The Duchess was the heiress of the old house of Scot, Earls of Buccleuch, and widow of the Duke of Monmouth. The Duke of Lennox's shield is further ensigned with the Garter, and the Duchess's with the *cordeliere*, then usual for widows in French heraldry, and occasionally adopted in our own island. A remarkable feature of the Lennox shield

[1] The names are catalogued by Mr. Dashwood in the *Norfolk Archæology*.

[2] In a copy of these *Insignia* in the library at Abbotsford Sir Walter Scott made a note, stating that one Walter Scott, goldsmith, of Edinburgh, was admitted into the fraternity of his craft in 1686, and another, using a similar signature, in 1701. On the 28th Aug. 1706, a daughter of *umquhile* Walter Scott was appointed to the Trades' Maiden Hospital; but the second of the name survived, being deacon of the incorporation for the two years 1706-7 and 1707-8. (Taylor, p. 204, from a communication of John Stuart, esq. Sec. S. Ant. Soc.) Other copies are at Drummond Castle and in the library of David Laing, esq. at Edinburgh: and one was possessed by the late Benj. Nightingale, esq. and sold with his museum at Sotheby's in 1862.

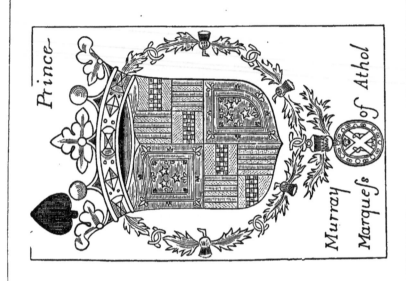

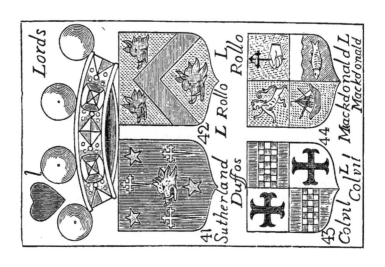

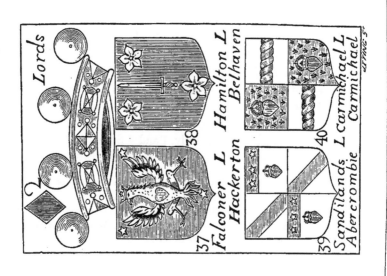

is, that the arms of Scotland, instead of those of France and England, are placed in the first and fourth quarters. This mode of marshalling the royal arms was then prevalent in Scotland, and has been maintained in some measure to more recent times; but it could not be legally justified in the case of the Duke of Richmond and Lennox, whose arms had been granted and officially blasoned by the English college.

THE PRINCE OF SPADES presents the arms of *Murray, Marquess of Athol,*—in the first and fourth quarters Murray within a tressure, in the second and third Athol and Stuart quarterly: ensigned with the collar of the Thistle.

The DEUCE OF DIAMONDS contains four Lords:—

37. *Falconer L. Hackerton.*[1] Azure, a crowned falcon displayed argent, charged on the breast with a heart gules, between three mullets of the second.[2]

38. *Hamilton L. Belhaven.* Gules, a sword erect proper between three cinquefoils argent.

39. *Sandilands L. Abercrombie.* 1 and 4, Argent, a bend azure, for *Sandilands*; 2 and 3, Argent, a heart gules, crowned or, on a chief azure three mullets of the field for *Douglas.*

40. *Carmichael L. Carmichael.*[3] Azure, semée de lis ermine, a heart gules, crowned of the second, for *Douglas* of Pittendriech (?); 2 and 3, Argent, a fess wreathy azure and gules for *Carmichael.*

The ACE OF HEARTS also contains the shields of four Lords:—

41. *Sutherland L. Duffos.* Gules, a boar's head erased between three mullets and three cross-crosslets fitchée or. (Composed of the coats of *Sutherland,* Gules, three stars or; *Chisholm,* Gules, a boar's head erased argent; and *Cheyne,* Azure, three cross-crosslets fitchée argent; which are marshalled quarterly, 1 and 4 Sutherland; 2 Cheyne, and 3 Chisholm, in Douglas's Peerage of Scotland, by Wood.)

[1] The eighth Lord Halkerton succeeded in 1778 to the earldom of Kintore, in which the former title has since been merged.

[2] The arms given to the peers on those cards are in various respects different from those usually stated. Douglas's *Peerage of Scotland* (edit. Wood) places a mullet argent in the arms of Lord Belhaven instead of the sword.

[3] Advanced to the earldom of Hyndford 1701. Lord Carmichael's ancestor, Sir John Carmichael (ob. 1600), married Margaret, daughter of Sir George Douglas of Pittendriech, sister of David, 7th Earl of Angus, and of James, Earl of Morton, Regent of Scotland. In addition to the crowned heart on an ermine field, Nisbet (i. 78) gives to the Pittendriech family a chief azure charged with three stars argent.

42. *Rollo L. Rollo.* Or, a chevron azure between three boar's heads erased sable.

43. *Colvil L. Colvil.* 1 and 4, Argent, a cross moline sable; 2 and 3, Gules, a fess checky argent and azure, for *Lindsay.*

44. *Mackdonald L. Mackdonald.* 1. Argent, a lion rampant gules ; 2. Or, a dexter hand couped in fess proper holding a cross-crosslet fitchée gules; 3· Or, a lymphad or galley sable; 4. Vert, a salmon naiant proper, and a chief wavy argent.

The company of Cardmakers of London was incorporated by letters patent of Charles the First, dated 22 Oct. 1629, by the name of *The Master, Wardens, and Commonalty of the Mistery of the Makers of Playing-Cards of the City of London.*[1] In 1739 it was governed by a Master, two Wardens, and eighteen As-sistants; but they had neither Livery, nor Hall to transact their affairs in.[2] The arms assumed by them were, Gules, on a cross argent between four ace-cards proper, viz. the aces of Hearts and Diamonds in chief and those of Clubs and Spades in base, a lion passant guardant of the first. *Crest*, on a wreath an arm embowed in armour proper, the hand holding a heart. *Motto:* CORDI ERECTO STANT OMNES.[3] *Supporters*, (as added in *Edmondson's Complete Body of Heraldry*, fol. 1780.), Two men in complete armour proper, garnished or, on each a sash gules. But we do not find these armorial insignia at all recorded in the College of Arms.

At the end of a little book of City ceremonials, printed when Alderman Barber (1710–17—) was City printer, is a list of eighty-four companies then existing, of which the Cardmakers and the Fanmakers stand the last in rank.[4] In a similar list of ninety-three companies in the 1755 edition of Stowe's *Survey* the Cardmakers are No. 72, " no Hall nor Livery." When the Company ceased we have not ascertained.

The English manufacturers were continually annoyed by a large importation of foreign cards, and it is stated that in 1631 (only two years after the incorporation of the Company) the

[1] Pat. 4 Car. p. 22, m. 6.

[2] Maitland, Hist. of London, 1739, p. 603.   Edit. 1775. p. 1243.

[3] We give the third word by conjecture : not having been able to find the motto except in Maitland, where it is misprinted ERAU.

[4] Seymour, Survey of London, ii. 413.

King created a monopoly for purchasing all cards, and selling them out at an advanced price.[1]   In 1638 it was ordered by proclamation that cards imported should be sealed in London and packed in new bindings or covers.   In 1684 the price of a pack of cards in England was four-pence, which is double that mentioned by Roger Ascham in 1545.   In the reign of Queen Anne, according to Mr. Chatto, they had become much cheaper, not more than a penny,—the wholesale price, one pack with another, being only three-halfpence.   There were then about a hundred cardmakers in and about London, who consumed annually 40,000 reams of Genoa paper.

The Cardmakers of Paris formed a guild, calling themselves *tarotiers*, in the sixteenth century.   There is a code of their statutes dated 1594.   By an ordonnance of the 22d May, 1583, the tax of *un sou Parisis* was laid on every pack intended for

CAEN.   LYONS.   MANS.

METS.   PARIS.   POITIERS.

THIERS.   TOULOUSE.   ROUEN.

[1] Macpherson, Annals of Commerce, i. 679.

home use. By another ordonnance 14 Jan. 1605, the exportation of cards was prohibited ; and, for the easier collection of the duty, it was determined that the manufacture should be limited to the towns of Paris, Rouen, Lyons, Toulouse, Troyes, Limoges, and Thiers in Auvergne. Shortly afterwards the like privilege was accorded to Orleans, Angers, Romans, and Marseilles; and, by way of recompence to other places, it was arranged that the revenue should be expended in the encouragement of manufactures. Subsequently, in 1751, it was devoted to the support of the Ecole Militaire.[1] The trade in 1847 was carried on by 129 makers, of whom sixteen were in Paris, employing 263 men, women, and children. In that year the stamp was placed on 5,555,807 packs,—an amount reduced 32 per cent. in the year following, in consequence of the population then finding employment for the time which they had before been spending in mere amusement.[2]

In common with other trading communities of the middle ages the Card Companies of France assumed armorial insignia; which were designed in very appropriate fashion, as will be seen by the annexed cuts, extracted from the recent work of Mr. Taylor. By the names it is evident that other towns obtained the privilege of the manufacture, besides those which we have mentioned on the authority of Chatto.

IRISH FAMILY HISTORY.

A History of the Clanna-Rory, or Rudricians, descendants of Roderick the Great, Monarch of Ireland : compiled from the ancient records in the libraries of Trinity College and the Royal Irish Academy, from our native Annals, the publications of several learned Societies, and other reliable sources. By RICHARD F. CRONNELLY, Constabulary Reserve Force. To which is added, by way of Appendix, a paper on the Authorship of the " Exile of Erin," by a Septuagenarian. Dublin, 1864. 8vo. pp. 135. (Price 18*d*.)

A History of the Clan Eoghan or Eoghanachts, descendants of Eoghan More or Eugene the Great, compiled from all the accessible sources of Irish Family History. By RICHARD F. CRONNELLY, Irish Constabulary Force. Dublin, 1864. 8vo, pp. xii. 137-267. (Price 18*d*.)

It may be observed by the pagination which we have noted above, that these two publications, though bearing distinct title-pages, form

[1] Chatto, p. 271.   [2] Taylor, p. 246.

Parts I. and II. of a work intended to be continuous, under the title of IRISH FAMILY HISTORY. The Introductory essay which is prefixed to the second of them offers some home thrusts, in answer to those who are inclined to cavil at what they may hastily regard as the visionary genealogies of the Irish and the Welsh. It is remarked with some show of truth that the extremely mixed race of which the modern English are composed, having lost the history of their remote ancestry, are prone to discredit such claims as they cannot advance on their own account. The shades of Hengist and Cerdic, of Creoda and Uffa, have faded (it is asserted) from men's sight, and are lost amongst the ruins of fallen kingdoms. The Saxon noble and the Saxon churl are alike untraceable: their generations were never recorded; they were swept from mortal ken by the Normans. With the Celts of Wales and of Ireland it has been different. Giraldus Cambrensis, in the twelfth century, wrote of them: " Generositatem vero, et generis nobilitatem, præ rebus omnibus magis appetunt; unde et generosa conjugia plus longè cupiunt quàm sumptuosa vel opima. Genealogiam quoque generis sui etiam de populo quilibet observat, et non solum avos, atavos, sed usque ad sextam vel septimam et ultra procul generationem memoriter et promptè genus enarrat. Genus itaque super omnia diligunt, et damna sanguinis et dedecoris ulciscuntur." Four centuries later the like observations were made by Sir Warham St. Leger: "As there is nothinge (he remarked) that the Irishe more esteme than the Nobilitie of bloud, preferringe it farre before eyther vertue or wealth, so abhorre they nothinge more than disparagement, more odious unto them than death." And now (adds the writer before us) after a further lapse of three centuries, the Irish are still apt to think it something for a poor man to have in his veins—and they are indulgent even if he boast of it —the blood of Heber Fionn, of Ir, of Heremon, or of Ith.

To meet a sentiment so generally diffused among the people at large, a work in a popular and accessible shape like the present is well suited. To all their countrymen the patriotism, the valour, the learning, and the piety of Irishmen of bye-gone ages are an inheritance, and therefore to all are these sketches, genealogical, historical, and biographical, presumed to be acceptable : but in an especial manner must they be dear to those families in whose veins still runs the blood of those saints and heroes whose pedigrees are commemorated. It is remarked in another page that even the pedigrees of the Norman colonists were more carefully kept in Ireland than those of their kinsmen and contemporaries who remained in England : of which as examples are cited the genealogies of the Fitz-Geralds, the Butlers, the De Courcys, the Barrys, and the Roches. We need not therefore be surprised that the genealogies of the native Irish chieftains were preserved with affectionate care. "The scrupulous accuracy with which every individual was placed at birth, and withdrawn at death, on and from the Sept Roll, owed its origin, not merely to the Celtic reverence for blood, but to a motive of worldly prudence, which to our English readers will appear more natural. That the ancient Irish (said the late learned Dr. O'Donovan,) should have been careful to preserve their genealogies need not be a matter of surprise; and that these are perfectly authentic may be expected, as they were entered on the local books of pedigrees, and preserved in the poems of family or hereditary bards. Those of the lowest rank among a great tribe traced and retained the whole line of their descent with the same care which in other nations was peculiar to the rich and great; for it was from his own genealogies that each man of the tribe, poor as well as rich, held the charter of his civil state, the right of property in the cantred in which he was born, the soil of which was occupied by one family or clan, and in which no one lawfully possessed any portion of the soil if he was not of the same race as the chief. This was also the case with the Welsh." (*Miscellany of the Celtic Society*, p. 144.)

We will now describe briefly how Mr. Cronnelly has arranged his account of 1. the descendants of Roderick the Great; and 2. the descendants of Eugene the Great.

Commencing "at the beginning," he first gives the genealogy from Adam, by fifty generations, to Rughraidhe Mor, or Roderick the Great, born A.M. 3352, and who, having reigned over Ireland for thirty years, died at Rath-beagh, on the Nore, in the county of Kilkenny, in the 80th year of his age. It was some fifteen generations earlier that Ir the son of Milesius had led his colonists to the land of Erin from the shores of Gallicia.

The families which claim descent from Roderick Mor are introduced by Mr. Cronnelly in the following order :—

1. MAGENNIS, "the senior family of the illustrious Irian or Rudrician race." The last notable chieftain of this name was Hugh Magennis, who died in 1595; but several of the race distinguished themselves in the army of James the Second, and afterwards shared the hard fortune of the Irish Brigade. Some of them were Colonels and Chefs de Bataillon in the service of France, and three became Knights of St. Louis. It is added that "The unhappy Dr. Magennis, who was committed for the murder of Mr. Hardy in June, 1783, was a senior representative of this family." Here "committed" is, we presume, a mis-

print for *convicted:* his trial and conviction took place at the Old
Bailey in London, on the 17th June, 1783, and is very fully reported
in *The Gentleman's Magazine* of that month, pp. 75-79.[1] It is there
stated that " The son of the unhappy Dr. Magennis's brother takes the
title of Lord Viscount Iveah of the kingdom of Ireland, but, on account
of some old outlawry, the title is not acknowledged by the House of
Peers. The last Lord Iveah, whose family name was Magennis, and
who sat in Parliament, was godson to King William III., and, what is
not a little remarkable, was murdered,"—the story of which is added.

In our own times, commercial enterprise and a princely munificence
have won a world-wide reputation for this ancient name, under a somewhat abbreviated form, for Mr. Cronnelly further states that

" BENJAMIN LEE GUINNESS, Esq., is one of the representatives of this ancient and
once powerful Sept ; but his pedigree is not yet satisfactorily traced."

2. O'MORE,—in Irish Mordha, and in English Moore.   Mordha,
from whom the name is derived, was thirty-first in descent from Roderick ; and there are records of many distinguished O'Mores, from the
date 1016, when Geathin O'More, a chieftain of Leix, was slain.

The famous *Rory O'More* of song and story was the head of the
insurrectionists of 1641.   His confederate chiefs Lord Maguire and
MacMahon, being taken prisoners, were brought to England, and hung
at Tyburn.   O'More buried himself in the woods of Ballyna, where he
soon after died.   This was the last of the native chieftains of Leix who
wielded much power : but after his death the leadership of the Sept
was assumed by Lewis O'More, a Colonel of the Catholic confedera-
tion ; whose great-grandson James O'More of Ballyna was father of
Letitia married to Richard O'Ferrall, grandfather of the present Right

---

[1] Mr. John Hardy was a hosier in Newgate Street, with whom Dr. Magennis
lodged, and the fatal event occurred during an accidental domestic fracas. Dr.
Daniel Magennis was a man of threescore years of age ; had been an army surgeon,
and had seen much service in the West Indies. The position in which his sudden
violence had placed him excited great commiseration, for he had many friends of
distinction who could speak to his character for humanity and gentleness of disposition. As witnesses to these qualities there came forward at the trial Mr. Daniel
Shiel, a West India merchant, who had known him for twelve years in Jamaica, Lord
Viscount Barrington, the Earl of Effingham, Major-Gen. Murray an uncle of the
Duke of Athol, no less a man than Edmund Burke, Major Fleming who had known
him for seventeen years, Mr. Alderman Sawbridge, and Governor Nugent of Tortola.
The judge (Willes) would not hear of an acquittal, and the jury, to the surprise of
the auditory, brought a verdict of Wilful Murder instead of Manslaughter. The Re-
corder in passing sentence declared he had never felt so much pain and affliction.
Qu. Was the sentence carried into execution ?

Hon. Richard More O'Ferrall of Ballyna. Of this family we observe that the modern genealogy may be seen in Burke's *Landed Gentry*.

3. O'CRONNELLY. The families of this name in Ulster and Connaught derive themselves from Cronghilla, who died in 935, and who was in the eleventh generation from Conal, 29th in descent (in M'Gennis's pedigree) from Roderick the Great. This Conal Cearnach, or the Victorious, left his name to the Conaille Murtheimhne, a large division of the province of Ulster, afterwards occupied by his descendants. There were also Cronnellys of Munster, but of a different race.

Our genealogist (p. 25) claims as an offshoot of the O'Cronnellys THOMAS CRANLEY, archbishop of Dublin, and lord chancellor of Ireland, temp. Rich. II. He says that

" Upon the defeat of the Ultonians in 1177, one of the chiefs of the family under notice was given as a hostage for the future fealty of the Conaille to the De Courcy, by whom he was sent to England, where he became the ancestor of the Cranleys of Cranley ; one of whom, a Carmelite friar. was elected Archbishop of Dublin, in 1397, at the instance of Richard II. This prelate came to Ireland in the following year, and was appointed Lord Chancellor by King Richard, who sent his *protegé* on a mission to the continent, and furnished him with letters of protection. He died at Farrington in England [Faringdon in Berkshire], on the 25th of May 1417, and was buried with great solemnity in the New College, Oxford, where a fair stone, adorned with brass plates, bearing the figure of a bishop clothed in his sacred vestments, was placed over his remains."

The fine sepulchral brass of Cranley, who was one of the wardens of New College, is well known: it has been engraved in the works of Gough, Waller, and Boutell. But we must demur to his being affiliated to the Cronnellys. We have places named Cranley both in Surrey and in Suffolk, from one of which the archbishop more probably derived his name and origin.

It is admitted that the O'Cronnellys sank into comparative obscurity at an early period of Irish history ; but, having settled in the county of Galway, they became through an heiress the coarbs or representatives of St. Grellan, the patron saint of the race of Colla da Crich, whose crozier was borne on the standards of the princes of Hy-Many, as is told in the Book of Lecain. "This crozier (says Dr. O'Donovan, writing in 1843,) was preserved for ages in the family of O'Cronghaile or O'Cronnelly, who were the ancient Comorbas of the saint. It was in existence so late as 1836, being then in the possession of a poor man named John Cronelly, who lived near Ahascra, in the east of the county of Galway." It is supposed to have been sold to some collector of antiquities, in which case it may probably still be recovered and identified. The arms of Cronnelly are two croziers in saltire.

Daniel O'Cronnelly, called Donal Buidhe or the yellow, was an officer in the army of Charles the First, and fought on the field of Edgehill and at Marston Moor. He is said also to have been at Worcester with Charles the Second; after which he repaired to his ancestral home at Killeenan near Rahasane, co. Galway, where he died about 1659, and was buried in the now ruined church of Kileely.

Intending to return to this important work, we close our review for the present with the following passage, at the end of which the author has introduced a very modest allusion to himself:

" According to a tradition in the family, the O'Cronnellys possessed the greater portion of the parish of Killeenen, together with the lands of Lavally, Ballynasteage, and Kileely, all in the barony of Dunkellin and county of Galway. These, however, have long since passed into other and various hands; and the lineal descendant of Matudhan, prince of Crich Cualgne, and of Donal of the Moor, holds the initiatory grade in the Irish Constabulary Force."

(*To be continued.*)

The Peerage, Baronetage, and Knightage of Great Britain and Ireland, for 1865, including all the Titled Classes. Twenty-fifth year. By ROBERT P. DOD, Esq. 12mo. pp. 770. (Price 10s. 6d.)

DEBRETT's Illustrated Peerage, of the United Kingdom of Great Britain and Ireland. 1865. 12mo. pp. xxxvi. 504. (Price 7s.)

DEBRETT's Illustrated Baronetage and Knightage, of the United Kingdom of Great Britain and Ireland. 1865. 12mo. pp. xxxii. 504. (Price 7s.)

These books being offered to our critical notice on the same day, and being compiled with the same aim and object, it is impossible to estimate them fairly without taking a comparative view of them : more particularly as they are now much more nearly assimilated in form and arrangement than they have ever been before. In the long review [1] which we presented last year of the whole series of this class of literature, past and present, we pointed out the change that had taken place in all successively having adopted the alphabetical form of arrangement, instead of that of rank and precedence, so as to furnish the ready reference of a dictionary without the intervention of an index. This plan has evidently been found useful and convenient, and is now carried out more entirely than ever.

The work of Captain Dod (whose premature death has recently occurred) has reached its twenty-fifth year, and is as closely compacted a manual of many thousand facts as the number of pages above mentioned could well be made to contain. It has arrived at this stage of completeness by the continued labour and attention of many years, and the new Editor is evidently impressed with the importance of maintaining that character

[1] Vol. II. pp. 348-363.

which Captain Dod so diligently acquired for accuracy and alacrity in recording every change incidental to the public or private lives of the subjects of the work. The leading articles of the book, in its first alphabetical arrangement, consist, not only of the Peers, Baronets, and Knights (of various orders), but also of the Privy Councillors, the Bishops (Irish, Scotish, and Colonial,) the Lords of Session, the Widows of Baronets and Knights, &c. In its second Part are contained the Junior Nobility bearing Courtesy Titles; with various tabular lists. Its further merits have been described at p. 358 of our last volume.

The two other volumes before us are really a new work on a similar plan, though they bear the name of one who had attained great popularity for works of the kind before the first appearance of Dod. We have related in the article before referred to, how that the Peerage and Baronetage of Debrett were formerly the standard manuals of the London booksellers, before their domain was invaded by "Lodge" or "Burke." The numerous editions of Debrett's *Peerage* are enumerated in our vol. ii. p. 352, the first having appeared in 1802, and the last in 1849; and in p. 354 those of his *Baronetage*, of which the first appeared in 1804, and the last in 1840. The revival of DEBRETT's *Peerage and Baronetage*, in 1864, was noticed in pp. 272, 355; and now we have to describe the expansion of that book into two, one a *Peerage* and the other a *Baronetage*, as in the days of old.

The arrangement of DEBRETT's *Peerage* is now as follows :—

After twenty-four pages occupied with an account of the Royal Family, historical and actual, the Peers of the three Kingdoms are arranged in one alphabet. This includes a genealogical account of all the living members of every family, omitting those that are deceased; accompanied by a list of the several creations of peerage that each enjoys, and the blason of their armorial insignia, which is illustrated by the woodblocks engraved for the former editions of Debrett (with the additions made necessary by new creations). Of the blason we may remark that its perspicuity is considerably impaired by a superfluity of punctuation.

The alphabet of Peers is interspersed by all the inferior dignities of peerage that are merged in others. This is very well, so far as regards the Courtesy Titles which are personally borne by sons or grandsons; but it would be better to confine the entries to that limit, perhaps with those by right of which peers of Scotland or Ireland sit in the House of Lords, the rest being otherwise given as we have already stated. Another presumed improvement that we still less appreciate is the insertion of the names of livings of which the peers are patrons. There is nothing of personal importance (except to clerks expectant) in this information. Some account of their estates or mansions would be more to the purpose, though perhaps not so readily procured, nor brought into available dimensions.

After this main division of the book, there follow,—1. The Lords Spiritual: Archbishops and Bishops in alphabetical arrangement; the Bishops in Scotland, the Colonial Bishops, and Retired Bishops, each arránged in like manner; and succeeded by a list of the Chaplains in Ordinary to the Queen,—we presume because some of them may be Bishops in embryo; 2. An alphabetical list of such Younger Sons of Peers, as either are married, or hold appointments in the army or navy, or learned professions, or have obtained degrees and distinctions in the universities; 3. A similar list of the Married Daughters of Peers; 4. A biographical list of the Judicial Bench, accompanied by engravings of their armorial bearings. The last is certainly a novel feature in a Peerage,—except that the Judges, as knights, have been included in Dod's book. Their marriages are given, but why not also their parentage? For the Bishops we are presented with their parentage, and not only their marriages, but their children also, which is something quite new. After these, follow mere nominal lists of the Privy Council, of Baronets, (might they not now be omitted from the Peerage?) Ambassadors, the Royal Households, and Convocation. Lastly, twenty-seven pages on Heraldic Distinctions and Armorial Bearings; and fifteen on the Orders of Knighthood.

The companion volume of DEBRETT's *Baronetage and Knightage* corresponds in the main with the Peerage, and is illustrated in like manner with wood engravings of armorial bearings. The preliminary matter as to the Royal Family and to titles, orders, and degrees of peerage, precedence, and dignity, appears to belong, on the whole, rather to the former volume. One great oversight that we notice is that the Baronets of Nova Scotia (or of Scotish families before the Union), though included, are not specially distinguished, nor are their armorial bearings charged with their appropriate badge. As is so usual in Scotland, they generally boast supporters.

The biographical *Knightage* occupies rather more than fifty pages of the latter part of the volume: it includes marriages, like Dod's, but not children. Of the final pages, six are occupied by accounts of the several orders of Knighthood, and nominal lists of their members; and then lists are also inserted of the present Sheriffs and of the House of Commons.

From the description we have now given, it will be perceived that these "Debretts" are very different from those of former days; for they contained genealogical histories of the families, as the work of Burke does now, whilst the present manuals are confined to living members, after the plans of Lodge and Dod. They are really new works, both in form and substance, adapted to the old name. We should have much more to say upon details, did not our limits now confine us to general criticism. We shall therefore only add, for the present, that whilst we consider Captain Dod's book one of the highest merit, as a compact aggregation of *biographical* facts, we think there may be room for *genealogical* manuals arranged on the plan formed by the new Editor of Debrett, and it is evident that to some people, both as regards price and convenience, they will be more acceptable than the very ponderous and gigantic tomes we have elsewhere described as genealogical encyclopedias. We hope therefore that he may be encouraged to bring his books to a state of further completeness in future years.

List of County Court Judges. Note on the Abolition of certain Franchise Gaols. London: C. W. Reynell, Little Pulteney-street. 1865. Royal 8vo. pp. 50.

This pamphlet, though neither heraldic nor genealogical, has a claim on our notice as a valuable contribution to legal biography. The List of Judges of the County Courts contains 103 names, with the dates of their appointments and of being called to the bar, and particulars of their other preferments and professional productions and performances. At the first institution of the County Courts in 1847, fifty-four Judges were appointed by Lord Chancellor Cottenham, and six by the Earl of Carlisle as Chancellor of the Duchy of Lancaster. The remaining forty-three have supplied the subsequent vacancies occasioned by deaths or resignations. To this list are appended Notes on the subjects of precedence, salaries, the amount of business in the several courts (of which some statistical tables are presented), and other matters of interest; and, finally, a relation, *How certain Franchise Gaols came to be abolished.* These lingering "Franchise prisons," which were abolished by an Act passed in 1858, were: 1, Swansea Debtors' Prison for the Liberty of Gower; 2, the Prison of the Liberty of Newark for Debtors; 3, Halifax Home Gaol for the Manor of Wakefield; 4, the Gaol for the Forest and Forest Liberty of Knaresborough, belonging to the Duchy of Lancaster; 5, the Gaol for the Borough and Township of Knaresborough, also belonging to that Duchy; 6, Sheffield Debtors' Gaol, for the Liberty of Hallamshire; and 7, Hexham Debtors' Prison. The steps which led to their abolition are stated to have originated at Swansea, first in a report made by Mr. Perry, Inspector of Prisons, in 1853; and subsequently, after the matter had been impeded by the death of the late and the coldness of the present Duke of Beaufort, by a more energetic remonstrance made in Jan. 1858 by Thomas Falconer, esq. Judge of the County Court of Glamorganshire. From this portion of the pamphlet, and from others, we gain our information of its author: the same gentleman whose writings on the law respecting Changes of Name we have before brought before our readers. Mr. Falconer has held the post of County Court Judge at Swansea from Dec. 1851.

GENEALOGICAL QUERIES.

Browne.—Are the Brownes of Elsing, co. Norfolk, extinct in the male line? In *The Paston Letters* (Ramsay's ed. vol. i. pp. 33, 64, vol. ii. pp. 124, 130, 137,) it appears that there were Brownes in Norfolk before the line founded by William Browne's marriage with the heiress of Hastings of Elsing. There have been Sir William Browne, knt. M.D. of King's Lynn, founder of Cambridge University prizes. J. Browne of Halveyate, John Browne of Tacolnestone [Morley Hall] and William Helsham Candler Brown of St. Mary Hall, Lynn. Were these of the Elsing family? One line of which, if not the family, is represented by the Batts and Astleys.

Hobart Town. Justin Browne.

SIR THOMAS FORTESCUE. Elizabeth eldest dau. of Ferdinando Cary is said to have married, 1st, Francis Staunton of co. Salop, esq. and 2nd Sir Thomas Fortescue. Who was the latter? C. J. R.

PRIDEAUX. In collecting information for a more detailed pedigree of the Prideaux family than any yet published, I met with a statement that one of the name named ARTHUR PRIDEAUX, of Lusan in the parish of Ermington, Devon, did for some time assume the name and arms of Parnell in compliance with the will of his maternal uncle, Nicholas Parnell of Lyons, gent. This Arthur Parnell was born about 1710. I wish to ascertain where or how I can confirm this statement; also what were the armorial bearings of Parnell that he assumed. GEORGE PRIDEAUX.

STANLEY. Who was Sir Hastings Stanley, knight, and to what family did he belong?

The will of "Dame Ellinor Stanley, widow, late wife of Sir Hastings Stanley, knt. deceased," is dated 7th June, 1614, and proved at York 11th March, 1615. She desires to be buried in the church of Haitefield, mentions her sons Hastings and Piercie, and her loving brother Mr. Bartholomew Fletcher. C. J.

[We do not find the name of Sir Hastings Stanley either in the list of Queen Elizabeth's knights or among those of James I. EDIT. H. & G.]

THOMPSON. I am told that, in some heraldric work or MS. of Legh, the Lancashire topographer, the following coat occurs:

"Per fesse embattled argent and sable, three falcons, belled, counterchanged, a canton gules. *Crest*, a demi-ounce erminois, collared, lined, and ringed azure. *Motto*, OPTIMA EST VERITAS."

In what book or MS. of Legh, is this coat likely to be found? I believe it is assigned to the family of Thompson, but to which branch, or where resident, I cannot ascertain. LANCASTRIENSIS.

In Burke's *General Armory* this coat and crest are assigned to Thompson of Yorkshire. [EDIT. H. & G.]

WESTON. I require the following particulars concerning BENJAMIN WESTON, youngest son of Richard 1st Earl of Portland.

The dates of his marriages (according to Burke he was twice married).

When and where he died, and if he left any issue.

It appears from Hutchins's History of Dorsetshire (new edition, vol. i. p. 32) that he was admitted a burgess of Poole, as "Benj. Weston, esq. son of the Lord Treasurer of England," Aug. 26th, 1630, and the name of Weston occurs after that time pretty frequently in the list of the Mayors of Poole up to the middle of the last century. C. H.

By Banks, *Dormant and Extinct Baronage*, 4to. 1809, iii. 609, he is mentioned as Benjamin, who married Elizabeth widow of Charles Earl of Anglesey, and daughter of Thomas Sheldon, of Hanley, in co. Leic. esq., but we do not find him named in Lodge's Irish Peerage as the Countess's second husband. [EDIT. H. & G.]

THE EFFIGY ATTRIBUTED TO GEOFFREY DE MAGNAVILLE,
AND THE OTHER EFFIGIES IN THE TEMPLE CHURCH.

FUIMUS TROES.

WHEN the inns of court, and particularly the Temple, formed an university for the youthful nobility of England, and when many an important transaction or serious consultation took place beside the pillars of the Round Church,[1] the cross-legged knights which lie in that remarkable area continually attracted the vague curiosity, and the extravagant conjectures, of those who were waiting to fulfil their appointments or loitering in mere idleness.

Hentzner, who visited England in 1598, gives vent to the amusing speculation that they were the figures of the Danish monarchs who once reigned in England.

It was a curiosity that was not readily satisfied, for it happened that no authentic information had been handed down for the due appropriation of these monuments of the præ-legal days of the Temple. To two or three only, of the whole, were names assigned by Camden, Stowe, and Weever, and the various London topographers who followed in their train.

In more recent times a name not mentioned by those authors has been attached to one of these effigies, which has thereby been raised into a position of such importance, in regard to the archæology of coat-armour, that it has especially suggested the present investigation.

This effigy has been assigned to Geoffrey de Magnaville, who was advanced to the earldom of Essex by King Stephen and the

---

[1] "Item, they have no place to walk in, and talk and confer their learnings, but in the Church; which all the terme times hath in it no more quietness than the Pervyse of Pawles, by occasion of the confluence and concourse of such as are suiters in the law." Description of the state of the Middle Temple in Cotton MS. Vitellius C. IX. f. 320 a. attributed to the reign of Henry VIII. by Dugdale, in *Origines Juridiciales*, p. 193. Nor was it otherwise two centuries later, when Hudibras was advised to

> Retain all sorts of witnesses
> That ply i' th' Temples, under trees,
> Or walk the Round with knights o' th' posts,
> Among *the cross-legged knights*, their hosts.

Empress Maud, and who died in 1144. Dallaway, writing in the year 1793, thus introduces it:—

" By many antiquaries the precise era of the introduction of ARMS into England is ascertained to have been in 1147, when the second Croisade was undertaken. It is observed by Mr. Gough, in his very accurate and judicious researches, that arms sculptured on the shield of Geoffry de Magnaville Earl of Essex in the Temple Church, who died in 1144, are the earliest which have yet been discovered." *Inquiries into the Origin and Progress of the Science of Heraldry in England*, p. 30.

And again, more vaguely and indefinitely,—

" It has been already observed, that the first instances of the sculpture of Arms upon the effigies placed as sepulchral monuments, now remain in the Temple Church, of the date of 1144." (Ibid. p. 105.)

The dictum thus asserted so positively by Dallaway has been adopted more or less decidedly by many subsequent writers, how far accurately or judiciously it is the object of the following pages to ascertain. Among others, Mrs. Ogborne,[1] who published in 1815 the first portion of an intended *History of Essex*, placed as a vignette on the engraved title a representation of this effigy, thus inscribed:—

Geofrey de Mandevile 1st Earl of Essex, created by K. Stephen 1139, founder of Walden Abbey, Buried in the Temple Church London, the first instance of Armorial Bearings on a Sepulchral figure in England.

When the late Sir Harris Nicolas began to search for the most ancient records of English armory, and could discover none of an

---

[1] Elizabeth Ogborne was the daughter of a physician of eminence and the wife of Mr. John Ogborne engraver. Her book, which is of some value for the Church Notes, and is illustrated with several portraits and other interesting plates, forms only a thin quarto volume, stopping short with the history of twenty-two parishes. As there is no Index to the book we will give an alphabetical list of them, with the pages at which each will be found: Barking 37; Chigwell 237; Chingford 219; Dagenham 57; Eastham 29; Epping 204; Havering 101; Hornchurch 138; Little Ilford 33; Leyton 76; Loughton 252; Nazing 226; Ongar 235; Romford 122; Theydon Bois 259; Theydon Gernon 261; Theydon Mount 272; Waltham 163; Walthamstow 83; Wansted 65; Westham 15; Woodford 71. Mr. Ogborne died at an advanced age, a pensioner of the National Benevolent Institution, Nov. 13, 1837; his widow survived, and died, also a pensioner of that charity.

earlier date than the reign of Henry the Third, he was met by this piece of apparently conflicting evidence, and he thus noticed it in his preface (written in 1829[1]) to the Rolls of Arms of the reigns of Henry III. and Edward III. at p. xxii.:

"Considerable doubt has been entertained as to the period when Heraldry was introduced; and it has been conjectured that if the science was known it was not generally adopted in this country until the reign of Richard the First. Arms, it is true, occur on the tomb of Geoffrey de Mandeville, Earl of Essex, who died in 1148 [1144], but this monument may not have been erected until some years after his death."

In 1845 Mr. M. A. Lower,[2] in his *Curiosities of Heraldry*, p. 40, still maintained the opinion, upon the authority of this effigy, that "Arms upon tombs are found so early as 1144;" but later authors have generally accompanied the introduction of this example with some scruples. Thus, in Parker's *Glossary of Heraldry*, 8vo. 1847, under the head of Escarbuncle:—

"The escarbuncle appears in perhaps the earliest remaining example of armorial bearings in England, upon the shield of Geoffry de Magnaville, or Mandeville, Earl of Essex, in the Temple church, London. He died 1144. It is, however, doubted whether the effigy is older than 1185, the date of the consecration of the church."

And Mr. Planché, in *The Pursuivant of Arms*, 1852, p. 129 —

"In like manner the arms of Geoffrey de Mandeville, Earl of Essex, are said to have been Quarterly or and gules, over all an escarbuncle sable; but a comparison of the shield[3] of the effigy in the Temple church, with that of William Earl of Flanders[4] and others of the same period, will convince you that the Escarbuncle did not become an heraldic charge till its use as a clamp became unnecessary from the alteration of the shape of the shield."

[1] Two years earlier, in an article in the *Retrospective Review*, New Series, vol. i. p. 92, Sir Harris Nicolas had expressed himself to the effect that the effigy in question "is perhaps the earliest instance which exists of the use of armorial bearings in this country."

[2] A woodcut copied from one of Mr. Edward Richardson's profiles of the effigy is prefixed to Mr. Lower's preface, but the scale of the diapering on the shield is so far magnified as to lose much of its due effect.

[3] A cut of the shield accompanies these remarks. It was not, however, made with an eye to Mr. Richardson's drawings, and consequently does *not* show the dancettes.

[4] Engraved in Sandford's *Genealogical History of England*, after O. Vredius.

Lastly, Mr. Boutell, in his *Heraldry, Historical and Popular,* (Third edit. 1864, p. 41), also when mentioning " the Carbuncle or Escarbuncle":—

"It appears upon the shield of Geoffrey de Mandeville, Earl of Essex, in the effigy attributed to him in the Temple Church, the date being about A.D. 1160 [qu. whence this date?]. This example, however, is earlier than the period in which any peculiar charges can be considered to have assumed definite and recognised forms."

By none of these writers is any suspicion expressed that the effigy in question might not really be that of the first Geoffrey de Magnaville, Earl of Essex; though it is now evident that such appropriation was altogether mistaken, as will appear in the sequel of this investigation.

None of the London historians [1] made any mention of the name of Geoffrey de Magnaville as belonging to one of the effigies in the Temple, before the publication, in 1786, of the first volume of Mr. Gough's *Sepulchral Monuments of Great Britain,* in which all the effigies were represented in Plates V. and XIX. Only Burton, in his *History of Leicestershire* 1622, had mentioned for them the names of " Vere Earl of Oxford; Mandeville, Earl of Essex; Marshal, Earl of Pembroke; Bohun, Earl of Hereford; and Lord Ross."

But this had been disregarded by the London historians, as will be seen in the review of them which we shall take presently.

Mr. Gough asserted without hesitation, (at vol. i. p. 23,) that " In the Temple church, London, is the figure of Geoffrey de Magnaville, first Earl of Essex, so created A.D. 1148 " [read 1141]; and the " long pointed shield " on his left arm is described as " charged with an escarboucle on a diapered field." It is afterwards added, " This is the first instance of arms on a sepulchral figure with us. They obtained in France 40 years before."[2]

Gough probably thought that he had substantial authority for his appropriation of this effigy in the chronicle of Walden abbey,

[1] The History of London, by John Noorthouck, 4to. 1773, gives an account of the Temple effigies at p. 646, but the only names mentioned are those of the three Earls of Pembroke.

[2] This allusion refers to an effigy at Mans, engraved in the *Monumens* of Montfaucon, and by Stothard, which is attributed to Elie Comte de Maine, who died in 1109.

which commemorates the same Geoffrey de Magnaville as its
founder. The story of the Earl's death and burial is there related: how that when he was killed at the siege of Burwell
castle in Cambridgeshire, some of the Knights Templars, putting
the habit of their order, with a red cross, upon his body, carried
it to their orchard in the Old Temple at London, and, coffining it
in lead, hanged it temporarily on a crooked tree, because he had
died under sentence of excommunication. Subsequently, that
when his absolution had been received from the Pope, they
buried him in the churchyard of the New Temple, in the porch
before the west door. And further, in another passage of the
same chronicle, it is stated that after Geoffrey was girt with the
sword of the Earldom of Essex, he augmented the arms of his
ancestors with a carbuncle—*postquam gladio Comitis accinctus
erat, arma progenitorum cum carbunculo nobilitavit.*[1] All this
was certainly sufficient to mislead an antiquary of the last century. It would even seem probable that the writer—at whatever
time he lived—knowing that the Earl was buried at the Temple,
may have had in his view this very effigy, the shield of which
displays so magnificent a "carbuncle." But the monastic chronicler was really no competent authority in such a matter. He
was evidently a man of a later age than that of which he was
writing. Our earliest armorial records recognise no carbuncle in
English coats.[2] In the roll of the reign of Henry III. we read for
Le Conte de Mandevile simply " quartele d'or et de goulez:"
which simple quarterly coat was long after held to be that of the
Earldom of Essex.[3] Moreover, we now know very well that, so

[1] Morant, in his History of Essex, vol. ii. p. 546, note [E], has, either by blunder
or design, transferred this statement to a subsequent Earl of Essex, Geoffrey Fitz-
Piers: and it may be noted that this error is inadvertently adopted by Sir Harris
Nicolas at p. xviii. of his Prefatory Remarks to the Rolls of Henry III. and Edward
III. where he states that Geoffrey (the IIId.), who succeeded to the earldom in 1212,
"is considered to have assumed the name and arms of Mandevile, *with an escarbuncle
over all,* which coat and name were adopted by his brother and successor in the Earldom, William, the last Earl." These and similar variations are often merely the
fancies of heralds in later times, when perhaps engaged in depicting (in stained glass
or otherwise) a series of Earls.

[2] We shall discuss the carbuncle in our next Part.

[3] As on the seal of Humphrey de Bohun, Earl of Hereford and Essex from 1297
to 1321.

far from "augmenting the arms of his ancestors," Geoffrey de Magnaville himself died before arms were as yet adopted.

In the very costly architectural renovation bestowed upon the Temple Church in the year 1842 the monumental effigies partook, when they were carefully restored by Mr. Edward Richardson:[1] and a very remarkable discovery was then made with regard to the effigy ascribed to Geoffrey de Magnaville; though, strange to say, it has never yet been publicly noticed. In his Plate III. Mr. Richardson gives a front and two profile views of this effigy, and it is accompanied by the following description:

This cross-legged effigy of Geoffrey de Magnaville, Earl of Essex, is of Sussex marble, and represents him in ring-mail. The hauberk and surcoat descend below the knee. This is believed to be the only example of a monumental effigy with the tall cylindrical flat-topped helmet over the hood of mail. King Henry the Second is represented, on his great seal, wearing such a helmet, with a similar appendage passing down each side of the face and under the chin. Strutt (about 1796) represented this helmet with a half-nasal, covering only the upper part of the nose. No part of it remained, though there is some appearance of a fracture. * * * The Chronicle of Walden Abbey says that on his promotion he augmented his family distinction by adding to his shield an escarbuncle, which is a charge consisting of eight rays, four of them making a common cross, and the other four a saltire. This charge is on the shield, and is represented raised on a diapered field, with three plain spaces left, somewhat resembling a fess dancetté. The head rests on a well-filled lozenge-shaped cushion. The upper lip is without any moustache, of the absence of which this and the effigy in Plate 10 are the only instances among these figures.[2] The legs, though thin and wasted, appear easy and natural.

Now, the little-heeded discovery to which we have alluded is this: that the "three plain spaces left" on the shield,[3] each of

---

[1] As described in "The Monumental Effigies of the Temple Church, with an Account of their Restoration, in the year 1842. By EDWARD RICHARDSON, Sculptor. 1843." Folio. Eleven plates in lithography.

[2] Except that in No. IV. the upper lip is not shown. See note in p. 110.

[3] The accompanying engraving is copied from Mr. Richardson's plate: which we have carefully examined with the original sculpture, and found to be very accurate. The bars are not cut in relief as the carbuncle is, but are formed by the cessation of the diapered pattern, the transverse lines of the diaper running level into the bars.

them resembling a dancette or bar dancetté, are in fact the arms of the person whom the effigy was intended to commemorate. The carbuncle, as it has been called, was nothing more than a constructional part of his shield; the diapering was a mode of ornamentation usual[1] at the time; but the bars dancetté were the distinctive coat-armour of the individual. It is perfectly clear he was not Geoffrey de Magnaville, Earl of Essex, nor any other member of that family. Who he really was it may be difficult to determine: but with our present knowledge of costume and of armour it may not be impossible to arrive at a proximate date for his death.

In one of the earliest rolls of arms, we have a coat Barry dancettée of six argent and gules given for Walter de Balun; and Barry dancettée of six or and sable for Roger Lovedai.[2] Either of these names might claim the effigy, could any connection between them and the Templars be established. Richard de Riveres bore Azure, two bars dancetté or,[3]—where the wavy or watery line was very probably intended to allude to his name.

Were we to regard the shield as an antique form of Undée, we have before us also the names of Achard, Amauri, le Blount, and Lovell. And at a later date three dancettes were borne by the family of Delamare,[4] another allusion to water, as *le mer*.

But since so little is known of the history of the Knights Templars, or their benefactors, we must turn from the coat-armour to the costume of this effigy.

One of its most remarkable features is its cylindrical helmet: upon which the following statements are made by Sir Samuel R. Meyrick:—

" The cylindrical helmet came first into fashion in England about *the latter part of the reign of Richard I.*; though Charles the Good, earl of Flanders, is represented in one on his seal so early as the year 1122; but it may be doubted whether it be the work of that period.[5] The

---

[1] A well-known and remarkable example of this is the effigy of Robert de Vere, third Earl of Oxford, 1221, at Hatfield Broadoak, Essex. Gough, vol. i. plate viii.

[2] St. George's Roll, printed in the *Archæologia*, vol. xxxix.

[3] Roll of the Society of Antiquaries, printed *ibid.*

[4] Brasses of the fifteenth century in the Lady Chapel at Hereford. Oliv. Vredius, p. 11.

Knights Templars, whose costume was appointed by Pope Eugenius in 1186, are represented on their official seal as wearing cylindrical helmets with aventailles, and *they are perhaps the earliest who so did*, Richard introducing it after his return from Jerusalem. The seal of William Earl Ferrers, in 1190, exhibits him in one of these helmets." *Critical Inquiry into Ancient Arms and Armour*, vol. i. p. 86.

"John is represented [on his great seal, 1199] with a cylindrical helmet, but without any covering over his face. The monument in the Temple church, attributed to Geoffrey Magnaville, and *which appears to be about this period*, has one very similar, except that in it the nasal is revived,[1] and there are cheek-pieces, &c." Ibid. p. 101.

Mr. Gough also compares the helmet of this effigy to that of Raoul de Beaumont, who founded the abbey of Estival in 1210, represented by Montfaucon.

On the whole, it would seem that this effigy is of a date very nearly, if not quite, half a century posterior to that of the death of the first Geoffrey de Magnaville, Earl of Essex, in 1144.

Having examined, for the object of this inquiry, all the successive descriptions that have been given of the Temple Effigies, it may be satisfactory to the reader that we should lay a brief abstract of them before him.

We have not discovered any notice of them earlier in date than that of Gerard Legh, in his *Accedens of Armory*, (first edition 1562, fo. 205,) where he describes himself as having " entered into a churche of aunciente building wherein were manye monumentes of noble personnages, armed in knightly habit, with their cotes depeinted on aunciente shieldes, whereat I toke pleasure to beholde."

Their shields were not improbably then actually painted in their proper tinctures,—afterward obliterated by rough usage, and

---

[1] As restored by Mr. Richardson, the helmet *has no nasal*. In his description Mr. Richardson says, " Strutt (about 1796) represented this helmet with *a half-nasal*, covering only the upper part of the nose. No part of it remained, though there is some appearance of a fracture." *Temple Church Effigies*, p. 18. To protect Mr. Richardson from the suspicion of having removed any indication of a nasal, we may point to Stothard's plate, where no symptom of it appears. Strutt perhaps imagined it when the figure was covered with paint: he did not engrave the effigy, but the helmet only, in his *Habits and Dresses*, vol. i. plate xliv.

concealed by coats of white paint, one application of which is
recorded in the year 1706.[1]

The first historical writer who describes them, so far as we are
aware, is Camden,—in the following passage, as it is given by
his earliest translator, Philemon Holland:—

—" having gotten in all places verie faire possessions and exceeding
great wealth, they flourished in high reputation for piety and devotion:
yea and in the opinion, both of the holinesse of the men and of the
place, King Henrie the Third[2] and many noble men desired much to
bee buried in their church among them. Some of whose images are
there to be seene, with their legges acrosse : for so they were buried in
that age that had taken upon them the crosse (as they then termed it)
to serve in the Holy Land, or had vowed the same. Among whom was
William Marshall the elder, a most powerfull man in his time, William
and Gilbert his sonnes Marshalles of England and Earles of Penbroch.
Upon William the elder his tombe I some yeares since read in the
upper part *Comes Penbrochiæ*, and upon the side this verse—

Miles eram Martis, Mars omnes vicerat armis."

Stowe, in his *Survay of London*, enlarges very little upon the
preceding account, but mentions one more name, that of Robert
de Ros:—

" In the Round Walk whereof, which is the west part without the
Quire, there remayne monuments of noble men there buried, to the
number of eleven. Eight of them are images of armed knights : five
lying cross-legged, as men vowed to the Holy Land, against the Infidels and unbelieving Jews; the other three straight-legged. The
rest are cooped stones, all of grey marble.

[1] "In the year 1706 the church was wholly new white-washed &c. &c. also the
figures of the Knights Templars were cleaned and painted, and the iron-work inclosing
them painted and gilt with gold." Seymour's *Survey of London*, fol. 1733, i. 79.

[2] There is documentary proof dated 27 July in the 19th year of his reign that
Henry the Third at one time announced his intention that his body should be interred
at the Temple, as appears by the *Registrum Hosp. S. Joh. Jerus. in Anglia*, in Bibl.
Cotton. fol. 25 a.; and his queen Eleanor, probably at the same period, made the like
promise, " with the consent and approbation of her lord Henry the illustrious King of
England, who had lent a willing ear to her prayers upon the subject." Subsequently,
having rebuilt the abbey church of Westminster, he desired by his will made in 1253,
to be buried there—"Sepulturam corpori meo eligo apud ecclesiam beati Edwardi
Westmonasterii, *eo non obstante quòd prius eligeram sepulturam apud Novum Templum
Londoniæ*." (Hearne, *Liber Niger Scaccarii*, ii. 532; Nichols, *Royal and Noble Wills*,
p. 15.) But his infant son William is said to have been buried at the Temple so late
as 1256. (Weever, p. 443.)

"The first of the crosse-legged was WILLIAM MARSHALL the elder, EARL OF PEMBROKE, who died in 1219.

"WILLIAM MARSHALL his son, EARL OF PEMBROKE, was the second; he died in 1231.

"And GILBERT MARSHALL, his brother, EARL OF PEMBROKE, slain in a tournament at Hertford besides Ware, twenty miles from London · he died in the year 1241.

"After this, ROBERT ROS, otherwise called *Fursan*, being made a Templar in the year 1245, died and was buried there.

"And these are all that I can remember to have read of."

The next account in order of date is that of Burton, who was a member of the Inner Temple, given in his *History of Leicestershire*, fol. 1622, p. 222:

"In the Round Walk at the west end of the church (he says) many of the said order lay buried, their portraits being cut in stone, some of them cross-legged, and who were of the chiefest houses of nobility; as Vere, Earl of Oxford; Mandeville, Earl of Essex; Marshal, Earl of Pembroke; Bohun, Earl of Hereford; and Lord Ross."

Whence Burton caught the names of Vere, Mandeville, and Bohun, does not appear;[1] none of them were adopted by the topographers of London until Mr. Gough made the identification of the effigy of Magnaville which we have now discussed.

John Weever, in his *Funerall Monuments*, fol. 1631, presents an apparently long account of the Temple effigies, but it is really a mere repetition of what had been already said by Camden and Stowe, amplified by biographical details. James Howell in his *Londinopolis*, fol. 1657, derives all his information from the same sources. There is a description of the Temple effigies in Dugdale's *Origines Juridiciales*, fol. 1666; but it is not very particular, nor perfectly accurate. It is as follows:

"Within a spacious grate of iron, in the midst of the Round Walk under the steeple, do lie eight statues in military habits, each of them having large and deep shields on their left arms; of which five are cross-legged. There are also three other gravestones, lying about five inches above the level of the ground; on one of which is a large escocheon, with a lion rampant graven thereon."

---

[1] Burton found some account of the monuments in the Temple in one of the Cottonian manuscripts, but which volume that was we are not now able to discover.

As no such stone as that last mentioned is elsewhere noticed, it may be supposed that the "lion rampant" was transferred from the shield of one of the effigies (hereafter, No. VII.)

We proceed to the account supplied by Hatton in his *New View of London*, 1708, which furnishes some fresh and interesting particulars:—

"In the middle of the area lie the marble figures of nine of the Knights Templars, some of them seven feet and a half in length. They are represented in the habit before described,[1] cumbant in full proportion, five in one rank, inclosed with iron railing, of which three are not cross-legged, and four in another rank, all cross-legged, and inclosed with iron railing, south from the last; but none (that I can find) shew the names of these knights, only that William Marshal, Earl of Pembroke, who died anno 1219, William his son, who died anno 1231, and Gilbert, the said Earl's brother, who was also Earl of Pembroke, 1241, and Robert Rouse, are represented in these images; and another, being the least, was brought from York by Mr. Serjeant Belwood, Recorder of that city,[2] about the year 1682, and is said to be the figure of one Rooce, of an honourable family."

In this account we may observe, that, since that published by Dugdale in 1666, the effigies had increased in number from eight

---

[1] This is imagination, the writer meaning the habit of the Order. Not any one of the effigies is attired in any such costume, but in ordinary armour and surcotes. This supports the tradition that they are rather the effigies of noblemen of high rank who were buried in the church, than of the regular members of the fraternity. No effigy of a Knight Templar has been discovered in England. Montfaucon (*Monumens François*, ii. 184,) represents one of Jean de Dreux, living in 1275. He is figured without armour in the mantle of the Order, with a cross, and wearing a beard. Hollis, in his *Monumental Effigies of Great Britain*, 1840, gives "a Knight Templar, in Walkerne church, Hertfordshire." The grounds of this designation seem to have been that the effigy is cross-legged, and bears otherwise a general resemblance to those in the Temple; but, unlike all of them, the face is wholly concealed by a helmet, of about A.D. 1225, as described by Hewitt, *Ancient Armour*, i. 280.

[2] Roger Belwood met the heralds at their visitation of York on the 21st March, 1665-6, and then described himself as " now a Student of ye Middle Temple, London, æt. 25 an." He was the son of Josias Bellwood of Leathley, co. York, and grandson of Roger Bellwood, a Master of Arts, of York, who died in 1646, or thereabouts. (Visit. of Yorkshire, edit. Surtees Soc. p. 213.) The books of the Middle Temple also record his admission on the 13th June, 1665, and that he was called to the degree of serjeant-at-law on the 11th of April, 1689. He does not appear in Drake's *History of York* to have been Recorder of that city; but he may have been Deputy Recorder to the Earl of Burlington, who was appointed Recorder in 1685. He died in 1694: Drake, p. 301, where he is miscalled *Robert*.

to nine, and they were now arranged in two groups, inclosed with iron railing, instead of being within one " spacious grate" as before. An addition had been made by an effigy brought from Yorkshire, of a member of the family of Roos, and that removal had probably been suggested by the opinion (mentioned by Burton) that one of the original Temple effigies belonged to the same family. On this occasion the effigies had been all shifted, a fact of which Mr. C. A. Stothard was convinced, and he remarks:

" It is almost conclusive from the situation of this figure that, whenever its removal took place, the whole of these statues received their present arrangement, and the two coped stones wanting were taken away and destroyed." *Monumental Effigies of Great Britain*, p. 12.

We add some further observations by Mr. Stothard:

" The most ancient of these statues are Nos. 1, 4, 7, [III. IV. and II. of the description hereafter given]. The first is said to represent Geoffrey Magnaville, and the other two appear to be of the same date with each other. The most remarkable circumstance that distinguishes these three figures arises from their wearing the sword on the right side; the repetition argues against its being accidental, and it is possible this may have been a fashion peculiar to the early Knights Templars, borrowed from their near neighbours, the infidels. *If the effigy called Geoffrey Magnaville really represents that nobleman*, this distinction in him on this ground would be easily accounted for, as he received from the Templars, when dying, the habit of the order. It may be added, as an argument for the high antiquity of these statues, that they are not like any others at present known."

This was written by Mr. Stothard in 1812, and accompanied by a Plate of the effigy, inscribed "GEOFFREY DE MAGNAVILLE, EARL OF ESSEX, in the Temple Church, London:" in which plate, however, the shield appears neither Quarterly nor Dancetté, but uniformly diapered over its surface, with the escarbuncle spread thereon: and so in the engraving by Ogborne.

Stothard, it will be observed, admitted in his description some doubt on the appropriation of the presumed effigy of Magnaville, whilst it was stated positively on his plate. His posthumous editor and brother-in-law Mr. A. J. Kempe, F.S.A., when continuing the subject, on the next page (but yet after an interval of nearly twenty years), after saying that " This effigy is *perhaps* rightly assigned to Geoffrey de Magnaville," and telling the story of his death and funeral (already inserted), suggests that the circumstances thereof "may account for the style of the effigy, which *does not appear to have been made before the latter end of the twelfth century.*"

It is therefore now pretty clear, from the concurrence of much judicious testimony, that Gough and Dallaway, and those who have followed in their track, designating this effigy as that of Geoffrey de Magnaville, Earl of Essex, bearing a shield of his Quarterly coat, surmounted by an escarbuncle, were totally mistaken. As a very early instance of armorial bearings it must still be regarded, but whether actually the earliest on a sepulchral effigy in this country may be worthy of further inquiry.

We shall conclude with a brief description of the Effigies, as they occur in Mr. Richardson's plates, noticing also which are etched by Stothard, and which by Hollis, in his continuation of Stothard's work.[1] We may premise that all the Knights are attired in chain mail and surcotes:—

I. A coffin-lid, *en dos d'âne*, its ridge terminated at the upper end by a lion's head, and at the lower by a lamb's. By Gough this coffin-lid was assigned to William the son of King Henry III. buried at the Temple in 1256. (*Sepulchral Monuments*, vol. i. pl. v.)

II. A knight with his legs straight, a large plain shield on his left arm. Sword at right side. (Engraved by Hollis.)

III. That attributed to Geoffrey de Magnaville.

IV. A knight with hands and legs both crossed, his forehead surrounded with a low cap or coif, his helmet coming over his cheeks and mouth,[2] but shewing his other features; a large plain shield. Sword at right side. (Engraved by Stothard, Plate 15.)

---

[1] There is a vignette representing the whole of the effigies on a small scale in Stothard's *Monumental Effigies of Great Britain*, p. 11. In Knight's London, (edit. 1842, vol. iii. 314) the two groupes are also represented—but without any indication of the dancettes on the carbuncled shield. In the accompanying description by Mr. J. Saunders that effigy is unhesitatingly assigned to Mandeville, and No. IX. to Robert de Ros (Fursan).

[2] The mouth of William Longuespée, Earl of Salisbury, (ob. 1226) in Salisbury cathedral,—an effigy of which there are many engravings, is covered in like manner.

V. Another, straight legs, his hands raised as in prayer: with features youthful, his mouth shown, and moustaches. Under each foot a grotesque human head. Large plain shield.

VI. Another, straight-legged: holding in his right hand the pommel of a sword, the point of which pierces the head of the leopard upon which his feet rest. A plain shield, not so large as the preceding. This is the effigy attributed to William Marshal the elder, Earl of Pembroke, who died in 1219. (Etched by Hollis.)

VII. A cross-legged knight, having both hands on his sword, as if sheathing it, his feet on a lion, and a lion rampant on his shield. The dexter corner of his shield is fancifully supported by a squirrel, which stands on his breast. His features are juvenile, and there seems to be no reason to doubt that this effigy is correctly assigned to William Marshal the younger, Earl of Pembroke, who died in 1231.[1] A pattern of battlements under the pillow of his head has been supposed to allude to the castles of Cardigan and Carmarthen, of which he was governor. (Engraved by Stothard, Plates 26, 27.)

VIII. A fine effigy of a young knight, represented as drawing his sword (the hilt of which is in the form of an escallop-shell) with both his hands: his legs crossed, and feet on a dragon. He has a large shield, but it is plain; and the guige by which it hangs is ornamented with small escucheons, but they are also plain.[2] This effigy has been commonly attributed to Gilbert le Marshal, Earl of Pembroke, who died in 1241: but if it had really been his we might have expected to have found the shield carved with armorial charges, like that of his brother William. They may however have been painted.

IX. A cross-legged knight, his right hand on his breast, with an acutely pointed shield.

---

[1] —"although (remarks Weever) the Annales of Ireland asserted him to be buried by his brother Richard, in the quire of the Friars Predicants in Kilkenny."

[2] There is a peculiarity in the attire of this effigy. "Between the hauberk and surcoat (as described by Richardson) is a plain thick under-garment, fastened with straps or clasps which appear under the arms; probably some kind of haqueton." Mr. Hewitt notices this more particularly as having been either made of leather, or, if of iron, the earliest example of a body-armour formed of two plates that Europe has to offer. *Ancient Armour*, &c. p. 271.

X. A cross-legged figure, the hood of mail let down on the neck, showing the head bare, with flowing hair; the hands raised in prayer, the legs crossed and resting on a lion. On his shield are three water-bougets. Mr. Richardson's plate is inscribed " ROBERT LORD DE ROS, died A.D. 1227;" but in his descriptive letterpress he admits that the costume is of the reign of Edward I. (This is also engraved by Stothard, Pl. 38.)

There is every probability that one of the preceding effigies is that of Robert de Ros, surnamed Fursan, who died in 1227 because it is stated of him that *factus est Templarius, et Londini est sepultus:* and his charter is still extant, by which he granted to the Templars his manor of Ribstone, together with his body for interment.[1] Burton's statement, also, shows that one of the effigies was traditionally attributed to a Lord de Ros.

The effigy No. X. however, was certainly the addition which was made to the series in the year 1682, as related in the extract from Hatton's *New View of London* already given. It is doubtless a de Ros, as shown by the three water bougets; and perhaps came from the priory of Kirkham in Yorkshire, where several of that family were interred.[2]

XI. The effigy of a Bishop, in a low mitre, his right hand raised in benediction, his left holding his pastoral staff, the point of which is thrust into the mouth of the dragon upon which his feet rest. This has been attributed by Browne Willis and others to Silvester de Everdon, Bishop of Carlisle, who died in 1247. (Engraved by Stothard, Plate 28.)

J. G. N.

[1] Monasticon Anglicanum, 1661, vol. ii. p. 557.

[2] It corresponds very closely in design to an effigy at Norton, co. Durham, engraved in Surtees' *History of Durham*, vol. iii. p. 155, and in Hewitt, *Ancient Armour*, plate lxx. Pennant, in his popular but often inaccurate work on London, gives the following absurd description of this effigy: " One of these figures is singular, being bareheaded and bald, his legs armed, his hands mailed, his mantle long, round his neck a cowl, as if, according to a common superstition in early days, he had desired to be buried in the dress of a monk, least the evil spirit should take possession of his body. On his shield are three *fleurs-de-lis.*" The baldness, the cowl, and anything like a monastic dress are altogether imagination, and the fleurs-de-lis a gross misapprehension.

THE LEES OF QUARRENDON.

This family is of very ancient origin, and came originally from Cheshire. It occupied a distinguished position at Wybunbury in that county in the thirty-eighth year of King Edward III., while from a member who settled at Quarrendon, co. Bucks, in the reign of King Henry VII., was descended Sir Henry Lee, the celebrated Knight of the Garter, *temp.* Queen Elizabeth. Sir Henry Lee, Knight, of Ditchley, co. Oxon, first cousin and heir of the K.G., was created a Baronet by King James I. 22nd May, 1611; and his great-grandson, Sir Edward Henry Lee, was by King Charles II. raised to the peerage as Earl of Litchfield, Viscount Quarrendon, and Baron Lee, of Spelsbury, co. Oxon, 5th July, 1674. This peerage became extinct on the death of Robert fourth Earl, in 1776; when the estates in the counties of Bucks and Oxon passed to Henry the eleventh Viscount Dillon, of Ireland, who had married, 26th Oct. 1745, Lady Charlotte Lee, the eldest daughter of George-Henry second Earl of Litchfield, and whose great-grandson now represents the main branch through the female line. Other representatives of the family exist, the intermarriages for many generations having been numerous; amongst them the following,—the Thorntons, of Brockhall, co. Northampton; the Dods, of Cloverley, co. Salop; Lord Clifford, of Chudleigh; the Nevills, of Holt, co. Leicester; Sir Piers Mostyn, Bart.; Lord Vaux, of Harrowden; Lord Palmerston; Sir Alfred Slade, Bart.; the Gore-Langtons, of Somersetshire; the Bishop of Manchester, the Rev. James Prince Lee, D.D.; Benjamin Lee Guinness, LL.D., of Ashford Park, co. Galway; the Lees, of Thame, co. Oxon; Henry Lee, esq., of Barna, co. Tipperary; Sir George Philip Lee, Knt., &c.

It will be the object of the writer of this paper to give as correct and reliable information as possible of the main and all other branches of this family, commencing formally with Benedict Lee, of Quarrendon, who settled there A.D. 1438. In the first place, however, the pedigree connecting this Benedict with the Lees of Cheshire will be set forth; and, in the second, it should be remembered that several recorded pedigrees of the College of Arms differ somewhat materially one from the other. The writer has the advantage of being able to consult four independent pedigrees, all transcripts of originals, possessed by different branches of the family; and thus may be able, in some degree, not only to reconcile certain existing differences, but to add from these and from other sources some valuable information with regard to a gentle, knightly, and noble family of considerable renown, and formerly of high position. The first pedigree, which will be referred to under the mark (A), is a transcript from one originally belonging to the 2nd Earl of Litchfield; the second (B), is copied from a MS. in the possession of Cosmas Nevill, of Holt, co. Leicester, esq.; the third (C), is transcribed from a most interesting original of the date A.D. 1611, at Brockhall, co. Northampton, the seat of the Rev. T. C. Thornton; and the fourth (D), from one formerly in the possession of John Lee, esq., great-grandfather of the late Rev. T. T. Lee, B.A. of Thame and Stokenchurch, co. Oxon. In pedigree (B) the Quarrendon Lees are thus connected with the Lees of Cheshire:—

Sir Walter At Lee, of yᵉ mannor of Lee, of⊤.... Lee Hall there in yᵉ parish of Wibenbury, in yᵉ County Palatine of Chester, yᵉ 36 of King Edward yᵉ 3, whose ancestors had been there seated for ages.

Sir John at Lee, of Lee Hall, 1 K.⊤Isabel, dau. to Sir Piers de Dutton, of Richard yᵉ 2d. | Dutton, com. Chester, kt.

John Lee, of Lee Hall, in Cheshire, esq.,⊤Elizabeth, dau. to Sir Thomas Foulshurst, of Crewe Hall, com. Chester, kt. King Henry yᵉ 4th.

Thomas Lee, of Lee Hall, in Cheshire, esq.,⊤Elizabeth, dau. to Sir John Aston, kt.[1] King Henry yᵉ 6th.

John Lee, of Lee Hall, in Cheshire, esq.,⊤Margerie, dau. to Sir Ralph Hocknell, of Hocknell Hall, com. Chester, kt. King Henry 6.

BENEDICT LEE, of Quarendon, com. Bucks, esq., a younger son; King Edward yᵉ 4th, K. Henry 7th.

Upon this it should be remarked (a), that in Pedigree A, Sir Thomas Foulshurst is called " Sir Thomas Fowlechurch," and that side by side with the John Lee who married Elizabeth Foulshurst are placed the names of two brothers not mentioned

[1] On an ancient silver seal of the sixteenth century, now in the possession of W. J. Legh, Esq., M.P. of Lyme Hall, co. Chester, which the writer of this paper recently inspected, and of which he took impressions, the ancient arms of Aston, co. Chester, appear in the second quarter, thereby connecting the Leghs of Lyme with the Leghs or Lees of Wibonbury. Lyme Hall contains some interesting ancient heraldic glass.

above, Richard Lee and John Lee; also (*b*) that in the same pedigree Sir John Aston is called " Sir John Astron of Astron, Cheshire," and that his daughter's name is given as " Alice," and not as Elizabeth.

The brothers of Benedict Lee, esq. of Quarrendon, stand as follows in Pedigree A.:—

John Lee, of Lee Hall, esq.—Margaret, dau. of Sir Ralph Hocknell, of Hocknell Hall, in Cheshire.

1. Tho-—Wini-   2. John Lee,—Grace   3. Wil-—Mary   5. BENEDICT—Elizabeth, mas Lee, freda   of Astron,   Bagot.   liam   Har-   LEE, of Qua-   heir of of Lee   Cotton.   in Stafford-   Lee, of   leton.   rendon,   John Hall.   shire.   Essex.   Bucks.   Wood,esq.

4. Robert Lee, of Astron, in Staffordshire.

In Pedigree C the information is slightly different, and given at greater length. On the latter account, therefore, it is worthy of being reproduced:—

Thomas   John Lee, of Lee, in the—Margery, dau.   Richard   William Lee.   parish of Wibonbury, in   of ....   Lee.,   Lee.   com. Chester.   Hocknell.

Thomas—Wyne-   John Lee,—Grace,   BENEDICT—Eliza-   Robert—....   Francis Lee, of   fred,   of Aston   dau.   LEE, of   beth,   Lee, of   Lee, Lee, in   dau. of   (*sic*), in   of ...   Quaren-   dau. of   Aston,   sixt Che-   ....   Stafford-   Bagot.   don, in   ....   in Staf-   sone. shire,   Cotton.   shire   com.   Woode,   ford- eldest   seconde   Buck.   of War-   shire, son of   sone.   fifte sone.   wicke-   fourth John.   shire.   sone.

William Lee, of Essex, thirde sone.—.... dau. of John Harleton.

Thus much, then, with regard to the descents as far down as Benedict Lee, the founder of the Lees of Quarrendon. The question now arises, what arms were borne by him? The ancient arms of Lee of Lee Hall were, *Argent, a chevron* (or *a fesse*, for both appear,) *between three leopard's heads sable*[1]. The following arms were also

ORIGINAL ARMS OF LEE OF CHESHIRE.

[1] The Leghs of East Hall, in High Lee, co. Chester, bear the following arms, allowed in 1566: *Argent, a lion rampant gules, armed and langued azure.* The Leighs of West Hall, in High Leigh, now bear the following arms, allowed in 1563: *Or, a lion rampant gules, armed and langued azure.* Originally this branch of the Leghs bore, *Gules, a pale fusillé argent.*

borne by the Lees of Wybunbury: *Gules, a lion rampant or*.[1]
These arms are found again and again repeated in either
the second or third quartering of the Lees of Quarrendon,
in the MS. description, now in the British Museum, of the
armorial bearings at (formerly existing in) St. Peter's Quarrendon, the family burying-place, by Nicholas Charles, Lancaster
Herald. In one shield of the Lees, for example, containing eight
quarterings—in the first of which appears the annulet, as a
mark of cadency—the arms, *Gules, a lion rampant or*, stand
second. [2]

It appears, however, tolerably certain that Benedict Lee, who
settled at Quarrendon A.D. 1438, and who, as is learnt from a
deed in the possession of Lord Viscount Dillon, was made Constable of Quarrendon in 1441, continued
to use the arms, as already given, which
the family had borne in Cheshire. He
married, as one of the above pedigrees
states, Elizabeth, daughter and heiress of
John Wood, of Warwickshire, esquire,
by whom he had issue three sons :

1. Richard Lee, styled "firmare" [far-
mer] in a deed dated 1472, was likewise,
like his father, Constable of Quarrendon,
and bore for his arms, *Argent, a fess*   THE ARMS OF WOOD,
between three crescents sable.   CO. WARWICK.

2. Edward Lee, Constable of Quarrendon from A.D. 1485 to
1486.

3. Robert Lee, Constable of Quarrendon from A.D. 1486 to
1496.

The arms borne by Richard Lee (whether by grant or by
assumption is not now easily determined, as there is no record
of such a grant at the College of Arms,) are undoubtedly those
which since his day have been invariably used by his descendants,

<hr>

[1] These arms appear in the first quarter of the arms of Sir Anthony Lee (wrongly
called Sir Henry Lee), impaling those of Wyatt, co. Kent, at fol. 104 of the MS. of
Nicholas Charles, Lancaster Herald (Lansdowne MS. British Museum, No. 874).

[2] The same arms and quarterings (the eighth being like the first) are likewise found
at fol. 78 of the Visitation of Bucks, 1575-1634. (Harleian MS. British Museum,
No. 1533.)

and by every branch of such, including both that more direct branch which was ennobled, and the other branches which sprung from the main stock during the fifteenth and sixteenth centuries. They occurred on every monumental memorial at Quarrendon; according to Nicholas Charles's MS., no less than thirteen times, either in glass or stone. Here and there other arms may have been used by individual members of the family—as for example: on one occasion by Sir Anthony Lee, already referred to, who reverted to the old Cheshire arms, and also by the widow of Sir Henry Lee, K.G., buried in the north transept of St. Mary's, Aylesbury,

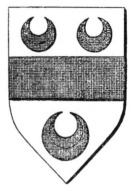

THE ARMS OF LEE, OF QUARRENDON, CO. BUCKS.

who bore the grant specially made to Sir Robert Lee in 1513 ; but the customary arms were those here represented.

Richard Lee married Elizabeth, daughter and co-heiress of William Saunders or Sanders, esq. of the co. Oxon. Arms of Saunders, Ar. a lion rampant azure within a bordure of the second, charged with fleurs de lys or. The Pedigree of Cope of Hampshire gives the arms " charged with eight estoiles or "in the Visitations of 1531 and 1575. Stephen Coape or Cope of Bedenham, in co. Southampton, married another of the co-heiresses of William Saunders, and the arms of Cope impaling Saunders are given by Nicholas Charles, Lansdowne MSS. No. 874, British Museum, as amongst " these four eschocons (which) stand in the north and south windowes of the chauncell" of St. Peter's Quarrendon. The above Richard Lee had issue, by Elizabeth his wife,

ARMS OF SAUNDERS, CO. OXON.

ROBERT LEE, of Quarrendon, Burston, and Hardwicke, co. Bucks, gentleman, sheriff of Bucks in 1521, afterwards knighted. He was Gentleman of the Privy Chamber to King Henry VIII. A special grant of arms was made to him by Thomas Wriothesley, Garter, and Thomas Benolt, Clarenceaux, dated London, April 18th, 1513, 4th of Henry VIII. He is styled "gentilhomme," and the arms are thus described in the grant: "D'argent a une fece d'asur entre trois testes de licorne rasees de sable, sur la fece trois lis d'or. A son tymbre ung laneret dor, ses esles becque et membres de gueules, saississant et repaissant sur une jambe de heron d'asur, assiz sur une torse d'argent et de pourpre, mantelle de gueules double d'argent."

ARMS OF SIR ROBERT LEE
OF QUARRENDON.

Sir Robert Lee married, first, Mary [some pedigrees say Joane] daughter of —— Cope, esq. of the co. Oxon, and by her had issue :

SIR ANTHONY LEE, Knt. of Burston, co. Bucks, commoner of St. John's College, Oxford, M.P. for Bucks, 1 Edw. VI. ob. circa 1550, buried at Quarrendon. Sir Anthony[1] married Margaret, daughter of Sir Henry Wyatt or Wiat, and sister of Sir Thomas Wyatt of Allington Castle, co. Kent. [Arms of Wyatt, Per fesse azure and gules, a barnacle argent.]

The following inscription existing at St. Peter's Quarrendon in 1611, transcribed verbatim from Nicholas Charles' Visitation, has not, we believe, been printed :—

> Anthony Lee knight of worthy name,
> Sire to Sʳ Henry Lee of noble fame,
> Sonne to Sʳ Robert Lee, here buried lyes,
> Whereas his fame and memory never dyes.
> Great in the fortune whence himself did run,
> But greater in yᵉ greatnesse of his sonne;
> His body here, his soul in heaven doth rest,
> What scornde the earth cannot with earth be prest.

In Charles' MS. the arms of Lee (eight quarterings) appear

[1] The arms of Sir Anthony Lee impaling those of Wyatt, may be found tricked at fol. 104, Heraldic Collections of Nicholas Charles, Lansd. MS. 874, British Museum. The old arms of Lee of Cheshire appear in the 1st and 4th quarters, and those granted to his father, Sir Robert Lee, in the 2nd and 3rd quarters.

to the left, and those of Lee impaling Wyatt to the right. Vide also Harleian MSS. No. 1533, A.D. 1575—1634, fol. 78.

He had issue,[1]

   1. Sir Henry Lee, K.G.

   2. Robert Lee.

   3. Cromwell Lee.

1. SIR HENRY LEE, Lord of Fleet Marston and Quarrendon, was born at Allington Castle, co. Kent, in 1531; married Anne, daughter of William, Lord Paget; died at Spelsbury, co. Oxon, in 1610, s. p. v.* and was buried at Quarrendon. Sir Henry's epitaph, as it appeared in Quarrendon Chapel, is given at pp. 114—116 of Mr. Jordan's *Parochial History of Enstone*, 4to. 1857; and again at p. 133 of the *Addenda to the Ædes Hart-welliana*, 4to. 1864, for a copy of which the writer is indebted to the kindness of Dr. John Lee, Q.C., of Hartwell Park. The fifth plate in this interesting volume contains engravings of certain monumental relics of the Quarrendon Lees in the Hartwell Museum, and a copy of Sir Henry Lee's arms as set forth in his garter-plate, still existing at St. George's, Windsor—restored by Sir C. G. Young, Garter. Sir Henry Lee's lady is buried in the north transept of St. Mary's Aylesbury, co. Bucks. On the tomb the arms stand as follows: Argent, on a fesse azure three lilies or, between three unicorn's heads erased sable, impaling, Quarterly, first and fourth Sable, on a cross engrailed arg. five lions passant of the first between four eagles displayed or; second and third Argent, two bars gules; in a dexter canton gules a cinquefoil or, in sinister chief a crescent: below on the dexter side the arms of the dexter impalement, and on the sinister

---

[1] In the Pedigree of the Lees in Lipscombe's *Bucks*, it is stated that Sir Anthony Lee married, secondly, Anne daughter and heiress of —— Hassell of ——, co. Chester, and had issue Jane or Elizabeth, but no authority is given for the statement. The MSS. in Caius Coll. Library, Cambridge, which *appear* to be referred to, contain no evidence of the fact. On the other hand, the Pedigree of the family of Lee, belonging to the Thorntons of Brockhall, co. Northampton (c), contains the following:—

——, daughter of S^r	Sir Anthony Lee of	Anne, daughter of
Thomas Wyat, Knt.	Burston, K. married	—— Hassall, seconde
first wife.	two wyves.	wyfe.

Sir Richard Lee, Knt. married the La.
Halls, and dyed without issue.

* The names of his children were John, Henry, and Mary.

those of the sinister impalement in a lozenge, for Lee of Quarrendon and Paget.[1] Sir Henry Lee was Master of the Ordnance to Queen Elizabeth, and Knight of the Most Noble Order of the Garter. His garter-plate still remains in his stall at St. George's Chapel, Windsor, whereon his arms are, Quarterly of seven (four in chief and three in base):

1. Argent, a fess between three crescents sable, *Lee*.

2. Argent, a fess between three unicorn's heads erased sable, *Lee of co. Bucks*.

3. Gules, a lion rampant argent, *Lee of co. Chester*.

4. Argent, a fess between three leopard's heads sable, *Wood of co. Warwick*.

5. Azure, an escocheon ermine, within an orle of eight estoiles or.

6. Vert, two wolves courant or.

7. Argent, a lion rampant within a bordure azure, charged with eight fleurs de lis or. Crest, out of a marquess's coronet, a column argent, upon the capital a bird's leg erased at the thigh, a cormorant preying thereon or. Supporters, On either side a lion sable, having a collar or charged with three crescents of the first. Motto (above the crest) FIDE ET CONSTANCIA, with the following inscription below:—

DV . TRESHONORABLE . CH'LR . HENRY
LEA . CH'LR . DV . TRESNOBLE . ORDRE
DE . LA . IARRETIERE . LE . XXIIII
DE . MAY . L'AN . 1597.

Not long after Sir Henry resigned his office as special champion of the beauty of Queen Elizabeth, he fell in love with her new maid of honour, Anne Vavasour, of an ancient and distinguished Yorkshire family, mentioned in a letter from Sir John Stanhope to Lord Talbot in November 1590, as a brilliant star at court,— " Our new mayd Mrs. Vavasoure florishethe like the lylly and the rose." "Though in the morning flower of her charms,"

---

[1] Having tricked the arms described above, Nicholas Charles writes : " On a fayre monument of Sir Henry Lee's wife, daughter of the Lord Pagett, wch woman died A° D'ni 1584, having issue, by Sir Henry Lee aforesaid, John Lee, Henry, and Mary." Fol. 70, MS. Lansdowne 874.

writes Miss Strickland, " and esteemed the loveliest girl in the whole court, she drove a whole bevy of youthful lovers to despair by accepting this ancient relic of the age of chivalry." Tradition reports that Miss Vavasour became Sir Henry's mistress ; hence the rhyming couplet :

> " Here lyes the old k^{nt} good Sr Harry,
> By her he lov'd, but ne'er would marry," etc.

It is also believed that after the erection of a monument to Sir Henry Lee and his mistress, in the chancel of Quarrendon church, the bishop of the diocese ordered it to be removed.[1] Two fragments of the figures, in alabaster, existed at Quarrendon so late as the year 1863, when that place was visited by the writer of this article. Nicholas Charles's MS. gives the following inscription as having been placed on the tomb:

> " Under thys stone intombed lyes a faire and worthy dame,
> Daughter to Henry Vavasor, Anne Vavasour her name.
> She living with Sr Henry Lee for love long tyme did dwell :
> Death could not part them but that here they reste within one cell."

Nicholas Charles gives the arms of Vavasour, on a lozenge, [Or,] a fesse dancetté [sa.] with a crescent for difference; crest, on a wreath or and sable, a cock gules ; as existing in Quarrendon church at his visit in 1611.

2. Robert Lee married Jane Restwold. Pedigree C states that Robert Lee married Jane, Lady Hastings, daughter of ———— Restwood. [Arms of Restwolde, co. Bucks, Gyronny of four, erm. and gu.] They had issue, according to Pedigree A, Barbara Lee, who married Richard Rogers, and had no issue ; according to Pedigree C. Barbara Lee married Edward Raynfforde.

3. Cromwell Lee, esq. of Holywell, Oxford, and of St. John's College, to which he was a very considerable benefactor, married Mary, the daughter of Sir John Harcourt, and relict of Richard Taverner, esq. [Arms of Harcourt, Gules, two bars or.] Cromwell Lee died A.D. 1601. His only son, John, is thus referred to at p. 802 of Wood's Athenæ Oxonienses, Ed. Oxon.: " June 1.— Doctor of Divinity, John Lea of St. John's College, and of the

---

[1] " This tombe is since erased and pulled downe. 1612." Nicholas Charles in MS. Lansdowne 876, p. 72.

gentile family of the Leas or Lees of Quarrendon, in Bucks, and
of Ditchley, in Oxfordshire; was chaplain to´ the most noble
knight, Sir Henry Lea ; was beneficed in the said counties, and,
dying about 1609,[1] was buried in St. John's Coll. Chappel, to
the adorning of which he was an especial benefactor. He gave
also many books to that Coll. Library." The Rev. J. B. Gray,
M.A., Fellow of St. John's, adds the following in a note to the
author of this paper :—" John Lee proceeded A.M. 1591, S.T.B.
1610. He was chaplain to Sir Hen. Lee and rector of Fleet
Marston, and afterwards of Wootton. He died a Fellow, and
was buried in the chapel. He gave *sexaginta et decem* pounds
for the choir, which, for some reason unexplained, was spent on
the ornamentation of the chapel."

Thus far, with regard to the issue of Sir Robert Lee of Quarrendon, by Mary Coape, Cope, or Coope, his first wife.

F. G. L.

[1] This date must be incorrect, as he proceeded to his degree of S.T.B. in 1610, and
possibly was not created S.T.P. or D.D. *per saltum.*

(To be continued.)

HATCHMENT OF THE SEVENTEENTH CENTURY.

A hatchment painted on oak panelling, in an oblong quadrilateral frame,
measuring 2 feet in width by 2 feet 3 inches in height, is now in the shop
of Mr. J. C. Hotten, in Piccadilly.

The armorial bearings which it displays, are these : Gules, on a chevron
between three spread eagles or as many torteaux, with the inescocheon of
Ulster ; impaling, Sable, a fess or, fretty of the field, between three fleurs
de lis and a bordure of the second. There is a crest over each coat : over
the baron side, an eagle's head erased argent gorged with a coronet or ;
over the femme, a wolf's head couped sable, collared or, and fretty on the
neck of the same.

These are the arms of Dycer impaling Styles. Sir Robert Dycer, of
Uphall, co. Hertford, who was created a Baronet March 18, 1660-1, married Dorothy, daughter of William Styles, esq. of Emingston, or Hemingstone, co. Suffolk. He died August 26, 1667, aged 72.

His son and successor of the same name died without issue about 1676,
when the title became extinct. (Courthope's *Synopsis of the Extinct
Baronetage*, p. 70; Burke's *Extinct Baronetcies*, p. 179.)

ANGLO-AMERICAN GENEALOGY—NORTH AND SOUTH.

THROUGHOUT the lamentable struggle which has afflicted the States of America during the last four years, nothing has been more remarkable than the sensitive anxiety manifested by either party to enlist on its own side the sympathies of Europe, and of England in particular. This was obviously at first suggested by the anticipation of a probable and indeed expected intervention: for, whilst the idea of control or dictation was spurned upon the instant, and the most friendly and benevolent mediation would have been as quickly misinterpreted, each antagonist confidently reckoned upon something more. Each imagined that England must of necessity take his part. The Northerners relied on her hatred of slavery, the Southerners on her hunger for cotton. As time wore on, these hopes, or fears, were continually deferred, or prolonged, until they can scarcely have been seriously entertained any longer,[1] and yet they have not ceased to tincture strongly the effusions of the public writers of America, from Mr. Secretary Seward downwards.

If England, as a nation, has done no more than sincerely lament this devastating conflict among those who derive their language and so much of their blood from herself, it has still been her misfortune to be greatly distrusted and misunderstood by both parties. And this has evidently arisen, in no slight degree, from the extraordinary misconceptions which are prevalent in America, in regard to the actual political condition of "the mother country." These popular delusions, founded upon a blind admiration of their own form of government, appear to proceed upon some such uninquiring argument as this: that, if a Republic and democracy afford the perfection of liberty, then a Monarchy and aristocracy must of necessity suppress it. They have, in fact, no adequate appreciation of the more than republican liberty which we really enjoy. In their view, England is rather a country as aristocratic as she was in the days of the Tudors or Stuarts. It was consequently a device of the Southerners to bid for her favour on the ground of their possessing a similar constitution of society. It is that line of argument

---

[1] " If the sympathy of England were now as desirable and *as strongly expected as it was two years ago* [*i. e.* about June 1861], I might urge the matter further. As it is, it seems sufficient to overthrow the claims of Southerners," &c. (This passage is from p. 48 of the pamphlet before us.)

which is encountered and combated by the pamphlet of which we now transcribe the title-page:—

THE CAVALIER DISMOUNTED: an Essay on the Origin of the Founders of the Thirteen Colonies.

"We are the Gentlemen of this Country."

ROBERT TOOMBS, in 1860.

"Our Plantations in America, *New England excepted*, have been generally, 1. by Malcontents with the Administrations from time to time; 2. by fraudulent Debtors, as a refuge from their Creditors; and by Convicts or Criminals, who chose Transportation rather than Death."   Dr. WILLIAM DOUGLASS, 1749.

By WILLIAM H. WHITMORE, Member of the Massachusetts Historical Society, and of the New England Historic-Genealogical Society.

Salem: Published by G. M. Whipple and A. A. Smith.   1864.   8vo. pp. iv. 48.

This essay appeared in the *Continental Magazine* for June 1863, the present impression being enlarged, particularly in the quotations by which the writer's arguments are supported. Two points are proposed for examination: 1. The proportion of native-born citizens in the United States descended from the inhabitants in 1790; 2. The origin of the ancestors of the Colonists. The discussion has been provoked by what are termed "the monstrous assertions of the leaders of the Rebellion."

"One of these was that which arrogates to the inhabitants of the Seceding States a superiority over their Northern brethren in respect to their Ancestry. Not only did they claim to be a nation peculiarly free from intermixture with foreigners, but they claimed one and all to be of English Parentage, and deduced their pedigree exclusively from one class of Englishmen,—the Gentry. The inhabitants of the Loyal States were described not only as mongrel in race, but the English portion of it was declared to be of the most ignoble extraction. * * * The cry of Cavalier and Puritan was again raised, and English sympathy was evoked in behalf of the oppressed Gentlemen.

" I propose in this sketch to prove the utter falsity of both assertions; to prove that the South is not homogeneous, and its English element is not of gentle origin; to show that New England is in the highest degree a purely English community, and that its colonists were not of the lowest rank.

" I shall confine myself to authorities whose statements were made long before the commencement of our civil war, in order that no reproach of partiality may attach to them; and in most instances I shall be able to use the words of Southerners, writing of matters in which they had a strong personal interest.

*   *   *   *   *

" That there has been a wide diversity in the construction of society, North and South, from the commencement of the colonies of Virginia and New England, is indisputable. Accident has brought these original peculiarities in antagonism, but we must not be misled as to their true significance.

" In the Southern colonies, as will be proved, society received a form somewhat analogous to that of the England of two centuries ago; an aristocratic form, a base and spurious imitation of a bad original, was imposed upon the infant settlements. In England in 1630 the rank of the Gentry was established, and it had a certain meaning and cause. This modified form of feudalism had a reasonable foundation. * * * The country Gentleman, whose family had been known and respected for four centuries, seemed a natural chief to those whose ancestors had during that period owned allegiance to the name. To this class had been confined nearly all of the wealth, valour, and culture of the nation.

" When Virginia and the other Southern Atlantic colonies were planted, however, the emigrants took with them but the empty form of their native customs. As will be proved, very few of them possessed any hereditary claim to the rank of Gentlemen, and even these were without the indispensable body of hereditary retainers, in whom a reverential submission was a matter of faith."

The writer proceeds to contend that the colonists of Virginia and the Carolinas never did establish an aristocracy of rank, but merely an imitation of such a class, which was liable to be invaded by any interloper that invested capital in slaves, and that " the slave-owners usurped the name of Gentlemen." He adds that it has only been in recent times that these Southern Gentry have claimed any superiority of race over the North.

" It has only been since our national prosperity has been so great, that these false aspersions have been indulged in, and a Cavalier has presumed to arrogate a precedence over a Puritan."

The meaning of the title of this pamphlet will now be perceived. Its object is to dismount " the Cavalier " from what is declared to be a false stalking-horse. For this purpose the author introduces a series of tables compiled from the official Census returns. These show: 1. that in the States in 1860, out of 27,706,425 white inhabitants, 19,976,762 were the descendants of those who in 1790 were citizens by birth; 2. that of the 19 millions of native-born citizens, New England has contributed nearly one third, and nearly one quarter of the entire population; 3. that by no conceivable chance can more than five-sixths of the population of the South be descended from the English Cavaliers. But, lastly, he proceeds to show from historical testimony that the Southerners were of divers races even at the commencement—all having a considerable proportion of French, Swiss, and German colonists. Several pages are then occupied by historical extracts which record that from the year 1619 even down to the Revolution of 1775 there was a large and constant stream of convicted criminals transported from England to the American colonies, particularly to Virginia and Maryland. Dr. Douglass, the same writer whose sweeping condemnation of the quality of the original colonists of America, *New England excepted,* has been already given as it appears on Mr. Whitmore's title-page, in another place distinguishes them with further particularity :—

"The settling of our sundry Colonies (he remarks) have been upon several occasions and from various beginnings. *New England* was first settled by people from England [who,] tenacious of their own Non-Conformist way of religious worship, were resolved to endure any hardships, viz. a very distant removal, inclemencies of the climate, barrenness of the soil, &c. in order to enjoy their own way of thinking, called Gospel Privileges, in peace and purity. Our *West India Islands* have been settled or increased, some of them by Royalists, some by Parliamentarians, some by Tories, some by Whigs, at different times fugitives or exiles from their native country. *Virginia* and *Maryland* have been for many years and continue to be a sink for transported criminals. *Pennsylvania* being the property of Mr. Penn, a Quaker, he planted it with Quakers; (as Lord Baltimore for the same reason at first planted Maryland with Roman Catholics;) it is lately very much increased with husbandmen swarming from Ireland and Germany." *A Summary, historical and political, of the first planting, progressive improvements, and present state of the British Settlements in North America. By* WILLIAM DOUGLASS, M.D. Boston, N.E. 1749.

The *original* settlement of Virginia is not here alluded to. Its Cavalier element is admitted, we presume, by all parties; but the proportion of that element is greatly reduced in the comments of the present writer, as will be perceived in the following passages:—

"It is shown by Bishop Meade, in his book especially devoted to the history of *The Old Churches and Old Families of Virginia,* that the records of the parishes have been lost, the churchyards destroyed, and few authorities save tradition remain. Even in the case of the Washingtons, a family whose records have been traced with sedulous care, there is now no evidence of the connections with an English family sufficient to satisfy Heralds' College. In short, there are two hundred families in Massachusetts having as great a claim, through traditions and the use of coats-of-arms, to the rank of Gentlemen, as the bulk of the Patrician families of Virginia.

"We have therefore to glean, here and there, little fragments of truth, to prevent our styling the entire claim of the Cavaliers a bold fabrication. A very few Virginia families can be thus proved to have sprung from the English Gentry. The book of Bishop Meade gives the following meagre list, and any other authorities are still wanting. He names the families of Ambler, Barradall, Baylor, Bushrod, Burwell, Carter, Digges, Fairfax, Fitzhugh, Fowke, Harrison, Jacqueline, Lee, Lewis, Ludwell, Mason, Robinson, Spottswood, Sandys, and Washington. I believe I have omitted none, and I have rather strained a point in admitting some. I do not, of course, mean to deny that others may exist, but until the proofs are submitted to examination there is no justice in presuming them to exist."

However, as a supplement to this enumeration of twenty families of Virginia whose gentle descent is allowed to be proved, we have a further list, from Meade's book, (vol. ii. p. 428,) of "some of the Old and Leading Families in Eastern Virginia, in Colonial Times and immediately succeeding the Revolution." These amount in number to two hundred and seventy, but upon them Mr. Whitmore makes this remark:—

"Most of the names in this list also occur in Savage's *Dictionary of the Settlers of New England.* Two thirds of them are to be found in both places. The proof is as ample in the one case as the other. If the Virginians were Gentlemen on account of their names, so were the Yankees."

One would scarcely have supposed that any claims to aristocracy would have been founded merely upon names: but Mr. Whitmore states that in America "it is often most erroneously supposed that the names of certain families is a proof of their gentle origin." We know how even at home the noblest names have subsisted for many centuries among the humblest classes. We have recently seen how unduly they have been assumed both in England and America. Mr. Whitmore certainly arrives at a just conclusion when he declares that, "unless the line of descent can be clearly proved, identity of name signifies nothing."

And even when names are apparently supported by coat-armour—we introduce here a point to which we know Mr. Whitmore's attention is now particularly directed,—it is essential to ascertain that such coat-armour is of hereditary right, and not merely fitted to the name, as for many generations has been done, and is even still doing, to a great extent in England, if there be any customers of the *soi-disant* Heraldic Offices, which are continually advertising their *Arms by name and county.* Records alone can be sure evidence either of arms or of descent.

On turning to examine the ancestry of the settlers of NEW ENGLAND, Mr. Whitmore at once confidently feels himself upon sure ground, and supported by records such as no other country can boast. With his account of those records we shall conclude this article, after first quoting the concise but perspicuous description of the settlement of this colony given by Palfrey in the introduction to his *History of New England,* viz.:—

"The founders of the Commonwealth of which I write were Englishmen. Their emigration to New England began in 1620. It was inconsiderable till 1630. At the end of ten years more it almost ceased.[1] A people consisting at that time of not many

---

[1] The motive of the Puritans for transportation to America was passed by after the change of affairs in England on the meeting of the Long Parliament. Hutchinson in his *History of Massachusetts*, 1764, states that "in 298 ships, which were the whole number from the beginning of the colony, there arrived 21,200 passengers, men, women and children, perhaps about 4000 families."

more than twenty thousand persons, thenceforward multiplied on its own soil, in remarkable seclusion from other communities, for nearly a century and a half. Some slight emigrations from it took place at an early day; but they were soon discontinued; and it was not till the last quarter of the eighteenth century that those swarms began to depart which have since occupied so large a portion of the territory of the United States."

The same facts are set forth in greater detail by extracts from *A Genealogical Dictionary of the Early Settlers of New England*, a very comprehensive work which has been recently completed by James Savage, formerly President of the Massachusetts Historical Society, and editor of Winthrop's History of New England.

" Mr. Savage's Dictionary consists of four volumes, embracing over twenty-five hundred closely printed pages. He attempts to give the first three generations of those who settled in New England before 1692. However imperfect the book may be in the record of the children, he has unquestionably obtained the names of nineteen-twentieths of those who settled here previous to 1640, the date when, as Hutchinson says, the immigration ceased ; and these names confirm entirely his assertion that the settlers were English. Of the 4000 heads of families one-third at least had taken the freeman's oath by that time, and their names are printed in the Massachusetts Records.

" Massachusetts, Plymouth, Rhode Island, and Connecticut have all issued volumes containing the early records of the respective colonies. Nearly all the older towns have their Histories carefully prepared and printed. Of those not yet published I believe hardly one can be named whose records have not been examined in aid of Mr. Savage, or for the use of our numerous genealogists. Our county registries of deeds, the records of births, marriages, and deaths preserved in every town, and the registries of the different parishes, are all very complete, are open to inspection freely and gratuitously, and have been consulted by hundreds of our writers. We have a Genealogical Society which has published seventeen annual volumes, averaging nearly four hundred pages each, devoted to the history of New England families. * * *

" When (continues Mr. Whitmore,) I published a *Handbook of American Genealogy* in 1862, the list comprised 222 genealogies, 16 tabular pedigrees, and 59 town histories and collections, and of the genealogies not half a dozen were of other than New England families. It is almost certain that there are extant more printed pages of genealogical information relative to the eight generations of families here, than there are relative to the history of English families since the Conquest.

" Is it too much to claim, therefore, that we are dealing with facts and not conjectures, when we say that, whatever was the case in other colonies, New England was thoroughly English and homogeneous? "

We cannot but add our conviction, that Mr. Whitmore proves his case with regard to New England. And when Virginia can advance her claims as pertinently, though not so completely, we shall rejoice to listen to them.

RECORDS OF THE FAMILY OF CARY: VISCOUNTS FALKLAND.

(*Continued from p. 54.*)

Wills from the Prerogative Court of Canterbury.

(Fenner 28.) *Sir Wymond Carye*, of Snettisham, co. Norfolk, knt. Dated Dec. 27, 1609.

To be buried in church of Snettisham. To said church 20s. To poor of Snettisham 10l. per ann. for 10 yrs. To my nephew Sir Henry Cary, kt., son and heir app. of my brother Sir Edward Cary, kt. and to his heirs for ever, my parsonage of Snettisham[1] and all my messuages, lands, tenements, &c. in or near Snettisham, whether freehold or copyhold, held of the manor of Snettisham, Dame Cicilies, Hawkyns, Ingalsthorpe, Rustings, Hitcham, or either of them; also to said Sir Henry Cary all my lands and terms of years in the manors and lordships of Snettisham and Hawkins in Snettisham, &c. To my nephew Sir Philip Cary, kt., the youngest son of my said brother, and his heirs for ever, my manor of Roydon Wingfield, and all my messuages, lands, and tenements in Marshland and Sharnburne, in co. Norfolk. To each of the daus. of my said brother 10l. To my said brother 4 of my best colts or horses, except my 2 coach horses, which I give to my niece the Lady Sydney, now wife of Sir Henry Sidney of Walsingham, kt., and to her said husband my nephew 2 colts. To Alex^r Roberts, preacher of the word of God, 5l., and appoint him supervisor of my will. To John Legitt 40s. To John Rogers, servant to my said nephew Sir Henry Cary, 10l. To Richard Metcalfe my servant 10l. and 40s. per ann. for life. To Margaret Grubb my servant 5l. and 20s. per ann. for life. To Wynyfred Rouse, so called before she married, and to Joan, dau. of Robert Brooke, of Newzed, my god-daughter, and to Beatrice Keble, a young girl about the age of 12 yrs. each 10l. Residue of all personalty to my said brother Sir Edward Cary, and my said nephew Sir Henry Cary; and appoint them executors. (Signed) " Wi: Cary."

[1] The manor was farmed by Sir Wymond Cary of Queen Elizabeth and James I., and, in consideration of 1,500l., was granted by the latter to Sir Henry Cary to be held in socage of the manor of East Greenwich, in Kent, by fealty. The manor afterwards passed to the Styleman family, an heiress of which carried it to the L'Estranges. H. L. Styleman l'Estrange is the present owner.

Proved in London at the C. P. C. April 20, 1612, by said Sir Edward Cary, kt., power being reserved to said Sir Henry Cary, kt., who also proved July 10, 1612.

(Lawe 12.) *Dame Catharine Cary*, of Flethall, in par. of Little Stoneham, co. Suffolk, widow. Dated 13 Feb. 1613, 11 Jac. Proved 1 Feb. 1614, at C. P. C.

To be buried at discretion of ex'or. To my loving mother Katharine Bellamy, widow, 10*l.* To my son Sir Rob. Crane, knt. a rounde hoope ringe of gould of the price or value of 3*l.* 6*s.* 8*d.* To my dau. his wife the like, and 1 pr. of fine sheets. To my loving nephew Sir Philip Knyvett, knt. and bart. one hoope ringe of like value. To my dearly beloved niece Dame Kath[e] his wife my ring of gold sett with 11 diamonds, and my best petticoat. To my dearly beloved sister Lady Hobert one ring of gold to be set with diamonds value 6*l.* 13*s.* 4*d.* To my very loving servant Hellen Gayle 50*l.* To my servant Frances Browne 100 marks. To my servant Johanna Springe 30*l.* To my nephew Frances Jarnegan 5*l.* To my cousin Bridgett Thimblethorpe my new gown. To my servant Martin 20*s.* To Thomas my coachman 20*s.* To Agnes Shellop my maidservant 20*s.* To Joane my cookmaid 20*s.* To poor of the parish where I shall be buried 5*l.* Residue to my very good friend Sir Thomas Hyrne, knt.,[1] and he to be my executor (he proved the will), forasmuch as I owe him divers sums of money, and he stands charged for payment of divers sums.

Witnesses, GREGORY SANDERSON.

Mark of ROBERT SEMAN.

(Meade 75.) *Sir Edward Carye*, of Aldenham, co. Herts, knt. Dat. Mar. 20, 1614-5. Codicil May 13, 1616. Proved July 21, 1618.

To my son Henry Carye all my household stuff and white plate, linen, brass and pewter, at my house in Great St. Bartholomew's, near West Smithfield, London, and at my house in Aldenham, co. Herts., my wife to have use of same during life or widowhood. To my said wife my carriage, coach horses, and 6 of my saddle horses; my son Henry to keep my said wife and her family at his cost and charge for 6 months after my decease. To my servt. Richd. Speed 50*l.* Poor of Aldenham and Great Berkhamsted, 10*l.* each; of Close of Great St. Bartholomew's 5*l.* Residue of all goods to said son Henry, and appoints him sole ex'or. ✷

Codicil.—Now of Gt. St. Bartholomew's, and Master and Treasurer

---

[1] Probably Sir Thomas Herne, who was connected with the Knyvett family. In 1613 Mr. Clement Hurne married Mary Knyvet, of New Buckenham, co. Norfolk.

of H.M. Plate and Jewels.   To my wife absolutely certain white plate.
To my dau. Manners and my dau. Barrett my gold buttons, to be
divided.   To my dau. Longvile 20*l.* or plate of that value.   To son
Philip 100*l.* or plate ; dau. Leeke 20*l.*; Lorenzo Cary, one of the sons
of my son Henry, and to John Cary, the eld. son of my son Philip,
each 50*l.* or plate.   To Margaret Monmouth 5*l.*   To my grandchildren,
Katherine Crompton and Frauncis Savell, each 10*l.*   For my funeral
200*l.*   For a tomb to be set up for me and my wife at Aldenham 200*l.*
    Proved by Sir Henry Cary, knt., son of decd. and ex'or named.
    (Swan 30.) *Dame Katherine Lady Paget,* dowager.   Dat. Nov. 18,
1622, proved April 9, 1623.
    To be buried at Aldenham.   Whereas there is due to me from
my son the Lord of Falkland, Lord Deputy of the Kingdom of
Ireland, 400*l.*; I dispose of the same as follows, viz., to Lucius
and Lorenzo, sons of my said son, each 100*l.*   To Adolphus, 2nd
son to my son Sir Philip Cary, Kt, 100*l.*; and 100*l.* to Edward,
youngest son of my said son Sir Philip Cary.   To my dau. the Lady
Manners my new couch and canopy in my bedchamber.   To my dau.
Lady Leake my cabinet.   To John Cary, eldest son of my said son
Sir Philip Cary, all my plate bought of my said son Viscount of Falk-
land, and a ring.   To Elizabeth Cary, one of the daus. of my said son
Sir Philip Cary, my clock, &c.   To Anne Cary, another of his daus.,
my diamond bracelet given me by my late decd brother Lord Knevet.
To said Elizabeth and Anne, the daus. of my said son Sir Philip Cary,
all my linen, to be divided.   To Pagett Latham, son of Nicholas
Latham decea, 10*l.*   To my servants as follows, viz., to Mrs. Bafford
10*l.*   To Katherine Matthew 5*l.*   To Philadelphia Williams 3*l.*   To
Margaret Elsden 3*l.*   To George Coleman 10*l.*   To Ambrose Marsh
10*l.*   To Robert Sowthwick 30*l.*   To Timothy Creston 10.   To Rice
Thomas 3*l.*   To Owen Thomas 3*l.*   To John Jarrett 3*l.*, and to Wm.
Burre 5*l.*   I leave the charge and providing for of Edward Ingley to
my ex'or.   To the poor of Aldenham 10*l.*; of Great Berkhamsted 5*l.*;
and of St. Olave's, in London, 5*l.*   I appoint said son Sir Philip Cary
sole ex'or.   (He proved.)
    (Coventry 21.) *Edward Cary* (Probate Act Book says died in parts
beyond the seas, bachelor).   Dated at Paris, January 3, 1640 (*sic*),
proved February 18, 1639-40.
    " For my loving brother, Mr. John Cary, Mr. Killigrew, Mr. Batty,
and to the twoe Ginde " cloth for mourning.   To Henry Bonnes 20*l.*
To Mr. Ayme 25*l.*   To St. John's College in Oxford, for the Library,

K 2

10*l*.   To Mr. Arne " the wache with the reveille matin." To Mr.
Quoy, my host, 20*l*.   To Mr. Paine 10*l*.   To the poor of Madlen par.
in Oxford, 10*l*.   To the woman who looks to me, Mary Aignan, 5*l*.

Second date, 24 Jan. 1640 (*sic*).

" I make my well beloved John Cary my sole heir and executor."
(He proved the will as brother.)

Witnesses, Thos. Killigrew, D. Smith, Williame D'Anisone, Robert
Diniy, Tege, and Galanach.

(Fines 92.)   *Lettice, Viscountess Falkland*, late wife of Lucius late
Viscount Falkland.   Dat. 25 May, 1646, proved 8 May, 1647.

To be buried at Gt. Tewe, co. Oxford.   To my mother Dame Marie
Morrison [1] 80*l*. per an. for life, and to my aunt Katharine Harrington
20*l*. per an. for life, both out of rents, &c. of the rectories or parsonages of Burford, Astall, and Fulbrooke, co. Oxon.; my estate to be
discharged thereof, however, if my son Lucius now Viscount Falkland
shall, when 21, make grants of said sums out of lands in fee simple.
Whereas my late husband in his lifetime granted 60*l*. per an. to my
aunt Ruth Harrington for life out of lands in or near Great Tewe, I
desire said son Lucius to confirm and continue said grant.   To my son
Henry the yearly rent of 80*l*., which is secured to me by the Lord
Capell out of the manor of Thorn Falcon and other lands in co. Somerset.   To my said son Henry 50*l*. more per ann. for life.   Residue of
the leases of said rectories of Burford, Astall, and Fulbrooke, and of
the manor of rectory of Gt. Tewe (whereof Doctor Sheldon and Doctor
Morley are trustees for me), and the manor and farm of Darneford
(whereof Thos. Hinton and Jno. Garrett, gents. are feoffees in trust for
me), and the monies thereupon due by Mr. Goodier, and residue of all
debts, goods, chattels, &c., to my said son Lucius, Viscount Falkland,
and I app[t] him ex'or, and during his minority I appoint said Thomas
Hinton and John Garrett to be my ex'ors.   (They proved the will.)

Overseers, Doctor Sheldon, Dr. Morley, Dr. Haman, and Dr. Earles.

2nd Adm'on, June 27, 1659.   To the R[t] Hon. Henry, Lord
Viscount Falkland, son of dec[d], of goods unadministered by said Hinton and Garrett by reason of the death of Lucius, Viscount Falkland,
the ex'or named, in his minority.

3rd Adm'on, Dec. 1, 1663.   To Lady Rachael, Viscountess Falkland, relict of Henry late Viscount Falkland, now also dec[d], during
minority of Anthony now Visc[t] Falkland, his son.

---

[1] Mary, daughter of Sir Henry Harington, knt., and widow of Sir Richard Morison,
knt., of Tooley Park, co. Leicester.

Will at C. P. C., but proved at Oxford.

Sir Lucius Carie, knt., *Viscount of Falkland*, in perfect health and memory. My soul to God, my body to earth to be buried as my ex'trix shall think fit. All my personal estate to my dearly beloved wife Lettice, Viscountess of Falkland, whom I appt. my extrx. she to have the education of my 3 sons, Lucius, Henry, and Lorenzo, and to bear the charges of educating my 2 younger sons, Henry and Lorenzo. Dated 12 June, 18 Charles, 1642.

(Signed) FALKLAND.

Witnesses, Robt. Stanior, Thomas Hinton. Proved at Oxford, 20 Oct. 1643, by Lettice, Viscountess Falkland.

Seal—Arms and crest of Cary, with a label of 3 points ; no coronet. The will, all but the signature " Falkland " and " Thomas Hinton," seems to be in Rob. Stanior's handwriting. With it is a copy altogether in one hand without seal, and the signature written " FAULKLAND." No notice of date or time of death.

(Lloyd 89.) *John Cary, of Stanwell, co. Middx. esq.* Dat. 10 Sep. 1685. Codicil 18 Sep. 1685 ; and 2nd codicil 20 Sep. 1685. Proved 1 Sep. 1686.

To Edward Cary, esq. my kinsman, son of Patrick Cary, esq. dec. the manor of Caldicott, Newton, and Magor, in co. Monmouth. All my manor and lordship of Stanwell, co. Middx. and all my farms, messuages, lands, and ten'ts in Minster, Isle of Thanet, co. Kent, and my rectories or parsonages of Llannarth and Llannina, in co. Cardigan, and my moiety of parsonage of Stanwell, and my manor of Skinnam, alias Skinnon, in co. Lincoln, my farm and lands in Naseby, co. Lincoln, and all my other manors, lands, and ten'ts, &c. whatsoever to John Grout, my menial servant, and to John Hall, of Gate Burton, co. Lincoln, gent. and to Wm. Whitlocke, of the Middle Temple, London, esq. in trust to settle and assure the glebe lands, tythes, tenths, &c. of said rectories of Llannarth and Llannina on the incumbents thereof for ever; said incumbents always to be fellows of St. John's College, Oxford. Same as to vicarage of Stanwell, co. Middx.,[1] the present Incumbent being George Calvert, clerk. Said trustees first to raise out of my estates 4,000*l.*, to be disposed as follows :—2,000*l.* to the children of Christopher late Lord Hatton[2] and the lady Elizabeth his wife, and

---

[1] This bequest does not seem to have been carried out. These livings are not now in the gift of St. John's College, nor ever have been.

[2] Lord Hatton married, 1630, Elizabeth, eldest daughter and coheir of Sir Charles Montagu (brother of Henry, Earl of Manchester).

the other 2,000*l.* to the children of Dudley late Lord North[1] and the Lady Anne his wife, to be distributed to said children according to a certain writing under the hand and seal of Dame Mary Baesh, my first wife, and dated Sep. 3, 1657 : rest of my said estates (except certain devises hereafter mentioned) to be held in trust for the Hon. Elizabeth Willoughby, my cousin and heir, sole dau. and heir of George late Lord Willoughby of Parham, my nephew, in case she be married[2] within 3 years after my decease, according to the practice of the Church of England, to Francis Lord Guildford, the eldest son of Francis late Lord Guildford, Lord Keeper of the Great Seal of England, lately deceased, for her life, and after her death for her eldest son by said marriage, &c. If such marriage do not take place as aforesaid, then the said estates in trust for use of the Rt. Hon. Anthony Cary, Lord Viscount Falkland, for his life ; remainder to his first son and other sons in succession ; remainder to the above-named Edward Cary, esq. and his heirs male ; remainder to my right heirs. I appoint as my ex'ors said Wm. Whitlock, esq. and Roger North, esq. brother to the late Lord Keeper. To my servant Joseph Bowry, my messuage or ten't and farm which John Wrenn now occupies in Stanwell, for life. To my kinswoman Mrs. Hester Hollingsworth[3] an annuity of 20*l.* for life, and same to her sister Mrs. Catherine Longvill. To my maid-servant Mary Fellowes annuity of 10*l.* for life. To my servant Nicholas Hersey the mess. or ten't where he now dwells in Stanwell, for life. To Sarah Mercer my late coachman's wife the mess. or ten't in Stanwell where she now dwells. To the Master and Fellows of University College, Oxford, 40*l.*, being a gift I promised Dr. Walker when he was Master of the said College. To the poor of Minster in the Isle of Thanet 10*l.* per annum for ever. 20*l.* for plate for the Commu-

---

[1] Lord North married, 1632, Anne, second daughter and coheir of the aforesaid Sir C. Montagu.

[2] This clause gave rise to considerable litigation. Elizabeth Willoughby did not marry Lord Guildford, and therefore this devise did not entirely take effect; but a compromise was made in 1697 by which Elizabeth Willoughby, then Mrs. Bertie, was allowed to enjoy the estate of Stanwell for her life, and the reversion was adjudged to Lucius Henry Lord Falkland, who accordingly succeeded to it in 1715, and sold it in 1720. See Lysons's *Environs of London* under STANWELL. A MS. copy of the pleadings in Chancery with reference to the estate is in the possession of G. E. Adams, Esq., Rouge Dragon.

[3] In the pedigree of the Longuevilles of Wolverton, given [by Sir B. Burke (Extinct Baronetage, 631), Sir Edward's eldest daughter Catherine is said to have married Thomas Gibbs, of Honington, co. Warwick ; and Hester, the second daughter, William Lawton, of Lawton, co. Chester.

nion Service at Stanwell; in the vault in the chancel of which said parish church I direct my body to be buried. To Sergeant Branch, 20*l.* To Stephen Stovell my cook 20*l.* To John Stevens my butler 20*l.* To my servants, Christ. Grout, Thos. Wakelyn, and James Broughton, each 20*l.* To Walter Owen, Richard Perry, and Wm. Fellowes, each 20*l.* To my maid-servants, Susannah Gander 30*l.*, Margaret Lorchin 20*l.*, and to Joane Crew and Rebecca Gray, each 10*l.* To John Ostler my porter, Charles Russell my postillion, and my servants Geo. Hurlocke, Thomas Mowdey, James Ashley, and Robert Hickman, each 5*l.* To Goodwife Ware, and Goodwife Trew her eldest dau., and Goody Stanny, each 5*l.*, &c., &c. I appoint Samuel Aldridge of Stanes, co. Middx., gent., to be steward of the Courts to be held for said manor of Stanwell for life.

1st Codicil appoints Simon Smith, esq., another executor; revokes appointment of John Hall as trustee; revokes bequest to Jno. Stevens his butler; and gives him an annuity of 10*l.* instead.

2nd Codicil desires Lady Wiseman, sister of the late Lord Keeper, to take care of the education of said niece Elizabeth Willoughby.

Proved by said Simon Smith, power being reserved to the other executors.

(Box 153.) *Anthony Cary, Lord Viscount Falkland.* Dated 30 Oct. 1691, proved 26 July, 1694.

Whereas Dame Rebecca Litton, widow, the relict of Sir Rowland Litton, knt., dec^d, by her last will dat. Jan. 7, 1685-6, devised all her messuages, lands, &c., which she had purchased of me, situate in Sandford or elsewhere, in co. Oxon., unto Sir Edward Atkins, knt., and Martin Folkes, esq., in trust to receive the rents &c. of the same during the life of her daughter, my wife, and dispose of the same to her separate benefit, and after decease of her daughter, my wife, then to the first and all the sons of her said dau. my wife; remainder to her daus., &c. And whereas Dame Rebecca Litton devised the residue of her estate, except an annuity of 500*l.*, to said Sir Edward Atkins and Martin Folkes, in trust to dispose of same to use of her said dau., my wife, and her sons and daus., with remainder as follows:—viz., one-third to Sir Thomas Hussey, nephew of said Dame Rebecca; one-third to her nephew Sir Berkeley Lucye, and the other third to me and my heirs. By death of said Dame Rebecca, I am entitled to the reversion, upon decease of my said wife without issue, of said messuages and lands in said co. Oxon., and said third part of the manors and lands to be purchased with the residue of said Lady Litton's estate. I now

devise all said messuages, lands, &c., in said co. Ōxon., and my reversion, &c., and all other property whatsoever to my said wife Rebecca,
Viscountess Falkland, dau. to said Lady Litton, and her heirs for ever,
and appoint her sole executrix. (She proved the will.)

The death of this Lord is thus noticed by John Evelyn, under the
date of May 30, 1694:—

"Lord Falkland, grandson to the learned Lord Falkland, Secretary
of State to King Charles I., and slain in his service, died now of the
small-pox.   He was a pretty, brisk, understanding, industrious young
gentleman; had formerly been faulty, but now much reclaimed; had
also the good luck to marry a very great fortune, besides being entitled
to a vast sum, his share of the Spanish wreck, taken up at the expense
of divers adventurers. From a Scotch Viscount he was made an English
Baron, designed Ambassador for Holland, had been Treasurer of the
Navy, and advancing extremely in the new Court.   All now gone in a
moment, and I think the title is extinct.   I know not whether the
estate devolves to my cousin Carew.   It was at my Lord Falkland's,
whose lady importuned us to let our daughter be with her some time, so
that that dear child took the same infection, which cost her valuable
life."[1]

(Young 28.)   *Anne Hamilton*, wife of Lord Archibald Hamilton.
Dat. 30 April, 1708, prov. 15 Feb. 1710-11.

Whereas the castle and lands of Confey and other lands in Ireland
are devised by my uncle Lord Lucas to Robert Thornhill, of Middle
Temple, London, Esqre, and John Walker, of Hillingdon, co. Middx.,
Esq., on trust for my sole and separate use; I devise the same to my
husband Lord Archibald Hamilton, subject to these legacies.   To my
daughter Ann,[2] Lady Grandison, 2,000*l.* in two years.   To Mrs.
Dorothy Potter 25*l.* a-year for life, payable in London.   If the land
is sold, then 300*l.* in lieu thereof.   To my son, Lord Viscount Falkland, 100*l.*   To my servant, Mary Hon, 25*l.*   My husband to be ex'or.
(He proved the will.)

Signed,   Ann Hamilton.
Witnesses, Jo. Marshall.
Wm. Rawlins.
E. Stables.

Seal.—Lucas, with a baron's coronet.
On the original will: "died Oct. 1709."

[1] Diary, edit. 1857, ii. 330.
[2] Evidently a clerical error for Frances.

Attached to the original will :—

Seal —Lucas, under a baron's coronet.

"These witness I, Lord Archibald Hamilton, impower my wife Ann Hamilton, to make a will of her real and personal estate left her by the late Lord Lucas for her separate use, and I consent to the same.

29 April, 1708.

Seal.—Arms, Quarterly, 1 and 4, Hamilton and Lorn.

2 and 3, Douglas.

Witnesses same as above.

(Box 42.) *Sir James Hayes* of Great Bedgbury, co. Kent, knt. Dat. 11 Jan. 1692, prov. 13 March 1721.

To poor of Goudhurst, co. Kent, and Great Tew, co. Oxon, 10*l.* each. To my dear brother John Hayes, my brother and sister Humphrey, my sister and my nephew Blake, and my good friend Mr. Arthur Moor, 10*l.* each. To my dear wife Rachel, Viscountess Falkland, all her jewels and plate, and all my plate, furniture, horses, &c. Debts to be paid in the way that my wife and said brother John Hayes and nephew James Blake and said Arthur Moor think fit, but not that of Sir John Champante, as not believing his transactions or those of Mr. Roberts. The debt to Sir Robert Dashwood, or other ex'or of George Dashwood dec^d, on acct. of undertaking to farm the revenues of Ireland, also not to be paid. To my dear dau. Rachell Hayes, 2,000*l.* at 21, or marriage, if with mother's consent; and she and my son James Hayes to be maintained. If she die, then the same to my son. Power to augment it to 3,000*l.* or abridge it. I hope my dear son William Hayes will be well provided for by the parsonage of Tew, and so leave him but 200*l.* My manors of Bedgbury, Goudhurst, and Foard and other lands, &c. to my son James Hayes for life, remainder to his issue in tail male, remainder to son William and his issue in tail male, rem^r to dau^s of said James Hayes, rem^r to daus. of said William, rem^r to my dau^r Rachel for her life, rem^r to her sons tail male, rem^r to her dau^s, rem^r to my brother John Hayes and his issue like way, rem^r to nephew James Blake and his issue like way, rem^r to my own right heirs. If I am indebted justly to Sir John Champante or Sir Robert Dashwood, it to be paid out of what is received from Sir James Shaen, who is bound to reimburse me. My wife, brother, and my nephew Blake, and said Arthur Moor, to be executors. My said wife to be the guardian of my children, and after her death my other ex'ors. In token of respect to Lord Falkland, son of my dear wife, and his lady, to whom I hold myself much obliged, I leave them mourning, and w^d have asked his lordship to have been ex'or, but considered he had so much business to look after. He to be consulted by my ex'ors, and hope he will look after the welfare of my poor children.

Witnesses.   ABRAHAM BLAKE.

JAMES SLOANE.

JACOB BOURDON.

JOHN WILSON.

Seal. Ermine, three escutcheons gules, for Hayes; impaling Hungerford. Over arms of Hayes, crest, an eagle displayed; over arms of Hungerford, a viscount's coronet.

Written on back of the original will of Sir James Hayes :

14 June, 1694. Rachel, Viscountess Falkland, one of the ex'ors, sworn. Proved by her 22 June, 1694.

13 Dec. 1721. Arthur Moore, esq. another ex'or, sworn. Proved 13 March, 1721-2.

Olim de Bedgbury in com. Kent, postea de parochia S^{ti} Jacobi Westmonstariensi, sed apud Kensington, co. Middx. defunct.

Sir James Hayes, having purchased the estate of Bedgebury from Thomas Colepeper, esq.[1] built a new house there, at a small distance from the ancient manor-house (in which Queen Elizabeth had slept in 1573). He placed the following inscription on the foundation-stone; together with the arms of *Hayes*, Ermine, three escucheons gules; impaling *Hungerford*, Sable, two bars argent, in chief three plates.

BENIGNITATE DEI

CVI PARENT OMNIA

SPOLIIS PROFVNDI ET ABSCONDITIS ARENAR' THESAVRIS

QVASI COELITVS LOCVPLETES FACTI

IACOBVS HAYES EQ. AVRAT.

SERENISSIMO REGI CAROLO II.

A SANCTIORIBVS CONSILIIS IN HIBERNIA

ET RACHEL VICECOMITISSA FALKLANDIAE UXOR EIVS

HANC DOMVM FOELICITER A FVNDAMENTIS

STRVXERVNT.

ANNO DOM. MDCLXXXVIII.

DA, PATER OMNIPOTENS, BONA QVI MIHI CVNCTA DEDISTI,

HIC PIETAS, HIC PRISCA FIDES, CONCORDIA, VIRTVS,

[1] Hasted, *History of Kent*, edit. 1790, iii. 36.

REGVM AMOR, ET PATRIAE MANEANT PER SECVLA CVNCTA,
ET BENE QVAESITIS VENIAT CENTESIMVS HAERES.

*Exemplar hujus Tabulæ in fundamentis ejus domus
Conditores Deum venerati posuerunt.*[1]

The house which Sir James Hayes erected still exists embedded in additions which Lord Beresford and Mr. Beresford-Hope have succes-sively made.

The descent of the property subsequently to Hasted's account is as follows. Mr. Cartier, formerly Governor-general of Bengal,[2] died Jan. 23, 1802, æt. 69, without issue. His widow, Stephana, daughter of Stephen Law, esq. of Broxbourn, formerly Governor of Bombay, succeeded, and died at Bedgebury Aug. 22, 1825, aged 80; leaving Bedgebury to her brother Archdeacon Law of Rochester (see again the Falkland pedigree, Table II.), who enjoyed it for less than two years, and left it to his son; he sold it in 1836 to Lord Viscount Beresford, on whose death in 1854 it devolved to Mr. Beresford-Hope.

Extract from the will of *Rachel, Viscountess Falkland.* All in her own handwriting.

(Browning 208.) To be privately buried. I appoint James Blake, esq., of Great Russell Street, and Mr. Thomas Bubb, of the Inner Temple, my ex'ors and trustees. To each of them 10 guineas. To Mr. John Lidgold 5*l.*, and to Mr. Crowther, of Cranbrooke, 5*l.* To Mrs. Elizabeth Fen, 15*l.* a-year for life. To my servant Katherine Springate, 5*l.* a-year, out of the general proceeds of my estate, or out of my right of mortgage due to me of Great Bedgebury. My real estate to my son James Hayes, esq. for life. Rem^r to such wife as he shall leave at his death for her life. Rem^r to his children; but, if none, rem^r to my dau. Rachel Hay (*sic*). Dated 19 Feby 1717. 4 George.

(Signed) Rachel Falkland.

Witnesses, Hen. Courthope, Robert Philip, Thos. Boorman.
3 June, 1719. James Blake, esq., one ex'or sworn.
30 June, 1719. Thomas Bubb, other ex'or sworn.
Proved 12 Nov. 1719, by both the ex'ors.
Seal—In a lozenge Cary, impaling Hungerford. All under a

---

[1] The brass plate bearing this inscription is now let into the wall of the Hall. The allusion in the third line is explained by the previous quotation from Evelyn.

[2] A memoir of him will be found in the *Gentleman's Magazine*, vol. lxxii.

viscount's coronet. Written on the original will: " Died 24 Feby 171$\frac{7}{8}$ at Bedgbury, in the parish of Goudhurst, co. Kent."

(Bellas 265.) *Sarah, Viscountess Falkland,* wife of Lord Henry Viscount Falkland, and relict of Henry Howard, Earl of Suffolk, only surviving child and heir of Thomas Inwen, esq. by Sarah his wife, late of St. Saviour's, Southwark, Surrey. Dated 25th May 1776, but stated in codicil to have been written many years before; contained in 23 sheets. She bequeaths to churchgoing poor of Widford, co. Essex, 200*l.*; Purleigh 100*l.*; Woodham Ferrers 60*l.*; Stow Maries 50*l.*; Woodham Mortimer 100*l.*; Writtle 100*l.*; Chignall Smalley 100*l.*; Boreham 100*l.*; Saffron Walden 600*l.*; Great Chesterford 100*l.*; Little Chesterford 100*l.*; Lewisham 200*l.*—to be entered in the register book as the gift of Sarah, daughter of Thomas Inwen, esq., late of Southend, in this parish, and relict of Henry Howard, esq. of Southend, and wife of Lord Henry Viscount Falkland 200*l.* To master of Dulwich College, for 6 old men and 6 old women 300*l.*; St. George's Hospital, Hyde Park Corner, 100*l.*; to Christ Church Hospital, as the gift of Sarah, daughter of Thomas Inwen, esq., late one of the governors, and relict of Henry Howard, Earl of Suffolk, also one of the governors, 3,000*l.* These charitable bequests amount to 5,210*l.*

To Servants, &c.:—To Margaret Turing, spinster, present waiting woman, 200*l.*; Thomas Cole, my late husband's old coachman, 60*l.*; Sarah Brands, widow, who lived with me as housekeeper at Beckenham, Kent, 30*l.*; besides 10 guineas each to every other domestic servant.

Legacies to Friends and Relations:—Margaret Hatcher, widow, of St. Margaret's Canterbury, 200*l.*; Mary, widow of the late Rev. Dr. Kemp, of Camberwell, 100*l.*; Mary Peck, spinster, sister of William Peck, of Sansford Hall, co. Essex, 100*l.*; Mary Howard, widow of Gen. Thomas Howard, of Savill Street, St. James's Westminster, 100*l.*; Catharine Howard, spinster, eldest daughter of Henry Howard, esq. and granddaughter of late Gen. Thomas Howard, in remembrance of the friendly notice the late Gen. Howard and his lady expressed to me and my late husband, 1,000*l.*; John Austen, esq. of Horsemonden, co. Kent, 100*l.*; Thomas Unwin, esq. of Castle Hedingham, Essex, 100*l.*; Rev. John Saunders, of Widford, Essex, 100*l.*; Francis Austen, esq. of Sevenoaks, Kent, 500*l.*; Sarah Hucks, widow of Joseph Hucks, of Great Russell Street, St. Giles's-in-the-Fields, 500*l.*; Mary Gibins, widow of Joseph Gibins, of St. George's, Southwark, 2,000*l.*; Richard Randall, brother of said Mary Gibins, 2,000*l.*; William Heberden, M.D. 100*l.*; Francis Motley Austen, esq. of Wilmington, grandson of the late Thomas Motley, esq. of Beckingham, co Kent, 500*l.*; to Viscount Falkland my husband 1,000*l.*

To be privately buried in churchyard of Widford, co. Essex. No escocheons at funeral; no achievements on any house or place of residence ; Thomas Cole, my late coachman, to drive the hearse to Widford. My tenants to attend, and to have 2 guineas each, their wives 1 guinea; the rector of Widford 3 guineas, and the parish clerk 1 guinea. An Egyptian pyramid to be built over my body in east front of churchyard [1] for 150*l.* like Mrs. Blackwell's at Lewisham, the inscription I have by me to be placed thereon and copied in register book. All my books, my two pictures of horses, and one of a dog, to the Rectory of Widford as heir looms, 30*l.* for the cost of fixing and moving them. Full-length picture of my late husband, of Southend, now in manor-house of Billingham in Southend, co. Kent, to Magdalene College, Cambridge; on it to be inscribed, " Henry Howard, Earl of Suffolk, Visitor of this College, born on New Year's Day 1706, died at his seat, Audley End, 22 April, 1745. The gift of Sarah, the wife of the said Earl, at the time of her decease." 30*l.* for expenses attending it ; 20*l.* to master of said college.

Recites that she had power by indenture made on late marriage to dispose of all her property failing issue of her body, and that since her marriage she had purchased many estates. The manor and lands of Widford Hall, Essex, and advowson (the lands let at 110*l.* a year) to William Hucks, son of late Thomas Hucks, esq. of St. Olave's, Southwark, subject to an annuity of 20*l.* for life to Lydia Vanderplank (youngest daughter of late Lydia Hucks Normandy, widow, of Dulwich) for separate use ; also my quit-rent and reverse of lease of a house in or near St. Saviour's, Southwark, and let to Roger Pindar. My trustees to present Rev. John Saunders to rectory of Woodham Mortimer, and subject thereto the said advowson, the manor of same and lands therein, now let at 73*l.* 10*s.* a-year, to Sarah Cope, widow, daughter of late Joseph Hucks, esq. of St. Giles's-in-the-Fields ; but if she die before me, then to William Hucks, son of said Thomas Hucks, in fee. To William Hucks, of Knaresborough, co. York, son of late Joseph Hucks, of St. Giles's-in-the-Fields, my manor of Barons and lands at Purleigh, co. Essex, now let at 125*l.* a-year. To Sarah Normandy, eldest daughter

---

[1] This injunction was carried out and the following inscription placed on it :—
" Sarah, Viscountess Falkland, wife of Lucius Charles Viscount Falkland, relict of Henry Howard, late Earl of Suffolk, and daughter and only child of Thomas Inwen, Esq., deceased, died the 27th May, 1776, aged 62."

of late Lydia Hucks Normandy, widow, of Dulwich, my manor of Woodham Ferrers, Purleigh, or Stow Maries, and lands now let at 33l. a-year ; but if she die before me, then same to William Harding, grandson of said Thomas Hucks, esq.

After my debts and the said legacies are paid, all other my lands in the counties of Essex, Kent, Middlesex, Bedford, Cambridge, Lincoln, or elsewhere, and all my real and personal property, in trust for my said husband Viscount Falkland for life, and then to sell and pay thereout :—to Robert Hucks, esq. of St. George's, Bloomsbury, 1,000l.; to Harriet Kelley, his sister, 500l.; to Sarah Noyes, also his sister, and if she die then to her issue, 3,000l. ; to Mary Gibins, widow above named, in like manner, 5,000l.; to Richard Randall, her brother, in like manner, 5,000l.; to William Hucks, of Knaresborough, in like manner, 4,000l.; to William Hucks, his eldest son, 500l.; to William Harding, grandson of late Thomas Hucks, esq, and if he die before me the same to Maria Harding, spinster, his sister, 2,000l.; to said Maria Harding 2,000l.; Sarah Cope, widow, daughter of said Joseph Hucks, esq. 1,000l.: Caroline Howard, spinster, granddaughter of late Gen. Thomas Howard, 1,000l.; Sackville Austen, second son of said Francis Austen, 500l.; John Austen, youngest son of said Francis Austen, 500l.; Sarah Normandy, eldest daughter of late Lydia Hucks Normandy, widow, 1,000l.   Residue to Francis Motley Austen, esq. absolutely.   My executors to be said Lord Falkland, Francis Austen, esq. of Sevenoaks, Francis Motley Austen, esq. of Wilmington, co. Kent, and William Hucks, esq. the son of Thomas Hucks, esq.

Signed " SARAH F." stated to be the " Signature and mark of SARAH, VISCOUNTESS FALKLAND."

Codicil of same date, with same witnesses, stating that a legacy of 2,000l. had lapsed by the death of the party, and bequeathing same to her husband, Lord Viscount Falkland.   ⁓

Seal effaced.

Proved 22 June, 1776, by Francis Austen, esq. and William Hucks, esq. two of the executors, power reserved to Francis Motley Austen, esq. and Lord Viscount Falkland, the others, the said Lord Viscount Falkland consenting.

On original Will: " Late of Blackheath in parish of Lewisham, Kent; died 27 May last."

(Ducarel 128.) *Lucius Charles, Lord Viscount Falkland.* Dat. 26 Nov. 1784, proved 5 Mar. 1785.

Desires to be privately buried in Audley Chapel, St. George's

Hanover Square, if he should die in or near London; if not, in the churchyard of the parish in which he should be resident. As to the capital messuage (now divided into two) at the corner of Great George Street, Hanover Square, and now in occupation of himself and Fish Bury, esq., and all other real estates, to eldest daughter Hon. Jane Cary in fee. To the said (*sic*) Dr. John Law 50 guineas, as a recompense for the trouble in assisting said daughter.

To daughters [Mary Law[1]] and Charlotte Chapman 20 guineas each. Residue to said dau. Jane Cary and Rev. Dr. John Law, whom he appoints executors.

Proved by said Rev. John Law, Archdeacon of Rochester, one of the executors, power reserved to Hon. Jane Cary, spinster.

ADMINISTRATIONS.

June 9, 1598. Administration of *Ralph Baesh*, late of Stansted, co. Herts, to the relict, Frances Baesh.

1631. July 4. *Sir Philip Cary, knt.*, late of St. Olave, Silver Street, London. Adm. granted to Sir Edward Barrett, knt., baron of Newburgh, in Scotland, and Sir George Manners, of Fulbeck, co. Lincoln, knt., during the minority of John Cary, Edward Cary, Elizabeth Cary, and Ann Cary, children of deceased.

(Marginal note.) These letters expired by reason of the arrival at full age of John Cary, one of the said children of deceased, to whom new administration was granted Jan. 1634-5.

This last administration, dated Jan. 3, 1634-5, to John Cary, son of Sir Philip Cary, knt., late of St. Olave's, Silver Street, London.

Nov. 4, 1633. Administration of *Lord Henry Carey, late Viscount Falkland*, to Lady Elizabeth Carey, Dowager Countess Falkland, relict of deceased.

July 10, 1663. Administration of *Lord Henry, late Viscount Falkland*, late of Tewe Magna, co. Oxon, to the relict the Viscountess Falkland.

Nov. 24, 1692. Administration of *Edward Cary*, late of St. James's Westminster, co. Middlesex, esq., to the relict the Hon. Anne Cary.

[1] Erased in original.

The following additions may be made to the Pedigree in p. 42:—

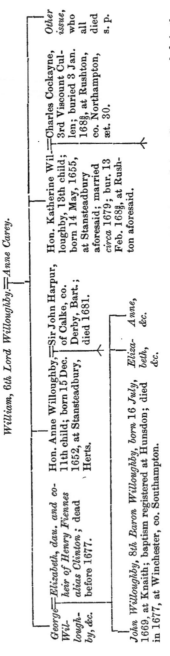

William, 6th Lord Willoughby.=*Anne Carey.*

George=Elizabeth, dau. and co-heir of Henry Fiennes alias Clinton; dead before 1677.
Willoughby, &c.

John Willoughby, 8th Baron Willoughby, born 16 July, 1669, at Knaith; baptism registered at Hunsdon; died in 1677, at Winchester, co. Southampton.

Hon. Anne Willoughby,=Sir John Harpur, 11th child; born 15 Dec. of Calke, co. 1652, at Stansteadbury, Derby, Bart.; Herts. died 1681.

Eliza-beth, &c. | Anne, &c.

Hon. Katherine Wil-=Charles Cockayne, loughby, 13th child; 3rd Viscount Cul-born 14 May, 1655, len; buried 3 Jan. at Stansteadbury 168 9/8, at Rushton, aforesaid; married co. Northampton, circa 1679; bur. 13 æt. 30. Feb. 168 8/7, at Rushton aforesaid.

Other issue, who all died s. p.

Note.—The dates and places of birth of the fourteen children of William Lord Willoughby and Anne Carey are recorded in the register at Hunsdon, Herts, although only the youngest child Mary was born and baptised there in July, 1656.

ADDITIONS AND CORRECTIONS.

P. 34. Chilton-Foliot was a manor in dower of the Queen of England temp. Hen. VIII and Edw. VI. From a survey taken on behalf of Queen Katharine, 19 Dec. 1548 (1 Edw. VI), it appears that Sir Edward Darell had obtained a lease of the principal manor, in 1546, for a term of 21 years; paying per annum 41*l*. 15*s*. 11½*d*., and 8*l*. 7*s*. 8*d*. new rent. Among the customary tenants (copyholders), at the same date, was Sir John Carie or Carye, who seems to have held an inferior manor, Sowley, in the parish of Chilton, together with a house containing "hawle and ketchinge, 2 chambers, and a stable," at the rent of xi*s*. per annum. (Communicated by the Rev. J. E. Jackson, Leigh Delamere.)

P. 35. Berkhamstead Castle and manor were recovered by the Prince of Wales in 1611, and remained the property of the Duchy of Cornwall till a few years since, when they were sold to the trustees of the present Earl Brownlow, who now holds them.

Ibid. The elevation of Sir Henry Cary to the Scotish peerage raised the question whether, as he had been chosen M.P. for Hertfordshire, Lord Falkland belonged to the Upper or the Lower House. (See *Court and Times of James I.*, vol. ii. 228.)

P. 37, line 12, *for* "perhaps in consequence," *read* "of the small pox."

Ibid. Evelyn states that he obtained an English barony (cf. infra, p. 136), but I have not been able to discover the date of the patent, nor indeed that any was issued.

Ibid. It would seem from a passage in Evelyn's Diary (vol. i. 156, ed. 1827,) that Patrick Cary became a monk early in life. Evelyn met him at Rome in November, 1644, and speaks of him as "an abbot, brother to our learned Lord Falkland, a witty young priest, who afterwards came over to our Church."

An interesting account of some of the writings of Patrick Cary may be found in *Notes and Queries* (29 Oct. 1853), and a reference is there made to a mention of him by Sir Walter Scott, in "Woodstock."

P. 38. Edward Cary was high bailiff of the city of Westminster, and his wife's burial is recorded in the registers of St. James's to have taken place in Oct. 1709. She is entered as "Mrs. Cary," and not as Lady Anne Hamilton. She is also so styled in the MS. Memoranda of Peter le Neve, Norroy, "Mrs. Cary mother of the present Visc*t*. Falkland dyed in Queen Street, Westminster."

P. 39. Thomas Cary of Chilton Foliot, ob. ante 1548.

Ibid. Joyce, widow of Sir John Cary. Cf. Machyn's Diary: " The vi. day of Aprell (1559) was bered at [Saint Clement's] without Tempyll-bare my lady Gray (Carey) the [wyfe of Sir John] Gray and the wyff also of Master Walsyngham, ... with ij. whyt branchys and iiij. grett tapurs and fo[ur] staff torchys, and ij dozen and di. of skochyons of armes [without] . . . . masse and or (*sic orig.*) communyon."

Ibid. Chamberlaine's Letter, dat. 6 April, 1609. " The small pox is very rife ... Sir Adolphus Cary died of them here in town about a fortnight since." (*Court and Times of James I.* vol. i. 96.)

P. 40. Sir William Uvedale was buried 3 Dec. 1652. His issue by his first wife will be given in the account of the Hunsdon line.

P. 43. Catherine, wife of Sir Henry Longueville, was buried at Wolverton, 10th May, 1611.

Ibid. The marriage between Jane Cary and Sir Edward Barrett seems to have taken place in 1609. (See *Court and Times of James I.* vol. i. 85.)

Additions and Corrections to the Register Extracts.

P. 47. ST. PANCRAS. The honourable Mrs. Cary was Anne, daughter of Hugh, Lord Clifford of Chudleigh, and widow of George Cary of Torre Abbey, co. Devon.

P. 49. WOLVERTON, CO. BUCKS.

1611. 10th day of May. The Ladye Longueville, junior, was buried.
1620. 17th day of May. Sir Henry Longueville, knt. was buried.

WYKEHAM, HANTS.

1642. William, son of Sir Wm. Uvedale and Lady Victoria, was born 5th May, 1642, and baptised in London. [He was alive in 1651, but dead before 1663, as appears by a family deed.]

1696. The Right Honourable Elizabeth, Countesse Dowager of y[e] R[t] Honourable Edward Earl of Carlisle, Lord Viscount Morpeth, Baron Dacre of Gilsland, was buried y[e] 30 day of Decr. 1696.

Victoria Cary married Sir R. Corbet in 1663 or 4, and was dead before 1683, as she is not mentioned in her husband's will, and her mother-in-law is appointed guardian of her children and executrix. (Communicated by Granville L. Gower, Esq. M.P.)

P. 132, line 3, *for* " 10 " *read* " 10*l.*"

REVIEW.

POPULAR GENEALOGISTS, OR THE ART OF PEDIGREE-MAKING.

Falsum committunt viri docti, qui hominibus de plebe nobilitatem, insignia, et antiquitatem generis adfingunt. . . . . Et potest profecto debetque
mercenariorum illorum pœna tunc, quum reipublicæ valde per eos nocitum,
atque fides monumentorum et historiæ turbata est, ad ultimum supplicium
proferri.—LEYSERUS, *Meditationes ad Pandectas*, Sp. DCXVI. 3, 4.
EDINBURGH : EDMONSTON AND DOUGLAS, 1865.   Crown 8vo. pp. 100.|

This is a small book, but very much to the purpose; and, though
the writer is anonymous, he is evidently one who possesses competent
knowledge of the matters of which he treats, and access to the best
sources of information.   He has been irresistibly provoked to speak out
when reflecting upon the contrast presented by the many excellent
examples of genealogical history which are an honour to the present
age, and the frequent instances of fiction and humbug that still venture
to show their heads like poppies in the harvest-field.

It has become an admitted fact that the history of the leading families of a country
is an important part of the history of that country.   A race of learned and accurate
investigators have sprung up, who, approaching genealogy in a critical spirit, have
brought entirely new resources to bear on it.   Rejecting all that is not borne out by
authentic evidence, they have applied themselves to the patient examination of the
national records, the archives and chronicles of the monasteries, and the contents of
private charter-chests.   Each source has yielded its quota of facts, and these facts
have been woven into genealogical biographies.   Heraldry itself, after having been
abandoned to coach-painters and undertakers, has again come into favour; having
been found to be a valuable, if not indispensable, aid to the knowledge both of family
and of national history.

England and Scotland have produced a succession of more or less excellent family
histories, some published and some privately printed, in the foremost rank of which
must be placed Lord Lindsay's delightful record of the House of Lindsay, the model
for all family histories in time coming.   In this change which has come over the
spirit of genealogy, it is pleasant to find that Scotland, once notorious for looseness
and credulity in matters of pedigree, has taken a prominent part.   It would not be
easy to overrate the value of the muniments which have been preserved and carefully
edited by the Maitland, Bannatyne, and Spalding Clubs.

While this genealogical revival cannot fail to be extremely gratifying to every lover
of historical truth, I propose in these few pages to make it matter of inquiry, how far
it has as yet extended to genealogical literature of a more popular kind, such as the
Peerages, histories of the " Landed Gentry," and similar works, which are in the
hands of every one, and daily referred to by the general public.

The writer proceeds to describe the various works that bear the name of Sir Bernard Burke; and which, he justly observes, have now an apparent stamp of authority, which they could not be said to possess before that gentleman, as Ulster king of arms, became the head of the heraldic establishment of one of the three kingdoms.   The *beau ideal* of a Genealogical History of our Nobility is first sketched.

It would presuppose high genealogical qualifications on the part of its author, including patience, carefulness, and a scrupulous regard to truth.   It would be based on an attentive examination of title-deeds, contemporary documents, and the public records, and its statements would be checked by reference to every available source of information.   While due weight would be allowed to conclusions arrived at by genealogical critics of tried skill and accuracy, no mere dictum of the representative of a family, however unimpeachable in point of veracity, would be received without investigation.   The heraldry would also be carefully checked and corrected by the records of the several Colleges of Arms.

The Peerage works of Dugdale and Collins in England, and of Crawfurd and Sir Robert Douglas in Scotland, written in an uninquiring and credulous age, were probably up to the highest mark of their time.   Since their day, the materials for arriving at truth have been so greatly extended, the public records have become so much more accessible, and so much light has been thrown on family history by the labours of genealogical antiquaries, that it is obviously desirable that these standard works should be replaced by others written under advantages which the older writers never possessed, and embodying the results of the genealogical literature which has been accumulating since their date.

The author then makes some critical remarks on Burke's *Peerage and Baronetage;* and alludes more particularly to an idea which "is found recurring in all Sir Bernard's writings, until it becomes a positive mania," that of introducing among the quarterings of families " the undifferenced royal arms of England, and still more frequently of Scotland, on the most frivolous grounds, and often on the score of an alleged descent from royalty that will not stand a moment's examination." (p. 10.)

The " lineage " presented by Sir Bernard's work is condemned very generally: " there are a few instances in which it is tolerably correct, and two or three in which it is extremely correct; but unfortunately these are exceptional cases." (p. 12.)   These are indeed sweeping charges, and must summon Ulster to his defence.

An average example, not worse than many others, is the pedigree of the Polwarth family.   Lord Polwarth is the representative of the family of Scott of Harden, a very early cadet of the house of Scott.   The representative of the male line, progenitor of Buccleuch, on marrying the heiress of Murdockstone in the thirteenth century, altered the original arms, the stars and crescent, by incorporating with them the Murdockstone bend, the old Scott coat being retained by the house of Harden, who branched off prior to the Murdockstone marriage :—

" An aged knight to danger steel'd,
　With many a mosstrooper came on :
And azure in a golden field,
The stars and crescent graced his shield,
　Without the bend of Murdieston."

The poet is fully borne out in this matter by the prosaic testimony of seals and charters. The Buccleuch succession went in the seventeenth century through an heir-female, Anne Duchess of Buccleuch, to her son by the attainted Duke of Monmouth, from whom the ducal house of Buccleuch are now descended, and are therefore not paternally Scotts. The male representation of Buccleuch passed to the latest cadet, Scott of Howpaisley, afterwards of Thirlestane, from whom descend Lord Napier and all the various Napiers who have deserved so well of their country, who are all paternally Scotts. So long as a male descendant of the Thirlestane branch is in life, or any male descendant of Sir Richard le Scot and the Murdockstone heiress, the Harden Scotts can never claim the male representation of Buccleuch.

Sir Bernard Burke, however, makes Lord Polwarth the heir-male of Buccleuch, and accomplishes this by putting forth Thirlestane as a cadet, not of Buccleuch, but of Harden, and assigning him for ancestor James fourth son of Sir Walter Scott of Harden, who "lived in the time of James VI." Yet, in the *Family Romance*, p. 27, (in a narrative called " The Heir of Thirlestane," which by the way is utterly apocryphal), the hereditary loyalty of the house of Thirlestane is enlarged on as already " attested by deeds of arms of ages " in the time of James V. ; and in the account of the Napier family in the *Peerage* we find the Thirlestane branch of the Scotts traced upwards—correctly enough—to William Scott of Howpaisley, whose grandson Walter fell at the battle of Pavia in 1525, more than forty years before James VI. was born.

I may state, as the result of my own experience, that any one who seriously attempts to use *Burke's Peerage* as a book of reference, will find himself involved at every turn in similar genealogical paradoxes.

Our author next remarks that one of the most unsatisfactory features of Burke's *Peerage* is its heraldry : into the examination of which however we will not now accompany him, having a more painful duty still to perform in reporting what is alleged of Sir Bernard Burke's other great and standard work, the *Dictionary of the Landed Gentry*. Respecting this, an account is first given of its four distinct issues, or editions, the first dated 1837, the second appearing from 1846 to 1849, the third in 1850, and the fourth in 1863.

Though we call these works different editions, each is to a great extent a new book, yet not always an improvement on those that were before it. While the *Peerage* may be to a slight extent improving from year to year, the *Landed Gentry* is deteriorating. The successive editions are marked by a gradual disappearance of families of *status* and historical repute, while their places are to a large extent filled by persons whose sole connexion with land arises from their having been purchasers of a few acres in a county where their very names are unknown. Surely Ulster does not consider the representatives of the Lords of the Isles, who had their due place in former editions, unworthy of being numbered among the lesser nobility, because their ancient possessions have passed into other hands. The excluded list comprehends also, it is difficult to divine why, other families of consideration, whose position as landed gentry remains unaltered, some of them (as the Bethunes of Balfour) being those whose genealogies were in former editions among the most elaborate in the work.

The immense majority of the pedigrees in the *Landed Gentry*, including more especially the Scottish pedigrees, cannot, I fear, be characterised as otherwise than utterly worthless. The errors of the *Peerage* are as nothing to the fables which we encounter everywhere. Families of notoriously obscure origin have their veins filled with the blood of generations of royal personages of the ·ancient and mythical world. There are not a few minute circumstantial genealogies of *soi-disant* old and distinguished families, with high-sounding titles, which families can be·proved by documentary evidence never to have had a corporeal existence. Other pedigrees contain a small germ of truth eked out with a mass of fiction, in the proportion of Falstaff's bread and sack ; while an extreme minuteness of detail is often combined with reckless disregard of dates and historical possibilities. Some of the anachronisms encountered are quite as bold as Mrs. Beecher Stowe's assertion [1] that Sir William Wallace received his education at the Grammar School of Dundee.

In proof of these admittedly strong censures, the author enters into a detailed examination of the genealogies of two families, one as an example of *the wholly fictitious Pedigree*, and the other of *the partially fictitious Pedigree*. We feel bound in honour to pursue his examination of the former of these, finding it to be none other than that of COULTHART OF COULTHART, our own account of which occupied some pages of our last Part. We there presented to our readers such a sketch of this marvellous genealogy as would at once intimate to any judicious apprehension how largely it partook of the legendary and poetical in its earlier generations; but we must confess that we ourselves were entirely unprepared for the intimation that, even up to very recent times, it is equally and throughout fictitious. Who the Mr. George P. Knowles, the "Genealogist and Heraldic Artist," who has solemnly pledged his faith to this performance in the presence of the Bishop of Manchester and another reverend magistrate of that city, may be, or have been, we are not informed; but we do not envy him the reputation, either professional or moral, living or posthumous, which he has thereby acquired.

Had we, by any accident, afforded the first facilities for the publication of such a composition, we should have been more anxious to make personal apologies; but such is by no means the case. This pedigree of Coulthart has now for nearly twenty years been pushed forward with remarkable pertinacity in every available vehicle, particularly in the works of Sir Bernard Burke.[2] It appeared first in the *Dictionary of the*

[1] *Sunny Memories of Foreign Lands,* Letter vii.
[2] Not so soon as the *General Armory* of 1842. In that work there are *no arms*

Commoners, in 1846, again with additions and expansions in 1849, and with further additions in 1863; also in *Illuminated Heraldic Visitations*, 1852; again in the *Visitation of Seats and Arms*, First Series, of the same date (where in the prior division of the volume is, at p. 123, a view of Croft House, Ashton under Line, "the seat of John Ross Coulthart, of Coulthart and Collyn, Esq., Chief of his name;" and in the latter division, at p. 39, the pedigree and an engraving of the Arms); and again in the Second Series of the same work, 1854, the Pedigree at still fuller length, with another plate of the arms.[1] Then, in Mr. Lower's *Patronymica Britannica*, 1860, a column is devoted to an account of this "most elaborate pedigree," together with an engraving of the seal (as in our p. 195), accompanied by a mystifying conjecture that " the name of the Scottish locality is probably synonymous with that of Coudhard, a village in the department of Orne, a few miles N.E. of Argentan in Normandy." And in the same year the crest of " a war-horse's head and neck, couped ar., armed and bridled ppr., garnished or," is furnished to the *Crests of Great Britain and Ireland*, collected by James Fairbairn, an engraver at Edinburgh, and inserted in his Plate 7 and fig. 12. Still more recently, the legend of the Coultharts has been again published in *Anecdotes of Heraldry*, by C. N. Elvin, M.A., 12mo., 1864; and in Walford's *County Families*,[2] John Ross Coulthart, Esq., is recognised as the " lineal heir male representative of the ancient Scottish family of Coulthart of Coulthart." We have, therefore, not merely to lament that we should in any degree have been deceived by wilful misstatements, but are required to assist in checking a wide-spread contagion.

It will be recollected that we undertook only to give an account, as an article of our *Bibliotheca Heraldica*, of a private volume of genealogy which Mr. Coulthart had produced at considerable expense, and which

---

whatever for the name of Coulthart. But in its " Third Edition, with a Supplement," 1844, they are, sure enough, inserted with three quarterings, crest, and supporters, as belonging to " Coulthart, of Largmore, co. Kirkcudbright, and Collyn, co. Dumfries, a family of great antiquity in the South of Scotland."

[1] " The *colt* and the *hart* meet us in every volume with the most ' damnable iteration,' and in one of the plates of the *Visitations* the SIGILLUM COULTHARTI occupies the centre, while round it are arranged the several quarterings of the Coulthart escutcheon." *Popular Genealogist*, p. 84.

[2] It is said (in p. 90) respecting Walford's *County Families*, that " its brief outlines of family history are filled with matter so extraordinary, that it is difficult to conceive from what source the writer could have collected it." Particulars, however, are not exhibited.

in that respect might rank with more important works of the kind,—though now unfortunately destined only to retain the bad pre-eminence of being the most extended fictitious pedigree ever printed.

We need not repeat our sketch of its earlier portions. When we refer the reader to page 18 of our last Part, he has only to peruse it, and it will carry its own convictions with it. It is perfectly unnecessary to quote the reviewer's assurance that Tacitus and Ptolemy and Bede, and all the early chronicles, would be searched in vain for even the names of the personages whose deeds and characteristics are set forth and described with unblushing confidence.

But when, in succession to such romantic history or tradition, an affectation of producing documentary evidence is assumed, the result is little less marvellous. We are told of a marriage settlement bearing date the *twenty-first* year of the reign of King Kennethus III., though that monarch has hitherto been supposed to have reigned only from 997 to 1005, and the very earliest written legal documents existing in Scotland belong to the closing years of the eleventh century. To make the matter still more absurd, the marriage was to be solemnised between two males, William de Coulthart and " one *Angus* de Cumin." Surely, Mr. George Parker Knowles was a little too wicked here!

Charters are put forth professing to be from the Scotish Kings, Robert I., David II. (a. r. 33), Robert II. (a. r. 12), and Robert III. (a. r. 2) all in favour of members of the family of Coulthart:

The constructor of those documents has, however, made a sad blunder. Instead of taking actual charters for his models, he has gone to the printed volume of the Great Seal Register, and, all unaware of the difference in form between the actual deed and the abbreviated record of it, he has transcribed four entries of charters *literatim* as they appear in the Register, and therefore in a form in which no charter was ever issued, changing only the name of the grantee and the designation of the lands. The record of the charter of Robert I. *Rot.* i. 32, " Alexandro de Meynies militi et Egiliæ secundæ sponsæ suæ," of the lands of Durrisdeer, is transformed into a charter, " Johanni de Coulthart militi et Elizabethæ secundæ sponsæ suæ," of the lands of Quhithurn, with the same date, and in the same terms; and Robert III.'s " Carta pro Mariota de Wardlaw et Andrea de Wardlaw filio quondam Gilberti de Wardlaw." *Rot.* x. 40, still more naturally becomes " Carta pro Mariota de Coulthart et Andrea de Coulthart filio quondam Gilberti de Coulthart," with all details scrupulously copied, letter for letter, down to the very verbal abbreviations, except the name of the lands, the identity extending to date, place of signing, and full name and designation of witnesses. The deeds of David II. and Robert II. conclude " Testibus etc.," without enumeration of witnesses,—an ending, it is needless to say, never found in any actual charters, though in accordance with the abridged form in which the charters of these two monarchs are entered in the Great Seal Register. But these mistakes are amply atoned for by the charming *naïveté* with which the designation " Willielmo de Coulthart gentis nominisque sui facile primario," comes into these fourteenth-century charters.

King David's genuine charter has no such fanciful phrase. It relates to the barony of Glencharny in the shrievalty of Invernys in the county of Moray, and was granted to Gilbert de Glencharny. Except the changing of that name to William de Coulthart *gentis nominisque sui facile primario!* and that of the locality to *baronie de Coulthart cum pertin' infra dominium de Wygtoun*, the remainder is taken unaltered, almost to a letter, including the date, as it may be read in the Register of the Great Seal of Scotland (one of the Record Commission publications), Lib. i. 20. Even the names of the baron of Glencharny's sister Christian and her husband, Duncan Fraser, are appropriated: but an amusing proof of the ignorance that has accompanied all this dishonesty is, that the contracted name, *Duncano fras'*, has been misinterpreted [1] into " Duncano-Francisco," a compound hitherto unexampled in the nomenclature of the fourteenth century.

As the second son of " Sir Roger de Coulthart," said to have been knighted by James I. at his coronation at Scoon, A·D. 1428, we are presented by the genealogist with the name of

Gilbert, who went in the train of Earl Douglas, lord of Galloway, to various European courts, A.D. 1449, and fought at the battle of Brechin, 18 May, 1452.

For this, in the Burke edition of 1849 (but omitted in the Private edition), the following authority is cited as a foot-note.

Thair was vtheris of lower estate, as Coulthart, Vrquhart, Campbell, Forrester, and Lowther, all knightis and gentlemen, whose convoy maid the Earle so proud and insolent, that he represented ane kingis magnificence quhair evir he came.—Lindsay's *Chronicles of Scotland.*

Will it be believed (asks the commentator) that the name here printed Coulthart is Calder in the original, the person alluded to by Lindsay of Pitscottie being doubtless Sir John Sandilands of Calder, ancestor of Lord Torphichen, who, as a far-off cousin of the Douglas, and his vassal in the lands of Calder, was naturally one of the high-born gentlemen who formed the Earl's train ?

Among the children of Sir Roger de Coulthart, the imaginary elder brother of the same imaginary Gilbert, are named

Walter, an admiral of the fleet.

Henry, who settled in Craven in the co. of York, and was ancestor of H.W. Coulthurst, D.D. late Vicar of Halifax.

---

[1] "Transcribed into unabbreviated Latin, 14 August, 1855, by the Reverend Edward Greswell, B.D. Fellow of Corpus Christi College, Oxford,"—a gentleman whose learning, it must be presumed, lies rather with classical than mediæval Latinity.

Upon these our merciless critic remarks that an Admiral of the
Fleet in Scotland in the sixteenth century would be "about as remarkable a phenomenon as a marriage contract in the tenth:" and that

It was a foolish and unaccountable act in the Vicar of Halifax thus to modify his
illustrious patronymic; but he had himself only to blame when the public forgot his
distinguished lineage, and imagined him to be the scion of a mere commonplace
respectable family of the Irish baronetcy.

But we have next to notice a fiction which affects a more historic
race than even the Coultharts could aspire to be.

Ever since the year 1852, Burke's Peerage has duly chronicled, in the lineage of
the Erroll family, among the daughters of the sixth Earl, "Elizabeth, m. first to Cuthbert Coulthart of Coulthart, lord of the barony of Coulthart, chief of the name, by
whom he had an only son, John (see Burke's *Landed Gentry*) ; 2dly to William lord
Keith, son and heir-apparent of William fourth Earl Marischal, by whom he had four
sons and four daughters."

Here we have the inky dye of this Manchester brooklet staining the
wider stream of a grand historic river. Such an irruption is enough
to turn any feelings of ridicule into indignation. In the accounts of the
Erroll and Marischal families given by Crawfurd and Douglas, Lord
Keith is stated to have been Lady Elizabeth's sole husband ; and the
writer before us (in his pp. 34, 35,) gives various proofs that their
statement is correct.

Besides this Erroll alliance, the Coulthart Pedigree affects to chronicle
numerous intermarriages with other historical houses,

—including Lindsays Earls of Crawfurd, Murrays of Tullibardine, Ramsays of Dal-
housie, the Earls of Breadalbane, the Lords Napier and Somerville, the Sinclairs of
Dunbeath, Anstruthers of that Ilk, Wallaces of Craigie, Baillies of Lamington, Hen-
dersons of Fordel, Chalmers of Gadgirth, Campbells of Skerrington, Muirheads
of Lauchope, Boswells of Auchinleck, and Boswells of Balmuto. The representatives
of all these families, as well as the Earls of Glasgow, are claimed as kinsmen by the
descendant of Coulthartus. It has hitherto been believed that Balmuto came to the
Boswells by an intermarriage in the fifteenth century with the heiress of Balmuto,
whose family name was Glen ; but we have here a Roger de Coulthart, in the reign
of William the Lion, marrying Margaret daughter of Boswell of Balmuto.

But even when we have travelled down this pedigree to its comparatively recent generations, there is still a strange amount of folly and
absurdity intermixed with its ambition and presumption. Thus, it
presents a "Captain of Royal Artillery" in the reign of James the
First, though no such corps in the British army has hitherto been discovered until the time of Queen Anne: it speaks of deeds with pendent
seals of lead at the beginning of the seventeenth century; and of a
Major in the army of Charles the Second, who never returned home

after he had been exiled by Oliver Cromwell. It speaks of Robert Coulthart, an officer in the R.N., who was killed 16 June, 1693, off St. Vincent, when fighting under Admiral Roche, against the French squadrons; and of William his brother, who represented the burgh of Wigtown in Parliament from 1692 to the Union. Now, the commentator shows that the latter personage was William Cultraine (not Coulthart), Provost of Wigtown, of whom various particulars are on record: and the naval officer must also be the duplicate of some other man, if not a being purely imaginary.

Lastly, and strangest of all, considering his propinquity, the Richard Coulthart, Esq., assumed to be the grandfather of the grandfather of the present " chief," and whom we have distinguished in p. 19 as having been " an eminent agriculturist and author of *The Economy of Agriculture*, long a favourite text-book of the farmers of Scotland," even this ancestor is not actually to be found, nor any trace of his " once celebrated work." When searching for it, our inquirer has merely had the fortune to encounter, as the production of one of the race, a book bearing a title at least somewhat in harmony with his object, viz. *The Quacks Unmask'd*, by P. COLTHEART, Surgeon, 1717.

There actually lived in the last century, in the suburbs of Kircudbright, a man named James Coltart, of whom M'Taggart, in a book called the *Gallovidian Encyclopedia*, (1824) gives some extravagant anecdotes, under the name of "*Laird Cowtart, or the obstinate man.*" It is suggested that if this person can be identified, as seems probable, with James Coulthart, Esq., of Coulthart and Largmore," who married " Grizel, daughter of MacTurk, Esq., of The Glenkens, co. Kircudbright," then we at last arrive at the first decidedly non-mythical person in this wonderful pedigree. The more sober facts of the case, and our author's reflections upon them, are as follows:—

The name of Coulthart or Colt-herd prevails among the peasantry of Cumberland, and is also not unfrequently found among the same class on the northern side of the Solway. No family of the name is mentioned in any of the chronicles or county histories, in any known charters, or other sources from which family history is derived, or in the public records. No such lands as those of Coulthart exist, or ever existed, in Wigtownshire or any other shire in Scotland ; and it is instructive to note that in the 1846-8 edition of the *Landed Gentry*, where the earliest trace is to be found of the family,[1] they are merely Coultharts " of Largmore," the territorial designation " of Coulthart " not having been thought of.

Had the framer of this pedigree been a Scotchman, he would probably have been

---

[1] Our author had not detected the notice we have quoted from the Supplement to the *General Armory*. (EDIT. H. & G.)

aware that the Register of Retours afforded a sure and easy means of testing its truth. Not only every minor baron, but every laird holding from the Crown, however small, before he acquires a right to his property by succession, must be served and " retoured " heir to it.   The retours are preserved in a register which is rendered peculiarly accessible to the public by an excellent printed index and abstract, easy of reference, which is to be found in every large public library of the kingdom; and notwithstanding day and date given, as above quoted, to the services of some of these Coultharts, neither the lands nor the surname occur once in this index ; whereas, had these " Lords of Coulthart " ever existed, every one of them would have appeared in his place.

Had they been even mere feuars, whom a vivid imagination had magnified into lairds and barons, they would have been found in another record, the Register of Sasines, where their names will also be looked for in vain.

The other alleged ancestral estate, Largmore, is a farm in the parish of Kells, shown by the Retours to have belonged first to the Gordons of Barskeoch, and afterwards to the Selkirk family, during the period when it is said to have been the property of the Coulthart chieftains. It is here that " Laird Cowtart " is reputed to have had his dwelling, and the popular belief on this subject is corroborated by the parish register of Kells.

We have still to make some important statements with regard to the shields of arms of which engravings were given in our last Part, and which have been erected, as the quarterings of Coulthart, in the west window of Bolton-le-Gate church.

First, as to the assumed arms of Coulthart,—Argent, a fess between three colts courant sable, borne, we are told, "in allusion to three horses that the Coultharts were anciently bound to furnish the sovereigns of Scotland in time of war, when required, for their barony of Coulthart in the county of Wigtown."[1] Now, this coat, including its tinctures, is simply the coat of Colt, a family "formerly possessed of very considerable estates in Suffolk and Essex,"[2] and which, having been raised to a Baronetcy in 1692, is still represented by the Rev. Sir Edward Harry Vaughan Colt, now Vicar of Hill in Gloucestershire.   In the Baronetages, its descent is traced from Thomas Colt, who was Chancellor of the Exchequer in the reign of Edward IV.: and therefore it may be presumed that the family bore these arms at least as early as that time. It appears that the same design, but with a field or, was granted by Camden, June 30, 1615, to Colfe of Canterbury;[3] and that it was

[1] Stated in Mr. Elvin's *Anecdotes of Heraldry*, to be confirmed by a charter from Malcolm Canmore—"a confirmation charter hardly less wonderful than a marriage contract of king Kenneth's time," and " a formal grant of arms in Scotland more than a century before the earliest germs of coat-armour in Normandy."

[2] Kimber's Baronetage.

[3] Morgan's *Sphere of Gentry*, 1661, book 2, p. 115.   Colfe or Coulf, not Colt or Coult, as in Burke's *General Armory*, and 1615 not 1613. See also the pedigree of

borne with an Ermine field, by another family of Colt in Essex; and also, with the field Argent and the fess Azure,[1] by a third Essex family of Colt. The like was granted to the name of Colthurst: to Colthurst of Somersetshire, Argent, a fess between two colts passant sable; but to Colthurst of Ardrum, co. Cork,—now represented by Sir George Conway Colthurst, Bart. (cr. 1744) M.P. for Kinsale, a coat still nearer to that of Colt, viz. Argent, on a fess azure between three colts courant sable, as many trefoils slipped or: and for crest, instead of the running colt of the Colts, a colt statant sable. We do not admire the taste of the heralds of former days, whoever they were, who allowed the arms of Colt, even so varied, to Colfe and to Colthurst: but it does not appear that, at any time, the arms of Colt were allowed, by official authority, to the name of Coulthart; whilst the crest of a " war-horse's head," and the canting Supporters of a *Colt* and a *hart*,—as Mr. Lower well remarks, " a unique instance of *canting supporters*,"—are additions for which the " heraldic artist " of Manchester must enjoy the entire credit.

But what is to be said of the seven quartered coats, which are blasoned in our p. 21, and engraved in pp. 22, 23 ? Our author describes them as " coats, some of which were never seen elsewhere, while the rest belong to other and really existing families."

One of these is the Glendonwyns of Glendonwyn. A well-known family of that name, whose history is to be found at length in Douglas's *Baronage*, long existed in Roxburghshire, owning also estates in Kirkcudbright; but these Coulthartian Glendonwyns are in Ayrshire, and their history and succession bear no resemblance to those of the real family.

The rest of these subsidiary families are purely fabulous. One of them, the Gordons of Sorbie, are said to have been owners of the lands of Sorbie from the time of David I. to 1552, (where were the Ahannays then ?) and their alliances during the fifteenth century are not quite what might have been expected of a Galloway family at that date. For example, one representative of the family, whose mother was " Millicent dau. of Sir William Knatchley," marries " Rachael dau. of Thomas Maltravers of Balgoram," while his daughters marry " Colonel Cavendish " (*sic*) and " Maclachlane of Drumore."

The arms assigned to the fabulous " ROSSES of Renfrew" are really those of the Lords Ross of Halkhead.

The " GLENDONYN " coat is slightly varied from the true coat of the Glendonwyns, which is Quarterly argent and sable, a cross indented counterchanged.

Colfe in the Kent Visitation of 1619, and as it is more fully displayed in the memoir prefixed to the *Catalogue of the Library of the Free Grammar School at Lewisham, founded by the Rev. Abraham Colfe, M.A., in the year* 1652 : by WILLIAM HENRY BLACK, 8vo. 1831, p. xvi.

[1] Burke's *General Armory*.

The coat given to the imaginary MACKNYGHTE OF MACKNYGHTE is that of Macnaught of Kilquharity [1]—to which family Mr. Knowles has attributed an utterly different coat at p. 14 of the Coulthart Genealogy, regarding a supposititious scion of that house.

The coat assigned to "CARMICHAEL OF CARSPHERNE" bears no resemblance to any Carmichael coat, the fess wreathed [2] being the characteristic bearing of the Carmichaels: a bend cotised, or still more cotised potentée, is utterly unlike Scotish armory.

The coat of "MACKENZIE of Craig Hall" is the true coat of Mackenzie, quartered with the insignia of Man,—borne by Mackenzie of Scatwell as representing the Macleods of Lewis. Whence the inescucheon *en surtout* may come from Mr. Knowles only could tell.

Of the two remaining coats, for "GORDON of Sorbie" and "FORBES of Pitscottie," it need only be said that they are purely fabulous.

It will now be thought, perhaps with some impatience, that we have expended sufficient space in exposing the genealogical fictions of Mr. George Parker Knowles. It is not to be imagined that his pedigrees of Ross, Macknyghte, nor the rest, are a whit more genuine than that of Coulthart. With regard to Carmichael we find that a remonstrance has already appeared (in *Notes and Queries*, Oct. 3, 1863), from Mr. Charles H. E. Carmichael, of the College, Isle of Cumbrae, complaining how variant were the statements in the *Visitation of Seats and Arms*, and in Lower's *Patronymica Britannica, s. v.* Carmichael, from anything he had previously read of his family. Indeed, we grieve to find that the pages of Mr. Lower are frightfully spotted with this Coulthart infection. Not only has his credulity been imposed upon in regard to the "Carmichaels of Carspherne;" but under the name of Glendonyn he has been induced to copy the fictions of Mr. Knowles, or (as they are attributed in this case,) of the deceased barrister, Mr. Alex. Cheyne. And again under the names of Forbes, Mackenzie, Macknyghte, and Ross, he everywhere quotes with confidence "Knowles's Genealogy of Coulthart."

Mr. Knowles's account of the Rosses of Halkhead is taken from Douglas's *Peerage of Scotland*, with a few apocryphal additions and interpolations. They were a Yorkshire family who acquired lands in Renfrewshire towards the close of the 13th century, and two centuries later the title of Lord Ross of Halkhead. Mr. Knowles copies Douglas

[1] The inescocheon has been altered from Checquy argent and azure to Checquy argent and or : but in the *Landed Gentry*, edit. 1849, it was exactly Macnaught of Kilquharity.

[2] See the Heraldic card engraved in p. 83 *ante*.

in stating that this dignity became extinct at the death of the 13th lord in 1754: yet he invents a younger son, " Randolph Ross of Rose-hill," to the second Lord Ross, from whom the Rosses of Dalton are said to be descended. If this were true, the peerage would not be extinct: but Mr. Coulthart's maternal grandfather was *de jure* Lord Ross, and his cousin is the present peer. But his audacity, or perhaps his discernment, does not push the pedigree-maker quite so far as to advance such a claim.

All the retours of the successive heirs, affected to be quoted by date, viz. of Patrick Ross of Rosshill in 1548, of William Ross of Rosshill 1594, Patrick Ross of Rosshill 1614, Ninian Ross of Rosshill 1631, Ninian Ross of Rosshill 1662, and John Ross of Keir 1701, are myths,—not one being found in the public records. The alleged permission to erect Rosshill castle in 1556, and an alleged confirmation charter under the great seal 1558, are alike non-existent.

There is evidence in the records of a Captain William Ross having acquired certain lands called—not Ross hill, but—*Rose-isle* in the latter part of the 17th century; to which his cousin Gulielmus Ros, *faber lignarius in Tayn* (filius fratris avi) serves heir in 1674; and on the death of this William soon after, Patrick Ros in Formeston (*nepos fratris proavi* of Captain William Ross) serves in 1676. These Rosses and this Roseisle were however in Dumfriesshire, not Ayrshire (the *locale* of the imaginary Rosshill Castle), and they do not bear the slightest correspondence to Mr. Knowles's Rosses.

One more audacious invention in the Carmichael pedigree may be noticed. It is that a certain Alice Carmichael married " Sir Richard Keith, ancestor of the Earl Marischal" about the time of King Robert II. There is no Richard in the line of Keith, and the Marischal at that period was Sir Robert Keith, a man of no little note in his days, whose first wife (ancestress of the Earls Marischal) was heiress of Troup, and his second Lady Elizabeth Lindsay of the Crawfurd family. Of the same date a Carmichael of Carspherne marries the "sister of the *Rev.* Canon Lawson, of St. Giles's church, Edinburgh"!

We have now pursued, from page to page, the critic's example of a *wholly fictitious Pedigree*, in order to redeem our own character after the additional circulation that was given to it in our last Part. We must more briefly state that his example of *the partially fictitious pedigree* is one entitled " BONAR of Bonare, Keltye, Kilgraston, and Kimmerghame," which occupies eleven closely printed columns of the *Landed Gentry* in the supplemental volume of 1849. This has been purposely selected as the account of "a family whose social position and high honourable principles preclude the idea of knowingly conniving at falsehood or fiction:" and yet so ignorant and careless about genealogy, as to allow their history to be written by one of those charlatans who seem to make a trade in writing for the *Landed Gentry*. The details of this composition both genealogical and armorial (exposed in pp. 55—82 of the Essay before us,) are quite as curious and extraordinary as those connected with the pedigree of Coulthart, but our space allows us only to make this allusion to them.

A few words are added regarding Sir Bernard Burke's other works, —the *Vicissitudes of Families* and *Family Romance*; and it is remarked that, " though at times they contain a correct enough sketch of some remarkable incident of family history, they are full of the same looseness and credulity in everything that relates to pedigree." As a sample, the history given in the former work of John Law, the great financier, containing a flourishing account of his estates and descent, is contrasted with the simple truth that he was the son of a working silversmith in Edinburgh, of no claim to gentle birth.

After noticing one more fantastic pedigree of the *History of the Landed Gentry*, that of Dearden of Rochdale, the writer draws to a close with the following reflections:—

In bringing this and similar genealogical fictions to the light of day, it is proper for me to add that no necessity exists for supposing that the late Mr. Dearden, or the other persons for whose glorification they were invented, had any complicity in the fraud. The presumption is that they had not. Profoundly ignorant of history and genealogy, and only interested in the latter in so far as it could be made to minister to their foolish vanity, a superabundance of this latter quality has probably led them to be eyed as promising subjects by one of these genealogical impostors who live on the folly and credulity of the public ; and, having once fallen into the hands of the charlatan, they yield as implicit a faith in his fables as does the unhappy patient to the nostrums of the quack doctor. As Mr. Coltheart exposed the medical charlatans of his day, and "set in a true light their pernicious and destructive practice, with some reasons why it ought to be entirely abolished," so have I thought it a duty, humbly following in the wake of that eminent surgeon, to "unmask" those "quacks" who deal, not in pills and potions, but in pedigrees, and whom a large portion of the community seem unable to distinguish from *bonâ fide* genealogists.

THE HOUSE OF SOMERSET:

IN THE DAYS OF EDWARD LORD HERBERT, EARL OF GLAMORGAN, AND MARQUESS OF WORCESTER.

THE LIFE, TIMES, AND SCIENTIFIC LABOURS OF THE SECOND MARQUIS OF WORCES-
TER. To which is added, a reprint of his CENTURY OF INVENTIONS, 1663, with a
Commentary thereon. By HENRY DIRCKS, Esq. Civil Engineer, &c. &c. London:
Bernard Quaritch, 15, Piccadilly. 1865. 8vo. pp. xxiv. 624.

The house of Somerset, descended in the direct male line from our
mediæval kings, though with two illegitimate links in the chain, has
maintained its dignity and high station throughout a duration of time
that has been seldom surpassed. In the long line of eighteen generations, extending from King Edward the Third to the present Duke of
Beaufort, the subject of the book before us occupies the tenth. He
lived in very perilous times: and by his profusion and temerity brought
the fortunes of the House of Somerset to the very brink of ruin,
though happily not past recovery. Very little has hitherto been
written in his praise, nor have the actions and events of his life been
placed in our ordinary biographical collections. Yet his name, or
rather his two successive titles of peerage, are sufficiently familiar, both
in political history and in the history of science. He is the EARL OF
GLAMORGAN of Clarendon and Carte, the MARQUESS OF WORCESTER of
those numerous authors who now write of Steam, that potent agent of
our daily progress.

But, if the Marquess of Worcester has not been enshrined in the
more popular temples of our English worthies, so neither has his
biography been altogether neglected. There is a memoir of him, by

Edmund Lodge, Norroy, in the *Portraits and Memoirs of the most illustrious Persons of English History;* and he had previously been noticed by Anthony Wood, in his *Athenæ Oxonienses;* by Granger, in his *Biographical History of England;* and by Horace Walpole, in his *Royal and Noble Authors.* These, however, in the opinion of the author before us, were tributes far inferior to the merits of a man whom he regards as " one of the most remarkable, interesting, and glorious benefactors of the country " (p. vii.), as "pre-eminent for his gifts in constructive ingenuity," and as unequalled " among the most eminent scientific celebrities of Europe, during the last two centuries." (p. iv.)

The origin of the book appears to be this. Mr. Dircks has been a student of the lucubrations of the Marquess of Worcester for thirty years. (p. vii.) He determined to prepare a new edition of the *Century of Inventions,* and this is incorporated in the present volume (pp. 343–552), accompanied by a running commentary, very diligently compiled : but, not satisfied with that, he undertook to investigate the personal history of the author, and this has given birth to "The Life, Times, and Scientific Labours of the Marquis of Worcester," of which the *Century of Inventions* now forms but a secondary feature.

The success of Mr. Smiles in rendering popular the triumphs of Engineering has evidently suggested the form and plan of the work; which is indeed a very handsome volume, and adorned with many beautiful illustrations, among which are portraits of the Marquess and both his wives, and numerous vignettes of the localities of his career and his more remarkable scientific contrivances. Mr. Dircks has collected his materials with diligence and perseverance, and he has had the advantage of deriving documents of very considerable importance from the family archives at Badminton.

Mr. Dircks differs, of course, *toto cælo,* from Horace Walpole, who termed the *Century of Inventions* " an amazing piece of folly," and from David Hume, who described it as " a ridiculous compound of lies, chimeras, and impossibilities." He differs also from Lodge, who remarks that the Marquess " was a statesman, a philosopher, and a mathematician, and in each of those stations a mystic. He was a man of parts or a madman, or both:" and afterwards describes the *Century of Inventions* as a "strange little book, which certainly savours much of a disordered imagination." Mr. Dircks differs equally from Lord Macaulay, who appreciated the merits of the Marquess feebly and defectively (pp. x. xi.), and from Mr. Muirhead, the biographer of James Watt, who has spoken of the Marquess and his inventions "in the most disparaging terms." (p. xviii.) The fact is that Mr. Dircks has become the champion of his hero with even more than the usual partiality of biographers, impressed with the conviction that the Marquess of Worcester "was a man of rigid honour and probity, remarkable for his modesty, virtue, and genius" (p. xii.); and, in regard to his "scientific labours," repeatedly employing such hyperboles as these—"his singular abilities, his versatile mechanical talent, and the fecundity of his inventive ingenuity." (p. 16.)

It would exceed our province, and far exceed our limits, to enter into a discussion of the merits of those philosophical labours of the Marquess of Worcester which our author admits (pp. x. 292) were so blindly "neglected by contemporaries," and have been so defectively estimated or depreciated by subsequent philosophers and historians. The subject, no doubt, will still be matter of debate in many a more appropriate arena : and we may therefore fairly take leave of it with the old maxim,—*Tractant fabrilia fabri.*

We may however remark that the researches of Mr. Dircks into the records of the Marquess's Water-Commanding Engine, which was set up at the manor of Vauxhall, form materials of a curious chapter in the history of that world-celebrated locality : and that other historical particulars relative to Worcester House in the Strand are a valuable contribution to our metropolitan topography.

The political conduct of "the Earl of Glamorgan" as the agent of King Charles in his negociations with the Roman Catholics of Ireland is a theme of still greater difficulty, and demanding a far wider space than is at our disposal. From Badminton the author has obtained several original documents that throw fresh light upon this subject, in addition to those which were published by the adversaries of the Marquess and his Sovereign when their designs were first discovered; to those which were edited by Carte in his *Life of James Duke of Ormond;* by Dr. Birch, in his *Inquiry into the Share which Charles I. had in the Transactions of the Earl of Glamorgan,* 1756, 8vo.; and by Mr. Bruce in *Letters of King Charles I. to Queen Henrietta Maria in* 1646 (Camden Society 1856); but Mr. Dircks has most unfortunately confused the arrangement of these documents, and impaired the perspicuity of his narration, by being perfectly unconscious of what is called the old style of the calendar; so that, in each successive year, nearly one-fourth of its events are presented to the reader before those to which they were actually consequent (the letters and papers of 1642-3 being taken to belong to 1641-2, and so on); and when at

last, on quoting some of his historical predecessors, the author falls
into their customary practice of notation, in which both the civil and
ecclesiastical years are mentioned, he actually is led on to speak of the
1st of April, 1644-5 (p. 112), and the 29th September, 1645-6 (p. 138).

This very material deficiency in one of the first points of knowledge
necessary for writing history has caused Mr. Dircks to head his Eighth
Chapter with this title, "The Earl of Glamorgan's *Second* Visit to
Ireland;" yet, in his Preface (p. xvi.), he admits his misgivings that
the Earl, after all, made only a single visit to that country. The same
misapprehension explains why, in p. 87, our author finds the statements
of Dr. Birch regarding the year 1644-5 "at variance" with the letters
of the year 1645-6, derived from the Carte papers.

The date of the birth of Edward Somerset has not been ascertained
with precision. It is supposed to have been in 1601, the year after
his father's marriage in June 1600. His grandfather Edward fourth
Earl of Worcester, Master of the Horse to Queen Elizabeth and King
James, and afterwards Lord Privy Seal,[2] lived to the year 1627-8 : up
to which time his father was Lord Herbert, and he only Mr. Somerset.[2]
He became Lord Herbert upon his grandfather's decease ; in 1644
King Charles designated him Earl of Glamorgan, by which title he
was known during his transactions in Ireland ; next, after his father's
death in 1646, he was called Earl of Worcester,—for the Parliament
would not acknowledge the higher title of Marquess ; and from the
Restoration in 1660 until his death in 1667 he was Marquess of
Worcester.

Scarcely any part of his earlier history has been recovered, except
the dates of his two marriages. His education appears to have been
chiefly, if not entirely, conducted on the Continent,—owing, no doubt,
to his father's zealous attachment to the Roman communion,[3] to which
his grandfather had also adhered: it being remarked by Fuller, or
some such sententious biographer, that "Q. Elizabeth excused his
faith, which was Popish; and honoured his faithfulness, which was
Roman." The Marquess himself writes of his education :—

Amongst Almighty God's infinite mercies to me in this world, I account it one of
the greatest that his divine goodness vouchsafed me parents as well careful as able to

---

[1] Mr. Dircks in p. 7 states that the Earl of Worcester was invested with the Garter
in 1604, an error for 1593.

[2] In writing of " the young Lord Herbert " in p. 12, Mr. Dircks is premature.

[3] Lord Herbert was scolded by James I. in 1620 for sending one of his daughters
to become a nun at Brussels. He died at last a Penitent of the Society of Jesus, as
declared in a paper drawn up by the Jesuits themselves, after the Restoration (p. 232).

give me virtuous èducation and extraordinary breeding at home and abroad in Germany, France, and Italy, allowing me abundantly in those parts, and since most plentifully at my master of most happy memory the late King's court.

But this statement is misunderstood by Mr. Dircks when he regards it (p. 11) as "making it almost conclusive that his education was considered as completed shortly prior to the King's decease, in 1625:" whereas the document from which it is extracted is assigned by Mr. Dircks himself, in p. 335, to the date 1663, or soon after, and therefore " the late King " whom it mentions was not James, but Charles.[1]

Our author has fallen into a more serious misapprehension just before, in stating (p. 11) that " His preceptor at Raglan Castle was Mr. Adams." That this error should be pointed out is the more necessary, as no authority is given for it; but we have discovered its origin at p. 141, in a document which unfolds an interesting picture of the household at Raglan Castle,[2] and the manner of living there established :

At the second table in the Dining-room sat Knights and honourable Gentlemen attended by footmen : Sir Ralph Blackstone, Steward; the Comptroller; the Secretary; the Master of the Horse, Mr. Delaware ; the Master of the Fishponds, Mr. Andrews; *my Lord Herbert's preceptor, Mr. Adams* ; with such Gentlemen as came there under the degree of a Knight, attended by footmen, and plentifully served with wine.

Now this was certainly not earlier than 1642, for Sir Nicholas Kemeys, Bart., who is subsequently mentioned in the same document as Governor of Chepstow (but misprinted Sir Mich. Keneys), was not created a Baronet before that year. It follows that the Lord Herbert to whom Mr. Adams was preceptor was Henry, afterwards first Duke of Beaufort, who was born in 1629.

The early predilection of Mr. Edward Somerset for philosophical amusements and engineering is shown by what he states in 1663 respecting a German who was then managing his "Water-Commanding Engine" at Vauxhall, and who is described as "the unparallel'd Workman both for trust and skill, Caspar Kaltoff, who hath been these

[1] Had Edward Somerset in his youthful days been about the court of James, or even elsewhere in England, his name would probably have been found among the Knights of the Bath made at the Creation of Henry Prince of Wales in 1610, at that of Charles Prince of Wales in 1616, or at the Coronation of King Charles. His three uncles had received that honour : Sir Thomas Somerset at the Creation of Charles Duke of York in 1604-5; Sir Charles and Sir Edward at that of Henry Prince of Wales.

[2] In the same paper Sir Toby Matthews, the son of the late bishop of Durham and archbishop of York, and a man well known in the annals of his times as a convert to the Church of Rome, is mentioned as the Earl's principal chaplain.

five and thirty years as in a school under me employed." This takes us back as far as 1628.

To the same early days belongs an anecdote connected with one of the " Century of Inventions." In p. 25, when speaking of the Marquess's "large wheel for exhibiting self-motive power," Mr. Dircks remarks that it was exhibited at the Tower of London whilst Sir William Balfour "was Lord Lieutenant,"[1] and he adds, that this wheel-experiment may have been made in 1638-9, prior to the decease of Lord Herbert's first lady. But her ladyship died in 1635 (p. 22), and the experiment may have been still earlier, for Sir William Balfour was appointed Lieutenant of the Tower on the death of Sir Allen Apsley, which took place in May, 1630. The Marquess of Worcester's own account of the circumstance is as follows :—

A most incredible thing if not seen ; but tried before the late King (of blessed memory) in the Tower, by my directions, two Extraordinary Ambassadors accompanying his Majesty, and the Duke of Richmond and Duke Hamilton, with most of the Court, attending him * * Sir William Balfore, then Lieutenant of the Tower, can justify it, with several others.

Beyond this little anecdote, all that Mr. Dircks has discovered of the Marquess's early life is confined to the dates of his marriages. He first married, in 1628, Elizabeth Dormer, grand-daughter of the first Lord Dormer, and sister to the first Earl of Carnarvon; and their eldest child Henry, afterwards Duke of Beaufort, was born in the following year. Her portrait, from a picture by Vandyck, is engraved in the volume before us by J. Cochran, we believe for the first time. The original at Badminton is minutely described by Mr. Dircks in p. 22. He mentions also Vandyck's portrait of Lord Herbert himself, and dates it as between 1621 and 1626; but Vandyck did not arrive in this country until 1632, and, as the picture represents Lord Herbert in armour and holding a baton, with a paper—perhaps a royal missive, in the left hand (as engraved in Lodge's series), we think it must be carried forward to more warlike times.[2]

---

[1] Mr. Dircks repeats this expression with respect to Sir John Byron in p. 59, evidently not aware that the meaning of Lieutenant of the Tower is merely *locum tenens* of the Constable of that fortress.

[2] There is an engraving of Vandyck's picture, by Faithorne, without an inscription; which is mentioned in the last edition of Granger's *Biographical History of England*, 1824, vol. iv. p. 163, under the name of Henry Duke of Beaufort : with the remark, " This has been mistaken for Edward, Marquis of Worcester, by Granger." It must, however, be the editor that is wrong; for, as Vandyck died in 1641, when the Duke of Beaufort was only eleven years of age, that painter could not represent him as a grown-up man, in armour.

It is not until these times arrive that Mr. Dircks has anything to relate of the subject of his biography, further than that he became a widower in 1635,[1] and was married secondly in 1639 to the Lady Margaret O'Bryen, second daughter and coheir of Henry Earl of Thomond. Accompanied by her, and by their only child, Lady Mary Somerset, who died in her childhood, he is represented in another picture at Badminton, which is engraved as a frontispiece to this volume. The Marquess is here attired in Roman costume, with a long flowing peruke out of curl, and without the moustaches shown in Vandyck's picture, looking, in Mr. Dircks' opinion, less young, and in ours less wise, than he need have done. The painter was Hanneman: and, whatever doubt there may be as to the date or identity of the two portraits by Vandyck,[2] the certainty of this is ascertained by the atchievement upon it of the arms of Somerset impaling O'Bryen.

It is in the year 1641 that we find Lord Herbert first drawn forth into public life. At that time King Charles, alarmed by the gathering storm, looked round for aid to all of his nobility upon whom he retained any influence. The Earl of Worcester was one who was better able to serve him in purse than in person. He had fallen into a gouty habit of body, which rendered him unwieldy and inactive.[3] The first original

[1] In Collins's Peerage this date has been misprinted 1665. Mr. Dircks has introduced (p. 23) her Ladyship's funeral certificate, prepared by George Owen, York herald. It records that she died at Worcester house in the Strand, near London, on Sunday the last of May, 1635; and that her body was honourably conveyed to Raglan, in the county of Monmouth, there to be interred.

[2] May not Vandyck's picture be one of the *second* Lady Herbert? The fashion of the hair in both pictures is identical, and the features, judging from the engravings, not dissimilar.

[3] " At the commencement of this period (remarks Mr. Dircks, p. 95.) the noble Marquess [Earl] would be in about the sixty-third year of his age, rather feeble, and a martyr to gout, which his fondness for claret may have aggravated; a pleasant story being related by his chaplain (Dr. Bayly) that, on the physician recommending abstinence from his favourite beverage, he declared he would rather incur the attacks of his old enemy than abandon his favourite claret." In regard to the age of the old Marquess we think that Mr. Dircks has differed on good grounds from former writers. Rushworth calls him eighty-four in 1646, and Lodge has consequently stated that " he was born in or about the year 1562:" but better evidence is offered by Anthony à Wood, who states that when William Lord Herbert (who died s. p.) and his brother Henry were at Magdalen College, Oxford, in 1591, they were of the respective ages of 15 and 14: this brings the birth of Henry to 1577.

It is remarkable that Granger, in the *Biographical History of England*, whilst adopting Rushworth's estimate of the Earl of Worcester's age, has given the very opposite account of his physical energies. He states that "The Earl of Worcester, when he was about eighty years of age, raised the first horse that were levied for Charles I. in

document now presented to us from Badminton is one dated Aug. 3, 1641, in which the King acknowledges "the good service of you and yours," but excuses the Earl's personal attendance to receive the royal thanks on account of his "indisposition of body." In December following occurs the King's first letter to Herbert. It was succeeded by many others, several of which are now published for the first time.[1]

They are a valuable addition to the history of the political transactions in which Glamorgan was involved; and little less so is the Autobiographical Statement of his Services and Expenses which he drew up after the Restoration, to be submitted to King Charles the Second and the House of Lords.[2]   But we must abstain from quoting them, for the reasons already assigned.   They show how profusely large were the contributions which he induced his father to make to the King's supplies,—to the extent of many hundred thousand pounds; and they also show how inefficient and painfully unsuccessful were his own military efforts, and how rash and desperate his expedition to Ireland, as, even with less complete evidence, it has always been considered by every judicious historian.

The King first addressed Lord Herbert as Earl of Glamorgan in 1644.   It was in June 1645 that the Earl landed in Ireland, and he remained there until the end of 1647,[3] when he passed over into

the civil war; *and entered into the service with all the ardour of a volunteer.   No man of his years seemed ever to have retained more of the fire and activity of youth; and the readiness and sprightliness of his wit are said to have been no less extraordinary.* * * * * * He was remarkable for the singularity of wearing a frieze coat, in which he was always dressed when he went to court." It is evident that the Earl and his son are here mixed together, and that the lines which we print in Italics relate to the latter. The allusion to "his wit" belongs to the Father, being founded on the anecdotes contained in Worcester's *Apophthegmata*, or Witty Sayings of the Right Honourable Henry (late) Marquess of Worcester. By T. B. a constant Observer, and no less Admirer, of his Lordship's Wisdom and Loyalty. 1650. 12mo. a scarce little book, from which extracts may be seen in Seward's *Anecdotes of Distinguished Persons*, and in Bliss's edition of the *Athenæ Oxonienses*, as well as in the volume before us.

[1] We believe there are still others, not introduced by Mr. Dircks. One at least of the most remarkable is that of which the original is in the British Museum (dated April 5, 1646), in which, after Charles had publicly disavowed Glamorgan's proceedings, he assures him *in cypher* to "be confident of *my making good all instructions and promises to you and* Nuntio." This is printed in Seward's Anecdotes.

[2] It occupies pp. 319-335 of Mr. Dircks' volume,—in modernised orthography: having been previously printed *literatim* from the original MS. in the possession of the Duke of Beaufort, by Charles Baker, esq. his Grace's Steward of the Seigniories of Gower and Kilvey.

[3] Mr. Dircks, p. 185, says he went to France in March 1647-8, with Father Leyburn, quoting Leyburn's Memoirs, p. 61; but Carte, in his Life of the Duke of

France. In July 1652 he returned to England as rashly as he had quitted her shores. He was again the forlorn hope of his sovereign, and as adventurous for the sake of the second Charles as he had been for his father. That at least is Kennett's account, who states that Charles "sent to England the noble Marquess of Worcester for private intelligence as well as for supplies; but the Marquess was taken up prisoner in London and sent to the Tower in September." This date, however, is wrong; for it was on the 28th July, 1652, that the House of Commons resolved, "That the Earl of Worcester[1] do stand committed to the Tower of London, in order to his trial." It was not thought necessary to proceed further; and, after Worcester had remained prisoner for two years and three months, he was released under the circumstances thus related in Burton's Diary of that Parliament.

The Petitioner was alleged to be a Papist, in arms in England, who had headed a party in Ireland, making a most dishonourable peace there, and had done many other disservices for which he was excepted from all mercy and pardon, his whole estate ordered to be sold, and all such to be banished. Yet, it was urged, he was an old man, had lain long in prison, and the small-pox then raging under the same roof where he lay; and he had not, as was said, done any action of hostility but only as a soldier; and in that capacity had always shown civilities to the English prisoners and Protestants. It was therefore ordered that he should be bailed out of prison.

His manifold errors and "disservices" were overbalanced by his long sufferings and unparalleled losses. His enemies could afford to pity him, and to admit that his faults had been those of the head, not of the heart. So this "old man," of about fifty-three years of age, was released from confinement, and allowed to go and amuse himself with his engineering at Vauxhall.

His son Lord Herbert, afterwards the first Duke of Beaufort, had now grown up into manhood; and it is evident that, taking warning from his father's errors, he had adopted a very different course of action. He had already established an interest with the ruling powers;[2] so far that on one occasion (from Edinburgh April 12, 1651,) Cromwell wrote to his wife as follows:

My Dearest,—Beware of my Lord Herbert his resort to your house; if he do so, may occasion scandal, as if I were bargaining with him. Indeed be wise: you know my meaning.

Ormond, states that the Duke went to Paris in March, and the Earl of Glamorgan had come thither a few months before him.

[1] The Commonwealth government, as before remarked, did not allow his title of Marquess.

[2] Mr. Dircks, p. 210, states that he "sat in the Cromwellian parliament."

Cromwell in fact bargained with him to the advantage of both parties, and the estates of the Somersets were apportioned between them. This was probably, in effect, the salvation of the family: for the old Marquess—or Earl, as he was then called—could never be taught, by all his painful experience, any worldly wisdom. In June 1655 he was glad to accept from Cromwell a pittance of three pounds a week; and all else that is learned of him until the Restoration is from papers which relate to his borrowing money from various parties. In 1655 he prepared his *Century of Inventions* for the press; but it was not published until the year 1663. He walked in the Coronation procession of Charles the Second; and died in London on the third of April 1667. The body of his father had been interred in 1646 in the family vault in the Beaufort Chapel at Windsor, the Parliament allow-. ing 500*l.* for the funeral expenses: but the second Marquess was conveyed to Raglan, as described in the Funeral Certificate,[1] as follows:

The Right Hon[ble] Edward Somerset, Marquess and Earle of Worcester, Earle of Glamorgan, and Baron Herbert of Raglan, Chepstow, and Gower, departed this mortall life upon Wedensday the third of Aprill 1667, and was conveyed with Fune-

---

[1] The quarterings placed at the head of this Certificate, are 1. Somerset; 2. Herbert; 3. Wydvile; and 4. Russell: viz.—

1. France and England quarterly, within a bordure gobonated argent and azure, *Somerset.*

2. Per pale azure and gules, three lions rampant argent, for *Herbert,*—the first Earl of Worcester having become Lord Herbert by his marriage with Elizabeth sole daughter and heir of William Lord Herbert, some time Earl of Huntingdon.

3. Argent, a fess and a canton gules, for *Wydvile,*—the wife of William Earl of Huntingdon just mentioned having been Mary sister and coheiress to Richard Wydvile, Earl Rivers.

rall Solemnitie from London to his Barony of Raglan in the county of Monmouth (accompanied with many Gentry of yᵉ Countys of Gloucester and Monmouth aforesaid,) and there interred in his Lordship's Chappell in the Parish Church, neare to the body of Edward Earle of Worcester, Lord Privie Seale, his Grandfather, (in a vault arched with stone,) on Fryday the 19. day of the same month. His Lordship married to his first wife Elizabeth Dormer, daughter of Sir William Dormer, knight, that dyed in the lifetime of his father, and sister unto Robert Earle of Carnarvon, by whom he had issue his only son Henry Lord Herbert, now Marquess of Worcester, at the time of the takeinge of this Certificate ; who, marrying with Mary daughter of that most loyall Nobleman Arthur Lord Capell, beheaded by the rebells upon the 9th day of March, 1648 (sister to Arthur Earle of Essex, &c. and widdow to Henry Seamour, Lord Beauchampe, that dyed in the lifetime of his father, by whom she had issue William now Duke of Somerset aged 15 years, and Frances and Mary dead, and Elizabeth Seamour third daughter now liveing,) had by the said Mary also issue Henry Somerset his eldest son dead, and buried at Windsor, Charles Somerset second son and heire, now Lord Herbert, about 6 years old; Edward Somerset, 3d son, dead also, and was interred at Raglan ; and Henry Somerset the yonger, 4 sonne, who departed this world about two dayes before his grandfather, and was buried at Raglan; Elizabeth Somerset, elder daughter, dyed young, and was buried at Raglan; and Lady Mary Somerset, younger daughter, is now liveing about a yeare and halfe old. Lady Anne Somerset, elder daughter to the defunct, was married to Henry Howard second sonne of Henry Earle of Arundell, and brother and heire to Thomas Duke of Norfolke, and by him hath issue Henry Howard, Thomas, Elizabeth, and Frances. Lady Elizabeth Somerset, younger daughter to the defunct, is the wife of William Lord Herbert of Powis, and by him hath issue William Herbert his only son, and four daughters.

---

4. Argent, a lion rampant gules, on a chief sable three escallops of the first, *Russell.* This quartering was inherited from the mother of the deceased, Anne daughter and sole heir of John lord Russell, (who died v. p.) son of Francis Earl of Bedford.

The Supporters are, on the dexter side, a Panther argent, spotted sable, azure and gules, sending forth flames of fire at his mouth, eyes, and ears proper [*otherwise blasoned as* incensed proper], collared and chained or; on the sinister, a Wyvern vert, devouring a hand couped at the wrist gules. .

The Crest of the Marquess (Sandford, *Geneal. History,* 1677, p. 344) was the same as is still borne by the Dukes of Beaufort,—a Portcullis or, chained argent. This well-known *badge* of the Beauforts—and through the mother of King Henry VII. of the Royal House of Tudor also—was evidently (remarks Mr. Willement, *Royal Heraldry,* 1821, p. 86,) the type of the castle of Beaufort in Anjou, where Dame Katharine Swinford gave birth to John Beaufort the first Duke of Somerset. But Charles first Earl of Worcester has on his seal (Sandford, p. 240) the more appropriate Crest of the royal line of England, a lion statant guardant, collared and chained.

The impalement for the Marquess of Worcester's first wife is, Azure, ten billets and on a chief or a demi-lion rampant issuant sable, *Dormer.*

That of his second wife is Quarterly of four: 1. & 4. Gules, three lions passant guardant, parted per pale or and argent, *O'Bryen;* 2. Argent, three piles gules ; 3. Gules, a pheon argent.

The said Edward Lord Marquess defunct married to his second wife the Lady Margaret O'Bryan, daughter and coheire of Henry Earle of Thomond, and by her had issue one only daughter named Mary, who dyed an infant, and was buried at Raglan.

This Certificate was taken upon the 24th of Aprill 1667 by Francis Sandford, Rouge Dragon, who served for Sr Edward Walker K^t. Garter Principall King of Armes, and the truth thereof attested by the subscription of the Right Ho^{ble} Henry Marquess of Worcester.

(*Signed*)　WORCESTER.

Examd F. R. S. D.
(i.e. Francis Sandford, Rouge Dragon.)

On the whole it will be seen that Mr. Dircks has added materially to the biographical particulars of the second Marquess of Worcester, but has formed a very exaggerated estimate of his abilities and performances. No wonder that he is angry with every one who has written about his hero ; and most of all with the unhappy Charles, who insanely entrusted the most hazardous enterprises to so weak a person. Lord Clarendon, who, at the time of those untoward events, told Secretary Nicholas plainly, " I care not how little I say in that business of Ireland, since those strange powers and instructions given to your [*i.e.* the King's] favourite Glamorgan, which appear to me inexcusable to justice, piety, and prudence: " yet, subsequently, in his History, looked back mercifully at the many failings of this generous but visionary enthusiast ; allowing that "he was one whose person many men loved, and very few hated ; that he was in truth of a civil and obliging nature, and of a fair and gentle carriage toward all men," as well as " a man of more than ordinary affection and reverence to the person of the King, and one who, he was sure, would neither deceive or betray him."

Edward Marquess of Worcester is, we may say, the Good-Natured Man of English History : one who followed the eager impulses of his affections, and the sanguine anticipations of an enterprising genius, at the sacrifice of every consideration of prudence, and with no reasonable prospects of success. These characteristics even Charles himself could not fail to perceive, though he was ready to catch at a broken reed, for he wrote to the Marquess of Ormond, " His honesty or affection to my service will not deceive you, but I will not answer for his judgment."[1]

The new dignities of peerage which the King conferred on the House of Somerset will form the subject of another article.

---

[1] This is a postscript added *in cypher* to Charles's letter to Ormond, then Lord Lieutenant of Ireland, dated Oxford, 27 Decemb. 1644.

WHO WAS ARNULPH DE HESDING?

To the Editor of THE HERALD AND GENEALOGIST.

SIR,—The name of Arnulph de Hesding appears in Domesday Book as the holder of large possessions in various counties, and he is mentioned in your vol. i. p. 202 as one of the companions in arms of the Conqueror.

Among his Gloucestershire possessions were the manors of Kempsford and Hatherop, the former of which, says Rudder (*History of Gloucestershire*), he about the end of the reign of William Rufus " *conveyed* to Patrick de Chaworth" (p. 510), and the latter, he says (p. 480), "probably passed to the Chaworths at the same time." Collinson, in his *History of Somersetshire*, confesses his inability to give any details of Arnulph's history further than that he was one of William's attendants, and that "about the latter end of William Rufus" certain hides in Weston, formerly his property, were also found to be in the possession of Patrick de Chaworth or Cadurcis.

From the list of donations to the monastery of St. Peter at Gloucester, given in Rudder, from the Monasticon, it appears that in the year 1126 Robert son of Walter and Aveline his wife gave to that monastery the church of Norton with the lands &c. as fully as Emeline the mother of Aveline some years since had given the same. A charter of Stephen, King of England, dated 1138, confirming certain gifts to the aforesaid monastery, enumerates, *inter alia*, "The church of Norton, with the tithes, &c., which were given by *Ernulph de Hesding and Emmeline his wife*." [1]

The same Arnulph also gave certain other lands in the year 1081, when Serlo was Abbot.

In the pages of Ordericus Vitalis, [2] we have a further trace of Arnulph. We learn that when Stephen laid siege to the Castle of Shrewsbury, anno 1138, FitzAlan the Governor made his escape privately, but Arnulph de Hesding his *Uncle*, "a bellicose and venturesome soldier, arrogantly refused the peace which the King offered him on several

---

[1] Under the head of "Norton" Rudder states that one "Elmelina" gave the advowson of the church to the abbey of Gloucester, and that the grant was confirmed by "her *grandson* Robert, son of Walter, and by Aveline his wife."

[2] Bohn's Edition, iv. 204.

occasions, and obstinately forced others who wished to surrender themselves to persist in their rebellion.[1] At last, when the fortress was reduced, he was taken amongst many others, and brought into the presence of the King, whom he had treated with contempt. The King, finding that his gentleness had lowered him in the eyes of the revolters, and that in consequence many of the nobles summoned to his court had disdained to appear, was so incensed that he ordered Arnulf, and nearly ninety-three others of those who had resisted him, to be hung on the gallows, or immediately executed in other ways. Arnulf, now repenting too late, and many others on his behalf, supplicated the King, offering a large sum of money for his ransom. But, the King preferring vengeance on his enemies to any amount of money, they were put to death without delay."

The FitzAlan here alluded to was William, son of Alan, son of Flaald, and ancestor to the great house of FitzAlan. Alan, son of Flaald, is said to have married Ameria the daughter and heir of Warine, Sheriff of Salop; so that, if Arnulph were really the uncle of William FitzAlan, he must have either been a son of Warine, or a brother of Alan. If it be true that Alan's wife was Warine's daughter and *heir*, of course she had no brother; and therefore (supposing all these statements to be strictly true), Arnulph de Hesding must have been another of Flaald's sons.

Mr. Eyton, however, in his account of the FitzAlans, after quoting the above passage from Vitalis, comes to the conclusion that FitzAlan's wife was not, as is usually supposed, a daughter of the Sheriff Warine, but one Aveline, Adeliza, or Adeline de Hesding; and this is corroborated by the foundation charter of Haghmond Abbey, wherein the mother of FitzAlan is styled Avelina.

This lady survived her husband many years, and, as is manifest from the passage above quoted from Rudder, was remarried to Robert, the son of Walter.[2]

Other proofs of connection subsisting between the families of FitzAlan and Hesding occur: Reginald de Hesding, probably a son of the second Arnulf, is a witness to the charter whereby William, son of William, son of Alan, at the request of Fulke Fitzwarren, grants the said Fulke's land at Alveston to Reginald de Le.[3]

Again we find a trace of Arnulph in the pages of Collins and Lodge, but this time he is a belted Earl—Henry de Novo Burgo, Beaumont,

---

[1] This "insolent soldier" must have been a son of the Domesday landholder.

[2] Who this person was I have yet to learn.

[3] Owen and Blakeway.

or Bellomonte, we are told, took to wife Margaret de Hesdene, "daughter of *Arnulph*, and sister to Rotro, *both Earls of Perche*."

Heylin (*Help to English History*) also makes the same statement on the authority of Milles, but adds that " Vincent, correcting Brooke, says she was daughter of Geoffrey Earl of *Moreton ;*" and gives the arms of this match as, Checky or and azure, a chevron ermine, the old Warwick coat. Now these arms are assigned in the heraldic dictionaries to the name of " Hesding," and are engraved in Burke's *Visitations of Seats and Arms*, 1st Series, vol. ii., as the arms of a family of Hedding, claiming descent from this very Arnulph. The pedigree there given states Arnulph to have been the son or grandson of Phœlice, daughter of Rohaud, Earl of Warwick, and wife of the celebrated Guy (Earl jure uxoris), and adds that these arms were assumed and ever afterwards borne by the Hedding family to commemorate their descent from the Saxon Earls of Warwick. The wife of Arnulph is stated to have been one Ameline,[1] "who gave to the Abbey of Bec Hellouin in Normandy the manor of Comb." He is said to have had a brother Ilbodus, who held vast possessions in Oxfordshire ; and finally he is made to be father of Rotro, Earl of Perche and Mortagne, who died 1123, whose daughter (by his first wife Maud, natural daughter of King Henry 1st) Margaret married Henry de Newburgh, and from whose second marriage with " a Saxon lady" springs the family in question. One daughter of Arnulph, Magdalen, is made to marry Marius IV. King of Navarre,[2] and another, by name Levitha, is stated to have been a nun.

Now the genealogy of the Counts of Perche and Montagne appears to be pretty well known. Rotro, Geoffrey, and other Counts of that family, are frequently mentioned by Ordericus Vitalis, but in no one instance is any relationship or connection with a family called de Hesding mentioned. Rotro Count of Perche is also called son of Arnulph de Hesding by Sandford,[3] but Vitalis distinctly states that he was the only son of " Geoffrey Earl of Moriton."[4]

[1] See the charter of Stephen, cited *ante.*

[2] Garcias King of Navarre married, according to Morèri, Margaret, daughter of Gilbert de Aquila, by Juliana, daughter of Geoffrey Earl of Perche.

[3] "Maud "a natural daughter of King Henry the First, was espoused to Rotrock Earl of Perch (called also Consul of Moriton) ... She was the first wife of this Rotrock, first of the name, *son of Arnolfe de Hesding also,* first Earl of that county ... She perished by shipwrack with her half-brother Duke William, upon Friday, the 26th of November, in the 20th year of her father's reign, and of grace M.CXIX." *Geneal. Hist.* p. 32, 1st ed.

[4] Bohn's edition, iii. 80 ; iv. 108, &c.

I subjoin a short pedigree of these Counts, derived principally from Moréri's Dictionary, which, it will be seen, is quite at variance with Burke's statements:—

Rotrou, Comte de Mortagne.⊤....

Geoffrey, "donna du se-⊤Beatrix,	Hugh, an-	Rotrou	Fulco-Elis,
cours à Guillaume le	dau. of	cestor of the	Sieur de	"*dont les*
Conquerant à son pas-	Hilduin,	Seigneurs	Montfort	*alliances*
sage en Angleterre,"	Comte de	de Châ-	dans le	*sont incon-*
died circa 1110.	Roucy.	teaudun.	Maine.	*nues.*"[1]

Juliana ux.	Margaret ux.	Heruise d'Ev-⊤Rotrou, Comte⊤Maud, natural
Gilbert de	Henry de Bel-	reux,[2] dau. of	de Perche,	dau. of Henry
Aquila.	lomont or Novo	Walter Earl	died circa	I., King of
	Burgo.	of Salisbury.	1149.	England.

Rotrou, died at the siege⊤.... Stephen, Archbishop   Philippa, wife of Elias d'Anjou,
of Acre, 1191.   of Palermo.   brother of Geoffrey Plantagenet.

Geoffrey, Comte de Perche et de Mortagne, died 1205.⊤.... Three sons, ob. s. p.

Thomas,[3] slain at the battle of Lincoln, s. p. 1217.

The whole question, says Mr. Eyton, in concluding his remarks, is worth the attention of any student of baronial genealogy. Hence I make no apology for occupying so much of your space with the few particulars I have been able to glean; indeed I trust the query propounded at the head of this article may be considered of sufficient general interest to induce your readers to lend me their aid in ventilating it. I should add, that I am personally interested in this question, one of my earliest ancestors having, according to constant family tradition, married shortly after the Conquest a great heiress, one *Ethelswytha de Hesdene, of the Saxon blood royal,* and for this match we quarter, whether rightly or wrongly I know not, the chequered shield and ermine chevron of the old Earls of Warwick.

This lady is supposed to have been a near relative of Arnulph, but in what degree she was related to him I am ignorant; indeed, the very name of her father is unknown.

I am, Sir, your obedient servant, H. S. G.

[1] *Sic* Moréri, but the Nugent family is said, I believe on pretty good authority, to derive from this Fulke. The name *Nugent* being taken from Nogent-le-Rotrou, the family residence of the Counts of Perche.

[2] The name *d'Evreux*, given to the Norman Earls of Salisbury, has been shown to have arisen entirely in error: see the *History of Lacock Abbey,* and a memoir on the Earldom of Salisbury in the *Archæological Journal.* (EDIT. H. & G.)

[3] See an anecdote of him in Topog. and Geneal. i. 312.

THE FAMILY OF MILLAIS,

AND THE CHIEF FAMILIES OF JERSEY.

THE LINEAGE AND PEDIGREE OF THE FAMILY OF MILLAIS ; recording its History from
1331 to 1865. Being an extract from an " ARMORIAL OF JERSEY," by J. BER-
TRAND PAYNE, Membre de l'Institut Historique de France, &c. &c. With Illustrations from Designs by the Author. London : Privately printed 1865. Imperial
4to. pp. 8.

Our readers will remember the account given in our first volume
(pp. 531-534) of *A Monograph of the House of Lempriere*, by the gentleman above named, who has devoted himself to the Genealogy of the
Island of Jersey, and who favoured us in our second volume (pp. 23-30)
with some brief notes on the principal *Jersey Families—Aboriginal and
Immigrant.* We have now before us a brief but sumptuously appointed
memoir, which, like the Lempriere Monograph, is an excerpt from Mr.
Bertrand Payne's great work, the *Armorial of Jersey,* now in progress
through the press.

The family of Millais is traced by records, among the lesser land-
holders of Jersey, for more than five centuries ; and is thought to have
existed there even before the Norman Conquest of England. A bold
range of hills to the north-east of the town of S. Helier is named Les
Monts Millais, and the Cuillette de Millais is one of the "gatherings"
or *vingtaines* of the parish of S. Ouen. In the *extente* or royal rent-
roll of Jersey of the year 1338 the name occurs under the form *Milayes;*
a bovate or *bouvée* of land in the parish of Grouville being held by
Gaufridus Milayes at 10 sols per annum. At other times the name
has been written Millays, Mylais, and Milès, and sometimes Millet.
About 1540 John Myllais, by his marriage with the heiress of the
family of Le Jarderay, became possessed of the estate of Tapon, in the
parish of S. Saviour ; of this ancient residence, which remained in the
family until the beginning of the present century, the book contains a
photographic plate.

The pedigree extends from John Millays, living circa 1331, to the
present representatives of the family : 1. John William Millais, esq.,
and William Henry Millais (his son), of Kingston, Surrey ; 2. John
Everett Millais, esq., R.A., of Cornwall Place, South Kensington
(brother to the last); 3. Henry William Millais, esq. (son of the late
George Henry Millais, esq., who died in 1864) ; and 4. Thomas Millais, esq., of Jersey.

The Memoir is illustrated by three armorial plates, representing the atchievements and alliances of William Henry Millais, esq., of the Royal Academician his brother, and of the late George Henry Millais, esq. A peculiar interest attaches itself to the second, which exhibits the coat-armour of the Royal Academician, whose works have rendered the name of Millais far more familiar to the world than it has ever been during the whole five centuries of his recorded pedigree. It is, that this plate was designed and etched by the hands of John Everett Millais himself: and we have to acknowledge ourselves under especial obligations to Mr. Bertrand Payne that he now affords us the pleasure of presenting an impression to our readers.

The bearings of the Millais atchievements are these:

1. Per bend for and azure, a star of eight points counter-changed, *Millais*; 2. Azure, a cross-passion argent, surmounted of an Eastern crown or, *Le Jarderay*; 3. Or, an orle azure, *Bertram*; 4. Argent, a palm-tree proper, *Pallot*; 5. Argent, a cock statant proper, *Faultrart*; 6. Argent, a cross sable between a Maltese cross gules in the first and fourth quarters, and a tent of the same in the second and third, *Baudouin*; 7. Argent, on a chevron sable four eagles of the field, between three mullets gules, *Morice de la Ripaudière*; 8. Ermine, a lion rampant gules, *Le Geyt*. Crest, a head gauntleted and apaumé, in pale, gules.

The marriage with the heiress of Le Jarderay we have already mentioned. The third quartering was brought in to the atchievement by the marriage of John Milays, early in the 17th century, with Jane daughter and heir of Benjamin Bertram; and the next four by that of his son Edward, in 1671, with Margaret daughter and eventual heir of the Rev. Joshua Pallot. It was Edward, grandson of the last, who married in 1728 an heiress of Le Geyt: and we may add, that the marriage of Mary, one of the offspring of that marriage with the Rev. John Dupré, Rector of St. Helier, introduces into the tabular pedigree a portion of the genealogy of that family; including Edward Dupré, D.C.L. also Rector of S. Helier, and Dean of Jersey, and John William Dupré, Attorney-general of Jersey, the Dean's son.

The arms impaled in the etching are those of *Gray*, Gules, a lion rampant within a bordure engrailed argent, a crescent for difference; the Royal Academician having married Euphemia-Chalmers, daughter of George Gray of Bowerswell, Perth, N.B. by whom he has issue three sons and two daughters.

The *Armorial of Jersey*, of which the *Lineage of the Family of Millais* is a chapter, contains the history and arms of the chief Jersey families, of which a list is subjoined:—

Amy.	De Quetteville.	La Cloche.	Mauger.
Anquetil.	De Vaumorel.	Langlois.	Messeroy.
Anthoine.	Duheaume.	Le Bailly.	Millais.
Bailhache.	Dumaresq.	Le Bas.	Mouraut.
Balleine.	Durell.	Le Breton.	Nicolle.
Bandinel.	Filleul.	Le Boutillier.	Payn.
Baudains.	Fiott.	Le Couteur.	Perrot.
Bertram.	Gabourel.	Le Feuvre.	Pinel.
Bisson.	Gervaise.	Le Gallais.	Pipon.
Boudier.	Gibaut.	Le Geyt.	Poingdestre.
Cabot.	Giraudot.	Le Gros.	Ricard.
Chateaubriand.	Godfray.	Le Hardy.	Richardson vel
Collas.	Gosselin.	Le Maistre.	Reserson.
Coutanche.	Gosset.	Lempriere.	Robin.
D'Auvergne.	Guerdain.	Le Montais.	Seale.
De Barentine.	Guille.	Le Quesne.	Simonet.
De Carteret.	Hammond.	Levrier.	Sohier.
De Gruchy.	Hamptonne.	Le Sueur.	Valpy.
De la Garde.	Hemery.	Le Touzel.	Vautier.
De la Place.	Hérault.	Low.	Vibert.
De la Taste.	Janvrin.	Luce.	
De Ste. Croix.	Jeune.	Malet.	
De S. Martin.	Journeaulx.	Marelt.	

To the account of most of these families, in addition to biographical notices of their chief members, the date of their establishment in the island, &c. is appended a tabular pedigree, compiled from family papers, parochial and royal court registers, and the ecclesiastical records of Jersey which exist at the departmental archives at S. Lo, in Normandy, with plates of the arms and quarterings borne by members of the houses whose histories are recorded. An endeavour has been made, in these plates, to chronicle the various styles of heraldic depicture from the earliest to the present time, and, although these number nearly 150, no two are identical in treatment.

The work will be completed in six Parts, to which will be added a Supplement, intended to contain the histories and arms of such families, not of native origin, which are either connected with the island by marriage or which possess property there. The work is printed for private circulation only, and has occupied its compiler ten years.

BIBLIOTHECA HERALDICA.

HERALDIC CARDS BY RICHARD BLOME.

Richard Blome was a very successful publisher of books by subscription, who produced the fourth and fifth editions of Guillim's *Display of Heraldry* in 1660 and 1679, and a variety of books illustrated by plates, of which the most magnificent were his *Britannia*, his *History of the Bible*, and his *Gentleman's Recreation*, all folio volumes. The plates of his works are dedicated throughout to his patrons, and are usually decorated with their armorial coats, now affording evidence of some importance of the heraldry of his contemporaries. He also produced an *Essay to Heraldry*, 1684, 12mo., re-published as *The Art of Heraldry* 1685 (but under the latter title unnoticed by Moule). This manual was illustrated with engravings of examples, most of which are marshalled on quartered shields, in the same way as those on the pack of cards now before us.

These cards have not hitherto attracted the attention of the bibliographer. We shall describe them from a copy on paper, mounted and bound in a volume, which is at present in the hands of Mr. J. C. Hotten, bookseller, of Piccadilly. The armories are coloured throughout. We copy (in part) the inscriptions literally, including errors.

HEARTS. *King.* His Maᵗʸˢ Royall Atchivement. The Royall Atchivemᵗ of his Sacred Maᵗʸˢ Charles, &c. &c.

Queen. The Atchivement of a woman not under femme in covert. She beareth in a Lozenge as a maiden Lady, B. a fess wavey between 3 Goates heads erazed A. by yᵉ name of sedney, & is yᵉ paternall Coate Armour of Mary sedney sole daughter & heyre of Sʳ Charles sedney of Southfleet in Kent, Barᵗ.

Knave. Navall things.—They are arranged in a shield of twelve quarterings.

Ace. Military things.—Another shield of twelve quarterings.

Deuce. Military things.—Another of fourteen.

Trey. The Atchivement of a Duke. The Rᵗ Noble Christopher Duke of Albemarle, E. of Torington, Baron Monck of Potheridge, Beauchamp & Teys, Kᵗ of yᵉ Garter, Lᵈ Leiutenant of Devonshire & Esses, one of yᵉ Gent: of his Maᵗʸˢ Bedchamber, & Lᵈˢ of his most Honᵉᵇˡ. privy Councell &ᶜᵗ. who beareth—his arms, crest, and supporters are described, after which these two lines :

To whose patronage these Armoriall Cards are humbly dedicated by his Grace most humble & obedient servant Ric. Blome.

Four. The Atchivement of a Marquess.—The like of Henry Marquess of Dorchester, a Privy Councillor.

Five. The Atchivement of a Earle.—John Earl of Bridgewater.

Six. The Atchivement of a Viscount.—Thomas Needham Lord Viscount Killmurrey,—Needham quartering Pearle, on a chiefe emerald a Taw between two mullets Topaz (*Drury.*)

Seven. The Atchivement of a Baron.—Lord Berkeley of Berkeley.

Eight. The Atchivement of a Baronet. yᵉ Augmentation of a Barᵗ is-always put in yᵉ most convenientest place of yᵉ shield. He beareth quarterly (1) G. 3 Kathèrin wheles O. on a cheife A. a Bulls head couped at yᵉ neck S. (2) B. a Lyon rampant O. yᵉ (3ᵈ) as yᵉ (2ᵈ) yᵉ 4ᵗʰ as yᵉ (1). in yᵉ midst of wᵗʰ is yᵉ Armes of Vlster wᵗʰ is yᵉ Augmentation of a Baronet viz in a Escocheon A. a sinister hand couped at yᵉ wrist G. mantled G. doubled A. & for his Crest on a helmet & wreath of his colours a Bulls head S. between 2 wings A. This Atchivement is thus borne by Sʳ. Phillip Mathews of Great Gobions near Rumford in Essex Barᵗ.

Nine. The Atchivement of a Knight. He beareth G. 3 Ducall Crowns O. on a chiefe of the second 3 laurell leaves erect pp. by yᵉ name óf Berkenhead, mantled G. doubled A. & for his Crest out of a Crown Ducall a dexter Arme pp. holding 3 Arrows O. This is yᵉ Atchivement of yᵉ Rᵗ worshipfull Sʳ Iohn Berkenhead Kᵗ. Master of Requests to his Maᵗʸˢ & Master of yᵉ ffaculties.

Ten. The Atchivement of an Esquire, wᵗʰ is yᵉ same as a Gentlemans.— That of Thomas Barrington, Esq. son & heir of Sir John Barrington, Bart.

Diamonds. *King.* The severall wayes of beareing of Lyons.—Arranged in fifteen quarterings.

Queen. Beasts, or four footed Animalls.—In twelve quarterings.

Knave. Flowers, and Fruits.—In twelve quarterings.

Ace. The Parts of a Mans Body.—In nine quarterings.

Deuce. Parts of Beasts.—In nine quarterings.

Trey. Parts of Beasts.—Nine more.

Four. Monsters.—Also in nine quarterings.

Five. Animalls.—In eleven quarterings.

Six. Birds and Flyes.—In twelve quarterings.

Seven. Fishes.—In fourteen quarterings.

Eight. Parts of Birds.—In nine quarterings.

Nine. Civill Artificiall things.—In twelve quarterings.

Ten. Civill Artificiall things.—In fifteen quarterings.

Clubs. *King.* The generall colours vsed in Armory are 6, & yᵉ hatches as thus exprest shew yᵉ Colours, but there are some others, as Purpure, Tenne, Tawny, and Murry, which being very rarely vsed in arms are here omitted.

Queen. Furrs.—In six quarterings.

Knave. The partes of Armes.—A shield with letters of reference to its several points.

Ace. Bordures.—In twelve quarterings.

Deuce. Formes of charges on wᶜʰ Rewards & Additions of honor are oftentymes placed in Coates.—In nine quarterings.

Trey. Abatments of honour for misdemenors & dishonourable actions. —In nine quarterings.

Four. Theire are severall crooked lines in Heraldry, &c.—Shown on a shield.

Five. The Honourable ordinaries.—In nine quarterings.

Six. The Crosses most usually borne in Heraldry.—In twenty-four quarterings.

Seven. The Chiefe is s^d to be given to those y^t by their high merits have procured them chiefe place and esteem amongst men.—Chiefs in six quarterings.

Eight. The fess is called ye Belt, or girdle of honor, &c.—Fesses and their diminutives, in twelve quarterings.

Nine. A Bend is said to represent a ladder set aslope to scale ye walls of a Citty, or Castle, and betokneth ye bearer to have been one of ye first y^t mounted vp ye enemys wall.[1]—Twelve examples quartered.

Ten. A Cheveron represents ye rafters of a hovse, & betokneth to ye bearer ye Atcheiving some signall undertaking.—Nine examples of the chevron and its diminutives quartered.

SPADES. *King.* A pale, &c.—In five quarterings.

Queen. The saltier was made ye hight of a man, and was driven full of Pinns, and served to scale ye walls of a Citty.—Four examples quartered.

Knave. The pile is an honourable bearing, &c.—In six quarterings.

Ace. A shield of six quarterings, an escocheon, orle, &c.

Deuce. Partitions and counter changes.—In fifteen quarterings.

Trey. Counter changes.—In four quarterings.

Four. A shield of six quarterings, the lozenge, roundel, &c.

Five. Two ordinaries in one shield, wch may be borne wth or betwen a charge.—Twelve examples quartered.

Six. Twelve more examples of the like.

Seven. A quartered shield of six examples of Paly bendy, &c.

Eight. Counter changes with charges on the field.—Twelve quarterings.

Nine. Celestialls.—A shield quarterly of twelve.

Ten. Vegetables.—Eleven quarterings.

1857.   1862.   1864.

Notices of the Ellises:

Of France (from the time of Charlemagne), and of England (from the Conquest) to the present time; and of the Synonymous Families (in France) of HALIS, ALES, ELIE, ELLIES, HELIS, ETC., *and (in England) of* ALIS, FITZ-ELLIS, ELLICE, EYLES, EALES, ALISON, ELLISON, ETC., *including the following Families of the same origin, viz.* MARSHALL *(Earls of Pembroke),* DEIVILL, DE LA MARE, DAMORY, CANTALUPE, *and*

[1] See Vol. ii. p. 245.

AUBERVILLE *(Barons)*, RALEIGH, VENOUR, PONTDELARCHE, PUNCHAR-
DUN, NORMAN, KIDDALL, FERBY, HAUVILL, AMUNDEVILLE, HELSHAM,
DAYVILL, DISNEY, DOISNEL, CERNE, PLUMSTEAD, BURNINGHAM, FITZ-
WALTER, REDISHAM, COMBE, ETC. By WILLIAM SMITH ELLIS, Esq.
Barrister at Law. No. I. March 1857, pp. 52. No. 2, September 1862,
pp. 53—108. No. 3, March 1864, pp. 109-184. *Not Published.*

From the title of this compilation, which is literally copied above, it will
be perceived that the author casts his net for a very large draught of fishes,
not limiting himself to the numerous families of Ellis, nor even to the
Eales, who, perhaps in allusion to their slippery character, bore three eels
for their arms, which have sometimes been taken for snakes (p. 14). The
fact is that Mr Ellis readily accepts, as a proof of families being connected,
either a similarity of sound in the name, or a similarity of bearing in the
arms: so that in one way or other his grasp is very comprehensive indeed.
Hence the concatenation which the title describes: to which we think most
of his readers will be disposed to give but partial and limited assent: particularly as (in a note in p. 5) he candidly admits that his genealogical
deductions in the earlier portion of his inquiries could, for the most part,
never have been made, except upon the assumption that hereditary arm
were in use long before the period of the Crusades: and he acknowleges
that "the belief in the existence for centuries before the Norman Conquest
of hereditary heraldic symbols, has been throughout the guide and clue to
the hypotheses and conclusions here made:" according to the views which
the Author has published in a pamphlet upon that subject which we have
before noticed in p. 2 of this Volume.

The introductory paragraph of No. I. is as follows:—"The object of the
following Essay will be to show that most of the Ellises of England descend
from a Norman ancestor, who came over with William the Conqueror, and
that he, in common with most of the Ellises, or synonymous families of
France, was descended from the early Kings of that country; and, as such,
bore the royal *fleurs de lis*, the name being originally Elias, or Louis."

The subject is divided into two Parts: the first (in pp. 1—34) treating of
the origin of the Ellises of England; the second (pp. 34—52) of those of
France.

The following names are then all taken as varieties of Ellis:

> Alis, Halis, and Hallis;
> Elias, and Helias;
> Elis, Ellis, Elles, Ellys, and Elys;
> Elice, Ellice;
> Hellis, Hellys, Hilles, Helles;
> Hollis, Holys, Holles;
> Iles, Ilys;
> Eyles, Eales.

Here we will venture to ask, if some of the name come from the Christian name Elias (in French Elie), have not others been derived from the female name Alice? Again, the French family of Alis took their name from a place called Alis or Alisay near Pont de l'Arche, according to the opinion of M. L'Echaudé D'Anisy, quoted in p. 4.

Sir William Alis, a Norman lord mentioned on three occasions by Ordericus Vitalis, is, says Mr. Ellis, the same person who occurs in Domesday Book and elsewhere as William de la Mare, William Fitz-Norman, William Dalmare, and William Pontdelarche; and he suggests also that Robert de Auberville, Robert le Marshal, Robert Fitz-Walter, and Robert Fitz-Halis, and Normannus Vicecomes, were different designations of Sir William Alis's father (p. 54). These few lines are sufficient to show how ready the author is to accept such identifications: accompanied by consanguinities furnished upon the presumptive, if not imaginary, evidence we have already described. We can scarcely consider it safe to adopt these so readily, as the general basis of early genealogical researches; though occasional discoveries of the kind, when worked out with severe caution, may have been among the triumphs of the most learned genealogists.

So, in regard to Armory, it is our grand maxim, that it has power to render the most efficient aid in early genealogical researches; but then it must be carefully ascertained, not accepted on mere "traditional" or legendary authority. In p. 55 we find it stated, of one of the most distinguished races of Ellis,—that resident at Kiddal near Leeds in Yorkshire—that "the great *traditional* ancestor of this family is Sir Archibald Ellis, a Crusader under Richard I., who *is said* to have first borne the crusading coat used by the family, viz. Or, on a cross sable five crescents argent; and to have first used their crest, viz. a woman naked, her hair dishevelled, proper, in celebration of his having captured a Saracen maiden, and, like another Scipio, left her honour inviolate." Now, it is very well known to more sober heraldic inquirers than Mr. Ellis that no such crest could have been adopted in the reign of Richard I. nor indeed for some centuries after. Neither, in fact, is there any proof whatever of the arms above blasoned having any claim to be classed as a "crusading coat." To determine their real date and origin, it should be ascertained on what rolls or other documents they are first recorded. And so, for the Crest, instead of accepting the romantic legend we have just repeated, it would probably further the history of the family much more materially to inquire in some other direction why the crest of a naked woman was adopted, a device which some of the name have varied to a mermaid. (p. 120.)

Nos. 2 and 3 of these "Notices of the Ellises" are occupied almost entirely with collections, from all quarters of the globe, of genealogical particulars of the various families of the name. They are somewhat fragmentary, and their arrangement confused, for which the compiler makes apologies,— his plans having changed during the progress of his labours. He states (p. 109) that he commenced by collecting what printed and accessible MS. sources furnished; which, joined to some specific and some incidental researches, and private communications, constituted a collection which he thought useful to be put in print. This he liberally undertook, at his private expense ; and, with the view of obtaining further information, sent copies to nearly two hundred persons of the name, such being the estimated number of the gentry bearing this appellation in the United Kingdom, so far as could be ascertained from calendars and directories. The communications he has received have induced him " to make these pages a Record of the Ellises of the present day, and of the recent as well as the remote past; in fact, as regards Families of One Name, to produce a Genealogical Visitation." In this respect his book resembles that on the Travers family, which we have noticed in a former page.

The circumstance that No. 3 consists so much of information supplementary to what had been given in No. 2, suggests that it will be desirable, before the volume is closed, to supply a synoptical table of Contents that will lead the inquirer to the several pages in which the same families are more than once noticed.

The Author has No. 4 in preparation, and it will probably be issued during the present year, to those who have intimated to him that his former Parts have been acceptable. It is to contain, *inter alia*, Additional Early Notices of the Ellises ; and the Descent of Families bearing *goat's heads*, of presumed cognate origin with the Alises. He solicits the communication of notices from Deeds, Wills, &c., and Monumental Inscriptions from churches and churchyards ; and any other additions or corrections to his pages already circulated ; which may be addressed to him at his residence, Hydecroft, Charlwood, Surrey.

THREE ROLLS OF ARMS of the Latter Part of the Thirteenth Century : together with an Index of Names and an Alphabetical Ordinary of the Coats. Edited for the Society of Antiquaries by WESTON STYLEMAN WALFORD, Esq. F.S.A. and CHARLES SPENCER PERCEVAL, Esq. LL.D., F.S.A. London : printed by J. B. Nichols and Sons, 25, Parliament Street. 1864. Printed in this form for Private Distribution. 4to. pp. 99.

These Rolls have been printed for the XXXIXth volume of the Archæ-ologia, the Second Part of which is on the eve of publication. The Ordinary is an addition peculiar to the separate copies, as will be presently explained.

The first Roll is edited by Mr. Walford. It is of the time of King Henry III. and is that which Mr. J. Wyatt Papworth, in his *Ordinary of British Armorials*, has quoted under the reference C. Its original has not been discovered ; but the copy by Nicholas Charles in the Harleian MS. 6589, from which it is now printed, was taken in 1606 from " a very antient Rolle, made, as may be supposed, in the year of K. H. 3." Mr. Walford considers it of not quite so early a date, but still not later than about 1280. It consists of about 180 coats, and is shown to be substantially the same as that given in Hearne's edition of Leland's *Collectanea*, vol. ii. p. 610' of which the present Editor has attached a collation.

The second and third Rolls of this series are also of the reign of Edward the First; and are edited, with some prefatory remarks, by Mr. Perceval.

One of these has, for many years, been preserved in the library of the Society of Antiquaries, but has never before been printed. It was in the year 1610 in the possession of that truly antiquarian herald and scientific heraldic antiquary, Nicholas Charles, to whose industry is due the transcription of nearly twenty rolls of arms preserved (in his handwriting) in the Harleian volume already mentioned. The Society's Roll, however, is not one of them; but there is a copy in the Harl. MS. 6137. In the Catalogue of the Society's Manuscripts, printed in 1816, it was entered as No. 17, and attributed to the fifteenth century: but it is now shown to be a copy from a Roll formed about the year 1300. It contains so many as 486 coats.

The third Roll is one which has gone by the name of Charles's Roll, and is quoted by Mr. Papworth by the letter E. It is known to exist only in two copies, preserved in the two volumes of the Harleian MSS. already named. That in the Harl. MS. 6589 (the work of Nicholas Charles himself,) is prefaced by this note: "This Roll, on the other side, was copied by the original, which Mr. Norry lent me An. D'ni 1607. NICHOLAS CHARLES." So that a more proper distinctive title for it is to call it St. George's roll, as Sir Richard St.George was the Norroy who possessed it.

These two rolls are ascertained to belong almost exactly to the same period. Of 677 coats which St. George's roll contains, nearly 300 are found agreeing in every respect with the other, whilst about 50 more occur in each roll with variations, sometimes as to Christian names, at other times as to *brizures*, with other discrepancies of various degrees of importance. The careful comparison which Mr. Perceval has carried out between them adds much to their value: and they together form a very large and important collection of arms between 1240-5, the date of the Roll of Arms of the reign of Henry III. edited by Sir Harris Nicolas, and 1300, the date of the Carlaverock Roll.[1]

The Editors have appended an Index of Names to the three Rolls; and to the separate copies is also added an Alphabetical Ordinary, to which is prefixed the following explanatory Note:—

NOTE.—Whilst engaged in preparing my text of Rolls E and F for the press, I found it necessary to compile, for my own use, an Ordinary of the Coats contained in those two Rolls. Mr. Papworth having digested the whole of these Rolls in his book, of which the greater part has already appeared, it seemed hardly justifiable to encumber the pages of Archæologia by printing my own Ordinary there. At the same time

---

[1] We have given, in our Second Volume, p. 377, an account of the poetic roll on the Siege of Carlaverock, and in p. 389 a note upon the other more regular, and longer, rolls of the arms present at the same siege.

it was thought that, with the addition of the coats comprised in Roll C, the compilation might be acceptable to that limited number of persons specially interested in the sub-ject, into whose hands the separate copies of the Rolls, and remarks thereon, might come. One hundred and twenty-five copies of the following pages have therefore been printed, for private distribution, at the joint expense of Mr. A. W. Franks, Mr. W. S. Walford, and myself.

Mr. Papworth's excellent arrangement has mostly been followed. In several in-stances a coat has been twice entered; once in its proper alphabetical order, and again in *italics*, either where the blazon is doubtful, or in order to bring one coat into juxtaposition with another, on which it either certainly is or may be conjectured to be founded.

December, 1864. C. S. P.

To those who appreciate the paramount value of contemporary evidence, we need say nothing further in estimation of the service conferred on the heraldic antiquary by making these Rolls accessible to ready reference: forming as they do a very ample storehouse of information for the earliest period of armory, dating next to the brief roll, of only 218 coats, edited by Sir Harris Nicolas in 1829.

REVIEW.

HERALDRY, HISTORICAL AND POPULAR. By CHARLES BOUTELL, M.A. Third Edition, Revised and Enlarged. 1864. 8vo. Pp. xvi. 547.

Having already on two occasions given our opinion upon this work, we have little more to say, on its third appearance, than to offer our congratulations. To enter into minute criticism is beyond our pur-pose, or indeed our available space: and it is a process which we are endeavouring to pursue, with regard to the whole field of Heraldry, more at large in the general scope of our miscellany. We attribute the success that has attended the work of Mr. Boutell at once to its moderate price, and to the good taste which the author has manifested in his artistic appreciation of the subject, and the selection of the best models among the remains of ancient heraldic design. Nor can we withhold from him a fair share of praise for the pains and diligence he displays throughout in working out the details of his subject, and availing himself in a candid and generous spirit of every aid which may be gained either from the communications of his friends or the animadversions of his critics. He assures his readers that

This Third Edition has been most carefully revised and corrected throughout; and it has received many additions of the greatest importance. To all points connected with heraldic rule, authority, and early usage, I have directed my especial attention. The

Chapters previously entitled *Marshalling* and *Cadency* now appear, enlarged and re-. arranged, severally bearing the following titles, *Marshalling and Inheritance*, and *Cadency and Differencing*. Chapter XIV. has been devoted exclusively to *Royal Cadency*, which has been treated in it in as systematic a manner as possible. The Chapter on the *Royal Heraldry of England* has been in part rewritten; and the Chapter on *Foreign Heraldry* has been considerably extended.

Again I have introduced several fresh Illustrations. They consist of twenty-four additional woodcuts, printed with the text : and four lithographic Plates, containing twelve examples : thus my Illustrations, in all, now number upwards of nine hundred and seventy examples. ·

Mr. Boutell pays a well-merited tribute of praise to the extraordinary spirit with which the shield of a knight who lies in effigy at Clehongre in Herefordshire is sculptured. The bars are carved in bold relief: the bend is brought to a still higher surface, and the leopard's heads have extraordinary animation. To this finely-sculptured effigy three plates (dated 1841) are devoted in *The Monumental Effigies of Great Britain*, by T. and G. Hollis. The person represented is there styled " A Knight of the Pembridge Family," and we think with great probability. The original and simple coat of Pembruge was Barry of six or and azure. To this coat Sir Henri de Penbruge, of Herefordshire, in the reign of Edward the Second, added a bend gules; and Sir Johan de Pembruge (whose name follows in the Roll of that date) added on the bend three mullets argent. Therefore we think it. highly probable that another of the family differenced again by leopard's heads in place of the mullets.

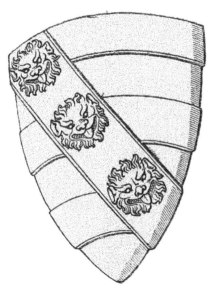

Thompson of Yorkshire; and of Lancashire?

To the Editor *of the* Herald and Genealogist.

Sir,—In the Harleian MS. 1394, folio 337, occurs this entry :

These armes, viz., Party per fece silver and sable, a fece batelle, three faulcons counterchanged of ye feild, the belles and beakes gould. The crest or badge an arme quarterly gold and azure, wth a gauntlett of the color of harneys, holding of tronchon of speare gould : set upon a wreath silver and sable ; were granted by Lawrence Dalton, al's Norroy King of Armes, to Henry Tompson, of Eshold, in the county of York, gentleman, and one of the King's Mat^s gentlemen-at-armes at Boloigne, by letters patent dated the 15. of Aprill in the first yeare of ye reigne of Queene Elizabethe.

It is to be inferred this Henry Thompson would not be admitted into the corps of gentlemen-at-arms of Henry VIII. unless he had some pretensions to what Sir Bernard Burke designates "gentilitial" origin; but, be this as it may, he is said (see Harl. MS. 1394, folio 211,) to have had a natural son by Ellen daughter of Lawrence Townley, esq. of Barnside. It is, however, rather in contradiction of this statement that, on an incised slab to the memory of this lady placed in the church of Colne in Lancashire, she is called Ellen " the wife " of Henry Thompson, esq.

The descendants of this Henry settled at Esholt, the lands of the dissolved priory there having been granted to him by his royal master. His son William married Dorothy daughter of Christopher Anderton of Lostock, Lancashire, prothonotary, and by her had two sons, Christopher and Henry. The former (born 1581) married Frances daughter of James Thwaites, of Marston, esq., about the year 1601, and had a son Henry, with other sons and daughters. The heir (Henry) married Mary daughter of Walter Stanhope, esq., and had only one child, a daughter, on whose marriage with Walter Calverley, esq., the estates passed from the Thompsons to the family of that name.

To return. Of Henry, the second son of William of Esholt, and the younger grandson of the grantee, nothing is stated in the documents (Harleian MSS. 1394, fol. 211, and 1487, fol. 310) from which these particulars are compiled.

The arms of Henry Thompson granted by Dalton, Norroy, are now used (quarterly) by Lord Wenlock, and, slightly differenced, by more than one branch of the wealthy Yorkshire family named Thompson, though none of them trace their pedigrees back to the original grantee of Esholt.

It is also remarkable that the same coat (or nearly the same) is assigned on anonymous authority (Harleian MS. 893, folio 31, date James I. and Charles I.), on the authority of Saunders (Harl. MS. 1468, fol. 109), on the authority of Randle Holmes (Harl. MSS. 1940, 1987, and 2040), and on that of Captain Booth of Stockport (Baines's MSS.) to Thompson of Lancashire, but that no place of residence is attached.

I would inquire, Was there any known Lancashire family in the sixteenth or seventeenth century to whom the arms in question were assigned,
and, if so, where were they seated ?   Baines, in his *History of Lancashire*,
in a catalogue entitled *Familiæ Lancastrienses*, mentions the name Thompson with a number of others of arm-bearing families; but adds that "no
residence is attached to any of them."   Would you, Sir, or any of your
correspondents able to throw light on this matter, oblige me by so doing ?
In the interesting letter of the late Mr. Markland, printed in your second
volume, it is related that, in a schedule to a kind of summons addressed by
Sir William Dugdale, Norroy, to the Bailiff of Salford, are inserted the
names of seventy-three Lancashire gentlemen, many of them members of
very ancient families, who had refused to make their appearance before
him to register their descents and justify their titles of Esquires and Gentlemen.   Does this circumstance account for the omission of residences from
Baines's list, the *Familiæ Lancastrienses ?*

In the lists of freeholders present or summoned to the Lancashire
weapon-shows in 1574, 1600, and 1613, several persons of the name mentioned appear; and, in the *Calendarium Inquisitionum post Mortem Ducatus
Lancastriæ*, published by the Record Commission, William Thompson is
recorded to have died possessed of lands in Lonsdale Hundred (1566),
William Tompson of land at Larbrick in the reign of Elizabeth, Henry
Thompson of land at Thistleton (1621), and others at places also named.
About the year 1580 also, among the Catholic families of Lancashire
having children in " Popish countries," who were ordered by the Bishop
of Chester to send for them in order that they might be educated at home,
was one named Thompson.   (See Gregson's *Fragments of Lancashire*.)

From the assignment of the arms of Thompson of Esholt to Thompson of
Lancashire by heralds or heraldry painters in the seventeenth century, it
seems probable descendants of the original grantee settled in the county
just named; or, if not, how do we account for the references already given ?

It is remarkable that the arms should have been recorded or entered in
so many lists, without being associated with a residence or assigned to
some particular person.   Probably some of your readers acquainted with
Lancashire pedigrees and armorial bearings may be enabled to clear up the
obscurity.   If they would do so they would oblige, Sir,

Yours obediently,
Genealogist.

FAMILIES OF ARTHUR.—At Wiggenhall St. Mary's in Norfolk, on the
28th November, 1655, died John Arthur, gent. and about the 20th March,
1656, his only child and heiress Anne Arthur married John Colby of
Banham in Norfolk, gent. whom she survived, and afterwards became the
second wife of Edward North of Benacre in Suffolk, Esq.   It does not
appear from the settlement made in contemplation of her first marriage,
that she derived any real property from her father, and the probability is

that he had only a casual residence at Wiggenhall. The question I want to ask is—to what family of Arthur did he belong? In the preceding century there was a family of that name located at Wisbech, from which Wiggenhall is not far distant; but they were of the Arthurs of Bishopsworth in the parish of Bedminster, Somerset, and bore for arms: Gules, a chevron argent between three rests or, while the coat added by Anne Arthur to the Colby quarterings is a very different one. It is shewn on a silver cup in the possession of my family, which now represents that of Colby, as—*Party per bend sinister gules and azure, a lion rampant argent*, and the same coat appears impaled with that of North on her tombstone in Benacre church. But that bearing has afforded me no clue whatever ; it is not to be found in any ordinary of arms or heraldic dictionary I have met with. Finding a match in 1704 between a John Arthur and a lady of my family, then in Cornwall but already allied in marriage with the Colbys and Norths, I hoped I had hit the right scent, but was again thrown out by the arms, the Cornish Arthurs being said to bear, Argent, a chevron engrailed gules between three choughs proper. If my family of Arthur can be identified by the peculiar bearing I have given, through the medium of H. and G. I shall be most grateful. GEO. A. CARTHEW.

BROWNES OF NORFOLK (p. 95). Of the extinction in the male line of the Brownes of Elsing there can be no reasonable doubt, and it is equally true that there were Browns and Brownes in Norfolk before the establishment of that line, which is now represented by the descendants of a female heir. There have also been more recently Browns of Norwich, Brownes of Lynn, Brownes of Tacolnestone, Brownes of Dereham, Brownes of Fulmodestone, Brownes of Blo Norton, Browns of Massingham, all of them distinct from the Elsing family, and from each other, and bearing different arms, and all of them, I believe, now extinct in the male line. Existing families bearing the name are legion ; but none of them claim descent from Elsing, nor any other of the families I have named, except through females. G. A. C.

Who was General RICHARD FORTESCUE, commander of the army in Jamaica in the time of Oliver Cromwell? He died there; and by his will, proved in the Prerogative Court of Canterbury July 29, 1657, bequeathed houses and lands at Bray and in Reading, Berks. His wife, Mary, was executrix. To what branch of the Fortescues did he belong? C.

P. 32. The name of SHOVELL has been perpetuated in the family of Brereton, of Brinton, co. Norfolk, of which there is an account in Burke's *Landed Gentry*. A niece of Admiral Sir Cloudesly Shovell was Anne daughter of Thomas Shorting, collector of customs at the port of Cley ; she was married to William Brereton esq. of Brinton, and her eldest son was Shovell Brereton, esq. who left only two daughters. John his brother, and successor, was father of another John; whose fourth and youngest son, now living, is the Rev. Shovell Brereton, M.A. of Briningham, impropriator and Rector of Great Poringland, Norfolk: who has two sons, the elder of whom is named Shovell-Henry.

WESTON (p. 96). Elizabeth Countess of Anglesey, who was remarried to Benjamin Weston, esq. was not the widow of Charles Earl of Anglesey, as stated by Banks in his *Dormant and Extinct Baronage,* iii. 609, nor of any of the Earls of the Annesley family, but of Christopher Villiers, Earl of Anglesey, younger brother of the favourite Buckingham. She is described by Dugdale, *Baronage,* ii. 432, as " Elizabeth, daughter of Thomas Sheldon of Houby, in com. Leic. Esquire," and Banks has previously named her, under the title of ANGLESEY (VILLIERS) at p. 11 of his same volume, as having been the daughter of Thomas, or William, Sheldon of that place. Nichols, *Hist. of Leicestershire,* iii. 265, shows that the Villiers family had some connection with Hoby, but the Sheldons were not seated there. It appears from the *History of Surrey, by Manning and Bray,* vol. ii. p. 767, that Christopher Earl of Anglesey resided at Ashley Park, in the parish of Walton-on-Thames; and that Benjamin Weston, esq., by marriage with the dowager Countess, became of that place. In *The Topographer,* 1791, vol. i. p. 304, is printed a letter written in 1728 by the Rev. Samuel Croxall, Vicar of Walton upon Thames, giving an account of the disturbance of the coffin of this Countess of Anglesey from a vault in that church in the year 1710; when the only portions of the interment that remained at all perfect or sound were some knots of ribbon, which were sent (with the letter) to the house of Sir John Shelley of Michelgrove in Sussex (as the presumed representative of the deceased); and they were seen by the Rev. Stebbing Shaw, the editor of *The Topographer,* at the house of Mr. Tomkins in Arundel, in 1790.

It is shown in the *Baronetages* that Sir Charles Shelley, the second Baronet (creation 1611), married for his first wife Elizabeth, daughter of Benjamin Weston, esq. of Walton upon Thames, by Elizabeth Countess of Anglesey; and that the subsequent Baronets have descended from that marriage.

THE INSTITUTION AND EARLY HISTORY OF THE DIGNITY OF BARONET.

FROM the earliest times of Chivalry in Europe we read of two grades of Knights, the Bannerets and the Bachelors:[1] the latter of whom carried penons terminating in a point or points: the former such as, from having the points cut away, became more like the standards of the sovereign chieftains, and were termed banners.

We shall not linger on the threshold of our present subject, by enlarging on this occasion upon the grade of the Banneret: although a very interesting topic, and one deserving of further investigation, in addition to what it has already received in Selden's *Titles of Honour*. We merely allude to Bannerets here, as having occupied in certain respects a rank between the Baron and the ordinary Knight during our mediæval times, and as having been occasionally, either purposely, or more frequently from etymological misapprehension, been styled Baronettus instead of Banerettus.[2]

When Baronets were first created by King James the First,

---

[1] *The Roll of Arms of the Reign of Edward the Second*, edited by Sir Harris Nicolas in 1828, is in the title-page termed a "Roll of Arms of Peers and Knights," and in its head-lines throughout "Les noms e les armes a banerez de Engleterre." But the names and arms of the bannerets, including those of the King, eleven Earls, and the Bishop of Durham, really extend over only the first thirteen pages; after which, the names and arms of the Knights of a lower grade, arranged under their respective counties, occupy seventy-six pages (pp. 14—89).

[2] There is an accord between the King and his Lords 9 Ric. II. in which occur the words " Contes, Barons et Baronettes, et sages Chevaliers. (Cotton MS. Nero, D. VI.) Selden quotes as examples the statute of Richard II. enjoining every Archbishop, Duke, Earl, Baron, *Baronet*, Knight of a shire, &c. to appear in parliament; an attaint 35 Hen. VI. in which a juryman challenged himself because his ancestors had been *Baronets et seigneurs de parliamént*; and a patent granted to Sir Ralph Vane so late as 4 Edw. VI. in which his grade of Banneret is latinised by *Baronettus*. The historian Walsingham, in like manner, describing the prisoners at the battle of Stirling, speaks of *Barones et Baronetti viginti duo, Milites sexaginta octo*, &c.

In a previous division of his great work, when discoursing of the Barons of Germany, Selden, after discussing the most probable derivation of *baro*, as a word equivalent to *vir*, makes these remarks—" But the Germans have also the name of *banner-heer* or *panner-heer* for a Baron, as if you would say *dominus vexillifer* or the like, or as the title of Banneret. The nearness and sometimes community of the title of *banneret* and *baron* in other states appears in due place hereafter." (*Titles of Honour*, Part II. cap. i. sec. 52.) "They that have the immediate title of *freeheeren*

the name therefore was not entirely new,—at least not in Latin records; nor was the rank, as representing the grade between a Baron and a simple Knight. The chief novelty was that the dignity of Baronet, when once conferred, was to be become hereditary, like a peerage, according to the terms of the letters patent conferring it.

During the reign of Elizabeth, on the whole so little martial, and so parsimonious in the bestowal of honours, the grade of Banneret had been allowed to die out in England: and in Europe generally the various Orders of Knighthood, like the Garter and the Bath in this country, and the Thistle in Scotland, had assumed the front of the ranks of chivalry. But " Order " had not been the English word in earlier times. We talked of the Company, Fellowship, or Fraternity of the Garter: the French word *ordre* was represented in English by " livery," and it meant, not the society or sodality of Knights, but their robes, their badge, their collar, their garter, or whatever we now term *insignia*.

It is therefore scarcely a correct application of the word Order to attach it, as has often been done, to this grade of our hereditary nobility. The Baronets do not owe their dignity to personal investiture with a livery or order, whether badge, star, or other insignia, but to a patent of creation which has raised them to a certain position of hereditary rank. At the same time it is true that this rank corresponds most nearly with Knighthood; that it is accompanied with the same titular designation of *Sir* and *Lady*; and that, up to a comparatively recent period, it possessed an inherent claim to the honour of Knighthood, with which in its earlier days it was usually associated.

Some of the leading circumstances connected with this institution are sufficiently well known, and have been repeated hundreds of times,—namely, that it was a device suggested by the low condition of the treasury of King James I.; that the dignity was avowedly sold (to persons of certain previous position and qualifications) for a stipulated sum of money; that the proceeds were professedly destined for the defence of the new plantation of

(or *banner-* or *panner-heeren*) and *barones* in Latin, in Germany, were such as in the Lombard Customs are called *valvasores regis* and *valvasores majores*, and *capitanei* also." (Ibid.)

the province of Ulster, but that they were almost immediately diverted to other still more urgent demands upon the Exchequer. Beyond these few prominent particulars, it is surprising how little has been hitherto collected regarding the origin of this dignity, or the early stages of its institution and progress. For such information we look in vain to the introductory pages of all the numerous works that set forth the genealogies of the existing families which enjoy it, or to the *Extinct Baronetages* of Courthope and Burke.

It may therefore be acceptable if we endeavour to collect somewhat of what—to use a favourite term of the elder D'Israeli, may be called "the secret history" of this institution.

It is to the year 1609 that our attention is first directed, when Robert Cecill, Earl of Salisbury, was Lord Treasurer and chief minister, and when the profuse expenditure that had attended the early years of James's reign was beginning to be seriously felt at the Exchequer. It was the unhappy object of the Stuarts, even from their first accession, to dispense as far as possible with Parliament, and consequently with parliamentary taxation. It was imagined that there were other ways and means which rendered that scarcely necessary, except on such emergencies as war. The revenues of the Crown were derived from a great variety of sources, among which were many of the nature of taxes that it was thought might be imposed by the royal authority alone. The hasty dissolution of parliament in Jan. 1610–11, made such courses more requisite; and the financial necessities of the day were such that the aid of every statist or projector whose talents or schemes were considered promising was summoned to assist in the undertaking: and the great record-antiquary of the day, Sir Robert Cotton, was desired to direct his attention to all the historical precedents that bore upon the inquiry, for which purpose he was allowed free access to the State Papers in the possession of the government.

The result was a methodical report or treatise[1] on "The Manner and Means how the Kings of England have from time to time supported and repaired their Estates :" in the course of

---

[1] Among the books made up by that busy book-maker James Howell, was one which he entitled *Cottoni Posthuma*, in 8vo, 1652. The treatise above mentioned is there printed, and the extract in the text is thence taken. Sir Robert Cotton's ma-

which it was suggested that among those means the sale of Titles
of Honour was perfectly legitimate, and authorised by precedent.
The passage is as follows :—

For Honours,

And That either by Power legall or Election.

Of the first it is only in respect of Land, whereby every man is to
give when the King shall require, that hath ability to be made a
Knight, and is not.   Of this sort there be plenty of examples.

The other out of choise and grace, as Hugh de Putiaco, bishop of
Durham, was by King Richard I. created Earle of Northumberland for
a great sum of money.   And I doubt not but many of these times
would set their ambition at as high a price.[1]

And for his Majesty to make a degree of honour hereditary, as
Baronets, next under Barons, and grant them in tail, taking of every

terials, and possibly his report itself (but in detached portions), is contained in a large
volume of his Library of Manuscripts, lettered *Collections relating to the Revenue of
the Crown,* and entitled on a fly-leaf *A Collection made by Sr Robert Cotton for his
Maties seruice in time of Extremytie.*   It is marked Cleopatra F. VI., and is a miscellaneous intermixture of many very valuable documents that were abstracted from
the archives of the country, together with the crude schemes and projects of his
own day, and the results of the researches and conclusions made by himself and
others on their examination of the public records.   Among other curious essays in
the volume (pp. 119-124) is one by Sir Francis Bacon in his own handwriting, being
*A proposition concerning the augmentation of the Kinges yearlye renewe, by the con-
vertinge of his Landes into a yearlye fee farme rent,* &c.

One portion, comprised in ff. 51-61, is intitled *Means to repayr the King's Estate
An° 10 Jacobi Regis,* 1612, *collected by Sr Robert Cotton for the Earl of Northampton,*
and is signed at the end Ro. COTTON, 1612, Sept. 15; but it is clear from the quotation in the text that Sir Robert's published Treatise—probably in the form in
which it is edited by Howell—must have been written before the institution of the
dignity of Baronet, that is in the year 1609 or 1610; and this remark is made by
Dr. Thomas Smith in his life of Cotton (in Latin) prefixed to the first edition of the
Cottonian Catalogue : " Licet enim ad finem libri predicti post nomen Cottoni, uti ab
initio aliena manu, adscribatur annus hujus seculi duodecimus [*i.e.* 1612], quo denuo
descriptus et recognitus videtur ; illud tamen ante institutum Ordinem quo de jam
agitur, *h. e.* circa annum M.DC.IX aut M.DC.X compositum fuisse constat, ex hac pro-
positione quam claris verbis profert, *Si Regiæ Majestatis,* &c." Dr. Smith then gives
a Latin translation of the passage in the text, *And for his Majesty,* &c. somewhat
amplified with the substance of the passages that precede it.

[1] It is not unknown that during the latter portion of the reign of James the First
this suggestion was acted upon, by the sale of Peerages.   The particulars would be
too large for the present note.   The price fixed upon a Barony was 10,000*l.* ; on an
Earldom 30,000*l.*; though in various cases reduced bargains were negociated.   The
former sum, given by Roper when created Baron Teynham, gave occasion for his
soubriquet of *ten-M*.   The larger sum was paid in full by Holles Earl of Clare.

one 1,000*l*. in fine, it would raise with ease 100,000*l*., and, by a judicious election, be a means to content those worthy persons in the Common Wealth that by the confused admission of many Knights of the Bath hold themselves all (*lege* at) this time disgraced.[1]

But before the scheme for creating hereditary Baronets had taken this definite form, there had been various proposals nearly resembling it. One was an idea [2] for making a new order of 500 Knights, of "gentlemen of ancient houses and sufficient abilities to take precedence." Another suggestion (of which the particulars will be given presently), was to form an intermediate grade of nobility between Baron and Knight by " the ancient and honourable title of Vidom." A third was to create " Knights of the Crown."

Sir Thomas Sherley of Wiston, a veteran but impoverished Knight of the previous reign, was, it is asserted, the actual inventor of "the devise for making of Baronets." He had been Treasurer at War in the Low Countries, but had become deeply indebted to the Queen, on which account her Majesty seized his estates and personal effects, excepting the manor of Wiston, which had been settled on his wife. He died in October 1612, before the end of the year following the institution of this dignity ; but so soon after as the 21st of Jan. 1615, his son of

---

[1] This censure, whether deserved or not, was certainly intended to apply to those Knights of the Bath who were made at the King's Coronation in 1603. On that occasion the number created was so many as sixty; and among them at first there were to have been three Earls and six Barons, as appears by a preliminary list signed by the Earl of Nottingham, of which the variations are described in the *Progresses, &c. of King James I.* vol. i, p. 221. One was " The Erle of Bedford; he was the last Nobleman [*i.e.* Peer] that made to be put out, because ther was non but him self." Several of those left, however, were sons of Peers, and eventually became Peers themselves, the foremost being Sir Philip Herbert, afterwards Earl of Pembroke and Montgomery. There were three subsequent creations of Knights of the Bath in James's reign, and on all those occasions they were either young Peers, or the junior members of the families of the peerage. Ten were made at the Creation of Charles Duke of York in 1604, twenty-five at that of Henry Prince of Wales in 1610, and twenty-six at that of Charles Prince of Wales in 1616.

[2] The draft of a Proclamation to this effect is preserved in the MSS. of Queen's College, Oxford, K. 4. It is possible, however, though perhaps not probable, that this was a scheme *subsequent* to the institution of Baronets. The document is undated. The MS. containing it belonged to Sir Thomas Shirley of Bottlebridge, the antiquary, not the Sir Thomas mentioned in the text. (He was a cousin of Sir Robert Cotton, whose mother was Elizabeth Shirley : see Stemmata *Shirleiana*, p. 57.)

his own name, one of the celebrated Three Brothers, in a brief of his claims presented to the King, asserted his father's merits on this score in the following positive terms :—

My Father (being a man of excellent and working wit,) did find out the device for the making of Baronets, which brought to your Majesty's coffers well nigh a hundred thousand pounds, for which he was promised by the late Lord of Salisbury, Lord Treasurer, a good recompense, which he never had. (Memorials and Letters of State relating to the History of Britain in the reign of James the First, edited by Lord Hailes. Second edition, 1766, p. 69.)

The proposal for making " Knights of the Crown " was part of a more extended project for a " Refined Militia." There is a paper regarding it in a volume of Sir Robert Cotton's own collections (Julius C. IX. p. 131), described in his table of contents as *Privat advertisementes of the title of honor.* The writer himself heads it, Priuat aduertisements, concerning a Suté to be framed, of perticular Hono^r, w^{ch} (besides ye inestimable benifite to ye publike) will accrewe by meanes of my Refined Militia (&c. &c.). And it thus commences :—

This sute is to be framed by an order of Knighthood handled in the sayde Militia, and tearmed by so honorable and extraordinary a titile as *Knights of the Crowne :*—a number lymited: a societie of gentillmen only of greate qualitie and value, professing armes: adorned wth Insignes of Hono^r according and peculiar to y^t Order, as is the Garter to that of St. George: honored wth precedence above all Orders, saveing of the Garter and Knights of the Previe Counsell: a dignitie to be exemplified wth all the privileges and immunities apperteyning under the King's Letters Pattens, wch everie Knight shall have as a record and monument of hono^r to all his Posteritie: in regard whereof, and to digresse from the vilitie of Knighthood now falne from reputatione into contempt, yt wilbe every man's indever to put himselfe in to so honorable a ranck, Whereunto never the less none can be admitted more than the stinted nomber here under inswing, and suche only whose abilities and desartes shalbe corresponding, according to the orders prescribed more at large in my *Treatise of the Refined Militia.*[1]

It would occupy too much space to transcribe all the details of the scheme here. It was to have a military organisation, of

---

[1] Whether this treatise is anywhere extant or not has not been ascertained.

which the Prince (Henry Prince of Wales) was "under his Majestie to be substituted as Generall": and it was to resemble the
Gens d'armerie of France. The number of Knights was to be only
forty-five in each shire one with another, and their fees of creation
were not to exceed 25*l*. The "office," with its profits, was to
be granted to A. B.—*i. e.* Sir Robert Cotton, supposing the offer
was made to him; and the Projector, styling himself C. D.,
claimed a certain proportion thereof, for which a blank is left in
the MS. On the whole, it appears to be exceedingly probable
that this is the original project of Sir Thomas Sherley submitted
to Sir Robert Cotton.

It is stated by Dr. Thomas Smith, the biographer of Sir
Robert Cotton, that the Earls of Salisbury and Northampton,[1]
the leading statesmen of the day, were divided in opinion regarding the new dignity, as they not unfrequently were upon other
subjects. Northampton (who was Lord Privy Seal), on the part
of the higher ranks of the nobility, feared that it might injuri-
ously affect the interests of their younger sons;[2] but Salisbury
deemed that such considerations were not to be regarded, in the
view of the great advantages it promised to bring to the treasury.

Dr. Smith further states[3] that the device of the hereditary

[1] " Comites vero Northamptoniæ et Sarisburiæ, licet pari Regis honorem patriæque
commodum promovendi zelo incitati, uti in plerisque consultationibus ita in hac quoque
discordabant : nam ille veritus, si novus hic ordo tantis juribus et privilegiis donaretur,
ne ea Magnatum filiis natu minoribus nobilissimæ prosapiæ fraudi forent, strenuè
admodum intercessit : hic vero, maximâ ex parte diligenti D. Roberti Cottoni et D.
Thomæ Sherley prensatione et ambitu adjutus, quasi absque hoc illicio nova dignitas
non tam avidè a pluribus captaretur, causam istam tum Regis tum suam (cùm fisci,
cui præerat, res esset,) acriter quoque tutatus est, et obtinuit." It must be observed
that in this passage Dr. Smith introduces the name of Sir Thomas Sherley, which in
all probability he had derived from some document different to that published by Lord
Hailes.

[2] It may be remarked, however, that Sir Robert Cotton is stated to have had
great influence with Northampton. That nobleman took a very active part in the
conduct of public business during the illness of the Earl of Salisbury, and was then
sanguinely aspiring to the treasurership ; though he was himself unwittingly approaching the close of his career, which terminated, after a short illness, on the 15th June,
1614. "He was so heart-whole and so little expected death, that he had not made
his will till the day before he died, and *Sir Robert Cotton, his old friend*, was the
man who put him in mind of it."—Mr. Chamberlain to Sir Dudley Carleton, June
30th, 1614.

[3] "Novos hosce Equites titulo *Equitum Coronæ* insigniendos aliqui contendebant :

Baronets finally triumphed, upon Sir Robert Cotton having discovered letters patent of the 13th Edw. III. in which that title was granted to William de la Pole and his heirs: and that in return for a sum of money of which the King and his army had been in great need. In the series of Domestic documents in the State Paper Office there are several which have been placed under the year 1611, because, though undated, they evidently have relation to this new rank of nobility. One of them is the proposal, already alluded to, for its institution under the name of Vidom. This was to be confined to two principal gentlemen in each county, a kind of ennobled Deputy Lieutenants, but we may conclude with hereditary succession, although that is not directly specified. This project is as follows —

[State Paper Office, Dom. James I. vol. lxiii. art. 61.]

The title of Vidom (in Latin *Vicedominus*) was an auntient and honorable title used in this kingdome of England both before and since the Norman Conquest: and is the next immediate degree of Honor under a Barron,[1] as Viscount is under an Earle. For in anno 948 in a Charter graunted by King Edred to the Abbey of Crowland, one Bingulph Vidom signed as a witness next after the Barrons before all Knights; and about the same time a Precipe was awarded by the King to Radboto Vidom of Lincolne, and to others our officers in that behalf, for the perambulation of the Ile of Crowland. Divers other presidents are extant to proove that the title of Vidom was frequent and Honorable in auntient times in this kingdome, and in France it continueth still, as the Vidom of Chartres, of Reims, of Amiens, &c.

If it might please the King's Matie to restore this Honorable title to the auntient dignitie and place, wth some additions of grace and favour,

sed mox itum est in sententiam Cottoni, qui literas patentes anno decimotercio Regis Edwardi III. signatas produxit, in quibus, præter opima prædia ad annuum quingentarum librarum valorem, titulus dignitasque Baronetti Gulielmo de la Poole et hæredibus conceduntur, ob pecunias ab ipso procuratas, quo tempore Rex ipse unà cum exercitu, deficiente pecunia, absque his subsidiis tum ingens periculum tum dedecus subiisset.''

[1] This assertion is untrue, and advanced upon a misapprehension. The fact with regard to a Vidome is that he was the representative of an ecclesiastical lord, whilst the Vicomte represented a temporal superior. Selden says, " As Viscounts had thus their original from being subordinate to the great Dukes or Counts of France, so the Vidames from being so to Bishops. And as the one so the other, being at first merely officiary, became at length feudal and honorary." *Titles of Honour*, Second Part, Cap. II, sect. 20.

and to conferr it onlye upon tow Principall Gentlemen of birth and Qualitie in everye shire of England, it would bring a great sum of monye into his Maties coffers wthin few months.

The favours whearwith it is desired that his Matie would be pleased to grace the title of Vidom are, that they may have place in the Lower House of Parliament as the Barrons have in the higher house, and that their persons may be free from arrest for matter of debt.

Indorsed, Project concerninge the conferringe the title of Vidom.

Another paper[1] (which is of considerable length) is headed *Distinctions and Differences of Barons*. It commences with the assertion that

Barons are of three sortes, but Lordes Barons are but of two, and the other only a *Baronett*,[2] but yet retayneth the appellation of a Baron by ancient custome.

The first and ancientest Lo. Baron is he that is summoned to Parliament by the King's writt of sommons, &c.

The second Lo. Baron is he that is created by the Kinges letters pattentes under his broad *or privie*[2] seale, &c.

The Baronett is he which is Baron by Tenure, holding mediat of another Lo. and not of the Kinge; and therefore ancientlie called a Baron, which appellation is continewed in them to this day. * * * *

Upon which definition the following remark is made by a second hand in a side-note:—

The name of Baronett hath not beene in use in England but corruptly for Bannerett.

This observation seems to be really the true view of the matter. However, the name Baronet was now approved, and the following paper contains the " Project " almost exactly in the terms in which it was subsequently carried into effect:—

[State Paper Office, Dom. James I. vol. lxiii. art. 64.]

A PROJECT for erecting a new Dignitie beetween Barons and Knights, in wch theese Circumstances are considerable:

What shall bee their name, and their place.

And upon what conditions they shall have itt.

---

[1] Article 63 of the same volume.

[2] The words printed in Italic are underscored by the same pen which made the remark on " the name of Baronett " printed in the text.

Name.

The partie that hath itt shall beare the name of *Baronet.*

Hee shall have the same given him by L'res Patents to him and to the heires males of his body.   Hee shall bee called *Sir* and his wife *Lady.*

Place.

Hee shall goe above all Knights Bannerettes, not made under the Kinges standard in the ffeild displaied in his owne presence, and above the Knights of the Bath [1] and all other Knights under them.

' The same place shall be retained by their wyves.   And their sonnes and their daughters shall likewise take their places above the children of all others that are to goe beneath their Fathers.

Condicions imposed upon the Partie that shall have the Dignitie.

Hee shall bee content to pay 30 foote after 8^d per diem for 3 yeares, towardes the service of Ireland and particularlie in regard of the plantation of Ulster, and that reason shall bee expressed in the Patent, *Honoris gratia.*

The King to bee pleased to covenant never to exceed the numbre of 200.

Thus much to bee expressed in the body of the Patent.

Cautions concerning the former Project.

1. That none bee admitted except hee have of certain yearlie revennewe of Inheritance, in possession 1000^{li} *per annum de claro*, or of landes of old rent good in accompt as 1000^{li} *per annum* of improovements, or at least twoo parts in three of landes to the vallewe as aforsayd and the third in revercion expectant upon one life only holding by Dower or in Jointure.

2. That none be received whose Grandfather by the Father did not beare Armes.

3. That whosoever shall bee received upon death of an other wthout issue, shall come in the lowest ranke.

4. That he must pay the mony downe for one yeares interteinm^t every yeare in hande.

·· And for the order to be observed in ranking those that shall receive this dignitie, although it is to be wished that those Knights wch have now place before other Knights in respect of the time of their creation may be ranked before others (*cæteris paribus*), yett, because this is a dignitie wch shall bee hereditarie, wherin divers circumstances are

---

' [1] Another of the papers in the same volume, Art. 62, contains "Notes to prove that the Knights of the Bath are not higher in dignity than the Knights Bachelors."   .

more considerable then such a marke as is but temporary (that is to say of being now in Knight in time before an other), It is his Maties pleasure that the LL. shall shall not be so precise in placing those that shall receive the dignitie, but that an Esquire of greate antiquitie and extraordinarie living may bee ranked in this choyce before some Knights. And so of Knightes a man of greater living, more remarquable for his house, yeares, and calling in the common wealth, [may be] now preferred before one in this dignitie that was made Knight before him.[1]

And lastlie, that it may appeare that the partie wch hath this dignitie hath not obtained itt by any sordid or base meanes, hee shall upon the delivery of his Patent take his corporall oath in the presence of the LL. Comissioners in manner and forme following, viz. I, A. B., doe sweare, that neyther I nor any other to my knowledge have, or hath, given, or promised, procured, or consented to give, or to bee given, any gift, or reward, directly, or indirectly, to any person or persons whatsoever, for procuring his Ma^{ts} favour in my behalfe to create me a Baronet, or ranke mee before any other (those summes of money wch by my Patent I am tied to pay for the interteinm^t. of 30 foote after 8^d *per diem* for 3 yeares in Ireland only excepted), And that I will not give, nor any wth my consent shall give, or consent to bee given, any gift or reward, directly or indirectly, other then that wch I am so to pay in manner as aforesayd. So help me God.

Indorsed, A Project for Baronetts.

This document (though itself previously unpublished) will be found to correspond with the Instructions[2] which were given to the Lords of the Privy Council who were appointed Commissioners for admitting such gentlemen as were willing to accept the new dignity.

Provided always, that you proceed with none, except it shall appear unto you, upon good proof, that they are men for quality, state of living, and good reputation, worthy of the same; and that they are, at the least, descended of a Grandfather (by the father's side) that bore

[1] The deficient words are supplied from the Instructions to the Royal Commissioners.

[2] The Instructions were promulgated at the time by royal authority, and are reprinted in Selden's *Titles of Honour* and in Wotton's *Baronetage*, 1741, vol. v. Further particulars respecting these and other documents belonging to the early history of the Order will be arranged in our second paper on this subject.

arms; and have also of certain yearly revenue," &c., &c., *as in the preceding* Project.

And so, for " the order of ranking " in precedence of creation,
the directions to the Commissioners are word for word the same
as in the " Project."

It is obvious that " the ranking " of the new Baronets in their
precedence *inter se* was the most arduous part of the Commissioners' task. The qualifications of each aspirant for admission
within certain limits as to birth and landed property would be
ascertained with little difficulty : but to arrange their relative
merits interchangeably, irrespective of any rank they had hitherto
sustained, but having regard at once to the antiquity of their
houses, their " greater living " (*i. e.* means of expenditure), their
services to the state, or other personal merits, must have brought
to the arbitration of the Commissioners a variety of embarrasing
and conflicting questions, the settlement of which would, after
all, be determined in great measure by individual interests, and
the private favour of the principal councillors. As the natural
result, some of the competitors would retire from the struggle in
disgust.

Such, certainly, are the inferences which may be deduced from
the few contemporary documents which we have been able to
discover relating to the earliest selection and admission of can-
didates for the dignity.

In the name of Sir Nicholas Bacon, who was placed first on
the list, and whose descendant still retains the position of Premier
Baronet, we may recognise a compliment very properly paid by
the Lord Chancellor to his eminent predecessor, the Lord
Keeper, who under the previous reign had attained no higher
rank than a Knight. Sir Nicholas (his son) was also well qualified for the new dignity as a wealthy man, and he must have
been now a " grave and reverend senior," for he had himself received knighthood in 1578, and in 1616 he erected a monument
to his wife, recording her death, after a union of fifty-two years,
at the age of sixty-eight.

In another instance we find the Lord-Treasurer earnestly so-
licited by his son-in-law, Lord Clifford,[1] for a gentleman who

---

[1] Henry Lord Clifford, only son of Francis fourth Earl of Cumberland, married in
1610 Lady Frances Cecill, daughter of Robert first Earl of Salisbury. He suc-

had lately been his associate in the Academy at Paris,[1] and was therefore evidently of youthful years.

[State Paper Office, Domestic James I., vol. lxiv. art. 32.]

My most honored Lord,—

⋅I have soe much enjoyed the good company and love of this gentleman heere, in the Academie, that I should be unthankful unto him for them both in denyinge him my letters unto your Lord^p, which hee soe earnestly requireth at my handes, and to entrete your favor unto him in the helpinge him unto that honor which hee for himselfe and I now in his behalfe doe most humbly and earnestly desire. To give the gentleman his due, hee hath beene allwayes soe observant of me that I coulde not doe lesse for him than now I doe, but his merit also is such, accompanyed with his quallity and menes, that I am in hope your Lo^p will helpe him to this dignity of Barronett as one who may bee fittinge for that honor. I therefore, beinge induced thus to doe by thes resons, as I am bould to pray your Lord^p to helpe to place him in that ranke as his menes and birthe shall require and deserve, and I shall not esteeme my selfe less honored by your L^p than hee if your L^p shall please to lett him know that I am an ernest suter for him. Thus, commending him unto your Lordshipp's

ceeded his father as Earl of Cumberland in 1641. It is remarkable that among the first seal of Baronets the thirteenth was Sir Gervase Clifton, of Clifton in Nottinghamshire, K.B., who subsequently became a brother-in-law of Lord Clifford. He was certainly not his brother-in-law in 1611, as the Lady Frances Clifford was the second of his *seven* wives, and the death of the Lady Penelope (Rich), the first of the seven, did not occur until the 26th October, 1613. It is not impossible, however, that Sir Gervase Clifton may have been the companion of Lord Clifford at Paris, and the person to whom his lordship's letter referred, rather than Sir Thomas Puckering, who is mentioned in the following note.

[1] In the printed Calendar of the State Papers, it is suggested that this may have been " Mr. Puckering," a suggestion which also appears on the document itself, in the handwriting of the late Mr. Lemon. Upon what grounds it was made does not appear. Thomas Puckering of Weston, in Hertfordshire, esquire, who was the son of Lord-Keeper Puckering, was created a Baronet seventeen months later, on the 25th Nov. 1612. He was educated at Paris, and not improbably at " the Academy "; of this Mr. Lemon may possibly have had some evidence besides the letter of his tutor Mr. Lorkin, written from Paris to Mr. Adam Newton (the tutor of Henry Prince of Wales), which is edited by Sir Henry Ellis, in his *Original Letters*, second series, vol. iii. p. 220, and presents a remarkable account of the arrangements of Mr. Puckering's education at Paris. The news-letters of Mr. Lorkin, which were subsequently addressed from England to Sir Thomas Puckering (then again abroad) are some of the most interesting that are extant for the latter part of James's reign : see *The Court and Times of James the First*, 8vo. 1848, i. 245.

favor and good assistance, with my most humble duty unto your LorP
I rest

Your Lord^{ps} most dutifull sonne in Law,

HEN. CLIFFORDE.

Paris, this 22th of June st. no.

We now come to a favoured client of the Lord Privy Seal.
This was a young gentleman of Suffolk, Lionel Talmach of
Helmingham, esquire, ancestor of the Earls of Dysart. Just on
the eve of the first creation of Baronets, the following letters[1]
were written to him by a kinsman in London, who seems to have
been also his legal agent.

" My very good cosin, I have bine sithence your departure out of
London thre times wth my lorde of Northhampton, and at the writing
heerof I came from his lo^{pp} becawse I would write to you of all cer-
tenty that his lo^{pp} woulde imparte to me; wch is that the business goeth
forwarde, but when any shalbe made his lo^{pp} could not tell me. I
pressed his lo^{pp} and tould him that I harde ther should be three made
nowe at the first. He towlde me that it was not concluded as yet howe
many should be first made, but saide ther was a speech that ther should
be three or fowre first made to leade the way. I desiered his lo^{pp} that

---

[1] For the communication of these letters we are indebted to Richard Almack, Esq.,
F.S.A., of Melford, Suffolk. The originals are now in the hands of Nathaniel C.
Barnardiston, Esq., of the Ryes.

Their writer was William Strode of Meavychurch, brother
to Sir Richard Strode, of Newnham, co. Devon; and who
afterwards, as M.P. for Beeralston, beacme celebrated as one
of the five members impeached by Charles the First in 1640.
He was cousin-german to the wife of Mr. Talmach, as shown
in the annexed pedigree. The arms of Strode, as they
appear on his seal, are, Argent, a chevron between three
conies sable.

Gregory first Lord Cromwell, son of⳨Elizabeth, dau. of Sir John Seymour, and sister
Thomas Earl of Essex (attainted). | to Edward Duke of Somerset, Lord Protector.

Henry second⳨Lady Mary Powlet, dau.	Richard Strode, esq.⳨Frances
Lord Crom- of John Marquess of	of Newnham, co. Cromwell.
well. Winchester.	Devon.

| Edward third Lord | Catharine, mar. Sir Lionel | William Strode, esq. of Meavy- |
| Cromwell. | Talmach. | church, *writer of the Letter.* |

In Dugdale's *Baronage*, ii. 375, Mr. Strode's father is erroneously named Edward;
and so in Banks's *Dormant and Extinct Baronage*, ii. 127. See the pedigree of
Strode in Westcote's *View of Devonshire*, 4to, 1845, p. 543.

you might not be forgotten, but that his lo^{pp} would place you as your selfe and the antiquity of your howse deserveth, wch was best knowne to his lo^{pp}. He saide to me that he would take all' the care he might for your advancement; wth many more protestations, and further saide that if he could bring you with the first making he would doo his best. But if it did not fall' out so for the first, he would so place you that it should be to your content, and saide I should not need to move him any more for it, for he could not nor would not forget you and your howse. This is all' I can write you of this matter; only I wilbe ready to doo my best in this or in anything else I may; so wth my moste loving commendations to your selfe, my good cosin your wife, and all' my cosins, I committ you to God, and rest

" Your moste assured loving cosin,
" From my lodging in littell'   " WILLIAM STRODE.
St Bartholmewes this xth
of May 1611.

" If you can conveyniently spare a hawke I will make bould to be a begger.

" I have not seene my lady Candish sithence your departure.

" To the right worp^{ll} my very ⎫
lovinge cosen Lionell Talmage ⎬ *This direction is in another hand.*
Esqr at Helmingham, dd." ⎭

" My very good Cosin, I hav receavd your Letter, and this day I hav bin wth my Lorde. Your patent is a writing, and ther wilbe of this newe creation at this time some tow and twenty, and the mony must be paide wth speed, wherfore if you please to cum upp you may see it done yourselfe, but I thinke it will go to the seale wth all speed, and then I will take order for the payment of the mony. Thus in hast, out of Westminster Halle, I committ you to God, and rest

" Your moste assured
" Loving Cosin,
" *London, this 24th of May*, 1611.   " WILLIAM STRODE.

" You may cum to London a littell the soner for this business.

" To the Right Wor^{ll} Lionell Talmach, Esq.
at Helmingham in Soffolke, geve these wth speed."

" My very good Cos^n. I have receaved your Letter, by the wch I understand you desire to know the certainty of this business. Ther ar sealed twenty and two patents, the names of them you shall see in the end of this letter, and as they stand in ther places as I am credibelly informed. I have not bin backward· in putting my Lord in minde for your place, and his Lo^{pp} saith he hath don his best for you. The patents are not as yet delivered to any, for I doo learn that the parties must cum upp to give securety for the payment of the two other payments, but whether you will cum upp nowe or when you shall hav notice I must leave to your liking. You shall here from me againe wthin these few daies. So I committ you to God and rest

" Your assured

" Loving Cos^n

" *London, this friday morning.*[1]   " WILLIAM STRODE.

" 1.*Sir Nicholas Bacon.
2.†Sir Richarde Mullinex.
3. Sir Thomas Maunsell.
4.†George Sherley, Esq..
5. Sir John Stradling.
6. Sir Francis Leake
7.†Thomas Pellam, Esq.
8.*Sir Richard Haughton.
9.†Sir Henry Hubbert.
10. Sir George Bouth.
11. Sir John Payton.
12. Lionell Tallmach, Esq.

13.*Sir Jarvis Clifton.
14.*Sir [Thomas] Gerrarde.
15.†Sir Walter Aston.
16. Sir Georg Trencherd.
17. Philipp Knevitt, Esq.
18. Sir John Strangwaise.
19.†Sir John St.John.
20.*John Shelley, Esq.
Sir Thomas Walsingham
and Sir Thomas Barnardstone ar
stayed.

" To the Right Wor^{ll} Lionell Tallmach, Esqr, at his Howse, Helmingham, Suffolk, geve these wth speed."

The family of Talmach, in its later generations written Tolle-mache, was certainly among the most ancient of those who were advanced to the new dignity. Mr. Talmach was the son and heir of Sir Lionel Talmach (who was christened during Queen Elizabeth's visit to Helmingham in 1561, her Majesty standing sponsor), by Susan, daughter of Sir Ambrose Jermyn of Rush-brook ; and his own wife was Catharine, daughter of Henry

[1] This last letter, in which the writer states that the patents " are sealed," but not yet delivered, was probably written on Friday the 31st of May; as in the second letter, written on Friday the 24th of May, he says that they " will go to the seal with all speed." Though the patents were dated on the 22nd of that month, they were evidently not actually sealed for some days after.

The Baronetcies are still existing in those five families which are marked with a * and also, merged in Peerages, in the six marked †.

second Lord Cromwell and grand-daughter of John Marquess of Winchester. The alliances of the family in other generations were of a similar character; and the fourth Baronet became, in 1697, Earl of Dysart, on the death of his mother, Elizabeth Countess of Dysart, (and by her second marriage Duchess of Lauderdale,) the heiress of that dignity in the peerage of Scotland. The baronetcy became extinct[1] in 1821, on the death of Wilbraham Earl of Dysart, the seventh who enjoyed it : but the Earldom survives, having passed to his sister Lady Louisa wife of John Manners of Grantham Grange, co. Lincoln, esq., whose issue have taken the name of Tollemache, rather than that of Murray, which was the patronymic of the first Earl.

The most remarkable point, perhaps, in the preceding letters, is the statement that two and twenty patents were originally sealed or intended for the first seal, but that two had been stayed, namely those for the families of Walsingham and Barnardiston. Subsequently, two others in the list were also stayed, namely, those for Trenchard and Strangways: so that, eventually, only eighteen were of the original creation of the 22nd May, 1611.

Sir Thomas Walsingham was the representative of an antient family seated at Scadbury, in the parish of Chiselhurst, Kent: the grandson of Sir Edmund Walsingham, sometime Lieutenant of the Tower of London, to whom the great Sir Francis Wal-

---

[1] In the *Baronia Anglica Concentrata*, 4to. 1843, by Sir T. C. Banks, (styling himself) Baronet of Nova Scotia, there is a list (vol. ii. p. 209) of Baronetcies then supposed to be dormant, and among them is this of Tollemache. But why it was placed in that list does not appear. It was probably a misapprehension. Sir William Manners, son and heir-apparent of Lady Louisa (Tollemache), by John Manners, esq. (mentioned in the text,) who died Sept. 23, 1792, was created a Baronet Jan. 5, 1793. He became by courtesy Lord Huntingtower on his mother's succession to the Earldom in 1821, and on that occasion he took the surname of *Talmash* only; dying during her lifetime in 1833. He was father of the present Earl; who in consequence is a Baronet, but of the precedence of 1793.

John Manners, esq. the father of Sir William, sometime of Buckminster Park, co. Leicester, was a natural son of Lord William Manners, second son of the second Duke of Rutland. When the Baronetcy was conferred, in 1793, the arms of the house of Manners were given to Sir William, differenced by a bordure wavy gobony argent and sable : the crest of a peacock in its pride, and the chapeau upon which he stands, being in like manner differenced by a bendlet sinister wavy gobony or and sable. (See the engraving in Debrett's *Baronetage*, edit. 1819, plate 35.) These have now been relinquished for the simple coat of Tollemache, Argent, a fret sable.

singham, Secretary of State, was nephew.[1]   Sir Thomas was the
son of Sir Thomas Walsingham, (knighted 1573, and died 1583,)
by Dorothy, daughter of Sir John Guldeford.   The junior Sir
Thomas Walsingham must have been knighted during the reign
of Elizabeth, as his wife Elizabeth, daughter of Sir Peter Man-
wood, K.B., was then already styled Lady.   The reason for his
not actually receiving the patent of Baronetcy that had so nearly
passed the great seal in 1611 we have no grounds to determine;
but it may be presumed that it was no loss of favour at court, as
his son and heir apparent, a third Sir Thomas, was knighted, at
Royston, so shortly after as the 26th Nov. 1613.   The father
survived to the year 1630, being then aged 69.

Sir Thomas Barnardiston was cousin-german to Sir Thomas
Walsingham, being the son and heir of Sir Thomas Barnardiston,
of Ketton, in Suffolk, by Mary, daughter of Sir Edmund Walsingham, of Chiselhurst, Lieutenant of the Tower.   He died Dec.
23rd, 1619, and has a fine monument, with his effigy, at Ketton.
His eldest son had died before him, in the year 1610; and at the
time when the old Knight received this affront in 1611, his heir
apparent was his grandson, Nathaniel, then about three and twenty,
and afterwards knighted, at Theobalds, Dec. 21, 1618.

Subsequently, in 1663, two brothers, Sir Thomas and Sir
Samuel Barnardiston, great-grandsons of Sir Thomas, were created
Baronets; but in the intermediate time, since 1611, the Bar-
nardistons had taken an important part in the events which had
brought grief to the royal Stuarts; having great influence, and
being generally in Parliament, for Suffolk or some of the
boroughs in that county.   Considered in connection with the
money payment required from those who accepted the dignity of
Baronet, it is remarkable to find that Sir Nathaniel Barnardiston,
in 1626, (who was grandson to the Sir Thomas upon whom the
baronetcy was to have been conferred in 1611,) "refused to lend
unto his Majesty;" and in February, 1627, the commissioners,
for the loan money, at Newmarket, were commanded to send
him (a prisoner!) to the Council, to be examined.   (See *Calendar of State Papers.*)   In March 1627, it was ordered by the

---

[1] The pedigree of this family has never been published: a defect which we propose
very shortly to supply.

King, being present in Council, that certain persons shall be " set at liberty from any restraint put on them by his Majesty's commandment," viz.,

> " Sir NATHANIEL BARNARDISTON,
> " JOHN HAMPDEN,
> " RICHARD KNIGHTLEY, &c." [1]

The *Insignia Dignissimi Dom: D:* NATHANAELIS BARNARDISTON, *Equitis Aurati*, placed upon a tree, the branches of which bear the names of his children (seven sons and three daughters) form the frontispiece to the Fourth Book of Sylvanus Morgan's *Sphere of Gentry*, fol. 1681, as an example of the atchievement of a Knight. He had died in the year 1653. In his life, which was written by Fairclough, and printed in Clarke's *Lives of sundry Eminent Persons*, fol. 1683, he is styled " one of the most eminent Patriots of his time, and the twenty-third Knight of his family."

In Dec. 1641, Samuel Barnardiston, a younger son of Sir Nathaniel, gave rise to the party term ROUNDHEAD, having been so called by the Queen, who saw him in a city procession that came to Whitehall, bringing a petition (see Rapin's *History of England*). This was the same Samuel who was created a Baronet in 1663, after having joined heartily in the restoration of Monarchy. However, the vengeance of the court again fell on him several times. In 1683 he was prosecuted for high misdemeanor (see *State Trials*), having said in an intercepted letter to Sir Philip Skippon, who had married his niece, that the brave Lord William Russell was lamented ; that the Earl of Essex had been murdered; and Algernon Sidney was about to be beheaded, &c. He was tried before Jeffreys, who in his address to the jury alluded to the *Roundhead* notoriety, and said, " The act of oblivion might have put Sir Samuel in mind that it was not fit any more to go down to Whitehall to make uproars and tumults and hubbubs." He was fined £10,000, which he refused to pay, and his estates were seized, and he suffered long imprisonment. The foreman of the jury, Thomas Vernon, was knighted " for his services in securing a conviction " (see *Lady Rachel Russell's Letters*, 3rd edition, p. 52).

[1] See Lord Nugent's *Life of John Hampden*, vol. i. p. 394.

P 2

In 1745, Sir John Barnardiston, the last male representative of the creation of 1663, died, being also the representative of the intended creation of 22nd May, 1611; but under such creation the male heir of Thomas, younger brother of Sir Nathaniel beforementioned, would have then become a Baronet, and the title would have descended to his lineal male heir, the present Nathaniel C. Barnardiston, of the Ryes, near Sudbury, whose pedigree is briefly given in Burke's *Landed Gentry*.

Sir George Trenchard and Sir John Strangways, the two others whose patents were also " stayed," were, like Walsingham and Barnardiston, persons nearly connected—the former being father-in-law to the latter.

The families of Trenchard and Strangways were both of high antiquity in Dorsetshire. Sir George Trenchard,[1] of Wolverton, had been knighted in 1588, and his daughter Grace was the wife of Sir John Strangways, of Melbury, in the same county.[2] Sir John was subsequently conspicuous for his opposition to the measures of the Court, and so early in the next reign as the years 1626 and 1627, he was confined to the county of Bedford for not complying with a loan. It is very possible that his first disgust was taken when his baronetcy miscarried.

J. G. N.

[1] There was another Sir George Trenchard, son of the above, who was knighted in 1603, but he was dead before the present date. He was the first of the three husbands of the Lady Penelope Darcy, of whom the story is told that, being courted by all at once, Sir John Trenchard, Sir John Gage, and Sir William Hervey, she told them that if they would have patience she would take them each in turn. Her first marriage had not taken place on the 21st April, 1610, as appears by a letter of Lady Darcy, her mother ; but Sir George Trenchard, junior, must have died during the same year, or early in 1611, as the Lady Penelope's marriage settlement with her second husband, Sir John Gage, of Firle, bears date the 28th June, 9 Jas. I. (1611). Sir Thomas Trenchard, the next surviving son of old Sir George, was knighted in 1613 : but the family never received the title of Baronet.

[2] The family of Strangways became extinct in the male line in 1726, and is now represented by the Earl of Ilchester, who bears their name in addition to Fox.

(To be continued.)

THE ORIGIN AND DEVELOPMENT OF COAT ARMOUR.

No. II.

BEFORE we proceed to investigate further the development of Armory,[1] we may still dwell with some advantage upon the era of its origin, it being most desirable to acquire some fixed opinions upon that primary point. Having refused to be misled by the visions of theoretic systems, or by data and examples[2] of which the true era has been misapprehended, let us form our judgment upon such reliable evidence as may certainly be attained by the study of contemporary documents whether of record or of art.

We welcome an excellent ally in Mr. John Hewitt,[3] who has unavoidably gathered for the heraldic antiquary many interesting facts, without attempting to set them forth in all their bearings upon the science of Coat-Armour, of which he has not professed specifically to treat. But, in perusing the following passages of his very elaborate and well-considered work, most readers will be sensible of a conviction how greatly preferable to the most ingenious theories are facts judiciously detected and faithfully related.

When speaking of the period extending from the Conquest to the end of the twelfth century, Mr. Hewitt remarks:—

The devices upon the shields in the earlier part of the period under examination are devotional[4] or fanciful. In the second half of the

---

[1] See the first paper of this series at the beginning of this volume.

[2] It has been objected to our former paper, that we cited some of our examples from the *Salle des Croisades* at Versailles, where they are positively attributed to persons who flourished *before* the middle of the twelfth century. We ought to have protected ourselves by saying, that we merely took them as examples of coats, *quantum valeant*, whatever the time of their origin. We do not believe that regular armorial coats can really claim a much earlier date in France than in England, but presume that the coats in question became those of the families to whose names they are attached at Versailles when such families first assumed arms.

[3] In his *Ancient Armour and Weapons in England: from the Iron Period of the Northern nations to the end of the seventh century.* 3 vols. 8vo, 1855-1860.

[4] By the term "devotional" we understand Mr. Hewitt merely as regarding the various forms of the cross in that light.

twelfth century heraldic bearings that became hereditary began to appear. The earlier shield-paintings consist of crosses, rounds or bezants, dragons, interlacing bands, flat tints bordered with a different hue, or simple flat tints; with some varieties which the pencil only can describe with clearness. Numerous examples of these in all their diversity will be found in the Bayeux tapestry, in Sir Frederic Madden's paper on the Isle of Lewis chessmen, (*Archæologia*, vol. xxiv.) and among the plates of Shaw's *Dresses and Decorations*.

The two seals of Richard the First very exactly mark the growth of the science of heraldry. In the earliest [1189] the monarch's shield is ensigned with the symbol of valour, a lion. But it is a rampant lion, and as the lower shield presents only one-half of its surface to view, it has been conjectured [certainly without substantial grounds] that the complete device would consist of two lions combatant. This device, whether of one or two lions, has passed away, among the serpents and knot-work of the earlier time ; but the bearing on Richard's second seal [1194], three lions [or leopards] passant gardant, retains its place in the royal escutcheon to the present day. In this second seal [1] of Richard I. the lion passant appears also in the helmet of the monarch.[2]

Another example of the repetition of a royal device is afforded by the seal of Alexander II. of Scotland (circa 1214), where the lion rampant figured on the shield is repeated on the saddle.[3]

The shields were often highly decorated with painting, and even, if we may interpret literally the evidences of chroniclers, with inlaid jewels. Examples of richly ornamented shields of the twelfth century may be seen in Shaw's *Dresses and Decorations*, and in Harl. MS. 2895, fol. 82. Robert of Aix, in the twelfth century, writing of the first crusade, tells us that the European knights carried shields *auro et gemmis inserti variisque coloribus depicti*. (Vol. i. p. 146.)

These evidences and proofs of what shields were at the very dawn of Coat Armour, are exceedingly valuable, for they offer many hints of that species of decoration from which Coat Armour took its early growth. In another page there are some further remarks of similar import:—

Armorial bearings are the usual adornment of the knightly shield

---

[1] Both seals are represented as the frontispiece to Mr. Hewitt's first volume.

[2] Mr. Hewitt enumerates other similarly ornamented helmets in p. 287. The devices are *not crests*, but placed on the surface of the helmet.

[3] We may refer to a beautiful representation of this seal by Mr. Edward Blore, among the seals of the Kings of Scotland engraved in Raine's *History of North Durham*. Seals, Plate II.

throughout this period [the thirteenth century], and the field was some-times richly diapered, as in this example [of a representation of the murder of Saint Thomas of Canterbury] from the window of the north transept of Oxford cathedral. Where heraldic devices are not found, a " pattern " generally takes their place : a cross, a rosette, a star, a fret, or some such simple ornament. In other cases *the face of the shield is painted of a single colour.* (Vol. i. p. 296.)

We learn from these statements that, before the rise of armo-rial charges, or the ordinaries as they are now called, shields were as richly ornamented as afterwards, and perhaps more richly—with gay colours, and ornamental patterns, and even valuable jewels.

There are proofs in the monuments of ancient Art that what is called DIAPERING was certainly coeval with, and probably ante-rior to, the earliest armorial charges. Diapering was a mode of decorating the surface of the shield independent of the actual device. The field might first receive from the hand of the carver or painter its ornamental pattern, and then be tinctured and charged according to the rules of armory; or the charges might be ornamented or diapered in like manner, if they pre-sented surfaces suitable for the purpose.

Mr. Planché, in his essay on the origin of Armorial Bearings, printed in the Winchester volume of the British Archæological Association, (and since amplified in his judicious and instructive volume entitled *The Pursuivant of Arms*,) has pointed out the fact that one of the shields of the Chessmen of the eleventh cen-tury, discovered in the Isle of Lewis, (and figured in the xxivth volume of *Archæologia*,) is (in the language of blazon) Party per pale, the sinister side being cross-hatched with oblique lines, evi-dently to represent a darker colour than that of the dexter side, which is left smooth, as being of some light colour, or Argent. He has placed, in juxtaposition, the round shield of a Mexican warrior, divided exactly in the same manner, from a native painting (circ. 1519) preserved in the Vatican.

Another shield of the Lewis chessmen is Quarterly of two colours, surmounted or divided by a plain cross. These were therefore evidently the primitive distinctions of shields before the superposition of charges.

Two of the most remarkable among our early sepulchral effigies have diapered shields. One is that which has been incorrectly attributed to Geoffrey de Magnaville, and is engraved in the present volume, at p. 103. The other is that of Robert de Vere, third Earl of Oxford (ob. 1221), at Hatfield Broadoak in Essex, which is engraved in Gough's *Sepulchral Monuments*, and also in Stothard's *Monumental Effigies*. His quarterly coat has two patterns of diaper: one for the first and fourth quarters, and the other for the second and third. See this shield also represented in Boutell's *Heraldry*, plate vi. together with two carved examples (circ. 1350) from the beautiful Percy monument in Beverley Minster.

Among the families bearing shields without charges is that of Ransow in Denmark. Its shield is like that of Waldegrave, party per pale, and of the same colours, but gules and argent, instead of argent and gules. This simplicity was claimed as an evidence of high antiquity, in the following epigram, which was written nearly three centuries ago:—

INSIGNIA RANSOVIORUM.

Ransovii rubra est clypei pars dextra, sinistra est
Candida: sed cassis cornua bina gerit.[1]
Cornua sunt robur: Martis color alter, et alter
Pacis, utrumque satos nobilitate decet.
Forma quid hæc simplex? simplex fuit ipsa vetustas;
Simplicitas formæ stemmata prisca notat.

HENRICI RANZOVII *de Conservanda Valetudine Liber*. 8vo. 1584.

The shield of Waldegrave, however, has not been always wholly uncharged. A junior branch of the family which resided at Lawford, between Colchester and Ipswich, and erected a mansion house there in the reign of Elizabeth, placed a large estoile in fess point.[2]

In regard to another biparted shield, that per pale indented, which was borne on the banners of the Montforts, and has been supposed (incorrectly as we have before remarked) to belong to the Honour of Hinckley, we should have stated that, not only Simon de Montfort, but his elder brother also, Amauri de Montfort, Constable of France, was represented in the cathedral of

---

[1] The crest is of two horns, argent and gules, resembling elephant's trunks.
[2] See drawing in Suckling's *Collections for Essex*.

Chartres in the manner already figured in p. 10: see Montfaucon, *Les Monumens de la Monarchie Françoise*, fol. 1730, tome ii.
pl. xxxiii. The counter-seal of Amauri in the same plate exhibits the same banner, evidently therefore belonging to the Montforts as a family, placed between two fleurs de lis, and surrounded
with the legend ✠ VERITAS. On the obverse of his seal he carries a shield charged with a lion, and a lion is on his horse's
housings, both before and behind,—its tail *not* forked, if we may
trust to the engraving.

An English family named Hickman, seated at Gainsborough
in Lincolnshire, and at Oken in Staffordshire, bore simply Per
pale indented argent and azure. This was the arms of the
family from which the present Earl of Plymouth is paternally
descended.

The family of Tuite, enjoying a baronetcy of Ireland, bears
simply, Quarterly argent and gules.

There are many other ancient bearings, which it is unnecessary to specify by name, that may be called coats without
charges, being simply Barry, Paly, Bendy, or Checky: though
some of them have been varied, by modern blasonry, into two
or three Bars, Bends, &c.

Another variety is Lozengy; or Masculy, as it was called in
the earliest times. The coat of Bavaria was once blazoned as
Masculy argent and azure; but its modern blazon is Barry
bendy. The well-known coat of Fitzwilliam is Lozengy argent
and gules; that of Burgh, Earl of Kent, was Lozengy gules
and vaire. And there are others in the old rolls. At Carlaverock in 1300 Ralph de Gorges (then a newly-dubbed knight)
had all his harness and his attire Masculy of gold and azure :

> Tout son harnois e son atire
> Avoit masclé de or et de azur:

whilst the good Richard de la Rokeley had his shield portrayed
Masculy of red and ermine.

The family of Grimaldi, princes of Monaco in Italy, bear
Lozenzy argent and gules, like our Fitzwilliam: and the late
Mr. Stacey Grimaldi (who derived his descent from them) was
disposed to trace this bearing to a very early date. He observed
that in the 15th plate of the Bayeux tapestry (as published by
the Society of Antiquaries) the Standard-Bearer, immediately in

advance of the Conqueror, has on his breast " a square, inclosing
some diagonal lines from right to left, as well as from left to
right, and thereby forming the figure commonly called diamond; "[1] and, when deducing the genealogy of the Barons of
Bec,[2] Mr. Grimaldi showed that Turstin, who was the Conqueror's Standard-Bearer at Hastings (and is afterwards mentioned
in the Domesday Survey as Turstinus filius Rolf), was, together
with his brother Goisfrid the Marshal, and his cousins William and
Gilbert Crispin, who all fought at Hastings, a grandson of Crispin
Baron of Bec (flor. 1000), who was a younger son of Grimoaldo
Prince of Monaco, by Crispina daughter of Rollo Duke of Nor-
many.   He adds that the armorial bearing of Goisfrid's family
was Lozengy, like that of Grimaldi: and these are associations
which certainly carry back the age of merely coloured banners,
or uncharged arms (as we may term them), used as distinctive
marks of gentilitial descent or alliance, to some generations before
the time when we first find coats bearing charges.

THE CARBUNCLE.

In discussing in a former article (p. 101) the armorial shield
on the effigy in the Temple Church, (erroneously) assumed to be
that of Geoffrey de Magnaville, Earl of Essex, we undertook to
make some remarks upon the Carbuncle, because that figure has
been supposed to be part of the arms of Magnaville; and, if so,
really one of the earliest armorial charges that was adopted.
We showed that the misapprehension is of no recent date, it
being actually asserted in the chronicle of Walden Abbey that
the said Geoffrey, *postquam gladio Comitis accinctus erat, arma
progenitorum cum carbunculo nobilitavit.*   And there is a correspondent passage in the chronicle of Wigmore priory, where it
said of Roger de Mortimer (circ. 1270) that, the Queen of
Navarre having fallen in love with him (from reputation), and
sent him a present of gold,

Ipseque dominus Rogerus ejusdem reginæ ob amorem carbunculum
armis suis ad totam vitam suam addidisse noscitur.

This second monastic story, however, like the former, is not

---

[1] Gentleman's Magazine, Dec. 1829, p. 499.   [2] Ibid. Jan. 1832, p. 27.

borne out by any seal of Roger de Mortimer, nor by the early Rolls of Arms.

The carbuncle appears to have become an armorial charge in some foreign coats: and its most honourable position was in that of the King of Navarre:

Le Roy de Navarre porte de goules ove une charboncle d'or. *Mr. Grimaldi's Roll, in Collectanea Topogr. et Genealogica, vol. ii.*

This is the key to the legend above presented, and explains why such an addition was fancied honourable.

As drawn more recently, and as familiar in representations of the arms of the united kingdoms of France and Navarre up to the time of the Revolution of 1789, the *escarboncle* had changed its appearance from that of a radiating star to a trellis-work of chains, said to be commemorative of the palisado begirt with chains, in which the Moors were intrenched at the battle of Tolosa, in 1211, and which was forced by the Christian warriors.[1]

The Counts and Dukes of Cleves, on the other hand, retained the more ancient form of the Escarbuncle, but for their arms it was blasoned as radiating from a small escocheon or orle placed in the centre—in fact, the original boss, or umbo, of the shield:—

Le Comtee de Cleve gules au escocheon d'argent un carbuncle d'or flurté. *Roll, Harl. MS. 6589.*

Comte de Cliffe de Alemain. Gules, an orle argent, surtout a carbuncle of eight rays or. *Society of Antiquaries' Roll, No. 7.*

As time ran on, the heralds gave this *escarboncle* a still fuller blason. It was described as being *pommétté et fleuretté;* that is, the former term was applied to its knobs or protuberances, and the latter to its terminations, which were drawn as fleurs-de-lis.

We have no hesitation, however, in affirming that originally these carbuncles were merely ornamental or constructional parts of the shield, and not strictly heraldic charges. The sepulchral effigy of William Count of Flanders (ob. 1227), son of Robert Duke of Normandy and grandson of William the Conqueror of England, furnishes a good example. This was in the church of S. Bertin at St Omer's, and may be seen figured in the work of Olivarius Vredius on the Counts of Flanders, and copied in

[1] Various noble houses of Arragon and Navarre assumed the same chains as part of their arms, as may be seen in Favine's *Theater of Honour*, quoting the Count de Lansarote.

Sandford's *Genealogical History of England*. The central boss is like a five-leaved flower, surrounded by eight short rays, and again by eight longer ramifications that dart out to the margin of the shield.

So, in Willemin's *Monuments Français*, pl. 73, will be seen a shield from the portrail de Notre Dame de Chartres, which is ornamented after the manner of the carbuncle, with eight bars radiating from a central boss, but with this difference that the bars run close up to the border. The border is studded as if with jewellery.

In the enamelled plate at Mans, engraved by Stothard, and by him assigned to Geoffrey Plantagenet, there is such a carbuncle: and it is accompanied by armorial bearings, (of which it forms no part,) viz. Or, eight lions rampant azure; in the same way as in the effigy at the Temple (engraved in p. 101) the carbuncle occurs together with the armorial charges of dancettes.

That the escarboncle did not become an armorial charge in England, as it did on the continent, is shown by the evidence of the three ancient rolls recently edited by Messrs. Walford and Perceval, as well as by others, in which it does not occur for any English coat.

It is true that a carbuncle appears on the seal of Hameline, Earl of Warren and Surrey, the natural brother of King Henry I.; and on the seal of John Earl Warren, his grandson,[1] 3 Edw. III. 1329, the carbuncle is worn as a crest both for himself and his horse. But this again we must refer to continental armory, the old arms of Anjou (of the house of Plantagenet) being blasoned as Gules, a chief argent, over all an escarbuncle of eight staves, nowed and flowered or. This coat is placed for Anjou on the monument of Queen Elizabeth in Westminster Abbey.

. We may here mention that, in the garter-plate of Ralph Lord Basset of Drayton, (ob. 1390), in the Chapel at Windsor, his escocheon is surmounted by this badge or cognizance,—On a roundel, per pale gules and azure, an escarbuncle of eight rays fleuretté or.[2]

The arms of some families of Thornton are three escarbuncles

---

[1] See both engraved in Watson's *History of the Earls of Warren and Surrey*.

[2] Beltz's *Memorials of the Garter*, p. 162.

on a bend, but these are modern variations of the more ancient coat, Argent, on a bend gules three Katharine-wheels of the field. The coat, Argent, on a bend gules three escarbuncles or, a fleur-de-lis sable for difference, was granted to Thornton of Middlesex, March 12, 1575.

If the escarbuncle be found in the quarterings of certain noble families, it will prove to be an imagination of the later heralds. Such it is in the quarterings of Sydney, for the very coat of " Magnaville Earl of Essex," which has led to this investigation.

And so one of the coats assigned to the abbey of Colchester is evidently formed in imitation of that attributed to Magnaville,— Quarterly argent and gules, a cross within a bordure or, over all an escarbuncle sable. We find this in Glover's Ordinary, with the name (or designation) Dapifer.[1]

On the whole, these exceptions help to prove the rule that the escarbuncle is not truly an armorial charge, but it is a misapprehension of the ornamental boss of the shield, which was antecedent to armory, and lasted for a certain period in conjunction with it. To conclude with one more quotation from our friend Mr. Hewitt, he states, vol. i. p. 295, that " The boss is still retained in some of the shields of the thirteenth century, though but rarely. It occurs in our woodcut No. 75, and on folio 4 of the Lives of the Offas." These historical shields were perhaps designedly drawn of an archaic fashion. The former belongs to a figure of Goliath, receiving on his temple the mortal wound from the sling of David. It is from a Hebrew MS. of the Pentateuch written in Germany about the close of the thirteenth century (Addit. MS. 11,639). " The shield retains (remarks Mr. Hewitt, p. xxi.) the boss and strengthening bands we have seen in examples from the Anglo-Saxon and Frankish graves."

" The boss and the strengthening bands "—writes Mr. Hewitt, perfectly innocent of any heraldic theory. But our own theory is that from " the boss " was developed the cross flory, and all the other endless varieties of crosses which are so abundant in armory, and from the other " strengthening bands " were derived the fess, pale, bend, chevron, and bars, which became the Ordinaries of the armorial system.

[1] It may be noticed that Dr. Charles Mandevile, Dean of Peterborough, received in 1722 a grant of arms founded upon the old traditional coat of Magnaville. It was Per saltire or and gules, an escarbuncle of eight rays sable ; and for crest, on a wreath, a

FEES PAID BY THE DUKE OF LAUDERDALE WHEN INSTALLED
AS A KNIGHT OF THE GARTER IN 1672.

[From the original account in the possession of Richard Almack, Esq. F.S.A.]

Fees payable by his Grace ye Duke of Lauderdale
at his Installation.

	£	s.	d.
To the Deane of Windsor, Register . . .	38	13	04
To the said Register for a Book of Statutes . .	03	00	00
To the Dean & Channons	10	00	00
To the Chore &c..	08	10	00
To the Poore Knights	10	00	00
	70	03	04
To Garter for [his] Grace's Upper Garment . .	55	00	00
To him for his Fee in Money . . .	35	00	00
To Garter & ye Officers of Armes for Proclayming his Stile	05	00	00
To ye Black Roodd	20	00	00
To ye Officers of Armes	20	00	00
	135	00	00

Fees & Gratuities to others his Mats Servants, vizt.

	£	s.	d.
To ye Wardrobe	03	00	00
To ye Trumpetts	06	00	00
To ye Serjeant Trumpetter . . .	01	00	00
To ye Musycians 4 Companies . . .	08	00	00
Knight Harbenger	03	06	08
Drums & Fifes	02	00	00
To ye Porters	03	00	00
Master Cooke.	01	10	00
Serjeant Porter	03	00	00
Vestry	01	00	00
Yeomen Harbengers	03	00	00
Vshers of the Hall	01	10	00
Groomes of the Chamber . . .	01	10	00
Yeomen Vshers	03	06	08
Quarter Waiters	04	08	04
Sewers	04	08	04
Buttery	01	10	00

	£	s.	d.
Pantry	01 : 10 : 00		
Celler	01 : 10 : 00		
To yᵉ Serjants at Armes lately added . .	05 : 00 : 00		

$$59 : 10 : 00$$

Totall . 264 : 13 : 04

EDW. WALKER, *Garter.*

Also yᵉ Painter's Bill for a Great Banner of his
Grace's Armes, Helmet, Crest, Sword & Plate of
his Armes, are to be paid to the Painter, amounting unto about yᵉ sume of . . . . 31 : 00 : 00
Besides Cloath of gold for the Mantle, Sattin to
line it, Velvit for a Cushion with Taffata to line
it, with Fringe & Tassells, are either to be delivered to yᵉ Painter to make up, or the Painter to
provide & make up yᵉ same . . . . *(blank* [1]*)*
Lastly, if the 3 other Noble Lords speedily to be Elected &
Installed shall think fitt to afford all yᵉ Officers of Armes who
attend them att their Installation, and who have received by the
Bounty of many Knights formerly installed each of them 5£ for
Hats, Feathers & Scarfes, his Grace hath promised that he will
Give his part of the sume of 60£ to yᵉ 12 Officers of Armes,
which is 15 for his part. EDW. WALKER, *Garter.*

Side note. The other 3 new Knights have paid each of them
15£. E. W. Gʳ.
Delivered May 25ᵗʰ 1672.

30ᵗʰ May 1672.

Received then by mee Edward Walker Knᵗ Garter
Principall King of Armes, of Mʳ John Lindsey,
the full sume of two hundred seventy nine Pounds
Thirteen shillings four pence being for the Instal-
lačõn Fees of his Grace the Duke of Lauderdale
according unto yᵉ before written Bill (excepting
the Painter's Bill) I say received the day & year
above written . . . . . . 279 : 13 : 4

EDW. WALKER, *Garter.*

June 3ᵈ 1672.

Works done & Money laid out for yᵉ Installation of yᵉ High
Mighty & Illustrious Prince John Duke of Lauderdale.

	£	s.	d.
Imprimis for one great Banner painted in Oyle & fine Gold with his Loᵖˢ Armes . . .	10 : 00 : 00		

---
[1] See the subsequent account.

	£	s.	d.
For a Socket for the Great Banner . . .	00	02	00
For a Staffe painted in Oyle for the Great Banner .	00	05	00
For an Helmet of Steele Gilt fitting his degree .	03	00	00
For a Sword with a Crossehilt Pomell & Chape Guilt	01	00	00
For Crest Carved & Guilt	02	00	00
For Carving Enameling & Guilding the Plate for the Stall	06	00	00
For 6 Scutchions guilt with fine Gold with his Grace's Armes and Titles at 15s p peece . .	04	10	00
For making the Mantles	00	10	00
For making the Wreath & finding Silk .	00	05	00
For making the Cushion . . . : .	01	06	08
For a pair of Knobs for the Mantle guilt .	00	02	00
For Cariage & putting up ye Acheivement .	01	10	00

For 7 yds & a Quarter of Silk and Gold Fringe for ye Cushion at 4s 6d	01	12	07
For 4 Silk and Gold Tassells for ye Cushions .	01	00	00
For 11 ounces Silk Fringe for ye Great Banner .	01	03	00
For 2 Tassells of Silk and Gold for ye Mantle .	01	00	00
	£34	07	01

Side note to the four last items. These have been formerly delivered with ye Velvet & Cloth of Gold, but now furnished by the Painter.

I have examined & doe approve of this Bill.

7 *June* 1672. EDW. WALKER, *Garter.*

June the 11th 1672.

Received then of Mr John Lindsey the sume of thirty four Pounds in full of this Bill. I say received p mee . . . . . . £34 : 00 : 00

ARTHUR BLACKAMORE.

Sir Harris Nicolas, in his History of the Order of the Garter, at pp. 388—393, has given various particulars in regard to the several items forming this aggregate of Fees; and the subject is still more fully discussed by Ashmole in *The Institution, &c., of the Order of the Garter*, pp. 455 —466. We are not aware of any bill of the whole payments for the Installation Fees that has hitherto been edited.

THE BEAUFORT PROGRESS THROUGH WALES,
1684.

NOTITIA CAMBRO-BRITANNICA: A Voyage of North and South Wales. Being various cursory Remarks touching their ancient Kings of ye North and South, Princes of ye British and ye English Line, Lords Presidents, Militia, Speeches, Entertainments, Seals of Corporations, Views of Churches, Funerall Monuments, Epitaphs, Inscriptions, Marbles, Roman Ara's, Fragments of Antiquity, Castles, Seats of Gentlemen, Coat-armors of divers British and other Families, Customes, Pedigrees, Sayings, Manners, Maps, Prospects, Landmarks, Havens, Market Towns, Faires, Wakes, Commodities of the respective Counties of Wales, with sundry other Observations in attending his Grace the Duke of Beaufort, in his Progres and Generall Visitacion of his Comands there, An° D'ni M.DC.LXXXIV. Intermixt wth some Historicall Observations, Annotations, and brief Notes from approved Authorities, Manuscripts of others, Records, ancient Charters, &c.

By T. D. *Gen.*

SPE LABOR LEVIS.

Edited from the Original MS. in the possession of His Grace the Eighth Duke of Beaufort, by CHARLES BAKER, His Grace's Steward of the Seigniories of Gower and Kilvey. Printed for Private Circulation. MDCCCLXIV. 4to. pp. vi. 284.

Among the archives of the Duke of Beaufort preserved at Badminton was found the original of the present volume—one of the MSS. of Thomas Dineley, a gentleman whose predilection for the study of genealogy and antiquities in general is commemorated by various volumes hitherto little known, but of which we propose to give some account. The present has been very handsomely printed at the expense of the Duke of Beaufort, under the careful supervision of Mr. Baker, and the impression is limited to one hundred copies.

Its contents resemble those of the Diaries of Richard Symonds which have been printed for the Camden Society. Symonds was a cavalier in the army of Charles the First, who during his marches, and in the intervals of the dangers and fatigues of active service, still pursued the bent of the taste he had acquired for gentilitial and armorial records by visiting the churches and mansions that lay in his way, and making notes of their memorials, whether inscribed in letters or in heraldic symbols.

Thomas Dineley, who accompanied the official progress which the Duke of Beaufort, as Lord President of Wales, made through the Principality in 1684, pursued a similar course, making the best use of the opportunity that more peaceful journey afforded him. Both works, in like manner, have two claims to attention, the one his-

torical, the other gentilitial; and though in the former respect the
Diary of Symonds may be considered as the more important from its
relation to the incidents of a great civil contest, yet that of Dineley
is also of a certain historical value, as showing not only that the Lord
President of Wales occasionally made a personal survey of his territory (as was customary with the Lord Lieutenant or Deputy of
Ireland), but also with what state and to what purposes he made it—
which seem to have been, principally, reviewing the militia, and
keeping up a loyal and political interest in the corporations.

The title of Lord President originated with a Council of which this
officer was the head, being appointed for the government of the Principality, in place of the ancient Lords Marchers.   That Council was not
constituted until the 17th Hen. VII. 1502.   It has sometimes been
supposed that at an earlier period John Alcock, Bishop of Ely, occupied
this position; because when Prince Edward, the son of King Edward
the Fourth, together with his uncle and governor Earl Rivers, were
sent to reside at Ludlow, Bishop Alcock accompanied them as their
chief councillor.[1]   That residence, however, must have been brief and
temporary.

WILLIAM SMYTH, Bishop of Lincoln (the founder of Brazenose), is
called " the first Lord President," by Humphrey Lloyd, in his History
of Wales; and his portrait at Brazenose College is inscribed PRIMVS
WALLIÆ PRÆSES.   He is stated to have accompanied Arthur Prince of
Wales to Ludlow, when that Prince went thither shortly after his
marriage in 1502, and upon the Prince's decease within a few months
he continued Lord President until his own death in 1513.[2]

The four next Lord Presidents were also Bishops.

2. JEFFREY BLYTH, Bp. of Coventry and Lichfield, appointed in 1513.

3. JOHN VOYSEY, Bishop of Exeter, appointed 1525.

4. ROWLAND LEE, Bishop of Coventry and Lichfield, appointed 1535.
During his time the principality of Wales was united to the kingdom

[1] Alcock was rather President of the King's Council, as well as Lord Chancellor.
He was so styled in the window of Little Malvern Church—" quondam Cancellarii
Angliæ, et Presidentis Concilii Edwardi Regis Quarti."

[2] The Council of the North, whose seat of government was York, was not established until 1526, when Henry VIII. sent thither his natural son Henry FitzRoy,
Duke of Richmond and Somerset, in the capacity of General Warden of the Marches
towards Scotland.   In the absence of any other male issue, it is certain that King
Henry had then some intention to make the Duke of Richmond his heir to the Crown,
though he did not exactly choose to place him in the definite position of a Prince of
Wales, because his hope of having a legitimate son, though long protracted, was not
abandoned.

of England by act of parliament. He died in 1543, and was buried at Shrewsbury.

5. RICHARD SAMPSON, Bishop of Coventry and Lichfield, succeeded Bishop Lee, and held the office until the second year of Edward VI., when he was removed.

6. JOHN DUDLEY, DUKE OF NORTHUMBERLAND, is then said to have held the office for a short time, but without visiting the seat of government; and he soon relinquished it to

7. WILLIAM HERBERT, EARL OF PEMBROKE, who held it until the King's death.

8. On the accession of Queen Mary, she returned to the former practice in Catholic times of appointing a Bishop to this office, in the person of NICHOLAS HEATH, Bishop of Worcester, who resigned in 1556.

The Earl of Pembroke was reappointed for a second time from 1556 to 1558; but Mary afterwards found another Bishop for the office in the person of

9. GILBERT BOURNE, Bishop of Bath and Wells, who was Lord President for the remainder of her reign.[1]

10. JOHN LORD WILLIAMS of Thame was appointed by Queen Elizabeth, and died in office at Ludlow on the 14th Oct. 1559.

11. Sir HENRY SYDNEY, K.G., was appointed in 1560, and held the office for six and twenty years. For a portion of that time he was also Lord Deputy of Ireland, and during his absence Whitgift, then Bishop of Worcester, was appointed Vice-President of Wales. Sir Henry Sydney died at Ludlow on the 5th of May, 1586.

12. HENRY HERBERT, second EARL OF PEMBROKE, was the next President, and so continued until his death in 1601. The Instructions given to him in 1586 are in the Lansdowne MSS. No. 49, art. 62.

13. EDWARD LORD ZOUCHE was appointed in 1602, and continued in office until 1606.

14. RALPH LORD EURE succeeded in 1607, and gave way to

15. THOMAS LORD GERARD, of Gerards Bromley, who was appointed March 7, 1616-17. He held the office for a very short time.

16. WILLIAM LORD COMPTON was appointed in 1617, and the Instructions given him are printed in Rymer's *Fœdera*, &c. He was created Earl of Northampton in 1618, and held this office until his death in 1630.

For the next two years the office was apparently vacant. Its duties were performed by the Lord Chief Justice, Sir John Bridgeman,

---

[1] His patent of appointment is in Cotton MS. Vitellius, C. I. fol. 173.

ancestor of the Earls of Bradford. He died in 1636, and was buried in Ludlow Church, where he has a monument.

17. JOHN EGERTON, EARL OF BRIDGEWATER, was appointed Lord President in 1633: and the Instructions issued to him also are in Rymer's collection. In the following year the memorable performance took place at Ludlow Castle of Milton's Masque of Comus. The Earl is believed to have nominally retained the office until his death in 1649 : but the Council itself "fell to pieces by reason of the civil wars,"[1] and it has been said that the King superseded the Earl by nominating his nephew Prince Rupert.[2] The Prince's commission was really as Captain-General of his Majesty's forces in Shropshire and North Wales, as that of the Marquess of Worcester was to be his Captain-General in South Wales and Monmouthshire.

18. After the Restoration, Charles the Second conferred this office upon RICHARD VAUGHAN, EARL OF CARBERY, extracts from whose Instructions are appended to the volume before us. The appointment of his secretary Samuel Butler to be Steward of the Court at Ludlow connects another eminent poet with the history of the castle, where the early cantos of Hudibras were composed. The Earl of Carbery survived until 1713; but he relinquished his office long before to

19. HENRY SOMERSET, MARQUESS OF WORCESTER, who was appointed in 1672, and created DUKE OF BEAUFORT ten years later. It is his stately progress in 1684 that has directed our attention to this subject ; and on the 23rd of August, 1686, he had the honour to receive his sovereign James II. at Ludlow Castle. The Revolution appears to have unseated him, together with his royal master, whose measures he had promoted with the hereditary loyalty of his race : and, though one more Lord President was nominated in the person of

20. CHARLES GERARD, EARL OF MACCLESFIELD, that appointment was probably only a preliminary to the extinction of the office; for in 1689 the Court of Marches was abolished by Act of Parliament (1 Will. & Mar. cap. 27,) as an institution which had operated too favourably in aid of arbitrary power.

[1] MSS. Salusbury of Erbistock, quoted in Parry's *Royal Visits and Progresses to Wales*, 4to. 1851, p. 335.

[2] Mr. Baker has appended to his volume, p. 272, the appointment of Henry Lord Marquis of Worcester to be President, " in as large, ample and beneficial manner &c. as Richard Lord Vaughan, Earle of Carbery, William Earle of Northampton, John Earle of Bridgewater, *our dear Cousin Prince Rupert*, or either of them, or any other person, formerly enjoyed &c. the same." We do not however regard this inexact enumeration of the former occupants of the office as decisive evidence.

We have drawn out this prefatory list of the twenty Lords President of Wales; because we think they are not readily to be found.[1]

Lord Macaulay, when noticing [2] the stately household and princely style of living of the first Duke of Beaufort, has alluded to the progress of 1684, as if it was an ordinary practice of the Lords President, and frequently repeated. We have no means of judging how far that was the fact; but it appears that Lord Macaulay founded his remark upon what he had gathered from the *London Gazette* regarding the Duke's perlustration of the principality in the year 1684; which, it seems to us, was rather an extraordinary measure, undertaken principally for political ends, and with the view of strengthening the dwindling loyalty of Welshmen towards the house of Stuart. During the journey his sole ostensible business seems to have been to review the militia of the several counties, and to receive the ovations of the corporations, one of which (Cardiff) is said to have surrendered to him its charter with very suspicious alacrity.

The Duke started from Chelsea on the 14th of July; rested the first night at Henley, the second at Chippen-Norton, and on the third at Worcester, having been met at Pershore by the Mayor, Sheriff, Dean, and many of the most eminent citizens of Worcester, who conducted him with all imaginable respect to the Bishop's palace. On the 17th, towards the evening, he arrived at Ludlow, where all the officers of his

---

[1] Only a few of the more prominent names are noticed by Mr. Thomas Wright, in his *History of Ludlow*, 8vo. 1852. We have extracted them from the curious and handsome volume entitled *Documents connected with the History of Ludlow and Lords Marchers*, 4to. 1841, a compilation formed by the Hon. R. H. Clive from the collections of T. F. Dovaston, Esq. and the Rev. J. B. Blakeway, and MSS. in the British Museum, with the assistance of Mr. John Martin and Mr. Thomas Moule, the author of the *Bibliotheca Heraldica*, by whose aid the arms of the Lord Presidents were drawn and blasoned, and a long series of arms and inscriptions in the castle and the Bull Inn at Ludlow fully described.

[2] History of England, 12mo. 1860, ii. 172. Lord Macaulay states that the Duke was Lord Lieutenant of *four* English counties. He was Lord Lieutenant of Gloucestershire, Herefordshire, and Monmouthshire. [See note hereafter, in p. 288.] The authors of the *History of Shrewsbury* (Owen and Blakeway), 1825, imagined that the Duke's progress was an inaugural one, making this remark : " He had held this distinguished office in an earlier part of the reign of Charles II. and appears to have been reappointed in this year (1684); on which occasion he made a tour through his jurisdiction. Hence the Peerages are to be corrected which attribute his second appointment to James II." It is true that Collins states that the Duke was by James II. made Lord President of Wales, quoting as authority *Bill. Signat.* 1 Jas. II.; and it thereby appears that he received a fresh appointment at the commencement of the new reign, though his tenure of the office was continuous.

Presidency waited his Grace's coming, and the order in which he made his solemn entry was thus marshalled :—[1]

First. The Quartermaster for ye Progress.

2. Four Sumpturemen in livery, well mounted, leading their baggage, covered with fair sumpture-cloaths of fine blew cloth, diversified and embroidered with the coat-armor of his Grace.

3rdly. Three helpers belonging to the stables, in livery, leading horses to supply accidents and defects of ye coach cavalry.

4thly. His Grace's Gentleman of the Horse, —— Lowe, Esq. well mounted and equipped.

5thly. Six Pages, in rich liveries, following him, 2 & 2.

6thly. Seven Grooms, in his Grace's livery, each with a led horse caparisoned, 3 stone and 4 gueldings, with stately sadles and houises, richly embroidered and embossed with gold and silver, some carrying a Portcullis subscrib'd with this motto in an escrowle, ALTERA SECURITAS, in high raised work, also of gold and silver.

. 7. His Grace's 4 Trumpeters, in very rich coats, having for badge his Grace's cypher in gold, under a ducall crown, on their backs and breasts, each with a silver trumpet, with gold and silver strings and tazzels, and crimson flowr'd damask banners, embroidered with ye coat armour of his Grace the Duke of Beaufort, viz. the souveraigne ensignes of France & England quarterly, with a bordure gobonated pearl and saphire, all within a garter, with his Grace's motto in a compartment,— MUTARE VEL TIMERE SPERNO.

8thly. Henry Chivers, Esq. Lieut.-Colonel of the Militia Foot in the county of Wilts, richly equipp'd, who led the cavalcade of his Grace's gentlemen, officers, and servants of his family.

9. Two Gentlemen at large.

10. The Yeoman of his Grace's Wine-cellar, Thomas Parson, gent. and Thomas Kemis, gent. Grome of the Chamber, in a breast.

11. The Cooks.

12. Mr. Smith and Mr. Nichols, a Master of Musick and Harper to his Grace.

13. Mr. Aldred and the Mareschall or Farier of ye Progress.

14. —— Wainman, gent. Clerk of the Kitchin, and —— Spiller, gent. in a breast, well mounted.

15. Captain Spalding and the Reverend his Grace's Chaplain.

16. The Steward of the House, and Steward outward.

17. Henry Crow, esq. his Grace's Secretary, and —— Harecourt, esq. his Grace's Sollicitor.

18. Mr. Lockwood and Mons. Claud, of his Grace's Chamber.

19. Mr. Rose and Mr. Blackmore.

20. Captain Lloyd and [William] Wolsley, esq. Steward of the Castle of Ludlow, Mustermaster of the county of Gloucester, and Governor of Chepstow Castle in Monmouthshire.

21. The Sergeant with ye Mace, Mr. Winwood with the White Rod, —— with ye Tipstaff, and other officers of the Court of Ludlow, as pursivants, &c.

---

[1] A copy of this procession has been previously published in Mr. Clive's volume, pp. 185—187, and in the *History of Shrewsbury*, but there are several *lacunæ* in it.

22. His Grace the Duke of Beaufort, &c. Lord President of Wales, himself in glorious equippage.

23. The Right Honourable Charles Earle of Worcester, and Sir John Talbot the High Sheriff of the county of Salop, with the Shropshire gentry, and a great number of the loyall gentlemen of the neighbouring counties.

These were followed by his Grace's chariot, and two other coaches and six horses each, wherein was her Grace the Lady Duchess of Beaufort, ye Countess of Worcester, ye most noble ladys her daughters, with their woemen, and with a greate retinue rideing by.

The cavalcade was received at the gate of Ludlow by the Bailiffs and Corporation; and "in the principall part of the town, neer ye high cross and publicque fountaine, his Grace was presented by them with a neat banquet of sweetmeats, consisting of half a dozen marchpanes, and wines."

The next day, being Friday, July 18, 1684, Sir Edward Herbert, Chief Justice of Chester, and all the judges and officers of the Court, waited on the Duke to the Chappel; after which his Grace, in his rich robes of Presidency, walked to the Court of Ludlow, where, the Chief Justice having given the charge, the rest of the forenoon was spent in hearing of causes, his Grace being upon the bench; which done, all the company was again enterteined at a magnificent dinner at the Castle, each person contending to outdo the other in manifestation of their loyaltie to his Majesty and due respect to his Grace.

Leaving Ludlow on the 19th, the Duke of Beaufort arrived that evening at the castle of Powis, commonly called Red Castle, having passed on the way in state through the town of Bishop's Castle, where he was welcomed by the corporation, and "an handsome banquett was lodged for his Grace at ye Palm-house[1] belonging to their church."

On entering the county of Montgomery, the Lord President was received by its militia, consisting of four companies of foot, with white colours flying, and one troop of horse. Their standard of damask carried a dexter arm, armed proper, and holding a heart gules, with this motto on an escrowle, PRO REGE, and tassels of gold silk and silver.

On Monday the 21st the Duke proceeded from Red Castle to Chirk, in Denbighshire, and at the confines of the two counties the Mont.. gomeryshire troop was relieved by the Militia of Denbigh and a great

---

[1] This term is new to us, but it appears to be synonymous with what architectural antiquaries now generally term a lych-gate. At p. 103, where Dineley gives a sketch of the church of Hay, he remarks, "The ascent to the Palmer's house whereof, marked A, is rocky." It is represented in the sketch as a shed covering the stile and gate in the churchyard wall. Perhaps in both these passages the true meaning is *palmer house*, a shelter for wandering palmers or pilgrims. The guild of the Palmers of Ludlow, founded temp. Edw. III. was the principal corporation of that town, and maintained the grammar-school: see Wright's Ludlow, p. 206.

number of gentry of that shire, who conducted him to Chirk castle, where a very magnificent and splendid entertainment was prepared by the owner, Sir Richard Middleton, Bart.

The like reception welcomed him elsewhere. On the 22nd he was entertained by Sir John Wynn, at Wynnstay, being there met  by the Bishop of St. Asaph (Dr. William Lloyd), and several knights and gentlemen of that. and the adjacent counties; on the 23rd by the magistracy of Wrexham; on the evening of the same day and during the 24th by Sir Roger Mostyn, at Mostyn; on the 25th at Conway; and on the 26th at Beaumaris in Anglesey. Here he was nobly entertained by the Lord Bulkeley, and, the next day being Sunday, attending service twice at Beaumaris church, was after evening prayers " collation'd according to his quality " at a house half a mile out of the town, which was the residence of the Lord Bulkeley's eldest son, the Captain of the County Horse; whose standard of crimson flowered damask was as is represented in the margin, with gold and silk fringe and tazzells. The militia of this county consisted of one troop of horse, and four companies of foot; the Beaumaris company having red colours with a red cross in the canton, and the other three blue colours.

On Monday the 28th the Duke came to Gwydir, a house that had been acquired by the Lord Willoughby of Parham, in marriage with Sir Richard Wynn's daughter and heir. Lord and Lady Willoughby were then from home; but their mansion accommodated " his sayd Grace, the Lord of Worcester, Lord Bulkeley, Sir John Talbot, and severall of the gentry of the neighbouring countyes."

Leaving Gwydir, on the following day, the Duke proceeded to Rhiwlas, about a mile short of Bala in Merionethshire. On his way thither he was met by its owner, Colonel Price, and some of the loyal gentlemen of that county; and at a convenient place on the way their party of horse was drawn up to attend his Grace, being well equipped. Advancing forward, in the avenue leading to Rhiwlas, the foot was found drawn in a line, with their officers in proper station. One of Dineley's neat sketches shows this military reception, as well as the aspect of the old mansion.

RHIWLAS, CO. MERIONETH.

The militia of this county consisted of one small troop of horse, and two companies of foot. The standard of the former bore this motto, in letters of gold upon silk :—

NON PALMA SINE PULVERE.

In Rhywlas hall, carved in the timber, is this,—

BYDB. DDADTHOLUDTRA VYCHYNY
MEDDIANTVAL IB OYSDORYT
PANE LYCH.

Which was explained to me—

Be Hospitable, as long as you are in possession of this House; so you leave somewhat behind you.

Another timber-beam carrieth,—

ANNO REMYNI REGINE ELIZARETHN VN-
DECCMO SEXTO : DEVM TIME.

This last date I believe was design'd for as good Latin as the advice in the rear.

Over ye Porch and principall entry is the Arms of England and France quarterly, subscribed IKRANIA D ELIZABETH. *ideo quære.*

The carver appears to have been no scholar, and to have blundered alike the Latin and his own language. We think, however, that the last inscription was clearly intended for *Insignia dominæ Elizabethæ:*

and the other in Latin is equally obvious for the 11th year of the Queen's reign, 1569. The Welsh should probably be read—

> Bydd dda d'th olud tra v'ych yn y
> meddiant, val y bo ysdôr y't
> pan elych.

Of which the following is the true version:

" Do good with thy wealth while thou possessest it; that there may be store [laid up] for thee when thou departest."

On the 30th the Lord President was at Lloydyarth, the seat of a gentleman named Vaughan, where a noble entertainment was provided, with good standing and provisions for above 90 horse: and from that place he began to retrace his steps. Having met the Duchess and ladies again at Powis Castle on the 31st, he stayed there during the next day; and on the 2nd of August, on his road to Ludlow, paid a somewhat unexpected visit to the town of Shrewsbury.

Yett his Grace was mett by a large troop of the most considerable and loyall gentlemen of Shropshire who were within notice; when, and at his Grace's arrivall, the Mayor of Shrewsbury and the Aldermen his bretheren waited upon him in their formalities, and the Town presented him with twenty dozen bottles of wine, and twenty chargers of sweetmeats. After dinner his Grace, accompanied with my Lord of Worcester, Sir John Talbot, and all the Gentlemen, visited the Schools, the Library, and the Castle; during which solemnity the people expressed their joy by ringing of the bells of ye severall churches of this town.

We have now followed the progress of the Lord President through the six counties of North Wales, and, without noticing so fully the particulars of his reception in the southern counties, which are very similar to those already detailed, it will be sufficient to say that he was entertained in Radnorshire at Presteign, on the 4th of August; on the 5th, having crossed the river Wye at Whitney Ford or Ferry, in his chariot, at the castle of Hay in Brecknockshire; and at the priory of Brecknock, where he stayed two nights, and in which town the author, among other gentlemen of the Duke's retinue, was admitted a Burgess; and on the 7th at " the Earl of Carberrie's famous seat called Golden Grove," having passed through the town of Llandinonaure, where, " for about an English mile, the road and streets were strewed with rushes, to receive him."

Among other remarkes at Golden Grove are seen ye Drinking Horn above exhibited, beautified with silver artifice, being the first vessell Henry Tudor Earle of Richmond, King of England (by the name of Henry VII.), drank out of after his landing at Milford Haven in Pembrokeshire, in order to the marrying the Lady Elizabeth and deposing Richard III.

This Horn was presented by himself to this noble family, now Earles of Carbery, where it hath remained ever since, and is kept among the noble Earles choicest raritys.   The foot is of silver in form of a mount, upon which stand a Dragon and Greyhound of the same mettall, in imitation of the Supporters of the Royall Arms of Henry VII. which are drawn below, shewing the dexter side a Red Dragon, the ensigne of Cadwalader the last King of the Britains, from whom by a male line

he derives his pedigree (according to the ·laborious Sandford's *Genealogy of Kings*, p. 434); and on the sinister· side a Greyhound argent, collared gules, which he gave in right of his wife the Queen Elizabeth of York, descended from the Nevils by Anne her grandmother, the daughter of Ralph Nevill Earle of Westmoreland, and wife of Richard Duke of York.   The Portcullis upon the lipping or rim of the mouth is in token of his descent through his mother from the noble family of the Beauforts.   To this devise on his mausole or royal sepulture at Westminster is added this motto—

ALTERA SECURITAS,

as who should say, As a Portcullis is a further security to a gate, so his [royal descent from the House of Lancaster through his] Mother corroborated his other titles.   From this devise he instituted a Pursivant at Armes, and named him Portcullis; as from the leading supporter the Red Dragon had been instituted by him also the Pursivant called Rouge Dragon.

The Roses on the rim I suppose to speake the Union of the two Houses, Lancaster and York, by his marriage.

Mr. Dineley inlarges further both on the heraldic and mystic import of this Horn, concluding with the additional information that its substance " is a fair horne of a beefe, a POCULUM CHARITATIS, famous for having seized the head of many a bold Britain." Whatever may have been its exploits in that respect, it is certainly a very interesting as well as beautiful piece of ancient plate, and very probably attributed correctly to the time of Henry VII.; though we may presume it was rather made during his reign, than in readiness for his first draught after landing at Milford Haven. We should be glad to learn whether it is still preserved at Golden Grove or elsewhere.

With regard to the greyhound adopted as a supporter by our Tudor sovereigns, it has been remarked by Mr. Willement,[1] that Sandford is probably mistaken in deriving it from the family of Neville; but that it properly belonged to the house of Beaufort. In the chapel of Canterbury Cathedral, in which the monument of John Earl of Somerset stands, there was formerly in the window his arms, supported on the' dexter side by a white greyhound, and on the sinister side by a white hind, the latter being the well known "beast" of his Countess the heiress of the Holands Earls of Kent. The same arms and animals yet remain on the ceiling of the same chapel, and the feet of the Earl's sepulchral effigy rest on a greyhound. On a chimney-piece erected by Bishop Courtenay, in the palace at Exeter, the arms of King Henry the Fourth were supported on both sides by greyhounds.

From Golden Grove the Duke of Beaufort journeyed forward, on the 8th of August, to Carmarthen, reviewing the militia of that county at Aberguilly, and on the next day that of Cardiganshire at Castle Emlyn. On Monday the 11th, entering Pembrokeshire, he came to Haverfordwest; and on the following day was "treated at sea" on board a yacht, in which he surveyed the historic bay of Milford Haven. On the 13th he was nobly entertained at dinner by Sir Erasmus Philips, at Picton Castle, and well collationed on the way by Wogan of Bolston. On the 15th he dined at Mudlescombe; and in the evening reached Swansea in Glamorganshire. On Saturday the 16th he was welcomed by Sir Edward Mansell, at Margam. In his progress of the 18th he

---

[1] *Regal Heraldry*, p. 59.

made a halt in the town of Cowbridge, and afterwards went out of his way to Cardiff, to receive a surrender of the charter of that borough, a ceremony said to have been made not only voluntarily, but with great manifestations of joy.   Probably to this medallion there was a reverse, to be read only in the next reign.   On the same evening the Duke arrived at the castle of Ruperra, part of the company halting at Keven-mably, both houses of Sir Charles Kemeys.

Whose loyall father had in the Standard belonging to his own troop this device and inscription in the British language : Issuing out of a cloud a dexter arm arm'd, holding a broad sword drawn proper, subscribed in an escrowle, which was thus explain'd to me,

Oes dalla hwn	If this holds
Gwaerpen crwn.	woe to the Roundheads !

On Tuesday the 19th, on the confines of Monmouthshire, the Duke was met by the troop of that county, commanded by his son Charles Earl of Worcester;[1] and was collationed in the market-town of New-port, where the streets were strewed with flowers and sweet herbs, giving our author the opportunity of quoting (as he was very fond of doing) one of the classic poets —

Floribus apricis et multicoloribus herbis.--MARTIAL.

The Lord President also made another halt at the town of Usk ; and in the evening arrived at Monmouth.   He lodged in the neigh-bouring mansion of Troy, the residence of his son the Earl of Wor-cester.   This " Progress and visitation of his commands in Wales " is now finished; and on the 21st of August he left Troy for his own seat at Badminton in Gloucestershire.

On resuming our notice of this interesting volume we shall direct our attention in the first place to the personal history of its author Thomas Dineley, and to some account of his Manuscript Collections; and then endeavour to estimate the value of the Church notes and other genealogical and antiquarian memoranda which he has handed down to us.

---

[1] It appears that he did not assume the designation of Marquess.

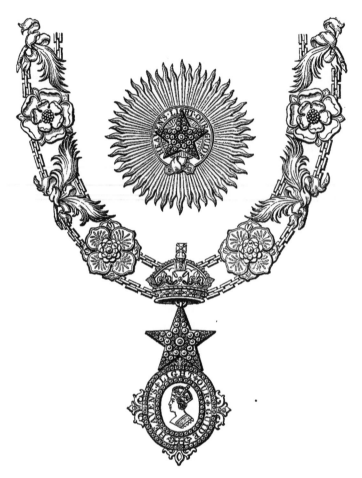

INSIGNIA OF THE STAR OF INDIA: FROM BURKE'S PEERAGE AND BARONETAGE.

PARSEE ARMORY IN BRITISH INDIA.

In his new edition of *Heraldry Historical and Popular* Mr. Boutell has given some engraved examples of armorial coats recently granted (we understand within these three years) by the College of Arms to natives of India, subjects of Her Majesty, which we are kindly permitted to extract from that work. They are interesting as specimens of the present taste in heraldic composition in this country, and further, when regarded as proofs of the cordiality with which the gentlemen of India are ready to adopt the ancient usages of the Imperial sway which they now acknowledge.

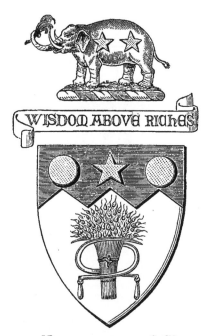

Mr. MUNGULDASS NUTHOOBHOY, of Girgaum House, Bombay, is a banker in that city. He bears, Argent, a garb of rice, environed by two sickles interlaced, all proper; on a chief indented azure, between two bezants, a mullet or. Crest,—On a. mound vert an elephant statant, holding in his trunk a palmbranch, all proper, charged on his side with two mullets in fess or. The lower portion of this heraldic composition intimates that the prosperity of the grantee has arisen from his father and himself having been laborious agriculturists: the bezants on the chief allude to his present profession as a banker; whilst the golden mullet or "Star of India" indicates the sphere of his exertions. It will be observed that in the insignia of the Order of the Star of India, the Star is in the form—not of an heraldic Estoile, but of a Mullet, covered with diamonds.

Mr. Cowasjee Jehangier bears, Azure, within an orle of
eight mullets, the sun in splendour or; on a canton argent the
rose of England and the lotus of India in saltire proper. Crest,—
On a mound vert, a low pillar, the base and capital masoned,
flames of fire issuing therefrom, all proper. The allusions in this
composition refer especially to the religion of the Parsees; including the crest, which seems to be the nearest heraldic approach
to a fire-altar. The rose and lotus united on the canton evidently typify the intimate union of England and India.[1]

[1] With the same feeling, the lotus and rose have also been adopted in a design which
Mr. Boutell has lately furnished for the Font of Bombay Cathedral. It resembles the

241

A·GOOD·CONSCIENCE·IS·A·SURE·DEFENCE·

Mr. CURZETJEE FURDOONJEE PARUK, also of Bombay, bears, Argent, a chevron gules between three ancient galleys sable; on a chief azure, between two estoiles, the sun in splen-

Norman style, in correspondence with the architecture of the church; the bowl is is supported by low clustered columns, the capitals of which are formed of the rose and lotus; a band of lotus-leaves encircles the base of the bowl; whilst another, of the lily of the valley, above, typifies baptismal innocence and also suggests the figurative image of the Saviour—"the Rose of Sharon and the Lily of the Valley." On the bowl are medallion bas-reliefs of the Baptism of our Lord, and that of the Ethiopian, the monogram IHS. and the date 1864. This font is of the finest Caen stone, the shafts being of Serpentine and Devon marbles. The plinth and steps have been prepared at Bombay in black basalt; but the other portions have been executed in London by Mr. James Forsyth. This font, which has been greatly admired as a fine specimen of modern architectural sculpture of the highest order, is of full cathedral proportions, and is the gift of an English gentleman long resident at Bombay, where he is deservedly held in great esteem.

dour or. Crest,—On a mound vert, a winged lion passant or, charged on the shoulder with an estoile azure, and behind him a palm-tree proper. Here again the devices have Parsee allusions: the galleys intimating the great Zoroastrian emigration in ancient days from Persia to Hindustan; and the winged lion, a well-known Persian emblem, is brought, in the crest, under the protecting shade of the Indian palm.

The gentlemen to whom these grants have been made are, to use their own expression, Zoroastrians: and the two latter have evidently taken a pride in selecting such armorial symbols as might typify their ancient descent, and commemorate the faith of their forefathers.

The two first-named are Fellows of the University of Bombay, and all are magistrates, and men of munificent liberality. One of the latest of the princely public gifts that these Parsee gentlemen delight in making, is a fountain to be placed in the centre of the new " Victoria and Albert Gardens " at Bombay. This fountain will cost £4,000, and it is the gift of Mr. Cursetjee Furdoonjee Paruk. It will bear the name of the " Frere Fountain," after Sir Bartle Frere, the present Governor of Bombay. The design, with the general superintendence of the execution of this important work, has been entrusted, through Dr. G. Birdwood of Bombay, to Mr. Boutell, who has called to his aid Mr. R. Norman Shaw, Mr. James Forsyth, and Mr. T. Woolner, the last named gentleman having undertaken a medallion portrait of Sir Bartle Frere. Mr. Forsyth, the sculptor, has made such progress with this fountain that it will be completed in the course of the present year.

The mottoes, which appear in the engravings, were selected by the grantees themselves, and by their desire are expressed in the English language. We cannot quite approve of a motto being placed, in the first engraving, *between* the Crest and the Shield. To place mottoes *above* the Crest is a recognised practice, particularly in Scotish heraldry, and in that way there are many instances of mottoes being attached both to the Arms and the Crest ; but, as there is here only one motto, it should be placed, as usual, below the shield.

These Indian coats are certainly more strictly heraldic than that of Sir Jamsetjee Jejeebhoy, whose father, the very munificent merchant, also of Bombay, was knighted in 1842, and created a Baronet in 1857. His armorial bearings, which are represented in the annexed vignette, are a pictorial landscape. They are blasoned as, Azure, a sun rising above a representation of Ghautz (a mountain near Bombay) in base, and in chief two bees volant, all proper. Crest,—A mount vert, thereon a peacock, amidst wheat, and in the beak an ear of wheat, all proper. Motto, By INDUSTRY AND LIBERALITY.

We believe that these are not all the coats that have been granted to natives of India ; but we have not hitherto met with the description or representation of any others.

IRISH FAMILY HISTORY.

By Richard F. Cronnelly.

(*Continued from p.* 92.)

4. O'Dugan.—The O'Dugans derived their descent and surname from Dubhagain, of the race of Soghan Salbhuidhe, *i. e.* of the Yellow Heel, son of Fiacha Aruidhe, prince of Ulidia. This Soghan settled, in the third century, in the country which now forms the barony of Tiaquin, in the county of Galway, and gave name to the families and lands subsequently known as the six Soghans, or Sodhans, the head chief of which was O'Mannion. The O'Dugans became the hereditary bards and historiographers of the O'Kellys, princes of Hy-Many, in the counties of Galway and Roscommon; and one of them was John More O'Dugan, author of a valuable poem on the Irish chiefs of the fourteenth century, who died in 1372, at the Abbey of St. John's of Rinndun, or Randown, on the Shannon. His family were the compilers of the Book of Hy-Many, "which is supposed to be in the collection of some English collector of rare books and manuscripts."

Of the same stock as the O'Dugans were the O'Morans, O'Lennans, and O'Casans of Sodan; but our author has found neither pedigrees nor memorials of them. We have still in London a prosperous family of Dowbiggin, which sounds to our English ears even nearer to the original Dubhagain than O'Dugan itself.

5. M'Gowan.—The MacGaibhnions were not only converted into the Anglicised orthography of M'Gowan, but directly translated into Smith. Felan M'an-Gowan was one of the authors of the Book of Hy-Many. Tadg Mac-an-Gowan was chief historiographer to the O'Connors towards the close of the fourteenth century; and at a much earlier date Angus the Culdee, Mac-an-Gowan, wrote lives of the Irish Saints and other treatises, in the eighth century. Of this race more learned men are enumerated; and they have a worthy modern representative in James Huband Smith, esq. of Dublin, M.A. and M.R.I.A.

6. MacWard.—The Mac-an-Bairds, or MacWards, were of the like literary class. They were hereditary bards to the O'Donnells, princes of Tirconel, and the O'Kellys, lords of Hy-Many, in Galway

and Roscommon; and the names of many of the race are com-memorated for that reason by the Four Masters.

7. M'Scanlan.—A family of note in Ulidia, or Down.

8. O'Kenny.—Also of Ulidia and Meath ; a different race from those of Galway and Roscommon.

9. O'Lawlor.—Formerly princes of Ulidia, of whom there are still several respectable families in the county of Tipperary, Queen's County, and county of Kildare, one of the chief representatives being Denis Shine Lawlor, esq. J.P. of Kerry.

10. O'Lynch.—The chiefs of Del-Araidhe, in Ulidia, and desig-nated by O'Dugan as

" The O'Loingsidhs of the haughty champions."

There were other O'Lynches in Mayo and Sligo, and others again in Tipperary.

11. O'Mainin, or O'Mannion.—Before mentioned under O'Dugan. Sometimes Anglicised into Manning.

12. Maginn.—Chiefly distinguished in the ecclesiastical annals of Dromore.

13. MacColreavy.—The descendants of Giolla Riabhach, twenty-seventh in descent from Conal Cearnach ; who was seventh from Roderick Mor. Their name has been further abridged into Macgreevy, M'Revy, and Gray ; but several respectable families of M'Colreavy are still existing in the counties of Roscommon, Leitrim, and Longford.

14. M'Cartan.—Cinel Faghartaigh was the tribe name of the M'Cartans, and also the name given to the district they inhabited. They are thus eulogized by the bard O'Dugan :

" To M'Cartan by charter belongs
The intelligent Cinel Faghartaigh ;
They are heroes who have been liberal to clerics,
The maintainers of hospitality are they."

They were descended from Artan, who was the son of Fahartaigh, of the race of Conal Cearnach. They continued a powerful family in Ulidia, down to the time of Elizabeth, when Acholy M'Artan, having joined the Earl of Tyrone with 250 horse and some foot, forfeited his estates, and they were granted to English and Scottish settlers.

15. O'Carelon.—The descendants of Cairbhalain, an Ultonian chief in the early part of the eleventh century. In the twelfth century they produced an archbishop of Armagh, and in the next several bishops of Tyrone and Derry. As late as 1542 Hugh O'Carolan was bishop of Clogher. Torlagh O'Carolan, the celebrated harper and bard,

who died in 1738, was born in 1670 at Newtown, in the barony of
Morgallian, co. Meath. The ancient barony of Glen-Dermot was
deserted by the head of the Sept towards the close of the seventeenth
century. He became possessed of a small estate in the co. Antrim.
About the same period several of the name, conforming to the Established Church, changed their name to Carleton. The senior representative of the family, Charles Carolan, Esq., was some years since
living in Abbey Street, Dublin.

16. THE CLAN FERGUS.—Descended from Fergus, son of Rosa Roe,
the fourth son of Roderick the Great. One line, called the Clan Ciar,
were lords of Kerry from Tralee to the Shannon, and for many generations went by the name of the O'Conor Kerry. They were finally
overthrown in the Cromwellian struggle, and Charles the Second in
1666 granted a large portion of their domains to Trinity College. One
of the chief representatives of the family at the present day is the
Commandant of Mantua, Daniel O'Connell O'Connor Kerry, now
Baron O'Connor, an officer high in favour with the Emperor Francis II.

17. Another branch is the CLAN CORC, named from Corc, son of
Fergus. From him descended the O'Conors Corc, whose progenitor
was Conchobhair, or Conor, son of Melaghlin, lord of Corcumroe, who
was slain in West Connaught in 1002. Their decadence is thus
pathetically and poetically told by our author :— ·

"The O'Connors of Corc fell into decay in the early part of the sixteenth century,
and their extensive possessions passed to the Fitzgeralds, Gores, Stackpooles, and
other English families, when the descendants of the Prince of Ullad, and of the
celebrated Meva queen of Connaught, became tillers of the fields of Corcumroe for
alien lords, and dwellers in miserable huts constructed in the shelter of the cloud-
supporting hills from whose gorse-clad slopes and cairn-crowned summits ten
thousand voices proclaimed their ancestors Kings of Cinel Ardga."

18. The O'LOGHLENS BURREN, another branch of the Clan Corc,
were formerly chiefs of Eastern Corcumroe, an extensive territory in
the county of Clare, having a harbour at Burren, in the parish of
Abbey. The present representatives of this Sept are, Sir Colman
M. O'Loghlen, Bart., son of Sir Michael, who was an eminent lawyer
and Master of the Rolls in Ireland, and his cousin, Colman Bryan
O'Loghlen, Esq., sub-inspector of the Irish Constabulary, son of the
late Bryan O'Loghlen, Esq., of Port, co. Clare.

19. The CLAN CONMAC is another tribe, which divides itself into
several branches; and our author notices first of them, O'KIELY of
West Connaught. That family derives its name and descent from
Cadhla, an ancestor in the twenty-fourth generation of Malachy

O'Kiely, who became Archbishop of Tuam in 1630, and was killed in 1645 in defending the town of Sligo from the forces of the Parliament.

"Conumacne Mara, *vulgo* Connemara, was the name given to the descendants of Conmac, son of Fergus, who settled along the western coast of Galway in very remote times. The adjunct *mara*, which signifies 'the sea,' was affixed to the tribe name that this family and their possessions might be distinguished from the inland Conmacne, such as the Conmacne Cuil Talaigh, or the Conmacne of the barony of Kilmain, the Conmacne of Dun-mor, the Conmacne of Magh-Rein, the Conmacne of Cinel Dubhan, &c."

20. M'SHANLEY, a name derived from Seanlaoich, a chieftain of the county of Leitrim, is frequently mentioned by the Irish annalists of the thirteenth, fourteenth, and fifteenth centuries, and maintained an independent position until forfeited by their adherence to James II.

21. The PRIORS of the same clan deduce their descent from the seven sons of Muireasgan Mac Raghnal, Prior of the Abbey of Cloone. They possessed an extensive tract of land in the barony of Carrigallen, co. Leitrim, down to the close of the seventeenth century, and some respectable families of the name are to be met with in that county at the present day.

22. One of the most dominant families of the Conmacne was O'FERRALL, which had its residence at a place now called White Hill, and more anciently Cluain-Bran, *i. e.*, the retreat of Bran O'Ferrall, whence the present name of the parish, Clonborne. The O'Ferralls were lords of Analy, in the county of Longford, and in p. 61 we are presented with a chronological table of their chieftains from 1030 to 1445. The constant state of warfare in which they lived is shown by their quick succession, for they are forty in number, of whom thirteen are stated to have been killed or slain. Nor was that the end of the bloodshed, by any means; for when William fitz John fitz Donal died in 1445, two rival chieftains were elected to succeed him, which led to a long and sanguinary struggle. At length Rossa son of Murtogh, lord of the fort of Longford, was settled in Upper Analy, and became ancestor of the O'Ferrall Buidhe, or the Yellow; whilst Donal Boy obtained Lower Analy, or the country north of Granard, and was progenitor of the O'Ferrall Ban, or the Fair. There were three other branches of some importance, and Mr. Cronnelly presents pedigrees of them all. O'Ferrall of Ballyna has been already mentioned as the present representative of the house of O'More.

23. O'RODDY.—Rodochan, thirty-sixth in descent from Rory the Great, left his name to the O'Rodachans, or O'Rodachaes, which name was Anglicised into Redington and Roddy. Tadg O'Roddy, who was

an excellent antiquary, and died at an advanced age in 1704, was representative of the hereditary Comorbas of St. Caillin, and possessed some very ancient manuscripts and other relics, among which was the *clog-na-righ*, or " bell of the kings," said to have been presented to St. Caillin by St. Columbkill.

The Redingtons of Kilcornan and Dangan, in the county of Galway, are claimed as descendants of the Rodachans; although some have stated them to descend from an English settler during the Protectorate; " but local senachies and tradition agree that they deduce their descent from a scion of the house of Fenagh, in the county of Leitrim, who settled in the parish of Ballinacourty, in the county of Galway, in or about A.D. 1624, and soon afterwards purchased the castle and lands of Cregana, whence his grandson, Thomas Redington, removed to Kilcornan on his marriage with the daughter and heiress of Christopher Burke, of Kilcornan House, the great-grandson of the celebrated Nora-an-Ouver-I-burc. The présent chief of Kilcornan (a minor) is the son of the late Sir Thomas Nicholas Redington, who was the son of Christopher, by his wife Frances, daughter of Henry Dowell, esq. of Cadiz."

24. M'FINVAR, or GAYNOR, as the name is now generally Anglicised. James MacFinvar, who died in 1792, was twenty-second in descent from Fionnbhair, or Finvar, of the race of Fergus M'Roy; and the antient territory of the Sept was the northern half of the barony of Granard. Mr. Cronnelly states that several families of this name are still extant in the counties of Galway, Roscommon, and Leitrim.

25. M'CORMICK, or CORMACK, derived from the house of O'Ferrall, and formerly chief of Corcard, co. Longford. Four bishops are commemorated of this sept—one of Down, one of Ardagh, and two of Raphoe.

26. The M'DORCHYS, Anglicised to Dorchy and Darcy, derive their name from Dubhchain, of the race of Fergus M'Roy. Their country, denominated Cinel Luachain, was co-extensive with the parish of Oughteragh, in the county of Leitrim.

27. MACRAGHNALL, or RANNALL, is a name now generally Anglicised to Reynolds. It is derived from Ragnall, son of Muirceardoig Maol, of the race of Conmac son of Fergus. They were chiefs of Muinter Eolus, otherwise the Conmacne of Magh Rein, a territory comprising the whole country of the present baronies of Mohill, Leitrim, and Carrigallen, co. Leitrim, and the parish of Killoe, co. Longford. In p. 75 Mr. Cronnelly gives a list of twenty chieftains of Muinter Eolus

concerned in the rebellion of 1641. One of them, Henry M'Rannal, of Annaduff, was the progenitor of several persons who have attained considerable notoriety in modern politics. Dr. Reynolds, the friend and fellow-patriot of Theobald Wolf Tone, in consequence of being implicated in the affair of Cockayne and Jackson in 1794, fled to America, and settled in Philadelphia, where he died about 1818. In another line from the same ancestor descended Henry Reynolds, esq. who, by Margaret, daughter of Richard Bulkeley, esq. M.D. of Nenagh, left issue—1. Thomas, born in 1793, Marshal of Dublin ; 2. John, born in 1797, now an alderman of that city, and late Lord Mayor; and 3. Henry Reynolds, esq. born in 1799. Of this Sept also, we are told, but not in what line, descended Thomas Reynolds, a silk-manufacturer of Dublin, who is "commonly called the Informer," because he contributed to the arrest of Lord Edward Fitzgerald in 1798. His political career is related by Mr. Cronnelly at considerable length.

At Lough-Scur, otherwise called Letterfine, resided in 1641 a Humphrey Reynolds, sixth in descent from whom was George Reynolds, esq. who was shot on the lands of Drynaun, near Sheemore, co. Leitrim, on the 16th Oct. 1786, by Mr. Robert Keon of the same county, an attorney, who was executed for that crime on the 16th Feb. 1788. The murdered man was the father of George Nugent Reynolds, esq. of Letterfine, (a very memorable person, as we shall see presently), who died without issue in 1802, leaving two sisters—1. Mary Anne, married first to Colonel Peyton, father of Reynolds Peyton, esq. and grandfather of the present Richard Reynolds Peyton, esq. of Letterfine, and secondly to Capt. Richard Macnamara, brother to the celebrated Major of that name; and 2. Bridget, married to Richard Young Reynolds, esq. of Fort Lodge, co. Cavan.

We must now notice the Appendix which is mentioned in the title-page of Mr. Cronnelly's book, and is entitled "A Paper on the Authorship of *The Exile of Erin*, by a Septuagenarian." It occupies thirty-seven pages, and is a very remarkable piece of literary history, in which one of the most distinguished poets of the last generation is seriously concerned.

The Septuagenarian relates that his memory of the ballad called *The Exile of Erin* carries him back to the Christmas of 1799, and he was then informed that its author was Mr. George Nugent Reynolds of Letterfine, to whom he was personally introduced in the autumn of the following year. Mr. Reynolds left his native country for England in the spring of 1801, and never returned to it; dying in the following year, at Stowe, the mansion of his relative the Marquess of Buckingham.[1]

Towards the close of 1810, the writer was astonished, on opening a new edition of the Poems of Thomas Campbell, to find *The Exile of Erin* there appropriated; and in the following January the circumstance attracted the attention of Thomas Stafford, esq. of Portobello, near Elphin, himself a relative of the deceased Irish bard. He immediately showed the writer a MS. copy which he had received from Reynolds's own hands in Nov. 1799, and it had only two various readings from the copy printed in Campbell's works.

"Mr. Reynolds was a gentleman of such high honour and feeling as to be totally incapable of so weak and disreputable an act as to pass off any other man's composition as his own, or to strut in borrowed plumes. He was besides regardless of literary fame or publicity."

On the other hand, the writer does not hesitate to say of Thomas Campbell, that, not content with the wreaths that already adorned his brow, he was in this case a shameless pilferer. Further proofs are added. Among others, Mrs. Macnamara, a sister of George Nugent Reynolds, makes deposition on oath that, to the best of her recollection, she copied and sang for her brother the song he called *The Exiled Irishman's Lament*, in the year 1792 : he also said that he intended it as a sequel to *Green were the Fields,* which he composed in the same year. This song described the affliction of a peasant turned out of his small farm for political reasons ; that he called *Erin Go Bragh*—the same as Campbell's *Exile of Erin*—was intended to depict the sorrow and sufferings of the same peasant dying on a foreign shore.

[1] How related the writer does not state; but we presume that he was actually second cousin to the Marchioness, as follows:—

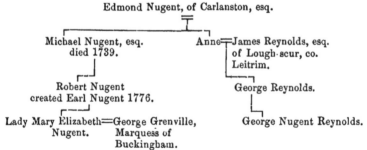

The Marquess of Buckingham, who was Lord Lieutenant of Ireland in 1782 and 1787, assumed the names of Nugent-Temple in 1779, and in 1788 succeeded his father-in-law as Earl Nugent by a special remainder, having been created Marquess of Buckingham in 1784.

Campbell was at last brought to account, but not until 1810. He was then able to deny some of the statements of the story, as it had been incorrectly related in the *Sligo Observer;* and he declared that " I wrote the song of *The Exile of Erin* at Altona, and sent it off immediately to London, where it was published by my friend Mr. Perry in the *Morning Chronicle.*" But this assertion helps rather to convict than to exculpate him. It is true that, at that period, Campbell was a constant contributor to the *Morning Chronicle,* and more than fifty of his songs and poems appeared in its columns, but with the never-failing advertisement that they were " By the Author of *The Pleasures of Hope.*" Mr. Reynolds's song was also printed in the *Morning Chronicle,* in the paper of the 28th Jan. 1801, but *anonymously,* and communicated, it is suggested, rather by some accidental possessor of a MS. copy, in the hope that it might excite a merciful feeling on behalf of the exiled rebels, rather than by the author himself.

There was never a clearer case of literary plagiarism. And what could have induced Campbell to commit it? It was that he had become intimate at Altona with a gentleman named Anthony M'Cann, a native of Dundalk, who had been banished for the part he took in the eventful '98; and, seeing the song in the *Chronicle* (with which his friend Perry supplied him), he took a copy of it, and in a moment of weakness and vanity passed it off as his own composition. The printed copy he probably cut out, and placed with his own compositions.

The discussion is closed by copies of Mr. Reynolds's two songs which we have named, together with some others of a similar character—all fully bearing out by their internal evidence his claim to the authorship of the disputed composition, the style of which, indeed, is different from that usual with Thomas Campbell.

MAGENNIS.—*Addendum to p.* 90.

A correspondent having expressed a wish to ascertain whether Dr. Magennis, whose unfortunate commission of homicide and harsh condemnation was related in the note at p. 90 of the present volume, was actually executed in pursuance of his sentence, we have the satisfaction to state that he was not, having discovered in the *Annual Register,* vol. xxvii. p. 236, the following paragraph : " 1785, July 16th. On Tuesday last Dr. Macginnis, who was convicted of stabbing Mr. Hardy the hatter in Newgate-street, two years ago, was discharged from his confinement in the King's Bench, and set off for the continent."

(To be continued.)

THE COULTHART ARMORIALS.

We are not at all surprised that in forming (in p. 151) our list of the books that during the last twenty years have been infected with the Coulthart plague-spots, we failed at once to discover the whole of them. The parties concerned have been so watchful to inoculate every heraldic or genealogical infant that was about to make its way in the world, that it is well-nigh impossible to detect all the ramifications of this disgraceful epidemic.

We now learn that there was a book published at Edinburgh in the year 1863, entitled *The Scottish Nation : or the Surnames, Families, Literature, Honours, and Biographical History of the People of Scotland*, by WILLIAM ANDERSON, in Three Volumes octavo, in which the Coulthart romance was heralded forth at considerable length in the Appendix, pp. 699-701 ; and recently there has been published (also at Edinburgh, in one volume, 8vo.) another work by the same author, entitled *Genealogy and Surnames : with some Heraldic and Biographical Notices.* In this book, in pp. 37-40, another edition of this monstrous fabrication is presented to the world, accompanied by an engraving of the window at Bolton-le-Gate, with its mendacious armory, and introduced by an amusing comment upon the name, which, so far as we know, is produced for the first time.

> " It would be useless (writes Mr. Anderson) to speculate on its original signification, beyond what is supplied in giving the name of its first recorded (!) possessor in Scotland, though we may add that all the earliest traditions and etymologies regarding it, and also all the armorial bearings belonging to it, refer the derivation to the prowess and valour of a Roman horse-soldier."

So that, after all, " Coulthartus, the Roman lieutenant of Julius Agricola," was so named because his charger was a *hardy colt !*

The compiler of this book, however, on the eve of his publication, appears to have smelt a rat : for the last paragraph of his Preface (dated April 1865) is as follows :—" The author thinks it proper to state that the account of the Coulthart family and Arms, inserted on page 37, rests entirely on the authority of the book quoted on page 38."

It has further been communicated to us that still another work of Sir Bernard Burke's, his *Authorised Arms*, published in 1860,[1] con-

---

[1] The full title of this work is " A Selection of Arms authorised by the Laws of Heraldry. With Annotations by Sir BERNARD BURKE, Ulster King of Arms, Author of *The Peerage and Baronetage, Vicissitudes of Families, &c.*" 8vo.

tains a brief sketch of the Coulthart genealogy, prefixed to an account of the armorial bearings, which opens forth a new chapter in their history. It is there stated that—

> " The Scottish Armorial bearings, viz., A fess between two colts in chief, and one in the base courant (*sic*), are registered in the Lord Lyon Office, Edinburgh ; but those annexed are recorded in the Heralds' College, London :—Arg. a fess between a horse courant in chief, and a water-bouget in base sable. *Crest,* a demi-horse argent, armed and accoutred proper, supporting a flagstaff also proper, therefrom flowing towards the sinister a pennon gules charged with a water-bouget arg. *Motto,* VIRTUTE NON VERBIS."

To which there is this, surely un-" authorised," addition—

> " The chiefs of the family of Coulthart of Coulthart and Collyn have always had *Supporters* by prescriptive right, in accordance with the usage in Scotland, authorised by Mackenzie and other heraldic authorities (! ! !) Those Supporters are Dexter, a war-horse argent, completely armed for the field proper, garnished or ; Sinister, a stag proper, attired and ducally gorged or.

We have now ascertained that the coat commonly displayed by Mr. Coulthart was granted to his father, and registered at the Lyon Office in November 1846—but without Quarterings or Supporters. We understand that, two years earlier, Mr. J. R. Coulthart had made application for leave to bear the coat of four quarters, which appears in Burke's *Heraldic Illustrations*, 1843, with Supporters,[1] but this had been refused ; and in 1849 Mr. Coulthart had a warning or remonstrance addressed to him by the Lyon Office that he was acting illegally in displaying Supporters and Quartered Arms, further than the coat granted to his father in 1846.

About 1857 or 1858 he made application to the English College of Arms for registration of the coat he had obtained at Edinburgh in 1846 ; which, being objected to as being the coat of a family of Colt,[2] was withdrawn.

Mr. Coulthart afterwards obtained of the English College a new coat, by a grant dated on the 17th January, 1859, wherein he was described of Coulthart, co. Wigtown, of Collyn, co. Dumfries, and of

---

[1] Burke's *Heraldic Illustrations*, Plate II. published in 1843, contains the arms of William Coulthart, esq. of Collyn, co. Dumfries, engraved as of four quarters, viz. the assumed arms of Coulthart, Ross, Macknyghte, and Glendonyn (though no names are there assigned to the quarterings,) accompanied by the supporters.

Again in the *Visitation of Seats and Arms,* vol. i. 1851, in plate iv. the same is repeated for John Ross Coulthart, esq. of Croft House, co. Lancaster, the only difference being a slight variation of the form of the cross in the fourth quartering.

[2] The Baronet's family, as we have stated in p. 156.

Ashton under Lyne, co. Lancaster, esquire, and in the commission of
the peace for that county ; without any reference to ancient right or
pretence to arms. The blason of that coat is, as we have already
detailed it from the volume of *Authorised Arms;* but, excepting in·
that work, it seems, from that time to this, to have been altogether
suppressed, and the usurpation of the arms of Colt perseveringly
repeated. Such is the history of "the Armorial Insignia of the Coulthart family."

The SIGILLVM COVLTHARTI (of which we gave an impression in p.
19,) is placed, certainly not without reason, in the title-page of
Popular Genealogists, as a symbol of the clumsy forgeries developed in
the pages of that work. It will be remembered that we made a
passing remark on the unexampled position and wording of the legend:
but the rest of the design is equally misconceived. The caparisons of
the colts are in the style of the last century, and the classical dentil
moulding which surrounds the whole is unlike any pattern of mediæval days.

Another piece of Coulthartiana has found admission into Mr. Anderson's new book, which is very characteristic, and deserves to be held
up for admiration. We see that the genealogical portions of it are
derived from the Coulthart Genealogies of Mr. Knowles's composition,
at p. 15 ; but Mr. Anderson's introductory observations of an etymological complexion appear to be peculiarly appropriate —:

> The surname of MacGuffie, sometimes written MacGuffy, is mostly confined to the
> south-west of Scotland and the north-east of Ireland. The epithet *Guff* in the Scot-
> tish language (*Goff* in the English), is still used as a synonym for fool, so that Mac-
> Guffie may be supposed to mean, as a correspondent suggests, the son of a fool; or,
> taking the terminal syllable of *og* or *oig* into account, as in the following name, the
> son of youthful folly. The name, however, has neither a Scotch nor an English
> derivation, being purely Celtic and Gallovidian, whatever may be its meaning.
>
> It is a name of frequent occurrence in Galloway, and there was a Colonel John
> MacGuffie, of Cubbicks, in the stewartry of Kirkcudbright, who was killed at Flodden
> 9th September, 1513. He left, by Felicia his wife, daughter of John Home, Esq., of
> Ardmillan, three sons and two daughters. The eleventh in direct heritable descent
> from this Colonel MacGuffie, of Cubbicks, is James MacGuffie, Esq., of Crossmichael,
> who married Margaret, only daughter of the late William Coulthart, Esq., of Coulthart
> and Collyn. The ensigns armorial used by MacGuffie of Crossmichael are, Argent,
> a fess sable between three boar's heads couped of the last. Crest, a boar's head, as
> in the Arms. Motto, *Arma parata fero.*

This MacGuffie pedigree, with the Colonel killed at Flodden at the
head of it, is a piece of exactly the same texture as that of the allied
house. We observe that the " eleven heritable descents " have been

drawn out in like fashion, and have been printed in the *Dictionary of the Landed Gentry*, edit. 1863, p. 747. What is more, we find on inquiry that "the Son of a Fool" is as apocryphal in his arms as in his lineage. There are in fact no arms whatever for this distinguished name. The nearest approach to it of a family actually entitled to arms is M'Guffock, whose totally different bearings are Argent, two crosiers saltire-ways azure between a man's heart in chief proper and three stars of the second. Crest, a dove proper. Motto, *Industria et labore*. This coat was registered in the Lyon office to William McGuffock of Rusco, in the year 1673. Mr. Anderson says (p. 71), "Although so similar, McGuffog and MacGuffie are distinct names :" we are inclined to believe that they are of one origin, in spite of the diversity of spelling. Indeed, Mr. Anderson himself has previously admitted as much (in the passage we have quoted),—" taking the terminal syllable of *og* or *oig* into account."

It ought further to be made generally known that, besides the window at Bolton-le-Gate, monuments to the imaginary line of the Coultharts have been erected in the churchyard of the parish of Kells, co. Kirkcud-bright, and in that of Kirkpatrick Fleming, co. Dumfries. They are both altar-tombs; and in the *Notes and Memoranda to the Coulthart and Ross Pedigrees*, printed in 1864, copies are given of their inscriptions. Upon the former are recorded personages supposed to have died in the years 1542, 1620, 1653, 1690, 1717, and 1775, being six lairds of Coulthart in succession, together with Griselda Macturk, the spouse of the last, supposed to have died 1767.[1] At Kirkpatrick Fleming, together with "the armorial insignia of the Coulthart family, beautifully sculptured within shields," are commemorated *Gulielmus Coulthart de Coulthart et Collyn arm. nominis gentisque suæ facile primarius*, who died in 1807; Janetta (McNaught) his wife, who died in 1832; and Alexander their son, who died in 1789. These last we believe to have been people who actually lived and died, but certainly without " armorial insignia."

With regard to the family of Henry William Colthurst, D.D. Vicar of Halifax, absurdly claimed by the Coulthart genealogist as an offset of the Coultharts, he is described in his epitaph in Halifax Church (a copy of which is printed in Whitaker's *Loidis et Elmete* at p. 39 of the Appendix), as " ab ingenuâ inter Cravenses stirpe oriundo ;" and in

---

[1] A rumour has just reached us, since the above was written, that the ancestral monument at Kells has recently disappeared ! Its brief existence will still be on record on the substantial vellum of *The Coulthart Genealogies*.

Dr. Whitaker's *History of Craven*, 4to. 1812, at p. 184, a pedigree of his family will be found. It had been resident at Gargrave from the reign of Elizabeth. The author of *Popular Genealogists* suggests that this was an offshoot of that family which, enjoying a Baronetcy, is seated in the county of Cork; but, so far as appears, these two families of Colthurst are distinct. The arms of Colthurst of Gargrave are Argent, a fess between two colts sable; those of Colthurst of Ardrum, co. Cork, Argent, on a fess between three colts courant sable as many trefoils slipped or.

ANGLO-AMERICAN COAT-ARMOUR.

The Heraldic Journal; recording the Armorial Bearings and Genealogies of American Families. Nos. I.—IV. Boston (Massachusetts.) 8vo. Published monthly.

This is a new periodical work, edited by Mr. W. H. Whitmore, and its object will be fully understood on perusal of the letter which that gentleman addressed to us a few months ago, and which was printed in our last volume, at p. 530.

The summary, from the pen of the same writer, of what has been done in America on the subject of Genealogy, quoted in our last Part, at p. 128, from his Essay entitled *The Cavalier Dismounted*, furnishes the English reader with a fair account of the extensive labours and accumulations of our American Cousins in that department of family history. And now we come to consider how far they have cultivated the science of Armorial Heraldry.

It is admitted that it has hitherto been neglected by them, and in fact allowed to fall almost into utter oblivion. Some families, entitled to hereditary coat-armour, have preserved and handed it down, but generally with no further appreciation of its peculiar meaning or value than they would attach to any other device on a ring or seal that was not armorial.

Others have taken up the notion that every person of the same name was entitled to the same armorial insignia.

Others again (as in the anecdote related in our vol. ii. p. 263) have regarded arms, when painted on a carriage or engraved on silver plate, much as they would any arbitrary patterns repeated upon paper hangings, on china, or other materials, which might be selected and copied by the public in general just as they pleased the eye.

In the introductory remarks which the Editor has prefixed to *The Heraldic Journal*, he has deemed it necessary to give his countrymen some elementary instruction on these matters. He apprises them that, " Notwithstanding the common error, coats of arms do not belong to all. the bearers of a name, but are a species of personal property inherited by the lineal descendants of the first owner, and belonging solely to them :" and that, " having been originally granted to individuals, their use is a distinct claim to a descent from the grantees." It is obviously requisite that these primary laws of Armory should be duly recognised, before it can take its proper place as an efficient accessory to the researches of Genealogy.

When, however, any early settler in New England can be shown to have used certain arms, Mr. Whitmore reasonably regards such evidence as of considerable importance. The arms then become a very serviceable clue towards the discovery of the particular family in the old country from which the settler was derived, and may save a world of trouble in prosecuting fruitless searches among families who, though bearing the same name, were of totally different race.

Mr. Whitmore further makes the following candid admissions :—

" Could we be assured of the authenticity of all the coats of arms in use here, our task would be light. We should simply have to record all the documents presented, and leave it to the persons interested to follow the clue abroad. Unfortunately we have no reason to presume that any such authority attaches to all remaining examples; we have on the contrary great reason for condemning whole classes as worthless. We see almost daily in this country seals engraved, arms emblazoned, and engravings published, which we know are assumed without proof or inquiry."

Rejecting entirely all recent assumptions of coat-armour, the Editor and his coadjutors propose to scrutinise critically all found to have been used in America prior to the year 1800. As the first colonists brought their seals of arms with them, that class of evidence is deemed of important value. But after the arrival of the time when seal-engraving and arms-painting were practised in New England by resident artists,—a date supposed to have commenced about 1730—1735, the confidence in contemporary usage is greatly impaired. In order to test the character of such artists, endeavours are made to ascertain their personal history : and notices of two of them are now presented to us,—Thomas Johnson, born in Boston 1708, died 1767 ; and Nathaniel Hurd, born in Boston 1729, died 1777.

The other contents of the Journal may be classed under the following descriptions :—

A series of arms derived from the official seals of the Governors of Massachusetts.

Documentary evidence,—such as a list of Esquires, residents in New England, 1736; extracts from Cotton Mather's *Magnalia*, descriptive of the ancestry of the colonists, &c.

Some brief genealogical memoirs, accompanied by evidence of various kinds in regard to their coat-armour.

Sepulchral inscriptions, to which armorial insignia are attached.

Heraldic Notes and Queries.

One of the most interesting memorials of the last century that is brought before our notice is a silver tankard, which was a marriage present received in the year 1728 by Dr. Ebenezer Miller, who built the Episcopal Church at Braintree, Massachusetts, and officiated therein for five and thirty years. He was a son of Mr. Samuel Miller, one of the earliest settlers at Milton, in the province of Massachusetts Bay, by Rebecca, daughter of Joseph Belcher of Boston. Having graduated at Harvard College, he came to England to pursue his theological studies, was ordained deacon in 1726, and priest in 1727, by the Lord Bishop of London; was thereupon appointed Chaplain to the Duke of Bolton, Lord Warden of the Cinque Ports; and received the honorary degree of M.A. from the university of Oxford; the several documents attesting which preferments are carefully preserved by his descendants. In 1728 he was appointed by the Society for the Propagation of the Gospel a missionary for New England, with the annual stipend of 100*l.*; and before leaving the old country he was married, at the church of St. Martin's-in-the-Fields, Westminster, to Martha Mottram, of a family resident at Addlethorp in Lincolnshire. The silver tankard bears the arms of Miller, Ermine, a fess gules between three wolf's heads erased azure; impaling Sable, on a chevron argent between three cross-crosslets [or?] as many quatrefoils [gules?]. Crest, a wolf's head erased, collared ermine.

We find these arms attributed to Miller of Oxenhoath in Kent, descended from Nicholas Miller of Horsenells Crouch in Wrotham, Sheriff of Kent 8 Charles I.

For the arms of Mottram, our American friends have not given the tinctures of either the cross-crosslets or the quatrefoils. Those we have supplied complete the blason as given in Burke's *Armory* for Mottram of Newcastle-upon-Tyne, except that we there read *cinquefoils* instead of quatrefoils.

Of the Mottram family, from which Mr. Miller took a wife, we find some particulars in Oldfield's *Account of Wainfleet and the Wapentake of Candleshoe*, 1829, Addlethorp being one of the parishes described in that work. It is there stated, at p. 115—

"The family of Mottram appear to have resided in this parish for a considerable period. The name of Thomas Mottram occurs in 1584. John Mottram from 1627 to 1663. John Mottram, jun. 1674. Samuel Mottram 1682 to 1710. The seal of John Mottram was a death's head, with the motto MEMENTO MORI."

But nothing is said of their having borne coat-armour; nor yet in p. 107, where are the epitaphs of John Mottram, gent. ob. 5 Jan. 1689, æt. 71; Samuel Mottram, gent. d. Feb. 9, 1710-11, aged 59; and Mary, eldest daughter of the last, and wife of John Andrews, gent.; she died Oct. 21, 1728, aged 31.

The arms here engraved are those of Mather: a family of great repute in New England as having produced several eminent clergymen, the authors of "many works, theological, historical, and political; the whole number being probably over seven hundred."[1] One of the best known of them was the Rev. Cotton Mather, the author of that important and very interesting historical work, the *Magnalia Christi Americana*, whose *Life* was written by his son Samuel, (Boston, 1729,) in which occurs the following passage :[2]—

[1] Handbook of American Genealogy, p. 61.

[2] "This passage," says our author, "has long been a puzzle to the reader." And no wonder, when it was printed after the following fashion :—"In our *Coat of arms*, we bear *Ermine Or, A Fess*, Wavy, Azure, three lions rampant; or, for a Crest, on a wreath of our Colours, a Lion Sedant, or on a Trunk of a Tree *vert*." This indeed is blason bewitched. It is corrected by our author, except that he has omitted the tincture of the lions. And *sedant* (though perhaps written by Mr. Mather) is not the correct heraldic term, but *sejant*. In the engraving, the " wreath of our colours "

" I have not great disposition to enquire into the remote antiquities of his Family, nor indeed is it matter of much consequence that in our coat of arms we bear Ermine, on a fess wavy azure three lions rampant or. For a Crest, on a wreath of our colours, a lion sejant or, on a trunk of a tree vert."

From other records [1] it is ascertained that Richard Mather, the first emigrant, was born at Lowton in the parish of Winwick, co. Lancaster, in the year 1596 ; that he was the son of Thomas, and grandson of John Mather of the same place. It is remarkable that this armorial coat, though not in Glover's Ordinary, has been found in a MS. of William Smith, Rouge-Dragon, now in America, entitled *Promptuarium Armorum*, 1602-15. It is there given for William Mather of co. Salop. In Burke's *General Armory* it occurs under the name of Madder, of Staffordshire. A simpler coat, viz. Ermine, a fess embattled gules, was granted to Mather of Secroft, co. York, Feb. 11, 1575.

The old burying-ground at Charlestown in Massachusetts furnishes ten coats of arms, others having perished. Those remaining are of the earlier part of the last century, and with two exceptions are of the same style of work. All are on stone, and nine of them are on the front of tombs built on the side of a slope. Five of these are shown in the accompanying engravings, representing the arms of Cheever, Greaves, Foster, Jenner, and Chambers.

EZEKIEL CHEEVER was born in 1692, the son of Thomas, and grandson of Ezekiel, "the famous school-master." He was styled " of Boston" in 1715, when he married Elizabeth Jenner of Charlestown. According to Savage's *Genealogical Dictionary* the family was from Canterbury in the mother country.

The coat and crest here assumed are, however, really those of a family wholly different, and not very closely resembling Cheever even in appearance. They belong to Chaytor, a house eminent among the gentry of the county of Durham : viz. Per bend dancetté argent and azure, three cinquefoils counterchanged. Crest, a stag's head erased lozengy argent and azure, the dexter horn argent, the sinister azure.

should not have been omitted : and the trunk of a tree should be described as " lying fessways :" for usually armorial trunks of trees are upright.

[1] Cotton Mather himself says (i. 443) : " It was at a small town called Lowton in the county of Lancaster, anno 1596, that so great a man as Mr. Richard Mather was born, of parents that were of credible and antient families." And in the Life of Richard Mather (1670) it is stated, " His parents, Thomas and Margaret Mather, were of ancient families in Lowton aforesaid, but by reason of some unhappy mortgage they were reduced unto a low condition as to the world."

CHEEVER.

GREAVES.

FOSTER.

FOSTER.

JENNER.

CHAMBERS.

On the next tomb, that of David Wood 1762, are carved, not the arms of Wood (which are said to be a lion rampant), but those of the Governor of the province, Sir William Phipps.

The Honble. Thomas Greaves, Esq. " departed this life in his sleep on the 19th of June, 1747, ætatis 63. He was a Beloved Physician, an Upright Judge, and a Wise and Good Man." There is an account of this family, of which the name is frequently spelt Graves, in Frothingham's History of Charlestown.

We find an eagle displayed borne, with various distinctions of the field, &c., by several families of Graves and Greaves. The little bird in the corner is doubtless intended as a martlet for difference, and should therefore be shorn of his feet.

The arms of Foster on the gravestone accompany several records of that family, one of which names the Honble. Richard Foster, Esq. who died August 29, 1774, aged 82 years, having " sustained the office of High Sheriff for the County of Middlesex for many years, and, upon his resignation, was appointed a Justice of the Court of Common Pleas for the same county, in which office he continued until his decease." He was the grandson of William Foster, who was of Charlestown about 1650, and is recorded as having been about 80 at his death in 1698. It is thought that he may have been the passenger in the Hercules from Southampton in 1634, and the son of Richard Foster of Romsey, baptised there 22 Jan. 1615. Various articles with the Foster arms are still preserved: among others, Mr. Edward I. Browne of Boston has a large tankard, on which they are beautifully engraved, with the colours, viz. Argent, a chevron vert between three hunting-horns sable.

The second coat of Foster is from another cemetery. It is upon an upright stone at Dorchester, recording Mr. James Foster, who died Oct. 4, 1732, in the 82nd year of his age, having been "member in full communion with the Church of Christ in Dorchester about 60 years." This gentleman was the son of Hopestill Foster, who died 1676, and brother to John Foster, of whom Blake writes that he was schoolmaster of Dorchester, and made the seal of arms of the colony, namely, an Indian with a bow and arrow, &c.

It is added that " he was the grandson of Hopestill Foster, who may not have come hither, though his family did in 1635 with their relative Rachel Bigg, of Kent." Among the many varieties of the coats of Foster and Forster that will be found in the ordinaries, composed of a chevron, bugle-horns, and leopard's heads, one is Argent, a chevron gules between three bugle-horns vert, on a chief of the second as many leopard's heads or (*Ordinary* in Edmondson); and one of the crests of Foster is An arm embowed, holding a broken tilting-spear proper. (Burke's *General Armory*.)

Another stone at Charlestown commemorates THOMAS JENNER, Esq., who died June 23, 1765, aged 72. He was the great-great-grandson of the Rev. Thomas Jenner of Weymouth. The armorial bearings are varied from some we find in Burke's *General Armory*, for Jenner of Essex, viz. Azure, a cross flory between four fleurs de lis or : with the like crest of a greyhound, sejant, argent. We do not quite understand the editor's remark that "the ornamentation of the border of the shield may be intended to represent it as engrailed, which it should be, according to English works on Heraldry." He alludes, we presume, to some coat of Jenner that we do not find; but the frame of the shield on the stone is certainly merely ornamental, not an heraldic bordure.

The last of the engravings is on a monument erected to the memory of CHARLES CHAMBERS, Esq., who died April 27, 1743, in the 83rd year of his age; having been for many years one of his Majesty's Council, a Judge of the Court of Common Pleas, and a Justice of the Peace for the county of Middlesex. On the same stone is added an epitaph in memory of Daniel Russell, Esq., who died Dec. 6, 1763, aged 78, having been for upwards of twenty years a member of His Majesty's Council for the Province of Massachusetts, a Commissioner of Impost, and for more than fifty years Treasurer of the county of Middlesex. He married a daughter of Thomas Chambers, and had a son named Chambers Russell. The arms are no doubt intended for Chambers; for, though we find no such coat in our ordinaries, there are some coats of Chambre and Chambers with a fess checquy. The hand in the crest, we presume, holds a palm-branch, which is alluded to in the motto JUSTUS UT PALMA.

These examples, it must be confessed, are not very encouraging in regard to the value of the sepulchral heraldry of America. Still, it is generally possible to test each instance that occurs, by other evidence, and such armorials are suggestive, if not authoritative. Being desirous to render our American friends any assistance in our power in their interesting investigations, we shall describe some of the other monuments when we resume this subject. We may now add that we find an account of a solitary funeral hatchment in p. 38 :—

"Addington Davenport, junior, was the first Rector of Trinity Church, Boston, and married Ann Faneuil. He died 8 Sept. 1746; and a hatchment bearing his arms impaling Faneuil was erected in the church. This has been preserved, perhaps the only remaining instance of such a memorial, and we understand that Bishop Eastburn has ordered its erection in a proper place in the church."

The arms in this case are not described.

We conclude for the present by extracting the following account of the family of THORNDIKE, compiled by Mr. A. T. Perkins from communications made by the late Lord Monson, Mr. H. G. Sowerby, and Mr. George Quincy Thorndike. The generations are shown by the small figures, a simple and ingenious method which the American genealogists find very useful.

William Thorndike, born in the reign of Henry VII., lived at Little Carlton in Lincolnshire, married there, and died in 1539. In his will he mentions six children,—Herbert,[2] William,[2] John,[2] and three daughters.

(2). Herbert Thorndike was lord of the manor of Little Carlton, and by his wife Janet had five sons, Nicholas,[3] Richard,[3] Herbert,[3] James,[3] George,[3] and five daughters.

(3). Nicholas married Frances Southrey, and had two sons, Francis [4] and Herbert,[4] and two daughters. The two sons signed their pedigree in the Visitation (? of Lincolnshire) in 1634.

(4). Francis married Alice Coleman, and left four sons,—Francis,[5] John [5] the first of the family in New England, Herbert [5] the Prebendary of Westminster distinguished by his theological writings, and Paul.[5]

(5). John, the second son, went to New England in 1633, married there, and had one son, Paul,[6] and six daughters. In the year 1668 John Thorndike returned to England on a visit to his brother Herbert, the Prebendary of Westminster, and took with him his son Paul,[6] and two of his daughters, Martha [6] and Alice.[6] He died in London not long after his arrival, and was buried in the cloisters at Westminster, Nov. 3, 1668.

(6). Paul Thorndike returned to New England, but his sisters Martha and Alice continued to live with their uncle Herbert until he died, when he provided for them in his will, on condition, however, "that they should neither return to New England their birthplace, nor yet, remaining in England, marry with any who went to the Mass or to the new Licenced Conventicles." Herbert Thorndike was a profound scholar and laborious author, and his works have been republished in the *Library of Anglo-Catholic Theology*, occupying six volumes, 8vo. 1844—1856.

Paul Thorndike,[6] son of John, on his return to New England, settled at Beverly, and married Mary Patch, by whom he left three sons, John,[7] Paul,[7] and Herbert,[7] and four daughters.

(7.) John Thorndike, the eldest son, married Joanna Larkin, and had Robert,[8] Paul,[8] John,[8] James,[8] Herbert,[8] Edward,[8] and two daughters.

(8). James Thorndike, the fourth son, married Anna Ober, and had Hezekiah,[9] James,[9] Jeremiah,[9] Paul,[9] Herbert,[9] and three daughters.

(9). Hezekiah Thorndike, eldest son of James and Anna, married Sarah Prince, and had Hezekiah,[10] Jeremiah,[10] and one daughter.

(10). Hezekiah married Abigail Chamberlain, and had one son, John Prince[11] Thorndike.

(11). John Prince Thorndike married Sarah Hill, and has John Hill Thorndike,[12] James F. Thorndike,[12] and George Quincy Thorndike.

S. Lothorp Thorndike, esq.[12] of Beverly, descends from John[7] through Herbert,[8] Nicholas,[9] Nicholas, junior,[10] and Albert.[11]

Augustus[12] Thorndike, son of Charles[11] and Mary Edgar Thorndike, descends from Paul,[6] Paul, junior,[7] Andrew,[8] Israel,[9] Augustus.[10]

The arms of Thorndike are, Argent, six guttées, three, two, and one, gules, on a chief of the second three leopard's faces or. Crest, a damask rose proper, with leaves and thorns vert, at the bottom of the stalk a beetle proper.

THE HOUSE OF PERCY.

Remarks on the far descended and renowned Title of Lord Percy. By ALEX-
ANDER SINCLAIR. 8vo. pp. 15.
More Percy Anecdotes, Old and New. pp. 12. 1865. (Privately printed.)

Mr. Sinclair (a member of a family well known in the literary world,
a son of Sir John the celebrated agriculturist, a brother of Sir George
a political writer, of Miss Sinclair the favourite novelist, and of our
own Archdeacon of Middlesex,) was the author of an elaborate dissertation on the subject of *Heirs Male* published nearly thirty years
ago, and has, it is well known, ever taken a lively interest in all
matters relating to pedigree and kindred topics. He has now been
again tempted into print by the fact that, on a death which has been
universally deplored, the Barony of Percy has recently been separated
from the English Dukedom of Northumberland to be absorbed in the
Scotish Dukedom of Athol. " The only question left open relates
to the *date* of the Percy peerage to which the Duke of Athol is heir
—which (Mr. Sinclair remarks) has been a subject of doubt for three
centuries, and involves many points of interest."

The real facts of the case are, however, to the best of our belief,
stated with perfect accuracy in Nicolas's *Synopsis of the Peerage*, nor
do we find that Mr. Sinclair's views differ from that authority.

The first summons to Parliament to a Henry Percy was dated on
the 6th Feb. 1299. It was his great-grandson the 4th Baron who
was created Earl of Northumberland at the coronation of King
Richard the Second. Attainders occurring in the reigns of Henry
IV. and Edward IV. were reversed: but there was a third eclipse
of the dignity in 1537, on the death s.p. of the 6th Earl, whose next
brother had recently engaged in Aske's rebellion, and suffered capital
punishment, leaving, in consequence, his son and heir under attainder.
When the wheel of Fortune again turned, and the time came for the
restoration of that heir, Queen Mary did not reverse the father's attainder, but she *created the peerage anew*. She made Thomas Percy a
Baron by patent, on the 30th April, 1557; and on the next day Earl
of Northumberland; each dignity with special remainder to his heirs
male, and then to his brother Henry and his heirs male.

On the accession of King Charles the First, in 1625, Algernon,
afterwards the 10th Earl, was summoned to Parliament as Baron

Percy: but this was regarded as one of those cases in which an heir apparent is summoned in his father's barony, and thereby no new peerage is created. His father was Baron Percy only by the creation of 1557: but the precedency of 1299 was, *in error*, conceded to the son.

When Josceline, the 11th Earl, dying in 1670, left an only daughter, that daughter, the Lady Elizabeth Percy, was believed to have succeeded to the barony of Percy and to other ancient baronies that had merged in the Earldom; but such was not actually the fact. The older titles had been forfeited in 1537, and not restored; and, had they existed, they might, at an earlier date, have descended in 1572 to the heirs of the 7th Earl, who left only daughters, but that he also died under attainder.

The Lady Elizabeth became Duchess of Somerset; and upon her death her son Algernon (afterwards 7th Duke of Somerset) was summoned to Parliament as Baron Percy, in 1722, under the erroneous supposition that he had inherited the ancient baronies, the original precedency of 1299 being again allowed.

And so again, on the death of Elizabeth (Seymour), Duchess of Northumberland, Dec. 5, 1776, her son (afterwards the second Duke of the creation of 1766) was summoned to Parliament in 1777 as Baron Percy, as if he had inherited a Barony by writ; and so he really had, but it was one originating with the summons of 1722, not the ancient barony of 1299, which was no longer in existence.

The summons in 1722, though made in error, had in fact, according to the present interpretation of Peerage Law, *created a new Barony by writ;* and it is this Barony of Percy, of the date 1722, which has now come to the Duke of Athol. His Grace is the grandson of John 7th Duke of Athol, by the Lady Emily Percy, Lady Glenlyon, sister of the two last Dukes of Northumberland, and the only one of her generation that has left children.

From Mr. Sinclair's supplementary notes we take the following:—

" Hugh the 3rd Duke got a shield of the quarterings of the families from whom the Percies were descended by heiresses or co-heiresses, numbering above nine hundred ! But there was an error in assuming the arms of Scotland with other eleven quarterings, as they did not descend from the Princess Margaret; and the arms and quarterings of Marshal, Earl of Pembroke,[1] amounting to eight, occur thirteen times by different lines, making one hundred and four."

---

[1] Mr. Sinclair's enumeration of the matrimonial engagements of the Marshals is extraordinary: " The Marshals, Earls of Pembroke, terminated in five brothers, all married, without children, by seven wives. The last died in 1246. They had five sisters, their co-heirs, all married. They had eight husbands, and one of these five

Where this wonderful aggregation of quarterings is to be seen we are not informed.[1] In Edmondson's *Baronagium Genealogicum*, Plate 267 represents the arms and quarterings of Percy, engraved at the expense of Elizabeth Countess of Northumberland circa 1765, or soon after. The number is there limited to one hundred and fifty.

Mr. Sinclair's second *brochure* of *More Percy Anecdotes* contains—

1. A notice of the family of Percy of Athol, proving that 500 years ago there was a family which lasted above sixty years under that title —being the reverse of the occurrence that has lately taken place.

2. A brief descent of the Strathbogie Earls of Athol, who were repeatedly forfeited both in Scotland and England, but were summoned to the English parliament for the three last generations (ending in 1373); also their share in the great Pembroke succession.

3. A deduction of the heirs of Thomas 7th Earl of Northumberland, who was forfeited, and executed in 1572, leaving daughters but no son; who, had there been one, would not have succeeded (on account of the Earl's attainder), though the entail in 1557 carried the Earldom, &c. to a brother.

4. The extraordinary history of Lady Dorothy Devereux's stolen marriage with Sir Thomas Perrott, which was dissolved, and after which, while Sir Thomas was living, she became the wife of Henry 9th Earl of Northumberland.

5. Explanation of the connection between the Earls of Egremont and the Percies, and how they derived their title and great estates— *i.e.* by creation in 1749, and the will of Algernon Duke of Somerset and Earl of Northumberland, who died in 1786—whereby the great Percy estates were divided between the families of Smithson and Wyndham.

had seven daughters, who had thirteen husbands. Thus the blood and arms of Marshal has been dispersed through various [and probably countless] channels for above six centuries."

[1] Since the above was written we have glanced at a copy of the shield alluded to. It is handsomely " Engraved by J. Leslie, 15, Oxendon Street, Haymarket," on a copper-plate, measuring 26 inches by 19½. The exact number of quarterings is 892. There is also a key-plate of the same, in outline; and four pages of letter-press in correspondent size, containing " *Surnames of the Heirs of Families.* London, printed by Wm. Nicol, Shakespeare Press." We found this plate in the collection of the late Mr. Robert Thomson, Joint Librarian of the London Institution, who is recently deceased, and his library sold at Sotheby's. Mr. Thomson was conversant with heraldry, having been in early life a clerk to the late Mr. Edmund Lodge, Norroy : and we are inclined to believe that he was concerned in the compilation of this grand Percy Atchievement.

Mr. Sinclair expresses some indignation that the Duke of Athol inherits so great a representation, and only a barren title. " On the former occasion (500 years ago) Northumberland took care that his sons the two Percies should, with the heiresses, secure the Athol estates, to which they had a right, in England. Now Northumberland, by cutting the entail, has succeeded in preventing his grand-nephew Athol from getting any Percy lands, on becoming Lord Percy." But this, we think, is scarcely surprising in the contemplation of the title being merged in the Dukedom of Athol. Should, indeed, it ever devolve to a Baroness Percy, estates will be required to support that dignity.

We have now one very important remark to make upon the tabular pedigree which Mr. Sinclair has given of the *Representatives of the Daughters and Coheirs of Thomas 7th Earl of Northumberland, beheaded 1572.* These representatives are drawn down to 1, Percy Woodroffe Paver, born 1829; 2, Henry Charles Gage, born 1854 (grandson of Henry Viscount Gage); and 3, Sir Stephen Richard Glynne, Bart. Now, it is true that the Lady Elizabeth Percy, the 7th Earl's eldest daughter and coheir, was married to Richard Woodroffe of Wolley in Yorkshire ; it is true that the descent given by Mr. Sinclair is set forth with full particulars in the *Baronia Anglica Concentrata* of Sir T. C. Banks (calling himself Bart. N. S.), 4to. 1845, p. 369 ; and it is true that even Mr. Beltz, Lancaster herald, was so far deceived as to state in his *Memorials of the Order of the Garter*, p. 158, that " Of [Lady] Elizabeth Woodruff William Paver was the heir-general in 1775." The *soi-disant* Sir T. C. Banks even presumed to say that Mr. William Paver, living at York in 1843, " is the eldest coheir of the Baronies of Percy and Poynings, and holds one entire moiety of the same, whereas the moiety of Lady Lucy, wife of Sir Edward Stanley, is divided and subdivided among several representatives of her ;" and to lament the sad fate of the said Mr. William Paver, as "the humble and depressed first co-heir of the unhappy Earl Thomas ;" though " possessing the honour of priority of blood over the present bearer of the ancient dignities," who was politely designated as " the pompous occupier of Northumberland House and Alnwick Castle."[1]

---

[1] In an earlier work, his *Stemmata Anglicana*, Banks had perversely endeavoured to back up the claims of James Percy, the Dublin trunkmaker, whose claim, after many years' investigation, was dismissed by the House of Lords, in 1689, as that of " the false and impudent pretender to the Earldom of Northumberland." We may add that the facts of the trunkmaker's claim were reviewed, and entirely exploded, by the present Garter in the *Collectanea Topogr. et Genealogica*, vol. vi. pp. 266—283;

The Historian of South Yorkshire was evidently unconscious of all this. He has, however, left an effectual contradiction to it in the following passage :—

"In Hopkinson, and in a better authority, Harl. MS. 6070, f. 123, it is shown that Richard Woodruff had issue by the co-heir of the Earl of Northumberland, who was beheaded at York, a son named Joshua or Joseph, who married Magdalene, daughter and heir of Roger Billings, esq. of Marthagare, near Denbigh, in Wales, by whom Charles, Joseph, Francis, Foljambe, and Mary. (Vol. ii. p. 387.)

Not a word of Maximilian Woodroffe, the "son and heir" of Richard and the Lady Elizabeth, said to have married a Paver; or of Maximilian his son that married another Paver; or Miliana the daughter and heir of the latter, who again married a Paver; whence the descent was deduced in the male line to the "son and heir" of William Paver, that was born in 1829, and named by his father "Percy Woodroffe Paver," in assertion of the Percy inheritance !

It was a clerk in the Will Office at York who was guilty of the fabrication. The particulars of it were fully exposed some years ago in a pamphlet on the Ecclesiastical Courts of Record written by Mr. Downing Bruce, now a member of the Chancery bar; but, as pamphlets are productions of which few copies are preserved, and are consequently difficult of access, we shall on this occasion republish the passage :—

"On 19th February, 1850, the author, accompanied by a friend, had occasion to visit the Will-office at York, for the purpose of making some researches among the early records. In searching the Index No. 76, for the years 1721 and 1722, they discovered, written in a modern hand, the name of John Paver. It appeared that a clerk in the office of that name claimed to be the representative of the house of Percy, and heir to all the ancient baronies of that illustrious family; this modern insertion caused a doubt in their minds, and the doubt was considerably strengthened by the production of the pretended will itself, dated 15th January, 1721. It actually recited that the testator, John Paver, had married Millian, only daughter and heiress of Maximilian Woodroofe, son and heir of Maximilian Woodroofe, who was the eldest son and heir of Richard Woodroofe, by Lady Elizabeth Percy, daughter of the Earl of Northumberland, and that the said John Paver, eldest son and heir, was then dead, and that William Paver, his grandson, was his eldest son and heir, and that his (Wm. P.'s) eldest child John was then living. The Earl of Northumberland was beheaded in 1572, and the last-mentioned John Paver died in 1760, so that this Will extended

including a curious account of the celebrated marriage of Thomas Thynne, of Longleat, with the Lady Ogle ; whilst in the second volume of that work, pp. 57—66, is some account (from the same high authority) of the actual younger branches of the house of Percy, several of whom would have succeeded to the Earldom on the extinction of the elder line in 1670, but for the attainder of Thomas seventh Earl in 1572. One of these was the family of Percy of Cambridge, descended from the Gunpowder Conspirator.

over no less than 188 years, and proved eight generations. It is fortunate for those persons having estates or titles depending on the records at York, that about this period the wills were all copied into volumes, which Mr. Protheroe describes as of "prodigious bulk, and requiring a man of herculean strength to move them;" for, on a most careful search made by both gentlemen, from 1719 to 1731, no such Will could be discovered in those books, which clearly proved that the Will had been placed in the office long since that period. Shortly after, several articles entitled "The Doom of English Wills" appeared in Mr. Charles Dickens's *Household Words*, on the subject. These had the effect of the removal or destruction of the pretended Will, and the erasure from the parchment Index Book, No. 76, of the name of John Paver; for, on a visit to this office by the same gentleman, on the 19th and 24th July, 1851, for the purpose of showing the document to a Barrister of high standing in his profession, no traces could be discovered, save the erasure from the Index under the letter P———." *An Account of the present deplorable State of the Ecclesiastical Courts of Record, with Proposals for their complete Reformation.* By WILLIAM DOWNING BRUCE, Esq., Barrister-at-law, F.S.A., 1854, p. 22. (The author proceeds to state that a real Will of John Paver had been destroyed, together with a leaf of the Register, and that subsequently a third (fictitious) Will, for John Paver, 1722, was substituted, with some other particulars, not now of importance.)

We are informed, that, whilst the pretended Will was on record, an official attested copy was obtained of it: but, after the publicity that has now been given to this transaction, there can be little chance of a dishonest advantage being taken of that copy hereafter;[1] or of future authors,—except by occasional inadvertence, as in the present case of Mr. Sinclair, assuming the Pavers to be cohiers of Thomas Earl of Northumberland.

We ought not to quit the subject of the House of Percy without remarking that in a work recently published under the title of *The Great Governing Families of England*, by JOHN LANGTON SANDFORD and MEREDITH TOWNSEND (2 vols. 8vo. 1865), the first essay is one upon "The Percies." It affords—in accordance with the general composition of those essays (which have recently appeared in *The Spectator* newspaper), an animated and effective sketch of the political history of the family. We will merely animadvert on the repetition it contains of the old legend as to the respective arms of Percy and Louvaine.

[1] There was also placed in the office at York a forged Will, purporting to be that of Maximilian Woodroffe, bearing date 14 May, 1652, and for probate 2 June in the same year. This Will, with some other fictitious documents relating to the pretended Paver descent from the house of Percy, were removed from the office, and were lately in the possession of Mr. Joseph Buckle the registrar, he having satisfied himself of their true character. William Paver, who had been clerk to a law stationer, and was the son of a working blacksmith at York, was dismissed from the office upon the discovery being made.

Josceline de Louvaine, who married the heiress of the elder line of Perci in the reign of Henry I, was brother to Adelisa, the King's second wife; and, it is added, was brought over by her " to marry the Percy under condition of accepting either her name or her arms. He chose the former, which was popular, substituting only his own arms for those borne, and probably invented, by Lord William the founder "—by which designation is meant William Perci, surnamed Alsgernons, who died in the Holy Land in 1096. Now this, as we have said, is the old and oft-repeated story : but that is no reason why any good opportunity of refuting such a legend, affecting the earliest origin of Armory, should not be taken. In the first place, then, we may remark, what we have frequently said elsewhere, that the era of Josceline de Louvaine is quite early enough for the very commencement of an armorial coat, and 1096 is nearly a century too early. Secondly, that all the most ancient rolls give for the arms of Percy the fusils, or millpicks as they were often termed, and which it has been supposed, not without probability, were allusive to the name. Lastly, in respect to the blue lion, said to have been the old arms of Brabant, or Louvaine, it was certainly not used by Josceline. Indeed Mr. Longstaffe tells us that the old story is erroneous on both the matters of which it affects to speak. Josceline always retained his paternal name of Louvaine, that of Percy being taken by his son. But, as to the arms, " neither in the main line of Percy, its offshoots, or its sub-feudatories, is there many traces of the blue lion until the reign of Edward I." (*The Old Heraldry of the Percys*, by W. HYLTON DYER LONGSTAFFE, Esq. F.S.A. 8vo., 1860, p. 6.)

It is in the *Siege of Carlaverock* 1300, and on the seal attached to the Barons' letter to the Pope in 1301, that we first meet with the blue lion on a golden field as the armorial coat of Henry de Perci, the first Baron of 1299. The change from the fusils or millpicks coincides remarkably with the marriage of this Baron to the daughter of the Earl of Arundel, his lord paramount, and their seals to the Barons' letter are very similar. The lion of the Arundels was borne in gold on a red field. They were descended from the same Queen Adelisa before mentioned, by her second husband William de Albini.

Mr. Longstaffe's essay is the most perfect monograph upon the heraldry of any great family that has hitherto been compiled; and we are pleased to observe in it a well-merited tribute to the labours of the great genealogist of the Percies, the Bishop of Dromore. After alluding to some mythic Earls of Caux and Poictiers before the Con-

quest of England, he remarks that, " saving the said early descent
and a few other apocrypha when the compiler was seduced by family
pedigrees and Pierpont's MS., the narrative detail of Bishop Percy in
the later editions of Collins's Peerage is wonderfully correct. The
light and glory of the house might well allow a total loss of the Earls
in Normandy if it could clearly and indisputably boast of Bishop Percy
as a scion." It was to the 1779 edition of Collins that the Bishop communicated his labours: they occupy there 211 pages, pp. 280—390:
and they were never reprinted at the same length, a fact which is worth
remembering. We may add that in the volume of *Testamenta Eboracensia*, which is now passing through the press for the Surtees Society,
the will of the Earl who was murdered in the insurrection at Thirsk
in 1489 is printed for the first time, and will be found an interesting
addition to the materials for his life.

" NOTICES OF THE ELLISES."

To the Editor of the HERALD *and* GENEALOGIST.

SIR,—The critique of my work—*Notices of the Ellises*—in your last
number induces me to request you will insert the following remarks :—

Conscious that the long title of my first Number might seem presump-
tuous, and that I had omitted the word " presumed " before the word
" origin," in the second and third Numbers I merely called my work
Notices of the Ellises. This you do not state; indeed, you were not bound

to do so : but if you had, it would have abated the pretensions of my work in the eyes of your readers as judged by its first title.

You have given my list of variations of the name of Ellis, which you mention " as taken" [for granted]. My words were, " investigation *proves*" that they are variations of one name, and I mean it.

I have no ambition of being reckoned among those "sober heraldic inquirers" who are contented to believe that " crests were not adopted for some centuries after the reign of Richard I." I can cite armorial seals of the twelfth century with crests; and Geoffrey de Vinsauf, in his Itinerary of Richard I., speaks of "helmets with crests" as seen in the ranks of the Crusaders serving under that monarch.

With respect to the naked female, it is found as early as Edward III. as the crest of the Ellises of Kiddall, for it occurs on a helmet of that date in stained glass in the church of Berwick-in-Elmete.[1] However, since the issue of my work, I have seen reason to give up the Crusading character of both coat of arms and crest, as also of most *other* "Crusading coats of arms." But in one of the copies of the Roll of Arms of Edward II.[2] the cross and crescents are given as the arms of Sir Henry Elys of Yorkshire—a copy that Sir H. Nicolas considers to have well-founded claims to genuineness. As to the crest, I believe it is as old as the coat, and my No. 4 will contain the result of my inquiries into the genealogy of all families bearing it, or anything like it—as the mermaid, maiden's head, &c.—so as, if possible, to get at its origin.

You ask, if Alis may not in some cases be the same as Alice. I admit that it may, as in the case possibly of Walter and Martin fitz Alice, Sheriffs of London 1201 and 13. But when I find " Rog' Alic'," temp. Hen. III. in connection with "Auditon," how can I refuse to identify that person with Sir Roger Alis, who is mentioned in deeds of that reign as owner of Auditon, or Allington, which, temp. Hen. II. I find, by the same evidence, was owned by William Alis, and, temp. Will. I. by another William Alis ?

When you mention Sir William Alis, " a Norman lord," you omit to state that he is named in Domesday, and was progenitor of a knightly race, who owned Allington, in Hants, till the time of Edward II.—an omission that would leave the impression that my derivation of the Ellises of England from the Alises of Normandy is entirely fanciful and unwarranted. This, and any mention of some not obscure persons and families of the name of Ellis and Fitz Ellis, you altogether omit, and have dwelt on my conjectures rather than stated my facts.

With respect to my "identification" of one with other Domesday tenants, if the evidence in No. 1 is insufficient, I trust in No. 4 very considerably to strengthen it ; and I think genealogists would elucidate many a pedigree by following my example in this matter.

[1] Harl. MSS. 1394.   [2] Harl. MSS. 4033.

You remark, that I readily accept a similarity of sound in a name as a proof of relationship. Now, all the Welch Ellises I expressly exclude from this bond of union, and do not apply it to other families of one name unless warranted by circumstantial evidence. As to similarity of arms in early times showing a common origin of the families bearing them (including female descent), I hold to that opinion as a general rule most tenaciously, and hope shortly to give you good grounds for it in a paper on "*Early Armorial Seals*," which will also strongly maintain my opinion which you quote—that "hereditary heraldic symbols were in existence for centuries before the Norman conquest."

I think a family established at the Conquest, and continued in the chief male line for nearly three centuries, must have thrown off many off-shoots, whose descendants must now be extremely numerous. Sir Roger Alis, temp. Hen. III. spelt his name also Elys, as did others of the family. It is not too much, therefore, to presume that "most of the Ellises of England" (not of Wales) descend from his Norman ancestor.

Alis-ay, near Pontdelarche, was a place where councils were held in the ninth century. It was evidently named after an Alis, and not conversely. It and Ferté-Alais in the twelfth century had the same owners. The name must, therefore, have been as old as the time of Charlemagne. I conclude it is the same as Louis and Elias. In De Brecquigny's *Receuil des Chartes*, 3 vol. folio, from the ninth century to the twelfth century the name of Elias occurs frequently at early periods; that of Louis never, except as the name of a French king. Nor is it met with in England or France at an early period, whilst Elie, as a Christian name, occurs frequently. What does this imply? I say boldly this: that during the tenth, eleventh, and twelfth centuries Elias in Latin and Elie in French were the synonyms or current forms of Louis.

Further, if in England and France at early periods families are found whose arms contain one or more fleurs-de-lis, and their surnames or prevalent Christian names are Elias, it is a remarkable coincidence at least, and can scarcely be accidental, but must point to a meaning. This is exemplified in my work. That fleurs-de-lis should be taken as *armes parlantes* by Alis, Elys, Fitz-Elys, &c. is, even if true, except originally, an insufficient explanation; for the families of Plumstead and Burlingham bore them, and places of these names were owned at the Domesday survey by "Elias." I am, Sir, yours, &c.

Charlwood, Surrey. W. S. ELLIS.

NORTON OF SHARPENHOE, CO. BEDFORD.

A GENEALOGY OF THE NORTON FAMILY, with Miscellaneous Notes. From the New England Historical and Genealogical Register for July 1859. Boston: Henry W. Dutton and Son, Printers, MDCCCLIX. 8vo. pp. 10.

An old pedigree of the Nortons of Sharpenhoe in Bedfordshire, having been preserved in America, in the possession of a junior branch of the family, is here edited by Mr. W. H. Whitmore, the indefatigable genealogist of New England. It is one of the performances of John Philipott, Somerset, anno 1632: but is evidently tainted with the romantic ingredients to which even the official heralds condescended at that period. To an experienced eye the title alone is sufficient: "This Genealogie of the Nortons of Sharpenhow in Bedfordshire, beginninge at NORVILE that married into the howse Valois, and came into England with Kinge William the Conquer^r, and was his Constable: whose posteritie, long time after, assumed the English name of NORTON, being the same in signification that Norvile is in French. For the proof whereof it is to be understood that this Pedigree agreeth with records remaining in the Office of Armes," &c. &c. The imaginary alliances—as we may make free without hesitation to term them, are,— into the house of Valois, the house of Barr, that of Dalbemonte, a daughter of Nevil of Raby, Joricia daughter of Sigr. Dampre de Court, the daughter of Sir John Hadscoke, and even we should say the daughter and coheiress of Monsignr. Bassingbourne, and the daughter of the Lord Grey de Ruthyn.

To the last two, however, it is true that some other testimony occurs. In the MS. Harl. 1546, p. 102b, is a pedigree which states that a certain Sir John Norton of Battle, in Sussex (the son of John Norton of the same place), married a daughter of the Lord Grey de Ruthyn, and was father of Thomas Norton, whose daughter Catharine was married to Thomas Windowt, alderman of London. But in the pedigree before us the father of Catharine is described as Thomas *Norland*, alderman of London, who became the second husband of Agnes, widow of Sir John Winger, alderman, that Agnes being daughter of William Walker by Joane Norton, daughter of " Sir John Norton alias Norvile, who married the daughter of the Lord Grey de Ruthyn." We suspect that about this there was some intentional mystification.

But, again, Philipott speaks of some armorial evidence shewing an alliance with Bassingbourne:—

In an ancient Mansion Hous in Fulham in the countie of Midd. sometime in the possession of Thomas Windowt, Alderman of London, and now *hoc anno* 1632 the possession of Mr. Williamson procurator in the Court of Arches, London, the armes of Norton are in manie places remaining, and the Bassingbournes armes quartered with theirs. There are also impailed the armes of Norland and Norton quarteringe Bassingbourn, and Walker impaled with Norton ; also the armes of Mr. Hill and Mr. Rice impaled with Norland.   Per JOHN PHILIPOTT, Somersett.

William Hill and Simon Rice are stated to have been the successive husbands of Lettice, another daughter of Alderman Thomas Norland, and sister to Catharine Windowt.

But this pedigree of Norton of Sharpenhoe is more remarkable because it is the hitherto unrecognised genealogy of Thomas Norton the Elizabethan poet, one of the metrical translators of the Psalms, and joint-author of *Gorboduc* with Thomas Sackville, afterwards Lord Treasurer and Earl of Dorset. When Mr. W. Durrant Cooper, F.S.A., prefixed a biographical memoir of Norton to the edition of *Gorboduc* printed for the Shakespeare Society in 1847, he failed to discover any pedigree,[1] though there actually is one, signed by his son Robert Norton, in the Visitation of Hertfordshire of 1634, and another signed by his nephew Graveley Norton in the Visitation of Bedfordshire of the same year. This is a copy of the former :—

Elizabeth, dau. of Robert Merry, of Northall, 1 ux.=Thomas Norton of Sharpenhow, co. Bedford.=Elizabeth, dau. of Robert Marshall, of Hitchin, co. Hertford, 2 ux.

Margaret, daughter of Thomas Cranmer, archbishop of Canterbury.=Thomas Norton, of Sharpenhow.=Alice, daughter of Edmund Cranmer.

Robert Norton, Esq. of Markeate-cell, esq. now living 1634.=Anne, daughter of Robert Hare of co. Lincoln.

Thomas, eldest son, s.p.　2. Robert, s.p.　3. Thomas.　4. Richard.　5. George.　Anne, wyfe of James Castle of London.　Elizabeth.

(*Signed*)　Rob't Norton.

We thus discover that the Poet twice married a Cranmer, and that by his first marriage he was son-in-law to the Archbishop.[2] Mr. Durrant Cooper

[1] — "in the visitations of Bedfordshire there are the arms of two families of Norton, without any pedigree." *Memoir*, p. lviii.

[2] The passage in Camden's *Annals*, 1635 (see note in p. 280) states that Margaret Cranmer was the Archbishop's only daughter. Finding that a will of *Margerie Norton* was proved in the Prerogative Court of Canterbury in 1572, we entertained a hope that we had discovered an interesting document in connection with that prelate's family. The lady proves however to be another person : she styles herself " Margerie Norton of Sharpenhoe, in the parish of Streatley, widow ;" and, we presume, must have been that " Margery, daughter of Wingar of Sharpenhow," as styled in Philipott's pedigree, who was the wife of Richard Norton, an uncle of the Thomas who married Margaret Cranmer. But the will shows her maiden name to have been Wingate, not Wingar. The pedigree gives her only two children, Thomas and William ; but the will opens many other genealogical particulars. She leaves her son Danyell 40*l*., two silver spoons at the age of 24, and other things. To her daughter Hill 30*l*.: if she died before her, the same to be equally divided among her children. To Marie Hill her goddaughter [and probably granddaughter] 10*l*.: if she die, the same to her brother Richard at 24. To her daughter Hill and her daughter Wynshe various articles of dress. To Margaret Wingate a petticoat. To Suzan Winshe 6*l*. 13*s*. 4*d*. on her marriage : if she died, the same to her sister Jane Winshe. To her daughter Winshe a silver salt. To Thomas Winshe her godson

subsequently[1] identified him with Thomas Norton, who was one of the members in parliament for London from 1571 to 1582,—"a man wise, bold, and eloquent,"—as well as City Remembrancer; having previously sat for Gatton in 5 & 6 Phil. et Mar. and 1 Eliz. He was (as stated by himself) "born a citizen," in the year 1532: became a student of the Inner Temple in 1552; counsel to the Stationers' Company in 1562; licenser of books by the Bishop of London 12th Dec. 1562; and the first City Remembrancer, on the institution of that office, 6th Feb. 1570-1. His father lived until the 10th March 1582-3; having in the previous year lost his third and last wife, who drowned herself. She had in her youth been brought up in the house of Sir Thomas More, and to that education the fancies which haunted her latter days, and drove her to distraction, are attributed in a letter of Fleetwood the Recorder.[2] She is not named in the Visitation; but, according to Philipott's pedigree now placed before us, she was the widow of a Mr. Osborne, and bore to Thomas Norton senior three sons, Daniel, Barnabas, and Isaac. It is probable that her sentiments were totally opposed to those of her step-son, who was a zealous Calvinist. On his father's death he came into possession of his estates; and in May 1583 he made a provision for his wife, by giving her the mansion of Sharpenhoe for life, with an annuity. He and his father had previously granted an annuity of 20l. out of the real estate to his brother Luke Norton, of the Inner Temple. The Remembrancer died at Sharpenhoe exactly a year after his father (March 10), making a nuncupative will,[3] which was proved April 14, 1584, by his brother-in-law Thomas Cranmer. When his inquisition post mortem was taken, Elizabeth his father's widow (and therefore his third wife) was residing in Holborn, and his own wife, Alice, was living at Cheston (i.e. Cheshunt), Herts. In Camden's *Annals*,

[and probably grandson] 50s. now in the hands of his father William Winshe. To John Wingate 3s. 4d. he owed her, and 6s. 8d. To her cousin [i. e. probably nephew] George Wingate, 48s. 6d. that he owed her. To every one of her daughter Winshe's children at home one sheep. To her brother Edward Norton [he is not in Philipott's pedigree] one sheep. To her brother Wingate 10s. To her sister Shorte 10s. To Mr. Watts, vicar of Streatlye, 3s. 4d. to make a sermon at her burial. Residue to her son William Norton. Witness, Thomas Norton. Executors, her son William Norton and son-in-law William Winshe. Overseers, her brother Edward Wingate and son-in-law Edward Hill. Dated 26th June, 1571, proved 25th Nov. 1572.

[1] See two papers in the *Archæologia*, vol. xxxvi. 1855, the first an account of a MS. by Norton on the ancient Duties of the Lord Mayor and Corporation, communicated to the Society of Antiquaries by J. Payne Collier, esq., and the second containing "Further Particulars of Thomas Norton, and of State Proceedings in matters of Religion, in 1581 and 1582," by W. Durrant Cooper, Esq.

[2] See Mr. Cooper's memoir, p. liii. Mr. Peter Osborne, mentioned in the same letter, was Remembrancer of the Exchequer, and a well-known person of his time. We may therefore presume that Mrs. Norton's former husband was a member of the same family, afterwards Baronets, of Chicksands, co. Bedford.

[3] Printed in Mr. Cooper's Memoir, p. lvii.

1635, he is stated to have left by her " a plentiful issue." And Philipott's pedigree supplies the names of their children, of which Mr. Cooper was unable to find any trace. They were—

1. Anne, married to Sir George Coppin, and had issue Robert and Thomas. Sir George was of a Norwich family, and knighted July 23, 1603. (Arms, Argent, a chief vaire.)

2. Elizabeth, married first to Miles Raynsford (his arms Gules, a chevron engrailed between three fleurs de lys argent), and had Robert and Garrett; and secondly to Simon Basell, by whom she had Simon.

3. Thomas, who died at Cambridge in his father's lifetime. Probably this was the Thomas Norton entered at Pembroke hall in 1565, and a graduate in 1569.

4. Henry, who was aged 13 years, 8 months, and 20 days at his father's death. (Inq. p.m.)

5. Robert,[1] who married Anne, daughter of Robert Heare, (or Hare, as in the Herts Visitation,) and had issue Thomas, Robert, Thomas, Richard, and Anne. He was living at Market Cell, near Dunstable, when visited by the Heralds in 1634.

6. William, who married Ruth Harding.

Norton's half-brother and successor, Luke, was admitted to the Inner Temple in 1583. In 1613 he was in possession of Sharpenhoe. He married Lettice daughter of George Graveley, and had issue three sons, Graveley, Benjamin, and Thomas; and six daughters.

In the Bedfordshire Visitation of 1634 is the following pedigree signed by Graveley Norton:—

Arms: 1 and 4. Gules, a fret argent, surmounted by a bend vaire or and of the field, differenced by a crescent; 2. Sable, a cross pointed argent, differenced by a crescent. *Graveley.*

Luke Norton, one of the Mrs of the Chancery, dwelt at Offley, in co. Hertford, Esqr. and Councillor of the Law of the Inner Temple.	Lettice, daughter and sole heire of George Graveley, of Hitchin, com. Hertford, a younger brother of Graveley, of Graveley, com. Hertford.	Thomas, of Sharpenhoe, co. Bedford, Counsellor at law.

Graveley Norton, of Sharpenhow, in the parish of Stretley, co. Bedford, and of the Inner Temple, Esq. liveing ao 1634, eldest son.	Ellen, dau. of William Angell, sergent of the Acatery to King James.	2. Benjamin Norton, of London, linnen draper.	3. Thomas Norton, of London, silkman in Lombard street.

Anne, wife to Eustace Nedham, of Little Wimondley, co. Hertford, esq.
Lettice, first wife to Robert Cheney, of Bramhanger, in Luton parish, co. Bedford; after to Richard Norton, of Cornhill, linnen draper.
Elizabeth, wife to Doctor Pierce, of Hitchin, divine.
Martha, wife to Thomas Coppin, of Markett cell, co. Hertford, gen.
Susan, wife to John Berners, of Tharfeild, co. Hertford, gen.
Talbot, wife to Thomas Rotheram, of Farley, co. Bedford, gen.

(*Signed*) GRA. NORTON.

(*From the original in the College of Arms.*)

[1] It does not appear why the estate of Sharpenhoe went to the half-brother of the

Mr. Durrant Cooper has noticed that the family of Norton continued owners of Sharpenhoe until the end of the 17th century or nearly so, although not resident. Richard Norton, esq. who lived at Mitcham in Surrey, by his will dated in 1686 founded at Sharpenhoe a school (still in existence) for eight children, and charged the manor with the annual payment of 10*l.* for its support: He left a son John; and a daughter Dorothy, who was the wife of Richard Laurence, and whose epitaph in Mitcham church is printed in the History of Surrey.

The emigrants to New England, in whose family this old pedigree has been preserved, were John and William Norton, sons of William Norton and Alice Browest; and grandsons of William Norton of Sharpenhoe, the son of Richard, a younger brother of the old man who died in 1583. Mr. Whitmore has briefly traced the descendants of John, (William having died

Remembrancer, and not to his son Robert. Robert Norton was, like his father, a man of letters. The Third edition of Camden's *Annals of Queen Elizabeth*, in folio 1635, was " translated by R. N. gent." and that he was this Robert Norton is shown by an insertion made by him at p. 254. This tribute of filial piety, which has not hitherto been recognised by Norton's recent biographers, is sufficiently interesting to induce us to copy it : —

" About the end of this yeare Thomas Norton of Sharpenhow, in the county of Bedford, Esquire, quietly rendered his soule into the hands of his Creator, who for his excellent gifts and able parts was by the grave citizens of London made Remembrancer of the same city and chosen one of their burgesses in divers parliaments. In which places he gave such proofe of his surpassing wisedome, remarkable industry and dexterity, singular piety and approved fidelity to his prince and country, that the most upright Lord Keeper Bacon, the most wise Lord Treasurer Burghley, the most sharpe-sighted subtile searching Secretary Walsingham, and the rest of the Queen's most honorable Privy Councell, taking notice of his sufficiencies, made use of his counsaile and employment in many weighty and important affaires of state. He most exactly translated into English that excellent booke of Master Calvin's *Institutions of Christian Religion*, and was the greatest helpe Mr. John Foxe had in compiling his large volume of *Acts and Monuments*. Besides many other pretty bookes he wrote corresponding with the times and tending to the promoting of religion, the safety of his Prince, and good of his country, to the advancement whereof he applyed his utmost studies and endeavours, his best credite in court and city, and his sundry excellent speeches in parliament, wherein he expressed himself in such sort to be a true and zealous philopater, that hee attained the noted name of ' Master Norton the Parliament man,' and hath left even to this day a pleasing impression of his wisedome and vertue in the memories of many good men. This short digression in pious memory of a good man, being all which the translator hath presumed upon the readers' patience to insert of his owne, he hopeth will not be distastfull to many, but pleasing to some, and excusable to most readers."

In 1604 was published " A Mathematical Appendix, containing many Propositions and Conclusions Mathematical, with an Easy Way to delineate Sun-dials. By Robert Norton." 8vo. And in 1628, with the same name, " The Gunner, shewing the whole practice of Artillery, and Artificiall Fireworks, as well for Pleasure and Triumphs, as for War and Service. London, 1628." Folio. But whether these were by the same Robert Norton we have not ascertained.

s. p.) down to Andrews Norton, now or recently Professor of Sacred Literature at Harvard College, and his son Charles Eliot Norton, esq. of Cambridge, Massachusetts, the present possessor of Philipott's pedigree. He
has also appended abstracts from the wills of some of the American members
of the family.

In his "Miscellaneous Notes" Mr. Whitmore alludes to the Nortons of
Norton Conyers in Yorkshire, and to others of the name in Kent. We
apprehend that none of these had any relationship to those of Sharpenhoe.
The former family, memorable for their devotion to the church of Rome,
which brought two of them to the scaffold as notorious rebels in the year
1570, was called Norton *alias* Conyers, and derived from the Conyers a
maunch for their armorial charge, their coat being Azure, a maunch
ermine, a bendlet gules.

The Nortons of Sharpenhoe bore for arms Gules, a fret argent, over all a
bend vaire or and of the field; and it is true that the same coat is attributed to the *sire de Norvyll* in Glover's Ordinary: but we are still uninformed *where* any such family of Norville may have flourished, and our
suspicions of its being entirely imaginary are not removed by the absence
of this coat from the ancient rolls of arms recently edited for the Society of
Antiquaries by Messrs. Perceval and Walford, as well as from those edited
by Sir Harris Nicolas.

THE COHEIRS OF SIR JOHN CHANDOS, K.G.— It is stated in the third
edition of Collins's Peerage, (*sub tit.* ANGLESEY, vol. ii.) that Sir John de
Annesley, knight of the shire of Nottingham temp. Edw. III. and Ric. II.,
married Isabel, *dau.* and coheir of Margaret, sister and co-heir of Sir John
Chandos, K.G. (but not mentioning who her father was), and was, by her,
ancestor of the late Earls of Anglesey and the present Viscount Valentia,
&c. Banks says Sir John de Annesley married the *sister* and co-heir of Sir
John Chandos, and left no issue by her; but in the Addenda to his work
he says she was Isabel, dau. of Sir John Ireland and *niece* of Sir John
Chandos, K.G., and again repeats he had no issue by her. Burke says she
was Isabel, sister and co-heir of the Knight of the Garter, and was ancestor
to the present families of Annesley. Which of these various versions is to
be preferred? A. H. Le B.

Note.—We add another and more circumstantial statement, from the
accurate pen of Mr. Beltz, given in his memoir of Sir John Chandos,
Memorials of the Order of the Garter, p. 74: "Sir John Chandos died unmarried (Dec. 31, 1369). The family inheritance devolved to his two
sisters Eleanor and Elizabeth, and his niece Isabel wife of Sir John Annesley, the daughter of another sister, Margaret. Eleanor Chandos was unmarried in 1371, when &c. She married, first, Sir John Lawton, who had
been 'the dear friend and companion in arms' of Sir John Chandos; and,
secondly, Roger Collyng, of Herefordshire, whose wife she was in 1391.

By Lawton she had a daughter, Elizabeth, who, in or before 1386, was affianced to Peter de la Pole, of Newborough in co. Stafford, and, in her right, of Radbourne. From this marriage descended Sacheverell Pole, of Radbourne, esq. who, in 1807, obtained the royal licence to prefix the surname of Chandos to his own. Elizabeth, the second sister, died unmarried in or before 1398, at which date Isabel Annesley was also dead without issue. So that the entire representation became vested in the family of Pole." See also the additions to Dugdale's *Baronage*, art. CHANDOS, by Francis Townsend, Windsor, printed in the *Collectanea Topogr. et Geneal.* vol. v. p. 142.

The names of Sir John Chandos's three co-heirs have been derived from an inquisition taken after the death of Sir Richard Damory, "supposed (says Mr. Beltz) to have been a son of Margaret by her husband Richard Damory;" and in that record (*Esc.* 49 *Edw. III.* p. 1, n. 36) the father of Isabel lady Annesley is not named;[1] which was the cause why Collins could not name him. A second inquisition on the death of Sir Richard Damory shews that Sir John Chandos had granted the manor of Headington, &c. to Damory for life only, with remainder to his own right heirs.

We have not been able to find the passage of Mr. Banks's *Addenda*, men-

---

[1] We are enabled to give the following abstract of the record in question : " Juratores dicunt quod Ric'us Damory Chr. defunctus tenuit die quo obiit M. de Hedington cum pertin' et hund' de Bolyndon et Northgate cum pertin' in co. Oxon. ad termin. vite sue et unius anni post mortem suum, revercione spectante rectis heredibus Johannis Chandos Ch'r. Et dicunt q'd predic' Ric'us obiit die Jovis prox. post festum annunc. beate Marie Virg. A°. sup'dicto. Et dicunt q'd Elizabetha Chandos, et Alianor Chaundos quam Rogerus Colynge duxit in uxorem, sorores pred' Joh'is Chandos, et Isabella fil' Margarete tercie sororum ejusdem Joh'is, quamquidem Isabellam Joh'es de Annesley Ch'r. duxit in uxorem, sunt heredes Joh'is predicti, et quelibet eorum etatis xxvi. annorum et amplius. (*Esc.* 49 Edw. III. p. 1, no. 36.) So that Eleanor was then already wife of Roger Colynge in 1375. 1377, 1 Ric. II. Another Inquisition taken on death of Sir Richard d'Amory further shews that he held the Manor of Hedingdon, &c. for his life by gift of John Chaundos, Kt. whose heirs were the sisters of said Sir John Chandos, which Sir John in 33 Edw. III. (1359) for his many services among other grants obtained the Manor of Hedingdon and the two bundreds of Bolendon and Northgate from the Crown. (Parker's *Architectural Antiquities in the Neighbourhood of Oxford*, p. 286.) 1399, 22—23 Ric. II. the King grants to Wm. Willicotes the Manor of Hedingdon and said hundreds in fee farm for 40l. yearly rent, which premises were formerly Sir John Chandos, and are now forfeited to the King for defect of payment of the reserved rent. (Ibid.) 1415, 3 Hen. V. Thomas Wilcotes, son and heir of William Wilcotes, who holds the Manor of Hedingdon, &c. accounts to the King in Michaelmas term for the reliefs of Eliz. Chaundos, Roger Colinge and Alianore his wife, John Annesley and Eliz. his wife, for the manor and hundreds aforesaid, due upon the King's pardon to them. (*Ashmole MSS. X.* p. 350.) This vol. of Ashmole's is No. 1106 in Mr. Black's Catalogue of the Ashmolean MSS. It contains collections for a history of the Order of the Garter ; and those for Sir John Chandos occupy from p. 349 to p. 360.—B. W. G.

tioned by our correspondent, in which the father of Lady Annesley is stated to have been Sir John Ireland. This statement should be verified,—it having, if true, escaped the notice of Mr. Beltz. Besides, a writer in *The Topographer and Genealogist*, vol. i. p. 179, names him as Sir Robert (not Sir John) de Ireland. We have further consulted the pedigree of Annesley in Lodge's *Peerage of Ireland* (edit. Archdall, 1789), iv. 103, but without obtaining additional information. He states indeed that Elizabeth Chandos was married to Thomas Berkeley of Cubberley; but in correction of that misstatement we may refer to a letter by B. W. G. in the *Gentleman's Magazine* for March of the present year, which shews that Elizabeth Chandos, who was married to Sir Thomas Berkeley of Cubberley, was not of the Radborne branch of the family, but of the Snodehull.

It may be further remarked that, notwithstanding R. Glover's opinion (quoted by Beltz and Townsend) that Isabel Annesley left no issue, that fact can scarcely be deemed to be thoroughly verified. Beltz in a foot-note (p. 75) clearly states that Elizabeth Chandos, who died unmarried, in 1386 settled her portion in Radborne on her niece Elizabeth Pole and the heirs of her body. This is no proof that her other niece Isabel Annesley left no issue: but it might be argued that this disposal of her estate has originated the assertion that Elizabeth Pole was the sole representative of Sir John Chandos: whilst, on the other hand, the Annesley family have continually assumed the quartering of Chandos, whether *per fas aut nefas*. So long since as the reign of Charles II. Arthur Annesley bore on his shield four quarters: 1 and 4. Annesley; 2. Vert, three battle axes or, Houscarle; 3. Or, a pile gules, Chandos. And his, and his grandfather's, descendants, have ever in the same way asserted their descent from the illustrious Sir John Chandos.

Sir John Archer, Justice of the Common Pleas in the reign of Charles II., married for his first wife Margaret, daughter of Sir George Savile, of Thornhill, by his second wife, Elizabeth, daughter of Sir Edward Ascough, of South Kelsey, co. Lincoln. Sir John Archer married secondly Eleanor daughter of Sir John Curzon, and had issue, which terminated in a female, and is assumed to be represented by Lord Wrottesley. By his first wife, who was buried at Great Ponton, in Lincolnshire (a manor possessed by Sir John Archer), he had a son, John. *Qy.* Was this the same John Archer who had an extensive grant of land in Jamaica in 1664? The Ayscoughs emigrated in great numbers to the West Indies in the 17th century; and in 1654 Sir George Ayscough published an Account of Barbados.

Gabriel Archer went to Virginia with Captain Gosnald in 1584, and published an account of the voyage in 1602.

Gabriel Martyn, of Jamaica, had by his wife Catharine Gallimore a son named Archer Martyn, who died in 1703. Jane Gallimore, sister to Catharine, was married to Matthew Gregory. John Archer in 1689 bequeaths to his nephew Gabriel Martyn.

Michael Archer, who is mentioned in the State Papers as having gone to Virginia, afterwards turns up at Cadiz, as Don Miguel Archer, a wine merchant. They were evidently one and the same.

The Virginian Archers of the 17th century were originally from Ripon, in England.

The following extract from the pedigree of a well-known Lincolnshire family is perhaps noteworthy :—

John Chaplin, of Blankney, co. Lincoln, had issue :

1. Anne, mar. *Thomas Archer* (son of Thomas Archer of Umberslade), ob. s. p. 1743. *Vide* Monument at Hale, near Salisbury.

2. Francis, ob. 1720.

3. John, ob. in *West Indies*.

4. Thomas, mar. *Diana*, youngest daughter of *Andrew Archer*, of Umberslade, and sister of the 1st Lord Archer.

5. Porter, mar. . . . . ? and had issue : 1. Elizabeth, mar. Edward *Ayscough*; 2. (Sir) John ; 3. Anne ; 4. Francis, mar. Charles Fitzwilliam.

(Compare these *coincidences* of names with the pedigree of the Coopersale Archers.)

There were twelve grants of land to, and purchases by, a John Archer, between 1664 and 1686, in Jamaica, and Sir Hans Sloane mentions in his work on that island " Archer's ridge."

There were certainly, however, at least two *John Archers* in Jamaica at the period in question. One died without male issue, and his line was eventually represented by a wealthy family named *Gregory*, from which descended the celebrated Monk Lewis.

The other John Archer had by his wife Dorothy Harvey a son named William, who settled at Wexford in Ireland.—Burke's *Landed Gentry*.

J. H. L.-A.

SIR HASTINGS STANLEY (p. 96).—In reply to the question "who was Sir Hastings Stanley, Knight, and to what family did he belong," I am enabled, by a search at the British Museum, to show that he was the son of Peter Stanley, of Womersley, co. York, by Margaret his wife, daughter of Thomas Wright and widow of Sir William Gascoign, of Gawthorpe, the said Peter Stanley being of the Stanleys of Hooton in Cheshire.

Sir Hastings would appear to have been "knighted by the French King in 1603," which may account for the absence of his name from the lists of knights made at home in the reigns of Queen Elizabeth and James I. His wife was Ellinor, daughter of Rooke Reresby, of Bunsham[1] in Huntingdonshire ; and though buried at Hatfield, co. York, in pursuance of her will, there is no memorial of her now to be found beyond the entry in the Register of Burials—

1614. " Novemb. Dᵃ Elinor Stanley, vii die."

[1] Probably Bluntisham, near St. Ives.

The pedigree of Stanley (Visitation of Yorkshire, 1612); of Mauleverer (Hunter's *South Yorkshire*, i. 297); of Gascoigne (ibid. ii. 484); and of Reresby (Harl. MS. 890, fo. 44b. and also 1174, fo. 140), may be referred to for confirmation of this account of Sir Hastings Stanley's family.

Peter Stanley, adm'on to his son,⊤Margaret, dau. of Thomas⊨l husb. Sir William
Nov. 1, 1600. │ Wright. Gascoigne.

Sir Hastings Stanley, of Womersley, knt.⊤Ellinor, dau. of Rooke Reresby.

Hastings Stanley, of⊤Margaret, dau. of John Lewis, of Marr,   Percy of Letwell,
Letwell, co. York. │ and widow of John Mauleverer.   gent. 1625.

Thomas Stanley, of Ful-   Darcy, buried at St.   .... wife of Timothy Scott,
wood's Rents, near Gray's   John's, co. York, in   of Bishopsdyke Hall, in Sher-
Inn, 1666.   1619.   burn, gent.

Having answered, I hope, fully the question of C. J., I would in my turn ask, on what occasion or for what particular service was Sir Hastings knighted by the French King?

Doncaster.   J. S.

CANTING SUPPORTERS.—When noticing (in p. 157) the fictitious SIGIL-LVM COVLTHARTI we remarked that the Colt and Hart had been truly designated by Mr. Lower as "a unique instance of *canting supporters*." A Correspondent demurs to this, reminding us that the Earl of Shrewsbury and Talbot has *Talbots* on both sides of his atchievement, and Lord Talbot of Malahide on the dexter; that the Earl of Ilchester and Lord Holland have *Foxes:* Lord Wodehouse has *Woodhouses* or wild men of the wood; Baring, Lord Ashburton, has two *Bears;* and the Babingtons once had *Baboons;* and there are perhaps other similar cases. Canting on his title, Lord Mounteagle has two Eagles, gorged with chains that carry a portcullis, the emblematic badge of the Exchequer; and the Eagles of Lord Godolphin, as the spread eagle in the coat of Godolphin, are derived from a Cornish word bearing that signification. But the idea of making a canting *rebus* of the two supporters—the *colt* and *hart*, remains, we imagine, "original" and unique, and the inventor must retain all the credit, such as it is, due to his perverse ingenuity.

HERALDIC CARDS BY RICHARD BLOME (p. 180). From the statement made in p. 180, viz. "The armories are coloured throughout," it might be inferred that these cards were printed in colours. This, however, was not the case, the tinctures being indicated by the lines and dots used for that purpose. I possess an exceedingly fine copy of these cards. The margins have not been cut off, and by placing them together I ascertained that they must have been originally printed in sheets, probably folio, the cards being arranged in two or three rows. I joined nearly all my pack in two pieces, but so as to lead to the impression in my mind that they were originally printed on two separate sheets. I purchased them some months ago from a country bookseller, for 5s.; they were bound in a little 12mo. book, which was in very bad condition. I have therefore had them remounted. GEORGE W. MARSHALL, LL.B.

THE AUTHOR OF THE WORKES OF ARMORIE.

Since I last wrote on this subject I have had an opportunity of looking through the early parish register of Stainton and have extracted the Boswell entries, and amongst them the burial of "John Boswell Gentleman" on 25 Oct. 1558. Was not this *John the heir* of Thomas B. of Stainton who died April 4th 1551, and *sixty years old* at the time of his father's death, as appears by a copy of the *Inq. p. mortem* now before me, and noted in Mr. Hunter's own copy of the South Yorkshire? *See Herald and Genealogist,* i. 115. If so, is it likely that he was the author of a book printed in 1572, when his age would be 81? Again, is it known that the author was alive when the reprint of his book was issued in 1597?

I have met with no Will or Administration of the John B. whose burial I have quoted above; and I fear the question "Who was John Bossewell the author of the *Workes of Armorie?*" must at present remain unanswered.

Doncaster. J. S.

ALLIANCES OF THE FAMILY OF FITZ-SIMON ALIAS SYMONDS WITH "THE LEES OF QUARRENDON," (p. 113).

According to the pedigrees of the Suffield (Norfolk) and Yeldham (Essex) branches of the Fitz-Simon alias Symonds family, it appears that William Symons, of Wendron, Cornwall, (elder brother of Simon Symons, rector of Taplow, Bucks, vicar of Bray, Berks, and prebendary of Lichfield), married, first, Margery, daughter of Thomas Fowler, of Ricot, Oxon, gent.; and secondly, Joan, a daughter of *Robert Lea,* of "*Quarenden,*" co. Bucks, Esq. He died in 1559, leaving by his *second* wife, an only son, Anthony Symons, of London, merchant, born in 1525, who married in 1571, Jane, sister of Giles Simonds, of Clay, co. Norfolk, (whose wife was *Katharine,* daughter of *Sir Anthony Lee,* of *Burston,* knt., M.P. for co. Bucks,) and died in 1586. His son John having predeceased him, he was succeeded in a small estate which he had purchased (Leigh, in Pillaton), by his nephew John, of Trelay, who died in 1615, leaving an only son, John, of Botus-Fleming, Cornwall, born in 1582, who married, in 1604, Agnes, younger daughter and co-heir of Robert Trepe, of Crediton, co. Devon, esq., and was ancestor of the Symonses of Hatt.

The arms borne by the above William Symons, of Wendron, were " Quarterly: 1st and 4th, Azure, a canton ermine; 2nd and 3rd, Argent three escutcheons gules," impaling " *Argent, a fesse between three crescents sable.*"

The arms borne by the above Giles Simonds, of Clay, were " Azure, three trefoils slipped or," impaling, " *Quarterly: first and fourth, Argent, a fesse between three leopard's heads sable; second and third, Argent, on a fesse....? between three unicorn's heads erased sable, as many lilies....?*"

The "Symonds" pedigree, of which I have a copy, having been made about 1587, when those marriages were but of recent occurrence, they are not likely to have been confused with *other* members of the Lee family. Probably, Robert "Lea," of "Quarenden," was father of Sir Anthony "Lee," of Burston; but I should like to know the dates of their marriages and deaths, as I cannot obtain any clue to them from *local* records. J. G. F.

HUTCHIN. Richard Hutchin of Dartmouth in Devonshire, died in 1808, and Hannah his wife in 1806. They had issue: 1. Henry, born in 1768, married, and had issue; 2. Charles, who settled in Newfoundland, who also married and had issue; 3. Hannah; 4. Margaret, married to Mr. W. Hasard, and lived at Brecon (issue Hannah and other children); 5. Susan, unmarried; 6. Mary.

A brother of the above Richard Hutchin died in 1813, aged 83, leaving issue: 1. the Rev. Robert Hutchin, Rector of Dittesham, co. Devon; and Chaplain to the E. I. Company at Penang; married at Calcutta May 10, 1818, to Elvira daughter of the late C. Phipps, esq. of Watton Court, Devon.

Amongst the collaterals of this family occur the names Spanke, Bramscomb, Montague, Trench, and Newman.

A branch of the family, spelling their name Hutchings, settled in Jamaica. Any information about them will oblige L.-A.

To TEMPLARIUS we reply, with thanks, that we were aware of the Memoir on the Temple Church by Joseph Jekyll, esq. M.P. F.R.S. F.S.A. in *Architectura Ecclesiastica Londini*, 1819; but the account it gives of the effigies will be found very confused and erroneous indeed. We should be very glad if any one would help us by a reference to "the collections made by a person studious of antiquities in Sir Robert Cotton's voluminous library," which were made use of by Weever.

LIEUTENANT-GENERAL TATTON.—Wanted the descent of this officer, whose son was Dean of Canterbury about the middle of last century, and whose daughter was the unfortunate Lady Abergavenny, wife successively of the 13th and 14th Lords, and mother of George 15th Lord.

229, Clarendon Villas, Plumstead. F. M. S.

P. 556.—W. G. condemns the two first lines of *le Siege de Karlaverock* as being clearly a spurious addition, because they speak of Edward the First as being *rois Edewars li ters.* But that objection is not decisive. King Edward I. was in legal documents called Edward only, or Edward son of Henry: but by historical writers of his own time or shortly after he was often called "the Third," they reckoning the two Edwards before the Norman Conquest, Edward the Elder and Edward the Martyr, as the First and Second.

Vol. II. p. 84.—In the title-page of his *Atlas Terrestris*, a book of maps of the world, John Seller is styled "Hydrographer to the Kings most Excellent Majesty." It was "to be sold at his shop at the Hermitage in Wapping, and on the Royal Exchange in London," but has no date. I have Mr. Bowyer's copy, full of his MS. notes.

In p. 16 of his *Heraldry Epitomized* he gives as the arms of *Seller*, Argent, a fess ermine and in chief three roses. This coat is not inserted in Burke's *General Armory*.   J. G. N.

P. 98.—Mrs. Elizabeth Ogbourne died 1853, the end of the year, in her 89th or 90th year, at 58, Great Portland-street, Oxford-street. She was not the wife, but the sister, of the engraver.

THE FIRST DUKE OF BEAUFORT.   Since the note in p. 229 of the present Part was printed, we have made further inquiry into the accuracy of Macaulay's statement that the Duke of Beaufort in 1685 "was President of Wales and Lord Lieutenant of *four* English counties." And again, in Dec. 1687, "the Duke of Beaufort, whose authority extended over *four* English counties and over the principality of Wales." We find these expressions derived from the random assertion of Roger North in his *Life of the Lord Keeper Guilford* that the Duke "was Lord Lieutenant of *four or five* counties and Lord President of Wales." The truth is that the Duke, besides being Lord President of Wales, was Lord Lieutenant of the *three counties* of Gloucester, Hereford, and Monmouth, also of the town of Bristol and of the Isle of Purbeck; and Lord President of Wales and of the Marches thereof, excepting the counties of Salop and Worcester,—Francis Viscount Newport being Lord Lieutenant of Shropshire and Thomas Earl of Plymouth being Lord Lieutenant of Worcestershire. At the Revolution the Duke relinquished not only the Presidency of Wales but all his Lieutenancies. The Earl of Macclesfield who was appointed his successor as Lord President, after the abolition of that office by act of parliament (as noticed in p. 228), continued virtually to exercise the same authority as Lord Lieutenant of North and South Wales, the counties of Gloucester, Hereford, and Monmouth, and the city of Bristol. After that nobleman's death in 1693, we find (in 1700) his son Charles the second Earl the Lord Lieutenant of North Wales as well as Lancashire, and the Earl of Pembroke and Montgomery the Lord Lieutenant of South Wales as well as Wiltshire, the Earl of Berkeley the Lord Lieutenant of Gloucestershire and the City of Bristol, and the Duke of Shrewsbury the Lord Lieutenant of Herefordshire. After the death of Charles second Earl of Macclesfield in 1702, the Earl of Derby succeeded him as Lord Lieutenant both in North Wales and in Lancashire. These particulars are derived from Chamberlayne's *Angliæ Notitia, or, The Present State*, &c. for the years 1684, 1687, 1700, and 1702.

THE LEES OF QUARRENDON.

(No. II.)

Continued from p. 122.

In addition to his three sons, Henry, Robert, and Cromwell, Sir Anthony Lee, according to a Pedigree of the Lees of Hatfield, co. York, had another son, Thomas; and from Pedigree C,[1] it appears that he had likewise four daughters—1. Lettice; 2. Joice; 3. Jane; and 4. Catherine. Of these, the eldest, Lettice, or Letitia, married Nicholas Cooke, of Linstead, in Suffolk, esquire. Joice married John Cheyne, of Chesham Bois, co. Bucks, esq., as the following extract from the parish register testifies:—"Maister John Cheyne, esquier, and Mistress Joice Lee, the daughter of Sir Antony Lee, Knight, were married the xxix. day of November, A° Dni 156j." We learn from the same source that "Joice, the wife of John Cheyne, was buried at Drayton Beauchamp, co. Bucks, July xi. 1579." The writer has been unable to discover anything concerning the two remaining daughters.

Sir Robert Lee, of Quarrendon, on the death of his first wife, married Letitia, daughter of Sir Thomas Penyston, Knt., and widow of Robert Knollys, esq., of Nether Winchendon, co. Bucks. [Arms of Penyston, of Hawridge, co. Bucks: Argent, three choughs sable.] "Robert Knollys was Gentleman of the Privy Council to King Henry VIII. and had from that monarch a lease for a certain number of years of the manor of Rotherfield Greys, co. Oxon. He married Letitia, daughter of Sir Thomas Penyston, Knt., Lord of Haurage or Hawridge and Marshall, in Bucks, and by her (who married secondly, Sir Robert Lee, of Quarrendon, in Bucks; and thirdly, Sir Thomas Tresham, Lord Prior of St. John), had a daughter, Jane, married to Sir Richard Wingfield, of Kimbolton Castle, and a son and heir, Sir Francis Knollys."[2]

---

[1] In the possession of the Rev. T. C. Thornton, of Brockhall, co. Northampton.

[2] MS. in possession of the writer. Francis Knollys of Thame, co. Oxon, Esq.—a member of this family, was created a Baronet 1 April, 1754. He was Sheriff of Oxfordshire in 1757 and M.P. for Reading in 1761. He married in 1756, Mary, daughter and heiress of Sir Robert Kendall Carter of Kempstone, co. Bedford, but dying without issue 29 June, 1772, the baronetcy expired.

By his wife Letitia [Penyston or. Knollys] Sir Robert Lee had issue three sons—1. Benedict; 2. Roger; and 3. John; and two daughters—1. Elizabeth; and 2. Mary.

1. BENEDICT LEE, of Hulcott and Bagginton, co. Bucks, who died 1574, married Elizabeth, fourth daughter of Robert and Elizabeth Cheyne, of Hulcott, co. Bucks.

2. Roger Lee married Isabel, fifth daughter of the said Robert and Elizabeth Cheyne.

3. John Lee (living 1520) married Alice, daughter of Robert Dalby, esq. and had issue the Lees of Yorkshire and of Binfield, co. Berks.

1. Elizabeth Lee married Sir Thomas Tresham, Knt.

2. Mary Lee married Thomas Lane, gentleman.

The following Pedigree of Cheyne and Lee, compiled from parish registers,[1] is authentic and reliable:—

ARMS OF CHEYNE, CO. BUCKS: Chequey or and az. a fesse gules fretty ar.

John Cheyne, Esq. Sheriff of Bucks 1505, and Sheriff of Beds 1520; died Jan. 1, 1535.	Margaret, dau. of Robert Ingleton, Esq. of Thornton, co. Bucks.		
1. Robert, mar. 1535; died 1532, aged 47; bur. at Chesham Bois.	Elizabeth, dau. of John Webb, Esq. of co. Hertford, widow of Fulke Odell, Esq.	2. Margaret, mar. Paul Dayrell, Esq. of Lillingston Dayrell.	3. Elizabeth, mar. William Fawconer, Esq. of Ashendon, co. Bucks.

| 1. John, his heir, mar. Winifred, dau. of John first Lord Mordaunt, of Turvey, co. Beds, who died July 8, 1561, and was buried at Chesham Bois; he mar. secondly, Joice or Jocosa, dau. of Sir Anthony Lee, Knt. of Quarrendon, co. Bucks. | 2. Catherine, mar. first, Christopher Lidcott, in Yorkshire, and secondly, Edward Maystyn or Mastyn. | 3. Margaret, mar. Richard Duncombe, of Marlow, co. Bucks. | 4. Elizabeth, mar. Benedict Lee, Esq. of Hulcott co. Bucks, A. D. 1529, brother of Sir Robert Lee, Knt. | 5. Isabel, mar. Roger Lee, of Pittson, co. Bucks, also brother to. Sir Robert Lee, Knt.[2] |

It should be mentioned here that some pedigrees (e.g. that at Brockhall, marked C) make Benedict Lee, of Hulcott and Bagginton, brother, and not son, of Sir Robert Lee, and give, as the issue of Sir Robert Lee and Letitia Penystone, simply—

1. Benedict Lee, of Bagginton, who married Margaret, daughter

---

[1] The author of this paper is indebted to the labours and assistance of the late Rev. Henry Roundell, M.A. sometime Vicar of Buckingham, an accomplished archæologian and genealogist, for several facts and references in compiling the above.

[2] At Chesham Bois, Bucks, there remains in the church the brass effigy of Benedict Lee, a chrysome child, with the following inscription:—" Of Roger Lee, gentleman, here lyeth the son, Benedict Lee, chrysome, whose soule Ihu pardon."

of Robert Packington, esq., by Catharine, daughter and co-heiress of Lord Chief Justice Baldwin, and had issue; and

2. Elizabeth Lee, " wife to —— Tresham, esq."

To render the differences intelligible — differences which appear in several visitations and records, both at the College of Arms and British Museum, it is necessary to give the descents for a few generations from Benedict Lee, of Quarrendon, the founder of the family, in Buckinghamshire, as far down as that of Sir Henry Lee, the first Baronet— from the four independent original pedigrees which have been used in the preparation of this article:—

PEDIGREE A.—LORD LITCHFIELD.

Benedict Lee.⸗Elizabeth Wood.

Richard Lee.⸗Anne Saunders.

Sir Robert Lee.⸗Lettice Penystone.

Benedict Lee.⸗Elizabeth Cheyne.

Sir Robert Lee.⸗Lucy Pigott.

Sir Henry Lee, Bart.

PEDIGREE B.—NEVILL OF HOLT.

Benedict Lee.⸗Elizabeth Wood.

Sir Robert Lee.⸗Lettice Penystone.　　Benedict Lee.⸗Elizabeth Cheyne.

Sir Robert Lee.⸗......

Sir Henry Lee, Bart.

PEDIGREE C.—THORNTON OF BROCKHALL.

Benedict Lee.⸗Elizabeth Wood.

Richard Lee.⸗Elizabeth Saunders.

Sir Robert Lee.⸗Lettice Penystone.　　Benedict Lee.⸗Elizabeth Cheyne.

Benedict Lee.⸗Margaret Packington.　　Robert Lee.⸗Lucy Pigott.

Sir Henry Lee, Bart.

PEDIGREE D.—LEE OF YORKSHIRE AND STOKENCHURCH.

Benedict Lee.⸗Elizabeth Woode.

Richard Lee.⸗Anne Sanders.

Sir Robert Lee.⸗Lettice Pennistone.

Benedict Lee.⸗Elizabeth Cheney.

Sir Henry Lee, Bart.

SIR ROBERT LEE, knt., of Hulcott, was the eldest son of Benedict Lee, esq., of Hulcott [by Elizabeth Cheyne]. He was born at Helstrapp in the parish of Drayton Beauchamp, co. Bucks, June 15th, 1545, and married Lucy daughter of Thomas Pigott or Pygot [1] of Beachampton, co. Bucks, and had issue eight sons and six daughters, viz.:

"SIR HARREY LEA."
(*See the blason before in p. 120.*)

1. Sir Henry Lee, Knight and Baronet, of Quarrendon, co. Bucks, and Ditchley, co. Oxon.

2. The Rev. Edward Lee of Merton College, Oxford, Rector of Hardwick, co. Bucks, to which he was presented by his brother Sir Henry, and instituted 2nd March, 1613; died Nov. 1641, buried at Hardwick. He was a liberal benefactor to Merton College.

3. Benedict Lee.

4. Thomas Lee.

5. George Lee.

6. Robert Lee.

[1] Arms of Pigott of Beachampton :—Sable, three pickaxes argent.

7. Richard Lee.

8. Anthony Lee.

1. Frances Lee, 2. Elizabeth Lee, 3. Mary Lee, 4. Margaret Lee, 5. Joyce Lee, 6. Alice Lee.

Sir Robert died at Stratford Langton in the county of Essex, and was buried at Hardwick, Aug. 20th, 1616, aged 78. On the north side of the sanctuary of St. Mary's Hardwick is a mural monument with statues of Sir Robert and Lady Lee with their children, all represented kneeling.

The following inscription stands on the upper part:—

NOBILIS HIC MILES GENERE ET VIRTUTIBUS ANNOS
CUM DECIES SEPTEM ET TRES NUMERASSET OBIT:
CUI VITAM UT RENOVET POSUIT CASTISSIMA CONJUX
HOC QUICQUID TUMULI EST SUMPTIBUS OMNE SUIS.
SIC VIVIT MORIENS: JUSTORUM VITA PERENNIS:
NON MORITUR QUISQUIS VIXERAT ANTE DEO.
MORS HO'EM UBIQUE EXPECTAT, UBIQ. ETIA' EXPECTAT EA'
AD VOCEM TUBÆ RESURGENT MORTUI.   [HOMO.
ANIMA MORITUR PER CULPAM, RESURGET PER GRATIAM,
CORPUS MORITUR PER PÆNAM, RESURGET PER GLORIAM.

And this on the part below:—

Here lyeth interr'd the Body of Sᴿ ROBERT LEE, kⁿᵗ, Sonne and heire of Benedict Lee of Huccott, in the county of Bucks, Esq., who was second brother to Sir Robert Lee of Birdsthorn. He was born at Helstrap in the P'ish of Drayton Beauchamp, Anº Dⁿⁱ 1545, June 15th, and married Dame Luce Piggott, Daughter to Thoˢ Pygot, of Beachampton in yᵉ County of Buckᵐ, Esq., by whom he had issue viii Sonnes, viz. Sir Henry Lee, Knt. and Baronett, Edward, Bennett, Thomas, George, Robert, Richard, and Anthonie; and vi. daughters, Fraunces, Elizab., Mary, Margaret, Joyce, and Alice; when he had lived married 55 yeares, he dep'ted this life in the faith of Jesus Christ at Stratford Langton in yᵉ county of Essex, and was buried at Hardwicke, Aº Dⁿⁱ 1616, Aug. 20, ætatis 73.

This inscription goes far to prove, therefore, that the pedigrees B and C are right in making Benedict Lee Sir Robert Lee's brother, and that pedigrees A and D are wrong.

1. Mary Lee, daughter of Benedict Lee and Elizabeth Cheyne,

married Sir George Tyrrell, Knight, of Thornton, co. Bucks. Burke calls him Sir *Edward*. (Arms of Tyrrell:—Argent, two chevronels azure within a bordure engrailed gules.) They had issue Edward, who was created a Baronet 31 May, 1627, and two daughters.

2. Jane Lee.

SIR HENRY LEE, Knt. of Quarrendon, eldest son of Sir Robert, was created a Baronet by King James I. 22nd May, 1611. He married[1] Eleanor, daughter of Sir Richard Wortley, Knt. of Wortley, co. York, died A.D. 1631, and was buried at Spelsbury, co. Oxon. In the year 1613 (10th James I.) Sir Henry Lee served the office of High Sheriff of the county of Oxford, on account of his tenure of the manor and mansion of Ditchley, Dytchlea, or Ditchlee, besides his property at Charlbury in the same county. He was Sheriff of Bucks in the year 1621. A note by Antony à Wood runs thus:—" Spelsbury,

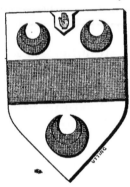

ARMS OF SIR HENRY LEE,
KNIGHT AND BARONET.

1675. On the north side of the chancel close to the wall is a faire table monument erected of black and white marble, with the statues of a man and his wife lying at full length, and divers children kneeling at the head and feet, to the memorie of Sir Henry Lee who married Eleanor Wortley. This Sir Henry Lee died 1633.[?] But this Eleanor married thrice after his death, viz. Ratcliffe

---

[1] Sir Henry Paget, brother-in-law of Sir Henry Lee, K.G. succeeded his father, William Lord Paget, and was the second lord, being summoned to Parliament in the 8th year of Queen Elizabeth. He married Catharine, daughter of Sir Henry Knevett, knt. and had issue Elizabeth, an only daughter and heiress, who married Sir Henry Lee, knt. and the same therefore, in all probability, as is mentioned above. By some the issue of this marriage is said to have been only one daughter ; others state that there were no children, the wife dying young, and this latter view is certainly confirmed by the fact that Thomas Paget succeeded his brother as third lord, and was summoned to Parliament in the 13th year of Elizabeth. This would not have been the case if his niece, the Lady Elizabeth Lee, had been alive, or had died leaving issue, for the title, being a barony in fee, would have passed to her or to her issue.— Vide Jordan's *History of Enstone*, p. 121, where these facts are given at length. On the other hand it is clear from the monument of Lady Lee at Aylesbury, that she had a grown-up daughter, Mary, and two infant sons, Henry and John, all represented on the monument, all of whom probably died before their mother.

Earl of Sussex, Rich Earl of Warwicke, Montagu Earl of Manchester." The monument referred to still remains at Spelsbury. From it we learn that his lady was the *fourth* daughter of Sir Richard Wortley, of Wortley, co. York, near which some of the Lees had continually resided, and that he had three sons, 1. Sir Henry, who was knighted at Woodstock, Aug. 26, 1614, but who died s. p. unmarried; 2. Francis; and 3, Henry Antony (died unmarried); and four daughters, 1. Bridget; 2. Anne; 3. Louisa; and. 4. Elizabeth.

1. Bridget, married Sir Francis Tryon, of Essex, Baronet; 2. Anne, married Sir Maurice Berkeley, Viscount Fitzhardinge.

SIR FRANCIS LEE, 2nd Baronet, married Anne, daughter of Sir John St. John,[1] of Lydiard Tregoze, co. Wilts, who survived her husband, and married, secondly, Henry Earl of Rochester. They had issue two sons, who in turn each succeeded to the baronetcy. 1. Henry Lee. 2. Francis Henry Lee.

SIR HENRY LEE, 3rd Baronet, married at Ditchley, June 4, 1655, Anne, daughter and heiress of Sir John Danvers of Dauntsey in Wiltshire. They had issue two daughters,—

1. Eleanor Lee, baptized at Ditchley June 3, 1658, married James Bertie, first Earl of Abingdon (created Nov. 30, 1682), and died May 31, 1691, leaving six sons.

2. Anne.

SIR FRANCIS HENRY LEE, 4th Baronet, married Elizabeth, co-heiress of Thomas Pope, Earl of Downe, (by Lucy, daughter and co-heiress of John Dutton, esq. of Sherborne, co. Gloucester), who married, secondly, Robert third Earl of Lindsey, and had issue—

1. EDWARD HENRY LEE, 5th Baronet.

2. Francis Henry Lee, who married . . . . daughter of . . . . . Williamson, esq. and had issue a daughter, Anne Elizabeth, baptized Sept. 22, 1687, at the Lodge in Woodstock Park, by the Rev. R. Rowlandson, Rector of Wootton, co. Oxon.

F. G. L.

(*To be continued.*)

[1] According to an ancient Court Roll of the manor of Spelsbury, for the year 1532-3, it appears that there was at that date a Sir John St. John, knt. the owner of lands and tenements in Ditchley, and, supposing this property still to belong to that family, the fact in all probability led to the marriage of Sir F. H. Lee with the daughter of Sir John St. John.

POSSESSORS OF THE MANOR OF HAMPTON POYLE FROM 1648 TO 1712.

PEDIGREE OF WEST.

ARMS: Ermine, a bend indented sable.

John West of London; afterwards of Hampton Poyle, and a Gentleman Pensioner in Ordinary to King Charles II.; purchased the manor of Hampton Poyle, etc. n 1648; ob. 8 Jan. 1695-6, aged 79; bur. in St. Aldate's Church, Oxford. M.I. = Mary, youngest dau. of Jarvis Kirke of Greenhill in Norton, co. Derby; ob. 8 May, 1686. M.I. in St. Aldate's Church, Oxford.

Charles West of London, merchant, in 1654.

Katherine Seaman, 1st wife; ob. 1668, s.p. = John West of Hampton Poyle; ob. mar.5 Jan. 1712. s.p. cir. 1664-5; = Elizabeth Palmer, 3rd wife; m. ante 1687; living a widow in 1717-8, s. p. = ..., 2nd wife, widow of Portington, ob.s.p.

Eliza-beth West, eldest dau.; living 1696. = ... Wil-liams, 2nd hus.; ...... Po-cock, 1st hus.

Henry Street, of Kidling-ton, 1st hus.; m. cir. 1671; ob. ante 1691, s.p. = MaryWest, 2nd dau. executrix of her father's will; living 1699. = John Conant, LL.D. of Ox-ford, 2nd hus.; m. ante 1693; living 1699.

Samuel Hunt, of Ox-ford; living 1696. = Kathe-rine West, 3rd dau.; living 1696.

Ann West, ob. un-mar. 9 Oct.1674; bur. in St. Aldate's, Oxford. M.I.

John West Pocock, ob. circa 1696.

Mary Pocock, under 18, 1687.

Elizabeth Williams, under 18, 1687; living 1696.

Ann, Katherine, Mary West. (All under 18, 1687.)

West Hunt, 1st son, under 21, 1687.

Street Hunt, 2nd son.

John Hunt, 3rd son; liv-ing 1696.

Mary Hunt, under 18, 1687; living 1696.

DESCENT of the MANOR and ADVOWSON of HAMPTON
POYLE, in the County of Oxford, in the Family of WEST,
from 1648 to 1712. By Benjamin Wyatt Greenfield, Esq.
Barrister at Law.

Since the article on this subject printed in the first volume of
the present Miscellany was completed, further documents have
enabled me to illustrate more completely the descent of the
Manor of Hampton Poyle, when in the possession of the Family
of West from 1648 to 1712.

Katharine Seaman, the wife of John West, (whose marriage on
5th Jan. 1664-5, is stated in vol. i. p. 333,) was daughter and
sole heir of Richard Seaman of Painswick, co. Gloucester, and of
Pantfield Priory, Essex, deceased, by his wife Katharine, daughter
of Martin Wright, an Alderman of the city of Oxford. She
inherited lands worth 240*l*. per annum, of which the manor of
Pantfield Priory formed part. The latter estate she brought in
marriage to John West the younger; and thereof, by indenture
tripartite of release, before marriage, dated 14th Oct. 1664, in
consideration of a jointure of 200*l*. to be settled on her by John
West the elder, and for other considerations, she covenanted to
levy a fine to John West the elder and his heirs, for the purpose
of paying 80*l*. per annum to Katherine, her mother, for life, and,
subject to that annuity, to the use of John West the younger,
her intended husband, and herself and the issue of their marriage,
and in default of such issue, then to the children of the survivor
of the husband and wife.

After her death without issue, John West the younger, on
7th Feb. 1669, conveyed the manor of Pantfield Priory to his
deceased wife's uncle and trustee, William Wright the elder, an
alderman of Oxford, who left it to his eldest son, William Wright
the younger, afterwards Recorder of Oxford in 1688, and appointed one of the Welsh Judges 15th Jan. 1714. He died in
1721, leaving the estate to his eldest son, Martin Wright of the
Inner Temple, who was made Sergeant at Law, 14th April, 1733;
King's Sergeant, 23rd Oct. 1738; Baron of the Exchequer, Nov.

1739, and a Knight; and one of the Justices of the King's Bench, Nov. 1740. He retired from the Bench in 1755, and died at Fulham on 26th Sept. 1767, possessed of Pantfield Priory.

John West the elder, being thus tenant for life, made his will, dated 2nd Sept. 1687, of which he made his second daughter, Mary, then Mary Street, widow, sole executrix, and appointed her his residuary legatee, who, as Mary Conant alias Street (being then wife of John Conant, LL.D. of Oxford,) duly proved the same, with a codicil dated 12th Aug. 1693, in the Prerog. Court of Canterbury, on 15th January, 1695-6. [Bond, 151.] He therein left various pecuniary legacies to his children and grandchildren and others, to the value of 3000l. and upwards. As he never made any specific appointment to whom the sum of 1300l., which by the settlement of 1664 was to be raised after his death and charged upon the Hampton Poyle estate, should be paid, that sum was claimed by his daughter Mary Conant as his executrix. He also bequeathed a yearly rent-charge of 6l. 10s. out of lands in Northmore, co. Oxford, to trustees to pay yearly to the minister of the parish of St. Aldate, in the city of Oxford, 60s., to preach three sermons in that church yearly, on the 8th May and 9th Oct —being the anniversaries of their deaths—in commemoration of his wife, and Ann West his youngest daughter, and on the day of the month on which he should die; and lay out on each occasion 20s. in a dole of bread to the poor men, women, and children of that parish who happen to be present; and apply the residue in payment of the clerk's dues, and for keeping clean the WEST aisle and monument erected by him in St. Aldate's Church, in which church he desires his body to be interred.

On his decease, which took place on 8th Jan. 1695-6, he was succeeded in the possession of the manor and premises of Hampton Poyle and Hundred of Ploughley and office of bailiff of the same, by his only son, JOHN WEST the younger, as tenant in tail male general under the settlement of 1664, whose first wife, Katharine Seaman, died without issue. John West the younger's second wife was a widow of the name of Portington. By her he had no issue; and he married, thirdly, Elizabeth Palmer, by whom he had no issue, and who was living as his widow in 1717.

He made his will on 30th April, 1712, and therein appointed
Elizabeth his wife sole executrix and residuary legatee, devising
to her all his copyhold lands in the county of Oxford called
Turley Farm, in the tithing of Haley and in the manor of
Witney, for her own absolute use; and leaving to her his manor
of Hampton Poyle, the Hundred of Ploughley, and office of
bailiff thereof, and two hams in Kidlington-on-the-Green, in
trust, to sell the same, and out of the monies thence arising to
pay and satisfy all his debts.

By Indentures of lease and release, dated 14th and 15th Feb.
1695-6, made between John West of Hampton Poyle, esq. son
and heir of John West, esq. deceased, of the first part; Joseph
Offley of the Middle Temple, London, esq. of the second part;
Edward Barry of Hampton Gay, and Winwood Serjeant of
Wickham, co. Bucks, esquires, of the third part, he made a
settlement of his estate tail in the manor and premises of Hampton Poyle, subject to a mortgage of 1000l., with interest at the
rate of 5 per cent. per annum, to the said Joseph Offley; and by
indenture tripartie, dated 20th July, 1698, between himself of
the first part; the said Winwood Serjeant, esq. and Thomas
Norton, of Clifford's Inn, London, and of the Six Clerks' Office
in Chancery, gentleman, of the second part; and the said Joseph
Offley of the third part, he made a further mortgage of the
premises (probably to meet the expenses of an action in the
Court of King's Bench mentioned below), for securing a further
sum of 250l. lent by the said Joseph Offley, with interest at the
rate of 6 per cent. per annum.

On the decease of John West the elder, Dr. Conant and his
wife took possession of the premises of Hampton Poyle, Mrs.
Conant, as sole executrix of her father's will, claiming the 1300l.
charged on the premises by the settlement of 1664, with interest
from the time of his death, and refused to give up possession
until the money was paid. Thomas Rowney and William
Wright esquires, who were the respective sons and heirs of the
surviving trustees under that settlement, likewise refused, the
former, to join in raising the 1300l. by mortgage of the premises,
the latter, to surrender his estate therein, without having a decree

of the Court of Chancery to protect them; consequently, in Easter term 1696, John West, esq. son and heir of John West, late of Hampton Poyle, esq. deceased, preferred his bill of complaint in the Court of Chancery against John Conant, LL.D. and Mary his wife, Thomas Rowney, and William Wright, esquires, and others, as to his having free possession of the capital messuage of the manor of Hampton Poyle with its appurtenances, the Hundred of Ploughley and office of bailiff of the said hundred, and as to the payment of the 1300*l.* charged thereon, in order that he might be relieved of the claim. The cause having come to full hearing in Michaelmas term following before the Master of the Rolls, it was ordered and decreed on 27th Oct. 1696, that the defendants, Dr. and Mrs. Conant, be paid 1300*l.*, with interest at the rate of 6 per cent. per annum from the time of the death of John West the father, together with their costs of suit, and discounting what Dr. Conant had received out of the profits of the premises,—the computation of what was due to Dr. and Mrs. Conant being referred to Sir Miles Cooke, one of the Masters in Chancery; that immediately upon payment being made at such time and place as the said Master might appoint, the defendants Conant and Rowney should execute an assignment of the term of 500 years to the plaintiff, or to such person as he might appoint; the defendants Conant and Wright deliver over to the plaintiff all deeds, evidences, &c. relating to the premises; and the defendant Wright execute a grant and surrender to the plaintiff of all the estate which he held in the premises under the settlement of 1664.

Accordingly, by indenture dated 27th Nov. 1696, and enrolled in Chancery 1st December following, between William Wright of Oxford, esq. son and heir of William Wright, late of Oxford, deceased, of the one part, and John West, of Hampton Poyle, esq. son and heir of John West, late of Hampton Poyle, esq. deceased, of the other part, Wright bargains and sells all right and title in the premises to West. [*Close Roll*, 8 *W. III. p.* 4, *No.* 5.]

On 25th Aug. 1697, the Master made his report, containing the following computation, viz.:

Principal sum	£1300	0	0
Interest at 6 per cent. from 8 Jan. 1695-6			
(on which day plaintiff's father died)			
to 30th Sept. 1697	134	14	6
Amount paid on the premises by the			
Conants	18	10	9½
Defendants' Bill of Costs £71 17s. 9d.			
taxed at	32	7	7
	£1485	12	10½
Less amount received by Dr. Conant			
out of the profits of the premises .	130	6	10½
Amount of balance due to Dr. and Mrs.			
Conant	£1355	6	0

Which amount, by order dated 16 Sept. 9 W. III. 1697, the Master appointed the plaintiff to pay to Dr. Conant at the Chapel of the Rolls on the 30th following; and at the same time and place the defendants Conant and Rowney to execute the assignment of the term of 500 years, as specified in the decree of the court.

In order to meet this payment, John West raised £1600 on a further mortgage of the premises, as is shown by the three following abstracts.

By Indenture quadripartite, dated 30th Sept. 9 W. III. 1697, between John West, of Hampton Poyle, esq. son and heir of John West, esq. deceased, of the first part; John Conant, doctor of laws, and Mary his wife, one of the daughters of the said John West deceased, and sole executrix of his will, of the second part; Thomas Rowney, of the city of Oxford, esq. son and heir of Thomas Rowney deceased, of the third part; and Christopher Clitherow of Boston, near New Brentford, co. Middlesex, and John Elwick of London, mercer, of the fourth part; in consideration of 1355l. 6s. paid to Dr. Conant by Clitherow (being part of 1600l. consideration money mentioned in the next noticed indenture), the Conants and Rowney, by the appointment of West, assign the term of 500 years in the premises to Elwick in trust for Clitherow; and by another indenture, of even date with the next above, between the said John West and Elizabeth his wife of the one part; and the said Christopher Clitherow and John Stevens of London, linendraper, of the other part; in consideration of 1600*l*. paid by Clitherow, the Wests grant and convey the reversion, freehold, and inheritance of the premises of Hampton Poyle to Stevens, in trust for Clitherow; with condition to be void on West's paying to Clitherow 1696*l*. being principal and interest for one year at rate of 6 per cent.

In Michaelmas term 1697 a fine was levied in corroboration of the above conveyance, between the said John West and Elizabeth his wife querents, and the said Clitherow and Stevens deforciants, after the said John West had been in possession of the premises; and on the 24th Nov. 1697, a deed indented was effected between the said John West and Elizabeth his wife of the first part, and the said Winwood Serjeant, esq. and Thomas Norton, gentleman, of the other part, for declaring the uses of the above fine levied to Clitherow and Stevens.

In Hilary term 1698, Mr. West brought an action in the Court of King's Bench, in the name of William Wright, esq. the representative of the surviving trustee under the marriage settlement of 1664, against Dr. Conant and his wife, as sole executrix of John West the elder, to enforce compensation for an unfulfilled covenant in that settlement that the jointure lands should remain of the yearly value of 200*l*. for ever, and obtained judgment: whereupon Dr. and Mrs. Conant filed their Bill in Chancery, 28th Nov. 1698, against West and Wright, and obtained an injunction restraining Mr. West, until Michaelmas term 1699, from executing a writ of inquiry as to what damages he had sustained. Accordingly, in that term the writ of inquiry was executed, when the jury gave Mr. West 200*l*. damages and costs; whereupon, in Hilary term, 1699-1700, Mr. West moved the Court of Chancery to dissolve the Conants' injunction.

By these protracted proceedings in law and equity, and other causes, Mr. West was forced to raise further sums of money on mortgage of the premises, as is shown by the following abstracts. By two indentures tripartite, dated 2nd Sept. 11 Will. III. 1699, the one between John West of Hampton Poyle, esq. son and heir of John West, esq. deceased, of the first part; the said

Christopher Clitherow and John Elwick of the second part; and William Lord Digby, Baron of Geashill in Ireland, and Edward Birch of Leacroft, co. Stafford, esq. serjeant at law, of the third part; the other between the said John West of the first part; the said Clitherow and John Stevens of the second part; and the said William Lord Digby and Michael Noble of the Middle Temple, London, esq. of the third part; for the purpose of raising 600*l.*, and transferring the mortgage for 1600*l.* from Clitherow to Lord Digby, in consideration of 2200*l.* advanced by Lord Digby, viz.: of 1600*l.* paid, at West's direction, by Lord Digby to Clitherow, and 600*l.* by Lord Digby to West, the inheritance in Hampton Poyle and Hundred of Ploughley with the appurtenances is, by the last deed, released and conveyed by West and Stevens to Michael Noble in trust for Lord Digby; and, as a further security, the term of 500 years in the premises is, by the first deed, assigned by Elwick—under the direction of Clitherow and ratification of West—to Mr. Serjeant Birch, in trust for Lord Digby; with condition to be void on payment of 2255*l.*, being principal and interest at rate of 5 per cent. for six months.

In May 1702, Mr. West raised a further sum of 2550*l.* by borrowing 6000*l.* of Sir Edward Sebright, bart. on mortgage of the premises, and transferring to him the mortgage to Offley for 1250*l.* and that to Lord Digby for 2200*l.* as is shown by the three following abstracts:

By indenture quadripartite, dated 22nd May, 1702, between the said John West, esq. of the first part; the said Joseph Offley, esq. of the second part; Sir Edward Sebright of Besford Court, co. Worcester, bart. of the third part; and Christopher Dighton of the Middle Temple, gentleman, of the fourth part; Offley, by the appointment of West, assigns his mortgage on the premises to Dighton, in trust for Sir Edward Sebright, for securing, with interest, 1250*l.* paid to Offley by Sir Edward Sebright.

By indenture quinquepartite dated 22nd May, 1702, between the said John West of the first part, the said Edward Birch of the second part, the said William Lord Digby and Michael Noble of the third part, the said Sir Edward Sebright, bart., of the fourth part, and James Wittewrong, of Lincoln's Inn, esq. of the fifth part, in consideration of 2,200*l.* paid by Sir Edward Sebright to

Lord Digby, Birch by the appointment and direction of West and Lord Digby, assigns the term of 500 years, and Lord Digby and Noble, by the direction of West, release the inheritance of the premises to Wittewrong to hold both in trust for Sir Edward Sebright and his heirs for securing the 2,200*l.*

By indenture tripartite of defeasance dated 22nd May, 1702, between the said John West of the first part, the said Sir Edward Sebright, bart., of the second part, and the said James Wittewrong and Christopher Dighton of the third part, the conveyance of the premises to Sir Edward Sebright and his trustees is to become void on payment by West of 6,000*l.* with interest at the rate of 5 per cent. per annum. This defeasance bears an endorsement, dated 23rd June, 1705, whereby West acknowledges to have borrowed a further sum of 1,000*l.* at 5 per cent. of Edward Sayer and John Coppyn, esquires, executors of the last will of Sir Edward Sebright, bart., deceased; 900*l.*, part thereof, being for three years' interest due, on 23rd May preceding, on the 6,000*l.* secured on the above mortgage.

Sir Edward Sebright died on 15th December, 1702, and was succeeded by his eldest son, Thomas Saunders Sebright, who was then under age. By his last will dated 9th Sept., 1699, he appointed Edward Sayer and John Coppyn, esquires, to be his executors and trustees of all his personal estate.

On 19th May, 7 Anne, 1708, a decree in Chancery was pronounced in a cause between the said Edward Sayer and John Coppyn, as executors of Sir Edward Sebright, bart., deceased, James Wittewrong and Thomas Barker, as executors of Christopher Dighton, deceased, and Sir Thomas Saunders Sebright, bart., an infant, plaintiffs, and John West and Elizabeth his wife, Thomas Norton and Winwood Serjeant, defendants, ordering computation of what was due to plaintiffs for principal and interest in respect of the 6,000*l.* secured on the above mortgage, no portion of the interest or capital having been paid up by West, and ordering West and his wife to pay the same within two years and a half from the date of reporting the computation. The Master, by his Report dated 23rd June, 1708, computed principal, interest, and costs of suit due to plaintiffs down to 23rd Dec., 1710, at 9,008*l.* 16*s.*, and ordered the same to be paid on 23rd

Sept. 1710, at the Chapel of the Rolls, which report was confirmed on 29th June, 1710. West and his wife not having complied with this decree, nor having paid any part of the principal and interest or costs, it was, by a subsequent order made on 2nd Feb., 10 Anne, 1711-2, ordered that the said John West should stand absolutely foreclosed and debarred of all right and equity of redemption of the mortgaged premises.

Sir Thomas Saunders Sebright, bart., on coming of age in 1715, took possession of Hampton Poyle, and exercised all the rights of lord of the manor.

By indenture dated 26th June, 1717, between Sir Thomas Saunders Sebright of Beechwood, Herts, bart. of the one part, and the Right Hon. Arthur, Earl of Anglesey, of the other part, an agreement is entered into between them, viz., for the consideration of 10,000l. the Earl of Anglesey agrees to purchase the manor and premises of Hampton Poyle with the appurtenances, the hundred of Poughlow alias Ploughley, and the office of bailiff of the said hundred from Sir Thomas, or from any other person seized or possessed thereof in trust for him, or for his father Sir Edward Sebright, bart. deceased; and Sir Thomas agrees to convey to the Earl an absolute indefeasible estate in the premises in fee, clear of all incumbrances. In pursuance whereof,

By separate indentures of bargain and sale enrolled, dated 16th Jan. 1717-8, and of lease and release of the same date and the day next before, made between Elizabeth West, widow, Edward Sayer of Berkhampstead, Herts, esq., and John Coppyn of Marketsell, Herts, esq., executors of the will of Sir Edward Sebright, bart. deceased, and Sir Thomas Saunders Sebright, bart., eldest son and heir of the said Sir Edward Sebright, bart. deceased, of the one part; Arthur, Earl of Anglesey, Francis Annesley, and Thomas Barsham, esquires, of the other part; the said manor and premises, hundred, and office of bailiff, etc. were granted, sold, and released in fee to the said Francis Annesley and Thomas Barsham, in trust for the said ARTHUR ANNESLEY, EARL OF ANGLESEY: which conveyance was further confirmed by fine levied in Easter term, 4 Geo. I. 1717-8, between the said Francis Annesley and Thomas Barsham, querents, and the said Elizabeth

West, widow, Edward Sayer, John Coppyn, and Sir Thomas Saunders Sebright, bart. deforciants.

Corrections and *Additions* to the DESCENT OF THE MANOR AND ADVOWSON OF HAMPTON POYLE. Vol. I.

P. 324, l. 5 from foot, *after* " commander," *add* He was knighted at Whitehall in 1604.

P. 325, l. 7. from foot, *after* " Knt." *add* She was eldest daughter of Sir William More of Loseley, near Guildford, Knt. Her first husband was Richard Polsted of Albury, Surrey, and her third Sir Thomas Egerton, Knt. Lord Keeper (afterwards Lord Ellesmere and Lord Chancellor); by neither of whom had she issue. She died in January, 1599-1600, and was buried beside her second husband in St. Paul's Cathedral.

P. 326, l. 2, *for* " 11 years," *read* 12 years.

P. „ , l. 3, *for* " 1584," *read* 1583; and *after* " Sir Francis Wolley," *add* was knighted at the Charterhouse 11th May, 1603; and

P. „ , l. 8 from foot, *dele* " Knt." and *add* being knighted at Theobalds 31st Oct. 1615.

P. 327, l. 3 from foot, *after* " 1596," *insert* The following scheme of descent contains particulars not recorded in Dugdale's Baronage under title: *Grey, E. of Kent :—*

Henry Grey, of Wrest, Beds, 1st husb. died v.p.⊤Margaret, sis-⊤Francis Pigott, of 20 March, 1545, bur. at Flitton, Beds.; son of | ter of Oliver, | Stratton, Beds, 2nd Sir Henry Grey, of Wrest, who died 24 Sept. | Lord St. John, | husb. marr. circa 1562 (brother and heir of Richard, Earl of | of Bletsho, | 1547 to Margaret, Kent, who died s.p. 1523), by Ann, dau. of | Beds. | who was his second John Blenerhasset. | | wife.

1. Reginald,   Winifred, 1st wife, sole dau. and heiress⊤John Pigott,⊤Winifred, 2nd
2. Henry,   of Thomas Sankey, Esq. of Edlesbo- | barrister-at- | wife, dau. of
3. Charles;   rough, Bucks, by Alice, dau. of Rafe | law, of Stud- | Ambrose Dor-
successively   Hawtrey, of Rislip, Middlesex, mar. in | ham, Beds., | mer, and wid.
Earls of   her 21st, and died in her 31st year, 12 | and Edles- | of Sir William
Kent.   May, 1592. | bro', Bucks. | Hawtrey, of
                                                | | Chequers, Knt.

1. Thomas,   Margery,   Frances Pigott, bo.   Catherine Pigott, bo. 3 July, 1596, co-
born 1586.   bo. 1584.   1590, mar. to   heir of her mother, mar. to Wm. Plais-
2. Henry.   Alice.   Henry Bruges.   tow, of Lee, Bucks, and died Aug. 1656.

P. 328, l. 10, *for* " 31st June," *read* 30th June.

P. 328, *dele* l. 12—16, and *after* " Plaistowe," *insert*, This she enjoyed for only 15 months, as she died in August or Sept. 1656, and administration of her effects, as " *Katherine Plaistowe, alias Pigott, late of Lee alias Ley, co. Bucks, deceased,*" was granted to [William] *Plaistowe, the lawful husband,*" in the Prerog. Court of Canterbury, on 15th Oct. 1656. Between 1628 and 1638 she married to William Plaistowe, of Little Hampden, Bucks, who for many years acted as steward to Mary Lady Wolley. He afterwards settled at Lee, near Little Hampden. They had issue two sons, Samuel and Thomas Plaistowe. The latter died 20th Sept. 1715, in his 87th year, and was buried at Lee. From him is descended Mr. Deering, the present proprietor of the estate at Lee.

P. 329, l. 3 from foot, *after* "inheritance," *insert* The following is a verbatim copy of General Fairfax's Original Passport to Sir Robert Croke, printed on parchment, and certified with his autograph signature at foot, preserved in the Public Record Office among the *Royalist Composition Papers.* Second Series, vol. xxv. p. 639:—

" Sir Thomas Fairfax, Knight, Generall of the Forces raised by the Parliament.

" Suffer the Bearer hereof, Sir Robert Croke, Kt. who was in the City and Garrison of Oxford at the Surrender thereof, and is to have the full benefit of the Articles · agreed unto upon the Surrender, quietly and without let or interruption, to pass your guards with his Servants, Horses, Armes, Goods, and all other necessaries, and to repaire unto London or elsewhere upon his necessary Occasion; And in all Places where he shall reside, or whereto he shall remove, to be protected from any Violence to his Person, Goods, or Estate according to the said Articles, and to have full Liberty at any time within Six Months to goe to any convenient Port, and to Transport himselfe with his Servants, Goods, and Necessaries beyond the Seas, And in all other things to enjoy the Benefit of the said Articles. Hereunto due obedience is to be given by all Persons whom it may concerne, as they will answer the contrary. Given under my Hand and Seale, the 24th day of June, 1646.

" To All Officers And Souldiers under my Command, and   " FAIRFAX.
to all others whom it may concerne."

P. 337, Table I. third descent from foot, Edward Gaynesford, of Idbury, *was living in* 1550.

P. 337, Table I. last descent but one, John Gaynesford, of Idbury, *was living in* 1574.

P. 337, Table I. last descent; besides Christian· there were three other daughters, viz., *Ann, Alice,* and *Lucy.*

Arms of John Gaynesford, of Idbury, as recorded by Richard Lee, Portcullis, in the Visitation of Oxfordshire, 1574 : Quarterly of four coats :—

1. Argent, a chevron gules between three greyhounds in full course sable, GAYNESFORD.

2. Argent, a saltire gules within a bordure sable bezantée, DE LA POYLE.

3. Argent, a chevron between three buckles, tongues fess-wise, sable, CROXFORD.

4. Sable, three garbs or, banded argent, NOWERS.

Crest : on a wreath argent and gules, a demi-woman sable, vested and crined or, in the dexter hand a chaplet vert, in the sinister a rose proper.

The presence, in an heraldic visitation in 1574, of the De la Poyle coat in the Gaynesford shield of quarterings may be accepted as further evidence of blood alliance of the two families.

P. 339, Table II. last descent, Susan Vanlore, wife of Sir Robert Croke : *after* " mar." *add* at St. Andrew's, Holborn, 29 July, 1634.

FAMILY OF VANLORE, p. 371, l. 27, *after* " Catherine, married," *add* at St. Alphage, Cripplegate, 21st June, 1619, to Sir Thomas Glemham, etc.

L. 29, *after* "Middlesex," *add* who died in 1625, s.p.

Southampton, May, 1865.   BENJ. W. GREENFIELD.

THE FAMILIES OF NICOLLS, PUREFEY, AND DUDLEY.

To the Editor of THE HERALD AND GENEALOGIST.

SIR,—In reading your article upon Mr. ADLARD's account of the American family of Dudley,[1] it occurred to me that I might be able to throw a glimmer of light upon the early history of the most interesting character in the family group, Governor Thomas Dudley of Massachusetts, the founder of the American line. I have for some time refrained from sending you the little information I am able to give in the hope that I might increase it by further inquiries, but I have not been able substantially to do so. My information relates to the families of Purefey and Nicolls, which are supposed to have been connected with that of Dudley.

The earliest protectress of Thomas Dudley is stated in Cotton Mather's account to have been "Mrs. Purfroy, a gentlewoman famed in the parts about Northampton for wisdom, piety, and works of charity;" and his later patron is said to have been "Judge Nichols, who, being his kinsman also by the mother's side, took more special notice of him." Mr. Adlard, without having clearly made out who Judge Nichols was, assumed that he was in some way connected with Mrs. Purefoy, and acting upon this assumption he appears to have hastily identified him with a Nicols of Devonshire, mentioned in the Purefoy pedigree to have married Dorothy, daugher of Michael Purefoy, of Caldecote, co. Warwick.[2] There can be no doubt, as you observe in your notice, that by Judge Nichols is meant Sir Augustin Nicolls, Justice of the Common Pleas 1612—1616;[3] who is well known to have been a Northamptonshire man, and whose connection with Mrs. Purefoy, or Purefey, I shall presently shew. I have taken considerable trouble to solve the question in what way Thomas Dudley was a kinsman of Sir Augustin Nicolls, but without success. In order to put Mr. Adlard in the way of further inquiry, I will furnish such information as I can of the connections and alliances of Thomas Dudley's protectress and patron.

---

[1] Herald and Genealogist, vol. II. p. 409.

[2] Nichols's History of Leicestershire, vol. iv. p. 601.

[3] Sir Augustin Nicolls's patent as justice, dated 26 Nov. 1612, is stated by Dugdale (Orig. Juridic. Chronica Series, p. 102) to have been recalled; but on his tomb he is said to have laboured in his calling of a judge for four years (Bridges, History of Northamptonshire, vol. ii. p. 95). This is explained by Mr. Foss (Judges of England, vol. vi. p. 172).

William Nicolls, the grandfather of Sir Augustin, is the first of his family whose name is remembered.[4] He was lord of the manor of Clay Coton, in Northamptonshire, of which he levied a fine, 4 Philip and Mary, 1557-8,[5] and appears to have resided at Ecton, in the same county; where his son Thomas was born, about 1530, and his grandson, Augustin, about 1560.[6] He died 7th Sept. 1575, aged 96, and is described upon his monument at Hardwick, co. Northampton, as 'Gulielmus Nicolls, generosus, pater Thome Nicolls, armigeri, defuncti.' No will of William Nicolls can be found, either at Doctor's Commons or at Northampton.

Thomas Nicolls, the father of the judge, is said by Fuller to have been a serjeant-at-law.[7] This I think is a mistake. His name does not occur in Dugdale's list of Serjeants,[8] and in his will, dated 25 March, 1568, three months before his death, and proved in the Prerogative Court of Canterbury in the same year, he describes himself as Thomas Nicolls of Pichelye, in the county of Northampton, gentleman. The same document however shows him to have been a lawyer, since he leaves to Edward Gryffyn, esquire, his two books of "Fitzharbert's Abrydgement and the Table to the same," and he directs the rest of his books, "as well such as concerne the law as others," to be divided among his sons. He appears to have resided a part of the year in London, for the purpose of his practice, for he directs his executors to dispose of the lease of his "house in the Old Bailie, in the suburbes of London, and all the hangings and joined works there, except only the bedstedes, chaires, and stools," for the payment of his debts. He disposes in favor of his sons of sundry estates in the counties of Northampton and Dorset, and devises to his wife Ann Nicolls the rectory and parsonage of Pichely, in which he then dwelt. He bequeaths to his singular good father William Nicolls a silver cup which he had of him, and also Sir Henry Compton's cup. He bequeaths ten shillings to the poor folks in Eckton, where he was born, as well as like sums

---

[4] In the pedigree entered in the Visitation of Northamptonshire, 1619, the name of William Nicolls is not given, but immediately above Thomas Nicolls, ". . . . Nicolls del North. temp. E. 4, et de Eckton in com. Northampton."

[5] Bridges's History of Northamptonshire, vol. i. p. 549.

[6] Fuller's Worthies, Northamptonshire.

[7] Fuller's Worthies, Northamptonshire. Serjeants' Inn, according to the obliging information of Serjeant Gaselee, the present Treasurer, and of my friend Serjeant Manning, whose learning respecting the antiquities of his order is so well known, is absolutely bare of any records capable of throwing light upon the point.

[8] Origines Juridiciales, ad fin.

to other parishes; and a ring to his servant and kinsman Edward Pell. He forgives to Mr. Mordaunt the arrears of the annuity of 6*l*. 13*s*. 4*d*. granted to the testator by my lord his grandfather and himself. This was probably one of those annuities *pro concilio impenso et impendendo*, which were so agreeably familiar to our early lawyers, and appears to shew the testator to have been retained by lord Mordaunt as of his counsel.[9] That Thomas Nicolls practised his profession with extraordinary success is proved by the fact that, although he died at the early age of thirty-eight and in the lifetime of his father, he left a very considerable landed estate in the county of Northampton and elsewhere. Among the creditors of Thomas Nicolls, mentioned in a schedule to his will, is William Nicolls, of Much Billing, the sum owed being 30*l*.; and William Nicolls 'phisitian,' (probably the same person) is a witness to his will. His children mentioned in the will were four sons, Francis, Augustin, Lewis, and William, and three daughters, Susan, Ann, and Margery. Thomas Nicolls died 29th June, 1568, and was buried at Picheley. It is probable, though I have not been able to obtain certain proof of it, that Thomas Nicolls of Pichelye was identical with Thomas Nicolls of the Middle Temple, who was Reader of that Society in 1566, and assistant at the Lent Reading in 1567, and whose arms (Sable, three pheons argent, the same as those of Sir Augustin Nicolls) are in one of the windows of Middle Temple Hall. The Register of that Inn, which ought to have contained the entry of Thomas Nicolls, is missing from 1524 to 1551, and in the entry of Sir Augustin Nicolls it will be seen that the status of his father is not very distinctly shown. The Reader of 1566 does not appear to have lived to attain the honour of a double Readership, which in the ordinary course of things he would have done about seven years after his first Reading.

Ann, the wife of Thomas Nicolls of Pichelye, is described in the Pedigrees of the family of Nicolls entered in the Visitations of Northamptonshire and Leicestershire in 1619, as daughter of John Pell of Eltington, co. Northampton. No pedigree of the family of Pell appears to have been entered; but some notices of them, derived from inquisitions *post mortem* and other records, are found in the manorial history of Eltington in Bridges's County History. Thomas Pell purchased a portion of that manor in 7 Edw. VI. and another portion 4

and 5 Phil. and Mar. and died 1 Eliz. leaving Edward Pell his grandson and heir. John Pell purchased a moiety of the manor 3 Eliz. and
died 23 Eliz. seised of lands in the tenure of Thomas Pell, leaving
Richard Pell his son and heir.[1] Mrs. Nicolls after the death of her
husband was married to Richard Purefey, who appears, if I rightly
understand an entry in the pedigree of Purefey which will be hereafter
mentioned, to have been the third son of Edward Purefey of Shalston,
co. Bucks.[2] That she was remarried to one of this family is proved
by her monument formerly existing at Faxton in Northamptonshire,
which was surmounted by the arms of Purefey (Gules, three pairs of
hands conjoined argent) impaling those of Pell, (Argent, a bend between two mullets sable), and in which she is described as "Ann . . . .
mother of Judge Nicholls, who . . . . day of February . . . . in the 82
yeare of her age;"[3] and still more conclusively by the will of her
son Lewis Nicolls, in which she is named as "my mother Mrs. Ann
Purifie." We find her name "Ann Purefey" as a witness to the baptisms of several children of her son William Nicholls, of Tilton, co.
Leicester, in the extracts from a family bible printed in Nichols's
Leicestershire, vol. iii. p. 1137, the last occasion on which her name so
appears being on the 3rd March, 1613. Richard Purefey, her husband,
was the purchaser of an estate at Faxton in Northamptonshire,[4] about
ten miles north of Northampton, where was afterwards her residence,
and that of her son Sir Augustin Nicolls;[5] and there can be little
doubt that this Mrs. Purefey was the gentlewoman famed in the parts
about Northampton for her piety and charity, to whom Thomas Dudley
was so much indebted in his early years. A religious temperament
was hereditary in her family, and her son Sir Augustin Nicolls, like
the other patrons and friends of Dudley, was attached to the Puritan
teaching. "His forbearing to travail on the Lord's day wrought a
reformation in some of his own order. He loved plain and profitable
preaching, being wont to say, 'I know not what you call *Puritanical*
Sermons, but they come nearest to my conscience.'"[6] Mrs. Purefey's
will, in which, if it could be found, some mention of Thomas Dudley

---

[1] Bridges's History of Northamptonshire, vol. i. p. 565.

[2] See Nichols's History of Leicestershire, vol. iv. p. 600.

[3] Bridges's Hist. of Northampt. vol. ii. p. 96 ; Nichols's Hist. Leic. vol. iii. p. 479.
The surname is defaced, but the first letter is given in both these accounts as B.

[4] Index to Chancery Proceedings, *temp.* Eliz. vol. ii. pp. 260, 326.

[5] Nichols's History of Leicestershire, vol. iii. p. 479.

[6] Fuller's Worthies, Northamptonshire.

might be expected, has been sought in vain at Doctors' Commons and in the Northampton Registry.

Francis Nicolls of Hardwick, co. Northampton, the eldest son of Thomas Nicolls, is said to have been governor of Tilbury Fort in 1588, and to have died 1st April, 1604, aged 47.[7] I have been equally unsuccessful in endeavouring to discover the record of his will either in London or at Northampton. His son Francis Nicolls of Hardwick was knight of the shire of Northampton in 1627, and sheriff of the county in 1631; was created a Baronet in 1641; and died 4th March, 1642. He married Mary, daughter of Edward Bagshaw, and stepdaughter of his uncle Sir Augustin Nicolls, and by her had issue, whose history I shall not now further pursue.

Sir Augustin Nicolls, the second son of Thomas Nicolls, was according to Fuller born at Ecton, co. Northampton, which was, as we have seen, the residence of his grandfather, William Nicolls. He was entered at the Middle Temple, when about sixteen years of age. The register of his admission is shorter and less formal than usual, having been omitted and subsequently inserted in the page, *ex relatione* the Treasurer or Reader who admitted him. It is as follows:

5 Nov. 1575. Mr. Augustinus Nicholls filius M[i] Nichols de Banco de Northampton admissus est. Per me Plm' Cole. Ex relatione sua propria.

Unless the words *de Banco* are a mere miswriting for *de comitatu*, they must, I think, be understood to mean a ' bencher of this Inn.' This description would be applicable to Thomas Nicolls the Reader of 1567. Benchers' sons were frequently admitted without ' fine,' or upon payment of a lower amount, and in all the formal entries the amount of fine or cause of exemption is stated. Of this nothing is said in the entry before us, and it is probable that Augustin Nicolls, as the first son of a bencher applying for admission, had the advantage of exemption. His brother William was admitted five years later, and is more formally entered, as follows:

1581, 26 Feb. Mr. Will[s] Nicholls nuper de Novo Hospitio generosus filius quartus Thomæ Nicholls de Picheley in comitatu Northampton admissus et obligatus una cum Augustino Nicholls fratre suo : dat de fine xx[e].

For a further account of Sir Augustin Nicolls I must refer to Fuller's Worthies, and Mr. Foss's Lives of the Judges. I may mention that we have among our manuscripts in Lincoln's Inn, " Les conceits *Augustini Nichols* sur le Statute 32 Hen. 8, de Devises," probably the notes of

---

[7] Nichols's History of Leicestershire, vol. iii. pp. 478, 480.

some reading in his Inn.   He is stated in the Pedigrees before referred
to, to have married Mary daughter ... Heming, or Hemings, of London,
and widow of Edward Bagshaw of London.[8]   Upon his monument
are the arms of his father and mother, Sable, three pheons argent,
Nicolls, impaling Argent, a bend between two mullets sable, *Pell;* and
his own arms, *Nicolls*, with a crescent for difference, impaling Gules,
on a fess between three mascles or, three escallops of the first, within a
bordure engrailed of the second semé with torteaux.   These arms appear
among those granted by Sir Christopher Barker, Garter King of Arms,
between 1536 and 1548, to Thomas Hemminge of Hitchine in the
county of Hertford.   The family of Heming does not occur among
the Hertfordshire gentry, and the grantee was very probably connected
with London.   There is in the Heralds' College a short pedigree entered
by a Roger Hemming (son of William) living in 1633, probably by a
different family,—by whom the same arms were claimed, but the claim
was respited for want of proof.

Sir Augustin Nicolls died without issue 3rd August, 1616, at Kendal
in Westmerland, while sitting there as Justice of Assize.   A handsome
monument with a long inscription was erected to him at Faxton, and
another with a like inscription at Kendal.[9]   His will, written in his
own hand, but without date, was proved by his nephew, Francis Nicolls,
on the 21st August, 1616, in the Prerogative Court.   He describes
himself as Augustin Nicolls of Faxton, co. Northampton, knight,
Justice of the Common Pleas, being well in health but moved to a
serious consideration of mortality by the late death of his wife, and
since of his mother, both within the year.   He directs his burial to be
in the chancel of the chapel at Faxton, and that a monument be made
like that of his wife at Bath, but with a figure of himself in his judge's
robes of scarlet.   He disposes of hereditaments at Broughton; settles
his manor and lands of Faxton upon his nephews Francis and William
and their sons in strict settlement; devises the rectory of Tilton to his
nephew William for life, with remainder to his wife Joyce, and to his
sons; and bequeaths the several legacies mentioned in a schedule to
his will.   This schedule, in which we might expect to find the name of
the judge's protegé Thomas Dudley, is unfortunately not registered
with the will, and being preserved, if at all, among the unsorted inventories, is not open to inspection.

[8] This lady died at Bath, 4 May, 1614, and was buried in Bath Abbey ; the inscription on her monument is given in Nichols's Hist. Leic. vol. iii. p. 479.

[9] Bridges's Hist. Northampt. vol. ii. p. 95 ; Nichols's Hist. Leic. vol. iii. p. 479 ;
Nicholson's Hist. of Kendal.

Besides Francis already mentioned, Sir Augustin had two brothers, Lewis and William. Lewis was a merchant of London, and died without issue. By his will dated 8th February, 1585, the testator is described as "bound for Barbarie in the affairs of Mr. Richard Gore." He leaves his brother Augustin his executor, bequeaths legacies to his sister Margerie Purefie and to his mother Mrs. Ann Purefie, and a ring "to his father-in-law, mother, and each of his brothers and sisters, brothers-in-law and sisters-in-law." As there is no mention of his wife either in his will or in the Pedigree, he may possibly mean by his father-in-law his step-father Richard Purefey. The name of Dudley does not occur in the will; which was proved by Augustin Nicolls, 2nd November, 1592, some years after its date.

Of the family of William Nicolls of Halstead in Tilton, co. Leicester, the other brother of Sir Augustin, a full account may be found in the History of Leicestershire, vol. iii. pp. 480, 1137. In his will, which was proved in the Prerogative Court in October 1625, there is no mention of the name of Dudley.

Sir Augustin had three sisters, who are all named in .the will of their father; Susan, married, according to the Pedigree of 1619, to Robert Manley of the county of Warwick; Ann, married, according to the same authority, to Edward Hesilrige, of Thedingworth, co. Leicester; and Margery (in the printed Pedigree in the History of Leicestershire incorrectly named Maria) married to Michael Purefey of Mussin (qu. Muston), co. Leicester.[10]

The Pedigrees of the various branches of the Purefey family given in the History of Leicestershire are taken from a manuscript in the Harleian collection, and, though copious, require considerable correction. In the pedigree of Purefoy of Misterton and Drayton (vol. iv. 599), Nicholas (qu. Michael) Purefoy, third son of George Purefoy of Drayton, is stated to have married Margery, daughter of — Nicholas of Pickley, Norfolk. This last name we may conjecture to be written in error for Thomas Nicolls of Picheley, co. Northampton. And in the pedigree of Purefoy of Shalstone (vol. iv. p. 600)), the second marriage of Ann Pell widow of Thomas Nicolls, which has been already mentioned, is found under a form still more difficult to recognise, Richard Purefoy, third son of Edward Purefoy of Shireford, being stated to have married — Pell, widow of Nicholas Foxton. Faxton was, as we have seen, the residence of Mrs. Ann Purefey and of her son Sir Augustin Nicolls.

---

[10] Pedigree in the Visitation of Leicestershire, 1619, in the College of Arms.

I think I have now set down all my information concerning these families which is not already in print. In all my researches I have not met with the name of Dudley. Mr. Adlard appears to have jumped rather hastily to the conclusion that the connection of Thomas Dudley was with the family of Purefey. The expression of his biographer is, that Judge Nicolls was a "kinsman by the mother's side." This would in strictness mean, either that Judge Nicolls's mother, Ann Pell, was of kin to Dudley, or that Dudley's mother was a kinswoman of Judge Nicolls, and therefore most likely to be found in the families of Nicolls or Pell. The judge was not, so far as I have found, related in blood to the family of Purefey, though doubly connected by the marriages of his mother and sister.

I am, &c.

Lincoln's Inn. FRANCIS NICHOLS.

SIKES OF DERBYSHIRE AND NOTTINGHAMSHIRE.

Great uncertainty obscures the origin of a family of this name, sometime of note in the counties of Derby and Nottingham; and this uncertainty is mainly attributable to the pertinacity of its late representative in putting forward inaccurate and (in some instances) irreconcilable statements on the subject. Led by these statements unchecked by any supervision of his own, Dickinson, in his *Antiquities of Nottinghamshire*, taking the earlier generations of the family of Sykes of Leeds, as recorded in Thoresby's History of that place, and suiting the orthography of the name to the occasion, brings them down to Richard *Sikes*, M.A., gives him for wife Martha daughter and heiress of Sir Francis Cavendish Burton knight (a myth), and for son, Joseph Sikes, afterwards of Derby; but, recklessly following his informant, Mr. Dickinson states the year of the father's death as 1686, and the year of the son's birth as 1696.

The object of this communication is to show that Richard Sykes, M.A. died unmarried, and therefore we must look elsewhere for the parentage of Joseph Sikes.

Mr. Burke, in his *Landed Gentry* (1833–38), under the head of " SIKES of the Chauntry House," states that Richard died in 1696, and that Joseph was born in 1686. Thoresby, who was nearly related by marriage to Richard Sykes, states distinctly that he died 10th Oct. 1686, *without issue*, and this is entirely corroborated by his will dated 11th Dec. 1684, and proved 10th Dec. 1686.

On the other hand, Joseph Sikes of Derby was evidently a man of some mark, apparently considering himself as having a common ancestor with the family of Sykes of Leeds, using the same arms, and the traditionary "branded bull" for crest, as specimens of his seals bear witness.

1. Argent, a chevron sable between three antique heraldic fountains or sykes, *i.e.* azure roundels, each charged with two bars wavy argent (the *modern* heraldic fountain being barry wavy of six, argent and azure).

2. Over the initials J.S., on a wreath, a bull proper. (One branch of the family of Sykes of Leeds uses the bull passant, *charged on the shoulder with an heraldic fountain*, as fully exemplifying the word "branded.")

This gentleman married Hannah daughter and heiress of William Chambers of Derby, and first cousin of Hannah Sophia Chambers (also an heiress) who married Brownlow eighth Earl of Exeter. He made his will 11th April, 1752, naming *inter alios* his sister Hannah Brough, his brother-in-law Mr. Thomas Ploughman, his brother George Sikes (abroad), his brother Edward Sikes, and an only surviving son, Joseph Sikes, who had already succeeded as heir-general, through his deceased mother, to the estates of the Burtons of Weston-under-Wood, on the death of Samuel Burton, Esq., 24th Oct. 1751,—the elder son, Samuel Sikes, having died previously.

The names George and Edward do not appear in Thoresby's account of the Sykes family, and the testator does not seem to have had any predecessors of his own at Derby, unless we accept as such John *Sixe*, who made his will 15th Nov. 1680, and does not name any male issue; but, singularly enough, speaks of his grand-daughter, Patience *Burton*.

At Anston, on the borders of North Derbyshire, a family named Sikes has been settled for
many generations ; and, although the baptismal
name Joseph is not known to have occurred in
it, Joseph Sikes of Derby may have been a member
of it, as his grandson, Joseph Sikes, LL.B. possessed an old seal
(engraved in the margin) of the arms of Clayton,[1] a family which
became extinct in the male line by the death of Vaughan
Clayton of Whitwell, near Anston, early in the last century.
Vaughan Clayton's will, dated 21st Jan. 1715, mentions his
cousin *Sich* (Addit. MS. Brit. Mus. 24,458, p. 472), which may
be only another variation of the name of Sikes.

The late Joseph Sikes, LL.B., was the inventor of the following stories: that Walter de Sike was returned among the
gentry of Cumberland early in the fifteenth century; that Robert
de Sike sued Daniel Fletwitch, &c. temp. Ric. III.; that a curious
picture of Henry Sike, temp. Eliz. *among others of little less antiquity*, is at the Chauntry House—all pure fiction; and he claimed
the "Heron and Crayle families" as his "collateral progenitors"(1)
(*vide* Curtis's *History of Nottinghamshire*, p. 198) merely because
his father had married for his first wife Jane Heron of Newark,
who died *issueless*, 28th July, 1778.

Q. F. V. F.

In regard to this subject, the following interesting and very characteristic letter of the late Historian of South Yorkshire has been placed
in our hands. It was addressed to Dr. Sykes of Doncaster:—

"30, *Torrington Square, May* 3, 1859.

"My dear Sir,

"To your main question I am quite unable to give any sufficient
answer, and I doubt whether you would obtain one in any quarter in
which you might apply. The question is, whether what Thoresby
states to be the origin of the family of Sykes of Leeds, which produced
several distinguished persons, is worthy of credit. I will tell you how
it appears to me. Thoresby's father must have been well acquainted

---

[1] Argent, a cross engrailed sable between four torteaux. Crest, a dexter arm, embowed, the hand holding a dagger, point to the dexter, all proper. (This may have
been the seal of Vaughan Clayton's grandfather, William Clayton of Whitwell, co.
Derby, who died 29th June, 1666.)

with the Richard Sykes who had accumulated a very considerable fortune and who was not far removed from his Cumberland ancestor, and the acquisition of such an estate would naturally lead to some curiosity respecting the origin of the family; and, again, Thoresby having married one of them would be in a favourable position for knowing what could be known respecting them. Again, there was no temptation to invent such a descent, and the very *unlikelihood* of it seems to me favourable to the truth of it. Thoresby had curiosity enough to seek out what could be known, and genealogical ambition enough to seek out a more showy descent if he was proceeding on insufficient information. See how he writes to Le Neve respecting the Sykes's. He even goes so far as to say, that this Richard gave his daughters ten thousand pounds apiece.

" So that it really appears to me that there can be no great reason to suspect the truth of his printed testimony, and I am quite sure that it will be very up-hill work for any one who shall attempt to show any other descent for the wealthy alderman. At the same time, one would like to know that there is or has been a Sykes Dyke in the neighbourhood of Carlisle; where a family of the name of Sykes resided in the earlier of the Tudor reigns. It is also quite clear that there were families of the name residing in a good position in the West Riding of Yorkshire, some one of whom might well be supposed to have strayed into Leeds, and he or a son to have acquired the wealth which it is manifest the alderman possessed. I could not but be struck with the support which the Wills you have shown me give to Thoresby's pedigree of Sykes; and this pedigree being so supported must, I think, for the present at least, be an impassable barrier to claims of descent from this family of the name; that is, *unless a person who has inherited the name* can show that he descends from one of the persons named in the Ducatus—which is still within the range of what may be expected from family recollections a little aided—he must give up all thoughts of being a descendant of the wealthy alderman. Yet there is a printed book of topography—one of Mr. Rastall's publications[1]—which deduces a family of the name, living at Newark I think, from one of the Sykes's whose will you have sent me; the latter showing plainly, when connected with Thoresby's negative testimony, that no such descent had any real existence. * * * * * * * * * but the disposition seems to be growing in the country of setting forth descents quite fictitious:—nor is it confined to England. Too many

---

[1] The *Antiquities of Nottinghamshire*, by Dickinson, who took the name of Rastall.

of our New England cousins do the same.   Some people seem to think
that there is a different law of veracity *in respect of Genealogy than in
respect of other subjects.*   I look upon Thoresby's pedigree as a very
important bulwark against intrusions such as these.   Here is one
family, with its borders well defined, living in the midst of countless
families of the name in various grades of social position.   But there is
nothing in regard to the insulation of this one family to discourage inquiry respecting other families who bear the same name; and something
would be found to reward research.   At the same time the wide diffusion of the name of which you speak, and the want of association with
any of the great landed estates, would make the search difficult and the
results uncertain.   There is even a possibility that a descent may one
day be proved from one of the Sykes's named in the alderman's will,
though not spoken of as relations by him, yet possibly being so.   I
quite agree with you that the name was in repute, early, in the Staincross and Agbrigg districts.   But I have no account of any family of
the name in those districts, or indeed in any part of Yorkshire.   I have
looked at my collections for any mention of the name that you might
like to add to what you have already collected, but all that I can find
is only what follows.   In the dispute between Christopher Wilson of
Broomhead and Thomas Barnby of Barnby, esq. respecting common in
Horndean, there are depositions taken in 19 Elizabeth, when Isabel
Sykes, wife of William Sykes of Cawthorne, servant to Thomas Barnby
and then aged 65, was one of the deponents on the side of Barnby.   My
notes are written short and are imperfect, but I rather collect from
them that she speaks of her father-in-law Nicholas Barnby having
made a pinfold in Horndean.   [*So far was written by an amanuensis.*]

Excuse me for having employed another hand.   I have a large collection of early Bretton deeds (that is, copies from originals), but I do
not observe the name either as principal or witness.   Nor, indeed, do
I in any of my Staincross or Agbrigg deeds.   Yet I conceive that the
name must have abounded, and have been of some note, in those parts of
Yorkshire.   The letter of Richard Sykes, in which he speaks of " Cousin
Beaumont," who must be he who was afterwards Sir Thomas Beaumont
of Whitley, proves a connection of the Sykes's of Leeds with that very
eminent family : how can it have originated ?   The printed pedigree
of Beaumont will not assist.   Who again was uncle and aunt Binns ?
The ' brothers ' of the latter were clearly Stocks, brothers of the
writer's wife.

" I have nothing of the name at Sandal.   They may be found, I suspect, at Holmfirth, and probably throughout the parish of Kirk Burton. But really the name is so abundant that there is probably hardly a parish in those parts without it. In the Sheffield Directory of 1797 there are 6 persons of the name, two of them, however, brothers. These were John and Dennis Sykes, both of whom I knew. You may perhaps like to know that this family of Sykes came to Sheffield from Derbyshire at the close of the 17th century, when Godfrey Sykes, son of John Sykes of Calver in the parish of Bakewell, mason, was bound apprentice in the Corporation of Cutlers of Hallamshire for eight years. This was in 1699, and on Dec. 21, 1710, he married Mary Sellick, by whom he had two sons: *John*, a filesmith, father of John and Dennis; and *William*, who died 24 Oct. 1809, aged 87. I knew many of the descendants of *John*, but not the descendants of *William*, whom I have always regarded as the Sykes's one reads of in the Lives of Mr. Wesley. I remember we spoke of this when I had the pleasure of seeing you at Doncaster. Very likely I might be quite wrong, as I have no notes of any authority, nor any very definite recollection of what I may have heard. John and Dennis had 5 married sisters; most of whom I knew. Dennis was the father of Mr. Godfrey Sykes, who became Solicitor to the Stamp Office in London. I knew also another family of the name at Sheffield, at the close of the last century, not related to the Sykes's just named. The family consisted of two sisters, one of whom married James Bramhall, and was mother of John Sykes Bramhall, who died some twenty years ago. The other sister never married. I remember hearing her speak of her descent as if there was something notable about it, but I never heard any particulars, so far as I recollect, and do not think there was much in it. Of the other Sykes's in the Directory I know nothing.

*   *   *   *   *   *   *   *   *   *

" Yours very truly,

" JOSEPH HUNTER."

VOL. III.   Y

BURY ST. EDMUND'S in 1741.

1. Church of St. Mary.
2. Church of St. James.
3. Ruins of the Abbey.
4. Abbey Gate. 5. Market House.

NORMAN TOWER AT BURY.

THE BRIGHTS OF SUFFOLK.

The Brights of Suffolk, England; Represented in America by the Descendants of
Henry Bright, Jun., who came to New England in 1630, and settled in Watertown, Massachusetts. By J. B. BRIGHT. For Private Distribution, Boston, 1858,
8vo. pp. xx. 345.

Among the many handsome genealogical works that have been produced in New England, this may deservedly be placed in the foremost
rank: whilst it has this peculiar characteristic, that it is wholly devoted
to the history of those members of an American family who either lived
before the emigration across the Atlantic, or who belonged to the
branches who still remained in England. It is profusely illustrated
with maps and views, chiefly of churches and mansion-houses in Suffolk:
and the town of Bury St. Edmund's, in particular, has in its pages an
epitome of its interesting history and representations of its very remarkable monastic monuments. The annexed copy of an old view of the
Town is a specimen of the neatness with which these illustrations are
executed: having been drawn and engraved by two young artists who
are natives of Waltham and Boston.

The Author takes a comprehensive survey of all the families of
Bright which have risen to any eminence. He has found the name in
most of our counties, though he states that it does not appear in the
records of the Heralds' College until the seventeenth century. The

Brights of Yorkshire, in their several branches, seated at Banner Cross, Whirlow, Graystones, and Carbrook, were described by the Historian of Hallamshire.   Colonel John Bright of Badsworth, born at Sheffield in 1619, after having been a distinguished officer in the service of the Parliament, was created a Baronet at the Restoration in 1660, but died without male issue.   His name and arms were assumed by his grandson John Liddell, (a younger son of Sir Henry Liddell of Ravensworth, Bart.) whose granddaughter Mary Bright became Marchioness of Rockingham; but she died without issue, and the Badsworth estates eventually passed by another heiress to the Earl Fitzwilliam.

Of other memorable persons of the name,[1] the Author describes—

1. Henry Bright, for forty years Master of the Grammar School at Worcester, and who was rewarded with a prebend in that church in the year 1607.   He is commemorated by Fuller, in his *Worthies*, as having in that border city equally contributed to the instruction of the youth of England and of Wales.   Dying in 1626, he was buried in the cathedral, and Fuller states that his Latin epitaph was written by the celebrated Dr. Joseph Hall, then Dean of Worcester.   It is set forth in the local works of Nash and Thomas, as well as in Willis's *Survey of the Cathedrals*.   Henry Bright married Joan Berkeley, one of the distinguished family of Spetchley near Worcester (*not* Sketchley, as in p. 299 of the book before us,) and his daughter, Dorothy, was married to John Dobyns, esq. an eminent barrister, who purchased the manor of Evesbatch in Herefordshire, and, dying in 1639, was also buried in Worcester Cathedral.

2. Thomas Bright, sometimes called " the second old Parr," a man considered to be a hundred and thirty years old in 1708, having his sight and strength to walk, and then living at Longhope in Gloucestershire.

3. Edmund Bright, of Maldon, who was remarkable for his size, weighing at his death in 1751, when only twenty-nine years of age, 5 cwt. 1 qr. 21 lbs.   His portrait is in *The Universal Magazine*, and in Caulfield's *Remarkable Characters*.

The fourth great man of the name is John Bright, M.P. for Birmingham, whose celebrity has now attained very large dimensions in the eyes of the men of America, as a consequence of his general sympathy with democratic institutions, and his particular advocacy of the North during the recent struggle.   When the book before us was

---

[1] Besides "the Brights of Suffolk," the author has collected various notes upon other families of Bright, in his pp. 2—5, 297—316, 323.

written eight years since, he was less known, and was thus briefly mentioned—

John Bright, Esq. recently the distinguished representative of Manchester in Parliament, is of the Society of Friends; but his family is unknown to us. (p. 4.)

At the general election of 1865 Mr. John Bright has been for the second time returned to Parliament for Birmingham. His brother Mr. Jacob Bright was a candidate for Manchester, but he was not successful. We are not aware what ancestry they can boast: except that Dod tells us they are the sons of Mr. Jacob Bright, of Greenbank, near Rochdale.

But we have now another senator of the name, Sir Charles Tilston Bright, who has been elected for Greenwich. He is an eminent civil engineer, and was knighted by the Lord Lieutenant of Ireland upon the first laying down of the Atlantic Telegraph: and we learn from Dod's *Peerage, &c.* that he is the son of Brailsford Bright, esq. by a daughter of Edward Tilston, esq. and was born at West Ham, in Essex, in 1832.

The wide diffusion of this name is obviously attributable to its having been personal with our Anglo-Saxon forefathers. They had it in composition in their favourite appellations, Egbert, Ethelbert, and Cuthbert, as we have it still in Albert, Gilbert, and Robert; and by itself in Beorht, from whence is evidently the modern Bright, as are possibly two other surnames, Brett and Burt. Our author has received the following comment on its import from Thomas Wright, esq. F.S A. " one of the best Saxon scholars in England : "—

The name Bright is an excellent Anglo-Saxon name. In the Saxon it was spelled BEORHT. It is the simple word *bright*; but was used then with much more extensive meaning, as signifying distinguished, excellent, surpassing in courage or anything else; as you would say now ' a *shining* fellow', we say ' a *bright* fellow,' more with reference to his intelligence. Hence the name means an excellent or distinguished man. Beorht was a common name among the Anglo-Saxons, and is often found in records.

To this we may add the remark that for a daughter the name of Beorht became Bertha, a name still not wholly disused, though not very common. We wonder that the Brights have not adopted it, though it might be bringing " sweets to the sweet."

The Suffolk family of Bright, from which the author derives his lineage, and which forms the principal subject of the work, was once very numerous in that county; but every branch of it that has been traced has run out, or entirely disappeared from Suffolk, and it is now believed to be extinct in England.   A single individual named Bright, living at Saxmundham, was ascertained to be of another race—that had come from Shropshire.

The first ancestor of the Suffolk family is discovered in 1539, when John Bright held leases in Bury St. Edmund's of the abbey, being described in one of them as a mercer.   He is supposed to have been the father of Walter Bright, from whom the pedigree has been satisfactorily and circumstantially deduced.

It is not without reason that the people of New England are invited to contemplate the map of Suffolk, and to read of its old personal and local names, from which so many of their own are derived :

This county is interesting to New Englanders, and especially to the people of Massachussetts, on account of the emigration from it to our State between the years 1630 and 1640, these emigrants being considered the best as to character that came to New England.   This State derived the names of many of its towns, viz. Acton, Boxford, Groton, Haverhill, Hingham, Needham, Stow, Sudbury, and others, from Suffolk.   Governor Winthrop, one of the first of the Suffolk Puritans that emigrated to Massachusetts, whose family was remotely allied by marriage to the Brights, came from Groton; and there were the Fiskes from Laxfield, Appleton from Little Waldingfield, Ward from Haverhill, Browne, Bond, and others, from Bury St. Edmund's, and numbers from differents parts of that county, many of whom were among the earliest settlers of Watertown and Waltham, where the names of Bright, Goldstone, Fiske, Pierce, Mason, Browne, Spring, Kemball, Mixer, Barnard, Coolidge, Livermore, and others, are found in the records.

The effect of this emigration from Suffolk on our topographical and genealogical nomenclature is everywhere manifest in our old and respected Commonwealth; and the good influence of these Puritans from the Eastern shores of the mother country, in shaping the destiny of the infant colony, is seen in its present elevated rank among its sister States of our Republic.   (p. 7.)

The author's thirst for information regarding his ancestors had existed from his early youth, but with little expectation of learning anything beyond what is afforded by such vague traditions as circulate among that portion of the population of New England which was composed of families mostly of English descent.   These obscure and unwritten family histories are wont to bear a certain resemblance to each other, and to tell how a progenitor fled with one or more of his brothers from the persecutions of his native country, to enjoy on the Western Continent that liberty of worship which was denied him at home.   Though implicitly believed, these traditions have often proved, on investigation, to be quite as erroneous as much of what is called history : and in Mr. Bright's case, " he regrets being forced to confess that investigation robbed him of the larger number of those objects of his youthful veneration; and that two out of the three brothers, whose supposed sufferings in the wilderness for conscience' sake had awakened his sympathy, never crossed the wide waters; but, having passed their whole lives in their native land, were gathered to their fathers, and now sleep in an ancient churchyard of that district of England whose shores are washed by the German Ocean."

The effectual clue to the real connection of the family with the mother country was accidentally furnished by the discovery, in the records of Boston, of payment of an English legacy to the first Anglo-Saxon ancestor. This led to the discovery of the will itself, in London; and, through it, to a knowledge of his family, and their once flourishing condition in Suffolk. The investigation was pursued in England by Mr. H. G. Somerby, a gentleman of much experience in such inquiries, who soon poured into the author's hands the materials which he has skilfully digested and arranged. After the genealogy itself was formed, upon the solid foundation of wills and other public records, some interesting family papers, consisting of letters and other documents, were recovered from the hands of Charles Tyrell, esq., of Haughley in Suffolk, into whose family the heiress of the Brights of Netherhall in Thurston was married. These documents occupy a considerable share of the volume : the letters being chiefly on affairs connected with foreign merchandise.

Two portraits are, for the first time, engraved. One is that of the heiress just mentioned (she died in 1753, and was buried at Stowmarket); the other is that of Thomas Bright, a public benefactor of the town of Bury, and son of Walter, before named. The original picture of him is preserved in the Guildhall of Bury, and bears the following inscription :

THOMAS BRIGHT, sometyme Draper of this Towne, a worthy Benefactor, who gave for the benefit of this Towne the inheritance of a portion of Thythes worthe x^{lb} per annum, and an equal part of his goods, as much as he gave any of his children, which amounted to ccc^{lb}. 1587.

As the testator left nine children, it will be seen that he was a wealthy man. His benefaction has not been kept distinct; but, together with the other town charities, to which his son Thomas and his daughter Lady Carew (hereafter mentioned) were contributors, it forms part of "the Guildhall feoffment," which in the year 1844 produced a yearly rental of 2,111*l.*

The arms of the family were first granted to Thomas Bright the younger, by Camden Clarenceux, on the 20th of May, 1615.[1] They are Sable, a fesse argent between three escallops or; and for crest, a dragon's head gules, vomiting flames of fire proper, collared and lined or.

Thomas Bright the elder, by his wife Margaret daughter of William Payton, of Risby, had in all fifteen children (enumerated in p. 49 of this history); and of the issue that he left alive, to share his property together with the poor of Bury, there were five that we may particularise:—

The eldest son, Thomas, was father of John, afterwards a captain in the Parliamentary army as well as alderman of Bury, who purchased Talmach hall in the parish of Bricet, Suffolk; and had issue William, whose daughter and heiress, Sarah, carried the representation of this eldest branch of the family to the name of Dawtrey; whence it came to Luther, one of whose co-heiresses was married to John Fane, esq. brother to the eighth Earl of Westmoreland, and the other to John Taylor, esq.[2]

In the church of Great Bricet the Parliamentary Captain was buried, under a slab of slate having this inscription:

John Bright of Little

Bricett Gent. Aged : 67: yeare

Departed this life the :17th

Day of March :1660.

[1] It is stated in Dr. Bond's *Genealogies and History of Watertown*, 1860, p. 102, "These arms were confirmed in 1615, (not then granted, as stated by Burke,) to Thomas Bright, Jr., showing that they had been in the family long before that period." And we perceive that in the American *Heraldic Journal*, (June 1865,) p. 82, the same idea is maintained, "These were confirmed in 1615 to Thomas and Robert Bright, uncles of the emigrant; and it is most probable that they had been long the inheritance of the family." But this latter account is entirely incorrect. It is clear that the arms were *granted* to Thomas Bright of St. Edmund's Bury in 1615, by Camden Clarenceux; and confirmed to Thomas Bright of Netherhall, nephew of the former, in 1643, by Sir John Borough. (*The Brights of Suffolk*, p. 66, quoting Gwillim's *Heraldry*.) Our American friends have been misled by the usual phraseology of Grants of arms, in which it was very usual to veil an original concession under terms of confirmation.

[2] Grandfather of the present John Taylor Gordon, esq. M.D. (Burke's *General Armory*, 1851.)

Twenty years later his son erected to his memory the monument here represented : when the mistake (never corrected) was made by the stone-cutter that he died *anno septuagesimo* of the century, instead of *sexagesimo*. That the inscription on the floor was the correct date is confirmed by the probate of the Captain's will.

But the monument exhibits another peculiarity, in the atchievement of arms with which it is crowned. The arms of Bright impale those of Style, of Hemingstone near Ipswich (where the father of Mrs. Bright built, in 1665, the manor-house which is still standing,) viz. Sable, a fess or, fretty of the field, between three fleurs-de-lis and within a bordure engrailed of the second; and on the sinister side of these, by an unusual arrangement,[1] are placed the arms of this lady's second husband. He was, as stated on the tablet, the Honorable John North, esquire, a son of Dudley third Lord North, of Catlege or Kirtling; and below the tablet his arms, Azure, a lion passant between three fleurs-de-lis argent, are more correctly marshalled, impaling hers.

William Bright, the son, also married, for his first wife, one of the same family, namely Sarah, daughter of Henry North, of Laxfield, son of Sir Henry North, of Mildenhall, a younger son of Roger second Lord North.

Robert Bright, the second son of old Thomas, was a citizen and salter of London, and founded the family at Netherhall in Thurston, of which we have already spoken as the last remaining in Suffolk. It is conjectured (p. 101) that he was identical with Robert Bright, "one of the coroners of Middlesex," who, in 1613, held the inquest on Sir Thomas Overbury, who died of poison in the Tower of London: but this may be doubtful.

Henry, the third son of the Benefactor, remained at Bury St. Edmund's, resident in the mansion which has since been the Angel Inn; and is found to have died in 1609, though neither will nor substantial record of him is preserved. It was his son HENRY BRIGHT, baptized at St. James's church, Bury St. Edmund's, Dec. 29, 1609, who became the settler in New England. There is reason to believe that he was one of the companions of John Winthrop of Groton in 1638: his name being the forty-eighth in the signatures to the Church Covenant

---

[1] When three coats are impaled in this manner, it is generally supposed that the central one is that of a husband, and those on either side the coats of his two wives. The former is termed the *baron*, and the others *dexter femme* and *sinister femme*. And that this practice has been adopted for nearly four centuries we have an instance presented by a sepulchral brass of the date 1486, still existing in the church of Salt. wood in Kent. It bears the following inscription:

"Here lieth the bowelles of dame Anne Muston late the wyf of Will'm Muston which dame Anne decessyd the vij[th] day of Septēber y[e] yere of o[r] lord M[l] iiij[c] lxxxvj. on whose soulles ihū have mercy."

Above is a demi-angel rising from clouds, holding with both hands the heart and bowels of the deceased, and below the inscription is a shield bearing the arms of Muston, a chevron between three swords erect; which is marshalled between two impaled coats, that on the dexter a chevron between three dog's heads erased, col. lared; that on the sinister three cross-crosslets.

at Charlestown. He emigrated a bachelor; but his future wife followed him four years after. Her name was Goldstone, and she came (with her parents) from the same county of Suffolk. Her father was Henry Goldstone of Wickham Skeith; her grandfather, the Vicar of Bedingfield, is called *Sir* William Goldstone; her great-grandfather, bearing the singular name of Roman Goldstone, was buried at Bedingfield in 1575. Their pedigree is given by Mr. Bright.

The last child we mean to notice of Thomas Bright the elder is his youngest, Susan, baptised at St. James's, Bury, Sept. 28, 1579. The name of her first husband is not ascertained. In her mother's will, 1599, she is named as Susan Barker, which it is thought may be an error for Barber, because one of her sisters, Katherine, is called Katherine Barber in the same document, having been really the wife of Bennet Barber. But in the Visitation of Surrey she is described as the widow of a merchant of London named Butler. Before the Surrey Visitation of 1623 she was married to Sir Nicholas Carew, alias Throckmorton, of Beddington in that county: who had married for his first wife

Mary, daughter of Sir George More of Loseley; and whose sister Elizabeth Carew was the wife of Sir Walter Raleigh. This was a

high alliance for the little maid of Bury St. Edmund's.   Of her further
history not many particulars have been ascertained.   Her character is
still commemorated upon the monument at Beddington, represented in
the preceding engraving, and by a benefaction which is thus recorded
by the historians of Bury :

> The Lady Carey, daughter of Thomas Bright, gave £100 for the purchasing of
> lands to the yearly value of £5, which was to be equally distributed to five poor
> widows.

The spelling Carey for Carew, which our author terms a mistake,
scarcely amounts to one, as the name Carew has been usually pronounced as it is thus written.   The late Right Hon. Reginald Pole
Carew (ob. 1835), who assumed the latter name on the extinction of
the male line of the ancient family of Carew, seated at Anthony in
Cornwall, thereby became, to ordinary ears, Mr. *Poole Carey.*

The Surrey Visitation of 1623 gives the lady only two children by
Sir Nicholas Carew, Thomas, who died in infancy, and Susan.   The
epitaph is in this respect ambiguous, in the phrase " *my* deare mother "
being first employed, followed by a mention of " her children."   Mr.
Bright infers from this " that other children than Susan survived
to mature age, and shared the duty of erecting this token of respect
to the memory of their parent."   She may possibly have had children
by her first husband : but we rather think those alluded to in the
epitaph are the numerous children of her husband by his former wife,
who would be called hers ; and it is exceedingly probable that the
monument was actually erected by her step-son Sir Francis Carew,
rather than by her daughter Susan, of whose surviving no record has
occurred.

As we have already intimated, the Author does not pursue the
history of his family after it became settled in America.   That has been
already done in Dr. Bond's *Genealogies and History of Watertown,*
1860, 8vo. (where the portraits of the Bright benefactor and the
Bright heiress are republished) ; and in Savage's *Genealogical Dictionary of the Early Settlers in New England.*   Henry Bright the
emigrant was for many years a deacon of the church at Watertown,
and held various town offices of trust.   He was seventy-eight years of
age in 1680 ; and yet his son Nathaniel, who continued the line in
America, did not marry until 1681.   He was the father of a second
Nathaniel, born in 1686 ; whose son, a third Nathaniel, was the father
of John Bright, born in 1754.   This John Bright married Elizabeth

Brown, and was father of Jonathan Brown Bright, the author of the handsome volume we have now had the pleasure to review.

He has introduced, in illustration of female descent, pedigrees of various ancient English families,—among which are Alston, of Newton, Saxham, and Boxford, in Suffolk; Dawtrey, of Sussex;[1] Fiske, of Rattlesden, in Suffolk; Forth, of Nayland; Honeywood, of Marks hall, in Essex; Luther, or Luter, of Essex; Mileson, of Suffolk; Salter, of Shropshire and Suffolk; and Tyrell, extending from the famous involuntary regicide, who shot William Rufus, down to Edmund Tyrell, esq. who married Mary Bright, and whose son Edmund Tyrell, esq. of Gipping, died in 1799, having devised his estates to his cousin, the father of the present Mr. Tyrell, of Plashwood, formerly M.P. for Suffolk.

[1] In the Dawtrey pedigree *Emle*, Chief Justice, is a misprint for Ernle. In the Forth pedigree there are these mistakes of names : Long *Malford* for Melford; *Clemham* for Glemham.; *Femley* for Fernley; *Crymble* for Grymble; *Hernegan* for Gernegan, *i. e.* Jerningham; and *Knewett* for Knevett. In the Tyrell pedigree there is *Hewy* for Hervey, an ancestor of the Marquess of Bristol.

THE ABBEY GATE,
BURY ST. EDMUND'S.

CHARTERS OF THOMAS FIRST LORD FURNIVAL.

By favour of a friend at Doncaster we are able to exhibit what
will be regarded as an extraordinary curiosity by such armorial
heralds as suppose that a lozenge shield has never been used except for
females.[1] It is the seal of Thomas Furnival, lord of Hallamshire, who
lived in the reign of Henry the Third, was first summoned to parliament as a Baron of the realm in 1274, and died before the 7 Edw. I.
1279. Two impressions are before us, attached to charters, which we
shall presently describe.

It is remarked by the late Historian of South Yorkshire, in his
earlier work *The History of Sheffield and Hallamshire* (p. 30), that
" there are fewer early charters than might have been expected in the
archives of the present noble lord of Hallamshire [the Duke of Nor-
folk], relating to his Grace's Yorkshire possessions:" and in a subsequent page the following passage will be found:—

In the fine collection of family evidences which descended with the estate of
Broomhead to its late proprietor, John Wilson, esquire, the oldest was a deed without
date of *Thomas son of Thomas de Furnival*, by which he conveys to John Wilson de
Bromhead forty-six acres of land in Wightwistle, &c. for a rent of sixpence yearly to
himself, and four shillings to his mother the Lady Bertha de Furnival, *d'næ Brette de
Furnivall*, yearly during her life, to revert on her death to the said Thomas and his
heirs. To this deed is appended a seal of greenish wax, exhibiting the arms of Furnival on a lozenge shield perfectly plain, and this inscription surrounding it,
S. THOMÆ DE FURNIVAL. *History of Hallamshire*, p. 34.

---

[1] There is one other contemporary example in what Sir Harris Nicolas terms " the
large signet of William de Paynell attached to the Barons' Letter to the Pope,
1301; displaying his arms in a lozenge,"—" the only instance of the kind " among the
seals attached to that document (*Archæologia*, vol. xxi. p. 222, and engravings in
the *Vetusta Monumenta*, vol. i.) The seal of the first Lord Furnival attached to the
Barons' Letter is different from that which we now publish. In another article upon
this family we shall give an engraving of it, together with the remarkable seal of his
great-uncle Gerard de Furnival, probably the first of the family who used arms.

We are disposed to think that this passage describes another impression of the same seal: notwithstanding that the copy of the inscription does not wholly agree. At any event it appears to have been a charter of the same person; whose mother Bertha is supposed to have been a Ferrars.[1]

On our seal the name is apparently spelt with an *o:* for, although both the impressions from which the engraving has been made are imperfect in the legend, in one of them part of an *o* seems to be left. The name is also spelt on the seal with a *w* in the last syllable, as it is in the following charter (which we transcribe *in extenso*) :—

Sciant presentes et futuri quod ego Thomas filius Thome de Furniwallo dedi concessi et hac presenti carta mea confirmavi Thome filio Rogeri de Haldwyrth et heredibus vel suis assingnatis exceptis viris religiosis et Judeis unam Bovatam terre et dimidium cum pertinentiis et edificiis superpositis in villa et territorio de Haldwyrth . quam quidem Bovatam terre et dimidium predictus Thomas de Haldewyrth de me tenuit in servicio Hastilar' . Jacentem videlicet inter boscum qui dicitur *Lockeslay* ex parte Orientali et Rivulum qui dicitur *Le Sputesyke* ex parte Occidentali et inter aquam qui vocatur *stene* ex parte australi et Moram que vocatur *Onesmor* ex parte boriali pro quadam summa pecunie quam predictus Thomas de Haldwrth mihi dedit premanibus Habendum et tenendum de me et heredibus meis sibi et heredibus vel suis assingnatis exceptis viris religiosis et Judeis libere quiete plenarie integre bene et in pace in feodo et hereditate cum omnimodis pertinentiis libertatibus [et] aysiamentis predicte Bovate terre et dimidio infra villam de Haldwrth et extra spectantibus. Reddendo inde per annum mihi et heredibus meis Duodecim solidos argenti ad duos anni terminos vid. medietatem ad festum Assumpcionis beate Marie virginis et aliam medietatem ad festum Annunciacionis ejusdem pro omnimodis aliis serviciis consuetudinibus exactionibus sectis curie et secularibus demandis.   Salvo forinseco servitio. Et salvis mihi et heredibus meis omnimodis appruamentis wasti mei infra limites de Hallumsyre sine aliqua contradictione predicti Thome de Haldwyrth vel heredum suorum.   Et salvis mihi et heredibus meis duabus sectis ad curiam meam apud Shefeud per annum, viz. ad proximam curiam post Pascham et ad proximam curiam post festum Sancti Michaelis.   Et quod molet bladum suum crescens super predictam terram ad quodcumque molendinorum meorum voluerit infra Hallumsyre et non alibi.   Ego vero predictus Thomas filius Thome de Furniwallo et heredes mei predictam Bovatam terre et dimidium cum omnimodis pertinentiis supradictis predicto Thome de Haldwyrth et heredibus vel suis assingnatis exceptis viris religiosis et Judeis pro predicto redditu contra omnes homines et feminas warantizabimus adquietabimus et imperpetuum defendemus.   In cujus rei testimonium huic presenti carte sigillum

---

[1] " A collector of the earlier part of the last century, Mr. Vincent Eyre of Dronfield-Woodhouse, in his account of the family of Furnival, represents Bertha the wife of Thomas as a daughter of William Ferrars the seventh Earl of Derby. It may be so, for Bertha was a family name among the Ferrarses; but no connection between the houses of Ferrars and Furnival appears in the laborious comments of Vincent on the work of Brooke." *Hallamshire*, p. 34.

meum apposui. Hiis testibus: Joh'e de Wyntewrth tunc senescallo. Thoma de Furneus. Elya de Midhop. Joh'e del Wyteley. Ricardo Moriz de Wyrhale. Nich'o Langus. Ricardo Ryuello. Will'o del Leyston. Thoma de Morwd' et aliis. (*Seal in green wax.*)

The second charter it will be unnecessary to transcribe, for its terms, except in any allusion to the *servitium hastilare*, are nearly an echo to those of that now printed; and it is evidently of almost the same date, as among its witnesses four names again occur: the whole attestation being, His testibus, Joh'e del Wytelye, Joh'e fil' suo, Rob'o le Rous, Ric'o Moriz, Nich'o de Langus, Ric'o Riuello, et aliis. By this charter Thomas de Furnivall, son of Thomas de Furnivall, (the name is now spelt with *u* instead of *w*), grants to Thomas son of Ralph sub monte (*i. e.* Underhill) and his heirs and assigns, except to religious men and Jews (as in the other case), one half bovate of land with its appurtenances and buildings, which John de Pillay once had to farm from Robert de Halddewrth: it lay between the field called Bilbeleye towards the south and the Moor towards the north, in its length; and the wood called Lockeslay towards the east and Le Bentelane towards the west, in its breadth. The rent was to be two shillings, and all the other conditions as in the former charter. Sheffield is written *Shefeuld*. On the fold of the parchment is written in a later hand: *que Will's Smalbihend tenet.* John Smalbyhynd was witness to a charter of William son of Thomas Ryvell of Haldworth in 1389. (Eastwood's *History of Ecclesfield*, p. 149.)

Two expressions in the first charter may require explanation. To one of them, indeed, an explanation is not readily to be found. The land that was granted to Thomas de Haldworth had it seems been previously held by him—the verb is *tenuit*, in the past tense,—*in servicio Hastilari*. We have been unsuccessful in searching for an explanation of this service: but find "half a bovate of hastler land" mentioned at p. 373 of Eastwood's *History of Ecclesfield*. It was evidently a military tenure, and we may presume was that rendered by a spearman.[1]

---

[1] A service rendered to the manor of Sheffield so late as the reign of Charles I. is thus described: " I cannot heere omitt a Royaltie that this manor hath above other manors, that is, upon every Sembley Tuesday (*i. e.* Easter Tuesday) is assembled upon Sembley Greene, where the court is kept, at least 139 horsemen with horse and harnesse provided by the freeholders, coppieholders, and other tennants, and to appeare before the Lord of this mannor, or the steward of this court, to bee viewed by them, and for confirmeinge of the peace of our sovereigne lord the Kinge." *Survey of the Manor*, taken by John Harrison in 1637, quoted by Eastwood, *History of Ecclesfield*, p. 466.

The term *Hastyllar* occurs frequently in a rental of the manor of Eckington, co.

It would seem that on the execution of this charter the *servitium hastilare* was to cease for land to which it relates, as the money rent of 12s. was to be paid " pro omnimodis aliis servitiis," &c.

The other remarkable term is *appruamentum.* This was the inclosure or cultivation of part of a common, wood, or pasture, on the part of the lord:

Domini vastorum, boscorum, et pasturarum *appruare* se possunt de vastis et pasturis illis, non obstante contradictione tenentium suorum, dum modo tenentes ipsi haberent sufficientem pasturam ad tenementa sua, cum libero ingressu et egressu ad eadem. *Statutum Westmonast.* 2, cap. 50.

The derivation of the term is " quasi in *provandam,* seu *prœbendam* sibi asserere [*i. e.* to raise provender for their own cattle], vel (forte) sibi *appropriare.*" See further in Ducange, *Glossarium Mediœ et Infimœ Latinitatis,* edit. Henschel, 1840, i. 338.

Next, as to the localities :

Haldworth is a vill in " the wide district called Bradfield." (Hunter, *South Yorkshire,* ii. 191.)   Some deeds relating to it are described by Mr. Eastwood (*History of Ecclesfield,* 8vo. 1861, p. 148).

" The wood called *Lockeslay.*" Mr. Hunter (*South Yorkshire,* ii. 191) mentions " the range of waste and rugged lands which formed the high ridge of Loxley Chase." This is also the name given to the stream which runs near Haldworth and Bradfield (see *South Yorkshire,* ii. 183), and the hamlet of Loxley is not far from Wadsley. (See Eastwood's *Ecclesfield,* pp. 5, 65, 231.) " Thousands know Locksley as one of the aliases of Robin Hood " (Ibid. p. 7), and " Locksley Chase being inhabited by fletchers, or arrow-makers, the tale would have peculiar attractions for this region " (p. 8). Dr. Ingledew, however, in his *Yorkshire Ballads,* p. 35, places the birth of Robin Hood at another Locksley in Nottinghamshire.

" The brook called the *Spute-syke.*" This was probably near *Spouthouse,* which will be found in the Ordnance Map to the north of Haldworth, and noticed by Eastwood, p. 486. A *syke* is the well-known local term for a spring.

" The water called *Stene.*" This is named in the Introduction to the *History of South Yorkshire,* vol. I. p. iii.

Derby, temp. Hen. VII. as, " a mese and j. oxg' land of the Hastyllar," and with it are mentioned other holdings, as " halfe a oxg'. land of the *Burdeland,*" " a oxg' of the *low hold.*"

Simon de Hashwell tenet quoddam tenementum in villa de Hashwell in com. Essex per serjantiam essendi Hastilarius Domini Regis, *i.e. the King's spearman.*—Blount's *Antient Tenures.*

" The moor called *Onesmor* " is to the north of Haldworth.

Then, in the second charter, *Underhill farm* still retains that name, and is to the west of Onesmoor and Haldworth, on the north of the river Don.

Pillay, from which "John de Pillay" derived his name, is in the parish of Tankersley: see *South Yorkshire*, ii. 306.

" The field called Bilbeleye."

" The Bentelane." Bents and Bentslane will be found south of Holdsworth: there is also a Bent Hill.

Lastly, with regard to the witnesses:—

The first witness is " *John de Wyntewrth* then steward " of Hallamshire. No name is more distinguished in the surrounding district in later times than that of Wentworth; but we do not identify this John, nor is there any list of the Stewards of Hallamshire. The same person, however, occurs among the witnesses to a charter of John de Carlton granting the manor of Penisal to Elias de Midhope (below mentioned) in 1284. (Hunter's *South Yorkshire*, ii. 195.)

Thomas de Furneus. This was one of the families, which, like De Ecclesall, Mountney, Wadsley, and Wortley, assumed an armorial coat resembling that of Furnival,—a bend between six martlets :—a very interesting chapter of heraldry which we purpose to develope in a future article.

Elias de Midhop. For the place from which this witness derived his name see *Hallamshire*, p. 282. Mr. Hunter says,

The lords of this manor had their residence within it, and were called de Midhope. We find the name in deeds from the reign of John to the time of Edward III. and most of the heads of the family bore the name of Elias. Several of them were knighted.

See also much more about the family in the *History of South Yorkshire*, ii. 194.

John del Wyteley. " Between Barnes Hall and Ecclesfield, about half a mile from the church, is the quaint old mansion of Whitley hall," which afforded a resting-place for one night to Mary Queen of Scots. (Eastwood, p. 421.)

Richard Moriz of Wyrhall. Probably Worral or Wirrall near Bradfield, in the byerlaw of Westmonhalgh or Westnal. (Hunter's *South Yorkshire*, ii. 191.)

Nicholas Langus, or *de Langus*, as in the second charter. Hunter in his *Hallamshire*, p. 271 (copied by Eastwood, *History of Ecclesfield*, p. 642,) mentions " Robert the son of Nicholas de Langers:" to whom Robert de Wadsley gave in 1294 land in Langers near the moor of

Wirrall. But Langus is the reading of the present charters,—qu. *Lang-us*, or "the long house," as Loftus is from Lofthouse, and Bacchus from Bakehouse.

Richard Ryvell, in the second charter *Rivell*. Mr. Hunter says,

At Revel-grange (in Stannington) resided from an early period a family of the name of Revel, whom we often meet in the old genealogies as connected by marriage with the superior gentry of the county of Derby. * * * Mr. Richard Broomhead of this place married the heiress of the Revels about the year 1740. *History of Hallamshire*, p. 273.

See also a pedigree of Revel of Whiston in *History of South Yorkshire*, ii. 180. The Ryvells were still at Haldworth late in the 14th century : see deeds quoted in Eastwood's *Ecclesfield*, p. 148.

William del Leyston. John de Leeston occurs in charters dated at Haldworth in 1379 and 1389. (Eastwood, pp. 148, 149.)

Thomas de Morwde. John de Morewod is also a witness to the same charters. See also several of the family in an inquisition of 9 Edw. III. printed by Eastwood, p. 124. They were afterwards a family of gentry at the Oaks in Bradfield : and subsequently at Alfreton in Derbyshire: for which county the three last representatives served Sheriff; John Morewood, of Alfreton, esquire, receiving a grant of arms of Vert, an oak-tree coupé in base argent, fructed or, in 1677. See their pedigree at full in Hunter's *Hallamshire*, p. 274.

———

Note. We cannot relinquish this opportunity of remarking that the "*History of the Parish of Ecclesfield* in the County of York. By the Rev. J. Eastwood, M.A. Curate of Eckington, Derbyshire, formerly Curate of Ecclesfield, (8vo. 1862, pp. xvi. 558,)" which has been so often quoted in the preceding pages, is one of the most elaborate and well-compiled topographical productions that has appeared of late years. Its author unfortunately did not long survive its production. From "A brief Memoir of the late Rev. Jonathan Eastwood, M.A. Incumbent of Hope. By the Rev. Alfred Gatty, D.D. Vicar of Ecclesfield and Sub-dean of York," (first published in *The Reliquary*,) we gather the following particulars:—

Mr. Eastwood was born on the 31st October, 1823. He was educated at Wakefield proprietary school and afterwards at Uppingham. At St. John's college, Cambridge, he graduated B.A. 1846 as eighth Senior Optime, and third in the third class of the classical tripos. He was ordained at York by archbishop Musgrave, and, being the only deacon who knew anything of the Hebrew language, was selected for preacher in the following year, when he proceeded to priest's orders. He was Curate

of Ecclesfield from 1 Feb. 1848 to 1 July 1854; when, on his marriage,
he became Curate of Eckington. In 1862 the Bishop of Lichfield
repeated an offer of preferment, and he accepted the church at Hope, in
the Potteries of Staffordshire. On his death it was reported to the
bishop by Sir Lovelace Stamer, the Rector of Stoke upon Trent, and
Rural Dean, that " In Mr. Eastwood the Church in the Potteries has
lost one of its most earnest, faithful, and judicious clergy—certainly its
most accomplished." He died at St. Leonard's on Sea, July 5, 1864,
aged 40. Mr. Eastwood married at Ecclesfield, August 3, 1854, Anne
Elizabeth, eldest daughter of William Frederick Dixon, esq. of Page
Hall in that parish, a magistrate for the West Riding, and had issue a
son, John Frederick, born in 1855, and two daughters.

Besides his History of Ecclesfield, Mr. Eastwood was the joint
author of " *The Bible and Liturgical Word Book.* By the Rev. J.
Eastwood, clerk, and W. A. Wright, Esq. Trinity College, Cambridge "
(announced for publication by Messrs. Macmillan). He was also a
frequent writer in *Notes and Queries* and in *The Reliquary.*

In the *History of Ecclesfield*, following in the steps of the Historian
of South Yorkshire, Mr. Eastwood availed himself of several sources of
information which were not open to that eminent antiquary: and we
must not terminate this brief notice of his work without remarking
that it contains at p. 372 a pedigree of the family of Hunter, Mr.
Hunter's great-grandfather having resided at Hatfield House in Ecclesfield. Mr. Hunter was buried, in accordance with a clause in his
will, on the north-east side of the churchyard; and the following
inscription has since been placed upon the stone:

H. S. E.

JOSEPHUS HUNTER, S.A.S.

Sacr. Scriniorum unus de Vice-custodibus,

qui cum in archivis nostris versaretur

summo rerum antiquariorum studio provectus

multa doctè, luculenter, accuratè scripsit.

Sed præsertim hujusce agri

annales labore exploravit historiæque mandavit.

Natus est Sheffieldiæ vi^{to} die Februarii

A° Salutis Humanæ ix^{no} die Maii

Anno M.D.CCC.LXI^{mo}

quo ipse vivens designavit loco

in pace deponitur.

THE INSTITUTION AND EARLY HISTORY OF THE DIGNITY OF BARONET.

(Continued from p. 212.)

At the institution of this hereditary rank, the most important documents relating to it were promulgated by royal authority:[1] but they have not been subsequently reprinted so often as might have been expected. Selden, in his *Titles of Honour*, copies the form of the original Patents of creation, and the Instructions given to the Commissioners appointed to admit the aspirants to the dignity, and to arrange their precedence; together with the substance of two subsequent Royal Declarations or Decrees on the latter subject. The same documents were reprinted in the *Analogia Honorum* attached to Guillim's *Display of Heraldry*, fol. 1677; in Wotton's *Baronetage* of 1741, in pp. 280-305 of the fifth and last volume; and in the *Baronetage* by Kimber and Johnson 1771; and the form of Patent is also given by Morgan in his *Sphere of Gentry*, Book 4, p. 12.

The Royal Commission for this business has never been re-

---

[1] In quarto pamphlets which bear the following titles:—

1. His Maiesties Commission to all the Lords and others of the Privie Counsell, touching the Creation of Baronets. Whereunto are annexed divers Instructions and his Maiesties Letters Patents containing the forme of the said Creation. Also the forme of an Oath to be taken by the said Baronets. Imprinted at London by Robert Barker, Printer to the Kings most Excellent Maiestie. Anno 1611. Title-leaf and pp. 44.

2. The Decree and Establishment of the King's Maiestie, upon a controversie of Precedence betweene the yonger sonnes of Viscounts and Barons, and the Baronets; And touching some other points also, concerning aswell Bannerets, as the said Baronets. Imprinted at London by Robert Barker, Printer to the Kings most excellent Maiestie. 1612. Leaf of Title, and pp. 14.

3. Three Patents concerning the Honourable Degree and Dignitie of Baronets:
   The first containing the Creation and Grant.
   The second: a Decree with addition of other Priuiledges.
   The thirde: a confirmation and explanation.
Imprinted at London by Robert Barker, Printer to the Kings Most Excellent Maiestie. Anno 1617. Title-leaf and pp. 5-39: there being no pages 1-4 either in the British Museum copy or in that in the collection upon "Baronets, Arms, &c." from Sir George Naylor's library, now in the Office of Arms.

The first and second articles of this third pamphlet are the same which were before published: the third is the Decree of 1616-17, which will be described hereafter.

printed since its first publication: and is probably known to few. It may therefore be acceptable if now reproduced:

His Majesties Commission to all the Lords and others of the Privie Councell touching the creation of Baronets.

James by the grace of God King of England, Scotland, France, and Ireland, Defender of the Faith, etc. To our right trustie and right wellbeloved Councellour Thomas Lord Ellesmere, Lord Chancellour of England, and to our right trustie and right well beloved cousins and Councillors Robert Earle of Salisburie, Lord High Treasurer of England, Henry Earle of Northampton, Lord Keeper of our Privie Seale, Loudovike Duke of Lenox, Charles Earle of Nottingham, our High Admirall of England, Thomas Earle of Suffolke, Lord Chamberlaine of our Household, Gilbert Earle of Shrewsbury, Justice in Eire beyond Trent northward, Edward Earle of Worcester, Master of our Horse, Thomas Earle of Excester, John Earle of Marre, Alexander Earle of Dunfermyline; and to our right trusty and right well beloved Councellours Thomas Lord Viscount Fenton, Edward Lord Zouche, William Lord Knolles, Treasurer of our Houshold, Edward Lord Wotton Comptroller of our Houshold, John Lord Stanhope, Vice-Chamberlaine of our Houshold; and to our trustie and right wellbeloved Councellours Sir John Herbert, Knight, our second Secretarie of State, Sir Julius Cæsar, Knight, Chancellour and Under-Treasurer of our Exchecquer, and Sir Thomas Parrie, Knight, Chancellour of our Dutchie of Lancaster, greeting. Whereas divers principall Knights and Esquires of sundry parts of this our Realme, mooved with zeale and affection to further the plantation of Ulster, and other like services in our Realme of Ireland, have offered and agreed every of them to maintaine thirtie footmen souldiers in the same our Realme at their owne proper costs and charges, after the rate of eight pence apiece by the day sterling during the space of three yeeres now next ensuing (by the imitation of which example that good worke, whereupon the establishment of religion and civilitie in place of blindnesse and barbarisme doeth so much depend, is likely to be so much advanced and supported as no reasonable meanes would be forborne that may cherish and encourage such an endeavour). Wee have been pleased, as an argument of our gracious acceptation of so remarkable a service, not onely to bestow upon them a dignitie newly erected and created by Us answerable to their estate and merit, which Wee have stiled by the name of BARONET, with divers privileges annexed thereunto, and the same have granted by Letters Patents to them, and the heires males of their bodies, to the end the memorie thereof may remaine to them, and their posteritie; but are determined to doe the like also to some such other selected persons as shall concurre in the same intentions, not exceeding a convenient number; and therefore, although Wee could not in reason forbeare to begin and conclude with some principall per_sons of especiall note and qualitie that first discovered their good affec_tions in this kinde, before Wee had made any publique declaration of our certaine resolution to proceed further, yet when We enter into consideration, that there may be divers other Knights and Esquires of all parts of this our Realme that are capable of this dignitie (respecting their estate and qualitie) and in whom there would be found a like affection to the said service if they could take notice of this course so soone as others that are not so remote in their habitations, We have thought fit hereby as well to notifie our pleasure to receive a conve-nient number to this dignity as to warrant and authorize you (when any that are moved with the same affections to the publique good, and are otherwise qualified as is fit, shall repaire unto you within the time limited for this our Commission,) to treat and conclude with them in maner and forme as you have done with others, and according to those Instructions, which for your better direction in a matter of this conse-quence Wee have annexed to this Commission. Know yee therefore that Wee have appointed you to be our Commissioners, and Wee doe by these Presents give and grant unto you all, or unto any eight or more of you (whereof you the said Lord Chancellor or Lord Treasurer to be always one, and you the saide Lord Privie Seale, Duke of Lenox, Earle of Nottingham our Admirall, Earle of Suffolk our Chamberlaine, and Earle of Worcester Master of our Horse, to be always two, who are so much the more able to judge of men's blood and antiquitie in regard you are Commissioners in the office of Earle Marshall,) full, free, and lawfull power and authoritie to commune and treat with any of our loving subjects whom you shall finde willing to give such pay and enter-tainment to such number of footmen as is aforesaid to be imployed in the said service, and for such time as aforesaid, and thereupon to informe your selves of their family, living, and reputation; and such and so many of the said persons as you or any such eight or more of you (as is aforesaid) shall find and approve to bee in all the respects aforesaid worthy such degree (not exceeding the number of two hun-dred, which We have covenanted in our Patents shall not be exceeded, but suffered to diminish as their issue shall faile,) to cause every one of them for himself to make payment or to give good and sufficient assurance for the due answering of so much as shall be sufficient for maintenance of thirtie souldiers footmen after the rate of eight pence apiece by the day for the terme of three yeeres as is aforesaid, and thereupon to give warrant and direction under any such eight or more of your hands as is aforesaid unto our Attourney or Sollicitor-Generall, for the drawing up of severall bills and grants to passe from Us unto all and every such person and persons as shall be so approved by you or any such eight or more of you,) as is aforesaid, for the making and creating of every such person Baronet, with all privileages of precedence, place, title, and all other things thereunto belonging according to the forme hereunto annexed; and these presents, together with such warrant and direction of you, or any such eight or more of you as is aforesaid, shall be from time to time to our said Attourney and Sollicitor Generall for the time being sufficient warrant for the drawing up and subscribing of every such bill or grant to passe from Us according to the true meaning of these presents; and our will and pleasure is that our Attourney or Sollicitor Generall shall draw, ingrosse, and subscribe the bills and grants to be made of the said dignitie of Baronet according to the directions and warrants by you, or any such eight or more of you, as is aforesaid; and the said bills and grants so drawen, ingrossed, and subscribed with the hands of our Attourney or Sollicitor Generall, or either of them, shall be a sufficient warrant and discharge to you our said Commissioners to subscribe likewise the said bills and grants with the hands of any such eight or more of you as aforesaid.

And furthermore, for the more easie and speady passing of the grants and letters patents to be made of the said dignitie, Wee are pleased and contented, and by these presents, for Us, our heires and successors, Wee doo grant, ordaine, and appoint that the bills for such patents prepared by our said Attourney or Sollicitor as aforesaid, and signed with the hands of you, or any such eight or more of you as is aforesaid, shall be a sufficient and immediate warrant to the Lord Chancellour of England or Lord Keeper of the Great Seale of England for the time being to passe the same grants and letters patents under the Great Seale of England without any other or further warrant from Us to be had or obtained in that behalfe; and this our Commission Wee have made to continue till the sixt day of July next comming after the date hereof, and then to cease and determine. In witnesse whereof, &c. Witnesse, etc.

The *Instructions* given to the Commissioners to guide their

conduct in the choice and ranking of Baronets correspond with
the contents of the original " Project" which we have inserted
at p. 201.

The *Patent of Creation*,—which was uniformly alike in every
case,—was composed by the learned Camden, as is commemorated
by Dr. Smith in his *Life of Sir Robert Cotton*. Its preamble
will be read with pleasure, as a specimen of the excellent ·
Latinity of its author :—

Rex omnibus ad quos, &c. Salutem.   Cum inter alias Imperii nostri
gerendi curas, quibus animus noster assiduè exercetur, illa non
minima sit, nec minimi momenti, de Plantatione Regni nostri Hiberniæ,
ac potissimum Ultoniæ, amplæ et percelebris ejusdem Regni Provinciæ,
quam nostris jam auspiciis atque armis, fœliciter sub obsequii jugum
redactam, ita constabilire elaboramus, ut tanta Provincia, non solum
sincero Religionis cultu, humanitate civili, morumque probitate,
verum etiam opum affluentiâ, atque omnium rerum copiâ, quæ statum
Reipublicæ ornare vel beare possit, magis magisque efflorescat: Opus
sane, quod nulli progenitorum nostrorum præstare et perficere licuit,
quamvis id ipsum multâ sanguinis et opum profusione sæpius tentave-
rint; In quo opere sollicitudo nostra Regia non solum ad hoc excu-
bare debet, ut Plantatio ipsa strenuè promoveatur, oppida condantur,
ædes et castra extruantur, agri colantur, et id genus alia; Sed etiam
prospiciendum imprimis, ut universus hujusmodi rerum civilium apparatus, manu armatâ, præsidiis videlicet et cohortibus, protegatur et
communiatur, ne qua aut vis hostilis, aut defectio intestina, rem dis-
turbet aut impediat: Cumque nobis intimatum sit, ex parte quorundam
ex fidelibus nostris subditis, quod ipsi paratissimi sint, ad hoc regium
nostrum inceptum, tam corporibus, quam fortunis suis promovendum:
Nos commoti operis tam sancti ac salutaris intuitu, atque gratos
habentes hujusmodi generosos affectus, atque propensas in obsequium
nostrum et bonum publicum voluntates, Statuimus apud nos ipsos
nulli rei deesse, quæ subditorum nostrorum studia præfata remunerare,
aut aliorum animos atque alacritatem, ad operas suas præstandas, aut
impensas in hac parte faciendas, excitare possit; Itaque nobiscum
perpendentes atque reputantes virtutem et industriam nullâ aliâ re
magis quàm honore ali atque acui, omnemque honoris et dignitatis
splendorem, et amplitudinem, à Rege tanquam à fonte originem et
incrementum ducere, ad cujus culmen et fastigium propriè spectat
novos honorum et dignitatum titulos erigere atque instituere, utpote à

quo antiqui illi fluxerint; consentaneum duximus (postulante usu Rei-publicæ atque temporum ratione) nova merita novis dignitatum insig-nibus rependere: Ac propterea, ex certâ scientiâ et mero motu nostris, Ordinavimus, ereximus, constituimus, et creavimus, quendam statum, gradum, dignitatem, nomen et titulum Baronetti (Anglicè *of a Baronet*) infra hoc Regnum nostrum Angliæ perpetuis temporibus duraturum. Sciatis modo, quod nos de gratia nostra speciali, &c. &c.

After thus setting forth the avowed object of the institution—the defence and maintenance of the Plantation of Ulster, and the royal desire to distinguish those who were well-disposed to assist in that design, the instrument proceeds to stipulate that every recipient of the dignity should furnish a contribution sufficient to maintain in the King's service thirty footmen for three years;[2] and to concede that the new Baronets should enjoy a rank above all Knights of the Bath, Knights Bachelors, and all Bannerets there or to be thereafter created, except such as should be made under the King's own standard, in open field of battle, and in the King's personal presence; that they should have the title of *Sir*, and their wives that of *Lady, Madam, Dame* (according to the mode of speech). Further, the King engaged, for himself, his heirs and successors, that the number of Baronets in the kingdom of England should never exceed two hundred, having precedency according to their order of creation; that he would create no other dignity intervening between those of Baron and Baronet; and that if any Baronet should die without heir male of his body or of the body of the grantee, the first number of two hundred should thereby be allowed to decrease, and be re-duced to a lesser number. To this last clause, however, it has been observed that King James did not pledge his "heirs and successors."

The Founder eventually created 204[3] Baronets; but it was alleged that he did not depart from his bargain: inasmuch as five vacancies had arisen, not by extinction, but by promotion to the peerage, viz. of Sir Robert Dormer to an English barony in 1615,

---

[2] At the pay of 8d. a day, as appears by the Instructions next mentioned : so that the total for three years amounted to 1,095*l.*; to which were added the cost of passing the patent and various fees of office.

[3] If Vavasour (see p. 352) be reckoned, they amount to 205.

Sir Thomas Ridgeway, Sir William Maynard, and Sir William Hervey to Irish Baronies in 1616 and 1620, and Sir Thomas Beaumont to an Irish Viscountcy in 1622. King Charles the First, however, had not long been on the throne when, relying on his royal prerogative as the Fountain of Honour, he disregarded the stipulated limitation of the number of Baronets. His father had virtually done the same thing by creating Baronets of Ireland,—except that, until the Union of 1801, all Baronets of Ireland ranked (in England) after English Baronets of whatever creation.

Among the documents relating to the early days of the dignity preserved in the State Paper Office is a *Warrant* for the nomination of a Baronet,—one that was not used, but prepared in readiness for use, having the autograph signatures of nine of the Commissioners:

[State Paper Office, Domestic James I. Vol. LXIII. art. 65*.]

After o^r very harty Comendations. Whereas of   in the County of   hath out of his good affection to his Maties service offered to charge himself wth the yearlye intertaynement of 30^{tie} foote for three yeares after the rate of 8^d *per diem* for the Plantation of Ulster. His Matie, having gratiously accepted of this his good service, is pleased in recompence thereof to conferr upon him the dignity and place of a Baronett; wth all titles, priviledges, and preheminences wch by his Maties favo^r is graunted unto others in like case. These shalbe therefore to require yow to drawe a bill for that purpose fitt for us to subscribe according unto the direction given yow and the authority wch we have received by vertue of his Maties Commission in that behalf. For wch this shalbe yor warrant. And soe we bid yow hartely farewell. From Whitehall this of   , 1611.

Yo^r very loving frendes,

T. Ellesmere, Canc.	R. Salisbury.	Lenox.
T. Suffolke.	Gilbert Shrewsbury.	E. Worcester.
W. Knollys.		Fenton.
	Jul. Cæsar.	

The payment of the 1095*l*. was divided into three annual sums. *The Receipt* given to Sir Thomas Holte, of Aston Hall, near Birmingham, whose patent was dated November 25, 1612, is still preserved by his descendant Charles Holte Bracebridge, esq. of Atherstone Hall, co. Warwick. It is as follows:

In Pello Recept' de Termino Mich'is anno nono Regis Jacobi, sexto Decembris. WARR'.—D' Thomas Holte Mil' et Baronett' trescent^r sexagint' quinq' libras de parte M^liiij^{xx}xv^{li}. per ip'm D'no Regi Jacobo dat' et conc' ad manutenend' trigint^a viros in cohortibus suis pedestr' in Regno suo Hibernie pro defensu ejusdem et p'cipue pro securitat' plantacōis Provincie Ultonie ib'm per spatium triū annorum subsequen' s'c'd'm ratam viij d. pro quolib't hujusmodi pedit' per diem duran' termino p'd' . . . . . . ccclxv^{li}. Sol.

Then follows the receipt for Michaelmas 1612, *and the like for Michaelmas* 1613—in plen' exon'ac' omni' on'um quor'cunq' sup' ip'm Baronett' hered' vel execut' suos posthac imponend' virtute duarum obligac' sive Recognic' capt' coram Joh'e Bingley ar' et Irrotulat' p' Ed'r'um Wardour ar' pro soluc' Dccxxx^{li} quinto Decembris 1612 et quinto Decemb' 1613 equis porc'o'ib's ultra ccclxv^{li}. p'manibus solut' ad usu p'd' Que quidem obligac' sive Irrotulament' eor' vel al' on'a quecumque pro manuten' d'c'or' xxx^{ta} pedit' vacua imp'p'm habeant^r.

Ex' p. ED. WARDOUR.

Mr. Bracebridge also preserves the original *Patent* of baronetcy granted to Sir Thomas Holte. It is not otherwise decorated than with a pen-and-ink initial of the King's portrait, seated, holding his sceptre and globe.

The names of the Baronets advanced to the dignity by the patents of the Second Seal, which was dated the 29th of June, 1611, were as follow. Though comparatively few remain on the roll of Baronets at the present time, yet nearly all will be recognized as having belonged to some of the most eminent families of our English annals.

(The names which are printed in Italics are those whose Baronetcies are still subsisting. Those marked * are those whose representatives are now Peers, or were so before their extinction.)

19. Sir John Savage, of Rocksavage, Cheshire, Knight.*
20. *Sir Francis Barrington, of Barrington Hall, Essex, Knight.*
21. Henry Berkeley, of Wymondham, Leicestershire, Esquire.

* *Dates of the Peerages conferred on Families of Baronets:*
19. Sir John Savage (second Baronet) succeeded in 1639 to the Earldom of Rivers conferred on his maternal grandfather Thomas Darcy in 1626. Extinct 1728.

22. William Wentworth, of Wentworth Wodehouse, Yorkshire, Esquire.*

23. *Sir Richard Musgrave, of Hartley Castle, Westmerland, K.B.*

24. *Edward Seymour, of Berry Pomeroy, Devonshire, Esquire.**

25. *Sir Moyle Finch, of Eastwell, Kent, Knight.**

26. *Sir Anthony Cope, of Hanwell, Oxfordshire, Knight.*

27. *Sir Thomas Monson, of Carlton, Lincolnshire, Knight.**

28. *George Gresley, of Drakelow, Derbyshire, Esquire.*

29. Paul Tracy, of Stanway, Gloucestershire, Esquire.

30. Sir John Wentworth, of Gosfield, Essex, Knight.

31. *Sir Henry Bellasyse, of Newborough, Yorkshire, Knight.**

32. Sir William Constable, of Flamborough, Yorkshire, Knight.

33. Sir Thomas Leigh, of Stoneleigh, Warwickshire, Knight.*

34. Sir Edward Noel, of Brook, Rutlandshire, Knight.*

35. Sir Robert Cotton, of Conington, Huntingdonshire, Knight.

36. Robert Cholmondeley, of Cholmondeley, Cheshire, Esquire.*

37. Sir John Molineux, of Teversal, Nottinghamshire, Knight.

38. Sir Francis Wortley, of Wortley, Yorkshire, Knight.

39. Sir George Savile, of Thornhill, Yorkshire, Knight.*

40. William Kniveton, of Mircaston, Derbyshire, Esquire.

41. *Sir Philip Wodehouse, of Kimberley, Norfolk, Knight.**

42. Sir William Pope, of Wilcot, Oxfordshire, Knight.*

43. *Sir James Harrington, of Ridlington, Rutlandshire, Knight.*

44. Sir Henry Savile, of Methley, Yorkshire, Knight.

45. Henry Willoughby, of Risley, Derbyshire, Esquire.

46. Lewis Tresham, of Rushton, Northamptonshire, Esquire.

22. Baron Raby, July, 1628; Viscount Wentworth, Dec. 1628; Earl of Strafford 1640: the two latter dignities extinct 1695. Again Earl of Strafford 1711. Extinct 1799.

24. Succeeded to Dukedom of Somerset 1750.

25. His widow Viscountess Maidstone 1623; Countess of Winchilsea 1628. Earl of Nottingham 1681.

27. Baron Monson 1728.

31. Baron Fauconberg 1627; Viscount Fauconberg 1643. Extinct 1815.

33. Baron Leigh, of Stoneleigh, 1643. Extinct 1786.

34. Baron Noel, 1617; succeeded his father-in-law Sir Baptist Hickes as Viscount Campden 1629. Earl of Gainsborough 1682. Extinct 1798.

36. Lord Cholmondeley of Kells (a Baron of Ireland) 1628; Lord Cholmondeley of Wich-Malbank 1645; Earl of Leinster 1645-6. Extinct 1659.

39. Viscount Hallifax 1668; Earl of Hallifax 1679; Marquess of Hallifax 1682. All extinct 1700. Baronetcy extinct 1784.

41. Baron Wodehouse 1797.

42. Earl of Downe, in Ireland, 1628. Extinct 1660.

47. *Thomas Brudenell, of Dean, Northamptonshire, Esquire.**

48. Sir George St. Paul, of Snarford, Lincolnshire, Knight.

49. Sir Philip Tyrwhitt, of Stanfield, Lincolnshire, Knight.

50. Sir Roger Dallison, of Laughton, Lincolnshire, Knight.

51. Sir Edward Carr, of Sleaford, Lincolnshire, Knight.

52. Sir Edward Hussey, of Honington, Lincolnshire, Knight.

53. *L'Estrange Mordaunt, of Massingham, Norfolk, Esquire.*

54. Thomas Bendish, of Steeple Bumsted, Essex, Esquire.

55. Sir John Wynne, of Gwydir, Carnarvonshire, Knight.

56. Sir William Throckmorton, of Tortworth, Gloucestersh. Knight.

57. Sir Richard Worsley, of Apuldercombe, Isle of Wight, Knight.

58. Richard Fleetwood, of Caldwich, Staffordshire, Esquire.

59. Thomas Spencer, of Yarnton, Oxfordshire, Esquire.

60. Sir John Tufton, of Hothfield, Kent, Knight.*

61. Sir Samuel Peyton, of Knowlton, Kent, Knight.

62. Sir Charles Morrison, of Cashiobury, Hertfordshire, K.B.

63. Sir Henry Baker, of Sisinghurst, Kent, Knight.

64. Roger Appleton, of South Bemfleet, Essex, Esquire.

65. Sir William Sedley, of Ailesford, Kent, Knight.

66. Sir William Twysden, of East Peckham, Kent, Knight.

67. Sir Edward Hales, of Woodchurch, Kent, Knight.

68. William Monyns, of Waldersham, Kent, Esquire.

69. Sir Thomas Mildmay, of Moulsham Hall, Essex, Knight.*

70. Sir William Maynard, of Eastaines Parva, Essex, Knight.*

71. Henry Lee, of Quarendon, Buckinghamshire, Esquire.*

On the 24th of September following, four others were added to the rank :

72. Sir Robert Napier, of Luton Hoo, Bedfordshire, Knight.

73. Paul Bayning, of Bentley Parva, Essex, Esquire.*

74. *Sir Thomas Temple, of Stowe, Buckinghamshire, Knight.**

75. Thomas Penyston, of Leigh, Sussex, Esquire.

47. Lord Brudenell 1627; Earl of Cardigan 1661; Duke of Montagu 1766 (extinct 1790); Now Earl of Cardigan.

60. Baron Tufton 1626 ; Earl of Thanet 1628. Extinct 1850. The present Sir Richard Tufton, being the natural son of the last Earl of Thanet, and heir of Hothfield and his other landed property, was created a Baronet in 1851.

69. Baron Maynard, in Ireland, 1620; Baron Maynard, in England, 1628 ; Viscount Maynard 1766. Extinct 1775. The Viscountcy conferred in 1766 (with a further remainder) still existing, the Viscount being also a Baronet of a creation 1681.

71. Earl of Litchfield 1674. Extinct 1776.

73. Baron Bayning 1628; Viscount Bayning 1628-9. Extinct 1638.

74. The fifth Baronet was created Baron Cobham 1714, Baron and Viscount Cob-

Sixth in precedence in this list, and having been up to this time a simple esquire, appears the name of Sir Edward Seymour of Berry Pomeroy, grandson of the Protector Somerset, and by seniority of birth actually his male heir, had not the remainders of the peerages which were conferred on the Protector given a preference to the offspring of his second wife Anne Stanhope. Two letters which at this period Mr. Seymour addressed to the Lord Treasurer are preserved in the State Paper Office, and the terms in which he expresses his appreciation of the honour conferred upon him by his admission into " the new order " are very remarkable as coming from a person of his birth.

In the earlier letter,[1] which is dated " Lupton, 12th June, 1611," after first thanking the Lord Treasurer for a prospect of obtaining the wardship of Mr. Parker (who had become the writer's son-in-law) if his grandfather should die before he became of age, he desires

" to intymate how much I stande further charged to your Lordship for your hon^{bly} conceaved good opinion of me and my house as to deeme me worthie to be ranckt amongst that newe intended order of Baronettes which (as it should seeme) is ment to none but such as are well deservinge."

Again, writing from Exeter on the 21st of July a similar letter [2] of thanks, Sir Edward Seymour a second time expresses his gratitude

" in that yt pleased yor Lo^p to holde me worthy to be ranckt in the nomber of Baronettes, and in that of havinge precedencye of many worthie gentlemen of the same creation, wch I cannot but be sensible to be by yor ho^{ble} meanes."

ham 1718. The former peerage became extinct on his death : the latter (by special remainder) was inherited by his sister Hester, wife of Richard Grenville, esq. and has descended to the present Duke of Buckingham and Chandos. The present Sir Grenville Temple descends from a younger son of the first Baronet.

[1] Domestic, James I. vol. LXIV.

[2] Ibid. vol. LXV. art. 48. He states in this letter that Mr. Parker's grandfather was dead since he wrote before. That was Edmund Parker, esq. who married Dorothy, daughter of Sir Clement Smith, Lord Chief Baron of the Exchequer. His grandson, Edmund Parker, of Northmolton and Boringdon, esquire, married Amy, daughter of Sir Edward Seymour, and was sheriff of Devonshire in 1622. His descendants have attained to the rank of Lord Boringdon (1784) and Earl of Morley (1815).

When it is remembered that the writer was grandson to a Duke, in remainder to the (then dormant) dukedom, and to the existing earldom of Hertford, and that his descendant (the sixth Baronet) actually succeeded to both those dignities in 1750, these passages are certainly worthy of notice, in proof of the estimation in which the dignity of Baronet was held in some quarters at its first institution. It happened that Mr. Seymour had never received knighthood. The present Duke of Somerset is the eleventh Baronet of the creation of 1611.

As a closely similar instance we may mention that of Edward Devereux, esquire,[1] of Castle Bromwich in Warwickshire, created a Baronet on the 25th Nov. 1612. He was in the remainder to the Viscountcy of Hereford; to which his son Walter succeeded, on the death of the Earl of Essex, in 1646.

Among other families that were to be raised to the dignity of Baronet by the patents of the Second Seal, there were three regarding which some delay arose; but whose precedency was eventually arranged with great precision, which shows how much importance was attached to that particular.

Charles Vavasour of Killingthorp in Lincolnshire, esquire, was not actually created a Baronet until the 22nd June, 1631; but he was then created with the precedency of the 29th June, 1611,[2] and placed between Monson and Gresley (Nos. 27 and 28). He died unmarried about 1665, when the title became extinct.

The Warrant for Sir George Savile of Thornhill did not pass until the 2nd July, 1611, and that for Sir George St. Paul not until the 5th of that month; but warrants were issued to date their patents of creation on the 29th of June last past, notwithstanding the Statute 18 Hen. VI., and they were ranked respectively as the 39th and 48th in order of creation.

J. G. N.

(To be continued.)

[1] The King knighted "Sir Edward Devereux of Warwickshire," in his summer progress of 1612. (*Progresses, &c. of James I.*, vol. ii. p. 462.) So he may have received that honour as a prelude to his advance to the Baronetcy, although designated as Esquire in the patent.

[2] This could only have been upon the ground of his having been accepted at the time, but by some accident "stayed." The particulars of the case have now disappeared : but may possibly at some time return to the surface.

REVIEW.

GENEALOGY AND SURNAMES: WITH SOME HERALDIC AND BIOGRAPHICAL NOTICES. By WILLIAM ANDERSON, Author of *The Scottish Nation, Landscape Lyrics*, etc. etc. Edinburgh, 1865. 8vo. pp. viii. 174.

Another addition to the multitude of rash and ill-considered works on this subject: a medley of hasty conjectures, trifling anecdotes, and empty humour. The author says, truly, in his preface, that "considerable attention has of late years been directed to the origin of Surnames:" and yet he betrays that he actually knows very little of what has been published. He acknowledges himself to be especially indebted to an American work on the subject by Mr. B. Homer Dixon, printed for private distribution, Boston, 1857, and yet he says nothing of another American book which has reached three editions, the *Suffolk Surnames* of the late Mr. Nathaniel Ingersoll Bowditch. He quotes the *Essays on English Surnames* by Mr. Mark Antony Lower, published in 1849, as being "as yet the only standard work on family nomenclature in the country," in complete ignorance of the same author's much more elaborate production, in a dictionary form, the *Patronymica Britannica*, completed in 1860.

It will not be worth while to examine Mr. Anderson's pages at much length. We shall be giving a general idea of them by copying the titles of the fourteen chapters into which his collections are distributed: 1. Original Significance of Names; 2. Personal or Distinctive Names; 3 Names from striking peculiarities; 4. Names from Colour and Complexion; 5. Surnames from Animals; 6. Surnames from Weapons and Insignia of War; 7. Surnames from Trades, Offices, and Occupations; 8. Genitive Names and Diminutives; 9. Surnames from Trees, Plants, Waters, and Rivers; 10. and 11. Surnames from Countries, Towns, and Lands; 12. Miscellaneous Surnames; 13. Change of Name; 14. Nomenclature in Scotland.

The penultimate Chapter is a very imperfect notice of a subject that has been recently much discussed;[1] whilst the last is the best part of the book, because it is actually the substance of a paper written by Dr. Stark, in the Annual Report of the Registrar-General for Scotland for 1860.

A hope is expressed in the Preface that the volume will prove acceptable, because "all mere theory or speculative conjecture as to the derivation of Names has been studiously avoided." But the performance is very opposite to this assurance. The glorious uncertainty of the etymologists of olden days is emulated to the full by Mr. Anderson with respect to personal nomenclature. The following is a specimen of his style of obscuring rather than elucidating the subjects of his inquiry:—

The name Mitchell is said by Lower (*Essays on Surnames*, vol. i. p. 140) to be

---

[1] See the various articles in our first volume, and the several essays there quoted.

derived from the Anglo-Saxon *Michel* or *Mucel,* meaning great; hence the Scotch *Mickle,* that is *muckle,* much or large. It may, however, have been derived from the Scandinavian *Modschiold,* Courageous Shield. I am inclined to think, from the crest of the Mitchells, a hand holding a pen, that it has its derivation in the German *Mit-schuler,* a disciple or scholar, literally " with a school."

Here is choice: but still omitting the most obvious derivation of all,— the baptismal name Michael, which has this soft pronunciation in French, and which the author (in p. 15) has already explained as signifying " Who is like God ?"

At p. 48, in like manner, three different derivations are offered for the name of Ellis; one, from Elias; another, from the town of Eliseux in Normandy; the third from the Cornish word for a son-in-law. No doubt some names, now perfectly alike in appearance, have had more than one origin: but then it would be much more satisfactory to give in each case an ascertained instance, than a variety of conjectures, however ingenious or plausible, unsupported by evident and authenticated deduction.

" It is strange (Mr. Anderson adds) how any family of the name should have chosen *eels* for their arms:" and yet he makes this remark at the foot of a page in which he has related how many families bearing the names of fish have canting coats, as Goujon, Delphini, Tarbet, Chabot, Garvie, Ged,— to which we might add Salmon, Herring, Roche, and others. It is apparent that he has never studied the late Mr. Moule's pleasing monograph on *The Heraldry of Fish.*

So little does he appreciate the symbolic system upon which, as we have elsewhere shown, armory was based from the earliest times, that he stigmatises it as *false* :

The Scotch name of Cockburn, in the true or rather false canting style of heraldry, also assumes three cocks in the shield, although the name itself has nothing to do with them, having been originally a corruption of Colbrand. (p. 47)

But was such the fact ? We are aware that the local name of Cockburnspeth on the Borders is traced as a corruption of Colbrandspath : but that derivation does not necessarily include the personal name of Cockburn.

On another well-known name the reader is offered the following absurd string of surmises :—

" The Scottish name of Stoddart is supposed to have been derived from the word *Standard.* It has also been conjectured to have been originally *Stout-heart,* to which the Anglified form of the name, Stothert, gives some countenance. An English family of the name of Studdard has for crest a demi-horse with a ducal coronet round its body." (p. 136)

—-implying, we presume, that its owner is a great *stud*-master!

The facts here asserted are as untrue as the conjectures are worthless. The " English family of the name of Studdard " (as the author designates it) is really named Studdert, and is seated at Bunratty castle, co. Clare : whilst that which is elegantly styled by Mr. Anderson " the Anglified form of the name Stothert," is to be found at Cargen in the county of Kirkcudbright.[1]

We do not know that the name can be properly termed " Anglified " or Anglicised under any form : but we have seen as eminent men in our own metropolis Dr. Stoddart, once the Editor of *The Times ;*[2] and Stothard the immortal Royal Academician, with his several clever sons.

But then, for the etymology of the name, is it not obviously one of the same class of which we have recently detected a memorable example in Coulthart ?—we mean a class descriptive of the herdsmen of the hills or open country.

Heard—a herdsman or keeper of cattle.

Colthart—the colt-herd.

Coward—the cow-herd.

Ewart—the ewe-herd.

Hoggard, and Hogarth [3]—the hog-herd.

Kennard—the kye or kine herd.

Shepherd—the sheep-herd.

Stothart—the stot-herd.

Swinnerd—the swine-herd.

Taggart, Teggart, and Tewart—the teg-herd.

Mr. Lower, in his *Patronymica Britannica*, adopts this origin for the name Coward, but still with some diffidence. He remarks,

" Although the popular derivation of this opprobrious word from *cow-herd* (whose occupation would be regarded with some disdain by the chivalrous in the middle ages,) is untenable,[4] I think it quite probable that the surname may be from that source, like Shepherd, Hayward, and other similar names."

---

[1] See Burke's *Landed Gentry* for both these houses.

[2] Afterwards Sir John Stoddart, Chief Justice and Judge of the Vice-Admiralty Court of Malta. He received the following allusive arms :—

Sable, two chevronels inclosing a Maltese cross between three estoiles argent, a bordure of the last. Crest, Fasces and the Oar of the Admiralty in saltire, placed within a wreath. Motto, *Justitiæ tenax.* He impaled Argent, a lion rampant gules, a chief ermine, for Wellwood (Book-plate), having married Isabella, eldest daughter of the Rev. Sir Henry Moncrieff·Wellwood, Bart. and sister to Sir William Moncrieff who died Attorney-general of Malta in 1813. Sir John Stoddart died Feb. 16, 1856, in his 85th year; and a memoir of him will be found in the Gentleman's Magazine for May following.

[3] In p. 31, Mr. Anderson says, " Hogarth is Dutch, and means high-natured, generous." But are any of our English Hogarths of Dutch ancestry ?

[4] " Coward is the past participle of the verb to *cowre* or to *cower*, a word formerly in common use," as stated by Horne Tooke : and adopted by Richardson in his *New English Dictionary*.

In the *Roll of Arms of the reign of Henry the Third*, edited by Sir Harris Nicolas, at p. 15, two contemporary knights, who bore the same name of John de Neville, are distinguished as John de Neville *Cowerde* and John de Neville *le Forrestier.* We are

But we can now present him with an instance of the name still written Cowherd at the beginning of the fifteenth century. In the register of archbishop Bowet at York there is recorded a dispensation granted in 1412 for the marriage of William son of Thomas de Fawxhed and Agnes daughter of *John Cowherd*, who were related in the third and fourth degrees.[1] In the *Promptorium Parvulorum* occurs COWHERDE, *vaccarius*, *vaccaria*, showing that this term was applied both to male and female servants. And somewhat later, " 16 Ap. 1618, Buryed Archie the cowhird of Goswick." Register of Holy Island, in Raine's *North Durham*, p. 151.

We do not, however, quite agree with Mr. Lower in combining the *Herd* and the *Ward*. We imagine there was this difference between the two. Whilst the Herd was a servant, like the Swain[2] (A.-S. *hyrd* and *swán*,) the Ward assumes the position of a public officer. The Hay-ward was the keeper of the hay or inclosure on the common for a whole community, the Wood-ward an officer who looked after a wood, the Bull-ward[3] the keeper of the parish bull, and so on.

Mr. Anderson (p. 44) says that "The surname of Swan has most likely been adopted at first from an innkeeper's sign,"—a similar misapprehension to that of deriving names from armorial bearings, instead of the former suggesting the latter. It is surely the original Anglo-Saxon form of Swain, which is still a frequent name as Swayne.

And so (in p. 76) " The surname Rose is evidently taken from the beautiful flower of the name ;"—whereas we suppose few can fail to perceive that Rose, together with Roos, and Rouse, is from *le Ros*, the Red-complexioned man, as Blount is from *le Blond*, the Fair man. This etymology of Blount and Blunt is correctly given by Mr. Anderson among his miscellaneous anecdotes (p. 121), but it is not included in his chapter on "Names from Colour and Complexion."

In p. 62 Mr. Anderson remarks that

The Church has supplied the names of Pope, Priest, Dean, Deans, Deacon, and Deakin ; Chaplin, Parsons; Abbot, Bishop, Prior, Monk, Friar, Fryer, and Frere ; Vicar, Vicars, and MacVicar (*Scotch*, son of the Vicar).

---

not aware whether any attempt has been made to explain these designations. In the preceding page Thomas de Moulton *le Forrestier* is thus distinguished from another Thomas de Multon.

[1] *Testamenta Eboracensia*, iii. 321 (a volume just published by the Surtees Society).

[2] The Swain was peculiarly the swine-herd. On the very ancient seal of Evesham, the swain from whom that town took its name is represented watching his swine, with this couplet—

"Eoves her wonede, ant was swon,
For wy men clepet this Eovishom."

See an engraving in the *Archæologia*, vol. xix. plate v.

[3] Bullard is still a surname : and within memory those who took an active part in the bull-fights at Stamford in Lincolnshire were called the Bullards.

To which may be added the lower clerical orders of Bennet and Colet (*i. e.* acolyte). Some of the former, as Pope, Bishop, &c. it has with probability been suggested, first adhered to the successful performers of such characters in the miracle plays, or in the mummeries of Christmas and other festivals. But Frere was a surname of a different origin, probably first given to distinguish two brothers that bore the same baptismal name, —as was frequently the case. We read of William FitzWarin le Frere in the reign of Edward the Third. It thus is of the same class as le Neve or Neve, *i. e.* the nephew; Fitz,—a well-known Devonshire family,—the son; Beaufitz,—a son-in-law; and Eyre, a name given to several races, the heir.

Altogether, this book is exceedingly imperfect, and full of errors, both historical and speculative, put together with a singular lack of knowlege and discrimination—and to criticise all its misstatements would occupy a greater number of pages than it contains.

We will not, however, part from Mr. Anderson without doing him the justice to admit that, to any one able to use his own judgment upon its contents, this book may be useful for occasional reference, particularly as it has a full *index nominum.* We would not pin our faith on all its genealogical information : but the following, at least, in which the author is personally concerned, we presume may be relied upon :—

As stated in a note to an article on the *Moral and Social Condition of Wales*, in Blackwood's Magazine for Sept. 1849, the leading scholars of Wales are all named WILLIAMS, viz. Archdeacon Williams,[1] and the Rev. Robert Williams, John Williams,[2] Rowland Williams,[3] Charles Williams, and another Robert Williams,—none of them relations. John Williams, author of *The Mineral Kingdom*, was also a Welshman, although the greater part of his life was spent in Scotland. He was the author's maternal grandfather. Well known in his time as an antiquarian and geologist, he was one of the twelve original members of the Antiquarian Society in Scotland. Having gone to Russia, on the invitation of the Empress Catherine, to survey for minerals in that Empire, he was on his way back to Scotland, having fulfilled his mission, after being two years and a half in Russia, when he was seized with a fever, and died at Verona in Italy, May 29, 1795.

[1] It is now sixteen years since this was written. It refers to John Williams, M.A. Archdeacon of Cardigan, Prebendary of St. David's, and of Brecon : who has been for some years deceased.

[2] The Rev. John Williams (ab Ithel), editor of the *Archæologia Cambrensis* and *The Cambrian Journal*, died Aug. 27, 1862, aged 51, and a memoir of him will be found in the Gentleman's Magazine for Feb. 1863.

[3] The Rev. Rowland Williams, M.A. Canon of St. Asaph, and Rector of Ysceifiog, one of the revisers of the Welsh translation of the Prayer-Book, died Dec. 28, 1854, aged 75.

BIBLIOTHECA HERALDICA.

1687.

GREGORY KING'S PEERAGE CARDS, TEMP. JAMES II.

By the favour of Evelyn Philip Shirley, Esq. F.S.A., we are now enabled to present our readers with some description of the Cards of the English Peerage edited by Gregory King, ~~Somerset~~ Herald, which were mentioned in our article on *Historical and Heraldic Cards*, in pp. 79, 80, of the present volume.

Though these Cards are now so exceedingly scarce as to be almost unknown, it is evident that there were several editions of them, and that consequently they must have had a considerable circulation.

The description we have quoted in p. 80 from Menestrier,[1] is that of a pack of cards of the Peers of England made before 1682, the year of the death of Prince Rupert, Duke of Cumberland. Whether that pack had been superintended by Gregory King does not appear; but its plan is identical with his, though the cards occupied by the several grades of the Peerage do not perfectly correspond.

Next, we know that Gregory King's set was published (or republished) in 1684 (see p. 80).

The same set, altered to the year 1687, is that we are about to describe from the copy lent us by Mr. Shirley.

And again, another edition was sanctioned by the Earl Marshal in 1688, as appears by the title or wrapper which we copied in p. 79.

Mr. Shirley's pack is remarkable, as showing the new dignities which James the Second had bestowed, chiefly upon noblemen of his own faith. The Garter is added to the shields of the Earls of Peterborough, Rochester, and Faversham, upon whom that honour had been conferred in 1685; but not to the arms of the Earl of Sunderland, who was elected K.G. in 1687. This pack includes, however, the King's natural son, James Duke of Berwick, so created on the 19th of March in that year.

Accompanying Mr. Shirley's pack is a List of the Peerage, in letter-press, copies of which had probably been provided to accompany the edition of 1684: it therefore furnishes the means of observing the alterations made by the engraver, which, considering the shortness of time that had elapsed, were very numerous, and involved the engraving of several new plates.

---

[1] Menestrier's description is evidently incomplete: as, besides the two Royal Dukes (of York and Cumberland), he mentions only three others,—Norfolk, Somerset, and Buckingham: and no Marquess. Now, the Duke of Albemarle was created in June 1660, and the death of Henry Duke of Gloucester did not occur until the following September. We should be very glad to be allowed to examine a copy of this pack of the reign of Charles II.

We will first make a copy of this *List of the Peers Spiritual and Temporal in the year* 1684,[1] omitting the armorial blason, which is sufficiently well known, and gives only single coats, without any quarterings or impalements. The mark * indicates a Knight of the Garter.

One Duke of the Royal Blood.

*JAMES Duke of York, only Brother to his most Sacred Majesty.

Three Great Officers who take place above all Dukes not of the Royal Blood.

Francis Lord Guilford, Lord Keeper of the Great Seal.
Laurence Earl of Rochester, Lord President of the Council.
George Marq. of Halifax, L. Privy Seal.

Two Great Officers who take place above all of their Degree.

Henry Duke of Norfolk, Earl Marshal of England.
James Duke of Ormond, Lord Steward of his Majesties Houshold.

Dukes XIII. and Duchesses II.

1. Henry Howard, Duke of Norfolk, (Earl Marshal of England.)
2. *Charles Seymour, Duke of Somerset.
3. *George Villiers, Duke of Buckingham.
4. *Christopher Monk, Duke of Albemarle.
5. *James Scot, Duke of Monmouth.
6. Henry Cavendish, Duke of Newcastle.
7. Barbara Villiers, Duchess of Cleveland.
8. Louisa de Queroüalle, Duchess of Portsmouth.
9. *Charles Lenos, Duke of Richmond.
10. *Charles Fitz-Roy, D. of Southampton.
11. *Henry Fitz-Roy, Duke of Grafton.
12. *James Butler, Duke of Ormond.
13. *Henry Somerset, Duke of Beaufort.
14. *George Fitz-Roy, Duke of Northumberland.
15. *Charles Beauclair, Duke of S. Albans.

Marquisses II.

1. Charles Pawlet, Marquiss of Winchester.
2. George Savile, Marquiss of Halifax (Lord Privy Seal.)

Two other Great Officers who take place above all of their Degree.

Robert Earl of Lindsey, L. High Chamberlain of England.
Henry Earl of Arlington, Lord Chamberlain of his Majesties Houshold.

---

[1] Catalogues of the Nobility temp. Charles II. were published by Nath. Brooke, 4to. 1660, and by Robert Pawley, 8vo. 1661 (see *Moule*, pp. 156, 160). One is also given in Sylvanus Morgan's *Sphere of Gentry*, folio, 1661. At p. 227, Moule describes "A Catalogue of the Nobility of England, according to their respective Precedencies, as it was presented to His Majesty [*i.e.* James II.] on New Year's Day, Anno 1684. To which is added, The Blazon of their Paternal Coats of Arms, and a List of the present Bishops. By Permission of the Duke of Norfolk. By JOHN DUGDALE, Esq. Norroy King of Arms. Printed at London, Anno 1685. A single Folio Sheet." (Reprinted in 1690.) This description tallies so completely with the Catalogue before us—to which the Duke of Norfolk's signature is attached, that we have no doubt that it is the same. The copy before us has no title: but is cut up

Earls LXVI. and I. Countess.

1.*Aubrey de Vere, Earl of Oxford.
2. Charles Talbot, Earl of Shrewsbury.
3. Anthony Grey, Earl of Kent.
4. William Stanley, Earl of Derby.
5. John Maners, Earl of Rutland.
6. Theophilus Hastings, Earl of Huntingdon.
7.*William Russel, Earl of Bedford.
8. Thomas Herbert, Earl of Pembroke.
9. Edward Clinton, Earl of Lincoln.
10. James Howard, Earl of Suffolk.
11. Charles Sackville, Earl of Dorset.
12. James Cecil, Earl of Salisbury.
13. John Cecil, Earl of Exeter.
14. John Egerton, Earl of Bridgwater.
15. Philip Sidney, Earl of Leicester.
16. GeorgeCompton,EarlofNorthampton.
17. Edward Rich, Earl of Warwick.
18. WilliamCavendish,Earl of Devonshire
19. William Fielding, Earl of Denbigh.
20. John Digby, Earl of Bristol.
21. Gilbert Holles, Earl of Clare.
22. Oliver St. John, Earl of Bolingbroke.
23. Charles Fane, Earl of Westmerland.
24. Charles Mountagu, Earl of Manchester.
25. Thomas Howard, Earl of Berkshire.
26.*John Sheffield, Earl of Mulgrave.
27. Thomas Savage, Earl Rivers.
28. Robert Bertie, Earl of Lindsey, (L. High Chamberlain of England.)
29. Henry Mordant, Earl of Peterborow.
30. Thomas Grey, Earl of Stamford.
31. Heneage Finch, Earl of Winchelsea.
32. William Pierpont, Earl of Kingston.
33. Charles Dormer, Earl of Carnarvon.
34. Philip Stanhope, Earl of Chesterfield.
35. Thomas Tufton, Earl of Thanet.

36. Thomas Weston, Earl of Portland.
37. William Wentworth,Earl of Strafford.
38. Robert Spencer, Earl of Sunderland.
39. Robert Leke, Earl of Scarsdale.
40. Edward Mountagu,Earl of Sandwich.
41. Henry Hyde, Earl of Clarendon.
42. Algernon Capel, Earl of Essex.
43. Robert Brudenel, Earl of Cardigan.
44. Arthur Annesley, Earl of Anglesey.
45. John Grenville, Earl of Bathe.
46. Charles[1] (now Edward) Howard, Earl of Carlisle.
47. William Craven, Earl of Craven.
48. Robert Bruce, Earl of Ailesbury.
49. Richard Boyle, Earl of Burlington.
50.*Henry Bennet, Earl of Arlington,[2] (L. Chamberlain of his Majties Household.)
51. Anthony Ashley Cooper, E. of Shaftsbury.
52. William Herbert, Earl of Powis.
53. Edward-Henry Lee,Earl of Lichfield.
54.*Thomas Osborne, Earl of Danby.
55. Thomas Lennard, Earl of Sussex.
56. Lewis de Duras, Earl of Feversham.
57. Charles Gerard, Earl of Macclesfield.
58. John Roberts, Earl of Radnor.
59. William Paston, Earl of Yarmouth.
60. George Berkeley, Earl of Berkeley.
61. ElizabethBanning,Countess of Shepey
62. Daniel Finch, Earl of Nottingham.
63. Laurence Hyde, Earl of Rochester, (Lord President of the Council.)
64. James Bertie, Earl of Abingdon.
65. Edward Noel, Earl of Gainsborough.
66. Coniers D'Arcie, Earl of Holderness.
67. Thomas Windsor, Earl of Plymouth.

---

into slips, which are pasted in a book. For the Peerage in the reign of William III. there is " An Exact Catalogue," by Robert Dale, Blanch Lion Pursuivant and Dep. Registrar of the College of Arms. 8vo 1697. Pp. 164. And, in succession to that, the catalogues given in the various editions of Chamberlayne's *Present State* may be usefully consulted.

[1] Charles first Earl of Carlisle died Feb. 26, 1684.

[2] The ordinary coat of Bennet, Gules, a bezant between three demi-lions rampant argent, granted by W. Dethick 1602, was altered to Gules, a *mound royal or* between

Viscounts IX.

1. Edward Devereux, Viscount Hereford.
2. Francis Brown, Viscount Mountagu.
3. William Fiennes, Viscount Say and Sele.
4. Thomas Bellassise, Viscount Falconberg
5. Charles Mordant, Viscount Mordant.
6. Francis Newport, Viscount Newport.
7. Horatio Townsend, Viscount Townsend.
8. Thomas Thynne, Viscount Weymouth.
9. Christopher Hatton, Viscount Hatton.

Barons LXII. and Baronesses IV.

1. George Nevill, Lord Bergaveny.
2. Mervyn Touchet, Lord Audley.
3. Charles West, Lord la Warr.
4. Thomas Parker, Lord Morley.
5. Robert Shirley, Lord Ferrers.
6. Charles Mildmay, Lord Fitzwalter.
7. Henry Yelverton, Lord de Grey.
8. Frances Sutton, Baroness Dudley.
9. William Stourton, Lord Stourton.
10. Coniers D'arcie, L. Coniers, Son and Heir apparent to the Earl of Holderness.
11. Vere-Essex Cromwell, Lord Cromwell (and Earl of Arglass in Ireland.)
12. Ralph Eure, Lord Eure.
13. Philip Wharton, Lord Wharton.
14. Thomas Willoughby, Lord Willoughby of Parham.
15. William Paget, Lord Paget.
16. Fran. Howard, L. Howard of Effingham.
17. Charles North, Lord North.
18. James Bruges, Lord Chandos.
19. Robert Carey, Lord Hunsdon.
20. John[1] (now Thomas) Petre, Lord Petre
21. Charles Gerard, Lord Gerard.
22. Henry Arundel, L. Arundel of Wardour.
23. Lady Catherine Stuart, Baroness Clifton of Leighton Bromswold.
24. Christopher Roper, Lord Tenham.
25. Foulk Grevil, Lord Brook.
26. Ralph Mountagu, Lord Mountagu.
27. John Lovelace, Lord Lovelace.
28. John Pawlet, Lord Pawlet.
29. William Maynard, Lord Maynard.
30. John Coventry, Lord Coventry.
31. Charles Mohun, Lord Mohun.
32. William Howard, L. Howard of Escrick
33. Henry Herbert, L. Herbert of Chirbury
34. Thomas Leigh, Lord Leigh.
35. Thomas Jermyn, Lord Jermyn.
36. William Byron, Lord Byron.
37. Richard Vaughan, Lord Vaughan, (and Earl of Carbery in Ireland.)
38. Francis Smith, Lord Carrington, (and Viscount Carrington in Ireland.)
39. William Widdrington, Lord Widdrington.
40. Edward Ward, Lord Ward.
41. Thomas Colepeper, Lord Colepeper.
42. Jacob Astley, Lord Astley.
43. Charles Lucas, Lord Lucas.
44. John Bellassise, Lord Bellassise.
45. Edward Watson, Lord Rockingham.
46. Robert Sutton, Lord Lexington.
47. Marmaduke Langdale, Lord Langdale
48. John Berkeley, Lord Berkeley.
49. Francis Holles, Lord Holles.
50. Charles Cornwallis, Lord Cornwallis.
51. Henry Booth, Lord De la mer.
52. Thomas Crew, Lord Crew.
53. Mary Lucas, Baroness Lucas, (and Countess of Kent.)

---

three demi-lions rampant argent, granted by Sir Edward Walker in 1664 to Sir Henry Bennet, Secretary of State, created Lord Arlington, of Arlington, co. Middlesex, (more properly Harlington,) in that year, and Earl of Arlington in 1672, K.G. also in 1672. He became Lord Chamberlain in 1674: and died without male issue in 1685. By a special remainder, his daughter, marrying the first Duke of Grafton, one of the sons of his Royal master, carried his dignities of peerage to that family.

[1] John Lord Petre died 1684.

54. Richard Arundel, L. Arundel of Trerice.
55. James Butler, Baron Butler of More Park, Grandson and Heir apparent to the Duke of Ormond.
56. Hugh Clifford, Lord Clifford.
57. Lord Richard Butler, Baron Butler of Weston, (and Earl of Arran in Ireland.)
58. Susan Airmine, Baroness Bellassise of Osgodby.

59. Richard Lumley, Lord Lumley, (and Viscount Lumley in Ireland.)
60. George Carteret, Lord Carteret.
61. George Legge, Lord Dartmouth.
62. John Bennet, Lord Ossulston.
63. Will.[1] (now Giles) Allington, L. Allington.
64. Ralph Stawell, Lord Stawell.
65. Francis North, Lord Guilford, (Lord Keeper of the Great Seal.)
66. Sidney Godolphin, Lord Godolphin.

Archbishops II. and Bishops XXIV.

1. Dr. William Sandcroft, Lord Archbishop of Canterbury, and Primate of all Engl.
2. Dr. John Dolbin, Lord Archbishop of York, and Primate of England.
3. Dr. Henry Compton, L. Bishop of London
4. Dr. Nathaniel Crew, L. Bishop of Durham
5. Dr. Peter Mew, L. Bishop of Winchester
6. Dr. Herbert Crofts, L. Bishop of Hereford
7. Dr. Seth Ward, L. Bishop of Salisbury.
8. Dr. Anthony Sparrow, L. Bishop of Norwich.
9. Dr. Thomas Wood, Lord Bishop of Lichfield and Coventry.
10. Dr. Guy Carleton, L. Bishop of Chichester.
11. Dr. John Pearson, L. Bishop of Chester.
12. Dr. Humphry Lloyd, L. Bp. of Bangor.
13. Dr. Will. Lloyd, L. Bp. of Peterborough.

14. Dr. Tho. Barlow, L. Bishop of Lincoln.
15. Dr. John Fell, Lord Bishop of Oxford.
16. Dr. Tho. Lampleugh, L. Bishop of Exeter.
17. Dr. Will. Thomas, L. Bishop of Worcester.
18. Dr. Will. Beaw, L. Bishop of Landaff.
19. Dr. Will. Lloyd, L. Bishop of S. Asaph.
20. Dr. Rob. Frampton, L. Bishop of Glocester.
21. Dr. Francis Turner, L. Bishop of Ely.
22. Dr. Laurence Womock, L. Bp. of S. David's.
23. Dr. Thomas Smith, L. Bishop of Carlisle.
24. Dr. John Lake, Lord Bishop of Bristol.
25. Dr. Tho. Sprat, L. Bishop of Rochester.
26. Dr. Tho. Kenn, L. Bp. of Bath and Wells. [Consecrated 25 Jan. 1684.]

The Archbishop of *Canterbury* takes place next to the Princes of the Blood, and above all the Nobility and Great Officers.

The Archbishop of *York* takes place above all the Nobility and Great Officers, except the Lord Keeper.

The rest of the Bishops take place next after the Viscounts, and above the Temporal Barons.

Whereof the Bishops of *London*, *Durham*, and *Winchester* do always precede the other Bishops, the rest taking place according to the Seniority of their Consecrations.

This Roll of Peers received the following *Imprimatur* from the Earl Marshal :—

William Lord Allington died in 1684.

Jan. 21, 1684.

I do Order and Appoint that this LIST be printed, and that none other be printed without my Allowance.

Norfolk and Marshal.

We now proceed to describe Gregory King's Cards:—

KING OF HEARTS. *Armes of England. Armes of Scotland.*
Two shields (the former encircled by a Garter) under one large crown.

KING OF DIAMONDS. *Armes of France. Armes of Ireland.*
Arranged in like manner.

KING OF SPADES. *Arch Bishops of Canterbury. York.*
Their two shields, under one mitre.

KING OF CLUBS. *Dukes of Norfolk, Somerset, Buckingham.*
Their three shields within one Garter, and under one ducal coronet.

QUEEN OF HEARTS. Dukes of *Albemarle* and *Newcastle;* and Duchesses of *Cleveland* and *Portsmouth :* the two former both encircled with Garters; the two latter in lozenges.

QUEEN OF DIAMONDS. Dukes of *Richmond, Southampton,* and *Grafton,* all within one garter, and under one coronet.

QUEEN OF SPADES. Dukes of *Ormond, Beaufort,* and *Northumberland,* arranged in like manner.

QUEEN OF CLUBS. Dukes of *St. Albans* and *Berwick* under one coronet.
These are the last of 15 DUKES AND DUCHESSES.

The plan of having one large coronet for each card is followed throughout the pack, as in that of the Peerage of Scotland, of which specimens were shown at p. 81 of the present volume.

The Prince of Hearts contains the shields of the MARQUESSES of *Winchester* and *Halifax :* and this memorandum : *Powis, Herbert, See his Armes among yᵉ Earles, No. 51,* his elevation having taken place in 1687, since the cards were first engraved.

The EARLES commence in the Prince of Diamonds. They agree with the printed list throughout twelve cards, that is down to No. 49. In No. 14 it may be remarked that the bordure has been taken out from the shield of Egerton Earl of Bridgwater : which corresponds with a remark made in the printed list, where that coat is thus blasoned :

Argent, a Lion rampant Gules, between three Pheons with a Bordure engrail'd Sable, (but the Bordure is now left off.)

In the 8 of Diamonds the shield of the Earl of Arlington, No. 50, has been taken out in consequence of his death s. p. m. in 1685. That of the Earl of Burlington was removed with it, and re-engraved in the centre, so that this card has only three shields instead of the usual number of four. *Shaftsbury* and *Powis* become Nos. 50 and 51 : and to the latter is added this memorandum, " now Marquess of Powis," that dignity having been conferred in 1687.

In the 8 of Spades, *Lichfield, Danby, Sussex*, and *Feversham* are altered to Nos. 52, 53, 54, and 55; and a Garter is added to the last, as already mentioned.

In the 8 of Clubs (the Nos. now being altered to the end of the Earls) the first shield, which had displayed the arms of the Earl of Macclesfield, is left blank. This is a remarkable memorial of the temporary disgrace of that nobleman—Charles Gerard, the first Earl (so created 1679) who was committed to the Tower in the year 1684, together with the Earl of Stamford and the Lord Delamere, on suspicion of having intended to raise a rebellion, but escaped attainder, and lived until 1693.

In the 7 of Hearts the arms of the Countess of Shepey have been taken out, and those of the Earl of Nottingham are engraved in the centre. According to Nicolas's *Synopsis of the Peerage* the death of the Countess of Shepey did not occur until 1690, but qu. ?

Lastly, to close the Earls, in the 7 of Diamonds is added the arms (on a lozenge) of the Countess of Dorchester, Catherine Sidley (or Sedley), the King's mistress, who had been so created on the 2nd Jan. 1685-6.

The VISCOUNTS occupy the 7 of Spades, 7 of Clubs, and 7 of Hearts, the last containing one shield only,—there being only nine Viscounts, and their names and arrangement the same as in the printed List.

The BISHOPS are thus arranged—

SIX OF DIAMONDS. *London, Durham, Winchester, Hereford.*

SIX OF SPADES. *Salisbury, Norwich, Coventry and Lichfield, Bangor.*

SIX OF CLUBS. *Lincoln, Exeter, Worcester, Landaff.*

FIVE OF HEARTS. *St. Asaph, Gloucester, Ely, Carlisle.*

FIVE OF DIAMONDS. *Bristol, Rochester, Bath and Wells, Chichester.*

FIVE OF SPADES. *Peterborough, St. David's, Oxford, Chester.*

(In every case the armorial coat of the See only is engraved.)

This was the precedence of the Bishops at the end of 1686, when Thomas Cartwright, Bishop of Chester, one of whose Diaries has been printed for the Camden Society, was the last member of the bench: except that Norwich is out of his place. There had been five changes since the printed list of 1684, by the deaths of Bishops Sparrow, Carleton, Pearson, Fell, and Womack. Dr. Lloyd, Bishop of Peterborough, had been translated to Norwich: but the shield of *Norwich* remains in its former place as for Bishop Sparrow. This must have been an oversight, as that very card (the 6 of Spades) has *Bangor* brought into it, omitting *Chichester* and *Chester*, the two intervening Bishops in 1684, and the four subsequent cards must have been all re-engraved.

The first four cards of BARONS correspond with the first sixteen names in the list of 1684, excepting that the number of *Howard of Effingham* is altered from 16 to 17, and at the foot of the card in a small lozenge is added 16 *Howard Baroness Stafford.* This lady was Mary Stafford, sole heir of the old barony of Stafford; whose husband Sir William Howard, created Baron Stafford (with remainder to his heirs male) Sept.

12, 1640, and Viscount Stafford on the 11th November following, had been attainted and beheaded in 1678. King James had now restored his wife to her ancestral dignity, and afterwards, on the 5th October, 1688, he created her Countess of Stafford for life, at the same time giving her son the dignity of Earl.

The next card, 4 of Clubs, still begins with another 17; and that and the 3 of Hearts correspond with the printed list. In the 3 of Diamonds *Lovelace* and *Pawlet* are altered to 28 and 29; and in the centre is inserted a small shield for 27 *Grey Ld Grey* [*of*] *Wark*. Why this nobleman had been omitted in the List of 1684 it is difficult to guess. Soon after, he was concerned in the rebellion of the Duke of Monmouth; but he managed to make composition for that error, and King William subsequently created him Earl of Tankerville.

In the next card, the 3 of Spades, there has been an alteration in the figures only. *Howard of Escrick* is numbered 31, and *Mohun* 32, as if their precedence had been found wrong, and corrected.

The next six cards correspond with the printed list as to names and shields: though in the first of them, the 3 of Clubs, there are indistinct traces of something having been inserted, and taken out again. And between that card and the next the number 37 is dropped: and consequently Nos. 38—57 inclusive correspond to Nos. 37—56 of the List.

The three last cards must have been re-engraved. They are—

ONE OF DIAMONDS. 58. *Armine Baroness Bellasise, for life.*
                 59. *Lumley Ld Lumley.*
                 60. *Carteret Ld Carteret.*
                 62. *Legge Ld Dartmouth.*
ONE OF SPADES. 61. *Bennet Ld Ossulston.*
                 63. *Allington Ld Allington.*
                 64. *Stawell Ld Stawell.*
                 65. *North Ld Guilford.*
ONE OF CLUBS. 66. *Godolphin Ld Godolphin.*
                 67. *Jermyn Ld Dover.*
                 68. *Churchill Ld Churchill.*
                 69. *Ieffreys Baron of Wem.*

The figures to *Ossulston* and *Dartmouth* it will be observed have been altered, reversing their precedence from the printed list. The three last Barons had been created in 1685,—Lord Dover, by patent dated May 13; Lord Churchill, afterwards the great Duke of Marlborough, by patent dated May 14; and the odious Lord Chancellor by patent dated May 15.

As it is very probable that any other set of these Cards that may happen to be preserved would prove to be of a different impression to that we have now described, it would be esteemed a favour if any of our friends that may be the fortunate possessor of a copy (whether perfect or otherwise) will allow us to examine it.

1865.

EVANS.

250 Copies.   Newcastle-upon-Tyne : Printed by J. G. Forster, 81, Clayton
Street.   For Private Distribution.   J.R.A. & M.C.J.   8vo. pp. 24.

The family of Evans, to which these pages relate, has long been settled
in the county of Montgomery.   Pedigrees of lines of the name flourishing
at Plas Duon, in Carno, and at Trecastle, in Llanwnog, both parishes in
that county, are given in Lewis Dwnn's Visitations of Wales (temp. Elizabeth), and in Protheroe's Collections of Welsh Pedigrees in the College of
Arms, as amongst the genealogies of families descended from a chieftain,

 Gwdhno Goron (or Gwyddno Garanhir), to whom the
Arms, *Argent, a lion passant between three fleurs de lis
gules*, were ascribed.   Vincent also states in his MSS.
that "of him Gwyddno Garanhir do descend men of the
Lordship of Keiveilior, in the county of Montgomery."
These arms (the lion being *sable*) have been worn in
common by families of Pryce, Pugh, and Evans, settled
in that shire, " a confusing and improper usage (as has
been well observed by an experienced genealogist,) as it is clear that only
the heir-at-law or co-heirs of some great *homo propositus* entitled to these
arms could wear them without substantial difference.   Some Cambrian
antiquary may be able to say who's who ; and all the Pryces, Pughs, and
Evanses besides should obtain differenced grants."

The particular family of Evans which constitutes the subject of this
memoir was resident in the parish of Guildsfield, co. Montgomery, where
they were tenants to the Herberts of Powis for nearly two centuries.   The
present head of the family is John Evans, Esq. long resident in Bartholomew Close, London, afterwards of Stoke Newington, but now of Leamington ; whose younger brother Edward Evans, esq., J.P., was Mayor of
Worcester in 1841-2.[1]

Their sister Elizabeth was married in 1806 to Morris Jones, esq. of
Welshpool, and afterwards of Gungrog in Montgomeryshire ; whose son
Morris Charles Jones, esq. of Liverpool, solicitor, and of Gungrog, is the
owner of the initials which, with those of J. R. Appleton, esq. F.S.A., are
attached to the present genealogy, and are a guarantee of the care with

[1] On the 7th August, 1865 (since the memoir before us was printed), at a meeting
of the Worcester City and County Banking Company, Richard Padmore, Esq. M.P.
in the chair, it was moved by Mr. Sheriff, M.P. and unanimously Resolved, " That
Edward Evans, Esq. *the founder*, and for many years the Managing Director of the
Company, be respectfully requested to sit for his bust in marble, to be placed in the
Bank."   It is intended as a companion to the bust of Mr. Padmore, which is already
there.

which it has been compiled, as indeed is amply shown by the circumstantial array of dates, with their authorities in each case annexed.

It may further be noticed that at p. 12 there is some account of the several families of Bickerton:[1] and at p. 13 a pedigree of Hill of Worcestershire, deduced from Humphrey Hill of Little Witley in that county, buried in 1712, to Thomas Rowley Hill, esq. now of Catharine Hill house, Worcester, who is the son of William Hill, esq. of that city, who died in 1859, by Elizabeth, daughter of Thomas Rowley of Stourport. Thomas Rowley Hill, esq. J.P. (who, like his partner and father-in-law Mr. Evans, has served the office of mayor of Worcester,) received a grant of arms on the 11th Aug. 1864, viz. Ermine, a chevron checquy or and azure, in base upon a mount a Cornish chough proper. Crest, on a wreath of the colours, upon a mount in front of a fern-brake proper a talbot or, collared azure, resting the dexter foot upon three annulets interlaced, also or. These arms were a compound of Hill and Rowley, and were registered with proof of pedigree.

Since the foregoing was written, we have received the following communication from one of the authors of the Evans pedigree:—

The circumstance mentioned on page 4, that "David ap Evan by his will dated in 1640 left 20s. to the poor of the parish of Llangadfan," was noticed by Thomas Nevill, Esq. (agent of the Earl of Powis), and it occurred to him that a branch of the family lived in that neighbourhood. In 1832 the late Lord Powis purchased some property in the parish of Llangadfan from Mr. Maurice Evan Evans, then of Holborn, London. The title-deeds (which by Mr. Newill's courtesy I have inspected) show Mr. Maurice Evan Evans's pedigree for eight generations from 1648, his ancestor then in possession of the property having been John Evan of Blouty. Lands called Tyddyn, &c. were settled by John Evan, by deed dated 20 Sep. 1648, and descended by heirship, or by virtue of several subsequent settlements, to Maurice Evan Evans, who sold to the late Lord Powis in 1832.

[1] The late Sir John Bickerton Williams, F.S.A. of Shrewsbury, and afterwards of the Hill, Wem, co. Salop, was the son of Mr. William Williams by Hannah second daughter of John Bickerton of Sandford hall in the parish of West Felton, co. Salop, and cousin-german to Catharine Bickerton, who married Edward Evans (Evans pedigree, p. 12.) He was the editor of the Life and Works of the Rev. Phillip Henry (the father of the Commentator, Mattbew Henry,) and author of a Life of Chief Justice Sir Matthew Hale. He died Oct. 21, 1855, and there is a memoir of him in the Gentleman's Magazine for December following, p. 656. He was the first Knight made by her present Majesty (July 19, 1837,) that honour having been promised by King William the Fourth, at the instance of H.R.H. the Duke of Sussex; and is said to have been the first Dissenter upon whom knighthood had been conferred since the accession of the House of Hanover. His friendship with the Duke originated in his presenting a very rare addition to his Royal Highness's collection of Bibles

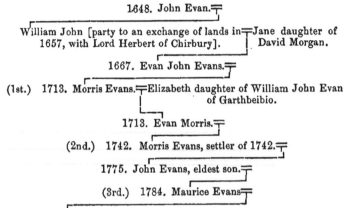

1832. Maurice Evan Evans, of Holborn (near Middle Row), London.

But what is more material to my present purpose is, that amongst the deeds there is one of the reign of Henry VIII. [the year illegible], being a Release from " Rees ap Jeuan ap Bedo and John ap Jeuan ap Bedo of Llangadfan, Brothers and Coheirs of Evan ap Bedo, unto Matthew ap Jeuan ap Bedo their elder Brother, another Son and Co-heir of the afore= said Jeuan ap Bedo (their Brother being then in possession) of all their right, &c. in four tenements in Garthbeibio, in the Lordship of Kereignion [Caereinion] called Tyddyn, &c." the same property that was settled by John Evan in 1648. The witnesses are, " David ap Jean Bedo, Griffith . . . ap Evan ap . . ., Matthew Bedo." " Jeuan " is identical with " Evan."

It is not possible that the " David ap Jean [or Evan] ap Bedo" could be the " David ap Evan," the Testator of 1640. But the bequest by the latter Testator of 20s. to the Poor of Llangadfan is a strong indication of his having sprung from that parish, and most probably from the " Evans " of Blouty there settled.

With reference to " Jeuan ap Bedo," the father of Matthew, Rees, John, and David, it seems probable that he was a brother of " Howell ap Bedo y Castell of Tre Castell in Llanwnog," which is a parish situate in the centre of Montgomeryshire, and not far distant from Llangadfan.

The name " Howell ap Bedo y Castle " commences the pedigree of " Tre Castle in Llanwnog," in Lewis Dwnn's *Visitations of Wales* (vol. i. 306), which is as follows :

```
Howell ap Bedo y Castell ap David  ap⟙Margaret urch Maurice David ap Evan
   David ap Meredith Benwyn.           |      ap Howell of Llandysal.
 ┌─────────────────────────────────────────────────────────────┐
David ap Howell⟙Catherine urch Thomas ap        Griffith ap Howell the father
           |        Evan Lloyd.                       of Henry.
           └─┐ Rᵈ Partyn ap Thomas Partyn⟙Elizabeth urch Robᵗ Richardson.
             Evan David, gentⁿ⟙Alson urch Rᵈ Partington.
          ┌──────────────┘ Wᵐ Griffith, M.A.⟙Mabel urch John Herbert of Kemaes.
        ┌───────────────┐
Richard Evans= . . . . . . urch Wᵐ Griffiths, M.A., and Parson of Kemaes.
```

This pedigree is also given with a little variation in Protheroe's collections in the College of Arms, vol. vii. 130, and vol. viii. 61.

I have since found in an old guide-book published in 1813 (*Cambrian Traveller's Guide*, p. 766,) the following :—

Near Llanerfyl [an adjoining parish to Llangadfan] is an uncommonly ancient mansion called Neuadd Wen. This was the seat of Meredyth ap Kynan, brother of Gruffudd ap Kynan, Prince of North Wales, who served the Princes of Powis, and was termed Lord of Rhiwhirieth, Coed-talog, and Neuadd Wen. The present name was probably given to the new structure, for there is a tradition that its former appellation was Llys Wgan. The brook which runs by is called Nant Wgan. Below this house on the side of the road once stood a stone whereon was a cross fleury, but it was lately broken by a silly wench in search of treasure.

Adjoining to Neuadd Wen lies the capital farm of Llyssin, sometime the estate of Jeuan ap Bedo Gwyn, descendant of a cadet branch of the family of Neuadd Wen, whose name appears amongst the bards. This estate was purchased by the Herberts ancestors to the Earl of Powis, and was the residence of some of its branches.

The statement that Jeuan ap Bedo, descended from Meredith ap Cynan of Neuadd Wen, was a brother of Howel ap Bedo, is confirmed by the pedigree given by Lewis Dwnn (i. 306) commencing "Howel ap Bedo y Castle ap David ap David ap *Meredith Benwyn*," if Meredith Benwyn was identical with, or a descendant of Meredith ap Cynan, *sed quære*.

I shall pursue the inquiry when time and opportunity permit; but the theory that springs to one's mind is, that, upon the purchase by Lord Powis's ancestors from the descendants of Jeuan ap Bedo of the farm of Llyssin—a remnant of their inheritance which had been divided into shreds by the operation of the custom of Gavelkind then prevailing in Wales— the Herberts provided farms for the descendants of the ancient owners of the soil, and amongst the rest for David ap Evan (Evans pedigree, pp. 3 nd 4,) in Tirymynech, and there the Evanses remained tenants for nearly two centuries (viz. from 1634 to 1817). This is consistent with the traditions of the Powis family, and with the circumstance mentioned on page 10 of the Evans pedigree.

Meredith ap Cynan is stated to have served the Princes of Powis. The intimate connection between his descendants and the owners of Powisland, who were the successors of the Princes of Powis, would seem to be evidenced by the circumstance that in a charter dated 1 Aug. 8 Hen. V. from Edward de Charlton, Lord of Powis, to the Abbey of Strata Marcella, the following are "Witnesses, John Fitzpier, Surveyor (*supervisor*) of our Lordship of Powis; David Holbach and Hugh Say, our Stewards there; *Matthew ap Evan* our receiver there," &c.

The result of the foregoing observations is to indicate the probability of this family of Evans in common with the Evans of Blouty in Llangadfan having sprung from Jeuan ap Bedo, who was a Brother of Howel ap Bedo mentioned in Lewis Dwnn's *Visitations*, and who is stated to have descended from a cadet branch of Meredyth ap Cynan of Neuadd Wen. Any information or hint on the subject would be highly esteemed. M. C. J.

1857.

MEMORANDA RELATING TO THE LANE, REYNER, AND WHIPPLE FAMILIES, Yorkshire and Massachusetts. Reprinted from the New England Historical and Genealogical Register, for April and July, 1857. By W. H. WHITMORE. Boston: Henry W. Dutton and Sons, Printers. 1857. pp. 22.

In America manuscript papers and letters of the seventeenth century are historical records of priceless value, regarded somewhat in the same light as we look upon charters of some five hundred years' earlier date. We make this remark with no disrespect; but with the very opposite feeling: for we admire the affectionate reverence which attaches itself to the earliest ancestral memorials that are available.

The primæval documents preserved in the pages before us are designated as the Lane Family Papers, preserved by descendants of Job Lane, who resided in "the old Lane Farm" near Boston, in Massachusetts, and whose descendants were commemorated in a previous number (Oct. 1856) of the magazine above named. They retained some property at Edstone, in the East Riding of Yorkshire, near Beverley, so late as 1796.

One of the longest and most curious letters among them is that written by John Dickinson of Gildersome near Leeds on the 6th of March, 1670, to his "Cozen Laine," then in America. We extract one or two remarkable passages:—

"Trading is bad; it's stolen out of England into Ireland, Germany, and Holland, that mightily impoverisheth England. Besides, there hath been great teynts and taxing in this land, that hath disabled tenants in too much money [i.e. deprived them of much money that might have supplied them with the means of paying their rents]. * * *

"I deal in oil and dye-stuffs. I have them from London: I am at London commonly every August, but write thither every week. * * *

"Old England is at a loss in sure things; the want of a liberty of preaching, ... , and that trade that hath been formerly in our country for cloath, which is much lamented."

Such were the causes that often provoked emigration : and, though these passages record but a temporary decadence of the great clothing trade of Yorkshire, yet they have an historical value. From a later letter of the same writer, dated the 1st April, 1679, we take another passage :

"Your uncle Boyes was slain in the war at a fight between the Lord Fairfax and the King's forces called Seacroft Fight, or Club Fight. It was called so because many of the countrymen went with the Lord Fairfax with clubs, and no other weapons. The Parliament party your uncle was in, and they was put to the run and he slain, between Seacroft and Leeds, within 2 miles of Leeds, in April 1643, now 36 years since."

The accuracy of this date we find confirmed by an entry[1] in the parish register of Leeds: "Buried 1st April, 1643, Captain Boswell, slain at

----
[1] Whitaker's *Loidis and Elmete*, p. 75.

Seacroft battel, and six soldiers." Though beaten at Seacroft, the Clubmen were on the whole an effective force, and their victories at Bradford, Leeds, and Wakefield were among the Republican triumphs commemorated in a contemporary news-tract entitled

The Rider of the White Horse and his Army: Their late Good Success in Yorkshire Or a true and faithful Relation of that famous and wonderfull Victory at Bradford obtained by the Club-men there, with all the circumstances thereof. And of the taking of Leeds and Wakefield by the same men, &c. . London, 1643.

Of which it is stated in the Catalogue of the library of Edward Hailstone, esq. F.S.A. at Horton hall (privately printed in 1858,) that not more than two or three copies are known to exist.

The other Lane Papers contain further particulars of the family of Boyes, who was also from Edstone,[2] and of the Reyners, who were from Gildersome, and whose entries have been procured from the parish register, and are appended.

JAMES HEYWOOD MARKLAND, ESQ. D.C.L., F.R.S., F.S.A.

On the 28th December last died at his residence, Lansdown Crescent, Bath, James Heywood Markland, esq. Hon. D.C.L. of Oxford (1849), F.R.S. and F.S.A. This gentleman has long been distinguished for his writings in support of the principles of the Church of England, and of the respect due to her sacred structures and their architecture and accessories: as well as for his general attachment to antiquities and literature. He was one of the original members of the Roxburghe Club (founded in 1812), and the last survivor of them. He was for nearly fifty-six years a Fellow of the Society of Antiquaries, having been elected on the 26th Jan. 1809; and for two years, from 1827 to 1829, its Director; and he was the contributor of several valuable papers to the Society, of which the first (published in the *Archæologia* in 1815) was connected with the subjects of our pages, being on "The Antiquity and Introduction of Surnames in England."

It is scarcely known, however, how much Mr. Markland's original bent was towards heraldry and genealogy. Whilst at school at Chester, and only fourteen, he compiled a treatise on *Lancashire and Cheshire Heraldry*, which is still preserved in manuscript: as are the fragments of some old family deeds, reaching back to the reigns of the Edwards, which about the same time he rescued from the scissors of a utilitarian housekeeper.

[2] Robert Ripley of Hull, who died about 1624, married Emmot, daughter of John Boyse of Egton (*i.e.* Edstone).—Dugdale's *Visitation of Yorkshire*, (Surtees Soc.) p. 130.

When a student in the Temple, in the year 1811, Mr. Markland communicated to the author of the *Life of Bowyer* some biographical particulars regarding the learned Greek scholar Jeremiah Markland, M.A. and his relative Dr. Abraham Markland, Master of St. Cross: the former having been one of the leading characters in Mr. Nichols's work. This communication was printed in the fourth volume of the *Literary Anecdotes of the Eighteenth Century*, pp. 657–661, accompanied by a sheet pedigree of the Marklands, formerly of the Meadows, &c. in the county of Lancaster.[1]

Mr. Markland was seventh in descent from Raufe Markland, of the Meadows, who about 1529 sat in Parliament for Wigan; near which town the family had held lands from the time of Edward III. The Markland family was one of the twenty concerning whom Queen Elizabeth ordered the Bishop of Chester to take heed that they sent not their children abroad to be brought up in the Popish persuasion.

When Mr. Ormerod (now nearly half a century ago) undertook his *History of Cheshire*, he received from Mr. Markland such assistance as elicited from him (in 1819) the following recognition:—

From J. H. MARKLAND, esq. F.R.S. and S.A. whose accurate pen has lately rescued the *Chester Mysteries* [some of which he edited for the Roxburghe Club,] from all aspersions on their well-grounded claim to remote antiquity, he has the pleasure of acknowledging many valuable communications and much friendly assistance.

Mr. Markland's eldest uncle John Markland, esq. took the name of Entwisle, on inheriting from his cousin, the last of that family, who died in 1787, the estate of Foxholes, co. Lancaster: his grandfather John Markland, of Pemberton, co. Lanc. esq. having married Ellen, eldest daughter of Bertie Entwisle, of Wigan, esq. Vice-Chancellor of the County Palatine of Lancaster. Mr. Entwisle was High Sheriff of Lancashire in 1798, and father of the late John Entwisle, esq. High Sheriff in 1824, and M.P. for Rochdale ; whose son John Smith Entwisle, of Foxholes, esquire, is the present representative of that family, and of the elder line of Markland.

Robert, the second son, succeeded to the small hereditary estate at Pemberton, near Wigan, and, becoming a merchant in Manchester, married Elizabeth daughter of Robert Hibbert, esq. of that town. James Heywood Markland was their fourth and youngest son, born at Manchester Dec. 7, 1788.

---

[1] An interleaved copy of this Memoir, enlarged by MS. additions and letters, was in the recent sale of Mr. Markland's library, lot 1094. It was purchased for 5*l.* 15*s.* by the Rev. C. R. Conybeare.

Mr. Markland married, in 1821, Charlotte, eldest daughter of Sir Francis Freeling, the first Baronet, one of his brother Roxburghers; and by that lady, who survives him, he had issue one daughter, Elizabeth-Jane, now the wife of the Rev. Charles Ranken Conybeare, M.A. Vicar of Itchen Stoke, third son of the late Dean of Llandaff. A short notice of Mr. Markland, written by his son-in-law, has been published in *The Gentleman's Magazine* for May 1865.

The memory of Mr. Markland will be preserved by a painted window to be erected in Bath abbey church, the proposal having emanated from the Bath Literary Club, of which he was the first founder and over which he long presided. This will be in accordance with the improved taste for sepulchral memorials which he did so much to promote, as well as a due tribute to his enlightened religious zeal, his many good works, and the warm interest he took in the restoration of the Abbey Church.

Mr. Markland, having previously parted with some of his more valuable books, left a large and gentlemanly library, which has occupied a whole week's sale at Sotheby's (May 29—June 3, 1865). It was rich in theology, history, biography, antiquities, and general literature, and included some volumes illustrated with interesting manuscript notes and autograph letters: but, as there were few lots of extraordinary rarity or value, its total proceeds did not exceed 1,636*l*. 4*s*. 6*d*.

Having mentioned that one of Mr. Markland's earliest printed memoirs was a communication regarding his family made to the elder Mr. Nichols, it is worthy of remark that, after the lapse of fifty years, one of his latest was the letter which he addressed to the Editor of *The Herald and Genealogist*, on "The Proofs of Arms required by the Heralds at their Visitations," and which was printed in our second volume, in pp. 149–154. The question he mooted was, how far arms of undoubted antiquity, but upon which the heralds have at any time expressed a doubt of "proof," and which have never received their official sanction, can be maintained as genuine and authentic. In this case it was mentioned that " a gold seal-ring with the arms and crest, pronounced by a competent judge to be of the age of Elizabeth, is still in the possession of the family."

Mr. Markland did not state the blason of his coat. It is simply Argent, a chevron between three martlets sable : and for crest, a lion's head erased. On his book-plate, which was engraved in wood, these arms appear, impaling Freeling: and we had obtained permission to append it to this article, but the block is unfortunately not forthcoming.

EDGAR OF AUCHINGRAMMONT, LANARKSHIRE.

There can be little doubt that one of the best claims to represent the Edgars of Wedderlie is that of the Edgars of Auchingrammont, who have moreover the double advantage of uniting another family of the same name by the marriage of Alexander Edgar of Auchingrammont (1740-1) and also styled, by himself (in the parish registers of Leith), "from Nether-houses."

The following facts contrasted will place the question more clearly before the reader, it being kept in view that there is no *proved representative* in the male line of Wedderlie.[1]

1. John Edgar, Laird of WEDDERLIE, was sued by Mr. Chieslie (vide Decree of Court of Session 1663) for the maintenance of his younger brother Alexander, then apprenticed to the said Mr. Chieslie, surgeon.

These lawsuits are continued till the close of the seventeenth century, and we gradually meet with suggestive cases, in the index to the records, in which the following appear almost interchangeably as litigants: Edgar, Chieslie, Osborne, Handasyde, Murray, &c.

On the establishment of the College of Surgeons of Edinburgh,[2] Alexander Edgar becomes a member, and that he is identical with the apprentice of Mr. Chieslie, and brother of John Edgar of Wedderlie, the order for him on record to settle the affairs of his late master Mr. Chieslie, at once shows.

The co-collegians of this Alexander Edgar were Mr. Purves (brother of Purves Hall), Colin Lauder (of the Hutton branch of the "Bass" family), ... Handasyde.[3] Then we find Minute Book, Register of Deeds):

16 June, 1663, Handaside to *Chieslie.*

[1] Captain F. Pemberton Campbell, 14th Hussars, the grandson and heir of the late Admiral Alexander Edgar, only surviving son of the last laird of Wedderlie, represents the direct line.

[2] "From the records of Inquisitions regarding the possession of property in Scotland and other sources of information, I can prove that, of the first 150 members of the Incorporation of Surgeons, nearly twenty were possessed of landed property. A great many more held property in houses, chiefly in Edinburgh; six at least were nearly allied by blood or marriage to the families of the nobility; three were members of the Parliament; and six were surgeons to the Scotch Kings."—*Sketch of the Early History of the Medical Profession in Edinburgh*, by John Gairdner, M.D. Edinb. Oliver and Boyd. 1864.

[3] Handasyde, I believe, is a Haddingtonshire name, and one would be inclined to examine the coincidences of names and dates in the family of Alexander Edgar, Commissioner for Haddington, "promoter of the Darien scheme," who was probably a son of Alexander Edgar of Westruther, Cautioner for Mary Edgar of Wedderlie, and probably her uncle.

It has been supposed that the Auchingrammont Edgars were of the Newton branch of Wedderlie, but this surmise seems rather applicable to James Edgar, father-in-law of Alexander Edgar of Auchingrammont.

2. Auchingrammont.—The various disjointed traditions of the family of Auchingrammont, supported by old-fashioned silver plate bearing the arms of Wedderlie, antique gold-enamelled snuff-boxes, &c. &c. appear to be as follows.[1]

They asserted that they were the descendants and lineal representatives of Edgar of Wedderlie, inasmuch as the father of the first Edgar of Auchingrammont was an Edgar of Wedderlie. That the latter took with him to Jamaica portraits of the Edgars of Wedderlie, which, being rolled up, were damaged, and so lost. That on his return he married a *cousin* (?) named Edgar, by whom he acquired property in the Luckenbooth and Lawn Market, Edinburgh, &c. and sent his sons early in life to the West Indies while he himself remained at home, and never returned there.

It is clear that in 1783 the Auchingrammont Edgars were intimate with Mr. Purves of Purves Hall, one of whose letters to John Hutton (afterwards a Doctor in the Army?) exists. John Hutton was the grandson of Alexander Edgar of Auchingrammont, and a correspondence exists in which he appears as candidate for the surgeoncy of the 56th regiment.

There was also an intimacy, as shown by old letters, with the family of Dr. Colin Lauder (son? of the Member of the College of Surgeons before named), with Hamilton of Dalzell, and with Stirling of Keir, but this last seems rather to have originated in Jamaica, and at a later period.[2]

It is worthy of a passing comment, that Alexander Edgar, then in possession of Auchingrammont, which he had now owned for many years, nevertheless *preferred* in 1754, the inferior designation of "from Netherhouses."[3] He was then living within the bounds of S. Leith, near Hillhousefield, and adjoining the village of the Water of Leith, both of which places are contiguous to the barony of Broughton, Restalrig, and other places,[4] mentioned in the "Inquisitiones Generales of 1599," as the property of a family named Edgar.

Early in the 18th century the Edgars of Auchingrammont owned pro-

---

[1] Armorial ensigns engraven on old family plate are by themselves no proof of a descent, but they may serve to throw a light on one obscure link, and show that at an early period, when money was scarce and books few, such articles belonged to a family assumed to have been descended from another bearing similar arms.

[2] There was a Scotch family of Edgar connected with Jamaica early in the 18th century which settled at Bristol, and their baptismal names were "*Preston, Alexander, Archibald,*" &c. The late Mr. Alexander Edgar of Bristol was J. P. for the co. Gloucester.

[3] Nethermills and Nethermains are common names. There are only, I think, altogether four Netherhouses mentioned in Gazetteers of Scotland. There is a place called *Nethermains,* which may possibly indicate the true locality in question.

[4] "Nicolaus Edger haeres Capitanei Jacobi Edger patris in terris *Patricii* Edgar merc. in burgo de Edin." &c.—"de Lymphoy"—"parte villæ et terrarum de Restalrig"—"Villæ et Aquæ de Leyth"—"In Baronia de Brouchtoun," "terrarum de Hillhousefield," &c.

perty in Jamaica, viz. Wedderlie plantation, and Osborne, in the parish of
St. George. This Osborne was so named after a *Mr. Osborne*, a *surgeon*,
who settled in Jamaica towards the close of the 17th century, and whose
seal bore the significant *Rhinoceros.*

Alexander Edgar, Fellow of the College of Surgeons, is again mentioned
in 1696. He *probably* married in 1697 the daughter of Mr. or Dr. Handasyde.

In an old silver-bossed family bible, the property of Margaret Edgar,
the last of her family who owned Auchingrammont, is the following entry :—
Alexander Edgar, born 1698. The locality of his birth is not given, and,
as parish registers in Scotland used to be very carelessly kept, it might not
be easy to find this entry of baptism, or that of Peter Edgar, a younger
brother ; but probably a positive proof of the parentage of both might be
obtained from some will of an Edgar between 1706 and 1750.

This Alexander[1] is stated to have returned from Jamaica in the record of
his purchase of Auchingrammont.

It seems reasonable to suppose that the sudden return of Alexander
Edgar, a young man only 26 years of age, from Jamaica, was caused by
the death of a parent in that year, and his not again going abroad seems to
confirm the inference.

His younger brother, Peter Edgar[2] (of Bridgelands) married in 1743
Anne, the daughter of the Rev. John Hay, minister of Peebles, and was

---

[1] 11 Oct. 1666. Disch. Edgar to Osburne, &c. &c. Alex^r Edgar ye bro: of
Wedderlie *contra* John Edgar of Wedderlie. If Alexander Edgar, younger brother,
of Wedderlie, was 15 in 1663, when Mr. Chiesly sued the latter (and probably he
was three years younger), he must have been born about 1648, in which case he was
50 years of age on the birth of his first (assumed) son Alexander in 1698. The
latter would therefore, let us say, be 17 years of age in 1715, and we may therefore
suppose that he had been scarcely six years abroad when his father died in 1723-4.
On receiving intelligence of the event he returned home, and with his father's personal property purchased Auchingrammont. The father therefore need only have
been 76 at the period of his death (assumed for the nonce) in 1723-4. This Alexander was not married till he was 43, and *his* son again, also Alexander, not till he
was actually 52.

From the Minute Book, Register of Deeds, Edinburgh.

16 June, 1663. Handiside to Chieslie.	20 June, 1667. Obl. Edgar to Hamilton.
23 Dec. 1664. Cont. Edgar and Edgar.	26 Jan. 1683. Obl. Edgar to Murray.
11 Oct. 1666. Disch. Edgar to Osborne.	

[2] *Peter* and *Patrick* are baptismal names continually interchanged in Scotland, and
very notable instances must be fresh in the recollection of Edinburghians.

Patrick from the earliest period was a family name constantly recurring amongst
the Wedderlie Edgars from *Cos-Patrick*, founder of the Earldom of Dunbar.

Peter Edgar appears to have been an episcopalian, for his marriage (with Ann
Hay) was solemnised by Mr. Kerr an episcopal clergyman, so that perhaps the
records of this family of Edgar are only to be found in the books of the episcopal
church.

father of Anne (the wife first of Count James Leslie of Deanhaugh, by whom she had a daughter Jacobina the first wife of Mr. Vere of Stonebyres, co. Lanark, and secondly of Sir H. Raeburn,) and of John Edgar, W.S., who died s.p. in 1799.   Peter Edgar ob. 1781, æt. 75 years.

In 1740-1 Alexander Edgar married Margaret (ob. 1791), the daughter of James Edgar, writer in Edinburgh, official clerk to Sir Gilbert Elliot of Minto, and who received the freedom of the City of Edinburgh in 1710 as a " Pewtherer Burgess."   James Edgar left no male issue.

The issue of Alexander Edgar of Auchingrammont by his wife Margaret Edgar, were: 1. Alexander, ob. 1820; 2. James, of Auchingrammont, ob. 1810; 3. Handasyde, M.D. ob. 1806 ; Priscilla, or Prudence ; Susan, ob. 1778, æt. 22.

According to a custom in Scotland, the eldest son is named after the paternal grandfather, the second son after the father, or the maternal grandfather, &c.   There are, however, numerous exceptions.

James Edgar of Auchingrammont also named a daughter Priscilla, in respect to the memory of his *grandmother* Priscilla Handasyde, but, as both grandfathers were Edgars it might be doubtful which of the two married a lady named Handasyde.   It is probable, however, that the wife of James Edgar, the maternal grandfather of James of Auchingrammont, was Eliza Lothian.   (Vide Par. Registers of Edinburgh.)   The latter James Edgar also had sons who died in infancy, named John, Alexander, James.

It is asserted that the patrimony of Alexander, the son of Alexander and Margaret of Auchingrammont, consisted of ground rents and tenements in the city of Edinburgh.   A reference to the Register of Sasines would of course set this question at rest.

I do not venture to assert positively that this is exactly how the question stands ; but I think that the references given would be ample to enable a clear case to be made out for the Edgars of Auchingrammont to compete with the Hutton and Newton Edgars, for the honour of representing Wedderlie; and if I have erred in my view of the case, I should only be too glad to be corrected, maintaining, however, and ready to prove, that the representation in the *male* line of Wedderlie is an open question.

The following particulars have come to my knowledge since the above was written, and are the result of a search in the *Register of Sasines*.

Although James Edgar *became* "of Auchingrammont," it was only by the breaking of the entail and surrender of Auchingrammont to him by his *elder brother Alexander*, who was returned their father's heir in 1777, and had seisin of the said property.   On the 1st March, 1783, there is a seisin or *sasine* in favour of James, as heir of his brother Alexander of Auchingrammont; but there is no sasine of a James as heir of his father of Auchingrammont.   L.-A.

MONUMENT OF CAPTAIN FRANCIS KNOLLYS.

We hear a great deal of the restoration of churches in the present day: and too often of that restoration being accompanied by a reckless destruction of sepulchral memorials. It is therefore a pleasant thing to be told occasionally of the restoration of a monument. An instance is just presented to us in the case of one of the ancient family of Knollys Earls of Banbury: to whom an inscription, with some quaint verses of the time of Charles I., was placed in the church of Stanford in the Vale in Berkshire. It has been restored by Mr. Byam his descendant and representative, and erected upon the wall of the chancel, within a mural monument of Gothic design. From an excellent photograph produced by the sculptors, Messrs. Tyleys, of Bristol, we take the following copy:—

ARMS. Quarterly, 1 and 4. Azure, crusilly and a cross moline voided or: 2 and 3. Gules, on a chevron argent three roses of the field; impaling Vaire argent and gules, on a canton or a stag's head caboshed vert, *Beecher.* Crest, an Elephant.

Near this place lies the body of Captain FRANCIS KNOLLYS, sonne of Richard Knollys esquire, brother to the late Earl of Banbury, who first married one of the daughters of Sir Charles Wiseman, of this County, and after her decease Alice, sister of Sir William Beecher, of Middlesex; by whom he left one Daughter and two Sonnes, and was by death taken from the command of the Train Bands of Abingdon Division, and here interred the 4th of August A.D. 1640.

> When stones break silence, and attention crave,
> Well may't be thought some wonder's in the grave:
> Reader, then stay, and marvell not if I
> (Though stone) relate what rare thing here doth lie.
> That noble name was his thou read'st before;
> Able itself to guild the Title o'er.
> That valor does but sleep within this bed
> Which never (but by death) was captive led;
> Whose ling'ring, slow, and coward-like delay
> Argu'd her fear of losing of the day;
> Since when, this place more than a grave shall be
> Where his bones are, 'tis an Artillerye.
> Thus I him praise, whose merit might denye
> The poor applause of fun'ral obsequie,
> But custom so prevails, that 'tis but just
> To polish diamonds, with their own dust.

Restored A.D. 1865 by Edward S. Byam, Esq. descended lineally from the "one daughter" above mentioned, viz. Dorothy Knollys, wife of William Byam, General of Guiana and Governor first of Surinam and afterwards of Antigua. The "two sons" William and Francis Knollys dying without issue.

Within the Communion-rails of this Church is placed a Marble slab to the memory of John Heigham, Esq. the maternal Uncle of the aforesaid Capt. Francis Knollys.

A brief biography of Governor Byam will be found in our first volume, at p. 377. He was son of the Rev. Edward Byam, M.A. Vicar of Dulverton, co. Somerset, and afterwards Precentor of Cloyne, whose elder brother was the more celebrated Dr. Henry Byam, Chaplain to King Charles I. We noticed in the same place a previous restoration, by the same pious hands, of Dr. Henry Byam's monument at Luckham or Luccombe, co. Somerset : and we may further mention that a mural monument has been erected in the church of Castle Lyons, co. Cork, to the Rev. Edward Byam, the Governor's father, which bears the following inscription :

Sacred to the memory of the Rev. EDWARD BYAM, M.A. of Magdalen Coll. Oxford, son of the Rev. Lawrence Byam, Rector of Luccombe, Somerset, and brother of the celebrated Henry Byam, D.D. of the same place. He married A.D. 1612 Elizabeth, daughter of the Rev. Anthony Eaglesfield, Rector of Walton and Prebendary of Wells. On resigning the vicarage of Dulverton, in his native county, Somerset, A.D. 1625, he became Vicar of Castle Lyons and Precentor of Cloyne. He died at Kilwillin 6th June, 1639, in the 55th year of his age, and was buried at Castle Lyons. His sons Lawrence and William were commanders of distinction in the service of King Charles the 1st, but more especially the latter, who rose to great eminence, and was General of Guiana, and Governor, first of Surinam, and afterwards of Antigua, where he died A.D. 1670.

This tablet was, A.D. 1864, raised to the memory of a respected Ancestor, by the Rev. Richard Burgh Byam, M.A. a Member of Council in Antigua, Vicar of Kew and Petersham in the county of Surrey.

ARMS.   Argent, three dragon's heads erased vert, each holding in his mouth a dexter hand, couped at the wrist, dropping blood, *Byam*; impaling, Or, three eagles displayed gules, a crescent for difference, *Eaglesfield*. Crest, a wolf passant or, collared and lined vert.

GORDONS IN IRELAND.

It appears to me that the following statement in the preamble to the pedigree of Gordon of Florida, as given in Burke's *Landed Gentry*, is a mistake, and that this family is a branch either of the Gordons of Earlston or of Knokespoch.

"Many years after the period of the settlement of the former (Irish branch) in the sister island, Lord Adam Gordon, a general in the army, fourth son of Alexander second Duke of Gordon, during a visit to that country, resided with his cousin (?) George Gordon of Florida ;" and, when the Irish branch afterwards visited Scotland, they were "received with much kindness by Alexander fourth Duke of Gordon, who *fully recognised the relationship.*"

Now, to have fully recognised the relationship he must have had either the PROOF, or simple faith ; but, as no such proof has ever been shown, it is more than probable that the duke was not a genealogist. In fact his recognition, as true, of a genealogical problem, was no more than any other person's recognition, without proof, and moreover it seems inconsistent that he should have agreed to a proposition which *his own pedigree ignores.* Thus much for *cousinship* or kindred. On the other hand it is quite possi-

ble that, in some obscure, remote, and now lost degree, a connection may
have existed between the two families, just as it may exist between any
families bearing the same surname; but these *secrets* of the past do not
belong to genealogy, which only recognises the definite, and rejects all else.

If I might venture to approach a more probable origin for this family, I
should be inclined to believe that, amongst the many children of Sir Alexander Gordon, second baronet of Earlston, who have been summarily dismissed from the pedigree of the latter family, would be discovered *Robert*
Gordon, the founder of the family in Ireland, and who died in 1720.

The Gordons of Florida were, during last century, connected both with
our western colonies and the army (50th regt.)

Now in Jamaica is found the monumental inscription of Colonel William
Gordon's wife Susannah who died in 1751. The arms of the former are
(no tincture) a roundle or annulet between three boar's heads couped . . .
impaling (no tincture) a bend between two wings. Crest, a dexter hand
grasping a sword.

The 50th regiment was for many years in Jamaica, where the monuments
or tombs of some of its officers still exist. Whether or no the . above
Colonel W. Gordon was of this corps, I cannot as yet say.

There were Gordons of Earlston in Jamaica, and Christiana Scarlett (of
Lord Abinger's family) married James Gordon in 1779, and was mother of
the fifth Baronet of Earlston.

Besides many distinct families of this name in Jamaica between 1700
and 1790, was that of *Harry Gordon* from Enniskillen, who married, 1st.
a (Lady ?) Mary Jones and 2nd. Anne Taaffe. By his second wife he had
a son, also named Harry, whose will is *dated* in 1788. In 1766 James
Gordon of Jamaica mentions in his will his "*brother Harry* Gordon in
H.M.'s service." A certain Lt.-Colonel *Harry* Gordon, Royal Engineers,
was in Liverpool (nearest English port to *Dublin*) in 1777, and was
deceased *before* the 1st Sept. 1787. He *served in the West Indies. Harry*
Gordon, grandfather of the first Gordon of Knokespoch, must have been a
contemporary with the above.

These are the only instances of the name *Harry* united to Gordon that
I have ever met with prior to 1800; and it seems clear to me that Lt.-
Colonel *Harry* Gordon of the Royal Engineers was *identical* with the Harry
Gordon, who by his wife Anne Taaffe had a son also named Harry.[1]

Whether these Gordons had been long settled at Enniskillen before they
emigrated (or *went*) to Jamaica it is impossible to say. Anne Taaffe was
the daughter of Christopher Taaffe, who appears to have been originally
from *Dromisken*, co. Louth, and it is not unlikely that the present proprietor of the castle of that name has papers which might show who these earlier Gordons were. *Vide* also Chancery Suits (Ireland) 1780-7.

L.-A.

---

[1] I have since discovered that another Harry Gordon is to be found in Douglas's
Baronage.

NOTES AND QUERIES.

ARMS OF RICHARD CŒUR DE LION.—In the extract from Mr. Hewitt's work, given in p. 214, the passage relating to the shield on the first seal of King Richard I. is marred by a misprint. It should read—"In the earliest (1189) the monarch's shield is ensigned with the emblem of valour, a Lion. But it is a rampant lion; and as the *bowed* shield presents only one-half of its surface to view, it has been conjectured that the complete device would consist of two lions combatant."

Our comment was "conjectured,—certainly without substantial grounds:" but this we must beg to modify. We made it, because we have observed that in similar contemporary instances the whole of an armorial coat is shown, although only part of the field of the shield may be visible: but in regard to this shield of King Richard the First, the remarks made by Mr. Planché ought not to be disregarded. They are as follow:—

"On the first seal of Richard I. we find a shield charged with a lion *counter-rampant*, that is, with his face *turned to the sinister or left side of the escutcheon*, and as the convex form of the shield enables us to see but half of it, Sir Henry Spelman, in his *Aspilogia*, conjectures there would be another lion on the sinister side, forming a coat that would be blasoned 'two lions combatant;' and that Richard, during the life of his father, bore, as his brother John did, more than one lion on his shield,[1] we have evidence in the verses of a contemporary poet, who makes William de Barr say he knew Richard by the grinning lions on his shield,

—— rictus agnosco leonum
Illius in clypeo :

establishing the plurality as strongly as John of Marmoustier has those of Henry I. or of Geoffry of Anjou." *Pursuivant of Arms*, p. 75.

These authorities certainly deserve some consideration, as tending to show that the device of Richard I. was not a single lion rampant. They do not, however, entirely convince us that he bore two lions counter-rampant or combatant. The visible lion being placed looking to the sinister favours that supposition: but it is not impossible that it only arose from the *gaucherie* of the seal-engraver, and that to the like cause, at that rude period of sigillistic art, we may attribute the appearance of only one lion instead of more.

SHERIFFS' SEALS. There is an interesting class of seals of which I think very little notice has hitherto been taken, though examples are not unfrequently occurring, and the number that once existed must have been very great. I allude to the Seals of Sheriffs, which were required, I scarcely know for what purposes, but should like to be informed.

[1] On the seal of John then Earl of Morton there are two lions passant: which appear entire, notwithstanding the convexity of the shield.

These seals are usually of a small circular form, and bear the representation of a castle, evidently denoting the power of imprisonment: and therefore it may be presumed that their chief employment was connected with the jurisdiction of the gaols. Accompanying this castle there is generally the coat of arms of the individual, a circumstance which gives them an important historical value.

In the *Gentleman's Magazine* for June 1787, Plate II. there is engraved such a seal : of which it is only stated : "Fig. 4 is an impression from a wooden seal, which wants decyphering."

It is in size about that of our old halfpenny, and represents a castle, on the walls of which appear two human heads (either alive or dead). Above, is a shield of two coats impaled : a chevron between three pheons ; and three boar's heads erased erect. In the margin are the initials P. H., and at the foot (as numismatists say, in the *exergum*), I. B.

In combination with these initials there can be little hesitation in attributing these arms to the names of Holman and Booth, which bore respectively, Vert, a chevron or between three pheons argent, and Argent, three boar's heads erased erect sable.

I think it most probable that in this case impalement does not typify marriage : but rather that this was the seal of some city or town that had two Sheriffs ; and I beg therefore to inquire whether in any list of Sheriffs the names of Holman and Booth are to be found serving in conjunction.

J. G. N.

In answer to A. H. Le B.'s queries—There is no doubt that the arms of Altham of Oxhey, Herts, were Paly of six ermine and azure, on a chief gules a lion passant guardant or; as they were thus quartered by the Annesleys Earls of Anglesey, &c. who were descended from the heiress of Altham by her marriage with Arthur first Earl of Anglesey.

We must refer A. H. Le B. to Lipscomb's *Buckinghamshire*, for the arms of Gayer of Stoke Pogeis ; but we think they are the same as the Gayers of Foxley, Berks.

Admiral Sir Charles Hardy, father of the late Mrs. Annesley of Bletchindon, was son of Admiral Sir Charles Hardy, knight banneret, and grandson of Admiral Sir Thomas Hardy, knt. of Queen Anne's time. He died in 1780 at Portsmouth, when in command of the Fleet.

We are not aware that there was any connexion between him and Nelson's flag-captain, the late Admiral Sir Thomas M. Hardy.

Probably the arms of Sir Charles Hardy might be met with at the Great Hall in Greenwich Hospital, as he was Governor at the time of his death in 1780.

JOHN BROWNE is mentioned in an Indenture dated 13 September, 1585 (Irish Archæologia, O'Flaherty's Iar Connaught) : the same person is supposed to be named in O'Luinin's MS. Pedigrees, vol. i. Office of Arms,

Dublin, and in a State Paper dated 18 April, 1585 (Hardiman's History of Galway, ed. 1820, pp. 10, 94, 95, and Notes). Is there an Inquisition upon the death of John Browne, dated 14 March, 1591, showing him to have béen killed in a fray in Connaught, 7 February, 1588? Does it give his arms, family, marriage, or heir, or style him of any place?

The lists of Inquisitions published by the Commissioners upon Irish State Records in 1816 to 1820 do *not* give this Inquisition, but do at p. 564, roll 68, give one of the same name taken at Dublin in the 25th year of Henry VIII.

- John Browne, "master of Awney," or Awny (co. Limerick), had ten daughters. The eldest, Annabella, was mother of the wives of Thomas Browne, knt. of Hospital, co. Limerick, head of the Kenmare family of Browne, and of Sir Richard Boyle, the first and great Earl of Cork (see Smith's County of Kerry, ed. 1774, pp 41 and 47, and notes; also County of Cork, ed. 1774, vol. i. p. 113).

What were his arms? had he any male heirs? or did Sir Thomas Browne, husband of his grand-daughter, inherit Awney?

Hobart Town, 19 *June*, 1865. JUSTIN BROWNE.

I should be glad to know whether there exists any copy of the now obliterated epitaph of Capt. Anthony Archer, who was buried at Shadwell, Middlesex, about 1680, and if any records of the name are to be found in the parish registers in connection with this surname. A.

John Hodges, a nephew of Bonella Hodges, mother of the first Lord Penrhyn, married Anne Blake (of a Jamaica family), in England, probably between 1760 and 1775. I should be obliged to any one who might be able to furnish me with the date and place of that marriage. One of the children of John and Anne Hodges was Robert Franklyn Hodges, who died in London either late in the last century or early in this. His wife, a daughter of Judge Lewis of Jamaica, was either divorced or separated from him. The story is curious, but unfitted for a note of this description. H.

Can any of your readers give me information respecting a family named *Handley*? More than one member of it was connected with the Court of Chancery during the last century, and I am inclined to think that the following extract (taken from a MS. Heraldic Painter's Book in the British Museum) has reference to the family in question.

"*Handley* and *Pickering* at Barnes, March, 1738."

Arms: (sketched) viz., Gules, a bend or between six mascles of the second, impaling Ermine, a lion rampant azure, crowned or. The Crest, a hand holding a bunch of quills proper. EQUITY, the motto.

The arms (which are quite different from any assigned to the name of Handley in Burke's *General Armory*) seem to allude to the connection which the family had with the Court of Chancery; the impalement is the ordinary coat of Pickering.

I find the names of Robert and Thomas Handley in the list of Sworn Clerks in 1766 and 1788. A son of the latter was Charles Peter Handley, of the Hon. E.I.C. Navy, who married in 1797 a Miss Dycé of Essex, and died in the year 1800. Closely connected (I do not know in what degree) was *Sukey Handley*, who married, 1st. Edward Norton, one of the six clerks and a brother of Fletcher Lord Grantley, and 2ndly, in 1755, Milward Rowe, chief clerk of the Treasury. She died in 1804, and was buried beside her second husband at Tillington, co. Sussex. Her sister *Anne Handley* married at St. Christopher's, in the West Indies, 16 July, 1757, Thomas Tomkyns of Buckenhill Park, co: Hereford, by whom she had, with other issue, Dr. Packington Tomkyns, chaplain to King George the Fourth.

There were families of the name of Handley in Nottinghamshire, Hertfordshire, and Buckinghamshire; but I have not been able to obtain many particulars of them. I believe it was from Thomas Handley of Great Marlow that the late Rev. H. Handley Norris, of Hackney, derived his second name; but on this point also my knowledge is somewhat conjectural.   C. J. R.

Vol. ii. p. 264.—Dr. James Lind the successful medical author and physician to Haslar hospital, and Dr. James Lind the genealogist and physician to the Household of Queen Charlotte, were evidently different persons: as the former died in 1794, and the latter printed his book in 1795. "1794. July 18 [not 11]. At Gosport, James Lind, M.D. formerly Physician to the Royal Hospital at Haslar, and deservedly celebrated as a medical writer." *Gentleman's Magazine*, lxiv. 767. The records of the Royal College of Physicians of Edinburgh show that one James Lind obtained his diploma at Edinburgh university 3 May 1748, and was admitted a Fellow of the College 1 May 1750; and another James Lind, also having an Edinburgh diploma, was admitted 6 Nov. 1770. The date of the genealogist's decease we have not ascertained.

PENELOPE DARCY.—Since the note in p. 212 was printed, the record of the first marriage of Penelope Darcy with Sir George Trenchard has occurred in the course of our reading. It is in the Parish Register of Clerkenwell:—1610: June 11. Sir George Trencher and Mrs. Penelope Darcey (*misprinted* D'urfey *in* Pinks' *History of Clerkenwell*, 1865, p. 46.)

THE FAMILY OF TEMPLE.

THE death of Lord Palmerston, whilst still at the summit of his power and popularity, has stimulated the pens of a legion of public writers throughout the civilised world; and the great length of his political career has carried back their reflections from the passing events of the day to those now far receding into past history. But whilst the late Premier had survived more than one generation of contemporary statesmen, he was also the last male survivor, in his own branch, of a family which has produced many men of considerable eminence during the last three centuries; the most illustrious among them having been Sir William Temple, the celebrated negociator, statesman, and essayist, who exercised great political influence during the reigns of Charles II. and William III. He was a brother of one of the late Premier's direct ancestors. It may therefore be interesting on this occasion to take some retrospect of the past generations of this family.

The name makes no prominent appearance in our earlier historical annals. It is not one that figures in the Chronicles or the ancient Rolls of Arms, nor even does it claim a place in Mr. Shirley's account of *The Noble and Gentle Men of England* who have retained the landed estates possessed by their ancestors before the year 1500. The race was one of those whose fortunes ensued after the changes of the Reformation.

And yet, like other new-made rich, when subjected to the patronage of flattering genealogists, the Temples have been furnished with ancestry of the most remote and most ambitious kind that this country has to offer. Their descent has been derived from the Saxon Earls of Mercia, and the fabulous arms attributed to those Earls have been prefixed (in the first quarter) to those which they originally assumed.

It is somewhat inconsistent with those pretensions when we find the same genealogists[1] asserting that the son of Earl Leofric, " living in the reign of William the Conqueror, was wrote Henry del Temple;" particularly when it is remembered that the order

---

[1] Collins, Peerage 1741, *tit.* Cobham; Lodge's Peerage of Ireland, edit. Archdall, . 1779, *tit.* Palmerston.

of the Templars was not founded until the year 1118, the same writers proceeding to state that the family derived their name from residence in one of the houses of that order.

In truth, this origin of the family is recorded upon very substantial evidence: but the genealogical descent is obscure, as the Temples did not rise above the rank of small gentry until the latter part of the 15th century.

Near the town of Market Bosworth in Leicestershire is a village named Whellesborough, which is a hamlet of the parish of Sibbesdon. " Within the hamlet of Whellesburgh," as described by Burton the old Leicestershire historian, but extra-parochial according to the usual privileges of the Templars, " is a mansion still called Temple Hall, which at an early date was granted to the Knights Templars,"—as Burton supposed, " by one of the old Earls of Leicester." [1] An inquisition taken in 7 Edw. I. (1279) showed this Temple to be then held by one Henry de Temple, who had evidently derived his name from his residence. The verdict to this inquisition is as follows:—

Templum est de feodo Wintonie, et Henricus de Templo tenet in eadem tres virgatas terre in dominico. Item in villenagio tres virgatas terre, quas quatuor servi tenent de eodem. Item in libera tenura tres virgatas terre, quas Willielmus de Templo tenet de eodem, una cum quadam cultura que vocatur Hongebur. Et dictus Henricus tenet dictam tenuram de Templariis de Balsall, et Templarii de heredibus Wintonie, et heredes de Rege. Dicti tamen Templarii tenent in pura elemosyna; et habent visum franciplegii et regale, et non dant scutagium. De warrena et aliis capitulis nihil.

The same Henry of the Temple also held of the Templars two virgates at Sibbesdon, in villenage, held of him by two serfs.

Burton states in another place that the manor of Shepey parva was the ancient inheritance of the family of Temple, and continued in that name until the latter end of the reign of Edward III. He notices also that John de Temple temp. Hen. III. gave lands at Shepey to the abbey of Miravall in Warwickshire. Burton observed, " at Great Shepey church, in the north-east window, very old, the picture of a man kneeling, under whom is written RICARDUS DE TEMPLO."

Two other generations of the family, both bearing the name

_____
[1] Whellesborough belonged to the fee of Leicester (Hist. of Leic. iv. 963*), but Temple to the fee of Winchester, as appears by the document next quoted.

Nicholas, occur in the year 1322; when Nicholas, son of Nicholas de Temple, of the county of Leicester, was one of the manucaptors for the good behaviour of Robert de Astele, of the county of Warwick, and other prisoners then discharged.[1]

Such are the scanty records of the family in those early times which we have been able to recover. They afford very little aid towards forming a pedigree: but in Nichols's *History of Leicestershire*, in which the genealogy of the family is far more fully detailed than anywhere, there appear (in vol. iv. pp. 958, 959,) the two following very contradictory lines of descent, both leading to Robert Temple, the husband of Mary Kingscote:

Visitation of Leicestershire, 1619, and that of *Bucks*, 1634.

Chetwynd MS.

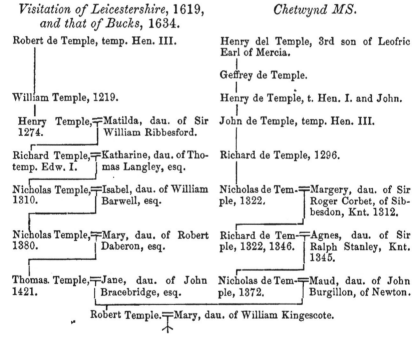

Robert de Temple, temp. Hen. III.

Henry del Temple, 3rd son of Leofric Earl of Mercia.

Geffrey de Temple.

William Temple, 1219.

Henry de Temple, t. Hen. I. and John.

Henry Temple,⊤Matilda, dau. of Sir 1274. | William Ribbesford.

John de Temple, temp. Hen. III.

Richard Temple,⊤Katharine, dau. of Tho- temp. Edw. I. | mas Langley, esq.

Richard de Temple, 1296.

Nicholas Temple,⊤Isabel, dau. of William 1310. | Barwell, esq.

Nicholas de Tem-⊤Margery, dau. of Sir ple, 1322. | Roger Corbet, of Sib- | besdon, Knt. 1312.

Nicholas Temple,⊤Mary, dau. of Robert 1380. | Daberon, esq.

Richard de Tem-⊤Agnes, dau. of Sir ple, 1322, 1346. | Ralph Stanley, Knt. | 1345.

Thomas Temple,⊤Jane, dau. of John 1421. | Bracebridge, esq.

Nicholas de Tem-⊤Maud, dau. of John ple, 1372. | Burgillon, of Newton.

Robert Temple.⊤Mary, dau. of William Kingescote.

It is not a question, to our mind, which of these discordant lines of descent should be preferred; for we deem them alike questionable, even though one has the sanction of having been entered by the heralds in their books of Visitation. Whether any of the alliances are gathered from presumptive evidence, or whether they are entirely imaginary, we cannot tell.

[1] Palgrave's Parliamentary Writs, &c. App. i. pp. 207, 209.

There was at the time in question a Sir Roger de Corbet, who married the heiress of Camvile at Sibbesdon.

Robert Temple, of Temple Hall, by his second wife Mary Kingscote, is stated to have had three sons: 1, Nicholas; 2, Robert; and 3, Thomas.

In regard to Nicholas we at last arrive at some substantial evidence. He was an esquire, and was buried in the church of Great Shepey, co. Leic. with the following inscription, the date of his death being 1506.

Hic jacet corpus Nicholai Templi armigeri, et Elizabethæ uxoris ejus, qui quidem Nicholaus obiit 1506.

This was accompanied by a shield of arms: Argent, on two bars sable six martlets or; impaling, Azure, two bars or, and a mullet in chief. The impaled coat is that of Burdet, an ancient Leicestershire family; and the pedigree recognises the lady as one of that name, adding that she was living in 1512.

The similarity of these two coats at once strikes our attention, and we are led to believe that there was something more than accident in that similarity. In the reign of Edward II. a Burdet had differenced his arms with three martlets on the upper bar—

Sire William Bordet, de azure, a ij. barres de or.

Sire Robert Bordet, meisme les armes, en la sovereyne barre iij. merelos de goules.

and in that of Henry VI. Sir Nicholas Burdet, who was great butler of Normandy, and slain at the battle of Pontoise in Bretagne, bore three martlets upon each bar.[1] In the latter example we have the complete design of the coat of Temple as it first appears on the monument at Great Shepey, and as it has been usually borne in modern times. Moreover, among various shields of Burdet which were in the windows of Great Shepey church, was one that displayed the six martlets upon the two bars. There are certainly, therefore, strong grounds for supposing that Nicholas Temple was the first to adopt these arms, deriving them, with merely a change of tinctures, from Sir Nicholas Burdet, who was probably no very distant relation of his wife.

Nicholas Temple left no legitimate issue. The subsequent branches of the family have sprung from the two other brothers, Robert and Thomas.

Robert, the second son, carried on the line at the ancient

[1] History of Leicestershire, vol. iii. p. 351.

Temple Hall;[1] and his posterity continued to occupy the spot from which they derived their name.

Burton and Wyrley have preserved memoranda of the epitaphs of two generations, at Sibbesdon, (and they are the only Temple epitaphs extant from that church [2])—

In eccl'ia de Sibbesdon per W. Wyrley et W. Burton a° 1603.

Richard Temple and Joyce his wife. He died 1556. Without any mark of arms.

Richard Temple, of Temple, alias Welsborow, and Elizabeth his wife. He died 1567. He bereth these tow cotes quartered and paled :

Arms.—Quarterly: 1 and 4, Ermine, on a chevron sable five martlets argent ; 2 and 3, Argent, three wolves passant in pale sable, *Lovett ;* impaling, Argent, on a fess engrailed gules, between three falcons rising azure, as many plates, each charged with a lion's head erased sable, for *George.*

Richard the son married Elizabeth, daughter of John George, of Baudington, co. Gloucester. He quartered Lovett for his mother, a coheiress of Lovett, of Welford, co. Northampton.[3] In his own coat, it will be observed, we have a great variation from that upon which we have already commented. We shall review the several changes of the family coat-armour hereafter.

At the Heralds' Visitation of Leicestershire in 1619 there were five brothers at Temple Hall, sons of Edmund Temple who had died three years before. Of these, Peter, the third, then aged nineteen, became the head of the family by the death of his elder brothers. In 1645 he was sheriff of the county (the first of his family that had filled the office), and in that capacity he took an active part in the defence of Leicester for the Parliament. This led to still graver charges and responsibilities. Thomas Coke, esq. one of the burgesses for Leicester, was ex-

[1] The Visitation of Leicestershire says, that Robert by gift of his father had lands at Barton under Needwood, co. Stafford ; and that Richard his son was also of that place, and died 22 Hen. VII. (Visit. in Coll. Arm. 127, p. 147.) Burton, having heard of this, was doubtful whether the Temple who came to Temple from Barton under Needwood was of the same race ; but this passage he afterwards cancelled : see Nichols's Hist. of Leic. iv. 958.

[2] These epitaphs are here given from MS. Coll. Arm. Vincent, 197, fol. 52. In Nichols's *History of Leicestershire,* vol. iv. p. 956, the arms are misdescribed : the quartering omitted : and the impalement said to be Langham instead of George, though correctly engraved in Plate CXLVII. fig. 26.

[3] In 1 Edw. VI. a fine was levied between Robert Warner, demandant, and Francis Temple, deforciant, of Lovett's manor in Welford. It was soon after sold to John Randolf. Bridges, *Hist. of Northamptonsh.* i. 594 ; that Francis being the only Temple there mentioned.

cluded from the House of Commons in November of the same year, whereupon Mr. Temple was elected to take his place; and, when subsequently the Republican party determined to sit in judgment upon their sovereign, the member for Leicester was one of those nominated upon that fearful commission. He became a close attendant during the trial, and signed the warrant for the King's execution. The following curious description of him is given in *The Character of the Regicides*, appended to *The Loyall Martyrology*, by WILLIAM WINSTANLEY, 1665.

LXVIII. *Peter Temple.* He was at first a linnen-draper, apprentice in Fryday-street, but his elder brother dying, he forsook his trade, and was possest of an estate of some four hundred pounds a year in Leicestershire, and being a person well affected to the Cause, was a recruit-chosen Burgess for that country-town, as colleage to Sir Arther Hazelrig, that furious Northern blast. He was made a Captain of a troop of horse, and besides was a great Committee-man; yet was a person of very weak parts, and easie to be led to act any thing to which the hope of profit called him; yet (as ill-gotten goods never prosper) so he thrived not, notwithstanding his gainfull trade, but was fool'd by Oliver into the snare, as he often afterwards confessed the same.

When the Regicides were themselves brought to trial after the Restoration, Peter Temple was one of those arraigned on the 16th October, 1660. He had previously pleaded Not Guilty, and he explained that plea on the ground that there were many things in the indictment of which his conscience could not accuse him, " for (he declared) I had not a malicious or traitorous heart against the King:" but he admitted his signature to the warrants. Being convicted, and asked why sentence should not be passed, he said that he had come in upon the Proclamation, and humbly begged the benefit of it. He was condemned, but not brought to execution, and is supposed to have remained a prisoner until his death.[1]

Thus terminated in disgrace the eldest line of the Temples, after having occupied for so many centuries the old preceptory of the Templars at Whellesborough. It is remarkable that the

[1] Another of those who signed the warrant for the King's execution was Colonel James Temple, whom Winstanley describes as "a Sussex man." He had obtained the estate of Sir Charles Shelley in that county; and appears to have been a nephew of the first Baronet of Stowe, and son of Sir Alexander Temple, of Chadwell in Essex, who was Knight of the Shire for Sussex in the second Parliament of 1625. Noble, in his *Lives of the Regicides*, does not attempt to identify either James or Peter; but he states that James was governor of " Banbury Castle in Sussex "—meaning Bramber. We shall notice him more fully hereafter.

Historian of Leicestershire did not, under the head of Temple Hall, recognise the cause of the family's removal, though in another place (under Shawell) he mentions the forfeiture of Peter Temple's estate.[1]

The Regicide married Phœbe, daughter of John Gayring, of London, and had three sons, Edmund, John, and Peter, born 1635. John died s. p. and of the two others nothing further is recorded.

The contemporary Baronet of Stowe, though a distant cousin, was also named Peter.[2] He also was nominated one of the commissioners for the trial of Charles the First (being then M.P. for Buckingham), but fortunately for him and the future Temples of Stowe, he did not take part in it.

TEMPLE OF BURTON DERSET, CO. WARWICK, AND OF STOWE, CO. BUCKINGHAM.

From Thomas, the third son of Robert Temple before mentioned, have proceeded those Temples who have risen to higher importance. The pedigree states that Thomas himself removed to Witney in Oxfordshire; and that William his son and Thomas his grandson were of that town;[3] that the last married Alice, daughter of John Heritage, or Eritage, of Burton Derset, co. Warwick, esq.; and that Peter, the second son of that marriage, purchased the manor of Burton Derset in 1560, and afterwards became owner of Stowe in Buckinghamshire.[4] The pedigree is still fragmentary, and embarrassing from the variety of its branches.

[1] " From the Bensons the reputed manor of Shawell passed to Peter Temple, who was a Regicide; and this estate, consequently, was confiscated by Charles II. who afterwards gave it to his brother James Duke of York." Hist. of Leic. iv. 337.

[2] Granger, Mark Noble, and other writers have confused the two, together with Sir Peter Temple of Stanton Barry, Knt., the Baronet's nephew.

[3] On the last page of Willis's *Hundred of Buckingham* is a slight memorial of the Temples of Witney. Anne Wenman, widow of Richard Wenman of Witney, a merchant of the staple of Calais (and ancestor of Lady Wenman), making her will Nov. 22, 1536, leaves to " Goodwife Temple " and other women of Witney small legacies.

[4] Besides this Peter, who was evidently the great raiser of the family fortunes, we meet, in the distribution of monastic property, with the recurrence of the old name of Nicholas. There was a Nicholas Temple (who has no place in the pedigree), to whom the manor of Cadeby, late belonging to Leicester Abbey, was granted in 1544 (Hist. of Leic. iv. 573); Nicholas Temple and Richard Andrews had a grant of Sele Abbey, in Sussex, which they sold in 1546; and the same parties occur with regard to other monastic property in Bridges's Northamptonshire, i. 160, 232, 584.

It here contains some brief particulars of a line of three generations descending from Robert,[1] an elder brother of Peter.

It is stated in the pedigree that Peter Temple " was owner of
Stowe in 1574." But this was not actually the case. Some
particulars stated by Browne Willis, at p. 275 of his *History of the
Hundred of Buckingham*, tend to place the position of the family
at this period in a truer light. That historian observes, " that
this family had been, as it seems to me, resident in this county in
Henry the Sixth's time; and were, as I find, lessee tenants to
Oseney Abbey [to which Stowe belonged][2] before the dissolution;" and he adds, that " Peter Temple occurs possessed of lands
in these parts anno 1554." In truth, he was one of those who
having had to do with monastic property, and knowing its value,
availed themselves of the opportunity of becoming its owners.
It was in 1553 that Peter Temple obtained from the Crown a
grant of the manor of Merston Boteler, in Warwickshire;[3]
and in 1560 he purchased the manor of Burton Derset, in the
same county. He was designated of that place when he received
in 1567 a grant of arms which will be particularly noticed
hereafter. It was so far considered the family seat, that, on his
death occurring at Stowe,[4] his body was conveyed into Warwickshire, and buried in the church of Burton Derset, with
the following inscription:—

Here under this stone lyeth the body of PETER TEMPLE, esquire, who departed out
of this world at Stow, in the county of Buckingham, the xxviij. day of May Anno
[1577] whose soule God hath in his blessed keeping.

It was not until the year 1590 that the Temples actually

[1] In 1597 the Augustine priory at Leicester was sold by Robert Temple of Leicester,
and Thomas his son and heir apparent, for 20*l.*, to Robert Heyrick, ironmonger. But
the Robert in the Pedigree has a son Cuthbert, and no Thomas.

[2] In the same page it is mentioned that among the ancient sepulchral memorials at
Oseney, was that of *Stephen de Templar*, who gave to Oseney a mill at Fullwell.

[3] His name occurs frequently in that character : see Dugdale, History of Warwickshire, pp. 326, 558, 612, Bridges's Northamptonshire, i. 5.

[4] His burial is recorded in the register at Stowe, under the date 28 May, according
to Willis's Hundred of Buckingham, p. 286; but, as in Lipscombe's History of
Buckinghamshire, iv. 296, " Peter Temple, esq. was buried y[e] 29th of May, 1577."
This probably records the commencement of the funeral ceremonies at Stowe, before
starting for Warwickshire. Lipscombe, in his pedigree of Temple, has a statement
(evidently unfounded), that the body was brought back to Stowe 11 May, 1603, the
date of the son's funeral.

became lords of Stowe. The estate up to that time had belonged to the bishopric of Oxford; but, during a vacancy of that see, Queen Elizabeth, by letters patent dated 27th Jan. in the 32nd year of her reign, granted the manor, &c. to Thomas Crompton, Robert Wright, and Gelly Merrick, who shortly after sold it to John Temple, esq. doubtless then the lessee, as his father had been before him.

John Temple, the purchaser of Stowe, was avowedly an opulent man, and his possession of many children, many friends, and much money, was commemorated in these epigrammatic lines appended to his epitaph :—

Cur liberos hic plurimos,
Cur hic amicos plurimos,
Et plurimas pecunias
Vis scire cur reliquerit ?
TEMPELLUS ad plures abiit.

The epitaph designates him as " of Stow, in the county of Bucks, Esquier, and one of the Lords of this Mannour " of Burton Derset,[1] where he was buried.[2] He died on the 9th of May, 1603, aged sixty-one ; having married the heiress of Thomas Spencer, of Everdon, co. Northampton, by whom he left five sons and six daughters.

Hitherto we have not met with a Temple who attained the order of knighthood; but the reign of the great Knight-maker James the First was now commenced, and in the very month after his father's death Thomas Temple went to support his neighbour Sir John Fortescue in the reception of that monarch at Salden in Buckinghamshire (when the King went part of the way on the North road to welcome his Queen on her first arrival in his new dominions), and on that occasion he became Sir Thomas Temple. Subsequently, when the order of Baronets was founded in the year 1611, Sir Thomas Temple was elevated

[1] Burton Derset was still in the possession of the Temples of Stowe in 1802, as appears by a letter of the Marquess of Buckingham written in that year, and printed in Lipscombe's History of Buckinghamshire, vol. iii. p. 87.

[2] Like his father it is evident that he died at Stowe, for his funeral is recorded among the burials there under the date of the 11th May. The epitaph will be found at length in Dugdale's Warwickshire, edit. Thomas, p. 525, together with an account of the armory surrounding the tomb.

to that dignity, the only other Buckinghamshire family thus honoured being that of Lee of Quarendon, afterwards Earls of Lichfield. Like his father, Sir Thomas had a numerous family, of whom four sons and three daughters lived to maturity; and so rapidly did their posterity multiply that it is said that the mother survived to see seven hundred of her descendants.[1] She was Esther, or Hester, daughter of Miles Sandys, esq. of Latimers, co. Buckingham; and after her the name of Hester was long perpetuated in many noble families. She died in 1656.

There were four Baronets in successive generations, of whom the last, Sir Richard, being a distinguished general in the campaigns of Marlborough, at length became a Field Marshal. He is the " brave Cobham " commemorated as a Patriot in the well-known lines of Pope, having been created Baron of Cobham in Kent in 1714, and in 1718 Baron and Viscount Cobham. The second patent included a remainder to his sisters, Hester wife of Richard Grenville, esq. of Wotton, and Christian wife of Sir Thomas Lyttelton, bart.,[2] and their male issue.

When Lord Viscount Cobham died in 1749, Stowe, with the peerage, passed to his sister Mrs. Grenville (her husband having died in 1727), and in the same year she was created Countess Temple. Thus it happens that the Duke of Buckingham and Chandos is also Earl Temple and Viscount and Baron Cobham, and bears the name of Temple as the first of his five conjoint

---

[1] " She had four sons and nine daughters, which lived to be married, and so exceedingly multiplied, that this lady saw seven hundred extracted from her body. Reader, I speak within compass, and have left myself a reserve, having bought the truth hereof by a wager I lost." Fuller's Worthies of England. She thus outrivalled by far her contemporary Mrs. Honywood. But we are not aware that the assertion has been proved (except to the satisfaction of Dr. Fuller). The posterity of Mrs. Honywood will be found enumerated and described in *The Topographer and Genealogist*, vol. i. pp. 397-411, 568-576.

[2] Their son was the first Lord Lyttelton (of Frankley, co. Worc.) so created in 1757, and the present Lord Lyttelton is now next heir presumptive to the Viscountcy of Cobham, the Duke of Buckingham and Chandos having only daughters. The title of Cobham was very remotely derived by Sir Richard Temple in allusion to the descent of his paternal grandmother, the wife of the second Baronet. She was Christian, sister and coheir to Sir Richard Leveson, K.B. of Trentham, co. Stafford, and daughter of Sir John Leveson, who was the eldest son of another Sir John by Frances, daughter and sole heir of Sir Thomas Sondes of Throwley, co. Kent, by Margaret sister to Henry sixth Lord Cobham, and last of that ancient line.

surnames.[1] He marshals the quarterly coat of Earl Leofric and Temple in his second quarter, has for his sinister supporter a horse argent, semée of the eaglets of the Saxon Earl, and gives for his motto TEMPLA QUAM DILECTA.[2]

Moreover, when his father was created Duke, in the year 1822, which was before the present Duke's birth, a fresh patent was also conferred of the Earldom of Temple, by which, failing the heirs male of the patent of 1749, it will be inherited by his granddaughter Anne Eliza Mary, and the heirs male of her body. In virtue of this remainder, that lady, who is now the wife of William Henry Powell Gore-Langton, esq. is at present the next heir presumptive to the title of Countess Temple.

When the representation of the Temples of Stowe devolved on a female, there were various junior branches in the male line, two of which have since successively borne the title of Baronet,—

[1] Earl Temple had the royal licence to use tbe names and arms of Nugent and Temple in addition to his own name of Grenville, Dec. 2, 1779.

[2] The canting motto TEMPLA QUAM DILECTA, which is used by the Duke of Buckingham, is evidently derived from the first verse of the 83rd Psalm, though the words in the Vulgate are *Quam dilecta tabernacula tua.* It has been observed, however, that in the epitaph of John, Abbot of Croyland, written about the year 1475, the words of the Temple motto are to be found. The abbot had painted and gilded the roof of his church, and it was said of him

Quam sibi dilecta fuerant sacra templa

Laudis in exempla demonstrant aurea tecta.

This motto TEMPLA QUAM DILECTA was also used by the late Lord Nugent, and has been adopted by the Baronets now represented by Sir Grenville Temple. The motto of the Lords Palmerston was FLECTI NON FRANGI, the opposite to the sentiment professed by the Levesons (Duke of Sutherland and Earl Granville), and by several other families, FRANGAS NON FLECTES.

We do not know when the motto TEMPLA QUAM DILECTA was first adopted, but it occurs in the engraving of the portrait of Richard Temple Viscount Cobham, made in 1732 by J. Faber, froṁ the painting of Sir Godfrey Kneller. It is scarcely fanciful to suppose that the ornamental temples in the gardens of Stowe were multiplied in reference to this sentiment. Browne Willis, in the introductory passage of his account of Stowe (*Hundred of Buckingham,* p. 273) after alluding to " the Mansion, Seat, and Gardens of its Lord " having been rendered " one of the Wonders of the Kingdom " by the addition of the ornaments of Art to those of Nature, expresses a hope that, to complete its beauty, " the tall Spire Steeple " of Buckingham might be re-edified, which beyond all other illustrations would dignify *the ancient Family Motto,* TEMPLA QUAM DILECTA.

the first having been represented by Sir William, Sir Peter, and Sir Richard, from 1749 to 1786; and the second by Sir John, and four Sir Grenvilles, from 1786 to the present time.

For nearly sixty years the various Baronetages, in their accounts of this family, were content to designate Sir William Temple as having been "the next heir male," without attempting to describe his actual descent; until by Mr. Courthope, the editor of Debrett's Baronetage in 1835, he was shown to have descended from Sir Peter Temple, of Stanton Barry, co. Buckingham, knt., son and heir of Sir John Temple, who married a co-heiress of Lee of Stanton Barry, and who was a younger son of the first Baronet.

Sir John Temple, who assumed the title in 1786, was stated, in editions of the Baronetage published before 1828, to have descended from the second Baronet. This could not have been the fact; or his branch would have inherited the dignity before those of Stanton Barry. Other lines of descent have subsequently been suggested for him, but none has been actually ascertained.

There were a great variety of junior branches of Temple at the commencement of the seventeenth century,[1] but there is the utmost confusion of statement regarding them in the several pedigrees of the family that have been published. In order to arrive at any satisfactory conclusions it will be necessary to examine each branch *seriatim*, for which we have not present space. We shall therefore defer this part of the genealogy to a future page, and then give some account of the two branches that have taken the title of Baronet, of the Temples of America, and of others: proceeding now to that branch, of still remoter origin (and, so far as appears, the most distant of the whole), which has produced the Viscounts Palmerston.

[1] The pedigree in the History of Leicestershire, vol. iv. p. 960, will give some evidence of this fact: though, like all others, it is imperfect and incorrect. It may be pointed out as a remarkable coincidence, that in p. 962 of that volume the pedigree of Pitt, Earl of Chatham, is given, in continuation from Grenville, and immediately below it is placed that of Temple Viscount Palmerston: so that the genealogy of our late Premier was printed some fifty years ago in the same page with that of William Pitt. It should also be noted, that the register extracts in p. 958 are not from Sibbesdon, as there stated, but from Stowe.

PARALLEL DESCENTS OF TEMPLE OF STOWE, AND OF TEMPLE, LORD VISCOUNT PALMERSTON.

PETER TEMPLE, Esq. of Burton Derset; died 1577.

John Temple, Esq. of Stowe; died 1603.

Anthony, of Coughton, co. Warwick.

Sir Thomas Temple, created Baronet 1611.

Sir William Temple, knighted 1622; died 1627.

Sir Peter, 2nd Baronet; died 1653.

Sir John Temple, Master of the Rolls in Ireland; died 1677.

Sir Richard, 3rd Baronet; died 1697.

Sir William Temple, P.C. the Statesman; created Baronet 1665; died 1698-9.

Sir John Temple, Attorney-General in Ireland; died 1704.

Sir Richard, 4th Baronet; Lord Cobham 1710; Viscount 1718; died 1749.

Hester, mar. George Grenville, Esq. Viscountess Cobham and Countess Temple 1749; died 1752.

Henry, created Viscount Palmerston 1722; died 1757.

Richard Grenville, Earl Temple, K.G.; died 1779.

Right Hon. George Grenville.

Hon. Henry Temple; died 1740.

George Marquess of Buckingham; died 1813.

Henry 2nd Viscount Palmerston; died 1802.

Richard-Temple-Nugent, Duke of Buckingham and Chandos 1822; died 1861.

Henry-John 3rd Viscount Palmerston, K.G.; died 1865.

Richard Plantagenet Campbell Temple-Nugent-Brydges-Chandos-Grenville, now Duke of Buckingham and Chandos, and Earl Temple.

Lady Anna-Eliza-Mary, wife of William H. P. Gore-Langton, Esq.; heir presumptive to the Earldom of Temple, created in 1822.

TEMPLE, LORD VISCOUNT PALMERSTON.

The line of Temple, of which the late Lord Palmerston was the last male representative, rose to distinction by filling various important offices in Ireland; whither his ancestor William repaired, on the ruin of his patron the Earl of Essex, in the year 1600.

William is supposed to have been a grandson of Peter Temple, esq. of Burton Derset, who died at Stowe in 1577. Of his father very little indeed is recorded. His name is said to have been (I.) ANTHONY; his residence Coughton, in the county of Warwick, and his wife a lady named Bargrave.

II. WILLIAM was elected from Eton to King's College in the

year 1573; and is said to have been for a time master of the free-
school at Lincoln.[1]

Having attached himself to the illustrious Sir Philip Sidney,
to whom he dedicated a Latin treatise, printed in 1581, he attended him as secretary to the Netherlands, and Sir Philip died
in his arms at Arnheim, on the 16th Oct. 1586. Sir Philip in
his will not only bequeathed to Mr. Temple an annuity of 30l.
for life, but recommended him to the service of the Earl of
Essex, who employed him in the same capacity until the rash
and fatal enterprise which terminated that nobleman's career.
In this event Mr. Temple was unavoidably compromised,[2] and
he was glad to escape more serious consequences by returning to
Ireland (where he had previously attended on the Earl of Essex
when Lord Lieutenant). His talents soon made a way for him
there. In 1609 he became Provost of Trinity College, Dublin,
at the request of Archbishop Ussher; and he held that office
until his death, together with a Mastership in Chancery, to which
he was appointed in the same year. He sat in Parliament for
Dublin University in the year 1613, and was knighted by the
Lord Deputy St. John in 1622. He died on the 15th Jan.
1626-7, and was buried on the 20th, under the Provost's seat in
his college chapel. Having married Martha daughter of Mr.
Robert Harrison[3] of Derbyshire, he left issue—Sir John, his
heir; Thomas, a divine, and the presumed ancestor of the

---

[1] There was a previous William Temple elected from Eton to King's in 1545, of
whom some account is given in the *Athenæ Cantab.* i. 116. It is possible that he
may have become the schoolmaster at Lincoln. No particulars are known of his
parentage.

[2] On the 17th Feb. 1600-1, he was indicted by the name of William Temple, late
of London, esq., for complicity in the treasons of the Earls of Essex, Rutland, and
Southampton. (Baga de Secretis, pouch 57, file 2.) In MS. Tanner 79, p. 229, is a
letter to him from Sir Philip Sidney testifying his great esteem. It is dated 29 May
1584. In MS. Tanner 75, p. 109, is a letter from him to Charles Blount, Earl of
Mountjoy, dated 7 May, 1604. We are not aware that these letters have been printed.
He is noticed in Zouch's Life of Sir Philip Sidney, pp. 240, 241, 266; Collins's
Sydney Papers, and Birch's Elizabeth, ii. 106; and will be more fully commemorated
in the *Athenæ Cantabrigienses.*

[3] Funeral entry in Ulster's office, printed hereafter. In Collins's Peerage this
name is altered to Harrington, and so in the pedigree in the History of Leicestershire,
and elsewhere. Lady Temple's family it may be presumed was not entitled to arms,
as the impalement on the funeral certificate is left blank.

Temples of Mount Temple in Westmeath (of whom hereafter);
and three daughters,—1. Catharine Lady Vell ; 2. Mary wife of
Job Ward, esq. (both of whose funeral entries will be inserted
hereafter) ; and 3. Martha, who died unmarried, and who was
very probably the "Mrs. Temple" buried at St. Werburgh's,
Dublin, in 1675.[1]

III. Sir JOHN TEMPLE, son of Sir William, born in 1600,
became Master of the Rolls in Ireland in 1640, and retained that
post until his death in 1677, throughout all the various influences
of those chequered times.   In truth, he inclined to the side of
the Parliament, and, after suffering a year's imprisonment on that
account, was much trusted in the business of Ireland by the Lord
Protector.   Yet he was continued in office at the Restoration, and
in 1663 obtained a reversionary grant of the same for his son. He
inherited the friendship of the Sydney family; and his wife, who
was a sister of the learned Dr. Henry Hammond, died and was
buried at Penshurst in 1638.   When Robert Sydney, Earl of
Leicester, was Lord Lieutenant of Ireland, Sir John Temple
enjoyed his utmost confidence: and from his intimate acquaint-
ance with the politics of those days, he was induced to write a
History of the Irish Rebellion, which was printed in 1646, and
was generally accepted as a work of the highest merit and importance.   On his death at Dublin, in 1677, he was buried with
his father; leaving issue two surviving sons, Sir William and
Sir John ; and two daughters, Martha the wife of Sir Thomas
Gifford, of Castle Jordan, co. Kildare, bart.,[2] and Mary wife of
Abraham Yarner, esq.

IV. His elder son, the second Sir WILLIAM TEMPLE, was,
until our own times, the most celebrated person of his race, and
his talents were widely recognised abroad as well as at home.
Eminently successful in political negociations, he was also highly
popular as an elegant writer.   His life is the subject of a work
by the Right Hon. T. P. Courtenay, 1836.   Succeeding to the

---

[1] See the funeral entry of that date. In Lodge's Peerage of Ireland (edit. Archdall)
v. 234, this entry is inadvertently applied to Lady Temple the mother.

[2] Lady Gifford wrote memoirs of her brother, and they were prefixed to the edition
of his Works published in 1741, but without those portions relating to his more private
life ; Mr. Courtenay availed himself of these in his Life, published in 1836. Lady
Gifford was buried in Westminster Abbey, Jan. 5, 1722-3, æt. 84.

Mastership of the Rolls in Ireland, he retained it until 1696; but
this was not incompatible with residence in England, where the
greater portion of his life was spent, taking a leading part in the
business of the privy council and parliament. He was created a
Baronet on the 31st Jan. 1665, but left no heir male; his only
son John Temple, esq. who was paymaster-general of the army,[1]
having drowned himself under London Bridge in the year 1691.
Sir William married Dorothy, second daughter of Sir Peter
Osborne, of Chicksands in Bedfordshire; his son married Mary,
the only daughter of M. Duplessis Rambouillet, a French Protestant,[2] by whom he had two daughters: Elizabeth, married to her
cousin John Temple, esq. next brother to the first Viscount
Palmerston; and Dorothy, married to Nicholas Bacon, esq. of
Shrubland in Suffolk. Sir William Temple died in Jan. 1698,
in his 70th year, at his seat, Moor Park, near Farnham in Surrey,
which became the property of Mr. John Temple, his granddaughter's husband. That gentleman had a numerous family,
but no surviving male issue at his death in 1752.

IV. 2. Sir JOHN TEMPLE, the younger brother, was succes-
sively Solicitor-General of Ireland 1660, Speaker of the Irish
House of Commons at the age of thirty, Attorney-General 1684.
His latter days he spent in England, and dying at a house he had
purchased at East Sheen, on the 10th March, 1704, in his 72nd
year, was buried in Mortlake church. He had married in 1663
Jane, daughter of Sir Abraham Yarner, Muster-Master-General in
Ireland; and she was buried at St. Michan's, in Dublin, in 1677.
Sir John Temple left two surviving sons,—Henry, created
Viscount Palmerston, and John, already mentioned; and several
daughters, of whom Jane, the youngest, was first the wife of
John Lord Berkeley of Stratton, and afterwards of William Earl
of Portland, under which name she was for many years governess
in succession to all the Princesses, daughters of King George the

---

[1] Mr. Courtenay terms this office "Secretary at War," and seems to have thought
the catastrophe occurred shortly after the accession of William and Mary. See what
he says on the subject in his vol. ii. p. 439: his authority being apparently the
Memoirs of Sir John Reresby, 8vo. 1735, p. 346. We give the date 1691 on the contemporary authority of Peter le Neve, MS. Baronets in Coll. Arm.

[2] Mr. Temple was in Paris in 1684, when the remarkable diploma or certificate of
nobility was granted to him, which is printed hereafter, p. 406.

Second. She died in London March 21, 1751, aged about 80 years.

V. HENRY TEMPLE, his son and heir, was appointed Joint Remembrancer of the Exchequer in Ireland as early as 1680, and held that office for some years in conjunction with his son, until the death of the latter in 1740.

In 1722 he was created Baron Temple of Mount Temple, co. Sligo, and Viscount Palmerstown, of Palmerstown, co. Dublin, with remainder to his brother John (who died however without surviving male issue). In the preamble to the patent the services of his father and grandfather were honourably acknowledged, and the more brilliant qualities of his uncle were also suitably commemorated, in the following terms:—

—— cujus Avus et Pater muneribus in Hiberniâ publicis eâ fide, prudentiâ, et abstinentiâ functi sunt, ut adhuc etiam grato animo recolant illius regni cives. Patruus vero periculis et negotiis ad exteras gentes legatus felicem Regi et Civitati operam navavit, atque rebus gestis juxta ac scriptis quod vivida vis animi possit ostendit. Virum itaque tali stirpe natum, priscâ fide et moribus antiquis præditum, cui nostra dignitas et salus publica maximè cordi sunt, libenter titulis insignimus.

The first Viscount Palmerston died at Chelsea in 1757, at the age of eighty-four.

VI. His elder son the Hon. HENRY TEMPLE had died before him in 1740 ; and his younger son, Richard Temple, esq. M.P. for Downton, died in 1749 without surviving issue.

VII. HENRY, the second Viscount, succeeded his grandfather, and was for many years a Lord of the Admiralty. His name occurs in literary memoirs in connection with Dr. Johnson, Sir Joshua Reynolds, and Madame D'Arblay, and it has been remarked that he was evidently a genuine Temple, but with the lighter qualities of the line in larger proportion than the solid ones. He died in 1802, and was the father and immediate predecessor of the late Premier.

VIII. HENRY JOHN, third and last Viscount Palmerston, thus succeeded to the title during his minority, and lived to enjoy it for sixty-three years. Altogether it has been held for the long period of 143 years by only three possessors. The last Viscount would doubtless have been rewarded with a British peerage, and of a higher grade, had the time ever arrived for him to relinquish

his commanding position in the Lower House of Parliament.
But to one who had no male heirs such promotion could scarcely
have offered any temptation.   He received from his grateful
Sovereign the personal distinction of the Garter, which was conferred upon him in 1856, and he had previously been created a
Grand Cross of the Bath in 1832.   The blue ribbon had never
before been conferred upon one who was only a Peer of Ireland;
nor since the days of Sir Robert Walpole has it been worn by
more than three members of the House of Commons: of whom
the first was Lord North, afterwards Earl of Guildford; and the
second Lord Castlereagh, afterwards Marquess of Londonderry;
both, like Lord Palmerston, occupying the foremost seat on
the ministerial bench.

Except in the possession of some Irish estates, the connection of
the Palmerstons with Ireland has been little after their elevation
to the peerage.   The first Viscount became a member of the
English House of Commons, sitting for various boroughs, and
his successors have done the same.   They resided for many years
at Mortlake, near London: and their marriages have been chiefly
with the families of eminent citizens.   The first Viscount married Anne daughter of Abraham Houblon,[1] merchant; and after
her death the widow of Sir John Fryer, bart., Lord Mayor in
1721, daughter of Sir Francis Gerard of Harrow-on-the-Hill,
bart.   The mother of the second Viscount was Jane daughter of
Alderman Sir John Barnard, and married during his mayoralty
in 1738.   His second wife, the mother of the late Premier,
was a sister of Benjamin Mee, esq. a Director of the Bank of
England.[2]

In reviewing the family history thus briefly sketched, we

---

[1] See our first volume, p. 173.

[2] The marriage of Lord Palmerston's parents is thus announced in the *Gentleman's
Magazine* for 1783: " Jan. 5, at Bàth, Ld. Visc. Palmerston of Ireland, M.P. for
Hastings, to Miss Mary Mee, second dau. of the late Benj. Mee, esq. and sister of
Benj. M. esq. one of the directors of the Bank."   Lady Palmerston's father is styled
" of the city of Bath " in Lodge's *Peerage of Ireland*, edit. Archdall 1779, v. 244.
Lord Palmerston was born on the 20th October in the following year, it has been
generally stated at his father's seat of Broadlands, near Romsey, but the con-
temporary authority of the Scots Magazine records his birth to have taken place in
Park Street, Westminster.   See further of the Mee family in p. 410.

gather as the general results[1] that Lord Palmerston came of a family of very ancient gentry, little connected in his own branch with the higher nobility, but frequently with the leading families of the commercial class; that it was a thoroughly English family, in spite of its Irish employments; that it has enjoyed nearly unintermitted intellectual distinction for 300 years; and that there has been a pervading likeness of character in the line all through. Practical statesmen or lawyers; always fond of literature, and sometimes famous in it; successful men of the world, and worldly, but kind-hearted, genial, and capable of high feeling; tough in constitution in spite of gout, and, for the most part, long-lived—the Temples were the natural forerunners and producers of the veteran who has just been laid in his grave. The old tree seems to have put forth all its energy and to have concentrated all its hereditary qualities to produce its last fruit, which has now fallen so ripe and yet so sound in surface and at core.

Lord Palmerston was the last of his own generation. He had one younger brother, Sir William Temple, formerly Minister at Naples, who died in 1856, and left a valuable collection of antiquities to the British Museum; and two sisters, Frances, married in 1820 to Captain Bowles, R.N.; and Elizabeth, married in 1811 to Laurence Sulivan, esq. Deputy Secretary at War. Mrs. Sulivan died in 1837; and Mrs. Bowles in 1838. Their husbands are still living: one as Admiral Sir William Bowles, K.C.B. and the other as the Right Hon. Laurence Sulivan,[2] having been sworn a Privy Councillor on his retirement from office in 1851. The latter only has children. His eldest son died at Lima in 1856. His only surviving son is the Rev. Henry Sulivan, now Rector of Yoxall in Staffordshire, who married in 1843 Emily Anne, eldest daughter of Lionel Ames, esq. of the Hyde, St. Alban's. There are three daughters, the eldest married to Henry Hippisley, esq.; the second to the Rev. Robert George Baker, Vicar of Fulham; and the third unmarried.

[1] In the ensuing remarks we avail ourselves of the conclusion of an historical summary, something of the nature of our own, which appeared in the Pall Mall Gazette.

[2] There was previously a Privy Councillor of this name, the Right Hon. John Sullivan, who held the office of Under Secretary of War from 1801 to 1805. But he was of a different family, spelling the name differently, and brother to Sir Richard Joseph Sullivan, created a Baronet in 1804.

FUNERAL ENTRIES OF THE TEMPLE FAMILY.

(From Ulster's Office at Dublin Castle.)

1626. Sr Wm Temple, knight, deceased ye 15 of January, 1626. He had to wife Martha, dau. of Robert Harrison of Darbyshire, by whome he had issue. (Vol. 5, p. 121.)

Arms : Argent, two bars sable, each charged with three martlets or; the impalement *blank.* But in the Will Books in Ulster's office, vol. iv. p. 222, accompanying a short pedigree derived from Sir William Temple's will, is a shield of the coat granted in 1576, a chevron ermine between three martlets, probably taken from his seal attached to the will.

1627. Mary, d^r of Sr William Temple, knight, deceased the 24 of December, 1627. She was mar. to Jobe Warde, by whome she had issue John. (Vol. 5, p. 123.)

Arms: In a lozenge, Azure, a cross flory or, a crescent for difference; impaling Temple (as before).

1642. Dame Katherin dau. of Sr William Temple, knight, and sometime Provost of Trinitie Colledge adjoyninge to the Cittie of Dublin. The said Dame Katherin was married to John Archdall of Archdall, in the county of Fermanagh, esquire, by whome she had divers children, but they are all dead. The said Dame Katherin was after marryed to Sr John Vell, knight, by whome she left issue 3 sonnes and 3 daughters, vizt, Gary Vell eldest sonne, John Vell 2^d sonne, Edward Vell 3^d sonne, Ann eldest daughter, Katherin 2^d daughter, and Martha 3^d daughter. The abovesaid Dame Katherin departed this mortall life the 13th of November, 1642, and was interred in St Warbrogh's church in Dublin the 15th of the same month. The trueth of the premisses is testified by the subscription of Sr John Vell, knight, aforesaid. Taken by me Albon Leveret, Athlone officer of Arms, to be recorded.

(*Signed*) Jo. Vell. (Vol. 10, p. 153.)

Arms: Argent, on a bend sable three wolves passant or, for Vell; impaling Temple (as before).

1662. Sr Thomas Gifford, of Castle Jordan, Baronett, deceased 4th of May, and was buried the 9th of the same month, 1662, in St Auden's church in Dublin. He had to wife [Martha] Temple, daughter of Sr John Temple, Master of the Rolles, and one of the Privy Councell of Ireland, but left noe issue. This certificate was taken by me, Richard St George, Esqr., Ulster King of Armes of Ireland, 1662.   (Vol. 10, p. 49.)

Arms: Gules, three lions passant argent, the badge of Ulster, impaling Temple (as before).

1663. Mr Alexander Temple[1] died 28th of November, and buried the 3^d of December, 1663.   He married Mary dau. of Calcot Chambre, by whom he had a son and a daug: now living named Mary. (Vol. 14, p. 57.)

Arms: Temple (as before) impaling Azure, a dexter arm embowed in armour or holding a rose gules slipt vert.

1675. Mrs Temple departed this mortal life the 6th of December, and was buried the 7th of the same month in St Warborough's church, Dublin, 1675.   (Vol. 14, p. 178.)

Arms: Two lozenge shields: 1. Temple (as before) quartering Or, an eagle displayed sable, " Kirhill"; 2. Temple alone (as before). This last, it will be observed, is the only case in these books in which the spread eagle occurs, and here it seems to have been mistaken for the coat assigned in Burke's *General Armory* to " Kirhiles or Kirhir, of Devonshire."

1677. Sr John Temple, Kn^t, Master of the Rolls, &c., in the Kingdom of Ireland, died the 12th and buried the 19th of November, in Trinity College. (Vol. 14, p. 196.)

Arms of Temple (as before).

[1] This appears, from Lodge's *Peerage of Ireland*, edit. Archdall, i. 278, to have been Alexander Temple of Ballinderry, esq., but his name does not occur in the same work *tit.* Temple Viscount Palmerston. His wife Mary was granddaughter of Calcot Chambre, of Denbigh in Wales, and Carnowe, co. Wicklow, esq. who " died 29 Oct. 1635, and was buried at Carnowe, leaving a son Calcot, whose issue were a son of that name who died childless, and a daughter Mary, who became sole heir to that estate, and by her first husband Alexander Temple of Ballinderry, esq. had an only daughter Mary, married in Nov. 1676 to Abraham, second son of Sir Abraham Yarner, in whose marriage articles the Wicklow estate was limited to the Countess of Meath and her heirs male." (Lodge, *ubi supra.*) The Countess of Meath was the younger daughter of Calcot Chambre, esq. the grandfather (whose elder daughter was Elizabeth wife of Francis Sandford, esq.), and hence the name of Chambre came to the Brabazon family, Chambre Brabazon her third son succeeding (after his two elder brothers) as fifth Earl of Meath.

A pedigree discovered since the foregoing note was written (in Harl. MS. 1533, fol. 68), shows that Mary, the widow of Alexander Temple of Ballinderry, was re-married to Henry Temple, esq. of Lincoln's Inn (unnamed by Archdall), the youngest son of Sir John Temple (*ante*, p. 399), and had issue a son, Chambre Temple, who died at 17 years of age. The same pedigree also shows that her first husband, Alexander, was a grandson of Sir Alexander Temple, of Longhouse in Essex, a younger brother to the first Baronet of Stowe : and of that branch some account will be given hereafter.

From the Peers' Entries in Ulster's Office.

The Right Hon'ble Henry Temple Viscount Palmerston, died in June 1757. He married first Anne, daughter of Abraham Houblon, esq. by whom he had five children, Henry, Jane, Elizabeth, John, and Richard, who all died before him. He afterwards married Isabella, daughter of Sir Francis Gerrard, of Harrow on the Hill, in Middlesex, Bart. widow of Sir John Fryer, Bart. by whom he had no issue. The eldest son, Henry, married first the daughter of Colonel Lee, by Lady Elizabeth Lee, daughter of the Earl of Litchfield; who dying without issue, he married Jane, daughter of Sir John Bernard, Knt. by whom he had one son, Henry, now Viscount Palmerston. The truth of all which is attested by the said Lord, this 1st day of May 1767. Pursuant to a Standing Order of the House of Lords, dated this 12th of August 1707.

(Signed)   PALMERSTON.

W. HAWKINS, Ulster.

Arms : 1 and 4, Or, an eagle displayed sable; 2 and 3, Argent, two bars sable each charged with three martlets or. *Supporters.* A lion pœan and a horse argent, maned, tailed, and hoofed or, both regardant. *Crest.* On a wreath, a hound sejant sable, collared or. *Motto,* FLECTI NON FRANGI.

DIPLOMA under the COMMON SEAL of the COLLEGE OF ARMS issued in 1684 to JOHN TEMPLE, ESQUIRE, then at PARIS, the son of the RIGHT HON. SIR WILLIAM TEMPLE.

This is an official certificate of the nobility of Mr. Temple granted by the College of Arms for the object of procuring him a proper reception in foreign courts. We are not aware of any similar document having been hitherto published; but the certificate from Sir John Borough, Garter, given to Marmaduke Rawdon of London when about to visit Spain in 1638, is described in our vol. I. p. 75.

[MS. Coll. Arms. L. 2, f. 163.]

Omnibus ad quos præsentes Litteræ pervenerint Nos Reges Heraldi et Pursuivandi Armorum florentissimi Regni Angliæ salutem. Cum nos juramento astricti et authoritate regiâ sub magno Angliæ sigillo muniti sumus genealogias virorum Nobilium una cum armis sive clypeis suis gentilitiis in Collegio nostro Armorum conservare et de eisdem quoties rogati fuerimus attestationem facere. Nos ex parte Johannis Temple Armigeri apud Luteciam Parisiorum in regno

Franciæ jam jam commorantis, Vobis notum facimus quod idem
Johannes genus suum ducit a nobili et perantiqua familia Templorum
quæ apud Temple-hall in agro Leicestrensi dicti regni Angliæ provincia
celeberrima per multa retro secula floruit.   Filius scilicet unicus
Domini Gulielmi Temple Baronetti nuper Legati Extraordinarii ad
Fæderatos Belgii ordines et Regiæ Majestati a sacris consiliis in Regno
Angliæ et Scriniorum Sacrorum Magistri in regno Hiberniæ et Doro-
theæ uxoris ejus filiæ D'ni Petri Osborne equitis aurati et nuper Guber-
natoris Insulæ de Gurnsey, qui quidem Dominus Gulielmus filius fuit
primogenitus D'ni Johannis Temple equitis aurati, Scriniorum Sacrorum magistri in regno Hiberniæ et ibidem Regiæ Majestati a sacris
consiliis, per Mariam uxorem ejus filiam Roberti Hammond de
Chertsey in com. Surrey generosi; filii et heredis domini Gulielmi
Temple equitis aurati et Marthæ Harrington [1] uxoris suæ; filii Antho-
nii Temple generosi (et uxoris ejus filiæ   Bargrave) secundo-
geniti Petri Temple de Byrton Dasset in com. Warwick generosi et
Milicentiæ filiæ Johannis Jykett [2] de Newington in com. Midlesex
generosi uxoris ejus; filii secundi Thomæ Temple de Whitney in agro
Oxoniensi generosi per uxorem suam Aliciam filiam Johannis Erytage
de Byrton Dasset prædicta; qui quidem Thomas fuit filius et hæres
Gulielmi Temple de Whitney prædicta generosi et Isabellæ uxoris
filiæ et hæredis Henrici Everton armigeri; filii et hæredis Thomæ
Temple de Whitney generosi et Mariæ filiæ Thomæ Gedney armigeri;
tertiogeniti Roberti Temple domini manerii de Temple Hall prope
Wellesbrough in com. Leicest. qui vixit aº 8 Hen. 6 Angliæ Regis et
duxit Mariam filiam Gulielmi Kingescote Armigeri.   Iste Robertus [3]
primogenitus fuit Thomæ Temple d'ni de Temple Hall prædicta aº
1 H. 6, et conjugis ejus Johannæ filiæ Johannis Brasbridge armigeri;
filii et hæredis Nicholai Temple domini de Temple Hall (aº 4ᵗᵒ Ric'i
2 Regis) et Mariæ filiæ Roberti Daberon armigeri; filii et hæredis
alterius Nicholai domini de Temple Hall (aº 24 Regis Edw. primi) et
Isabellæ filiæ Gulielmi Barwell armigeri; primogeniti Ricardi Temple
domini de Temple Hall aº 3. Edw. primi prædicti et Katharinæ uxoris
ejus filiæ Thomæ Langley armigeri. Qui quidem Richardus filius et
hæres fuit Henrici Temple (aº 3 Edw. I.) et Matildæ filiæ Johannis
Ribbesford armigeri; filii et hæredis Roberti Temple de Temple Hall in
parochia de Sibsden prope Wellesbrough in com. Leicestr. qui Rober-

---

[1] So in MS: see p. 398.   [2] An error for *Jekell*.
[3] From this point the pedigree will be found to ascend in conformity with the line
already given from the Visitations in p. 387.

tus ibi floruit imperante Henrico tertio Angliæ Rege prout per Genealogiam suprascriptam plenius apparet. Ac etiam Insignia sive tesseras
gentilitias antecessorum ejusdem Johannis Temple ritè et legitimè
spectantia in hiis tabulis delineari curavimus. Quæ omnia ex Regis-
tris nostris in Collegio Armorum Londini remanentibus vobis pro veri-
tate perlucida et indubitata per præsentes significamus et attestamur,
rogantes ut præmissis fidem debitam adhibeatis. In quorum omnium
testimonium sigillum commune Collegii Armorum prædicti præsenti-
bus apponi fecimus. Datum Londini tricesimo primo die Julii aº
regni prepotentissimi et excellentissimi Monarchæ Domini nostri Caroli
2di Dei gratia Angliæ, Scotiæ, Franciæ et Hiberniæ Regis, Fidei Defen-
soris, etc. 36°, Annoque Salutis 1684.

At the foot of the document two shields of arms are drawn. One is
quarterly: 1 and 4, Sable, a chevron ermine between three martlets
argent, differenced by a crescent, for *Temple;* 2 and 3, Argent, three
boar's heads erased sable, for *Everton;* and an inescocheon of Ulster,
with the inscription:—

Insignia Domini Gulielmi Templi Baronetti quarteriatim cum scuto familiæ de
Everton, ex cujus hærede Isabella genus suum duxit.

The second shield contains the same quartered arms, with a crescent
in centre point, and in chief a label of three points, with this inscription:—

Insignia Johannis Temple armigeri, filii et hæredis Domini Gulielmi Temple Baronetti, prout opportet eum gestare durante vita patris secundum leges armorum apud
Anglos, scil. Lemnisco triplici distincta.

This is the only instance that has occurred of the adoption of the
quartering of Everton; for which the heralds went so far back as the
marriage of William Temple of Witney (mentioned in the preceding
page), which took place in the 15th century.

By his Will dated Nov. 22, 1864, Lord Palmerston has left his real
and leasehold estates in England and Ireland to Lady Palmerston for
life, and after her decease to her Ladyship's second son, the Right Hon.
William Francis Cowper; expressing his earnest wish, but without
imposing an obligation on the devisee, that he will, immediately upon
coming into possession of the estates, apply for Her Majesty's licence
and authority for him and his descendants to take and use the surname
of TEMPLE, either in substitution for, or in addition to, that of Cowper,
but so that Temple be the final name, and that the family arms of
Temple be quartered with those of Cowper.

TEMPLE, OF MOUNT TEMPLE, CO. WESTMEATH.

We have further to acknowledge, among the favours we have received from Ulster's office, the following pedigree of the branch of Temple, seated at Mount Temple, co. Westmeath. In a note to Archdall's edition of Lodge's Peerage (vol. v. p. 234) it is stated that Robert Temple, esq. was descended, it is presumed, from Thomas Temple, B.D. sometime Fellow of Trinity College, Dublin, and afterwards Minister of Battersea, in Surrey (1641), a frequent preacher before the Long Parliament: the date of whose death and place of burial are not stated. He had an assignment of 750 acres of land in the county Westmeath; and Robert, who married a Surrey lady in 1693-4, was not improbably his grandson. The name of TEMPLE has been twice assumed by his heirs in the female line. The pedigree is as follows:

Dorothea, 1st wife, sister to William Cock, of Letherhead, co. Surrey, widow of Mr. Needham; mar. March 11, 1693-4. ＝ Robert Temple, of Mount Temple, co. Westmeath, Esq. ＝ Catharine, 2nd wife, sister to John Jephson, Esq.

Two children, who died young. | Gustavus Handcock, of Waterstown, co. Meath, Esq. M.P. for Athlone; died at Bath, 5 Sept. 1751, or 25 Oct. 1754. ＝ Elizabeth, only dau. and heir, bapt. Aug. 29, 1701; mar. July 1725.

Robert Handcock, of Waterstown, Esq.; born 15 April, 1728. ＝ Elizabeth, eldest dau. of Sir John Vesey, Lord Knapton; mar. 4 July, 1751. ＝ Edmond Sexten Pery, created Viscount Pery, 1786; 2nd husband. | Catharine, only dau.; died April 2, 1746.

Gustavus Handcock, of Waterstown, Esq.; born in Sackville Street, Dublin, 9 June, 1754; assumed the name of TEMPLE. ＝ Mary, eldest dau. of William Henry Moore, of Drumbanagher.

Robert Handcock Temple, Esq. of Waterstown. ＝ Louisa, dau. of William Stearne Tighe, Esq. of South Hill, co. Westmeath. | Edmond, of the Navy Office. | Gertrude, wife of William James Alexander, son and heir of Robert Alexander, of Seamount, co. Dublin. | Henry. | Charles, in East India Company's Service. | Gustavus. | Vesey. | Louisa, wife of John Lushington Reilly, of Scarvagh, co. Down.

1 w. Eliza Serena Anne Dick. ＝ William George 2nd Lord Harris. ＝ 2 w. Isabella Helena, only child.

George Francis Robert now Lord Harris. | Hon. Robert Temple Harris, born 1830, took the surname and arms of TEMPLE only by Royal Licence 1852.

LORD PALMERSTON'S MATERNAL ANCESTRY.

THE FAMILY OF MEE OR MEY is of considerable antiquity in Hereford-shire and Gloucestershire. John Mey was Mayor of Hereford A.D. 1406. Members of the same family were Mayors temp. Edw. IV. and Hen. VII. Richard Mey was Vicar of Hempsted, co. Glouc. 1428, appointed by the Canons of Lanthony Priory. The following Pedigree has been furnished by the Rev. Samuel Lysons, M.A., F.S A.:

Thomas Mee described as citi-═Elizabeth, dau. of Thomas zen of London, born 1636, set-│Pierce, of Gloucester, mayor tled in Gloucester. Marriage │of that city in 1661. She settlement dated 15 Chas. II. │was born 1640; died 1721, 23 Aug. 1663, ob. 1711, æt. 75. │æt. 81.

Thomas Mee, born 1664, ob. 1722.

Samuel Mee, born Oct. 7, 1668,═Anne, dau. of Thomas Trye,[1] ob. Aug. 3, 1749, æt. 81, High │Esq., of Hardwicke Court, co. Sheriff of county of Gloucester │Glouc.; born 1668, ob. 1706; 1731. │mar. at Hempsted, co. Glouc.

Mary, b. 1704, d. 1705. Anna, mar. J. Viney, Esq.

Thomas═1. Anne, dau. of ... Savage, Esq. Mee, b. │by whom three children, Eliza-1700, d. │beth, Anne, and Samuel, died 1757. │young. │2. Barbara, dau. of ... Nest, Esq.

Eliza-═Daniel Ly-beth │sons, Esq. Mee, │of Hemp-born │sted Court, 1702. │co. Glouc.

Mary, born 1739.

Samuel Benjamin, born 1740.

Benjamin ═ ... ThomasMee, │dau. Esq. b. 1742.│of ..

Thomas, Anne. born 1743.[2]

Daniel Lysons, Esq. LL.D. ob. s.p. 1802.

Rev. Samuel Lysons.

Mary Mee, ═Henry, 2nd mar. Jan. 3, │Viscount 1783, died │Palmers-1805. │ton.

Rev. Daniel Lysons, of Hemp-sted Court, Rector of Rodmarton, and joint author with his brother of many archæological works.

Samuel Lysons, Esq., F.R.S. F.S.A. Keeper of H.M. Re-cords, ob. 1819, s.p.

Henry John, 3rd Viscount Palmerston, died 1865.

Elizabeth, m. Rt. Hon. Lawrence Sulivan.

Rev. Samuel Lysons, M.A. F.S.A. of Hempsted Court, and Rector of Rod-marton, Gloucestershire.

Colonel Daniel Ly-sons, C.B., D. Quar-ter-Master-Gene-ral, Canada.

Rev. Henry Sulivan (see p. 403).

Arms of Mee : Gules, a chevron ermine between three goat's heads erased argent, horned or.

[1] The Tryes, a most ancient and honourable family of Trie in Normandy, connected with the royal family of France. Among them were the Comtes de Dammartin, several Grand Admirals and Grand Constables of France, an Archbishop, Duc de Rheims, &c.

[2] The children of Thomas Mee and Anne Savage were baptized at St. Mary de Lode, Gloucester. Thomas Mee was Mayor of Gloucester in 1793 and 1804. His sister Anne was married to the Rev. Richard Raikes.

THE ENGLISH LADIES OF PONTOISE.

(*Continued from p. 66.*)

NAMES OF ALL THE RELIGIOUS OF THE CHOIR AT PONTOISE

(*except the Abbesses already mentioned*).

The initial M. in this catalogue signifies Mary, an additional conventual name assumed in honour of the B. Virgin. The appellation *Lady* is applied to the Abbess, and *Mother* to the Prioress. *Dame* is the title of all Choir Nuns, in distinction to the Lay Sisters.

The Pedigrees which are appended (in pp. 417 *et seq.*) will be found to explain the relationship of many of the ladies.

Dames—

Lucy Perkins, from Northamptonshire: her mother, N. Icomme, died 1662, aged 57.

Margaret Markham, daughter of George Markham, of Ollerton, Notts, and Judith Withernwick Fitzwilliams, heiress of Claxby, &c. died 25 July, 1717, aged 104.

Clara Vaughan, daughter of Richard Vaughan, of Courtfield, in Monmouthshire, and Bridget, daughter of John Wigmore, esq. of Luchton, died 1687, aged 49.

Gertrude Turner, daughter of Thomas Turner, esq. of Little Audley End, in Essex, and Alice, sister to Lady Abbess Wigmore. She died 1691, aged 59.

Mary Jane Butler, daughter of Toby Butler, of Collin, in Ireland, esq. nearly related to Duke of Ormond. Her mother was Anne Audley, who was co-heiress to an estate in Essex. Dame Butler afterwards became Abbess of Ypres, and died 1723.

M. Frances Elliot, daughter of John Elliot, of Bellos, in Essex, and Catherine, daughter of John Scrimshaw, esq. of Norbury, in Staffordshire (this lady was nurse to James II.); died 1698, aged 66.

Helen Hammerton, daughter of Philip Hammerton, of Monkroode, in Yorkshire, esq. and Dorothy daughter of . . . Young, esq. of Burn, in Yorkshire, near Selby; died 1707, aged 68.

Anna Catharine Bruning, sister to Dame Mary; died 1668, aged 27.

Mary Bruning, daughter of Anthony Bruning, esq. of Wimmering, Hants, and Mary Hyde, of Pangbourn, Berks; died 1709, aged 72.

Mary Roper, daughter of Edmund Roper, esq. of Hartcliffe, Kent, and Anne, daughter of Henry Noble, who was coheir to an estate in Essex. She died 1690, aged 48.

Placida Roper, sister to Dame Mary; died 1709, aged 65.

Catherine Roper, sister to Dames Mary and Placida, and coheir with them to their father's property; died 1700, aged 51.

Justina Timperley, daughter of Michael Timperley, esq. of Hintlesham, Norfolk, and Frances, daughter of Sir Henry Bedingfeld, Bart.; died 1684, aged 43.

Aloysia Elliot, sister to Dame M. Frances; died 1722, aged 82.

Benedict Hammerton, sister to Dame Helen; died 1679, aged 45.

Anna Maria Talbot, daughter of John Talbot, Earl of Shrewsbury, and Frances, daughter of Lord Arundell of Wardour; died 1692, aged 51.

Dorothy Calvert, daughter of John Calvert, esq. of Lincolnshire; died 1665, aged 25.

Angela Riddell, daughter of Sir Thomas Riddell, of Fenham, in Northumberland, and Barbara, daughter of Sir Alexander Davison, of Newcastle; died 1709, aged 65.

Mary Teresa Swift, daughter of Mr. Henry Swift, of Magborough, Devon, and Margaret Lismore; died 1720, aged 85.

Barbara Philpott, daughter of George Philpott, esq. of Compton, Hants, and Winifred, daughter of Gilbert Welles, esq. of Brambridge, Hants; died 1696, aged 56.

M. Winifred Philpott, sister to Dame Barbara; died 1737, aged 88.

Mechtilda Smith, daughter of Edward Smith, esq. of Ash, near Durham, and Margaret Boulemore; died 1708, aged 64.

Alexia Smith, sister to Dame Mechtilda; died 1666, aged 19.

Xaveria Collens, daughter of John Collens, of Diricksteed, Kent, and Mary, daughter of Sir N. Best, of Maidstone, in Kent; died 1668, aged 22.

Scholastica Bruning, daughter of Edmund Bruning, of Wimmering, esq. and of Anne, daughter of Henry Winchcombe, esq. of Bucklebury, Berks; died 1713, aged 65.

Mary Gertrude Cone, daughter of Mr. Francis Cone, and Susan, daughter of Thomas Wiseman, of Canfield Hall, Essex; died 1686, aged 43.

M. Ignatius Champion, daughter of Thomas Champion, of Champion Court, Bucks, esq. and of Elizabeth, daughter of Mr. George Paterson; died 1717, aged 78.

Anna Catherine Thorold, daughter of Sir Robert Thorold, Bart. of the Haugh, Lincolnshire, and Catherine, daughter of Sir Henry Knollys, of Grove Park, Hants; died 1707, aged 54.

M. Magdalen Warren, daughter of Arthur Warren, esq. of Thorpe Ernold, Leicestershire, and Catherine, daughter of Sir Rowland Rugley, of Dunton, Warwickshire; died 1683, aged 36.

Victoria Longueville, youngest daughter of Sir Edw. Longueville, of Wolverton, Bart., and of Margaret, daughter of Sir Richard Temple, of Stow, co. Bucks, Bart.; she died 1674, aged 26.

Eugenia Greene, daughter of Sir Edward Greene, Bart. of Sandford Hall, Essex, and of Anne, daughter of Sir George Simmons, of   , Oxfordshire; died 1709, aged 73.

M. Christina Whyte, daughter of Sir Andrew Whyte, Bart., naturalised in France, and afterwards made Comte *d'Albie* by Louis 14 (because Whyte was too difficult a name for the French), and Anastasia, daughter of Sir James Walsh, Bart. of county Waterford. Dame Christina died at the convent at Ipres in 1683, aged 29.

Anne Neville, daughter of Henry Neville, esq. of Holt, in Leicestershire, and Ursula, daughter of William Clopton, of Clopton, in Warwickshire, esq. (See the account of her journey to Ireland with M. Markham in a future page.) She died at Milford Haven, 25 September, 1687, aged 30.

Alexia Weston, daughter of John Weston, esq. of Sutton Court, Surrey, and Mary, daughter of William Copley, esq. of Burnthall, Surrey; died 1674, aged 18.

Mary Brooke, daughter of John Brooke, of Madeley, in Shropshire, esq. and Elizabeth, daughter of Edward Guildford, esq. of Hempsted, Kent; died 1714, aged 57.

Maura Gifford, sister to Lady Abbess Gifford; died 1691, aged 33.

Ursula Hammerton, sister to Dame Dorothy; died 1691, aged 31.

Dorothy Hammerton, daughter of John Hammerton, esq. of Purston, Yorkshire, and Dorothy, daughter of Mr. Richard Lockwood, of Soersbie (Sowerby) in Yorkshire; died 1705, aged 49.

M. Susan Fletcher, daughter of Mr. Richard Fletcher and Mrs. Mary Furs, of Ashford, Kent; died 1689, aged 40. She died at the new establishment in Dublin, for which see a future page.

M. Lawrence Lawson, daughter of Sir John Lawson, of Brough, Bart. and Catherine, daughter of Sir William Howard, of Naworth, in Northumberland; died 1728, aged 71.

M. Stanislaus Culcheth, daughter of Thomas Culcheth, esq. of Culcheth, and Anne, daughter of James Bradshaw, of Haigh, esq. in Lancashire; died 1704, aged 48.

Francisca Culcheth, sister to the above; died 1717, aged 59.

M. Catherine Tichborne, daughter of Henry Kemp, esq. of the house of Slindon, in Sussex, and of Mrs. Anne Coope. Dame M. Catherine was widow of Michael Tichborne, of Sheffield, Hants. She died 1689, aged 69.

M. Carola Selby, daughter of Sir George Selby, of Whitehouse in the North, and of Mary, daughter of Lord Viscount Molyneux; died 1721, aged 60.

Mary Anne Tichborne,[1] daughter of Sir Henry Tichborne, Bart. and Mary, daughter of William Arundell, esq. of Wardour; died 1734, aged 73.

Augustine Bruning, sister to Dame Scholastica; died 1741, aged 80.

Constantia Heneage, daughter of George Heneage, esq. of Hainton, Lincolnshire, and of Faith, daughter of Sir Philip Tirwhitt, of Stainfield, Bart.; died 1717, aged 59.

Mary Petre, daughter of John Petre, esq. of Fithelres, in Essex, and of Mary, daughter of Sir Francis Mannock, of Gifford's Hall, Suffolk; died 1733, aged 70.

Justina Greene, daughter of Sir Edward Greene, of Sandford Hall, Essex, and Catharine,[2] daughter of Mr. Pegg, of Bradley, in Shropshire. She died 1717, aged 50.

[1] Some interesting particulars of this Lady will be found in a subsequent page.

[2] Katharine Pegge, the wife of Sir Edward Greene, was the daughter of Thomas Pegge of Yeldersley, co. Derby, and Katharine his wife, eldest daughter of Sir Gilbert

Anne Bodenham, daughter of Thomas Bodenham, esq. of Rotherwas, and Catherine, daughter of Edward Guildford, esq. of Hempsted, Kent.   She died 1717, aged 51.

Henrietta Pound, daughter of Henry Pound, esq. of Bernons, Hants, and Dorothy, daughter of Arthur Warren, esq. of Thorpe Ernold, Leicestershire; died 1745, aged 78.

Appollonia Belasyse, daughter of Sir Rowland Belasyse, of Smithells, in Lancashire, Knight of the Bath, (second brother and heir presumptive to the now Viscount Fauconberg,) and of Anne, daughter and heir of James Davenport, of Sutton, in Cheshire, esq.; died 1741, aged 77.

Mary Margaret Belasyse was only sister of Dame Appollonia; died 1742, aged 71.

Ignatia FitzJames, daughter of James 2—Mrs. Churchill. Professed 1690, died 7 November, 1704, aged 30.

Benedict FitzRoy, daughter of Charles 2—Duchess of Cleveland. Professed 1691.   Was made Prioress of St. Nicholas's Priory at Pontoise in 1721, and died there 6 May, 1737, aged 53.

Cecilia Stanihurst, daughter of Henry Stanihurst, esq. of Godoff,[1] in Ireland, and Henrietta Maria, daughter of Sir Joseph Van Colster, of Colster, in Germany, Bart.; died 1746, aged 73.

Agnes Arthur, daughter of Sir Daniel Arthur, of   , Ireland, and of Catherine Smith, of Crabett, in Sussex; died 1752, aged 71.

Kniveton, of Mercaston and Bradley, co. Derby.   By King Charles the Second she had two children: 1. Charles Fitz-Charles, born 1647, for some time known as Don Carlos, and created Earl of Plymouth in 1675: of whom and his wife Lady Bridget Osborne, afterwards remarried to Dr. Bisse, Bishop of Hereford, see further in Nichols's *Literary Anecdotes*, vi. 224; 2. a daughter, who became a nun at Dunkirk, as noticed in the pedigree, p. 419.   Having become the third wife of Sir Edward Greene, of Sampford in Essex, Bart. Katharine Pegge was also the mother of Justina the nun at Pontoise, who was born in 1667, being 50 at her death in 1717.   Sir Edward Greene died in Flanders in December 1674 (or 1676?) leaving no heir to his title, and having ruined his estate by gaming and extravagance.   Lady Greene probably died in 1678, as in a letter dictated by Nell Gwynne (and addressed to Mr. Hyde) it is supposed in the June of that year, there is this passage " Mrs. Knight's Lady mother is dead, and she has put up [for her] a scucheon no bigger than my Lady Green's scucheon." (*Camden Miscellany*, vol. v.)   Mrs. Knight was a singer of great celebrity, and another competitor for the tender regards of Charles II.

[1] Richard Stanihurst, esq. of Court Duff, who was historiographer of Ireland, died at Brussels in 1618.   See Lodge's *Peerage of Ireland*, (edit. Archdall,) 1779, v. 46.

Anna Maria Constable, daughter of John Constable, of   ,
in Lincolnshire, and of Elizabeth Harper; died 1756, aged 74.

The Necrology finishes here.

List continued from Lady Abbess Clavering's list of names
(only), and the word "niece," but without further explanation.

Catherine Maurin.	Scholastica Haggerston.
M. Joseph Clavering.	Maura Tyrrel.
M. Austin Oxburgh.	Elizabeth Preston.
M. Placida Whetenhall.	Anne Preston.

M. Agatha Hunloke, niece to the eighth Lady Abbess.

M. Benedicta Belasyse, niece to ——

Pélagie Brown, professed at a French House at Rouen, and
lived with us 21 years.

M. Bernardine Haggerston.

M. Mag. Belasyse, niece to yᵉ ——

M. Téresa Armstrong (from Dunkirk).

M. Joseph Fothringham.

M. Xaveria Semmes.[1]

M. Henrietta Jerningham.

M. Scholastica Preston, niece to ——

Anna Maria Thickness.

M. Placida Messenger (from Dunkirk).

M. Winifred Clarke (from Dunkirk).

M. Frances Markham (from Dunkirk).

M. Scholastica Belasyse, niece to ——

M. Ann Austin Innes.

In a list of the Religieuses printed by the Abbé Trou the three
following names appear which have not hitherto occurred:—

Marie Anne Lincoln.

Marie Pety Chaulle [Pattishull?]

Anne Marie Byard.

Agnes Morgan + at Hammersmith. Two lay-sisters came to
us from Pontoise. One died at Dunkirk, the other at Hammersmith. The 1st was Agnes Morgan; the 2nd Margaret Evans.

---

[1] Mary Xavier Semmes was an American. She removed to Paris, and there died
from a cold, engendered on the breaking of the great frost which had lasted all
December and January in the winter of—1813-14 ?

PEDIGREES IN ILLUSTRATION OF THE ENGLISH LADIES OF PONTOISE.

I. ROPER, OF ELTHAM, LORDS TEYNHAM.

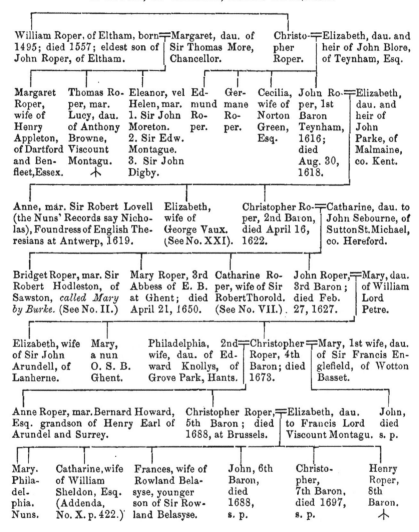

William Roper, of Eltham, born 1495; died 1557; eldest son of John Roper, of Eltham. ⊤ Margaret, dau. of Sir Thomas More, Chancellor.

Christopher Roper. ⊤ Elizabeth, dau. and heir of John Blore, of Teynham, Esq.

Margaret Roper, wife of Henry Appleton, of Dartford and Benfleet, Essex.

Thomas Roper, mar. Lucy, dau. of Anthony Browne, Viscount Montagu.

Eleanor, vel Helen, mar. 1. Sir John Moreton. 2. Sir Edw. Montague. 3. Sir John Digby.

Edmund Roper.

Germane Roper.

Cecilia, wife of Norton Green, Esq.

John Roper, 1st Baron Teynham, 1616; died Aug. 30, 1618. ⊤ Elizabeth, dau. and heir of John Parke, of Malmaine, co. Kent.

Anne, mar. Sir Robert Lovell (the Nuns' Records say Nicholas), Foundress of English Theresians at Antwerp, 1619.

Elizabeth, wife of George Vaux. (See No. XXI).

Christopher Roper, 2nd Baron, died April 16, 1622. ⊤ Catharine, dau. to John Sebourne, of Sutton St. Michael, co. Hereford.

Bridget Roper, mar. Sir Robert Hodleston, of Sawston, *called Mary by Burke*. (See No. II.)

Mary Roper, 3rd Abbess of E. B. at Ghent; died April 21, 1650.

Catharine Roper, wife of Sir Robert Thorold. (See No. VII.)

John Roper, 3rd Baron; died Feb. 27, 1627. ⊤ Mary, dau. of William Lord Petre.

Elizabeth, wife of Sir John Arundell, of Lanherne.

Mary, a nun O. S. B. Ghent.

Philadelphia, 2nd wife, dau. of Edward Knollys, of Grove Park, Hants. ⊤ Christopher Roper, 4th Baron; died 1673. ⊤ Mary, 1st wife, dau. of Sir Francis Englefield, of Wotton Basset.

Anne Roper, mar. Bernard Howard, Esq. grandson of Henry Earl of Arundel and Surrey.

Christopher Roper, 5th Baron; died 1688, at Brussels. ⊤ Elizabeth, dau. to Francis Lord Viscount Montagu.

John, died s. p.

Mary. Philadelphia. Nuns.

Catharine, wife of William Sheldon, Esq. (Addenda, No. X. p. 422.)

Frances, wife of Rowland Belasyse, younger son of Sir Rowland Belasyse.

John, 6th Baron, died 1688, s. p.

Christopher, 7th Baron, died 1697, s. p.

Henry Roper, 8th Baron.

II. HUDDLESTON.

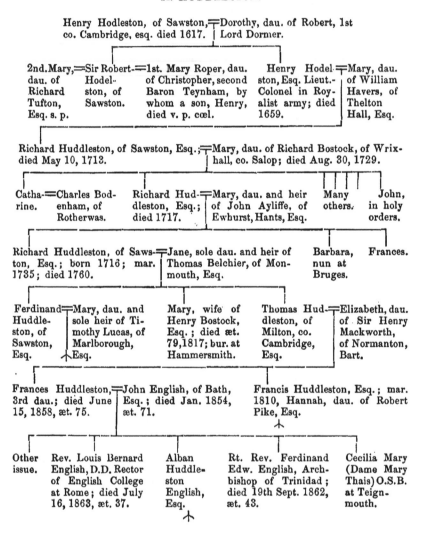

Henry Hodleston, of Sawston,⊤Dorothy, dau. of Robert, 1st
co. Cambridge, esq. died 1617. | Lord Dormer.

2nd. Mary,═Sir Robert-═1st. Mary Roper, dau.   Henry Hodel⊤Mary, dau.
dau. of   Hodel-   of Christopher, second   ston, Esq. Lieut.- | of William
Richard   ston, of   Baron Teynham, by   Colonel in Roy- | Havers, of
Tufton,   Sawston.   whom a son, Henry,   alist army; died | Thelton
Esq. s. p.   died v. p. cœl.   1659. | Hall, Esq.

Richard Huddleston, of Sawston, Esq.;⊤Mary, dau. of Richard Bostock, of Wrix-
died May 10, 1713. | hall, co. Salop; died Aug. 30, 1729.

Catha-═Charles Bod-   Richard Hud-⊤Mary, dau. and heir   Many   John,
rine.   enham, of   dleston, Esq.;| of John Ayliffe, of   others.   in holy
         Rotherwas.   died 1717. | Ewhurst, Hants, Esq.   orders.

Richard Huddleston, of Saws-⊤Jane, sole dau. and heir of   Barbara,   Frances.
ton, Esq.; born 1716; mar. | Thomas Belchier, of Mon-   nun at
1735; died 1760. | mouth, Esq.   Bruges.

Ferdinand⊤Mary, dau. and   Mary, wife of   Thomas Hud-⊤Elizabeth, dau.
Huddle- | sole heir of Ti- Henry Bostock,   dleston, of | of Sir Henry
ston, of | mothy Lucas, of   Esq.; died æt.   Milton, co. | Mackworth,
Sawston, | Marlborough,   79,1817; bur. at Cambridge, | of Normanton,
Esq.   ⋏Esq.   Hammersmith.   Esq. | Bart.

Frances Huddleston,⊤John English, of Bath,   Francis Huddleston, Esq.; mar.
3rd dau.; died June | Esq.; died Jan. 1854,   1810, Hannah, dau. of Robert
15, 1858, æt. 75. | æt. 71.   Pike, Esq.
                                                    ⋏

Other   Rev. Louis Bernard   Alban   Rt. Rev. Ferdinand   Cecilia Mary
issue.   English, D.D. Rector   Huddle-   Edw. English, Arch-   (Dame Mary
         of English College   ston   bishop of Trinidad;   Thais) O.S.B.
         at Rome; died July   English,   died 19th Sept. 1862, at Teign-
         16, 1863, æt. 37.   Esq.   æt. 43.   mouth.
                                  ⋏

III. HENEAGE.

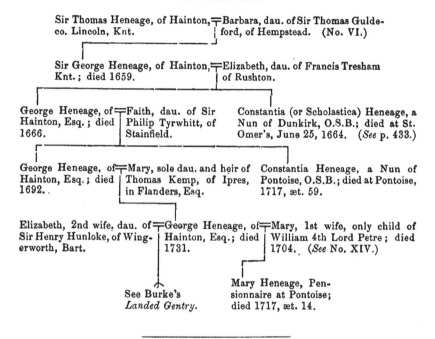

Sir Thomas Heneage, of Hainton,⹋Barbara, dau. of Sir Thomas Gulde-
co. Lincoln, Knt. | ford, of Hempstead. (No. VI.)

Sir George Heneage, of Hainton,⹋Elizabeth, dau. of Francis Tresham
Knt. ; died 1659. | of Rushton.

George Heneage, of⹋Faith, dau. of Sir   Constantia (or Scholastica) Heneage, a
Hainton, Esq. ; died | Philip Tyrwhitt, of   Nun of Dunkirk, O.S.B.; died at St.
1666. | Stainfield.   Omer's, June 25, 1664. (*See* p. 433.)

George Heneage, of⹋Mary, sole dau. and heir of   Constantia Heneage, a Nun of
Hainton, Esq.; died | Thomas Kemp, of Ipres,   Pontoise, O.S.B.; died at Pontoise,
1692. . | in Flanders, Esq.   1717, æt. 59.

Elizabeth, 2nd wife, dau. of⹋George Heneage, of⹋Mary, 1st wife, only child of
Sir Henry Hunloke, of Wing- | Hainton, Esq.; died | William 4th Lord Petre ; died
erworth, Bart. | 1731. | 1704. (*See* No. XIV.)

See Burke's   Mary Heneage, Pen-
Landed Gentry.   sionnaire at Pontoise;
    died 1717, æt. 14.

IV. GREENE, FITZROY, AND FITZCHARLES.

Rooke Greene, of Little Sandford, co. Essex,⹋Eleanor, dau. of Wm. Fitch,
Esq.; died 9 April, 1602. | of Little Canfield.

William Greene, died⹋Katharine, dau. of Thos. Timperley, of
11 July, 1621. | Hintlesham. [*See* No. V.]

John Greene, born 14 Sept. 1575;⹋Frances, dau. of Sir John Russell, of
ob. vit. pat. | Strensham, co. Worcester.

1st wife, Jeronima, dau.⹋Sir Edward⹋2nd wife, Mary, dau.⹋3rd wife, Anne, dau.
of Sir Wm. Everard, of | Greene, cre- | of .... Tas- | of Sir George Sim-
Linstead. | ated Ba- | burgh. | mons.
     | ronet 1660. |

Six daughters.   Barbara ⟍ KING ⟍ Katharine, dau.⹋Sir Edward   Eugenia
    Duchess ⟍ CHARLES ⟍ of Mr. Thomas | Greene,   Greene,
    of Cleve- ⟍ THE ⟍ Pegge, of Yel- | died in   a nun O.
    land. ⟍ SECOND. ⟍ dersley. (See | Flanders   S. B. of
                   note in p. 414.) | 1676.   Pontoise.

Benedicta Fitzroy, born   Charlotte or Katharine Fitz-   Justina Greene,   Two other
1672; died Prioress of   Charles or Fitzroy (Dame   a nun O.S.B. at   daugh-
Hotel Dieu at Pontoise,   Cecilia), O. S. B. at Dun-   Pontoise; died   ters.
May, 1737.   kirk; died 1759, very aged.   1717, æt. 50.

2 E 2

V. TIMPERLEY.

Thomas Timperley, of Hintlesham, Suffolk;=Awdry, dau. and heir of Sir Nicholas
died 1600; bur. at Hintlesham. | Hare, of Burford, Knt.

Katherine Tim-=Wm. Greene, of Little   Nicholas Timper-=Anne, dau. and coh. of
perley.   Sandford.   ley, of Hintles- | William Markham, of
[*See* No. IV.]   ham, esq. | Little Oakley, Esq.

Sir Thomas Tim-=Elizabeth, dau. of Sir John   Lucy Timperley, wife of Antony
perley, of Hintle- | Shelley, of Michelgrove, co.   Bedingfield, of Scots, co. Suf-
sham, Knt. | Sussex; died 1611.   folk.

Michael or=Frances, dau.   Nicholas.   Anne and Ellen: one of them was probably
Thomas | of Sir Henry   Elizabeth Timperley, 2nd Superior of the
Timper- | Bedingfield.   Blue Nuns or Conceptionists of Faubourg
ley.   St. Antoine at Paris.

Sir Thomas Timperley.   Justina, a nun O. S. B. at Pontoise.

VI. GULDEFORD, AND GIFFORD.

Sir Thomas Guldeford, of Hempstead,=Elizabeth, dau. of John Shelley, of
co. Kent.   Died June 15, 1575. | Michelgrove, co. Sussex, Esq.

Elizabeth, wife of   Sir Henry=Lady Elizabeth Somerset,   Barbara, wife of Sir
Thomas Gage, of   Gulde- | dau. of Edward Earl of   Thomas Heneage, of
Firle, Esq.   ford, Knt.| Worcester.   Hainton. *See* No. III.

Edward Gul-=Catharine, dau. of   Robert=Catha-   Sir Henry =Mary, dau.
deford, of | Thomas Petre, Esq.   Gulde- rine   Gifford, of | of Baynham
Hempstead, | son of John 1st   ford. Gif-   Burstall, co.| Vaughan, of
Esq. | Lord Petre.   ford.   Leic. Bart. | Ruerdean, Esq.

Mary, wife of Sir Samuel   Edward=Anne, dau.   Elizabeth, wife of   Lady Abbess
Tuke, of Cressing Tem-   Gulde- | of Sir Robt. John Brooke, of   *Anne Xaveria*
ple, co. Essex, Bart.   ford, of| Throck-   Madeley, co. Sa-   and *Dame*
Catharine, wife of Thomas   Hemp- | morton, of   lop; their dau.   *Mary Maura,*
Bodenham, of Rother-   stead, | Coughton,   Mary Brooke, O.   both nuns
was; their dau. Anne   esq.; | Bart.   S. B. at Pontoise, O. S. B. at
Bodenham, O. S. B. at   died   died 1714, æt. 57.   Pontoise.
Pontoise, d.1717, æt. 51.   1678.   (*See* p. 61.)

VII. THOROLD.

Dorothy, dau. of Thomas Leeke, Esq., of Hallom, Notts; 1st wife. = William Thorold, Lord of Marston and Blank-ney, co. Lin; died Nov. 24, 1569. = Mary, lau. of Sir Robert Hussey, of Linwood, co. Lin; 2nd wife.

Margaret, dau. of Sir Anthony Tho- = Anne, dau. and coheir of Sir John 1. Sir Edmund Tho- = Eleanor, dau. 2. Robert Tho- = Agnes, dau.
Henry Sutton, Esq. rold, Sff of Mo, of Kinalton, 2nd wife; rld, Kt. of the High and coheir of rold, of the and coheir
of Wellingore, co. Lincol ire 13 by whom a daughter Winifred mar. Hall, in Haugh, co. William de Low Hall, of William
Lincoln; 1st wife. Eliz. George Clifton, Esq. of Clifton. Li rdn. ley, of Haugh. Haugh. Audeley.

Martha, My, 1. Thomas = Anne, dau. of Sir 2. Wil- Frances, 4. Sir = Alice, Alexan- = Christian, Antho- = Catharine, Wini-
wife of wife of Thorold; rpe Pierpoint, of liam du. of John Tho- dau. and der Tho- dau. of Ro- ny Tho- dau. of fred,
Sir Philip John died s. p. Holme Pierpoint; Ta- Sir Ro- rd, Kt. heir of rld, rd, of nyTho- rold, of Edward 2nd wife
Tyrwhitt, M- m.; his two mar. 2nd Francis rold, bert Tyr- of Co- Tmas bert Bru- the Hasel- of Robert
Kt. of rn, Esq. daughters Beaumont, of ace Esq. witt, ringham Cranham well, of High Maidwell- wood, of Mark-
Stain- of Sedge- died in his Dieu, co. Kt. of and Cranmer, Hall; Doding- Low ham, of
field. nk. time. died 1598. Kettleby. Cawnton. of Aslac- died ton, Hall. Maidwell. Cotham.
ton. 1616. Hunts.

Sir Wil- = Anne, dau. Sir An- = Elizabeth, Two Martha, Edmund Tho- = Jane Sir Robert Tho- = Katharine Ro-
liam of John thony dau. of Tho- other mar. Joshua rold, of Thorold. rold, created per, dau. of
Tho- Blytlie, Tho- mas Moly- daugh- Whichcote, Haugh; died a Baronet Christopher
rold. Esq. of rold, neux, of ters. of Haver- 31 August, 14 June, 2nd Lord
Grantham. Kt. Haughton. tte. 1653. 1644. Teynham.

A daugh- Sir William Thorold, = Anne, dau. of Lady Eugenia Tho- Sir Robert Tho- = Catharine, dau.
MaryThorold, mar. 1629 ter died of Haugh; knighted by Sir Charles rold, Abbess of Pon- rold, Bart. of of Henry Knol-
to William Lord Wid- unmar- Sir Wil- Charles II. 1666. Dalison, Kt. toise; died 1667, Heath; died lys, of Grove
drington; slain at Wigan ried. liam æt. 44. 1695. Place, Hants.
in royal cause 1651. Tho-
rold. Their son died an infant.

(See No. XX.) Anne Catharine, O. S. B. at Pontoise; died 1707, æt. 54.   Sir Robert Thorold, Bart.; died s. p. 1706.

VIII. HUNLOKE.

Margaret, dau. of═Henry Hunloke,═Edith, dau. of Sir Lionel Reresby,
Nicholas Walker, | Esq.; died 1612. and widow of George Markham,
Esq. | Esq.; died s. p.

Henry Hunloke, of Wingerworth, Esq.;═2nd wife, Anne, dau. of Richard Alvey, of
died 17 Aug. 1624. Corber, co. Derby.

Sir Henry Hunloke, created Bart.;═Mariana, dau. of Dixey Hickman,
1642; died 1648. of Kew, Esq.

Sir Henry Hunloke,═Catharine, only dau. and | Thomas Windsor Hun- | Mariana,
2nd Bart.; died | heir of Francis Tyrwhitt, | loke; died at Trèves, | O. S. B. at
1715. | of Kettleby. | 1672. | Brussels.

Sir Thomas Windsor | Elizabeth, 2nd wife | Lady Marina, Abbess of E. B. at
Hunloke, 3d Bart.; | of George Heneage, | Pontoise; educated at Hammer-
died 1752. | of Hainton, Esq. | smith with two sisters, who died
⋏ | [No. III.] | cœl. (See p. 62.)
 | ⋏ |

IX. MONTAGUE.

Sir Edward Montague, Lord Chief Justice═3rd wife, Eleanor, dau. of
of King's Bench; died 1557. | John Roper; died 1563.

Elizabeth Montague, mar. 1st | Sir Edward═Elizabeth, dau. | Eleanor Monta-
Richard Cave; 2nd, William | Montague, | of Sir James | gue, ma. George
Markham, of Little Oakley; | died 1602. | Harrington, of | Tyrrell, of
their dau. Anne, mar. Nicho- | | Exton, Knt.; | Thornton.
las Timperley. [No. V.] | | died 1618. |

Sir Edward M. | Sir Henry Mon-═1st wife, Catharine, dau. | James, Bishop of Bath
created Lord | tague,1st Earl of | of Sir William Spencer, | and Wells, then of
Montague. | Manchester. | of Yarnton; died 1612. | Winton; died 1618.
⋎ |
The Dukes of | Walter, second son, Abbot of St. Martin's, Pontoise
Montagu. | (see p. 55); died 1670.

ADDENDA TO SHELDON PEDIGREE (IN THE OPPOSITE PAGE).

Edward Sheldon, etc.═Mary, dau. of Lionel Wake, etc.

Ralph Sheldon, equerry═Elizabeth, dau. of | Magdalen Sheldon, | Teresa Sheldon, a
to James II.; died in | Daniel Dunn, of | a nun, O. S. D. at | nun O. S. A. at
France in 1723, æt. 90. | West Heath, co. | Brussels; died in | Louvaine; died in
 | Worcester. | 1699, æt. 59. | 1724, æt. 84.

Hon. Catherine Roper, dau. of═William Sheldon, only son,═Anastasia, dau. of Bar-
Christopher 5th Lord Teyn- | of Ditchford and Winchester, | tholomew Smith, Esq.;
ham (see No. I.); d. 1714. | Esq.; d. 19 Sep. 1748, æt. 74. | ob. 11 March, 1744-5.

Catharine Sheldon, a | Mary Sheldon, sometime a | Three | Elizabeth Sheldon, a
nun O. S. B. at Cam- | novice at Dunkirk, but was | sons. | nun O. S. B. at Cam-
bray; died in 1763, | professed a nun O. S. B. at | | bray; died July 14,
Sept. 22. | Cambray, where she d. in | | 1808, æt. 89.
 | 1756. | |

Edward Sheldon, of Beoley,=Elizabeth, eldest dau. of Thomas Markham, of Ollerton
co. Worcester.   and Kirby Bellars, Esq.

2. Ralph Shel-=Bridget, dau. of An- | Jane Sheldon, mar. | 1. William Sheldon, | =Elizabeth, dau. of | 3.Edward Sheldon,=Mary, dau. of Lionel
don, of Steeple | tony Morgan, of Hey- | Sir Henry Appleton, | born 1588-9; died | Wm. 2nd Lord | born 1599; died | Wake, of Antwerp,
Barton, co. Ox- | wood, co. Northamp- | of Jarvis Hall, co. | 1659. | Petre, of Writ- | 1687, æt. 88. | and Peddington, co.
ford. | ton; died 1670. | Essex, 2nd Bart. | | tle. [No. XIV.] | | Northampton.

Edward =Catharine, | Ralph=Sin, | Henrietta | Katharine, mar. Edmund | Edward | Ralph Sen. | Katha- | Mary Sheldon, mar. Sir Samuel
Sheldon, | dau. of | Shin, | aMa, | Ren, Esq. "The | Sheldon, | (See opposite page.) | rine | Tke, of Cressing Temple, 2d Bt.;
of Stee- | Philip | of Wes- | dau. of | Auncient Mrs. Pu- | of O. S. | Dominick, General | Shel- | Lady Tke was Lady-in-waiting
ple Bar- | Constable, | ton; bo. | Thas | den." | B. at | in French army. | don, | to Katharine of Braganza, and
ton; bo. | of Ever- | 1623; | Sant | Faith, bo. 1619; mar. | Douay; | Rev. Lionel, O. S. B. | living | followed her to Portugal; thir
1624; | ingham, | died | Rock- | Sir Thas Gacoigne, 3rd | died | Chaplain to the | 1704. | only son, Sir Charles, died of
died | co. York; | 1684 | Savage; | of Barnborough, | Apr.16, | Duchess of York; | Tke | wounds received at the Battle of
1676. | died 1681. | s. p. | d. 1663. | Bart. | 1685. | died 1678. | in p. | the Boyne, Aug. 10, 1690.
 | | | | | | Edward. | 427.

Ralph Sen, of=Mary Anne, dau. of | Mary Sheldon, a | Elizabeth, O. S. A. at Louvaine; | Philip
Steeple Barton | Humphrey Eliot, | nun, O. S. A. at | died 1685. | Sheldon.
and Wm; died | Esq.; died Nov. 9, | Louvaine; died | Anne Sheldon.
1720. | 1707. | 1727, æt. 66. | Frances Sheldon.

Ralph Sel- | Edward Shel-=Elizabeth, dau. of | Katharine Shel- | Frances Shel-=Simon Scrope, | Margaret Scrope,
len, S. J.; | don, born | Sir John Shelley, | don, O. S. B. at | don, 2nd | of Danby, co. | mar. John Mes-
died at | 1679; died | of Michelgrove; | Dunkirk; died | wife; died | York, Esq.; | senger, of Foun-
Liege,1741. | 1746. | died 1766. | 1717. | 1733. | died 1723. | tains Abbey, Esq.

Henry Shel- | Edward Sheldon, born | 1. Catherine, | 2. Mary, a nun | 3. Barbara? a | Frances, mar. 1. | Dame Mary
don, S. J.; | in 1716; a priest. | a nun O.S.B. | O. S. B.at Dun- | nun O. S. B. | Henry Fermor, | Anne Scrope,
died at Rome, | Ralph Sheldon, a mer- | at Ghent; | kirk; died at | at Dunkirk; | of Tusmore, | O. S. B,
1756. | chant; died cœlebs. | died 1791, | Hammersmith | died 1784-5, | Esq.; 2. Sir | Dunkirk,
 | Henry Sheldon, ob. | æt. 75. | Convent 1798, | aged 60. | George Browne, | died before
 | cœlebs. | | æt. 78. | | Bart.; died 1790. | 1759.

William=Margaret Frances,
Shel- | dau. of James
don, | Rooke, of Bigs-
born | were, Esq.; died
1715; | 1776.
d. 1780.

Seven sons. Margaret Frances, wife of Hon. Francis Talbot, of Witham Place, son of 14th Earl of Shrewsbury.

XII. WALDEGRAVE AND FITZ-JAMES.

Sir Edward Waldegrave, of Boreley. Essex;⊤Frances, dau. of Sir Edward Neville,
   died 1561. æt. 44, a prisoner in the Tower. | " Baron Bergavenny."

Catharine Walde-	2. Charles⊤Jeronima,	1. Nicholas	Magdalen Waldegrave,
grave, wife of	Walde-	dau. of Sir	Waldegrave,	wife of Sir John South-
Thomas Gawen, of	grave,	Henry	mar. Catha-	cote, of Witham; their
Norrington, Wilts;	Esq.	Jerning-	rine, dau. of	dau. Elizabeth South-
their dau. *Dame*		ham, of	Wistan	cote, O. S. B. at Brus-
Frances Gawen, 1st		Cossey	Browne, of	sels, died 1631.
Abbess of E. B. of		Hall.	Abbot's Ro-	Mary Waldegrave, wife
Cambray, d. 1640.			ding.	of John 1st Lord Petre.

Sir Edward Waldegrave,⊤1st wife, Eleanor, dau. of Sir Thos.
   created a Bart. 1643. | Lovell, of Harling, co. Norfolk.

2nd wife, Catharine, dau.⊤Sir Henry Waldegrave,⊤1st wife, Anne, dau. of Edward
of Richard Bacon, gent. | died 1658, æt. 60. | Paston, of Appleton, Esq.

Six sons and	Theodosia Waldegrave,	Sir Charles.⊤Eleanor, dau. of Sir	Six other
five other	Abbess of E. B. at Brus-		Francis Englefield,	sons and
daughters.	sels; died 1719, æt. 71.		of Englefield.	four daus.

KING JAMES II.⊤Arabella Churchill.

Ignatia Fitz-   Henrietta⊤Sir Henry Walde-
James, O.S.B.   Fitz- | grave, died 1689,
at Pontoise.   James. | at Paris.

James, 1st Earl Waldegrave.   Arabella, a nun.

XIII. TICHBORNE.

Sir Benjamin Tichborne, of Tichborne, Sheriff of⊤Amphillis, dau. of Richard
Hampshire 1603; created Bart. 1620; died 1629. | Weston, Esq. of Skreenes,
(Epitaph in Gent. Mag. Apr. 1810.) | [No. XV.]

liza-	Sir Ben-	Sir ⊤Mary, dau.	Sir Richard⊤1 w. Ellen,	Sir Henry⊤Jane,	Anne
eth	jamin,	Wal-	and coh. of	T. ma. 2 w.	dau. and	T. died	dau.	T. m
·ma.	died s. p.	ter,	Robert	Susan, dau.	coh. of Ro-	1667, 4th	of Sir	1 W
at	3rd son.	2nd	White, of	and coh. of	bert White,	son.	Robt.	Broc
¹obert		son.	Aldershot.	Wm. Wal-	of Alder-		New-	2 Sir
arth,				ler, of Old-	shot.		comen	Wm.
sq.;		Francis Tichborne,	stoke, Esq.			Bart.	Tim-
nd,		of Aldershot and				died	per·
Villiam		Frimley, Esq. an-				1664.	ley.
wen,		cestor of the pre-					
sq.		sent Baronet.		TICHBORNE of Beau-	
				lieu, co. Louth.	

usan,	Anne, wife of Charles	Sir Henry Tich-⊤Mary, dau. of the Hon.	Amphillis, wi
ied	Tasburgh, of Flixton,	borne, 3d Bart.	William Arundell, of	of Sir Lawrenc
œl.	co. Suffolk, Esq.		Horningsham, Wilts.	Hyde, Knt.

¹ary Anne, O. S. B.	Lettice, mar. Henry	Sir Henry Joseph Tich-	Sir John Hermengil
ᵗ Pontoise; died	Whetenhall, of	borne, 4th Bart.; ob.	T. 5th Bart.; a pries
⁷34, æt. 78.	Peckham, Kent.	s. p. m. 1743.	S. J.; d. at Ghent 174

XIV. PETRE OF INGATESTONE.

John Petre, 1st Lord Petre, of Ingatestone.=Mary, dau. of Sir Edward Waldegrave, of Boreley.

1. William Petre, 2nd Lord; died 1637.=Catherine, 2nd dau. of Edward Somerset, Earl of Worcester.

2. John Petre, of West Henyngfield; died Jan. 2, 1622-3.=Catherine, dau. of William Lord Morley and Monteagle.

3. Thomas Petre, of Cranham, Essex; died Oct. 3, 1625.=Elizabeth, dau. of William Baskerville, of Wanborough, Wilts.

Robert Petre, 3rd Lord; died Oct. 23, 1638.=Mary, dau. of Anthony Browne, Viscount Montague.

Six other sons.

Mary, mar. John Roper, Lord Teynham.

Elizabeth, mar. William Caryll, Esq. of Harting.

1. Sir Francis Petre, Knt. of Cranham.=Elizabeth, dau. of Sir John Petre, Knt. of Cranham.

Catharine Petre, mar. Edward Gage, of Firle, Bart.

2. William Petre, of Stanford Rivers and Belhouse; born 1602; died 1677.=Joy, dau. of Sir Ferdinando, Knt.; died 1679.

Eliza=beth, 1st wife, dau. of Thomas Pordage, Esq.

John Petre, of Fidlers, co. Essex, Esq.=Elizabeth, 2nd wife, dau. of John Pincheon, Esq. of Writtle.

Seven sons. (a)

Two daughters.

2. John, 5th Lord; died cœl. 1684.=1. Elizabeth Savage, 1st wife, dau. of John Earl Rivers; died s. p.

Wm. Petre, 4th Lord; died in the Tower 1683.=Bridget, 2nd wife, dau. of John Pincheon, Esq. of Writtle.

3. Thomas, 6th Lord.=Mary, dau. of Sir Thomas Clifton, of Lytham.

John Petre.=Mary, dau. of Sir Francis Mannock, of Gifford's Hall.

Robert Petre, a Priest S. J.; died July 17, 1726, æt. 60.

Thomas Petre, a Priest S. J.; died Sept. 7, 1729, æt. 66.

John Petre, a Priest S. J.; died Aug. 9, 1738, æt. 77.

Mary, sole child, born 1697; mar. George Heneage, of Hainton, Esq. [No. III.]

Dame Mary Petre, O.S.B.Pontoise; died 1733, æt. 70.

Winifred, Anne, } Nuns. George.

Catharine, 1st wife, dau. of Sir William Andrew, Bart.=1st Joseph Petre, died 1721.=2. Dorothy Throckmorton.

(a) Edward Petre (the celebrated "Father Petre," Clerk of the Closet to James II.), the eldest of these seven sons, was born in London in 1631 ("ex familia prænobili primogenitus"), joined the Society of Jesus in 1652, and died on May 15, 1699, æt. 68. His younger brother Charles was also a Priest S. J., and died in 1712.

XV. WESTON, EARL OF PORTLAND.

Richard Weston,of Skreenes, Judge⊤1st wife, Wilburga, dau. of Michael Catesby,
of the Common Pleas; died 1572. │   of Seaton, co. Northampton.

Amphillis, mar. Sir Benj.   Sir Jerome Weston, of Skreenes,⊤Mary, dau. of Anthony
Tichborne, Bart. [No.   parish of Roxwell, Essex, Knt. ; │ Cave, of Chicheley.
XIII.]   died 1603.

1st wife, Eliza-⊤Sir Richard Weston, of Skreenes,⊤2nd wife, Fran-   Dorothy Wes-
beth, dau. of │ Lord High Treasurer; created │ ces, dau. of Ni-   ton, mar. Sir
William Pin- │ Baron of Stoke Nayland and │ cholas Walde-   Edward Pincheon, of Writ- │ Earl of Portland ; died 1635, │ grave, of Bore- cheon, of
tle, Esq.   │ æt. 57.   │ ley. [No. XII.]   Writtle.

Mary Weston, mar.   Nicholas.   Anne, mar. Basil Lord   Jerome⊤Frances
Walter, son of Lord   Benjamin, mar.   Feilding.   Wes- dau. of
Aston of Forfar.   Elizabeth Shel-   Frances, mar. Philip   ton, Esmé
Richard Weston, died don ; died s. p.   Draycote, of Paynes-   2nd   Stuart
s. p., v. p.   mas.   ley, co. Stafford.   Earl of D'Aubig-
Elizabeth Weston, m. Mary, died cœl.   Catharine, ma. Richard   Port- ny, D. of
Sir John Netterville, Thomas, fourth   White, of Hutton, Es-   land. Lenox
s. and h. of Nicholas Earl ; died cœl.   sex; died 1645, bur.   and
Viscount Netterville.   at Rome.   Rich-
A daughter.   mond.

Charles, 3rd Earl,   Henrietta-Maria. ⎫
fell in naval action   Frances.   ⎬ All Nuns.
with the Dutch, s.p.   Katharine.
1665.   Elizabeth.   ⎭

In the Records of the Poor Clares of Rouen *(Les Gravelines)* are mentioned
" tres filiæ Comitissæ Portlandiæ " amongst the foundresses of the Convent in 1651,
" unà cum tribus Dominæ Gage, quarum omnium quatuor postea in eodem parthe-
none monasticam vitam amplexæ sunt." They were daughters of the second Earl, as
appears from Dugdale's MS. additions to his *Baronage*, printed in the *Collectanea
Topogr. et Genealogica*, vol. ii. p. 332.

Richard Weston, of Skreens (whose name heads this pedigree), used as his armorial
bearings,—Ermine, on a chief azure five bezants, with a martlet for difference. His
grandson Sir Richard Weston, on being elevated to the peerage, adopted a different
coat, viz. Or, an eagle regardant and displayed sable. The first coat decorates the
monument of Sir Benjamin Tichborne, in Tichborne church, A.D. 1621, and the
second occurs on the monument of the first Earl, in Winchester cathedral, A. D. 1635..

XVI. SMITH ALIAS CARINGTON, AND PHILPOTT.

John Carington changed his name from Carington to Smyth, in order to escape the resentment of King Henry IV., on having taken part with the Earls of Huntingdon, Salisbury, and Kent. Returning to England from the Low Countries, whither he had fled, he was courteously entertained and provided for by his kinsman the Abbot of St. Osyth, in Essex. His descendant

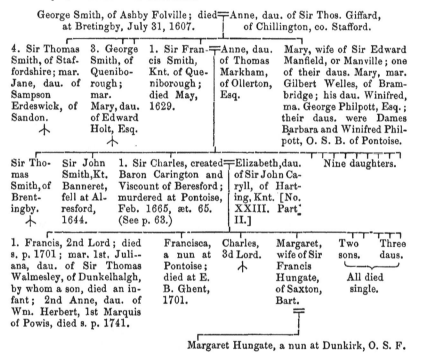

George Smith, of Ashby Folville; died at Bretingby, July 31, 1607. = Anne, dau. of Sir Thos. Giffard, of Chillington, co. Stafford.

4. Sir Thomas Smith, of Staffordshire; mar. Jane, dau. of Sampson Erdeswick, of Sandon.

3. George Smith, of Queniborough; mar. Mary, dau. of Edward Holt, Esq.

1. Sir Francis Smith, Knt. of Queniborough; died May, 1629. = Anne, dau. of Thomas Markham, of Ollerton, Esq.

Mary, wife of Sir Edward Manfield, or Manville; one of their daus. Mary, mar. Gilbert Welles, of Brambridge; his dau. Winifred, ma. George Philpott, Esq.; their daus. were Dames Barbara and Winifred Philpott, O. S. B. of Pontoise.

Sir Thomas Smith, of Brentingby.

Sir John Smith, Knt. Banneret, fell at Alresford, 1644.

1. Sir Charles, created Baron Carington and Viscount of Beresford; murdered at Pontoise, Feb. 1665, æt. 65. (See p. 63.) = Elizabeth, dau. of Sir John Caryll, of Harting, Knt. [No. XXIII. Part II.]

Nine daughters.

1. Francis, 2nd Lord; died s. p. 1701; mar. 1st, Juliana, dau. of Sir Thomas Walmesley, of Dunkelhalgh, by whom a son, died an infant; 2nd Anne, dau. of Wm. Herbert, 1st Marquis of Powis, died s. p. 1741.

Francisca, a nun at Pontoise; died at E. B. Ghent, 1701.

Charles, 3d Lord.

Margaret, wife of Sir Francis Hungate, of Saxton, Bart. =

Two sons.

Three daus.

All died single.

Margaret Hungate, a nun at Dunkirk, O. S. F.

Note to p. 423.—Katharine Sheldon, daughter of Edward Sheldon and Mary Wake, was living in London in 1694 and in 1704, when she was called Mrs. Catherine Sheldon. It also appears that she was sometimes called *Mrs. Catherine Stevens*, for instance in 1698. She lived in troublesome times, and her family were staunch supporters of James II.; consequently it was expedient for her to shield herself under an assumed name at times, more especially as she was continually engaged in sheltering and rendering assistance to the poor and persecuted priests of the Catholic church.—(*Communicated by Francis Joseph Baigent, esq. of Winchester.*)

XVII. SALVIN, AND STRICKLAND.

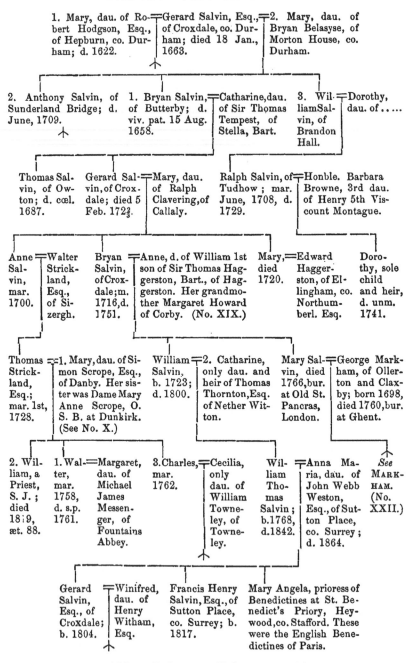

(These Pedigrees will be continued.)

ANGLO-AMERICAN COAT-ARMOUR.

(Continued from p. 265.)

The Heraldic Journal; recording the Armorial Bearings and Genealogies of American Families. Nos. I.—XI. Boston (Massachusetts.) 8vo. Published monthly.

The old burying ground at Dorchester in Massachusetts contains four monuments that are decorated with armorial bearings. The earliest in date bears the following inscription :

HERE LIETH BURIED YE BODY OF

MR. WILLIAM POOLE, AGED 81 YEARS,

WHO DIED YE 25TH OF FEBRVARY, IN

YE YEARE 1674.

The sister of this gentleman was the chief promoter of the settlement at Taunton in Massachusetts : and on a monument which was erected to his memory in 1771 she was described as "of good family, friends, and prospects." The coat, semée de lis and a lion rampant, has been borne, differently tinctured, by several families of Poole or Pole; and, as the carving gives no tinctures, this coat can afford no information unassisted by other evidence. But should such evidence be found, the mullet, as the distinction of the third house, may prove a valuable confirmation.

On the tomb of WILLIAM STOUGHTON, Esq. sometime Governor of Massachusetts, and Chief Justice of the Higher Court, and still more celebrated as the Founder of the Stoughton College—his highly eulogistic Latin epitaph is placed before us, showing that he died in 1701,—is carved the atchievement here represented. We find its blason thus given, as for *Stoughton of Kent :* Argent, on a saltire gules between four tenter-hooks—*aliter* door staples—sable an escallop or. The lion holding an escallop in the Crest is engraved minus his legs, because they are perished in the stone.   In Berry's

Kentish Genealogies a family of Stoughton, which was resident at Ashe near Sandwich, is commemorated,[1] and carried up (through two generations) to Sir John Stoughton, Lord Mayor: but the only Lord Mayor of such a name, Sir John Stocton in 1471, had the very different coat of Gules, a chevron vaire argent and sable between three mullets of the second.

The next shield accompanies these lines :

· Here lyeth yᵉ body of WILL. ROYALL, of North Yarmouth, in the Province of Maine, who departed this life Novᵇʳᵉ 7th, 1724, in yᵉ 85th year of his age.   This stone is erected to yᵉ Pious

Memory of his Father by his eldest son Isaac, as a last act of dutifull remembrance." After which follows a much longer commemoration of "the Honᵇˡᵉ Isaac Royall, Esq." (the son) who died at his seat in Charleston, June 7, 1739, aged 67. Williamson in his *History of Maine*, i. 692, has noticed one generation still higher : William Royall, of Casco, 1636, who purchased land at Wescustogo, now Royall's River, in North Yarmouth : and was in the same year an Assistant under William Gorges's administration of New Somersetshire. Isaac, the grandson, was a member of Council for twenty-six years ; and founded the first law professorship at Harvard university. Being a Loyalist, he fled to England ; and died here in 1781: his sister marrying Henry Vassall, and his daughters respectively Thomas Savel and Sir William (Sparhawk) Pepperrell. Further particulars of the family will be found in the *History of Medford*, Massachusetts, 1855.   We are unable to find, however, any blason for the shield of the three garbs. ·

The fourth shield at Dorchester, that upon the monument of Mr. JAMES FOSTER, we have already introduced in p. 261.

---

[1] See also Mr. Planché's recent History of that Parish.

One of the early settlers in Massachusetts was SAMUEL SYMONDS, uncle to the Cavalier Richard whose valuable *Diary* was printed for the Camden Society in 1859. To that volume is prefixed the family pedigree, derived from the same author's MS. Collections for the county of Essex, which are preserved in the College of Arms. It traces the ancestry of Richard the antiquary's grandfather, through six generations, resident in the counties of Salop and Stafford, up to John Symonds of Croft, co. Lancaster, and his wife a daughter of Sir William Lording. Richard Symonds the grandfather was one of the Cursitors of the Chancery, and so were all his three elder sons, John, Edward, and Samuel. Edward, the second of them, was the father of the antiquary. Samuel (writes his nephew in his pedigree,) " bought y⁰ place in Toppesfield in Essex called Olivers ¹, 100*l.* per ann." but afterwards " went into New England." He had married for his first wife Dorothy, daughter of Thomas Harlakenden of Earl's Colne : and her cousin Roger Harlakenden also went out to New England in 1635. By Dorothy, Samuel Symonds had a son Richard, " student of Greyes Inn," and four other children, " Dorothy, Samuel, Harlakenden, and Elizabeth, which he carried with him to New England."

The American genealogists have ascertained that Samuel Symonds had subsequently two more wives. His second is clearly shown by *The Winthrop Papers* to have been Martha, daughter of Edmund Reede, of Wickford in Essex, and widow of Daniel Epes : by her he had probably three or four children.

His third wife, to whom he was a fourth husband, was Rebecca, daughter of Bennett Swayne, of a family long seated near Salisbury. Her will, on file at Salem in Massachusetts, bears a seal with the arms of Swayne, Azure, a chevron between three pheons or. A pedigree of her family will be found in Sir Richard C. Hoare's *South Wiltshire*, Addenda, p. 49.

The arms of Symonds are drawn in the Harleian MS. 1542, with this testimonial :

The auntient Armes of Richard Symonds of Great Yeldham, in com. Essex, son of John Symonds of Newport, in com. Salop, gent. wᵗʰ the guifte of this creaste; all wᶜʰ Sʳ Ri. St. George, Knt. Clarenceux King of Armes, exemplified by L'res pattent, dated in the First year of King Charles the xᵗʰ day of January aᵒ 1625, to the said Richard Symonds and to his posterity for ever.

---

¹ Oliver's, from a previous owner : see Morant, *History of Essex*, ii. 362. The name is misprinted Olmers in *Symonds's Diary*. In the *Heraldic Journal* a note is added, " He more probably inherited it." What may have suggested this remark we do not know, but we should presume that his nephew Richard must have written upon competent knowledge.

Richard Symonds resided at the Poole, an ancient seat in the parish of Great Yeldham, and married Elizabeth, second daughter of Robert Plume of Great Yeldham Hall, gentleman. She died in 1611, and he in 1627; and both were buried in Yeldham church, where their figures in brass still remain, accompanied by a shield of arms: Quarterly, 1 and 4. Azure, a chevron engrailed between three trefoils slipped or; 2. Three eagles displayed; 3. On a bend three eaglets displayed; impaling, Ermine, a bend vaire or and gules, cotised vert, for Plume. The crest of Symonds is, Out of a mural crown or, a boar's head argent, tusked or.

The *Heraldic Journal* is continued monthly with regularity. Its latter numbers have contained a variety of interesting articles, upon several of which we shall hereafter make remarks; particularly the series of the Seals of the Governors of New England.

There is a curious account of an herald-painter named John Coles, who, with his son, is said to have produced the greater part of the armorial paintings now extant in New England, and " it is evident established a fashion for these pictures." It is related by the Rev. Dr. Jenks of Boston, who knew him well, that—

Mr. Coles's authorities for his drawings of coats of arms were very scanty, being, as I have supposed, confined to Gwillim's folio volume. And he was in the habit of giving arms to applicants, whenever he found them assigned in that book to the family name of his employer, without much, if any, genealogical research or inquiry. If no crest were found in Gwillim, he did not hesitate to raise on the torse our national flag. His charge for furnishing such drawings, of folio size, was, I recollect, a guinea.

The career of this artist was closed about half a century ago: that of his son, John Coles junior, in 1826.

The *Gore Roll of Arms*, which is printed in Parts VIII and IX. and furnishes ninety-nine examples of arms, appears to have been the compilation of an earlier trader in such distinctions. It was the work either of John or Samuel Gore at the beginning of the last century, or perhaps was partly filled by others of the family; for successive generations seem to have been carpenters and housewrights, sometimes employed to paint a carriage, sometimes to engrave coffin-plates, and supply hatchments and funeral banners. The earliest dates the roll contains are 1701 and 1702, the latest is 1724. It is valuable as bearing testimony to contemporary usage, though otherwise of insufficient authority.

THE HISTORY OF CLERKENWELL.

The History of Clerkenwell. By the late William J. Pinks, Author of "Country Trips," "Curiosities of Clocks and Watches," "The Streets of Clerkenwell," &c. With additions by the Editor, Edward J. Wood. Illustrated with nearly two hundred Engravings [on wood]. London: published by the Proprietor, J. T. Pickburn, Myddelton House, Myddelton Street, Clerkenwell, E.C. 1865. 8vo. pp. xx. 800.

In turning over the pages of Topography it is obvious to what a wide and almost boundless variety of subject this useful class of literature adapts itself. It is not only descriptive of localities in their natural features, and of the changes which the hand of man has wrought upon their surface,—his monuments of religion, of industry, or of taste ; but it is further the history of all the generations of man himself that have successively occupied those localities, or have been connected with them. The topographer may say, even more entirely than the satirist,

> Quicquid agunt homines, nostri est farrago libelli.

And this is more especially the case with a great suburban district, such as Clerkenwell. Very much more is here presented to the attention of the historian, than the mere descent of property, or the genealogy of families, which form the staple of the manorial and parochial annals of our County Histories. In such districts families are seldom of long endurance: but a vast number of persons, of various degrees of celebrity, and in all ranks of life, appear for a brief period upon the stage, and leave some faint remembrance of their names behind them. The book that chronicles all these becomes essentially biographical and anecdotical, and is one more interesting to the general reader than the graver topography of the higher class. A *History of Islington*, produced some twenty years since by Mr. Lewis, in a handsome quarto volume, answers to this character: and the present work on the contiguous parish of Clerkenwell, with which much of the history of Islington is intermixed, well deserves to take a place by its side.

There has been a previous *History of Clerkenwell*, by Thomas Cromwell,[1] and this new book has of course been constructed upon its

---

[1] But frequently going by the names of the artists J. and H. S. Storer, by whom it was undertaken, and illustrated with very neat line-engravings, in 8vo. 1828. Some account of the Messrs. Storer and their publications, produced in Chapel Street, Clerkenwell, is given by Mr. Pinks in p. 546; but we do not find in his pages any biographical notice of his predecessor Mr. Cromwell. He had previously written a History of Colchester, in 1825.

basis : but it is carried out to a far ampler extent in every department, particularly in describing all the features of modern improvement, and is very creditable to the reputation of a young man who was
evidently a person of considerable intelligence and very great diligence,
though of scarcely sufficient scholarship for the antiquarian portions of
his task.   William John Pinks was a native of Clerkenwell, born on
the 29th Sept. 1829.   He was apprenticed to a bookbinder; but, after
attaining manhood, he gave up that trade for literary work on Mr.
Pickburn's journal, called *The Clerkenwell News*, to which, among other
papers, he contributed some on the great local manufacture, entitled
" Curiosities of Clocks and Watches."   Another was a series of " *Country
Trips*," afterwards collected into a small volume.   But for the last six
years of his life he was chiefly engaged on the History before us, which
was originally published in parts.   He died on the 12th Nov. 1860,
and was interred in Highgate Cemetery, where a stone, " erected by a
few admirers of the departed," commemorates his name as " The Clerkenwell Antiquarian."

In the history of Clerkenwell we trace an ever-changing locality,
from the early days when it was a small village, surrounded by its
meadows, and separated from London by the open area of Smithfield,
until the present time, when it has become a closely packed section of
the metropolis itself.   It has borne in succession very different aspects,
but all characteristic of its suburban position.   At first we have its
ecclesiastical age, when its quiet and its propinquity to the town were
equally advantageous to the religious orders.   Then, when they were
gone, their commodious houses and flourishing gardens were occupied
by the nobility, who at that time did not require to go further from
the town to obtain the products and beauties of the country.   These also
have long since all passed away.   Next, we have the period of popular
entertainment, when this was the favourite area of public gardens, particularly where mineral springs rose to the surface, such as Bagnigge
Wells and Sadler's Wells,—the latter of which became widely famous
as a place of dramatic performances,—with the Rotunda or New Pan-
theon by Spa Fields, and the bear-baiting and cock-fighting at Hockley
in the Hole.   Closely pressing upon these comes the age of labour,
which chokes up the neighbourhood with offensive manufactories, whilst
the quieter streets are full of industrious artisans, particularly watch-
makers.   Lastly, but intermingling with the remnants of the foregoing,
which still in some measure distinguish Clerkenwell from other parts of
the town, we come to our own age of engineering, which has made

Clerkenwell a great locality of prisons,—we should remark that the County Sessions House was placed there so early as the reign of James the First,—of reservoirs for the supply of London with water, and of the Metropolitan Railway, which has burrowed its way through the soil once percolated by so many springs, and has put to flight the ancient Turnmill Street, in order to make room for its giant terminus.

Among all these various aspects of Clerkenwell it is our special province to direct our attention to its relations with noble families. A modern popular writer has described Kensington as "the old Court Suburb," to which designation it was perhaps entitled during the last century, when the royal palace there was occupied by our sovereigns, and for some time after. But the annals of Clerkenwell and of other parishes show that at an earlier date the aristocracy were not driven so far west. They remained more in the city, or its northern precincts ; and in the reign of Charles the Second the following are found in the parish of Clerkenwell :—[1]

In 1666,—Earl of Carlisle, Earl of Essex, Earl of Aylesbury, Lord Berkeley, Lord Townsend, Lord Delamere, Lady Crofts, Lady Wyndham, Sir John Keeling, Sir John Cropley, Sir Edward Bannister, Sir Nicholas Stroude, Sir Gower Barrington, Dr. King, Dr. Sloane.

In 1667.8,—Duke of Newcastle, Lord Baltimore, Lady Wright, Lady Mary Dormer, Lady Wyndham, Sir Erasmus Smith, Sir Richard Cheverton, Sir John Burdish, Sir Goddard Nelthorpe, Sir John King, Sir William Bowles, Sir William Boulton.

But the parish registers—from which extracts are given in pp. 46— 49, offer many other great names besides these, during the whole previous century, and would doubtless furnish still more if examined with care. We see in the extracts several names that are evidently misread, but we shall not now enter upon their examination, as it will sufficiently occupy our present space to notice those families of the foremost rank which took the place of the Religious Knights and Nuns of Clerkenwell.

The priory of the Knights of St. John was retained by Henry the Eighth in his own hands, and was preserved from immediate destruction by being made the storehouse for the King's tents and toils, as well for

---

[1] Communicated by Dr. Edward F. Rimbault to *Notes and Queries*, I. i. 180, "from a MS. in the late Mr. Upcott's Collection." We have altered, with certainty, in the first list, the names of "Dellawar" to Delamere, and "Wordham" to Wyndham; and in the second "Cliverton" to Cheverton. And we also suspect that "Burdish" is a misreading for Bendish. From notes in pp. 9, 11, of Mr. Pinks's volume, we find the original authority for these names to be the parochial rate-books of those dates, but the same errors occur in the names.

war as for the chase. In the reign of Edward the Sixth its church
was in great measure destroyed, at the time when the Protector Somerset
made the old religious edifices of London his quarries for the erection of
Somerset House: but the other buildings were still preserved, and became
the town mansion of the Lady Mary, of whose presence there several
particulars are extant. It thus happened that this was one of the few
cases in which that princess had the power, when she came to the
throne, to indulge her religious sentiments by the re-erection of conventual establishments: she restored the house to the Knights of Saint
John, and Sir Thomas Tresham became their Prior.

On the accession of Elizabeth, the priory returned to its former des-
tiny as a royal storehouse, particularly for the offices of the Tents and
Revels, and they remained there until the middle of the reign of
James I. when the house of St. John's was, in 1610, given to Lord
Aubigny.

It does not appear, however, that it was long the abode of that nobleman, if at all, for within a few years the property passed into the
hands of the Earl of Exeter, whose Countess, Elizabeth Drury, repairing the ruined choir of the church, converted it into what Dr. Fuller,
writing in 1655, describes as " one of the best private chapels in
England, discreetly embracing the mean of decency betwixt the ex-
tremes of slovenly profaneness and gaudy superstition."[1] This had
been effected in 1623, when the celebrated Dr. Joseph Hall preached
at its re-opening on St. Stephen's day, taking for his text Haggai ii. 9,
" The glory of this latter House shall be greater than the former, saith
the Lord of Hosts." This prediction, however, has never been accomplished. After being relinquished as an adjunct to the mansion, but
retaining its name as Aylesbury Chapel (after the Earl of Aylesbury,
its recent owner), it became a meeting-house of the Presbyterians (in
which capacity it was despoiled by a Sacheverell mob in the days of
Bishop Burnet), until, having been purchased for the Established
Church, it was reconsecrated by Bishop Gibson on Saint John's Day
in 1723, and is the present Saint John's Church, Clerkenwell.

Before that date marriages, and perhaps baptisms, had sometimes
been celebrated in this church or chapel, as we find that

John Fenwicke, Esq. the sonne of Sir William Fenwicke, and Lady Mary Howard,
daughter of the Earl of Carlisle, were married together in the Earl of Elgin's chapel,
July 14, 1663. (Register of the parish church.)

---

[1] Church History, book v.

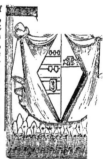

Here lyeth interred Elizabeth, Countess Dowager of Exeter, daughter of Sir William Drury, of Hawstead, in the county of Suffolk, knight, and coheir of Robert Drury, her brother. She was married to William Cecil, knight of the most noble Order of the Garter, Lord Burghley, Earl of Exeter, and grandchild to the illustrious William, Lord Burghley, Lord Treasurer to Queen Elizabeth. By the said Earl she had three daughters and coheirs : — Elizabeth married to Thomas Howard, Viscount Andover, Earl of Barkshire : Diana married first to Henry, Lord Vere, Earl of Oxenford, and after his death to Thomas, Lord Bruce, Baron of Whorleton, Earl of Elgin ; Anne married to Henry, Lord Gray of Grooby, Earl of Stamford. She died at her house called St. John's, the 26th day of February, 1653; her age was about 80 years : leaving behind her an example for piety, wisdom, bounty, charity, and all goodness, fit for imitation of all ladies of honour and virtue.

ARMS: Barry of six argent and azure, over all six escucheons sable, three, two, and one, each charged with a lion of the first, for *Cecill;* impaling, Argent, on a chief vert a tau between two mullets pierced or, for *Drury.*

but all interments had taken place in the parish church of Saint James, which had been also that of the Nunnery.[1]

Thus it happened that the Countess of Exeter was not interred in the church which she had partly restored, but in that of Saint James. Her tomb was affixed to the wall at the east end of the south aisle, and is described as "a beautiful monument of white marble;" but the barbarous iconoclasm of the last century consigned it to the vaults of the present church, where it still remains, as represented in the engraving above given.

[1] The church of the nuns appears in ancient records as *Ecclesia S. Mariæ,* and our author remarks (p. 28), "it is not apparent at what time the church of Clerkenwell was dedicated to St. James." The probability is that, as in other cases, the conventual and parochial churches were contiguous, and indeed under the same roof, but had separate dedications.

Close by this tomb there was a painted board, setting forth that this lady was honoured and beloved by all for her hospitality and charity to the poor, and freedom from all pride, that she left great legacies to her servants (to some annually for life), and was grandmother to thirty-two children, and great-grandmother to thirty-three.

Of the great-grandchildren two were buried near her: William Booth (ob. 1661), the eldest son of George Lord Delamere by the Lady Elizabeth his wife, daughter of the Earl of Stamford; and Anne Booth, his sister (ob. 1667). The former had " a neat white marble tablet," still it seems " affixed to the wall in the vault" (p 66), and the latter "a monument of the Ionic order, adorned with a pediment, whereon were two cupids weeping."

It is remarked by Collins in his *Peerage*, that when David third Earl of Exeter succeeded his uncle William in his honours in 1640, he found the family estate much diminished by the fortunes of three coheirs, and the dowers of two widows, his grandfather's and his uncle's. The three coheirs were the ladies mentioned in the epitaph on the tomb at Clerkenwell; and it was to the second, the Lady Diana, Countess of Elgin, that the Priory of St. John's was apportioned. It then probably took the name of Elgin House, as it certainly subsequently did that of Aylesbury House, after Robert second Earl of Elgin had been created Earl of Aylesbury in 1663. When this house was at last destroyed, or subdivided,[1] we are not precisely informed. The street named Aylesbury Street does not actually occupy its site, but was built on the north side of its garden wall; but there is also Aylesbury Place, which certainly stands within the inclosure of the old domain.

We do not find that any of the family of Bruce had monuments at Clerkenwell. But there were, in the old church, several of greater interest than those we have yet named, which were either ruthlessly destroyed, or dismissed to the lower regions,[2] in the good old days of George the Third. Among them was that of the very JOHN WEEVER who, in the former century, had exerted himself so industriously in the commemoration of our sepulchral antiquities. It was in this church

---

[1] In p. 276 our authors, whilst expressing an opinion that Aylesbury house "was adapted out of the monastic buildings of the Priory," fail to perceive its absolute identity with the former mansion of the Earl of Exeter. In 1720 it was spoken of as being "still standing, but let out in tenements."—Strype's Stow.

[2] "The floor of the vaults is overlaid with monumental slabs, the inscriptions on which are nearly effaced." (Pinks and Wood, p. 66.) That of Bishop Burnet "was discovered a few feet below the surface," when the ground was excavated in 1822 for the interment of Mr. Sinnot, a dust contractor. (p. 67.)

that the author of the *Funerall Monuments* was himself interred, in the year 1652 :

WEEVER, who laboured in a learned strain
To make Men long since dead to live again,

*   *   *   *   *

For where so ere a ruin'd Tomb he found,
His pen hath built it new out of the ground.

And yet, with shame be it spoken, the epitaph of which these lines form portions, itself no longer exists.   It is said that

When the church was taken down, the Society of Antiquaries, with a very proper zeal for the preservation of this tablet, ordered a diligent search to be made for it, but without success, as it had been taken from the church a few years previously by some person or persons unknown.   (p. 42.)

Weever dates the prefatory epistle to his work " From my house in Clerkenwell close this 28 of May, 1631."

It might be imagined that, as against " Tom Hearne," the destroyer Time cherished a particular spite against John Weever, and the edifice in which his zeal was commemorated.   The church was summarily condemned in the year 1788, as being too small and choked up with galleries (which was doubtless true), and as hastily demolished,[1] without any proper regard being paid to the interesting memorials of the illustrious dead which it contained.

One of the most remarkable was the monument of Sir William Weston, the last Prior of the Knights Hospitallers of Saint John, before the suppression of that Order in England.   " It fortuned (writes Weever) that on the 7th of May, 1540, being Ascension Day, and the same day of the dissolution of the house, he was dissolved by death, which so strooke him to the heart at the first time when he heard of the dissolution of his order."   It may be supposed that the Lord Prior had previously prepared his monument, and erected it in his own conventual church of St. John's, and that it was thence removed to the parish church, though it is not remembered when.   It was already considerably injured when thus described by Weever:—

---

[1] " I was sorry to hear that the parishioners had been so precipitate as to take down the old church before they had made a contract for a new one.   The materials produced above 800*l.*   A great part of them is now working up into houses in St. George's Fields."   (Gentleman's Magazine, Oct. 1788, p. 853.)   A view of the interior, during the progress of demolition, is introduced at p. 49 of the volume before us.

In the north walle of the chancell is a faire marble tombe, with the portraiture of a dead man lying upon his shroud, the most artificially cut in stone that ever man beheld. All the plates of brass are stolne away, onely some few pieces remaining, containing these words :—

𝔥ospitalitate inclytus, genere praeclarus.
𝔥anc urnam officii causa.

In the centre, on another plate, in Old English characters, was

𝔖pes me non fallat quam in te semper habebam
𝔙irgo da facilem botis natum (qu.)

And on another

𝔈cce quam cernis semper tuo nomini debotum
𝔖uscipe in sinum birgo 𝔐aria tuum. ·

In the engraving, the matrices of the brasses appear in shadow on the wall of the recess, but too indistinctly to form a conclusion upon their design. It would seem almost as if there had been two kneeling figures, and two objects of their adoration. The Virgin was possibly represented as Our Lady of Pity, sustaining the dead body of her Son.

In the lower compartment of the monument, as it were deposited in the tomb, and appearing behind a range of five twisted columns, was an effigy in stone representing the body of the deceased in decay, lying on a shroud and mat. On the five twisted pillars were shields of arms, which, being of brass, were stolen away, as were five others from the canopy. In the centre of the canopy remained the atchievement of the Lord Prior carved in stone, surmounted by a singular cap or helmet, above which was his crest, of a Saracen's head, full-faced;[1] and wreathed, surrounded by mantling. In the cornice were roses and small shields of the cross of Saint John, placed alternately. The motto of the Lord Priors of Saint John, SANE BARO, seems to have been corrupted in this instance to ANY BORO.[2] The Lord Prior of Saint John's took precedence as the Premier Baron of England, and this motto appears intended to assert that privilege.

The arms (which are not distinctly shown in the engraving,[3]) were quarterly, 1. and 4. Ermine, on a chief azure five bezants, for *Weston;* 2. and 3. Or, three camels sable, for *Camell;* in chief, in token of his office, Gules, a cross argent. The arms

---

[1] "A Saracen's head affronté, with a band round the neck or, couped at the neck proper, wreathed about the temples argent and azure:" as blasoned in *Excerpta Historica,* p. 331, for the standard of Sir Richard Weston, an elder brother of Sir William,—and Master of the Court of Wards. He was the builder of the fine mansion still standing at Sutton Place near Guildford.

[2] The motto is printed "Ani boro" for Sir Richard Weston in *Excerpta Historica,* p. 331. (To Sir Richard it did not really belong, as it was the official motto of the Lords of St. John.) It would seem to have been often misunderstood, or regarded as unintelligible. In the Gentleman's Magazine for 1755 is a letter in which a writer, after stating that he had found an ancient inscription SANCTE BORO on one of the windows of the Preceptory at Dynmore in Herefordshire, proceeds at great length to discuss and explain those words as if they had been English.

[3] We annex a cut of the same from the hall of Temple Balsall in Warwicksbire. (See the Gentleman's Magazine for Sept. 1838, p. 268.) In this, however, the tinctures are not correctly indicated, the original having been apparently repainted with improper colours.

of Camell were derived from Sir William's mother, who was Catharine, daughter and heir of John Camell, son and heir of Robert Camell, of Shapwick, co. Dorset.

It is stated by our authors (p. 39) that " in 1788, when the old church was destroyed, this noble monument was removed, it being purchased by Sir George Booth, and conveyed to Burleigh." We fear that this is altogether a mistake: for it is elsewhere mentioned (p. 95) that when Pennant, in his walks through London in 1793, visited the former residence of the Duke of Newcastle at Clerkenwell, it " was in the occupation of a cabinet-maker, and scattered over the garden were the remains of the monuments of Sir William Weston and others, shamefully ruined, removed from the old church." And as the emaciated effigy, which was the most remarkable portion of the monument, is still remaining in the vault of the new church (engraved in the volume before us, p. 66), it is not probable that the other parts of the monument were taken elsewhere.[1]

In the Gentleman's Magazine, vol. lviii. p. 501, is a letter from Mr. Matthew Skinner, of Camden Street, Islington, who had witnessed the removal of Sir William Weston's monument on the 27th of April, 1788, and who proceeds to describe the state in which the mortal remains of the lord prior were found, deposited in a leaden coffin, which was moulded to the shape of his head, and marked on the breast with the cross of his Order, as figured in an accompanying plate.[2]

[1] We have traced the statement to one of the letters which appeared at the time in the Gentleman's Magazine (Oct. 1788, p. 853) as follows: " Prior Weston's is gone down to Burleigh, having been purchased by Sir George Booth, but the principal figure on it, the skeleton, is left in Mr. Mallet's garden." This must have been a misapprehension, which perhaps may have arisen from the writer having heard some conversation on the probability of the Countess of Exeter's monument being removed to Burghley, which he misapplied to that of Sir William Weston.

The Rev. Sir George Booth, Bart. mentioned above, was a gentleman connected with the parish of Clerkenwell, where his father John was buried in 1725, as was his mother in 1742, and his sisters in 1715, 1723, and 1743. (Baronetage, 1771, i. (39).) He had no connection with Burghley; but, as the last heir-male of the ancient family of Booth, of Dunham Massey, co. Chester, he succeeded to the Baronetcy (of the first creation in 1611) on the death of Nathaniel third Lord Delamere in 1770. On his own death in 1793 the baronetcy also became extinct. The account of his family in Courthope's *Synopsis of the Extinct Baronetage* includes his name; but it is omitted in Burke's *Extinct Baronetage*. In the Baronetage by Kimber and Johnson, however, 1771, is the fullest history of the family, 22 pages having been interpolated into the first volume for the purpose, contributed by George Booth Tyndale, esq. barrister at law.

[2] This account is quoted in the work before us (p. 39), but with no other authority except that it was written by " a contemporary." It is probable that Mr. Pinks was unaware from whence it really came, as he is elsewhere careful in naming his autho-

With regard to the more ancient interments at Clerkenwell, Stowe
has recorded in his *Survey* that, besides Jordan Briset, the founder of
the Benedictine Nunnery (circ. 1100), and Muriall his wife, buried in
the Chapter-house there,—"more buried in this church were, John
Wilkes esquire and Isabel his wife, Dame Agnes Clifford, Ralph
Thimbleby esquire, Dame Jahan Baronesse of Greystocke, and Dame
Jahan Lady Ferrar." We hear of no memorials of these surviving the
time of the dissolution; but it is remarkable that the church contained a
monument to the last Prioress of the Nunnery, as well as that to the last
Prior of the Preceptory of St. John's. This lady was Dame Elizabeth
Sackville, who, enjoying a yearly pension of 50*l.*; died at an advanced

rities. But the several contributions which Mr. Skinner made to the Gentleman's
Magazine in illustration of the antiquities of Clerkenwell should not be forgotten.
We find him first writing (vol. liv. p. 409) respecting Prior Weston's monument, and
stating that one arm of the emaciated statue had been lately broken off, in the year
1780. Next, he sends a drawing of one side of the Nunnery cloister, which is
engraved in the Magazine for Dec. 1785, together with what was then left of the
sepulchral brass of the prioress Elizabeth Sackville. In the number for June, 1787,
is a letter from Mr. J. Henn, of Hoxton, communicating various particulars regarding
the monuments, accompanied by an engraving of the arms on that of Lady Berkeley.
In June, 1788, is the letter from Mr. Skinner, which we have mentioned in the text;
and in the following month another, giving further particulars; in that for October
following is a letter, signed VIATOR LONDINENSIS (probably the draughtsman Schneb-
belie), furnishing copies of the inscriptions on the four old bells, and an engraving of
the oldest, together with the armorial carvings placed by prior Docwra on St. John's
Gate; succeeded by a communication from W. & D. (the Rev. Samuel Denne,
F.S.A.), containing biographical particulars of prior Weston; and again in Dec.
1788, is another letter from Mr. Skinner, describing various relics of antiquity found
during the demolition of the church, accompanied by engravings of a stone coffin, an
inscribed beam, and the panelling of an old monument. Notwithstanding the numerous engravings of the new History, none of these are copied, though most of them
might have been with advantage, and particularly the interesting view of the Nunnery
Cloisters. We find that the Editor has mentioned most or all of these matters in his
Appendix, but we observe that he has mistaken (p. 601) Mr. Skinner's very rough
sketch of the emaciated effigy of Prior Weston for a representation of the appearance
of his "skeleton" as discovered in 1788.

In the Gentleman's Magazine for March, 1846, p. 247, is engraved a handsomely
carved bench, formerly in the church, having raised partitions or arms that divided it
into four seats, with this inscription:—

HOC OPVS PERFECTVM FVIT ANNO DOMINI 1534.

It was copied from a drawing of John Carter, F.S.A. and in the same page is given a
list of other drawings made at Clerkenwell, by the same artist.

Another view of the Nuns' Cloister, looking along its extent, is given in Mr.
Pinks's work, at p. 96, but it represents *seven* bays or arches, instead of six, which we
have little doubt is an error, as the view in the Gentleman's Magazine for Dec. 1785
is accompanied by a ground plan.

age, in the twelfth year of Queen Elizabeth, to whom she was not very remotely allied, for she was a sister of that John Sackville who married Margaret Boleyne, and Margaret was aunt to Queen Anne Boleyne, and great-aunt to her Virgin Majesty. In her will, which is extant, Dame Elizabeth Sackville desires to be buried in the church of Clerkenwell, and requests her cousin Lord Buckhurst to become the overseer of her testamentary injunctions. In 1785 the upper half of her (whole-length) sepulchral brass remained, together with the arms of Sackville in a lozenge,—as represented, unfortunately not very carefully, in the Gentleman's Magazine, vol. lv. p. 935; but these had entirely disappeared two years later (ibid. vol. lvii. 460).

We fear we must also regret the loss of a sepulchral brass that formerly commemorated one of the last nuns of Clerkenwell, whose name occurs in the pension lists as receiving an annuity of 4l. and who survived the last Prioress for nearly seven years. This was at Dingley in Northamptonshire; and she was represented praying at a table, and uttering the words *Jesu, Jesu, Merci*, with this inscription:

Here resteth the bodye of Anne Boroeghe, second daughter of Nicholas Boroeghe of Stanmer in the countye of Middlesex esquier, sometyme professed of Clerkenwell nere London, who died the 9th of April in the yere of our Lord God 1577, after she had lived 75 years, to the great losse of the poor, who divers ways were by her relieved.

This is described in Bridges's *History of Northamptonshire*, ii. 306; but, as it is unnoticed in the Rev. Herbert Haines's *Manual of Monumental Brasses*, 1861, it would be an agreeable surprise to us to hear that it is still preserved.

There is, however, now in the possession of the Editor of this miscellany, the monumental brass, once at Clerkenwell, of Doctor JOHN BELL, some time Bishop of Worcester, who, having resigned his see in 1543, died during the reign of Queen Mary at Clerkenwell, in 1556. This is slightly engraved by Malcolm, in his *Londinium Redivivum*, and should have been copied in the present work.

Even for a far more distinguished Bishop, and who had not then rested in his grave much more than seventy years, the Clerkenwell churchwardens of 1788 showed little more respect. Gilbert Burnet, the Historian of the Reformation, and of His Own Times, was, during the latter years of his life, a resident in Saint John's Square. In his will, made on the 24th Oct. 1711, he desired " that my body be decently but privately buried, in case I die at Salisbury, in the south isle of the Cathedral, where two of my children lie buried: And in case I die in any other place, in the church or churchyard of the parish where I may happen to die." His death occurred at his house in Clerkenwell,[1] on Thursday, the 17th of March, 1714-15; and on the Tuesday following his body was deposited in the church of that parish, near the Communion table. The pall was supported by six Bishops,— Dr. Talbot of Oxford (who became his successor at Salisbury), Dr. Wake of Lincoln (afterwards Archbishop of Canterbury), Dr. Trimnell of Norwich, Dr. Hough of Lichfield and Coventry, Dr. Evans of Bangor, and Dr. Fleetwood of Ely.

His monument, which is now in the vestibule of the church, was erected (it is stated by Mr. Pinks, p. 59), at the expense of the parish, in pursuance of the following resolution :—"At a vestry held November 13th, 1715, It was moved a monument should be erected to Bishop Burnet, in consideration of twenty guineas paid to the Poor.—Granted." We do not understand this entry as Mr. Pinks has done: it shows, as we take it, that the monument was erected by the Bishop's executors, and that *permission* for its erection was granted by the parish, only upon consideration of receiving twenty guineas towards the relief of the poor. The monument is of white marble ; in fact, a tall mural tablet, having a long Latin inscription, under a pediment carved in alto-relievo, with books and scrolls, and surmounted by an armorial escucheon of the arms of the see of Salisbury

[1] The same house was afterwards the residence of Dr. Joseph Towers, a dissenting minister of some theological and some political notoriety, who died there May 20, 1799. It is still standing. There is a view of it in the Gentleman's Magazine for June 1817, another in *The Mirror* 1837, and a third (taken 1858) in the volume before us. It is said to be now divided into twenty-three apartments, occupied by numerous families, exercising a great variety of trades.

impaling Burnet, encircled by the Garter (as Chancellor of that Most Noble Order), and crowned by a mitre. This monument remained in the vault with the rest until the year 1814, when it was rescued through the interference of Mr. S. Warner.

"On going into the vaults of St. James's church, about the year 1814, I discovered the monument of Bishop Burnet. Felt considerable regret at finding it in such a place, and immediately set about to make interest with some of the Board of Trustees, for the purpose of getting it removed to some more suitable place. The result was its removal to the place it now occupies." (MS. Notes on Clerkenwell.)

The grave of Burnet was disturbed in 1788. It is related that his corpse was found in a leaden coffin, the outer one of wood being decayed. Through an aperture at the top of the coffin the skull and some hair were visible. (p. 60.) The blue slab which covered the grave was carried down with others to the vault, and there it still remains. It bears the arms shown in the annexed engraving, which were carved by Mr. Stanton, a stone-cutter, next door to St. Andrew's church in Holborn,[1] and this inscription :—

---

[1] P. 687, from a MS. of Le Neve in the British Museum. But *qu.* is not the monument meant?

Here lies interred the Right Rev. Father in God, GILBERT BURNET, D.D., Lord Bishop of Salisbury, Chancellor of the Most Noble Order of the Garter, who departed this life March 17, 1714-15, in the 73rd year of his age.

The arms of Burnet are Argent, a hunting-horn sable garnished gules, in chief three holly-leaves vert. We find the following anecdotes relating to them in Mr. Seton's *Scottish Heraldry*. (p. 118.)

A keen dispute for chieftainship between the Burnets of Barns, in Peeblesshire, and the family of Leys in the North, is said to have been decided, about the middle of last century, in favour of the former, by Sir Robert Douglas (author of the *Peerage* and *Baronage of Scotland*), to whom the charters of the two families were submitted for examination. While the Barns' coat-armour is blazoned Argent, three holly-leaves vert, and a chief azure, the Baronets of Leys carry three similar leaves in chief, and a hunting-horn in base sable, garnished gules; the horn, and also the supporters (a highlander and a greyhound), having reference, according to Sir George Mackenzie, to the fact of the family being the King's Foresters in the North. Both families, however, use the same crest and motto, viz. a hand with a knife, pruning a vine-tree proper, surmounted by the words, VIRESCIT VULNERE VIRTUS. This crest and motto owe their origin to Mary Queen of Scots, and were probably intended to allude to her own unhappy condition. When she was in England (says Bell in his Life of the Scottish Queen,) she embroidered for the Duke of Norfolk a hand with a sword in it, cutting vines, with the motto, VIRESCIT VULNERE VIRTUS.

Several other varieties of the coat of Burnet will be found in Burke's *General Armory*. The leaves are there in every case blasoned as holly-leaves; but by Dale, in his *Catalogue of English Nobility*, they are termed burnet leaves.[1]

The Burnets are stated in their genealogy to have been originally Burnards, and it is remarkable that we find leaves upon two very early seals for persons of this name. We quote them from charters (without date) relating to Arlesey, co. Bedford, printed in the sixth volume of the *Collectanea Topographica et Genealogica*, where will be found many particulars of the descendants of Burnard, who occurs in Domesday book as a mesne tenant of William de Ow in the several counties of Bedford, Hants, and Wilts.

[1] Burnet is said to be the *poterium* of Pliny. In Ainsworth's Latin Dictionary we find " Burnet, pimpinella."

Bishop Burnet was a nephew to the first Baronet of Leys, co. Aberdeen (so created 1626), his father having been a judge of Session by the title of Lord Crimond. The Bishop had a son (his third and youngest) who became an English judge, and who was buried by the side of his father at Clerkenwell, his coffin-plate being inscribed:—

The Hon. Sir THOMAS BURNET, knt. one of [the Justices of] his Majesties Court of Common Pleas, died 17th May, 1753, in the 59th year of his age. (p. 60.)

The coffin of a granddaughter, Mrs. Mary Mitchell, was found lying upon that of the Bishop.

There is a long memoir of Sir Thomas Burnet in the *Biographia Britannica* and in Chalmers's *Biographical Dictionary:* as well as some account of his two brothers. William, the eldest, was Governor first of New York and the Jerseys and afterwards of Massachusetts and New Hampshire, and died at Boston Sept. 7, 1729, having married two wives, of whom the first was a daughter of Dr. George Stanhope, Dean of Canterbury. The second son bore his father's name; and was the Rev. Gilbert Burnet, M.A. Chaplain to King George I. and Rector of East Barnet, where he was buried in 1726, having died a bachelor. He had attained some distinction in literature.

It happened that not many years later another Gilbert Burnet, M.A. became connected with the parish of Clerkenwell, and has been sometimes confounded with the last; but he is said to have been no relation to the Bishop. He was elected Minister of Clerkenwell in 1743,[1] in succession to the Rev. Charles Lee (p. 69); but was probably Curate before, as two of his children had been previously christened at the church,—Elizabeth in 1734, and Gilbert in 1736. (p. 47.)

This Rev. Gilbert Burnet was an able preacher, and soon after his death were published two volumes of " Practical Sermons on various subjects, by Gilbert Burnet, late Vicar of Coggeshall, and Minister of St. James, Clerkenwell." He had before published, in three vols. 8vo. 1737, an abridgment of Boyle's Philosophical Lectures, which was translated into French.

[1] In the *Gentleman's Magazine* for June 1817 it is stated by T. P. (Thomas Prattent) that " In 1743, the Rev. Gilbert Burnet was curate of St. James's, Clerkenwell, and is said to have had 20 brothers and sisters living. He was born in Scotland, the native place of the bishop ; but it is believed he was no relation. In 1788, the bishop's grandson, Thomas, lived at Chigwell, Essex. In 1811, a Mrs. Mary Burnet, upwards of 80 years of age, was buried in the bishop's vault, from Chigwell, where she died." We find her death thus recorded in the Gentleman s Magazine :— " Aug. 27, 1811. At Chigwell, aged 83, Mrs. Margaret Burnet, widow of Thomas B. esq. surgeon, who was the last of the ever-memorable family of Gilbert Burnet, Bishop of Salisbury."

THE INSTITUTION AND EARLY HISTORY OF THE DIGNITY OF BARONET.

Continued from p. 352.

On the 13th of November, 1611, Mr. John Chamberlain wrote to Sir Dudley Carleton (then Ambassador at Venice), that " The Baronets multiply but slowly ; yet there be some few lately come in, as Sir Marmaduke Wyvill and Mr. Englefield."[1]

The number of those made at this time was actually seventeen, and their patents bore date on the 25th Nov. 1611.[2] We append their names, in continuation from the former list (p. 350)—the Italics marking, as before, the only one which is not extinct[3]

---

[1] Mr. Chamberlain continues, " In the mean time, divers of them walk under protection, as Sir Thomas Monson, Sir Roger Dallison, Sir Richard Houghton, Sir Harry Goodere, Sir Michael Sands, Sir Hugh Beeston, as well Baronets as bare Knights; which breeds some mislike that Protections grow so frequent. Indeed money is become very scant, as well in Court as in company," &c. &c. Four of those named were Baronets—presuming Sir Miles Sandys to be intended by " Sir Michael :" Sir Henry Goodyere and Sir Hugh Beeston were only Knights.

[2] In all lists of the Baronets these creations will be found placed under the date of the 25th Nov. 1612, instead of 1611; and so also with the four made on the 24th September preceding (named in p. 350,) they likewise have been misattributed to 1612. This error crept into the lists on some very early occasion, and has never hitherto been duly corrected.

As regards Sir Marmaduke Wyvill it was detected, " From examination of the original patent, the date whereof has hitherto been erroneously printed (by Dugdale, and in other catalogues of Baronets,) Nov. 25, 1612. Ex Inf. Dom. Mar. Wyvill, Bar." (*The English Baronetage*, 1741, i. 232.) But this discovery being confined to the Wyvill patent, the only result was an undue removal of the article of *Wyvill* from its proper precedence, to a place before that on the family of *Gostwick*. And in the Baronetage of 1771 Wyvill is further advanced before Temple, created Sept. 12, 1611, —the latter being misassigned to 1612.

There are various incidental circumstances which upon this discovery became intelligible, but were previously embarrassing. Sir Edward Devereux was styled Esquire at his creation; and he was knighted in the summer progress of 1612; where before mentioned in p. 352, the year in the text may be altered to 1611, and the conjecture advanced in the note is rendered unnecessary. Sir John Wray was knighted in Sept. 1612—probably as the eldest son of a Baronet (Sir William). The Receipt given to Sir Thomas Holte (printed *antea*, p. 348,) is dated 6 Dec. *anno nono* (*i.e.* 1611); and his name is the last upon the list now before us.

[3] The last Baronet of these seventeen families who died bearing that title was Sir Henry Charles Englefield (the 8th Baronet of his house,) an eminent antiquary, whose death occurred on the 21st March, 1822. And the last of another of the seventeen was an antiquary not less distinguished, Sir Joseph Ayloffe, (the 7th Bart.) who died April 19, 1781.

(though now merged in a higher title), and the (*) denoting those families which subsequently attained a peerage:

76. Sir John Portman, of Orchard Portman, Somersetshire, Knight.
77. Sir Nicholas Saunderson, of Saxby, Lincolnshire, Knight.*
78. Sir Miles Sandys, of Wilberton, Cambridgeshire, Knight.
79. William Gostwick, of Willington, Bedfordshire, Esquire.
80. Thomas Puckering, of Weston, Hertfordshire, Esquire.
81. Sir William Wray, of Glentworth, Lincolnshire, Knight.
82. Sir William Ayloffe, of Braxted Magna, Essex, Knight.
83. Sir Marmaduke Wyvill, of Burton Constable, Yorkshire, Knight.
84. John Pershall, of Horsley, Staffordshire, Esquire.
85. Francis Englefield, of Wotton Basset, Wiltshire, Esquire.
86. Sir Thomas Ridgeway, of Tor, Devonshire, Knight.*
87. William Essex, of Lambourne, Berkshire, Esquire.
88. Sir Edward Gorges, of Longford, Wiltshire, Knight.*
89. *Edward Devereux, of Castle Bromwich, Warwickshire, Esquire.*
90. Reginald Mohun, of Boconock, Cornwall, Esquire.*
91. Sir Harbottle Grimston, of Bradfield, Essex, Knight.
92. Sir Thomas Holte, of Aston, Warwickshire, Knight.

Regarding one of the creations in this list, that of Sir William Essex of Lambourne, in Berkshire, a letter is still preserved amongst the correspondence of Sir Robert Cotton. It appears to have been written by Robert Bowyer, Clerk of the Parliament (ob. s. p. 1634), who was son of William Bowyer, Keeper of the Records in the Tower of London,[1] and, like those which have been already laid before the reader, its object was to procure as good a precedence as possible for the party whose interest it advocated :—

[1] It will be remarked that the representatives (though not male descendants) of No. 76 and No. 91 are also now Peers: in the persons of Lord Portman and the Earl of Verulam. The Baronets advanced to peerages were :—

77. Viscount Castleton in the peerage of Ireland, 1627; Earl of Castleton, 1720. Extinct 1723.

86. Baron of Gallen-Ridgeway in the peerage of Ireland, 1616; Earl of Londonderry, 1622. Extinct 1713.14.

88. Baron of Dundalk in the peerage of Ireland, 1621.

89. His son Walter succeeded as fifth Viscount Hereford (on the death of the Earl of Essex) in 1646, and was ancestor of the present Viscount.

90. Baron Mohun, of Okehampton, co. Devon, 1628. Extinct 1712.

[2] See pedigree of Bowyer in Dallaway's *Rape of Chichester*, p. 61.

[Cotton. MS. Julius C. III.]

Sir,—My happe was to come to your lodginge on Satterdaie last, being a daie after your departure foorth of London : my errant speciallie was to entreate you to have commended my cosen Essex his name to be in the list of the next Baronetts, and one cheife point of our suit is, that he mai be rancked as high as by your good meanes maie be, which as wee hope maie be foremost of anie of his counterie, because as yet none of that shire, viz. Barkeshire, is come in. This will much raise his reputation in that place, which, by your kindnesse and the honorable favour thorough your meanes shewed him, hath ben both there and elsewhere supported, when otherwyse yt had fallen. If you shall thincke good to wright to anie person honourable or other, in your absence, for the present fartherīng of this matter, I shall be vearie willing to be the deliverer of your letters, and sollicitor of the business : otherwise, if you know that at your returne yt mai be dispatched to as good advantage of precedence as at this time, we shall then rest on your cominge. Wherefore I pray you let mee herein receave your direction as soone as convenientlie you mai. I pray you direct your letters to be left for mee at Mr. Garrettes shop, a goldsmyth over against St. Dunstanes Church in Fleetestreet, for so will thei be sent foorthwith to mee, whether I be at Tower hill or at Westminster, which is uncertaine.

Thinges are heare so still that wheare I become is no mencion of newes : and to lett you know that I wish you much happiness is no more than I hope you know alreadie. And so God keepe you, and send us a good meetinge. Your well assured, whome you maie commande,   Ro. Bowyer.

I must commend unto your frendlie regard the rememberance allso of my frende Mr. Bannynge.   R. B.

14 *Aug.* 1611.   *Westminster.*

The gentleman mentioned in the postscript was Sir Paul Bayning, created a Baronet on the 24th of September, 1611 (see p. 350), and afterwards Viscount Bayning.

After these creations there were no more for three years and a half. During that interval considerable difficulties arose from two causes. The first was a warmly disputed question of precedence ; the other, an effort made in the Parliament of 1614 to overthrow and unmake the new Order altogether. Of the former contest we now proceed to give some account : reserving the second for our next paper.

THE QUESTION OF PRECEDENCE. 1611-12.

The claim of Precedence advanced by the Baronets was, that they should take rank before the Younger Sons of Viscounts and Barons; but such claim was vigorously resisted by the parties concerned. The first notice of the controversy that we have met with is in the letter written by Mr. Chamberlain to Sir Dudley Carleton, on the 31st Dec. 1611 :—

[Domestic, James I. Vol. LXVII. art. 117].

The new Baronnetts have a question for place with Barons' Younger Sonnes, which is hotly followed by Sir Moyle Finch, Sir William Twisenden, Sir John Wentworth, and Sir Robert Cotton. The matter was lately brought to the Counsaile table, where by the Earle of Northampton and other Lords yt was decreed against them; but they have appealed and made petition to the King, who promiseth to reverse yt as they geve out.

Sir William Twisden, who took a leading part in this matter, was the father of the learned antiquary Sir Roger Twisden; and he was himself an accomplished scholar. He was son-in-law of Sir Moyle Finch (the progenitor of the Earl of Winchilsea), who had been created a Baronet at the same time with him (see pp. 349, 350), and who joined in asserting the claims of the new Order. Others who are mentioned in the proceedings were Sir George Gresley and Sir Thomas Brudenell, and it is somewhat remarkable that among the very few families that still survive of the original Baronetage, these early champions of its importance have still their representatives. Sir Thomas Brudenell was himself in middle life advanced to the peerage (in 1627), and he was Earl of Cardigan before his death, at the age of eighty, in 1664. Sir George Gresley is commemorated[1] as a man of good parts, and an encourager of learning; and as the person to whom Sir William Dugdale in some measure owed his rise, from having introduced him to the notice of the Earl of Arundel, Earl Marshal, on his first coming to London. Sir Walter Aston, who is also mentioned, was a cousin of Sir George, for the wife of Sir William Gresley, his grandfather, had been Katharine Aston, of the Tixall family. Sir Henry Savile was the Baronet (created June 29, 1611), seated at Methley, in Yorkshire—not the better

---

[1] Wood, Fasti Oxonienses.

known Sir Henry Saville, the learned Provost of Eton. Among the manuscripts preserved at Queen's College, Oxford, is a Petition from the North-country Baronets, of which Sir Henry Savile of Methley was the prime mover. It relates to Precedence among the Council of the North, which held their sittings at York; whether it should go by rank or office.

We have to describe the earlier question between the Baronets and the Younger Sons of Viscounts and Barons. The arguments and records adduced on either side are preserved in one of the volumes at the Public Record Office.[1] The Baronets seem to have been led to believe that their rank was not new, but one that was frequently mentioned, both in the records and the chronicles of earlier times; and it was upon this point that they chiefly insisted.

The Lords of the Council gave a second decision against their claims on the 8th of January :—

The same day [Sunday, January 8] the new Baronnetts had there [at the Council Table] a second defeat in the cause of precedence with Barons' Younger Sonnes ; for yt was told them that howsoever the words of theyre patent might seeme to carry a contrarie construction, yet yt was never the King's intention, which he will shortly declare by proclamation; whereupon they being not satisfied, but still urging the words and validity of their patent, and how in that consideration they had paid theyre monie, yt was aunswered by the Lord Treasurer (Salisbury) that yf any of them misliked his bargain he shold have his monie againe.—Mr. Chamberlain to Sir Dudley Carleton, Jan. 15, 1611-12.

[1] Domestic, James I., vol. lxvii. art. 19. The document consists of forty leaves, written on both sides, but still is not perfect. On more than one leaf is written in pencil, *ex lib: D'ni H. St. George.*" At fol. 1 is The Humble Petic'on of yᵉ Baronetts to yᵉ King's most Excellent Maᵗⁱᵉ : commencing, Finding by some speech cause of doubt, &c. At fol. 2, The Petition of the Visconts and Barons. Fol. 3, dorso, arguments, Whither Baronetts ought to have Precedency before the yonger sonnes of Barons. These continue to fol. 16, which is headed For yᵉ Barons' yonger sonns.

Art. 120 in the same volume is a paper of " Reasons " on the part of the Baronets, of which one clause is—" and therefore Mr. Camden in his Booke might well say as he dothe *Baneretti qui aliis Baronetti.*" Art. 160 in the same volume is a paper of arguments regarding the precedence of the offices of the Navy, among which are clauses, " To shew that the Patent of a Baronite doth not extend itselfe to take away the priviledges of offices;" and " To shew yᵗ the words of a Baronite's Patent to take place of all Knights are not universall."

The King was at his hunting seat at Royston, but the deputation of Baronets followed him thither and obtained an audience, the result of which is described by Sir Thomas Lake (the Secretary of State) in a letter written to the Lords of the Council in London about the 9th of February.

[Domestic, James I. Vol. LXVIII. art. 60.]

Those former points having filled up my paper, I thought good to writt the matter of the Baronets by itselfe.   This afternoon, coming by his Ma^{ts} appointment to have my byls signed for the Pyrates, (which herewith I send to your Lordships,) I found with his Highness fowre of the Baronets, Sir Thomas Brudenell, Sir William Twisden, Sir George Greisley, and Sir Gervase Clifton, who had delivered a Petition to his Matie with a copie of that which they had presented to your Lordships.   There was much altercation, and his Majestie defended his act very stiffely, and stood upon these termes, that *in ambiguis ejus est interpretare cujus est condere,* and he had never intention to give them precedency before Noblemen's sonnes.   Their plea was,—the wordes of their Patent ; the right of the place of a Baronett of aunsient tyme ; their own intentions in taking the degree.   His Majestie replied with many witty and strong arguments.   They were as earnest and vehement. The disputation was about an howre.   And when his Majestie wold have sent them to your Lordships of his Councell, they refused, and prayed to be heard when he was present.   So as, after his Majestie was retired and had dismissed them, he gave me direction to lett your Lordships understand that he could not refuse to heare them, the rather for that they said they had not been fully heard before your Lordships. His Majestie thought if they had no more to say then they had uttered here, he should aunsweare them well enough ; but yet could not refuse to heare them.   In the mean tyme, seing he was so soone to be there, your Lordships might prepare the Proclamation, a draught of which you had in hand, and at his Majesties comming he wold putt it to a point.

The King gave the Baronets another hearing in London on the 25th of March : but they were disappointed of the presence and support of Sir Robert Cotton, upon whose aid they had greatly relied to establish the validity of that historical evidence which they advanced to show that they formed a revival rather than a new grade of nobility.   Sir Robert had found himself in a position of great embarrassment.   On the one hand the Lords of the Council viewed him as the chief promoter of the new institution, and in some measure answerable for the success of a measure which he had himself recommended, and the machinery of which had been partly entrusted to his management. On the other hand, many of the Baronets had, more or less, been led to occupy their new status at his instigation, or by their estimate of his historical knowledge; and by accepting a place among them himself he had become a partaker of their destinies. Unwilling to offend either party, he retired to his country house. It was feared that he had been sent out of the way by the Earl of Northampton; and the Baronets, half thinking that they were betrayed, addressed to him with some indignation the following objurgatory epistle:—

[Cotton MS. Julius C. III.]

SIR,—We weare yesterdaye heard verye gratiouslye and att large by the Kinge, with soe muche judgment and indifference [*i.e.* impartiality] as wee did all admire, His Majestie beinge pleased to utter many gracious speeches that gave us great cause of comfort, And withall expresslye to deliver that there was noe intention or purpose in hym, one way or other, concerninge the place of Barons' Younger Sonnes. Upon Monday next in the afternoone a newe hearinge is appointed, wherein they of th'other side are to object what they can. Itt will certainly stand much upon the Patent, which wee doubt not to make evident to be fullye for us. And a great point which they will insist upon will be whether Banneretts have had and in right ought to have the place of Barons' Younger Sonnes, wherein your knowledge and presence will stand us in much steed. And therefore wee all desire you not to fayle to be heare by the day; which if you should, besides the prejudice to the common cause, weare like to turne much to your owne disreputation, as if you betrayed, as much as in you lay, the honour and dignitie not onlye of your selfe butt of your Posteritie after you, which wee doubt not but you will be most tender of; and soe, expectinge your cominge, we bidd you farewell.

Your very lovinge friends,

WA. ASTON.
MOYLE FINCH.
H. SAVILE.
PHILLIP TIRWHITT.
WM TWISDEN.

Mr Godfrey's Chamber, this Thuresday ten a clock 26 Martij in ye morninge.

Sir William Twisden was the last to sign, but he was not the man who felt least ardent in the cause. It occurred to him to write in addition a second letter, in order, if possible, to stimulate still further the truant antiquary. He therefore hastily penned the following, got his father-in-law Sir Moyle Finch to join in signing it, and despatched it by the same messenger:—

[Cotton. MS. Julius C. iii.]

S^r: Out of our speciall respect unto you whose advises have ever agreed: we have particularly sent our l're to you, beside the general, to intreat you not to fayle to come as you respect your and our owne (*sic*) and our desire, who have much relied on your understanding herein, and many things we know you can speake and none but you. No more, but we recomend our love unto you, and rest,

Your very loving frends,

Lond. this 26 of March.   MOYLE FINCH. W. TWISDEN.

We had warning at tenn at night on Tuesday night (S^r Mo: Finche at Copthall, my selfe at Peckham, 25 mile out of towne) on Wedensday to be by 2 in the afternoone before the K. We were there: my self not at all knowing of it untill 7 on Wedensday morninge.

Notwithstanding these urgent missives, Sir Robert Cotton esteemed it to be more prudent to remain in the country. He was informed of the progress of the suit by Nicholas Charles, Lancaster herald, who on the 2nd of April made the following report:—

[Cotton MS. Julius C. iii. fol. 86.]

Right Wo^{pll}: Sir, my duty remembred, I have made bould to trouble you with this script, conteyning some of the occurrences and buisines of the Baronettes since your going out of towne. The matter hath bin heard on both sides, wherein by the Baronettes was shewed the promiscuous using of Baronett and Bannarett, and their proofes held for litle and nothing worth, being accompted monkish stories, and so made but a mistake in all ages. Withall it was urged that if they could shew a Baronett made formerly, and afterwards corruptly called a Bannarett, that then it were a good instance to proove them all one. This and some other such like argumentes, too long to be written, were used of eyther part on two severall dayes of hearing, and the last day it seemed to leane toward the Baronettes side, that they should be declared Bannarettes; but with proviso to give place unto Barons' yonger sonnes;

and we have delivered in a note to the Lordes of the Privileges and Immunityes of a Bannarett, but what they will allow I cannot yet heare of; but on Saturday next the finall determination is expected, if some troublesome spirit do not hinder it: which end I wish were well made, and am glad that you are not seen in it at this tyme. And no doubt it wilbe to the content of you and other understanding gentlemen. Thus wishing to your worᵖᵖ all health and prosperity, I take my leave. From my Lodging in the Office of Armes, Thursday the 2d of Aprill A° Dni. 1612. Your Worshipp's bounden to be commanded,

NICH. CHARLES *Lancaster.*

The final result is thus described by Mr. Chamberlain, the 29th of April, 1612 :—

[Domestic, James I. LXVIII. art. 104.]

After three or fowre times audience the King hath determined that the Baronnetts shall not take place of Lordes' Younger Sonnes; but in requitall hath geven them three or fowre additions,—that, first, they shall quarter or beare in a canton the Armes of Ulster, which is a hand in a bloudie feild : but many thincke this so far from Honor that yt may rather be taken for a note of disgrace to shew how they came by yt. The next is that they shalbe knighted of course at 21 yeare old. The third that they shall fight in the feild under the King's standerd and neere his owne person; and the fourth that they shall have fowre (or sixe) Knights assistants at their funerall. The cause was argued with much vehemencie and contestation; insomuch that Sir W. Twi-senden charged the Earl of Northampton with sending Sir Robert Cotton out of the way, who was furnished with theyre best reasons and records; which he denieng, Sir W. urged Sir Henry Savile to deliver what aunswer he had from him by his man that he sent to him into the countrie for that purpose; which he did in these wordes—that Sir Robert Cotton saide his brother Baronetts must pardon him, but yf my Lord Privie-seale did send for him he wold come with a tan-tara. The King asked my Lord what he could say to this; who aunswered he could say no more but that he was glad to understand that his frend the antiquarie was become so goode a trumpetter: which made them all merrie.

The Royal Decree was promulgated on the 28th of May; and confirmed by the great seal.[1] It will be found printed at length in Selden's *Titles of Honour,* and in the *Baronetage* of 1741 ;

[1] Rot. Pat. 10 Jac. I. p. 10, m. 8.

but we must here state its provisions somewhat more precisely than Mr. Chamberlain was informed of them. After stating that the King had "in person heard both parts and their learned counsel three several days at large," had taken information from the Heralds, and duly considered such proofs as were produced on both sides, the precedence of the Younger Sons of Viscounts and Barons before the Baronets was affirmed; but it was further declared, that the said Younger Sons and the Baronets should take precedence before all Bannerets, except such as were made under the royal banner displayed, and in the King's presence, as before-mentioned in the Patent, and except also, " for a singular honour to the person of the most high and excellent prince, Henry now Prince of Wales,"—and, we may add, in regard to his martial aspirations,[1] to such Bannerets as might be made by that Prince, "under the King's standard displayed in an army royal in open war, and the said Prince personally present."

The additional boons which the King granted to the Baronets by this Decree or Declaration were:—1. That he would knight the present Baronets who were not already Knights,[2] and that the honour of knighthood should be conferred on the heirs male of their bodies, on their respectively attaining the age of twenty-one, and making application for that purpose to the Lord Chamberlain or Vice-Chamberlain of the Household;[3] 2. That the Baronets should bear in their coats of arms, either in a canton or in an escucheon, at their election (or choice), the arms of Ulster, that is, in a field argent a hand gules, or a bloody hand ; 3. That in the armies of the King they should have place, in the gross, near the Royal Standard ; 4. That, at their funerals, they should have two Assistants of the Body to support the pall, a Principal Mourner, and four Assistants to him, being the mean betwixt a Baron and a Knight.

---

[1] Six months later, and that gallant spirit was no more! His strong warlike pre-dilections are well known. Sir Robert Cotton had been employed (in 1609) to write in deprecation of them : see Birch's *Life of Prince Henry*, p. 186.

[2] Several instances occur, in the course of the next few years, of those who were already Baronets receiving the honour of knighthood.

[3] This privilege was withdrawn by King George the Fourth, by letters patent dated 19 Dec. 1827, having latterly been seldom exercised, and in the few recent instances perhaps not acceptably. It is still maintained in Ireland.

THE ORIGIN OF SYKES OF LEEDS.

To the Editor of THE HERALD AND GENEALOGIST.

SIR,—The letter upon this subject, written by the late accomplished Historian of South Yorkshire, which is printed in your last Part (p. 317), will have been perused with admiration by every reader, as the effusion of a man who was full of antiquarian and genealogical lore, and it claims the respectful attention of those who are interested in its contents. It was, however, avowedly poured forth in haste, and is rather suggestive of further inquiry and research. than invested with that judicial character which demands implicit deference and acquiescence. Mr. Hunter had a due respect for Thoresby and Dugdale, and others of his laborious predecessors; but he would have been the last to maintain the authority of their *dicta* when inconsistent with authentic evidence of the same nature as that upon which they themselves were mainly disposed to rely. In a note to Thoresby's Diary, vol. i. p. 110, he has left some remarks which show his true feelings in such questions :—

" Hopkinson owed much to the labours of Flower, Glover, and St. George, the visiting heralds in 1585 and 1612, and still more to Sir William Dugdale's Visitation in 1665 and 1666. He has followed too much in the track of the Heralds, and has admitted, without examination, whatever received their sanction. His work cannot be regarded as at all a critical disquisition. He has, however, some pedigrees which are illustrated by reference to charter-authority. Thoresby owed much to this volume. Many of the pedigrees in the *Ducatus* are nothing more than transcripts from Hopkinson."

Mr. Hunter's proposition, that Thoresby had particular advantages in the compilation of his account of the Sykes family, may be readily admitted so far as *contemporaneous* points are concerned (as in the case of Richard Sykes, M.A. under the heading of " Sikes of Derbyshire and Nottinghamshire," at p. 315 of the present volume), but, in regard to details belonging to an antecedent period, he, like the family itself, accepted the pedigree entered at the Visitation of Yorkshire in 1665 as sufficiently conclusive as to its *origin*.

As to the " main question," Did the Sykes' of Leeds originate at Sykes Dyke, near Carlisle, or at Flockton in the West Riding? Mr. Hunter professes to be " quite unable to give any sufficient answer."

To his pertinent remark, " one would like to know that there is, or has been, a Sykes Dyke in the neighbourhood of Carlisle," the only available reply is of a negative character, viz. that such a place is not mentioned as existing or having existed there in any topographical work relating to Cumberland; nor has any reference to it been found among the authentic documents recently brought to light, the discovery of which called forth Mr. Hunter's letter. The first named omission is, perhaps, not very significant; but the second appears fatal to the theory of its existence as the original location of the Sykes's of Leeds.

Mr. Hunter proceeds to say: " It is quite clear that there were families of the name residing, in a good position, in the West Riding of Yorkshire, some of whom might well be supposed to have strayed into Leeds." To this assertion there need be no demur, as the sequel will shew.

Further on Mr. Hunter speaks of the " possibility that a descent may one day be proved from one of the Sykes's named in the alderman's will, though not spoken of as relatives by him, yet possibly being so." These were his nephews, William, John, and James Sykes, baptized, respectively, at St. Peter's, Leeds, 9 June 1606, 11 Sept. 1609, and 24 Aug. 1611. John Sykes was of Woodhouse Lane, Leeds, and died about 8 Nov. 1660, leaving at least eight children; and this paragraph in Mr. Hunter's letter is noticed for the purpose of shewing that, though no descent may have been proved from either of the alderman's nephews, it may partly account for the redundancy of the name of Sykes in and about Leeds at the present time.

But to revert to the main question, Mr. Hunter says: " I quite agree with you that the name was in repute early in the Staincross and Agbrigg districts. But I have no account of any family of the name in those districts, or indeed in any part of Yorkshire." Again, " I have a large collection of early Bretton deeds (*i. e.* copies from originals) but I do not observe the name either as principal or witness. Nor indeed do I in any of my Staincross or Agbrigg deeds." Here it is only fair to note that an interval of thirty years, assiduously employed in various researches of moment, must have obliterated so relatively small a matter as the quotation below from Mr. Hunter's recollection; though, had opportunity occurred for drawing his attention to the fact at the time, it is equally fair to assume that it would have materially influenced his deductions on this subject in 1859. But it was not until after Mr. Hunter's decease, in 1862, that the valuable manuscript from which this quotation is taken became available for general inspection.

It is from one of the volumes of his own collections, now happily deposited in the British Museum: " FLOCKTON : Sciant, &c. Alicia fil' Add fil' Emme de Floketon in mea viduitate, &c. dedi, &c. Henrico Erl de Wakefield et her. ejus, an annual rent of 3s. 5d. to be taken from my tenants at Floketon, of *John del Syke* 2s. 4d., of Wm. fil' Mich'l' 7d., of John fil' Tho. (much decayed). Test. Will' Ingreys de Emeley, Hum' de Floketon, Joh'ne fil' Math' de Floketon, Will' fil' Pet' de ead', Paulino de Emeley, Theo' fil' Joh'n' de Floketon, . . . Kay, and others. 1 Edw. fil' Edw." And, " Sciant, &c. Alicia ux' quondam Joh'nis de Panall in pura viduitate mea, dedi, &c. Joh'ni de Methelay her. et ass' 4d., annual rent from a mess. and 3 acres in Floketon. Test. D'no Joh'ne de Thornhill, Nich'o de Wurteley, Jordano Deney, Will' fil' Petri de Floketon, Ada del Cote de ead', Mich' del Hov'hale, *Joh'ne del Syke*, et al. Dat. apud Thornhill, 1319." This is from Addit. MS. 24,467, which is entitled, in brief, " Wilson's Yorkshire Deeds . . . Copies or Abstracts made by me, Joseph Hunter, F.S.A. in the years 1825—1829."

The Lansdowne MS. 900 informs us that the wapentake of *Agbrigg* contains, among other towns and hamlets, Bretton, Chevitt, Emley, *Flockton*, Horbury, Liversedge, Shelley, Thornhill, and Wakefield; the point to be noted here being that the family of Sykes, in olden time, was more or less connected with all these places.

To conclude, existing evidences prove that, (1) William del Sicke had lands at Floketon temp. Hen. III.; (2) Agnes del Sicke acquired the " Estecroft " at Floketon about the year 1270, Sir John of Horebyry being principal witness to the transfer; (3) John del Syke, of Floketon, was engaged to pay to Henry Erl of Wakefield, annually, 2s. 4d., in 1308; (4) witnessed a charter at Thornhill, in 1319; (5) quit-claimed hereditary lands at Floketon to Michael del Syke, his son, in 1345; (6) Robert del Syke witnessed a transfer of lands at Shelley in 1416; (7) Robert Syke, of Flockton, was a retainer of Sir John Nevill, of Chevitt, in 1526; (8) Robert Syke, of Flockton, son of the former, left *two* sons named John (after the Nevilles of Liversedge and Chevitt), in 1548; (9) John Sykys, of Flockton, conveyed tenements and lands there, with remainder to his elder son Charles, and second son William, in 1550; (10) William Sykes was living at Leeds, having, beside one who had pre-deceased, four sons, James, William, Richard, and Edmund, in 1576; (11) Charles Sykys sold certain pastures at Flockton in 1577; (12) Nicholas Syke, son of the last-named, was plaintiff in Chancery for recovery of lands at Flockton in 1601;

(13) Richard Sykes, alderman of Leeds, son of Richard and grandson of William, purchased lands, before-named, at Shelley, in 1638; (15) Richard Sykes, of Kirk-Heaton and Leeds, purchased lands at Flockton, of which he died seised in 1652; (15) and these lands passed to the family of Kirshaw, by the will of Micklethwaite Sykes, in 1697, a representative of Rebecca Kirshaw, née Sykes,—the Rev. Canon Hopper being now in possession of many of the documents enumerated, including some, not named, of scarcely less interest.

About forty years ago a lady of the Kirshaw family, in ignorance of their value, destroyed others of these documents; otherwise the series might have presented an *unbroken* continuity, but hardly a more convincing proof that, in genealogies going back beyond the certain knowledge of those who relate them, "charter-authority" is entitled to more credence than official statement, and that the *latter*, in such a case, should always be based upon the *former*, or its more modern equivalents.

I append a copy of the letter of the "Parson of Kirk-Heaton" to his father, referred to by Mr. Hunter:—

"Most Lovinge Father,

"I have sente y^w a peece of venison: it hath made an vnlucky proofe wch I am not a little sorry for: it vexeth mee more than the venison is worth that it proves noe better: but I see beggers must be noe choosers, otherwise I had spedde better. I desire y^r kinde acceptance of it as it is, and hope the Cooke may helpe it. I have made bolde to inuite my Cos. Beaumont, of Whitley (the benefactor of the venison, who I perswade myself colde not helpe it), and his good wife to y^r feast. He cannot come, but shee purposeth, God willinge: as also my Brother Joseph, and his good wife, and Brother Alexander. I doubte you have forgot Vnckle and Aunt Binnes, but I will eyther goe or sende this daye to inuite them. Soe wth my most humble duety ever remembred to y^r selfe, as alsoe my good Mother, and hearty affecc'on to all Brothers and Sisters,

"I ever rest y^r obedient son till death,

"K. Heaton, August 22th, 1637.   "RICHARD SYKES.

"To His ever approved, most loveinge, and most carefull Father, Mr Richard Sykes, these p'sent in Leedes."

The "connection of the Sykes' of Leeds with the very eminent family of Beaumont of Whitley," to which the letter refers, may be accounted for in the following way: Sir Thomas Beaumont was the descendant of two inter-marriages of the Nevilles and Beaumonts, and

Elizabeth Mawson (mother of Richard Sykes, writer of the letter referred to by Mr. Hunter, and dated 22 Aug. 1637) was descended from the marriage of Elizabeth, daughter and heir of John Neville of Cudworth, with Roger Leghe of Middleton, temp. Hen. VII. Another instance of the extended sense in which the same Richard Sykes used the term " cousin " occurs in his accompt-book for the year 1643, wherein is an entry referring to his " cos. Gilb. Cowp." who descended from the marriage of Frances Leghe with John Cowper of Leeds, 8 Nov. 1547. " Uncle and aunt Binns" were father and mother of the wife of Richard Sykes's *deceased brother* John, this phrase affording another curious example of the comprehensive sense in which the terms of relationship were then commonly used.

It only remains to be added, if further corroboration of the origin of the Sykes' of Leeds (as now stated) be necessary, that the tradition of the " branded bull " was evidently derived from the Nevilles, whose retainers they had been ; and that the " crescent for difference," given with the arms in the *Ducatus Leodiensis*, is equally in accordance with exactly ascertained fact, and with the recognised laws of heraldry.

Q. F. V. F.

The following is an abstract of the Will of Richard Sykes, M.A. (grandson of the writer of the letter above printed,) cited in p. 316:—

" Richard Sykes, Master of Arts, of Sydney Sussex College, Cambridge," made his will Dec. 11, 1684, giving his real estate at Kirk Burton, Leeds, and Kirk Smeaton, to his brother Micklethwaite Sykes, charged with the yearly payment of 6*l* to testator's goddaughter Elizabeth Kershaw during her minority; after attaining her full age of 21 years to have the whole sum of 100*l*. To testator's aunt Rebecca Kershaw he gives certain lands at Thorpe Arch for her life, remainder to said Micklethwaite Sykes. " Also I give and bequeath to my cousin Sarah Kershaw, of Leeds aforesaid, one diamond ring, and to my cousin Rebecca Kershaw one ruby ring, both which are now in the custody of the said Sarah Kershaw." Residue to brother Micklethwaite Sykes, whom he made executor. Signed in the presence of George Bannister, Samuel Kirke, Thomas Dinsdale, Jun[r]. Proved Dec. 10, 1686.

As a negative proof that the testator had no wife nor child, but only a brother, Micklethwaite Sykes, this document adds strength to the statement in the former article that there was no issue of that Richard Sykes from whom the Sikes's of Chauntry House claimed descent.

Doncaster. J. S.

PERCY, WOODROFFE, AND PAVER.

To the Editor of THE HERALD AND GENEALOGIST.

Sir,—You have performed (in p. 269) a painful but not unnecessary service to the cause of historical truth by laying bare the hollowness of the pretensions advanced by Mr. William Paver to representation of the House of Percy, as a coheir of Thomas seventh Earl of Northumberland. This fallacy having been advocated by Banks, and inadvertently admitted by authors so worthy of attention as Beltz Lancaster and Mr. Sinclair, might well be adopted by other less cautious writers if proper warning were not held out. Mr. Paver has been a ready correspondent upon genealogical matters, and I have noticed some warm acknowledgments of his favours in the books of our Transatlantic friends. The late Sir Cuthbert Sharp also was one who was ready to accept with thankfulness Mr. Paver's assistance, and it may be as well to notice that at p. 349 of his *Memorials of the Rebellion of* 1569 (8vo. 1840) he admitted a note affirming that William Paver of York, esq. was the lineal descendant of John Paver, who married the great-granddaughter of the marriage between Richard Woodroffe and the Lady Elizabeth Percy.

Sir Cuthbert Sharp, perhaps, was too ready to catch at any striking incident or anecdote that he fancied would enliven his writings, and there were instances in which such things were specially fabricated for his enjoyment: as, for instance, the story of Hilton the celebrator of clandestine marriages, which embellishes his *History of Hartlepool.*

A friend has handed me copies of the pretended Wills which you have mentioned in p. 271, namely, one purporting to be that of Maximilian Woodroffe in 1652, and the other that of William Paver in 1721. As they will not occupy much of your valuable space, I will request you to " gibbet " them *in terrorem.*

In the name of God, amen. I, Maximilian Woodrove, of yᵉ Citye of Yorke, gentleman, being seke in bodye but of good minde and memorie, praised be yᵉ name of God for yᵉ same, do make my last and onlie Will and Testament, to wit: I doe give and bequeathe unto Richard Woodrove my younger broder and unto Joseph Woodrove of Cardiff mye youngest broder, if he be still alive, to each of them the sum of five pounds, and I do give and bequeath unto Maximilian yᵉ sonne of Richard Woodrove of Awtofts, my father cosin, the sum of two pounds, and I doe give and bequeath yᵉ Ring yᵗ mye deare mother gave me yᵗ longid to her father the Earle of Northomberlande unto Milliana ye only child of Maximilian my late deare sonne and heire, and I doe give and bequeath unto her Milliana all ye rest of my monyé, goods, and chattils, and I appoint her Executor of my Will and Testament. Witnesse mye hande and seale ye fourteenth day of May 1652.

> In ye presence of us
> Thomas Metcalfe,   M. WOODROFFE. L.S.
> George Dallman.

In ye name of God, amen. I, John Paver, of College Acaster, in ye countye of Yorke, Farmer, doe give and bequeath all my estate and effects unto my son William, and I appoint him sole executor of this my last Will and Testament. In witness whereof I have hereto set my hand this twentyeth daye of February, 1721.

> Signed in ye presence of   John Paver,
> John Brown.   x
> Thomas Smith.   his marke.

The first of these is more ingeniously conceived than the other: which is indeed a beggarly substitute for the bold fabrication that had previously been inserted in the same place, among the Testamentary Records at York, and of which you have given the substance in the quotation (p. 270) from Mr Downing Bruce's pamphlet.[1]

Yours, &c.   VINDEX.

EDGAR AND LAUDER.

Perseverance in the inquiry regarding the connection of the Edgar and Lauder families (see before, pp. 374-377) has procured me information which enables me to construct the following pedigree of a collateral branch of the family of Dick-Lauder, baronets.

At the same time the following extract from Burke's *Peerage and Baronetage* may serve to explain or give a clue to the origin of any doubt about the Christian or baptismal name of the first member of the collateral branch. "Richard Lauder of Lauder, a senator of the College of Justice by the title of Lord Lauder" (ob. about 1575). "He married Mary,

---

[1] Notwithstanding the thorough exposure of the fictitious pretensions of Mr. Paver that had been made in 1854, as quoted in p. 270, we observe that his unfounded assumptions were recognised so recently as 1860, in Mr. C. N. Elvin's *Handbook of Mottoes*, in which occurs the following—

"*Faded, but not destroyed.* PAVER, of Braham Hall, co. York. *Crest*, A tree proper.

"This motto doubtless refers to the crest as well as to the old barony of Percy, of which this family is coheir."

It is evidently not unnecessary to caution authors from unwittingly assisting in the propagation of such misrepresentations; nor, perhaps, can the caution be too often repeated. When weeds of this nature have been industriously scattered over the field of history for some years, it is difficult thoroughly to eradicate them. (EDIT. *H. & G.*)

daughter of MacDowall of Mackairston, by whom he had his *eldest** son,"
Robert Lauder of Lauder, "whose line *terminating* by the death of his *son*
and *grandson*, the direct line was carried on by Richard's second son," &c.

Qy. What were the names and dates of decease of the *son* and *grandson*
alluded to ?

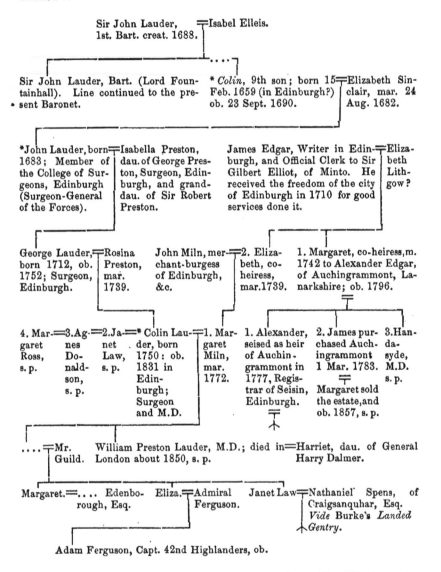

Sir John Lauder, ═Isabel Elleis.
1st. Bart. creat. 1688.

Sir John Lauder, Bart. (Lord Foun-   * *Colin*, 9th son ; born 15═Elizabeth Sin-
tainhall).   Line continued to the pre-   Feb. 1659 (in Edinburgh?)   clair, mar. 24
• sent Baronet.   ob. 23 Sept. 1690.   Aug. 1682.

*John Lauder, born═Isabella Preston,   James Edgar, Writer in Edin-═Eliza-
1683 ; Member of   dau. of George Pres- burgh, and Official Clerk to Sir   beth
the College of Sur- ton, Surgeon, Edin- Gilbert Elliot, of Minto. He   Lith-
geons, Edinburgh   burgh, and grand-   received the freedom of the city   gow ?
(Surgeon-General   dau. of Sir Robert   of Edinburgh in 1710 for good
of the Forces).   Preston.   services done it.

George Lauder,═Rosina   John Miln, mer-═2. Eliza-   1. Margaret, co-heiress, m.
born 1712, ob.   Preston, chant-burgess   beth, co-   1742 to Alexander Edgar,
1752 ; Surgeon, mar.   of Edinburgh,   heiress,   of Auchingrammont, La-
Edinburgh.   1739.   &c.   mar.1739.   narkshire ; ob. 1796.
                                                            ═

4. Mar-═3.Ag-═2.Ja-═* Colin Lau-═1. Mar-   1. Alexander,   2. James pur-   3.Han-
garet   nes   net   der, born   garet   seised as heir chased Auch-   da-
Ross,   Do-   Law,   1750: ob.   Miln,   of Auchin-   ingrammont   syde,
s. p.   nald-   s. p. 1831 in   mar.   grammont in   1 Mar. 1783.   M.D.
         son,   Edin-   1772.   1777, Regis-   ═   s. p.
         s. p.   burgh ;   trar of Seisin, Margaret sold
                         Surgeon   Edinburgh.   the estate, and
                         and M.D.   ═   ob. 1857, s. p.

.... ═Mr.   William Preston Lauder, M.D. ; died in═Harriet, dau. of General
      Guild.   London about 1850, s. p.   Harry Dalmer.

Margaret.═.... Edenbo-   Eliza.═Admiral   Janet Law═Nathaniel Spens,   of
          rough, Esq.   Ferguson.   Craigsanquhar, Esq.
                                                    Vide Burke's *Landed*
                                                    Gentry.

Adam Ferguson, Capt. 42nd Highlanders, ob.

Dr. W. P. Lauder bequeathed to his eldest niece, Mrs. Edenborough,
the portraits of his ancestors marked *. The first portrait represents

an elderly man in a black gown and large flowing wig. The second is in a scarlet uniform.

According to the records of the College of Surgeons, Edinburgh, the following are the only Lauders surgeons, so far as Colin Lauder, with the dates of *entry: John* Lauder, 23 Feb. 1683; John Lauder, 1 July, 1709; George Lauder, 20 April, 1737 ; Colin Lauder (M.D.), 31 August, 1772.

It would be desirable to refer to the baptism of *Colin* Lauder (recorded in Edinburgh), stated to have been the ninth son of the first baronet.

Dr. Colin Lauder was an intimate friend of the second Alexander Edgar of Auchingrammont, whose brother Handasyde Edgar was his fellow collegian.

The family connection between Lauder and Edgar is clear; between *Preston* and Lauder it is also clear; but between *Preston* and *Edgar* it is obscure, though the following coincidences seem significant, and I should be glad to be assured that Alexander Edgar, Fellow of the College of Surgeons, Edinburgh, still alive in 1697, was the father of Alexander Edgar, the first of Auchingrammont, and who returned from *Jamaica* and purchased that estate in the earlier part of last century. Alexander, F.C.S. Edinburgh, had a son named *John* (after his grandfather John Edgar of Wedderlie), also a F.C.S. Edinburgh, who appears to have died about 1722.

From these Edgars came probably the *Scotch* family of Edgar of Bristol, in which city the wills are, I am told, recorded of Archibald and *Preston* Edgar. The latter's son, John Edgar, has a monument in Falmouth church, *Jamaica*. He died in 1805.

There has been no connection as yet surmised however between Thomas Edgar (baillie of the barony of *Grange*, owned by the Dicks) and his fellow collegian, Alexander Edgar, brother of John Edgar of Wedderlie. The family of Dick formerly owned the estate of *Preston*field, near Edinburgh, now possessed by the Cunninghames. Here then we find a group of names and dates converging towards the point where a clearer light is required, with a curious suggestiveness, when it is remembered that Edgar is a very uncommon surname.

Bristol, as the commercial nurse of the West Indies, early in the last century received an influx of Scotchmen from those once flourishing colonies.

There remains one other doubt, namely, whether Alexander Edgar the first of Auchingrammont was not the son of *John* Edgar, F.C.S. (ob. 1722), son of Alexander Edgar, F.C.S. and consequently *grandson* of the latter.

J. H. L.-A.

JUNIOR BRANCH OF DEVEREUX, AND THE RIGHT OF QUARTERING ARMS.

To the Editor of THE HERALD AND GENEALOGIST.

DEAR SIR,—According to a MS. Pedigree of this family in a copy of Duncombe's *History of Herefordshire* in my possession (inserted, as I suppose, by Mr. John Blount, to whom the book formerly belonged,) Sir George Devereux of Sheldon (brother of Walter Viscount Hereford, who died in 1676,) had by Blanche his wife, daughter and heiress of John Rudge of Rudge, co. Salop, three children, viz. George, from whom springs the present Viscount; Walter, of Coleshill, co. Warwick; and Anne, wife of Valence Sacheverell, of New Hall. The second son, Walter, it is stated married Mary, daughter of James Bitton, D.D. and had issue :—

1. Walter, of Coleshill, who by his wife Anne, daughter of Bryan Janson, of Daventry, had two sons, George and William.

2. James, of the New Exchange, milliner, living 1710. He married Isard, daughter of Anthony Farrington, of the Exchange and Battenhurst, Surrey, and had issue :—

  James, aged 21 in 1710; Essex, aged 15 in 1710; and three daughters, Farrington, Frances, and Mary.

3. Arden Devereux, who died without issue.

4. Samuel Devereux, who, by his wife Mary, daughter of   Jordan, of Warwick, had two daughters—

  Mary, wife of   Lloyd, who was living in Virginia in 1710; and Anne, married to   Hill, stocking-seller in the Exchange.

5. Robert, living at Coleshill in 1710, who had issue—his wife's name is not mentioned—two sons, George and Robert, and a daughter, Elizabeth, wife of   Smith, of Coleshill.

I send this extract to you for publication, because I have not hitherto seen these persons mentioned in any account of the Devereux family. In Collins's Peerage the younger sons of Sir George Devereux are stated to have been *Walter*, *Arden*, Edward, William, *Samuel*, and *Robert*, and in Mr. C. E. Long's "Genealogical List of the several Persons entitled to Quarter the Arms of the Royal Houses of England," 1845, occur the " descendants (*if any*) of Walter, &c. younger sons of Sir George Devereux, of Sheldon." The pedigree in question, however, only enumerates the three children I have mentioned, and Walter, Arden, Samuel, and Robert are stated to have been sons of Walter.

Of course nothing would be more natural than for Walter Devereux to give his children the same baptismal names as their uncles; but it would be interesting to know if this was really the fact. From one of these sons of Walter may have descended George Devereux, Esq. of Cefyn Werfa, co. Montgomery, who left a legacy to his relative, Martha, daughter and co-heir of a John Devereux, gent. and wife of Richard Hickman,* by virtue of which match the Hickmans quarter the Devereux arms.

* She was married to Mr. Hickman in 1788.

By the way, there is a passage in the Brochure recently reviewed in your miscellany— *Popular Genealogists*—which is surely a little too sweeping : " No one, it is stated, is allowed to quarter his arms with those of another family (irrespectively of the case of sovereign families) *without the permission of the King-at-Arms*."

It is of course a well-known law of heraldry that the arms of another family can only be quartered in those cases in which there is representation as well as descent, but it is quite new to learn that the permission of the King of Arms is necessary.

With more especial reference to the Royal Arms, this writer lays it down that no person, even if he be a representative or co-representative of any of the Plantagenet Princes, can quarter the royal coat with his own unless he obtains a proper authority from the Heralds to do so. " I allude to this matter more particularly (he continues) because, throughout the *Peerage* and the *Landed Gentry*, and all Sir B. Burke's writings, the same idea is found continually occurring until it becomes a positive mania . . . . The same cool assumption of right to *bear* the royal arms meets us *passim* in the *Vicissitudes of Families*." He then cites the case of Mr. Smart, butcher, and others, stated in that work to be " entitled to quarter the royal arms," and asks, " did it ever occur to Sir B. Burke what the persons here enumerated are to quarter the royal arms *with* ?" adding, " that no one can quarter any coat of arms if he have not in the first place a coat of his own, so as to be in the heraldic sense a gentleman."

This latter remark is manifestly true and just; but, suppose by way of argument Mr. Smart had a paternal coat of arms, or took out a grant, could he not then place among the quarterings to which he is entitled the ensigns of Edmund of Woodstock, of whom he is a co-representative?

The case of Mr. Smart, I may remark in conclusion, is " no sinister nor awkward claim." The butcher has been, however, long gathered to his fathers, but the family still exists in very good circumstances at Halesowen.

Yours, &c.

H. S. G.

We should be happy to assist a SUBSCRIBER who writes from the Junior United Service Club for aid in making researches, did we not foresee that to undertake to do so would expose us to more trouble and responsibility in such matters than we feel able to undertake. We must refer him to Advertisements that are frequently appearing, particularly in the pages of *Notes and Queries*, and at the same time caution him to be careful with whom he deals.

ARCHER OF HALE, CO. SOUTHAMPTON.

In the small church of Hale in Hampshire, not far from Salisbury, is a monument bearing the following inscription:

Sacrum Memoriæ THOMÆ ARCHER, Armigeri, filii natu minimi Thomæ Archer, de Umberslade in agro Warwicensi Arm, SS^{tæ} Trin. Coll. Oxon. nuper Alumni, ubi per tres annos studiis academicis adolescentiam excoluit, et postea quadriennii peregrinatione perpolivit. In Angliam redux, eximiâ corporis formâ insignis, ingenuisque artibus apprimè ornatus, in Aulâ Regiâ emicuit juvenum pulcherrimus, flos, ac decus: constitutus fuit Groomporter Serenissimæ Annæ Reginæ A.D. 1703, et Præfect. Custumar. apud Newcastle A.D. 1715. Rura hæc quæ cernis, Lector, vicina eodem emit anno, sedemque istma amœnissimam ab integro extruxit, et hanc ecclesiam vetustate collapsuram stabilivit propriisque sumptibus exornatam ampliavit. Duas duxit uxores, fœminas lectissimas, 1^{am} Eleonoram filiam unicam et heredem Johannis Archer de Welford[1] in agro Bercheriensi Arm. quæ, primo connubii anno nondum completo, variolarum lue, proh dolor! in ipso fere puerperio, prærepta est. In secundis nuptiis habuit Annam, filiam unicam Johannis Chaplin de Tathwell in com. Lincoln. Arm. e quâ nullam suscepit prolem. Conjugibus prædilectis hoc supremum amoris fideique conjugalis pignus, sibique monumentum, vivens posuit A.D. 1739. Vir fuit summis negotiis par, titulis superior; patriæ valdè amans, nec minus patriæ amatus, pauperibus largus, divitibus gratus, miseris amicus, omnibus charus.

Obiit 22^a die Maii Anno $\left\{ \begin{array}{l} \text{D'ni 1743,} \\ \text{Ætat. suæ 75,} \end{array} \right.$

peccatorum vere penitens; ac certâ spe resurgendi in Christo Deoque humillimè confidens, Qui divino favore tamdiu in terris fœlicem servaverat, in cœlis fœlicissimum servet in eternum!

The tablet bearing this inscription is placed underneath three life-sized figures of Thomas Archer and his two wives; and above it is a shield bearing Azure, three arrows in pale, 2 and 1, points downwards, or; impaling Ermine, on a chief azure three griffin's heads or.

A second monument consists of another life-sized figure of a lady holding a sepulchral urn, and a tablet thus inscribed:—

---

[1] John Archer, of Welford in Berkshire, esquire, was the son and heir of Sir John Archer, justice of the Common Pleas, whose marriages have been already stated in the present volume, p. 283.

" To the memory of HENRY ARCHER, Esq. pious, just, charitable, in his Country's service steady, an affectionate Husband, this marble is erected by the R^t Honble Lady ELIZABETH ARCHER, a much afflicted widow."

On the urn—

" After 24 years of conjugal harmony, he died March 16, 1768, aged 68. Farewell!"

On the latter monument are two oval escutcheons, one apparently quartered, but now effaced; the other bearing the coat of Archer of Umberslade, with a crescent for difference.

This Henry Archer, Esq. was the nephew to the first wife of Thomas' being younger son of Andrew Archer, Esq. M.P. for Warwickshire, by Elizabeth daughter of Sir Samuel Dashwood, Lord Mayor of London in 1702; and brother to Thomas created Baron Archer of Umberslade in 1747. He was M.P. for Warwick in several parliaments; and married Lady Elizabeth Montagu, sister to George Earl of Halifax, but died without issue.

TAAFFE PEDIGREES.

From the residence of the head of this family abroad arises probably the comparatively little interest that has been taken in it, and consequently, notwithstanding its historic note, its various branches remain to this day a problem unsolved.

Even generally recognised pedigrees differ, and some of the discrepancies are sufficiently striking to invite inquiry.

Thus Sir Bernard Burke in his *Peerage and Baronetage* gives the following descent :—

1. Richard Taaffe of Ballybraggan was succeeded by his son

2. Sir William Taaffe, who by his wife Ismay daughter of C. Bellew, esq. had a son

3. Sir John Taaffe, the first Viscount Taaffe.

Should not the following however be considered the true descent?—*Vide* Lodge's *Peerage of Ireland*, &c.

1. Peter Taaffe (1559) who married and had three sons, viz. :

John, the eldest.=	(Sir) William,=Ismay ob. 1630.	Bellew.	Peter, of Peppardstown.
Christopher, in= .... the rebellion of 1641.	Mary, mar. to John Taaffe, of Arthurstown, co. Louth.	Sir John=Anne, Taaffe, cre- dau. ated a Peer of first of Ireland Viscount Aug. 1, Dillon. 1628.	Eleanor.=Richard Taaffe, of Cookstown, co. Louth.
1. John of Braganstown. 2. Christopher.			

This, the first Viscount Taaffe, had according to "Ulster," "*with other issue*," 1. Theobald, 2. Lucas, 3. Francis, who *married an Italian lady and* HAD A SON, 4. Peter, 5. Jasper, 6. William, who married Margaret, daughter of Connor *O'*Kennedy *Roe*, and had issue Nicholas, who succeeded as sixth Viscount.

Now, in the case submitted to the Lords (1859-60), these sons are thus given in the tabulated pedigree, viz. 1. Theobald, 2. *Luke*, "died without issue," 3. Francis, "*died without issue*," 4. William, married Margaret *Kennedy*, not "*O'*Kennedy *Roe*." Further on, at page 4 of the same case, these are styled the first peer's "*eldest four sons*," which may probably be a misprint for "*four elder sons*," as at page 8, the issue of Sir John Taaffe, first Viscount, is stated to have been "*eleven* sons and *three daughters*." I have seen elsewhere however, but have unfortunately mislaid the reference, that Sir John first Viscount Taaffe had no fewer than *fourteen sons*, besides the three daughters.

With regard to remote branches of this family the following remarks may be taken for what they are worth.

A Christopher Taaffe, of Mansfieldstown, and other places in the county Louth, was attainted in 1691, at Ardee, and in consequence lost all his *real* estate. He was an adherent of James II. in whose own regiment of Infantry[1] he was a lieutenant.

The *chattel* property of a Christopher Taaffe, probably the above officer, was sold at public auction in 1725, at Ardee. This Christopher died in Dublin, and bequeathed by will dated in 1736 to "*Theobald Taaffe* of Dowanstown, co. Meath," his new gun, case of pistols, and "two crossbows," likewise trifling legacies to those who nursed him when ill at Drogheda. The testator is designated "gentleman."

Now, this unfortunate soldier appears to be identical with a certain Christopher Taaffe, who is mentioned by the Rev. Arthur Taaffe, in his will dated in Jamaica, 1750, and registered 30 Jan. 1752, as "his father Christopher, of the kingdom of Ireland, *if still alive*." The testator also mentions his brother Henry Taaffe, and his *nephew* Henry Gordon. The Rev. Henry Taaffe, in his will registered in 1771, also in Jamaica, appoints John Gordon guardian of his four sons, 1. Arthur-Rodger, 2. John-Armistead, 3. Richard-Brownrigg,[2] 4. Thomas-Wheeler.

Henry or Harry Gordon[3] in his will, dated Jan. 18, 1788, also recorded in Jamaica, says, "I give and devise all my estate real and personal or

---

[1] *Vide* Mr. Dalton's valuable annotations on the Irish Army List of King James II.

[2] Sir Richard Brownrigg, G.C.B. married Elizabeth, daughter of William Lewis of Jamaica.

[3] I believe this Harry Gordon to be identical with the Lieut.-Colonel Harry Gordon who was superseded as dead on 1st Sept. 1787, and who served in the West Indies. The name *Harry* Gordon is exceedingly rare, and moreover James Gordon of Jamaica in his will dated in 1766 mentions his brother "Harry Gordon in His Majesty's service."

mixed, arising from my claims in the kingdom of Ireland," *i. e.* in right of his mother Anne Taaffe, and his father Harry Gordon.

There are two other wills recorded in Jamaica which bear upon the same question, viz. registered in 1762, that of Michael Taaffe, who mentions his mother then residing in the parish of Dromisken, co. Louth, and his sister married to Peter Clinton; and the will of Susanna, wife of Theobald Taaffe, of Hanover Square, Middlesex, dated May 3, 1754.

If the Irish property of these emigrant Taaffes be identical with the lands in the parish of Dromisken, co. Louth, granted to Theobald Taaffe, first Earl of Carlingford, in 1668, it seems highly probable that the former were descendants of John Taaffe, uncle of Sir John the first Viscount Taaffe, if not of his sisters, who also married gentlemen bearing the same name.

It is supposed however that Arthur and Henry Taaffe of Jamaica, sons of Christopher, had another brother in Ireland named George, who settled in Roscommon.

To return once more to the pedigrees given by Sir Bernard Burke, and to that submitted to the Lords, it must strike a casual reader that the assertion made by Ulster, that Francis third son of the first peer married an Italian lady and had a son, has not been disproved. It seems to be tacitly admitted that such a marriage existed, but it is not clearly shown how the conclusion was arrived at by the petitioner that he "died without issue." On whom lies the *onus probandi*—on Sir Bernard, or on the representative of the first peer? Whence came the information of either? The latter accepts to a certain extent the assertion of the former, but sets it aside arbitrarily. Is not this like an open question still?

No one indeed is likely to dispute this peerage; but at the same time, merely selecting it for discussion from its singularity, does it not seem as though senior lines were somewhat hastily disposed of? Younger sons go abroad and are lost sight of. Their grandchildren mingling with a lower grade of society, and perhaps speaking another language—without heirlooms or houses in which to keep them—in the course of little more than half a century may be totally unrecognisable, and yet after all they nevertheless exist, although summarily cut off from all future connection with the parent stem.

There are numerous similar cases of more or less interest.

L.-A.

BIBLIOTHECA HERALDICA.

GIFT-BOOK, OF THE ARMS AND QUARTERINGS OF NORTH : in the Possession of the Baroness North, at Wroxton, co. Oxford.

Gift Books, containing Illuminations of the Arms of the Families to whom they were presented by the Heralds, were not unusual during the Seventeenth Century, and were sometimes accompanied by verses descriptive of the different arms and quarterings. The following example has been lately found among the papers of the North family.

The original is a small 4to. on vellum of seven leaves, and bound also in the same material, and the arms are well drawn, and coloured. It is the work of "MERCURIUS PATTEN Bluemantel," who occupied that office from 1597 to 1611.[1] The Title is in Latin :

Honoratissimi Do: Dom: Dudley: Northe Baronis de Kirtling, alias Cartlige, in co-
    mitatu Cantabrigiensi, Armorum Descriptiones, Gallicè et Anglicè, atq: carmine
    Heroico.

Then follows a beautifully executed shield, displaying the arms of North, quartered with Dale, Caldecott, and Newport, and the two Crests on separate helmets, according to the taste of the age, of North and Dale, the first on a torse or and azure, a Dragon's head erased sable, collared or ; the second on a torse argent and sable, a Wolf rampant ermine, collared or. The Supporters, two Dragons sable collared or : The Motto, " PERAGE."

On the next page is the single coat of North, Azure, a lion passant or, between three fleurs de lis argent, and this verse :

Hic leo solaris gradiens clarescit asurro :
Hoc etiam splendent clypeo tria lilia lunæ.

We have on the next page the coat of Dale, Argent, on a bend sable three wolves passant of the first, thus described :

Nigrens banda lupos gradientes continet albos
Tres niveo scuto.

The arms of Caldecott on the following page, are, Sable, a chevron between three withered plants, or trees, "arrached" or, and the verse

Auratum tignum campo gestavit in atro,
Avulsas plantas tres siccas inter, et auri.

The last is the coat of Newport, Sable, on a chevron between three pheons argent [*called in this MS.* darts or brode arrowe hedds] as many mullets gules, described :

Molettas rubeas tignus tres possidet albus
Saturni clypeo
Inter telorum tria ferrea spicula lunæ.

[1] Having been set down by Lord Burghley as a proper person for the office of Rouge Croix or Bluemantle, he was created a Pursuivant by the latter name, Oct. 22, 1597; but his patent was dated 8th May 2 James I. (1603). He sold the office to his successor Henry St.George, who was created Bluemantle Dec. 23, 1611.

The Book concludes with a description of the Crests and Supporters in French, Latin, and English, and is signed

Honori tuo humilime devotus

MERCURIUS PATTENUS *Blumantel.*

[*Communicated by* E. P. SHIRLEY, ESQ. M.A. F.S.A.]

ON THE SEALS AND ARMS OF THE CITY OF WORCESTER. Being the substance of a Paper read at a Meeting of the Worcester Archæological Club, by RICHARD WOOF, F.S.A., Town Clerk of Worcester. (Reprinted from the Reports of the Worcester Diocesan Architectural Society, 1865.) 8vo. pp. 10, with two lithographic plates.

The seals described in this essay are three in number: 1. The Common Seal of the City of Worcester: SIGILLUM COMMVNE CIVIVM WIGORNIE. It is not improbably of the reign of Henry III. and is ascertained to have been used as early as 1298. The device is intended, apparently, for a representation of the city: though somewhat conventionally indicated, by a gate surmounted by a spire, and side-scenes of windows, arcades, roofs, and pinnacles, the whole begirt in front by a battlemented wall. The buildings might be taken for a representation of the cathedral only; and Green the Historian of Worcester fancied that the design was "meant probably to typify the ancient ecclesiastical power as pre-eminent over the civil;" but we do not perceive anything to support that idea.

A considerable portion of Mr. Woof's paper is occupied by the history of a duplicate of this seal, of modern fabrication; but by which an antiquary of no less experience than Mr. Albert Way was for a time deceived. He met with it at Rouen in the year 1843, and was induced to purchase it for 2*l.* or something less: he afterwards heard that the late Rev. G. C. Gordon, the Historian of St. Neot's, had seen it at a chateau near Saint Lo, in 1836, where it was offered him for ten Napoleons. We have ourselves met with some fictitious matrices of the like manufacture. They are betrayed by the elaborate and inappropriate handles that are given them, generally castings derived from some modern inkstand or paper-weight, of French design, or perhaps even copied from a Greek or Egyptian model. Let us contrast such devices with the simple apparatus of the genuine seal of Worcester, which has never left the custody of its legitimate guardians. "It is a fine circular seal of brass, two and a half inches in diameter, and of a quarter of an inch in uniform thickness, having a small projecting piece from the edge, perforated, as if to receive a ring for suspending it from a ribbon or chain."

2. A smaller seal, also circular, an inch and a quarter in diameter, is perhaps of the same antiquity. It is the seal of the Bailiffs: Worcester having no Mayor until the year 1622: s. BALLIVORVM CIVITATIS WYGORN.

The device an embattled gate, standing between two oak trees, above which appear the moon and the sun.

The purposes to which these and similar municipal seals were applied are thus distinguished by the author:

The one was probably used by the Bailiffs to give the necessary official character to any document which they were required to execute in their individual official capacity, in a similar manner to that in which the Mayors of this day authenticate by their signature and the common seal the execution of deeds and other documents intended for foreign use.

The other was the Common Seal of the City, used for the execution of leases, and all other deeds and documents which it was necessary should be effected as the act of the Bailiffs, Aldermen, and Citizens combined; in fact the act of the City as distinguished from the individual official act of the Bailiffs.

3. The third seal is of comparatively modern date. It is THE SEALE OF THE STATVTE MARCHANT OF WORCESTER, and has the year 1654 engraved on its handle. Its device is an embattled gate, between two vines. The purposes for which such seals were provided, in the recognizance of commercial debts, are clearly explained by Mr. Woof: but we need not enter upon them, as they have no relation to our special inquiries.

None of the seals indeed have any armorial relations. The inquiry, *What are the proper Arms of the city of Worcester?* has to be pursued upon other evidence. The earliest authority seems to be the Heralds' Visitation of Worcestershire in the year 1569: where the arms of the city of Worcester are thus given: *Quarterly sable and gules, a castle-triple-towered argent.* In the subsequent Visitations of 1634 and 1582-3, the same is repeated as "the ancient arms," with a second coat as "the modern arms" of the city, viz. *Argent, a fess between three pears sable.* In more recent times it has been usual to combine these two coats, by placing the latter as a canton upon the former.

No official authority, however, has been discovered for any of these assumptions. There is a tradition that Queen Elizabeth added the three pears to the city arms on her visit to Worcester in 15.. This device has not however been traced earlier than one of the half-crowns coined at Worcester whilst the mint of Charles I. was established there during the civil war. This has one pear on the obverse, and three pears on the reverse, as mint marks. Shortly after, in 1659, a token was struck having *three pears, two and one,* on a shield, and more than thirty tradesmen's tokens of the age of Charles II. bearing the same arms are represented in Green's *History of Worcester.* It has not been discovered when the coat of *Argent, a fess between three pears sable,* originated: but at the Heralds' Visitation of 1682 this was entered as the "modern armes" of the city.

Mr. Woof does not approve of the more recent practice of placing the "modern arms" as a canton upon the ancient coat: but would retain them both "borne on separate shields united by a scroll or ribbon." For so doing the Visitation of 1682 may be pleaded as official authority: but it is remarkable that no regular grant of either one or the other coat has been discovered. Two passages of the poet Drayton are cited, in which he represents a pear or pear-tree as the cognizance of Worcestershire; but it would be more satisfactory to obtain some earlier evidence of that fact. We are told that the pear-tree is now borne by the Worcestershire regi_ment of Volunteer Rifles ; having been adopted, on the authority of Dray_ton, as the badge which the Worcestershire men wore at Agincourt.

Mr. Woof states that "the shield of the pears is placed over the entrance to the County Gaol, and it has been frequently, and as I believe errone_ously, used for county purposes." At the same time he remarks, that " Counties, except such as the Palatinates of Chester and Durham, had no arms; though in many cases they adopted the arms of their capital town, or of the ancient kingdom they represent; the White Horse of Kent for example." (p. 3.)   Subsequently (p. 10) he informs us that

The County of Worcester appears to have adopted a coat of arms. The earliest date at which I can learn its public use is 1838, when it was displayed upon the iron cast_ings of Powick Bridge: it is now used by all the great public establishments of the county,—the Clerk of the Peace, the Police authorities, the County Gaol, and (im_paled with the City arms) the County and City Lunatic Asylum. I am unable to meet with a correct blazon of these adopted arms; and the engraved examples, which differ considerably, in no instance afford sufficient detail for a description. The shield is parted per fess : in the upper portion is a river, on the sinister side a boat in full sail and distant hills, and in dexter chief a beehive and bees ; on the fess point a cornu_copiæ : in the lower part two coats, which may be intended for those of Kidderminster and Bewdley, occupy the spaces of the third and fourth quarters. Motto : DEO JUVANTE ARTE ET INDUSTRIA FLORET.

This is altogether a curious account of the growth of corporate arms, without legitimate authority, in modern times.   There is a vast quantity of the same kind, continually produced for the use of public works (such as railways, &c.) and commercial companies, not in the Office of Arms, but in the shops of the Seal-Engravers.   But surely Counties and Cities might pursue a more dignified course in such matters.

NOTES AND QUERIES.

GENEALOGICAL TRADITIONS—FAMILY OF COWPER.

SIR,—In your Number for last May you have an excellent article on fictitious pedigrees.   I was glad to see it, because "the Art of Pedigree-making," as very largely practised at present, cannot be too unsparingly exposed.   Will you, however, allow me to make your remarks an excuse for offering a few words on the opposite side of the case.

I cannot help thinking that there is a tendency in our day to believe too little ; to attach little or no weight to probability and to family traditions ; to accept the omission of names as proof of the non-existence of the persons to whom they professedly belonged.   Let me give an instance.

I am acquainted with a lady, now upwards of 80, but in the perfect possession of her memory, whose father, a wealthy clergyman, bore the same name as the poet Cowper, was intimate with and corresponded with him as " Cousin." Owing to an accident which befel the eldest son at sea, this correspondence, and other documents which would have proved the relationship, and with it the community of ancestry, are lost.

The poet Cowper and Earl Cowper descended from two brothers, as is well known; but in all the Peerages which I have consulted the younger (the poet's) branch is, as usual, scantily given, and its younger members disposed of as " dying young," and so forth, probably as the elder branch have chanced to remember, or *fancied* that they remembered. Now, Sir, will any of your readers tell me how the descent of this lady and her family is to be established? In another generation the tradition will be still further weakened, and in a comparatively short time it will, according to our growing theory, be treated as utterly untrustworthy. The lady was twenty years old when her father died.

The clergyman to whom I allude was the Rev. William Cowper, Rector of Harwich, Dovercourt, and Ramsay; died Nov. 1809.

31 *Oct.* 1865.   ·   Yours, &c.   W. M. H. C.

ARMS AT BAGENDON IN GLOUCESTERSHIRE.

In the east window of the small church of Bagendon, near Cirencester, is a shield of arms : party per pale ; dexter, Sable, a chevron argent between three pheons or; sinister, Argent, on a chevron between three birds sable (shovellers?) a mullet argent. This coat has a border, which appears to be merely ornamental, in the nature of diapering, having no tincture. The dexter coat appears, like the other, to have had a mullet for difference, but a fracture has carried away nearly the whole of it. I should be glad to be informed to whom these armorial bearings belong.

In the spandrils of the same window are two other smaller shields : one Argent, an escallop-shell gules, belonging to Prelatte of Cirencester : the other is similar to the sinister bearing above, but has no border.

From the character of the glass I believe the date to be about 1450. I learn from Atkyns *(Present and Ancient State of Gloucestershire)* that about that date William Nottingham and Elizabeth his wife levied a fine of lands in Bagendon, 20 Hen. VI. Sir William Nottingham was seized of the manors of Coates and Trewsbury, 1 Rich. III., and died in the following year seised of the manor of Saperton, which he devised for life to Elizabeth his wife. She married secondly Richard Pool of Coates.

Atkyns also states that the manor of Bagendon belonged to the Chantry of the Holy Trinity in the parish church of Cirencester, which Chantry was founded by Sir William Nottingham, Baron of the Exchequer. He adds " that there is an inscription upon a marble slab in the south isle for Sir Wm. Nottingham and his wife : he died in 1427." This is probably an error : for on a brass plate in the south aisle there is still a monumental in-scription commemorating William and Christina Nottingham, who probably were parents of Sir William, and died respectively 1427 and 1433. As every monument on the floor of Cirencester church has been removed for *the Restoration* it is now undergoing, it is not unnecessary to be thus par-ticular.

I have dwelt on the family of Nottingham, because I fancy they may be commemorated in the armorial bearings at Bagendon, though I have no means of identifying the family with the arms.

William Prelatte, who died 1462, is commemorated with his two wives by effigies and inscriptions on brass in Cirencester church.   W. D.

HUBERT OF LE MANOIR AND HUBERT HUSEE.

The late Sir F. Palgrave, in his *History of Normandy and England*, vol. iii. pp. 212—214, gives a graphic account of the flight of William Duke of Normandy, in 1047, from Valognes to Falaise, to escape from a con-spiracy of his Barons, headed by Nigel de St. Sauveur, and he concludes the narrative thus : " The road through which William escaped still retains the name of *la voie du Duc*." Where can I find a detailed account of this flight ?

It seems that William, being awakened in the dead of night by the Court Jester Golet, fled from Valognes to the river Vire. There, close to Isigny, he tarried at the church of St. Clement ; thence he went, not to Bayeux, but made for " le Manoir," and, " ere the sun had cleared the horizon, William had arrived at *Hubert's* door. The narrative then goes on, " Hu-bert's sons conducted the Duke to palatial Falaise." Who was this Hubert ? Can he have been Hubert Huse, patriarch of the English branch of the Husseys, whose arms, and an extract from whose pedigree, appeared in your pages, vol. i. pp. 524—526 ? My reasons for venturing on such a conjecture are as follows.

In the ancient copies of the Husey pedigree, Hubert Huse, temp. Will'mi Conquestoris, is described as " a nobleman near to Cæsarsburg." (Cher-bourg.) He married Hellena, one of the two illegitimate daughters of Richard III. Duke of Normandy. In a note in the body of the pedigree, said to have been copied from a document found in Glastonbury at the Dissolution, and written in what is popularly known as Norman French, it is stated that he was brought over to England by the Conqueror, " with all his brethren according to the flesh," and " got great substance," &c. Add to this the fact that the family of Huse, or Hose, certainly was widely spread and largely estated in the Cotentin at an early period.

Putting these facts together, it seems to me highly probable that Hubert of the " Manoir " and the first Hubert Huse were the same person, or at least father and son ; and, in this latter case, that Hellena's husband was one of the " sons " who conducted William to Falaise. It was most natural that William, in his flight, should take refuge in the dwelling of his kinswoman's husband; and it was equally natural, that, having been thus sheltered and aided in his hour of need, he should afterwards provide for Hubert in his newly-acquired kingdom. ·   W. M. H. C.

Upon a picture (Elizabethan) containing portraits of a lady and (female) child, the following arms are emblasoned :—

Quarterly, 1st and 3rd, Azure, a cross between four leopard's heads or.

2nd and 4th, Ermine a chevron and a chief sable, over the point of the chevron a leopard's head or.

Any information with a view to identifying the portraits will be acceptable.

Qy. Kingston, of the co. Leicester, and Pourdon, of co. Derby ?

R. W.

Marshalling of Quarterings with an Inescocheon.

Considerable technical difficulties occasionally arise in marshalling and delineating quarterings ; as, for a familiar example, it is difficult to place eight quarterings within a lozenge, particularly if the coats themselves are not of simple composition.

But what is to be done when quarterings are surmounted by an inescocheon? Suppose an atchievement of twelve quarterings, over which has to be placed an inescocheon, itself bearing four quarterings, and consequently of considerable dimensions. Is the inescocheon to be allowed to *conceal* those quarterings which happen to fall in the centre of the principal shield?

Suppose another case, and indeed the actual case which prompts me to make these inquiries. I have a shield of ten quarterings only, upon which I am required to place an inescocheon of four quarterings. May I be allowed to arrange the ten coats as

1 2 3 4

5   6

7 8 9 10

so that the inescocheon shall really conceal non-entities ?   Pictor.

[Such inquiries as these have so completely to do with modern practice and modern arrangements only, that we can only promulgate them, with a hope that they may be answered from competent experience of their solution. With regard to the principles of ancient Quartering, it is evident they were very different from the modern ; and, so far as we are aware, they are now perfectly unknown. We have commenced some collections upon the subject, which we shall endeavour to arrange at a future day, for it can only be by diligent scrutiny and comparison of such a series of examples that it will be possible to ascertain either why certain quarterings were marshalled in a certain manner, or why they were adopted at all.

Edit. H. & G.]

THE LEES OF QUARRENDON.

(No. III.)

Concluded from p. 295.

SIR EDWARD HENRY LEE, fifth Baronet, was, in the reign of King Charles II., by letters patent dated 5 June, 1674, created Baron Lee of Spelsbury in the county of Oxon, Viscount Quarrendon of Quarrendon in the county of Bucks, and Earl of Litchfield. In the reign of King James II. he was Lord Lieutenant and Custos Rotulorum of the county of Oxford, Lord Lieutenant of Woodstock Park, High Steward of the borough of Woodstock, one of the Lords of His Majesty's Bedchamber, Colonel of a Regiment of Foot, and afterwards Colonel of His Majesty's First Regiment of Foot Guards. His lordship married Charlotte FitzRoy[1] (daughter of King Charles II. by Barbara Duchess of Cleveland), who died 17 Feb. 1718, aged 55.

He had issue: 1. Charles, who died young.—2. Edward Henry, born in 1681, died Oct. 21, 1713.—3. James, born Nov. 12, 1682, married Sarah, daughter of John Bagshaw, esq.[2] of London, and died without issue at Brazil in 1711, having been captain of the Litchfield man-of-war.—4. Francis, born Feb. 26, 1684, died in infancy.—5. Charles Henry, born June 5, 1688, died unmarried Jan. 3, 1708.—6. GEORGE HENRY, second Earl, of whom hereafter.—7. Francis-Henry FitzRoy, baptized Sept. 17, 1691, died young.—8. FitzRoy Henry, born Jan. 2, 1699, died 1750 (a Vice-Admiral).—9. William, died young.—10. Thomas, died young.—11. John, died young.— 12. ROBERT LEE, of Charlbury, Oxon, born 1706, afterwards fourth Earl of Litchfield, succeeded 1772.—13. Charlotte, baptized March 13, 1678, married on the second of January, 1698, Benedict-Leonard Calvert,[3] [Lord Baltimore in Ireland].—

---

[1] See the notes of the Baptisms of her children appended to this article.

[2] " James Lee, married to Sarah, d^r of Bagshaw, a seller of East Indian goods in Bishopsgate St."—*Le Neve's Memoranda.*

[3] " Benedict-Leonard Calvert [who succeeded as 5th Lord Baltimore Feb. 21, 1714-15], only son of the Lord Baltimore, turned Protestant, received the sacrament

14. Anne.—15. Elizabeth,[1] born May 26, 1693, married first to
Colonel Lee, and secondly to the Rev. Edward Young, D.C.L.,
Rector of Welwyn, co. Herts.—16. Barbara, born March 7,
1696, married in May, 1725, George Browne, esq., afterwards
created a Baronet,[2] only son of Sir Charles Browne, of Kiddington, in Oxfordshire.—17. Mary-Isabella, died young.

2. GEORGE HENRY LEE, second Earl,[3] born March 19,

in St. Anne's Church, Westminster, at the hands of the Bishop of Hereford " [Dr.
Bisse].—*Le Neve's Memoranda.*

[1] Lady Elizabeth⊤1. Colonel⊤2. In 1731, Rev. Edward Young, D.C.L.
    Lee, died at │ Lee. │ son of the Dean of Salisbury, Rector of
    Lyons in 1736. │ │ Welwyn, co. Herts, and author of " Night
                        Thoughts."

1. Eliza-=Hon. Henry Temple,   2. Caroline.=Gen. Willam Ha-   Frederick
beth.   son of 1st Viscount   viland, of Penn,   Young.
        Palmerston.   co. Bucks.

1725.
Sir George Browne, Bart. of=Lady Barbara=Edward Gore, esq.
        Kiddington.   Lee.   died in 1801.

1748.
Sir Edward=Barbara 1. William=Bridget, dau. and heiress 2. Charles,=Harriet
Mostyn, Browne. Gore. of Joseph Langton, Esq. in holy Little.
Bart.   of Newton Park.   orders.

1780.
1. Sir=Barbara 2. Charles, who 1. Wil-=Jacintha- 2. Edward. 1. Montagu
Pyers. Slaugh- assumed the liam. Dorothea, 3. John. Gore, M.P.
    ter, of name and arms only child 4. Frances- for Barn-
    Ingate- of Browne; ma. of H. Matilda. staple.
    stone, 1. Elizabeth Powell- 2. William
    co. Witham, and 2. Collins, Charles.
    Essex. Miss Tucker. esq. of 3. George.
                Hatch
                Beau-
                champ.

1808.
Sir Edward.=Frances, dau. Charles Brown William-Henry=Lady Anna-Eliza-
    of Nicholas Mostyn, mar. Powell-Gore- Mary Grenville, da.
    Blundell, Mary, dau. of Langton, esq. of the Duke of
    esq. George Butler. M.P. Buckingham and
                Chandos, K.G.

Sir Pyers.=Hon. Frances G. Fraser, George Brown Mostyn, now Lord
    2nd dau. of Lord Lovat. Vaux of Harrowden.

Hon. G. C. Mostyn, mar. Mary Monk, dau. of the
late Bishop of Gloucester.

[3] A fine portrait of the second Earl is let into a panel on the right-hand side of the
entrance-hall of Dytchley House, Oxfordshire. A miniature in oil of the same is in

1689, succeeded in 1716, married Frances, daughter of Sir John Hales of Woodchurch in Kent, Baronet. His lordship's marriage with this lady was, for some cause or another, kept secret for some time. (Arms of Hales of Woodchurch: Gules, three arrows or, feathered and bearded argent.) He died Feb. 15, 1742, and had issue:—

1. GEORGE HENRY, third Earl, born May 21, 1718, died 1772.—2. Edward-Henry, born June 3, 1719, died July 1721. —3. Edward-Henry, born Dec. 1723, died Aug. 4, 1742.— 4. Charles-Henry, born Feb. 20, 1732, died July 7, 1740.— 5. CHARLOTTE, of whom hereafter.—6. Frances, born Nov. 1721, bap. Dec. 16, 1721, at Enstone, co. Oxon, died 1723.— 7. Mary,[1] born Dec. 17, 1722, married, 1742, Cosmas H. J. Nevill, esq. of Holt, co. Leicester, died March 25, 1758.— 8. Frances, born Jan. 21, 1721, died unmarried.— 9. Harriett, born 1726, married 1749, John Lord Bellew, died April 30, 1752.—10. Anne, born Jan. 1730, married, 1749, Hugh Lord Clifford of Chudleigh,[2] co. Devon.

GEORGE HENRY LEE, third Earl of Litchfield, born in 1718; as Viscount Quarrendon, was elected M.P. for the co. of Oxon. in Feb. 1739; afterwards became successively High Steward and Chancellor of the University of Oxford;[3] married Diana, daughter and heiress of Sir Thomas Frankland of Thirkelby, co. York, Bart. (Arms of Frankland: Azure, a dolphin naiant embowed or, on a chief of the second two saltires gules.) His lordship died without issue in 1772, aged 54; the countess died in 1779. They were both buried at Spelsbury, Oxon, where a handsome monument is erected to their memory.

On the death of the third Earl of Litchfield, the title and estates passed to his lordship's uncle,—

the possession of the writer of this paper, representing his lordship in the later years of his life.

[1]   Lady Mary Lee.⊤C. H. J. Nevill, of Holt, co. Leicester, esq.

       Cosmas Nevill, esq. F.S.A.⊤Annabella-Maria, dau. of W. Gardiner, esq.

Charles Nevill, esq.⊤Lady Georgiana Bingham, dau. of Richard 2nd Earl of Lucan.

              Cosmo Charles George Nevill, of Holt, esq.

[2] This Lord Clifford was great-great-grandfather of the present peer.

[3] An excellent portrait of his lordship is preserved in the Bodleian Library.

ROBERT LEE, fourth Earl of Litchfield, born 1706, succeeded 1772; who had married in 1747 Catharine daughter of Sir John Stonehouse of Radley, co. Berks. Bart. (Arms of Stonehouse:— Argent, on a fesse sable, between three hawks volant azure, a leopard's face between two mullets or.)

Upon the death of the fourth Earl, without issue or heirs male, the estates in Bucks, Oxon, and elsewhere, passed to Henry the eleventh Viscount Dillon of the co. of Sligo, who had married the lady Charlotte, eldest surviving daughter of the second Earl of Litchfield. The present (the fourteenth) Viscount, Theobald-Dominick-Geoffrey Lee-Dillon, who was born 5 April, 1811, married in 1856 Sarah-Augusta, daughter of the late Alexander Hanna, esq.

————

We now turn to other branches of the family of Lee. The first is that of LEE OF HATFIELD, co. York. Sir Anthony Lee of Burston, co. Bucks, married Margaret Wyatt (vide p. 150, Art. I. Lees of Quarrendon), and had issue, as appears by a Pedigree p. 177 of Hunter's *South Yorkshire*, as follows:

1. Sir Henry Lee, K.G.[1]—2. Robert Lee[2] of Hatfield, also of Quarrendon, who married Jane, daughter of Edward Restwolde of the Vache, Aston Clinton, co. Bucks., and widow of Sir Francis Hastings.—3. Thomas.—4. Cromwell.

The said Robert had a natural son, Henry Lee [alias Wareing] of Hatfield, who was buried in the church of Hatfield,[3] having married Elizabeth, daughter of William Fletcher of Campsal, esq. They had issue: 1. Robert Lee of Hatfield, son and heir, will proved 8 Aug. 1663, who married a daughter of—Lent-

---

[1] Sir Henry Lee was keeper of the park of Hatfield.

[2] " Robert Lee resided at Hatfield and Dunscroft. His conduct in his office of justice of the peace for the West Riding gave too much occasion for scandal. ' He is a notable open adulterer, one that giveth great offence and will not be reformed. He uses his authority as well to work private displeasure as to serve other men's turns. A very bad man and doth no good. Better put out than kept in.' This was the character given him by his diocesan Archbishop Sandys, in his report of the state of the magistracy in the West Riding, made in 1587. His marriage with the Lady Hastings connected him extensively with the gentry in this part of the kingdom. By her he had only female issue. But there was a family living at Hatfield for a few generations descended of an illegitimate son."—*Hunter's South Yorkshire*, p. 176.

[3] A few monuments, with the inscriptions much defaced, still remain here.

hall, esq.—2. Susan Lee, who married John Routh of Pollington.

Robert Lee, above, had two sons, (1) Thomas Lee of Hatfield, esq. 1667, died 1699.—(2) Cornelius Lee, gent., of Hatfield, cornet of horse in the King's army in the Civil Wars, living 1700; and two daughters, (1) one married to Edward Sandys, esq. a captain in the Earl of Oxford's regiment; and (2) another, married to John Walker of Mansfield. Vide also, for intermarriages, Dugdale's Visitation of Yorkshire,[1] " Pomfret, 7º April, 1666," in which Sir Philip Hungate of Saxton, who died in 1665, is said to have married " Dorothy daughter of — Lee of Hatfield in com. Ebor. widow of Andrew Younge of Bourne in com. Ebor." Sir Philip's sister Mary married Sir Henry Browne,[2] of Kiddington, in com. Oxon. Bart., connections of the Earls of Litchfield.

We now revert to John Lee of Warwick, esq. who married Alice daughter of Robert Dalby, esq. A.D. 1535 (vide p. 290' Lees of Quarrendon), and had issue, 1. ROBERT LEE OF BEACONSFIELD, co. Bucks, esq., who married Katharine, daughter of —— Daubenny, esq. 2. John Lee, of Pocklington, co. Ebor. esq., first cousin of Sir Henry Lee, K.G. who married a daughter of —— Pigott, esq. 3. Edmund Lee of Pightlesthorne, esq. married Arnicia, daughter of   .
4. Alice Lee.

Robert Lee, as above, had issue, 1. Robert Lee of Binfield, co. Berks, esq. who married Joyce, daughter of John Sweyne of

[1] See also in Dugdale's Visitation, Lee of Pinchingthorpe, D'Arcy of Richmond, Lee of Batley, Moreton of Spouthouse, Green of Leversedge, and Lee of Pocklington. Also MS. pedigree in possession of the Rev. T. C. Thornton, of Brockhall, Northamptonshire, and Douglas's Peerage of Scotland, Wood's edition, vol. ii. pp. 537, 538. Edinburgh.

[2] Anthony Browne, of Kiddington, co. Oxon, knighted at the coronation of King Edward VI., was advanced to the peerage, as Viscount Montagu, Sept. 2, 1554, in which year he was Master of the Horse, and was subsequently made a Knight of the Garter :—

Anthony Browne.┬Lady Jane Radclyffe, dau. of the Earl of Sussex.

| 1. Anthony, mar. Mary, dau. of Sir William Dormer, Knt. | 2. John. | 3. Dorothy, mar. Edward Lee, of Stantonbarry, co. Bucks. [The Rev. F. Lee was Rector of Stantonbarry for some years.] | Two, other daus. |

Binfield, èsq. 2. William. 3. Richard. 4. Peter. 5. Philip.
6. Richard. 7. John. 8. Agnes, married to Brian Johnson of
Bassetbury, co. Bucks. esq. High Sheriff of Bucks, 1615.

The above JOHN LEE,[1] OF POCKLINGTON, had issue by ———
Pigott, his wife, John Lee, esq., who married Dorothy ——,
and had issue, 1. John Robert (?) Lee, who, dying without issue,

was buried at Pocklington in 1636. 2. Humphrey Lee,[2] of the same place, baptized Aug. 10,
1630; married, temp. Commonwealth, Mary,
daughter and heiress of Frederick D'Arcy [or
Darcie], esq. of co. York, first cousin to Sir
Robert D'Arcy, knight banneret, Gentleman of the Privy Chamber
to King Charles I. afterwards created a Baronet. (Arms[3] of
D'Arcy: Argent, three cinquefoils gules, with a crescent for difference.) Mr. Humphrey Lee had issue a son, John Lee, baptized March 19, 1671, who married Mary, daughter and heiress
of the Rev. Dr. Timothy Newmarch, of Buckinghamshire, a
noted Jacobite; and had issue a son, John, who married Mary
Tripp, great-great-aunt of the Rev. Dr. Tripp, Rector of Spof-
forth, co. York, and had issue two sons: 1. Timothy Newmarch
Lee, baptized 18 Nov. 1745, at Pocklington, married Elizabeth
daughter of William Simons, gent. and died at Thame, co.
Oxford, 1794, leaving issue a son in holy orders,[4] and a daughter. 2. Thomas Lee, who in 1789 married Jane, daughter of
Richard Hudson, gent. of North Dalton, co. Ebor.

We return at this point to ROBERT LEE OF BINFIELD, who
by Joyce his wife had issue: 1. Robert Lee, esq. son and heir, of
the Middle Temple, London, married Eliza daughter of.— Arch-
dale of London, and had issue, (1) Robert, and (2) Judith,
who married Henry 4th Earl of Stirling.[5] 2. John Lee. 3. Philip

---

[1] The following memorial, somewhat defaced, remains at Pocklington : " Here .
lyeth . ye . bodie . of . Iohn . Lee . of . this . prish . beeng . ye . sonne . of . Iohn .
Lee . of . Warwick . and . Alicia . hys . wyfe . ye . wch . deceesed . ye . 21st of
Ianuarie . 1601. W . M. + H . M."

[2] A fine portrait of Mr. Humphrey Lee is in the possession of the writer of this
paper.

[3] Represented in glass in the S. transept or aisle of Pocklington church, impaled
with the arms of Lee.

[4] Rev. T. T. Lee, B.D. Vicar of Thame 1795.

[5] Buried at Binfield, co. Berks.

Lee. 4. Catharine Lee, who married Charles Dod,[1] of Clover-ley, co. Salop, and of Lea, co. Worcester, esq. 5. Agnes Lee, who married Henry Lee, merchant of London, great-great-grandson of Richard Lee, of Quarrendon, esq.

The issue of Henry Lee, by Agnes Lee his wife, taken from the pedigree of Thornton of Brockhall, is as follows:

1. William, married Mary daughter of William Ambler of London, and had issue William Lee of Cold Ashby, who in turn married Frances, daughter of Robert Apreece, esq., having issue Frances Lee, daughter and heir, who married Thomas Thornton of Brockhall, co. Northampton, esq. (now represented by the Rev. T. Cooke Thornton of the same place) ; 2. John Lee; 3. Richard Lee; 4. George Lee; 5. Thomas Lee; 6. Philip Lee; 7. Martin Lee; 8. Herbert Lee; 9. Frances Lee; 10. Joyce Lee, wife to Richard Ryves of London, son of Richard Ryves of Shaftesbury in Dorsetshire ; 11. Anne Lee, wife to Richard Wescombe, son of Clement Wescombe of Exeter in Devonshire; 12. Margaret, wife to Nicolas Warren of Devonshire.

The writer of these papers has now completed his task. He might have entered more into detail in many particulars, but has preferred doing so only with reference to the ennobled branch of the ancient and honourable family of Lee of Quarrendon, leaving to others, who are interested either directly or by intermarriages, to supply that which is wanting here in regard to the junior branches of the same. F. G. L.

[1] Now represented by Whitehall Dod, of Cloverley, esq. who married Matilda, daughter of Lieut.-Gen. Sir H. M. Vavasour, Bart.

SEAL OF HUMPHREY LEE, ESQ.
From a matrix still existing. (For the quarterings see pp. 116—118.)

BIRTHS IN THE FAMILY OF LEE.

These notes are taken from a MS. volume in the handwriting of the first Countess of Litchfield, in the possession of Lord Dillon of Dytchley:—

FitzRoy Lee borne ye 10th of May 1698 in James Street, Westminster.

FitzRoy Henry Lee borne ye 2 of Jan. '99 in James Street, Westminster.

William Lee borne ye 24 of June 1701 in James Street, Westminster.

Thomas Lee borne ye 25 of Aug. 1703 in James Street, Westminster, a quarter afore nine in the morning on Wednesday.

John Lee, borne ye 3 of Dec. 1704 in James Street, Westminster, a little affore 4 in ye afternoune.

Robert Lee borne ye 3 of iouly a little before six in the morning 1706 at our house in Jeames Street, Westminster.

John Lee godfathers lord Gillford, Mr Charles Villars, Mrs St John.

Robert Lee godfathers Earle of Killdare, Mr Roger Northe, Lady Candish.

Charlotte Lichfield hir book.

Charlotte Lee.   K. C. ye 2nd, D. of Cleavland, C. of Lindsey.

Charles Lee.   K. C. ye 2d, P. Rupert, C. of Rochester.

Ed. Henry Lee.   ·D. of Grafton, E. of Lindsey, C. of Sufolke.

James Lee.   D. of Richmond, Lord Grandison, Dutchesse of Grafton.

Francis Lee.   D. of Northumberland, Sr W. St. John, C. of Rochester.

Ann Lee.   P. A. of Denmark, L. Fitzharding, E. of Sunderland.

Chas. Hen. Lee.   L. Godolphin, Mr. F. H. Lee, C. of Sandwich.

Jorge [sic] Hen. Lee.   L. Feaverchim, Mr. Charles Berty, Lady Mary Ratliff.

Francis Hen. Lee.   B. of Southampton, Sr Rafe Verney, P. St. John.

Elizabeth Lee.   D. of Northumberland, Ldy Peterbrow, Sr Richard How.

Barbrey Lee.   Dutchess of Deavencher [Devonshire], Mrs Graham Ld Sussex.

Mary Easibella. C. of Arlington, Lady Goodrick, D. of S. Albance.

Fitzroy Lee. Duke of Grafton, E. of Yarmouth, and C. of Susex.

Fitzroy Henry Lee. Ld Fanchawe, Sr Richard Dutton, and Lady Grandison.

William Lee. Sr John Talbott, Sr John Verney, Lady Francklin.

Thomas Lee. Lord Derwentwater, Sr Charles Orby, Lady Dartmouth.

Charlotte Lee was borne at St. James's Park the 13 day of Marche 1678.

Charles Lee was borne at Winsor the 6 day of May 1680.

Edward Henry Lee was borne at Winsor the sixt day of june 1681.

Jeames Lee was borne at St. Jeames parke the 13 day of November 1682. Frances Lee was borne in St. Jeames' Parke one Saturday the 14 day of Febwarey 1685.

Ann Lee was borne at Winsor the 29th of june 1686 on a Tuesday at wone aclock.

Charless Henry Lee was borne at St Jeames Parcke the 5 day of joune 1688 on a tuesday a littell after twilfe.

Jorge Henry Lee was borne in St. Jeamesis parke one the 12 of Marche 1690 about 5 a clock in the afternoune.

Francis Henry Lee was borne the 10 of Sep. '92 about half anoure afoor 12 in the morning at oure House in Jeameses street Westminster.

Elizabeth Lee was borne ye 26 of May one a friday half anoure affor 6 in ye after noune at our house in Jeames street Westminster in the year 1694.

Barbrey Lee was borne at our House in Jeames Street Westminster one Sunday betwene one and tow in the afternoune Marche 3, 1696.

Sep. ye 6. Marey Easabella was borne at the House in Jeames Street Westminster at one aclock in the morning in ye year 1697.

My deare brother the Duke of Grafton died the 9th Oct. ye yeare 1690, half a noure after 3 in the afternoune. he was shot at the taking of Corke in Iarland the 28th of September.

THE QUINS AND THE WYNDHAMS.

MEMORIALS OF ADARE MANOR, BY CAROLINE, COUNTESS OF DUNRAVEN. WITH
HISTORICAL NOTICES OF ADARE, BY HER SON THE EARL OF DUNRAVEN. Printed
for private circulation, by Messrs. Parker, Oxford, MDCCCLXV. 4to, pp. xii. 303.
(31 lithographic plates and 55 woodcut vignettes.)

The contents of this handsome volume are chiefly of an historical
and topographical nature, and its illustrations are in correspondence
therewith. Adare is a beautiful sylvan valley in the county of
Limerick. The village contains the ruins of three priories and of two
churches ; an ancient bridge ; and a castle of the Earls of Kildare,
popularly called Desmond Castle. The ruins of the Augustine Priory
were, sixty years ago, restored for a Protestant church, and those of
the Trinitarian Priory for the Catholics. The manor came to the
Crown on the attainder of the " silken " Earl Thomas, in 1536. The
manor-house dated only from the close of the seventeenth century, and
it has been entirely re-edified by the late Earl of Dunraven, who began
the work in 1832, and left it nearly finished at his death in 1850. On
the east front is this inscription :

In memory of JAMES CONOLLY of Adare, mason, and faithful servant of the
EARL OF DUNRAVEN, and builder of this House from A.D. 1831 till his death in
1852.

On the south front the following :

This goodly House was erected by WINDHAM HENRY, EARL OF DUNRAVEN, and
CAROLINE his Countess, without borrowing, selling, or leaving a debt. A.D. 1850.

The Earl was his own architect until his death. In 1850 Mr. P. C.
Hardwick was consulted, and completed the south and west fronts.
The works, both in stone and timber, were entirely executed by the
mechanics and labourers of the neighbourhood, and proved an inestimable blessing to them during the years of famine.

We could not refrain from quoting these interesting facts, but we must
relinquish the pleasure of dwelling upon the architectural beauties of
the mansion, further than by extracting the description of its armorial
decorations, which will at the same time exhibit the descent of the
Quins and the Wyndhams, the ancestors of the authors of this handsome volume.

Some confusion has existed relative to the different families of
O'Quin or Quin. There were three distinct families of that name of
chieftain dignity in Ireland, namely, 1. O'Quin of Moy-ith, in the
plains of Raphoe, in Ulster (this O'Quin is of the race of Eoghan, the

fourth son of Niall of the Nine Hostages); 2. O'Quin of Muinter Gilla-gan, in the county of Longford, in Leinster; and 3. O'Quin of Muinter Ifearnain, in the county of Clare, in Munster. The last were settled in very early times at Corofin, near the lake of Inch-iquin, and from their name was derived that of the barony of Inchiquin, *i. e.* the Island of O'Quin. They traced their genealogy from Cormac Cas, ancestor of the Kings of Thomond and Munster. Ifernan (*Anglicè* Hellhound!) was the fifteenth in descent from Cormac Cas, and from him the clan name was taken. From the twentieth, Conn, was derived the surname O'Cuinn, now written O'Quin and Quin.

The following notice relative to the O'Quins, and the serpents which figure in their arms, was written by the late Professor O'Curry:—

Cas had thirteen sons, from whom the Dalcassian tribes descend. Of these sons, Aengus-Cenn-Nathrach (Aengus of the Serpent Hill or Head), and Aengus-Cenn-Aitinn (Aengus of the Furze Hill) were two. From the former descends O'Dea and other tribes of the now Barony of Inchiquin (Insi-ui-Chuinn, or O'Quinn's Island); and from the other descend the O'Cuinn (or O'Quin) and Inghean Baith (the daughter of Baith), who founded Kilnaboy, and was the patroness of the O'Quinn and his co-relatives.

Mac Firbis appears to think that Aengus of the Serpent Head and Aengus of the Furze Head were but one person. There is little doubt that the Serpent Head was remembered in the banners of the tribe in after times, and was not an invention of Dermod O'Conor's, nor of Terry; and, excepting the Red Hand of Mac Enis, which the O'Neils usurp, it is perhaps the oldest and most historical coat of arms or clan emblem in Ireland. Motto: *Cenn Nathrach Aboo!* The Serpent Hill was one of the Royal residences of the Kings of Munster. See the "Book of Rights."

The arms of the O'Quins and the O'Deas are registered in an old MS. authority in Ulster's Office in Dublin, entitled Smith's Ordinary of Arms. The subjoined sketches of the same arms are copied from O'Connor's edition of Keating.

ARMS OF O'DEA.   ARMS OF O'QUIN.

Sir Richard Carney, Ulster King of Arms, granted, Nov. 29, 1688, the coat of *Vert, a pegasus passant ermine, a chief or*, to Thady Quin, Esq. of Adare, under the misconception that he derived his descent from the northern O'Quins, who had the pegasus for arms. To rectify this error, and to perpetuate the ancient arms of O'Quin of Inchiquin, chief of Munster Iffearnain, the family from which the Quins of Adare really descend, the present Ulster King of Arms has issued a patent, giving authority to the Earl of Dunraven and his descendants to bear quarterly, with the arms assigned by Carney, the coat of the O'Quins of Inchiquin, as marshalled in this engraving :

ARMS OF THE EARL OF DUNRAVEN.

Quarterly : 1st and 4th grand quarters, quarterly, 1st and 4th, Vert, a pegasus passant ermine, a chief or—Quin; 2nd and 3rd, Gules, a hand couped below the wrist grasping a sword proper, on each side a serpent, tail nowed, the heads respecting each other, or; in chief two crescents argent—O'Quin of Inchiquin: 2nd and 3rd grand quarters, Azure, a chevron between three lion's heads erased or, with a mullet for difference—for Wyndham. Crest, A wolf's head couped at the neck. Supporters, Two ravens proper, plain collared and chained or.

The seven latest generations of the Quins and the Wyndhams are represented in rows of shields placed between the corbels which support the beams of the oak ceiling in the vestibule or entrance hall at Adare. Those on the west side are :

I. QUIN, with O'RIORDAN on an escucheon of pretence.

[Donogh Quin, or O'Quin, of co. Clare, (whose ancestors, the O'Quins of Inchiquin, were chiefs of Hy-Ifearnan, and descendants of Cormac Cas, son of Olioll Olium, Monarch of Ireland,) married a co-heiress of the old Celtic family of O'RIORDAN, which derived its descent from Riordan (*i.e.* " the undaunted,") son of Dungal, ancestor also of the MacCarthys, Kings of Munster and Princes of Desmond.]

II. QUIN impaling MERONY.

[Thady Quin, esq. of Adare, co, Limerick, married Catherine, youngest daughter of Pierce Merony, esq. of Clounmeagh, co. Clare, by Margaret his wife, daughter of Theobald Butler, esq. The O'Meronys, or Meronys, claimed descent from Dermot Roe, and were an old Celtic family of Clare.]

III. QUIN, with WIDENHAM on an escucheon of pretence.

[Valentine Quin, esq. of Adare, married Mary, elder daughter and co-heiress (with her sister Alice, wife of Price Hartstronge, esq. eldest son of Sir Standish Hartstronge, Bart.) of Henry Widenham, esq. of Court, co. Limerick, and Mary his wife.]

IV. QUIN impaling DAWSON.

[Windham Quin, esq. of Adare, married Frances Dawson, sister of Thomas, first Lord Cremorne, and third daughter of Richard Dawson, esq. M.P. of Dawson's Grove, co. Monaghan, by Elizabeth his wife, daughter of John Vesey, Archbishop of Tuam.]

V. QUIN impaling STRANGEWAYS.

[Sir Valentine Richard Quin, Bart. of Adare, afterwards first Earl of Dunraven and Mount Earl, married Lady Frances Muriel Strangeways, daughter of Stephen first Earl of Ilchester. By this alliance the subsequent Earls of Dunraven derived a Royal descent from King Edward III. through the families of Manners and St.Leger; Henry Strangways, esq. the direct ancestor of Lady Frances, having married Margaret, daughter of George Lord Roos, son of Sir George Manners, Lord Roos, by Anne his wife, daughter and heir of Sir Thomas St.Leger, knt. by Anne of York his wife, sister of King Edward IV.]

VI. QUIN, with WYNDHAM on an escucheon of pretence.

[Windham Henry Quin, second Earl of Dunraven and Mount Earl, married Caroline, daughter and sole heiress of Thomas Wyndham, esq. of Dunraven Castle, co. Glamorgan, a lineal descendant of Sir John Wyndham, Knt. of Orchard Wyndham, ancestor, through his eldest son, of the Earls of Egremont.]

VII. QUIN impaling GOOLD.

[Edwin Richard Windham Wyndham-Quin, third Earl of Dunraven and Mount Earl, married Augusta, third daughter of Thomas Goold, esq. a Master in Chancery, son of John Goold, esq. (of the family of Goold of Old Court, Barts.) by Mary his wife, daughter and eventually heiress of Valentine Quin, esq. of Rosbrien, the representative of a junior branch of the Quins of Adare.]

The shields on the east side are:—

I. WYNDHAM, with DAVY on an escucheon of pretence.

[Sir George Wyndham, Knt., of Offords, near Cromer, co. Norfolk, son of Sir John Wyndham, Knt., of Orchard Wyndham, by Joan Portman his wife, married Frances, dau. and co-heir of James Davy, Esq., of Suffield, in the same county.]

II. WYNDHAM impaling DAYRELL.

[Francis Wyndham, Esq., of Cromer, married Sarah, daughter of Sir Thomas Dayrell of Shudy Camps, co. Cambridge, by Sarah his wife, daughter and co-heir of Sir Hugh Wyndham, Bart., of Pilsden, co. Dorset.]

III. WYNDHAM, with EDWIN on an escucheon of pretence.

[Thomas Wyndham, of Clearwell, married, first, Jane, daughter and heiress of John Wyndham of Dunraven Castle, co. Glamorgan, Serjeant-at-Law (but had no issue by her); secondly, Anne, daughter of Samuel Edwin, of Llanmihangel, co. Glamorgan.[1] Her brother, who married Lady Charlotte Hamilton, dying without issue, she succeeded to the large estates of Llanmihangel and Coity.]

IV. WYNDHAM impaling ROOKE.

[Charles Wyndham, who took the name of Edwin, married Eleanor, daughter of General Rooke, of Bigswear, co. Gloucester.]

V. WYNDHAM, with ASHBY on an escucheon of pretence.

[Thomas Wyndham, Esq., of Dunraven Castle, married Anna Maria, daughter of Thomas Ashby, Esq., by Charlotte his wife, daughter of Robert Jones, Esq., of Fonmon Castle, co. Glamorgan.]

VI. QUIN, with WYNDHAM on an escucheon of pretence.

[Windham Henry, second Earl of Dunraven and Mount Earl, married Caroline, daughter and sole heiress of Thomas Wyndham, Esq., of Dunraven Castle.]

VII. QUIN of Adare (modern) and O'QUIN of Inchiquin (ancient).

[The latter resumed and confirmed by patent, bearing date Dec. 20, 1862, as already stated.]

---

[1] Sir Humphrey Edwin, who was Lord Mayor of London in 1698, was descended from the ancient family of the Edwins of Hereford and Holmer. The annexed pedigree traces the line down to the marriage with the Wyndhams:—

Sir Humphrey Edwin, born 1642; died═Elizabeth Sambrooke, died 22 Nov. 1714; 14 Dec. 1707; bur. at Llanmihangel. │ bur. at Llanmihangel.

Samuel Edwin, died═Lady Catherine, dau. of Robert 3rd Earl of 1722. │ Manchester, d. 1731; bur. at Llanmihangel.

| Charles Edwin, nephew and═Charlotte, dau. heir of Thomas Edwin, of Headley, co. Surrey; was M.P. for Glamorganshire 1747, 1754; died s.p. 29 June, 1756. | Charlotte, dau. of James 4th Duke of Hamilton; died 1777, aged 74. | Catherine, died unmarried before 1777. | Thomas Wyndham, of Cromer, co. Norfolk, and of Clearwell.═Anne. |

Charles Wyndham, Esq. who took the name of EDWIN, and was grandfather of Caroline Countess of Dunraven.

Having passed through the Great Hall, the visitor of Adare enters into the Great Gallery, which is the favourite sitting-room of the family. Its dimensions are—in length 132 feet 6 inches, in breadth 21 feet, in height 26 feet 6 inches. It has five very large bay windows, in which the personages described below are commemorated by large shields of painted glass : the central part of the western window containing the following explanatory inscription :—

The stained glass of these windows, illustrating the pedigree of the ancient and noble family of Wyndham, was designed and executed by Thomas Willement of London, F.S.A., in the year of our Lord one thousand eight hundred and thirty-eight, and erected by Windham Henry Wyndham, second Earl of Dunraven, in the love and honour of Caroline Wyndham his Countess.

WEST WINDOW.

Ailwardus de Wymondam,[1] 1139.	Thomas de Wymondam, 1197.
Hugo de Wymondam, 1152.	John de Wymondam, 1223.
Edricus de Wymondam, 1170.	Rodolph de Wymondam, 1250.

NORTH WINDOW (No. 1).

William de Wymondam, Johanna de Castell,	1284.	John de Wymondam, Katherine Redshaw,	1357.
John de Wymondam, 1335.		Thomas Wyndham, Margery Walcot,	1386.

NORTH WINDOW (No. 2).

Full-length figures of

John Howard, Duke of Norfolk, in his robes of state.	Sir John Wyndham, in complete armour.

NORTH WINDOW (No. 3).

John Wyndham, Elizabeth Sherrington,	1415.	John Wyndham, Margaret Clifton,	1456.
John Wyndham, Margaret Segrave,	1440.	Sir John Wyndham, Margaret Howard,	1502.

EAST WINDOW.

Sir Thomas Wyndham, Eleanor Scrope,	1535.	Sir John Wyndham, Joan Portman,	1645.
Sir John Wyndham, Ellen Sydenham,	1574.	Sir George Wyndham, Florence Davy,	1671.
John Wyndham, Florence Wadham,	1572.	Francis Wyndham, Sarah Dayrell,	1694.

[1] Ailwardus, a noble Saxon, assumed soon after the Conquest the name of de Wymondham, from his property in the county of Norfolk.

WEST WINDOW. (Second Series).

| Thomas Wyndham, Catherine Edwin,[1] | } 1751. | Thomas Wyndham, Anna Maria Ashby, | } 1814. |
| Charles Wyndham, Eleanor Rooke, | } 1801. | Windham Henry Wyndham, Caroline Wyndham, | Earl and Countess of Dunraven. |

In the central compartments of these windows are the following shields of arms, illustrative of the royal descent of the Wyndhams, through Howard and Mowbray, Earls of Norfolk, as well as of their Scrope ancestry —

WEST WINDOW.

I. KING EDWARD I., encircled by the legend " Le Roy Eduard Premier."
II. ENGLAND impaling CASTILE, with the legend " La Reine Eleanore."
III. ENGLAND impaling FRANCE, with the legend " La Reine Margarite."
IV. THOMAS DE BROTHERTON, impaling DE HALYS, with the legend " Thomas Comte de Norfolke."

NORTH WINDOW (No. 1).

V. BARON SEGRAVE, with the legend " John Baron de Segrave."
VI. SEGRAVE impaling BROTHERTON, with the legend " Margaret Duchesse de Norfolke."
VII. MOWBRAY impaling SEGRAVE, with the legend " John Baron de Mowbray."
VIII. MOWBRAY impaling FITZALAN, with the legend " Thomas Duke de Norfolke."

NORTH WINDOW (No. 2).

IX. HOWARD impaling MOWBRAY, with the legend "Sir Robert Howard Eques."
X. HOWARD impaling MOLINES, with the legend " John Duke de Norfolke."
XI. WYNDHAM impaling HOWARD, with the legend " Sir John Wyndham Eques."
XII. SCROPE, with the legend " Sir William le Scrope."

NORTH WINDOW (No. 3).

XIII. SCROPE impaling DE ROOS, with the legend " Sir Henrye Scrope."
XIV. SCROPE impaling DE LA POLE, with the legend " Rycharde Baron Scrope."
XV. SCROPE quartered with TIPTOFT, with the legend " William Comte de Wilts."
XVI. SCROPE impaling NEVILLE (Earls of Westmerland), with the legend " Roger Baron Scrope."

EAST WINDOW.

XVII. SCROPE impaling SCROPE, with the legend " Henrye Baron Scrope."
XVIII. SCROPE impaling FITZ HUGH OF RAVENSCROFT, with the legend " Rycharde Baron Scrope."
XIX. SCROPE impaling WASHBOURNE, with the legend " Syr Richarde Scrope."
XX. WYNDHAM with SCROPE on an escucheon of pretence, with the legend " Syr Thomas Wyndham."

---

[1] This is a mistake : it should be Anne, as already stated in p. 494.

The Wyndhams have been a very widely-spread family, ramifying into numerous branches. There are pedigrees denoting those branches, but not detailing all of them, in Hutchins's *History of Dorsetshire*, second edit. 1813, iii. 330, and in Sir R. C. Hoare's *History of Salisbury*, p. 815.

The branches which have flourished in modern times are almost all sprung from the sons of Sir John Wyndham of Orchard Wyndham, co. Somerset (ob. 1645, aged 87) : who himself was very nearly deprived of the whole of his long life and the chance of perpetuating the family, according to an anecdote of his mother, which is thus related in Collinson's *History of Somersetshire*, iii. 490 :

> John Wyndham, of Orchard, married Florence, sister and co-heir of Nicholas Wadham, of Merifield, in this county, esq. founder of Wadham College in the University of Oxford. It is said that this lady was, the year after her marriage, 1562, buried, having in a sickness lost all appearance of life; but the sexton hearing some noise in the coffin, as he was closing the vault in the church of St. Decuman's, she was happily taken up, and soon after delivered of Sir John Wyndham.

Sir John Wyndham married Joan, daughter of Sir Henry Portman, and among their numerous family of nine sons and six daughters were the following :—

1. John, ancestors of the Earls of Egremont, extinct in 1845—the last Earl leaving his estates to his natural son, now Lord Leconfield.

2. Thomas, ancestor of the Windhams of Felbrigg, co. Norfolk, of whom the last was the Right Hon. William Windham, Secretary of War, who died in 1810: when the name was taken by Admiral Lukin (son of his maternal half-brother), from whom a second house of Windham of Felbrigg (but not inheriting any representation in blood) has subsisted until the present time.[1]

From this branch also descends Mr. Smijth Windham of Waghen, co. York, a brother of Sir Edward Bowyer Smijth, Bart.; who assumed the name of Windham in 1823, as representative of the Windhams of Earsham, in Norfolk.

3. Sir George Wyndham, of Cromer in Norfolk : the lineal male ancestor of the Earl of Dunraven, as already shown in p. 494.

4. Humphrey, ancestor of Wyndham of Dunraven Castle, co. Glamorgan, and of Clowerwall or Clearwell in Gloucestershire.

5. Sir Hugh Wyndham, of Silton, co. Dorset, successively a Baron of the Exchequer and a Justice of the Common Pleas, whose daughters

---

[1] William Frederick Windham, esq. grandson of the Admiral, after a career of great but unhappy notoriety, died on the 2nd Feb. 1866, at the age of twenty-five.

and co-heiresses were married to Sir Nathaniel Napier and John Earl of Bristol.

6. Sir Wadham Wyndham, of Norrington, co. Wilts, a Justice of the King's Bench, ancestor of the Wyndhams of Norrington, Dinton, Salisbury, and Hawkchurch, and grandfather of Sir Thomas Wyndham, Lord Chancellor of Ireland, created Lord Finglas in that kingdom (ob. s. p. 1745). A pedigree of Wyndham of Dinton will be found in Sir R. C. Hoare's *South Wiltshire*, hundred of Dunworth, p. 108, and Addenda, p. 66: and the existing family is described in Burke's *Landed Gentry*.

RICHARD WYATT, CITIZEN AND CARPENTER.

Genealogical Memoranda relating to Richard Wyatt, of Hall Place, Shackleford, Citizen and Carpenter of London: with an Account of the Almshouses of his foundation at Godalming, under the care of the Worshipful Company of Carpenters, the Governors. Compiled by EDWARD BASIL JUPP, F.S.A. Clerk of the Company. *Privately printed*, 150 *Copies.* 8vo. pp. 53.

Richard Wyatt followed the usual course of a prosperous London citizen in the olden time. Born in the country—at Slindon in Sussex, in the year 1554, probably the son of the parson of that parish, he was apprenticed to Roger Sheers, citizen and carpenter,—but not until the unusually advanced age of eighteen, and in due time married his master's daughter. He subsequently became deputy alderman of the ward of Queenhithe, residing in a messuage or tenement called *The Robin Hood*, now known as Trigg Wharf. It was a house belonging to the Company of Armourers, whose custom it was to take their barge there on public occasions: and it was leased to Wyatt with that condition, and also with a stipulation that they should have the use of the kitchen, parlour and hall, being the ground floor of the said capital messuage, for keeping their breakfast upon every Lord Mayor's day.

Richard Wyatt filled the office of Master of the Carpenters' Company three several times, in the years 1604, 1605, and 1616; and on his death, in 1619, he bequeathed to that fraternity the trust of his charities. He had acquired property in various places; and among others the mansion of Hall Place at Shackleford, in the parish of Godalming, which remained in his family until about 1748. Near that spot, on the old Portsmouth Road, between Guildford and Godalming, he destined by his will a site for the erection of Almshouses.

Item my will is that my Executors shall get lycence to.builde Tenne Almshouses for tenne Poore to dwell in, to be sett up in some convenient place near Godall. mine, upon some parte of Prismarch. For the building of them, with a convenient place to saye prayers in every daie, I give five hundred pounds. My desire is that, with the advise of some councell to take advise howe to doe it, soe as it may be to the glory of God and the benefittinge of such poore as I shall appointe hereafter to be placed there from time to time for ever. Looke on the orders of Mr. Lamberd's Hospitall at Greenwich, and follow them yf you shall thinke it good. When it shalbe finished, then my will is that there shalbe placed there five poore men of the parish of Godallmine, two of the parish of Putnam, one of the parish of Hambledon, one of the parish of Compton, one of the parish of Downsfould.

The prototype to which allusion was made was the Hospital built at Greenwich by William Lambarde, the Kentish antiquary, and which was completed in 1576. It is said to have been the first founded in Protestant times.

Wyatt's Almshouses were erected accordingly in the year 1622, and they still do credit both to the taste and the workmanship of the builders of that day. " They are (remarks Mr. Jupp) strongly built of red brick, and harmonize well with the landscape that surrounds them." The chapel stands in the centre, and within it is a brass plate, representing Richard Wyatt with his wife and six children, as shown in the engraving in p. 501.

The usual residence of Mr. Deputy Wyatt was however at Isleworth in Middlesex, and there some of the Wyatts remained until towards the close of the seventeenth century; as well as the descendants of his daughter Jane, the wife of Gideon Awnsham, esq. son of Sir Gideon Awnsham, sometime lord of the manor of Cranford.[1] Richard Wyatt died and was buried at Isleworth, and a monument to his memory still remains in Isleworth church, with kneeling figures of himself and his wife, an engraving of which occupies the next page.

The arms of Wyatt at the head of the monument are, Gules, on a fess or between three boar's heads couped sable a lion passant between two pheons sable. These arms are recorded in the Visitations of Surrey and Sussex in the year 1662, at which time the elder branch of the worthy Carpenter's descendants was still seated at Shackleford

---

[1] Lysons states that Sir Gideon Awnsham sold the manor of Cranford in 1604; but the epitaph to his widow Dame Anne Awnsham (who died 1613) formerly in the church of St. Benet Fink dated his death in the year 1600, according to the copy which is printed in Stowe's Survey. It would seem that his son Gideon, Mr. Wyatt's son in law, was also knighted before his death, as his interment is thus recorded at Isleworth: "Sr Gideon Aunsham, Knt. buried Ap. 23, 1631." Aungier's *History of Syon House, Isleworth, and Hounslow*, 8vo. 1840, p. 174; or April 28, as printed by Mr. Jupp, p. 45.

HERE SLEEPETH IN Y LORD RICHARD WIATT, ESQ SOMETIME CITIZEN OF LONDON &
FREE OF Y WOR COMPANIE OF Y CARPENTERS WHO WAS BORNE AT SLINDEN IN Y
COVN OF SVSSEY. HE MARRIED MARGARET Y DAVGHT OF ROGER SHEERS. BY WHO
HE HAD X CHILDREN WHEREOF VI ARE YET LIVING. III SONNES VID HENRY ROGER &
FRANCIS & III DAVGHT MARGAR. JANE & ELIZAB. VNMARRIED AFTER HE HAD LIVED
RELIGIOVSLY IN Y FEARE OF GOD & FAVOR OF ALL GOOD MEN FOR TEMPERANCE
VPRICHTNES & DEEDS OF PIETIE. AS Y HOSPITALL W HE FOVNDED AT GODLYMĀ IN
SVRREY FOR X POORE MEN & HIS GVIFT OF VII POVNDS YEARELY TO BE GIVEN
TO XIII POORE WIDOWES MAY GIVE SVFFICIENT TESTIMONY HE DEPARTED THIS LIFE
IN Y 65 YEARE OF HIS AGE IN Y YEARE OF OVR REDEMPTIŌ 1619
WIATVS
VTVIVAS

THIS ALMES-HOVSE WAS Y̆ GIFTE OF RICHARD WYATT GENT: CITTEZE OF LONDON & FREE OF Y̆ COMPANY OF Y̆ CARPENTERS, WHO DIED Y̆ 8 OF NOV: 1619.

in Godalming, and the younger at Horsted Keynes in Sussex. Mr. Jupp has introduced into his volume the pedigrees then entered.[1]

Over either of the columns of the monument is an impaled shield of which no explanation is furnished by the inscription; but Mr. Jupp concludes (p. 5) that these are " the arms of Sheers impaling Butler." He adds that

Mrs. Wyatt's will contains bequests to persons of the name of Butler; from which we conclude that his father Roger Sheers, or one of his ancestors, married into a family of that name. The extracts from the Slindon registers (see Appendix) confirm this supposition.

Mr. Jupp here alludes to the marriage of a John Sheere with Joane Butler that took place at Slindon in 1561: but this is evidently unsatisfactory, as Richard Wyatt was himself born in 1554, seven years before the marriage in question.

On referring to the account of the monument in Aungier's *History of Isleworth* we find it suggested that these were " the arms, it is probable, of the heir or executor by whom the monument was put up." And the will of Richard Wyatt, which is now published by Mr. Jupp, proves that suggestion to be near the truth.

The arms do not belong to Sheeres. If that family had boasted any arms, they would have been impaled with those of Wyatt. But they

---

[1] A silver-gilt tankard is still existing in the possession of W. Cosier, Esq. bearing this inscription

Richard Wyatt Citizen and Carpenter of London in the yeare 1619.

The arms of Wyatt are engraved thereon (as represented at p. 13 of Mr. Jupp's book) but the lion is guardant and the crescent omitted.

are the arms of Trevor, Per bend sinister ermine and argent, a lion rampant gules: the impalement being Butler, Sable, a chevron argent between three covered cups or.

Now, Wyatt had no executor. He left his wife sole executrix of his will. But he added,

Alsoe I desire my good friends Mr Trevor and Mr Duncombe to bee Overseers, and to helpe to see this my Will in all poynts performed. And I doe give to each of them, for their paines, tenne pounds a peece.

Mr. Duncombe is again mentioned in the will of Margaret Wyatt, the widow of Richard, made in 1634:

Item I give and bequeath to George Duncombe Esquier five pownds to make him a Ring. And I intreat him to be Overseer of the true performance of this my Will and Testament.

And, though we do not find Wyatt's other " overseer " again mentioned in Mr. Jupp's volume, we are able to identify him satisfactorily. He was a councillor of the Inner Temple, who very shortly after Wyatt's death was knighted (at Greenwich) on the 18th of May, 1619, being then Solicitor to Charles Prince of Wales, and became afterwards (in 1625) a Baron of the Exchequer.[1] He married for his first wife Prudence daughter of Henry Boteler, esq. of London, and she was buried at St. Bride's, Fleet Street, January 6, 1614.[2]

Mrs. Trevor was no doubt a kinswoman of Mrs. Wyatt, and of the other Butlers named in Mrs. Wyatt's will. We consider it certain, therefore, that the arms of Mr. Trevor were placed upon Wyatt's monument because it was erected by his order, as overseer of the will of the deceased. It is interesting to remark this fact, as it may suggest a clue in other instances to the explanation of arms occurring upon monuments. And we can point to a second example of this kind. It is the monument of Sir Peter Carew in Exeter cathedral, which was erected in 1576 by his friend and biographer—but no kinsman—John Vowell alias Hooker, the well-known Devonshire antiquary; which, besides a long display of shields representing the alliances of Carew, bears also on its brackets two shields of the arms of Hooker. An engraving

---

[1] See his memoir in Foss's *Judges of England*, vi. 367—where the time of his knighthood is misstated. The Lord Chief Justice Sir John Trevor (temp. Anne) and his descendants the Trevors Viscounts Hampden have descended from Sir John Trevor, of Trevallin, co. Flint (also knighted 1619) elder brother of Sir Thomas.

[2] See the epitaph of the Trevor family at St. Bride's in Seymour's *Survey of London and Westminster*, fol. 1734, i. 781; also the epitaph of Sir Thomas Trevor, at Leamington Hastings, co. Warw. in Dugdale's *History of Warwickshire*, (edit. Thomas,) p. 319.

of this may be seen in Mr. Maclean's edition of Vowell's *Life of Sir Peter Carew*, 8vo. 1857.

We have only to add that Mr. Jupp's appendix is copiously stored with documentary evidence ; consisting of the funeral certificate of Richard Wyatt, his will, and those of his widow, his sons Francis and Henry, and his grandson Gideon Awnsham esquire (of Heston in the county of Middlesex); with extracts from the parish registers of Slindon, Godalming, Puttenham, and Isleworth ; extracts from the accounts of the Carpenters' Company ; monumental inscriptions of the Wyatts at Horsted Keynes and Lindfield, and extracts from the registers of those parishes and Cuckfield. To these are added the pedigrees of Bysh, from the Surrey Visitations.

Those who have not the good fortune to obtain a separate copy, will find the substance of this Memoir in the recent volume of the Surrey Archæological Society.

THE CROWNED HEART OF DOUGLAS.

The arms of the illustrious house of Douglas are remarkable from the heart, which has rendered them easily recognised even by those who know little of the science of armory. The residence of the clan was originally far north in Morayshire, and, like the Morays and Inneses, it had a Flemish origin.

FRESKIN, ancestor of the Morays, Sutherlands, &c. had no surname. He is said to have come from Moravia in the east of Europe, and the late Lord Mansfield was deeply interested in having got tidings that there is still a tradition there of Freskin's departure on his pilgrimage about 1100. His descendants in the second degree took the name *de Moravia*, afterwards transformed into Murreff and Moray or Murray, and, when coats of arms began, they bore *Azure, three stars* (afterwards *mullets*) *argent*.

BEROALD the Fleming was the ancestor of the family who took the name of Innes, and adopted three stars like their patrons.

THEOBALD the Fleming, from whom is derived the far-famed family of Douglas, had no surname in the district of Moray; but he got a grant of some lands on the water of DOUGLAS, whence his children took the name; but they kept up the connection with Morayshire for several generations, and his second son Bricius was Bishop of Moray in 1203. Friskin's great-grandson, Walter de Moravia, also became transferred to Lanarkshire by obtaining Bothwell about 1240.

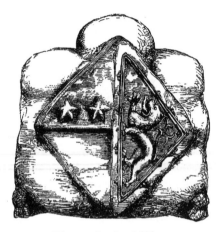

From the Monument of James Earl of Morton, ob. circ. 1498.

The Douglases, according to the system of those days, took their arms from the great family in the neighbourhood, at first *Azure, three stars argent:* but they soon pushed up the whole into a chief, which thus gave room for the subsequent addition of the heart below.

The seal of William Lord Douglas appended to his deed of homage to King Edward I. in the year 1296 (remaining in H. M. Record Office) is represented in the annexed engraving.[1] The shield, which bears the three mullets on a chief, is surrounded by three lizards, or wyverns, after the fashion of that period. The legend, s' D'NI WILLELMI DE DVGLAS.

The first great division of this family was when the ancestor of the Douglases of Laudon, Dalkeith, Earls of Morton, &c. came off the parent stem about 1230 in the person of Andrew nephew of the Bishop. This branch took a similar coat, but changed the tincture, making the arms, *Argent, on a chief gules two stars of the first*—sometimes there were three stars. None of their descendants had the heart till, a daughter of James third Earl of Morton marrying James Douglas of the Angus branch, he became the Regent Earl of Morton, and the future Earls of the Lochleven branch, though not descended from that family, took up the quartering after an interval.

On a monument in the ruinous choir of the parish church of Dalkeith, upon which are two recumbent effigies, supposed to represent

---

[1] Made for the forthcoming Second Volume of the *Catalogue of Scottish Seals*, by Mr. Henry Laing.

James Douglas first Earl of Morton (ob. circ. 1498) and his wife Johan, third daughter of King James I. are the lozenges of arms represented on the opposite page.[1] That at the Earl's head bears the arms of Douglas of Dalkeith only, namely, two mullets on a chief (the chief occupying full one-half of the lozenge); that at the head of the Countess bears the same coat impaled with the royal lion and tressure of Scotland.

This partition happened a century before King Robert Bruce commissioned the good Sir James Douglas to convoy his heart to the Holy Land. Though he had no lawful posterity, his immediate relations all adopted this memorable distinction from him. But the question now arises, When was the heart crowned? Even those acquainted with the family will not be prepared to find that it was only after the Union of the Crowns in 1603 that this exhibition of royalty began.

The chief family towards the end of the 16th century was undoubtedly that of the Earl of Angus, and he in 1589 bore the heart uncrowned, as appears by his seal.[2] When Queen Elizabeth erected in Westminster Abbey a magnificent tomb to her cousin Margaret Douglas, Countess of Lennox, the Angus arms are given, and there is no crown. And when King James succeeded in 1603 he added a similar memorial to his grandmother Queen Mary, where the Douglas arms are given in full, but still with no crown. –

But the Earl of Angus in 1617 had a seal with the heart crowned,[3] perhaps to enlighten the English as to the dignity of the heart he exhibited. It is thus evident from the family seals and the royal tombs that down to the union of the crowns the Earls of Angus never ensigned the heart with the crown, and that soon afterwards their family and gradually the other branches began to use this tardily adopted additional display.

At Crathes Castle, Sir James Burnet's, there is a handsome wardrobe commemorating the marriage of his ancestor Sir Thomas Burnet about 1620 with Margaret daughter of Sir Robert Douglas of Glenbervie, where the arms are Burnet of Leys impaling Douglas, having the heart without the crown, quartered with Auchinleck of Glenbervie. Sir Robert was brother of William Earl of Angus, from whom came the Marquesses and Duke of Douglas.

On the house of Stenhouse in Stirlingshire, there is a coat of Sir

[1] We are favoured with these engravings from the *Proceedings of the Society of Antiquaries of Scotland*, vol. iii. p. 27.
[2] Laing's Ancient Scottish Seals, p. 48.   [3] Ibid. No. 255.

William Bruce, Bart. impaling the arms of his wife in 1655, viz. Helen daughter of Sir William Douglas of Cavers ; but even there no crown is added.

It is uncertain when the Queensberry family assumed the crown upon the heart; but probably they only followed the example of the Earl of Angus, who by position was head of the house. Douglas of Cavers and Douglas of Drumlanrig, afterwards Queensberry, were descended from two brothers, natural sons of the hero of Otterburn, James Earl of Douglas and Mar, killed in 1388. It is remarkable that Cavers took the arms of Douglas alone, while Drumlanrig quartered Mar,—Azure, a bend between six cross-crosslets fitchée or. ·They both had a bordure to signify their irregular origin. Cavers had a plain bordure gules, said to have been at first azure; but Drumlanrig had ·a bordure engrailed gules. After Drumlanrig was made Earl of Queensberry, he was permitted to amputate the engrailing and change the colour to *or*, to make his coat more honourable ; and his descendant when made Marquis of Queensberry was authorised to adorn his bordure by placing upon it the double tressure of Scotland with the eight fleurs de lis, thus converting it into a great additament of honour.

Without entering into further particulars, the result is that the crown did not surmount the heart in the coat of Douglas till some years after 1603.   ALEX. SINCLAIR.

In illustration of the remarks with which our much-esteemed correspondent has favoured us, we take the opportunity to add a reference to the many interesting seals of the house of Douglas which are described in Mr. Henry Laing's valuable *Catalogue of Scottish Seals*, 4to. 1850, particularly those of the fourth, fifth, eighth, and ninth Earls of Douglas; of the fourth, fifth, sixth, eighth, ninth, and eleventh Earls of Angus; of the third, fourth, and fifth Earls of Morton; with various others of inferior note. Those of Isabel, Countess of Mar (1404), and of Archibald Douglas, Earl of Moray (1452), are represented in wood engravings, which were previously published in Drummond's *History of Noble British Families.* (See also the heraldic features of some of the Douglas shields copied in Seton's *Scottish Heraldry*, plates xii. xiii.)

In the second volume of Mr. Laing's Catalogue, which is now passing through the press, several other Douglas seals will be described and engraved. Among them is that of Archibald third Earl of Douglas and Lord of Galloway 1401, from a charter in H. M. General Register House, in which the armorial bearings are, Quarterly, 1. and 4. the heart, and on a chief three mullets, for Douglas; 2. and 3. a lion rampant crowned, for Galloway; on an escutcheon surtout, three mullets for Murray of Bothwell. This is said to be " perhaps the earliest Scottish example of the armorial ensigns of an heiress being carried on an escutcheon surtout:" the Earl of Douglas having married Jean, daughter and sole heiress of Thomas Murray, Lord of Bothwell.

In the seal of Archibald fourth Earl of Douglas, 1421, who was also Duke of Touraine and Earl of Longueville in France, the arms are marshalled: Quarterly, 1. three fleurs de lis, for Touraine; 2. the heart and three mullets on a chief, for Douglas; 3. a saltier and chief, for Annandale; 4. a lion rampant, crowned, for Galloway.

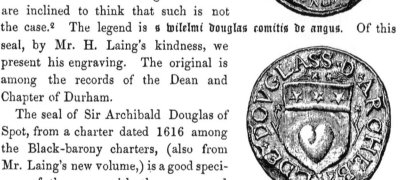

In a seal of William Douglas, second Earl of Angus, 1429, the coats of Galloway and Douglas are quartered with an escucheon surtout of some lordship which has not hitherto been explained.[1] The base of the shield is cut off from the quarterings, and it has been imagined that it bears some charge: but we are inclined to think that such is not the case.[2] The legend is s ᚦᚱᛁᛚᛖᛚᛗᛁ ᚦᚩᚢᚷᛚᚪᛋ ᚱᚩᛗᛁᛏᛁᛋ ᚦᛖ ᚪᛝᚢᛋ. Of this seal, by Mr. H. Laing's kindness, we present his engraving. The original is among the records of the Dean and Chapter of Durham.

The seal of Sir Archibald Douglas of Spot, from a charter dated 1616 among the Black-barony charters, (also from Mr. Laing's new volume,) is a good specimen of the arms with the uncrowned heart, at a late period.

---

[1] It cannot be Murray of Bothwell, with which the Angus branch of Douglas had nothing to do. The only coat of a bend in connection with them was Bonkill, and the charges upon the bend (which are indistinct upon the seal) were probably intended for the buckles of that family.

[2] In the seal of William Earl of Angus 1617 there is a similar base under four quarterings. It is charged with a cross counter-company, perhaps not an armorial quartering, but signifying some order of knighthood. See Laing's Catalogue, vol. i. No. 255.

THE ENGLISH LADIES OF PONTOISE.

(*Continued from p.* 428.)

One of the sisters of Pontoise who fled from that town to Dunkirk was Dame Mary Frances, by birth *Catharine Markham,* one of the two daughters and coheiresses of George Markham, esq. of Claxby, co. Lincoln. She was one of those living at Dunkirk when Mr. Lodge wrote his notes to his *Illustrations* [1] in 1791 ; and at the same time the other sister, Mary, was the widow of Marmaduke Tunstall, esq. of Wycliffe, co. York.[2]

Her great-aunt, *Margaret Markham,* had also been a very useful member of the sisterhood, and was further remarkable for having lived to a great age. Of these two ladies the following biographical particulars will be found interesting :

(*From the Pontoise Necrology and other MSS.*)

Dame Margaret Markham was daughter of George Markham, esq. of Olerton (or Allerton), in Nottinghamshire, in the forest of Sherwood. There was another house belonging to their family called Querbie (Kirby Bellers), which was " substracted" from them for being Roman Catholics, for which, upon false and unjust accusations, they underwent many heavy penalties and banishment.

Dame Margaret's mother was Mrs. Judith Withernwick FitzWilliams, of one of the most ancient and best allied families in England, inherited of Claxby and Normanby, and many other fair tenements.

Dame Margaret was professed at the Benedictine Convent at Ghent, on 27th December, 1639, at 22 years old, my Lady Eugenia Pulton being Abbess.

In 1652 she was sent with four Choir Religious and a lay sister to assist in the foundation of a convent of the order at Boulogne, and went very cheerfully through the many difficulties that occurred in the new beginning. But continual rumours and frights of wars, and the insults they were exposed to in a frontier town on the sea-side, together with

---

[1] Illustrations of British History, 4to. 1791, vol. ii. pp. 417, 418.

[2] See a memoir of Marmaduke Tunstall, esq. F.R.S. and F.S.A. in Nichols's *Illustrations of the Literature of the Eighteenth Century,* vol. v. p. 511.

constant want of health in the community, obliged them to seek a more inland residence.   They left Boulogne on 9th May, 1658, and arrived at Pontoise, by Dieppe, and Rouen, in six days; where, by the credit of Abbot Montague (Lord Walter Montague, brother to the Earl of Manchester the warm adherent of the Rebellious Parliament), a convert, then Abbot of St. Martin's, the Benedictine abbey near Pontoise, and almoner to Queen Henrietta Maria, they obtained letters-patent for their settlement from the Court of France, and their munificent founder Sir Richard Forster, father of one of the community, bestowed upon them a house, with an inclosure of 14 acres, and a gift of 30,000 livres.

At Pontoise, Dame Margaret, "our most dear and saintly mother" (as the Necrology terms her), "ever gave proofs of great charity and very exemplary humility, having been subject to seven Abbesses, and comporting herself towards them all with great submission and cheerfulness, so as to be much esteemed and loved by them ; and, under their government, going through all the chief offices much to their satisfaction, the advantage of the community, and the true edification of all. She was several times elected Prioress, and in 1687 was sent with three other Religious, at the request of Lord Tyrconnel, then Viceroy for James II., to found a royal convent in Dublin.

Dame Margaret undertook this obedience with much humility, and, taking leave of the community with many tears on both sides, commenced her journey, during which she was to act as Superior to the other three, starting on the 29th July, 1687, for Rouen, where she and her companions took ship for Ireland.

Their journey was a very hard one, and their voyage of two months was attended by great dangers and terrible storms, which cast them into several havens ; and in that of Milford Haven, one of the Religious, Dame Anne Nevill (of Holt), got her death by a fall, and was buried there.

On their arrival in Dublin, where Lady Abbess Butler [1] and Dame Mary Joseph O'Ryan were awaiting them, Dame Margaret and her companions were most kindly received by Lord and Lady Tyrconnel and many others,[2] and everything seemed to promise a happy settle-

----

[1] Mary Jane Butler, once a nun at Pontoise : see p. 411.

[2] They were joined by a small sisterhood from Ypres, of which the history is as follows : Mary Beaumont, an English Benedictine of Ghent, was in 1655 permitted by her superiors to attempt to establish a community at Ypres, to which purpose she took along with her three gentlewomen of the same order, Flavia Cary, Helena White,

ment.   Dame Margaret here celebrated her jubilee of fifty years' profession with great splendour.[1]

But at this time the unhappy revolution took place, and divine Providence permitted that King James the Second, who, after the Dutch usurpation had made his way back from France, and had spent about two years in Ireland (during which time he had encouraged the new establishment, in which many persons of quality had placed their children for education), should be at last forced to withdraw, and with him the hopes of the Catholic party and of the new establishment fell. It was deemed necessary for the community to disperse immediately,[2] and Dame Margaret returned with the other religious to the convent at Pontoise; from which she was again sent, in quality of Prioress, to Yprès, on the 28th November, 1700, in company with Dames Scholastica Bruning, Eugenia Green, and Lawrence Lawson. Here she professed several religious, and, having obtained leave to return to Pontoise, was again there at the beginning of October, 1702 ; where, after edifying all by her sweetness and consideration to inferiors, submission to superiors, and severity to herself, having been Prioress at different times no less than twenty-four years ; having in her last sickness been strengthened with the sacraments of Holy Church, she died on the 25th July, 1717, in the 105th year of her age,[3] and the 78th of her religious profession.   *Requiescat in Pace.*

(*From Preface to the Oratorian Life of Ste. J. de Chantal, and from the Pontoise Necrology.*)

Dame Mary Frances Markham was the second daughter of George Markham, esq. of Claxby in Lincolnshire, and received in baptism the name of Katharine.   She and her elder sister Mary were educated in

and Viviana Eyre.   They remained at Ypres till 1687, when they removed to Dublin chiefly under the conduct of Dame Margaret Markham and Dame Mary Butler, two discreet nuns of the monastery of Pontoise, who were ordered to attend that new establishment.

[1] In the presence of King James, according to another account.

[2] Their house having been plundered, and their best effects carried off by the rabble.   (Ibid.)

[3] In the different papers, some variations occur in date.   One has it, that Dame Margaret was professed in 1639, another in 1640, and her age at this time is, after several erasures, set down at twenty-two, which, if she were 105 at her death in 1717, cannot be correct ; she must have been twenty-seven at her profession in 1639 (two papers give this date) and she would have been seventy-eight years professed on 27th Dec. 1717.   Her portrait, having been brought from Pontoise by Dame Frances Markham, is still preserved by the community.

different convents abroad, and were for some time at that of Pontoise, where Lady Ann Catharine Haggerston, their great-aunt, was 9th Abbess. Their mother,[1] who was now a widow, accompanied them, and affectionately watched over their education.

The elder sister was some time after married to Marmaduke Tunstall, esq. of Thurland, and Wycliffe Hall in Yorkshire, and, becoming a widow in 1790, spent her time and fortune in succouring the emigrant clergy and distressed Religious and others driven from their country or convents abroad. She was the foundress of the English Convent of the Visitation.

Katharine Markham, who was co-heiress with her sister to their father's large property, was professed at Pontoise on the 23rd April, 1776, at the age of 23; and it is said that much of her portion was spent in building cloisters, &c. to the convent. But in 1784 they were forced to leave it; and Dame Mary Frances, with Lady Clavering and three other choir nuns, and two lay sisters, joined our community at Dunkirk, and at our expulsion from thence shared in all our trials, and with the rest settled at the convent at Hammersmith on the 8th May, 1795. She was a bright example of a fervent Religious, always first at choir, and every discharge of the various offices in which she was employed. In her last illness she was strengthened with all the rites of Holy Church, and died on the 25th February, 1824, aged 70.

Perhaps the only epitaph from the church of the English nunnery at Pontoise that has been preserved, is the following, which still exists upon a marble tablet now fixed against the west wall of the cathedral church of Nôtre Dame. It commemorates not a nun, but one of their pupils, *Mary Heneage*, who died in 1717, in the fifteenth year of her age. She was the only child of George Heneage, esq., of Hainton, co. Lincoln, by his first wife, the hon. Mary Petre, as shown by the pedigree, p. 419.

Cy gist Damoiselle MARIE HENEAGE, fille de George Heneage de Hainton, Ecuier, et de Marie Petre son Epouse, Fille et heretière de my lord Guillaume Petre, Paire d'Angleterre, pensionnaire dans ce Monastère, décédée l'onzieme janvier, l'an de Grace 1717, et de son âge le quinzième. *Requiescat in Pace.*

---

[1] Mary, daughter of Bryan Salvin, esq. of Croxdale, by Anne, third daughter of William Haggerston, esq. son and heir of Sir Thomas Haggerston, of Haggerston, Bart.

An aunt of this young lady, Constantia Heneage, was a nun at Pontoise (see p. 414); and a great-aunt, another Constantia (otherwise called Scholastica), was a member of the Dunkirk community, and the circumstances of her death are thus recorded :

" When our first Abbess was blessed (consecrated), the ceremony was appointed by the Bishop to take place at St. Omer's, and one of the nuns who accompanied Lady Abbess Caryll was our Dame Constantia Heneage. She was however taken so ill that Rev. Peter Caryll, who accompanied his sister, kindly offered to forego the interesting ceremony to attend poor Dame Constantia, to whom he administered the last holy sacraments. She survived to the following day only, dying on the 25th June, 1664. She had come from Ghent [1] to found the convent at Dunkirk, and had been professed twenty years."

[1] There had been among the nuns at Ghent one Ursula Heneage, who died in 1638.

Note to the Pedigree of Bruning, in p. 519.

Anthony Bruning of Wymering, esq. lived at the old manor house of Woodcot, in the parish of Bramdean. His will is dated March 26, 1663, and proved on 23rd April, 1663. In 1648 he is named with Swithun Wells, esq. Sir William Courtney, knight and baronet, and dame Mary his wife, as one of the heirs of Gilbert Wells of Bambridge, co. Hants, gentleman, deceased. He had a family of nine sons and four daughters living at the time of his death; of the sons six were priests, and two of the daughters became nuns. Three of the sons were christened Francis, and were designated in his will as " my son Francis Bruning the elder," " my son Francis Bruning the second of that name," and " my son Francis the third of that name." The names of the other sons were Edmund, Charles, John, Gilbert, Anthony, and George. The two elder daughters were Martha, married to —— Winchcombe, and Anne, married to —— Tempest. One of the Francis' (the second I believe) was also a priest of the Society of Jesus (by the name of Francis Hyde), admitted in 1670, and died Nov. 23, 1714, aged 66.

In addition to the following Pedigrees, we have in preparation for our next Volume a very complete one of the once wide-spread family of Caryll; and a second pedigree of Tichborne, which will be accompanied by some interesting documents relative to that family, recently extinct.

lo. cu hut vol.

(Pedigrees continued from page 428.*)*

XVIII. CLAVERING OF CALLALY.

Sir John Clavering, of Callaly,╤Anne, dau. of Sir Thomas
co. Northumberland, Knt. │ Riddell, of Gateshead.

Rev. John Clavering, Confessor to E. B.   Robert,   2. Ralph╤Mary, dau. of Wil-
Pontoise; died Jan. 24, 1694, "a very   died   Claver- │ liam Middleton, of
old man."   s. p.   ing.   Stockeld.

John Clavering,╤Anne, dau. of William 3rd   Mary Claver-╤Gerard Salvin, of
born 1659.   │ Lord Widdrington.   ing.   │ Croxdale.

Ralph Clavering,╤Mary, dau. of Nicholas Stapleton, of   Anne Claver-═F. Maire,
born 1695.   │ Ponteland, and Carleton, co. York.   ing.   Esq.

Mary Anne, Lady Abbess of Pont-   Ralph Claver-   Rev. Nicholas Clavering, Con-
oise; born 1731; died 1795; bur.   ing, born 27   fessor to E. B.; born 1728; died
at Hammersmith. (See p. 62.)   June, 1727.   1805; bur. at Hammersmith.

XIX. HAGGERSTON.

Sir Thomas Haggerston, of Haggerston,╤Margaret, dau. of Sir
2nd Bart. (his sister Ellen mar. William │ Francis Howard, of
Selby, of Biddleston.)   Corby; 1st wife.

Edward═1. Mary, dau. of   William╤Anne,   Thomas,   Henry,S.J. Anna
Hagger- Gerard Salvin,   Hagger- │ dau. of   died in   John, S.J. Cath'ne,
ston,   of Croxdale.   ston,   │ Sir Phi- service of Francis.   9th Lady
died   2. Mrs. Fitz-   died   │ lip Con- James II.   Abbess of
s. p.   herbert.   viv. pat. stable.   s. p.   Religious. Pontoise.

Anne╤Bryan Sal-   Sir Carna-╤Elizabeth Mid-   .... Haggerston,   Two
Hag- │ vin, of   by Hagger- │ dleton, of   mar. Thomas   daugh-
ger- │ Croxdale,   ston,3d Bt. │ Stockeld   Clifton, of   ters
ston.│ Esq.   died 1756. │ died 1769.   Lytham, Esq.   cœl.
     │ (No. XVII.)   died s. p.

Mary Salvin.═George Markham, Esq.

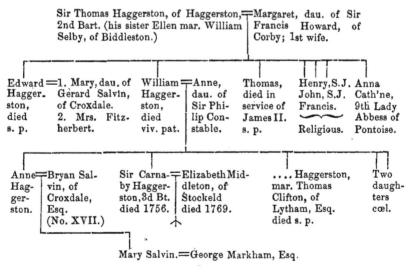

XX. WIDDRINGTON, OF WIDDRINGTON.

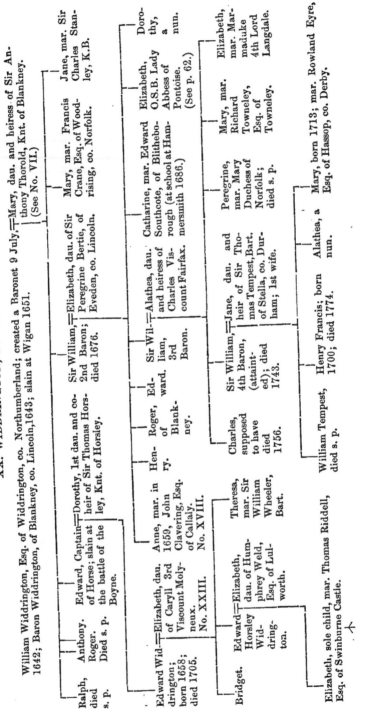

William Widdrington, Esq. of Widdrington, co. Northumberland; created a Baronet 9 July, = Mary, dau. and heiress of Sir Anthony Thorold, Knt. of Blankney. 1642; Baron Widdrington, of Blankney, co. Lincoln, 1643; slain at Wigan 1651. (See No. VII.)

Ralph, died s. p.

Anthony. Roger. Died s. p.

Edward, Captain = Dorothy, 1st dau. and co-of Horse; slain at heir of Sir Thomas Hors-the battle of the ley, Knt. of Horsley. Boyne.

Sir William, = Elizabeth, dau. of Sir 2nd Baron; Peregrine Bertie, of died 1676. Eveden, co. Lincoln.

Mary, mar. Francis Crane, Esq. of Wood-rising, co. Norfolk.

Jane, mar. Sir Charles Stan-ley, K.B.

Edward Wid- = Elizabeth, dau. drington; of Caryll 3rd born 1658; Viscount Moly-died 1705. neux. No. XXIII.

Anne, mar. in 1659, John Clavering, Esq. of Callaly. No. XVIII.

Roger, of Blank-ney.

Henry.

Edward.

Sir Wil- = Alathea, dau. liam, and heiress of 3rd Charles Vis-Baron. count Fairfax.

Catharine, mar. Edward Southcote, of Blitheborough (at school at Ham-mersmith 1686.)

Elizabeth, O.S.B. Lady Abbess of Pontoise. (See p. 62.)

Doro-thy, a nun.

Bridget.

Edward = Elizabeth, Horsley dau. of Hum-Wid- phrey Weld, dring- Esq. of Lul-ton. worth.

Theresa, mar. Sir William Wheeler, Bart.

Charles, supposed to have died 1756.

Sir William, = Jane, dau. and 4th Baron, heir of Sir Tho-(attaint- mas Tempest, Bart. ed); died of Stella, co. Dur-1743. ham; 1st wife.

Peregrine, mar. Mary Duchess of Norfolk; died s. p.

Mary, mar. Richard Towneley, Esq. of Towneley.

Elizabeth, mar. Mar-maduke 4th Lord Langdale.

Elizabeth, sole child, mar. Thomas Riddell, Esq. of Swinburne Castle.

William Tempest, died s. p.

Henry Francis; born 1700; died 1774.

Alathea, a nun.

Mary, born 1713; mar. Rowland Eyre, Esq. of Hassop, co. Derby.

XXI. VAUX, NEVILLE OF ABERGAVENNY, SIMEON, AND SHELLEY.

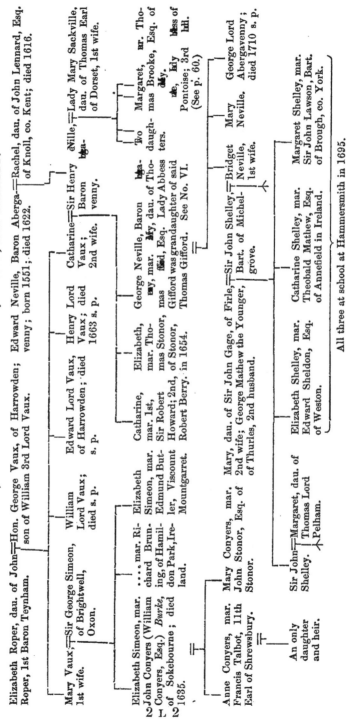

All three at school at Hammersmith in 1695.

2 L 2

XXII. MARKHAM, AND NEVILLE OF HOLT.

Sir John Markham, Lord Chief Justice of King's Bench, =Margaret, dau. and co-heir of Sir Simon Leeke, of Cotham.
of Sedgebrook, co. Lincoln.

Katharine, dau. of Sir Anthony Babington, =Sir John Markham, of Cotham, Lieutenant=Anna, dau. of Sir John Strelley, widow of Sir Richard Stanhope, Knt.; 3rd wife.
Knt.; 1st wife. of the Tower temp. Hen. VIII.

Frances, mar. Henry Babington of Dethick. Their son Anthony was executed for high treason in the reign of Queen Elizabeth.

Thomas Markham, of Ollerton, co. Notts; Standard Bearer to Queen Elizabeth.
=Mary, dau. and heiress of Rice Griffin, Esq. of Dingley and Braybrooke, co. Leicester. Her mother Elizabeth Brudenell, of Dean.

William Markham, of Little Okeley, co. Northampton; died 1571.
=Elizabeth, dau. of Sir Edward Montague and widow of Richard Cave, of Stanford. Their daughter and heiress married Nicholas Timperley, of Hintlesham. See No. V.

Isabella, 2nd wife of Sir John Harrington, Knt. of Kelweston, near Bath.

Sir Griffin Markham, Knt. of the Golden Spur; in Ireland under Earl of Essex; was banished and died at Rouen. Had no male issue; married Anna, daughter of Peter Roos, Esq. of Laxton.

Anne, mar. Sir Francis Smith, Knt. of Wotton; their son Charles created Baron Carrington. No. XVI.

Charles Markham, mar. Bridget Ford; had one daughter, married 1st, Thomas Waterton, of Waterton; 2nd, Sir John Middleton, Knt.

Elizabeth, mar. Edward Sheldon, of Beoley; died 1643, æt. 83. (No. X.)

George Markham, Esq. of Ollerton.
=Judith, dau. and heiress of John Withernwick, Esq. of Claxby, co. Lincoln, by Judith Fitzwilliams, of Claxby.

Robert, died at Rome a priest.

Eight sons.

Four daughters.

a

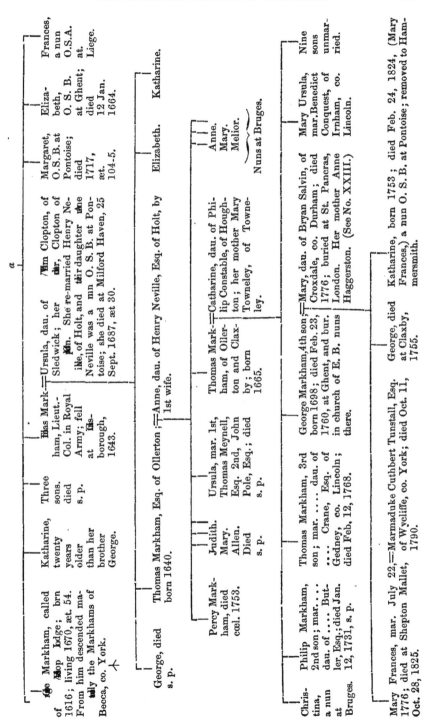

a

Frances, a nun O.S.A. at Liege.

Eliza- beth, O. S. B. at Ghent; died 12 Jan. 1664.

Margaret, O.S.B. at Pontoise; died 1717, æt. 104-5.

Katharine.

Elizabeth.

Anne.
Mary.
Melior.

} Nuns at Bruges.

Mary Ursula, mar. Benedict Conquest, of Irnham, co. Lincoln.

Nine sons unmar- ried.

───Geo. Markham, called of Mop Idge; brn 1616; living 1670, æt. 54. From him descended ma- inly the Markhams of Becca, co. York.

Thos Mark-══Ursula, dau. of ham, Lieut.- Sledwick; her Col. in Royal 2un. She re-married Henry Ne- Army; fell ville, of Holt, and their daughter the at Has- Neville was a nun O. S. B. at Pon- borough, toise; she died at Milford Haven, 25 1643. Sept. 1687, æt 30.

Wm Clopton, of dir, Clopton of the

Thomas Markham, Esq. of Ollerton;══Anne, dau. of Henry Neville, Esq. of Holt, by born 1640. 1st wife.

Thomas Mark-══Catharine, dau. of Phi- ham, of Oller- lip Constable, of Hough- ton and Clax- ton; her mother Mary by; born Towneley, of Towne- 1665. ley.

George Markham, 4th son;══Mary, dau. of Bryan Salvin, of born 1698; died Feb. 23, Croxdale, co. Durham; died 1760, at Ghent; and bur. 1776; buried at St. Pancras, in church of E. B. nuns London. Her mother Anne there. Haggerston. (See No. XXIII.)

Katharine, born 1753 ; died Feb. 24, 1824, (Mary Frances,) a nun O. S. B. at Pontoise; removed to Ham- mersmith.

Katharine, twenty years older than her brother George.

Three sons, died s. p.

George, died s. p.

Ursula, mar. 1st, Thomas Meynell, Esq. 2nd, John Pole, Esq. ; died s. p.

Judith. Mary. Allen. Died s. p.

Thomas Markham, 3rd son; mar. .... dau. of .... Crane, Esq. of Gedney, co. Lincoln; died Feb, 12, 1768.

George, died at Claxby, 1755.

Christ- tina, a nun at Bruges.

Percy Mark- ham, died cœl. 1753.

Philip Markham, 2nd son; mar. .... dau. of .... But- ler, Esq.; died Jan. 12, 1731, s. p.

Mary Frances, mar. July 22,══Marmaduke Cuthbert Tunstall, Esq. 1776; died at Shepton Mallet, of Wycliffe, co. York; died Oct. 11, Oct. 28, 1825. 1790.

XXIII. SELBY OF BIDDLESTONE.

Sir William Selby, of Biddleston; knighted=Ellen, dau. of Sir Thomas Haggerston, of Haggerston. Her mother Alice, by James I. 1603. | dau. of Henry Banaster, Esq.

Charles Selby, of Biddleston, Esq.=Elizabeth, dau. of . . . Gilibrand, of Chorley, Esq.

Roger Meynell, of North Kilvington,=Mary, dau. of Sir John Middleton, Knt. 2nd Esq. born 1639. | son of Sir Peter Meynell, of Stockeld.

Thomas William Selby, of Biddleston, Esq.=Barbara, dau. and died 1755; bur. at Old Street, Pancras. | heir of Christopher (See Vol. II. p. 224.) | Percehay, Esq.

Roger=Anne, dau. of Edward Mey- | Charlton, of Hesley Side; nell. | died 1748.

Thomas Meynell, son and heir, mar. Ursula, dau. of Thomas Markham, of Claxby; died s. p.

Eliza-=John Lawson, Esq. 3rd son of beth | Sir Henry Lawson, of Brough, Selby. | Bart. by Mary, dau. of Sir John | Shelley, of Michelgrove, Bart.

Eleanor, 2nd wife,=Thomas Selby,=Mary, 1st wife, dau. of dau. and co-heir | of Biddleston. | Roger Meynell, Esq. of Ni . . . das . . . | of Ni . . . | Esq.

Mary Selby, died unmar.

Barbara=Roger Selby, | Meynell, mar. | of N. Kil- 1735. | vington.

Margaret Anne. O. S. B. at Dunkirk.

Mary, m. Thomas Selby, Esq.

1. John Lawson, of York, M.D. 2. Thomas . . . in . . . orders. 3. Henry . . . 4. Elizabeth, m. John . . . Weston, of Sutton Place, Surrey.

Catharine,=Thomas dau. and | Selby, heir of Ralph | of Biddle- Hodshon, | ston, of . . ., | obm Esq.; died | 1753. 1826, æt. 62.

2. Nicholas-Tuite, born 1754, by his 3rd wife Frances, dau. of . . . Walmesley, of Sholley, Esq.

3. Robert Selby, m. . . . sister to Charles late Earl of Shrewsbury.

1. Roger, died cœl. 2. Thomas, S. J. obm 1737. 3. George, died cœl. Edward. Two daughters, died cœl.

Walter Selby, of Bid-=Alicia, dau. of dleston, Esq. mar. | Thomas Swar- 1817. | breck, Esq.

Catharine, mar. 1819 John Aloysius Clavering, of Callaly, Esq.

Henrietta (Mary Placida), Lady Abbess of E. B.; now at Teignmouth.

Mary Anne=Sir Charles Selby. | Wolseley, | Bart.

XXIV. BRUNING OF WYMERING AND HAMBLEDON, CO. HANTS.

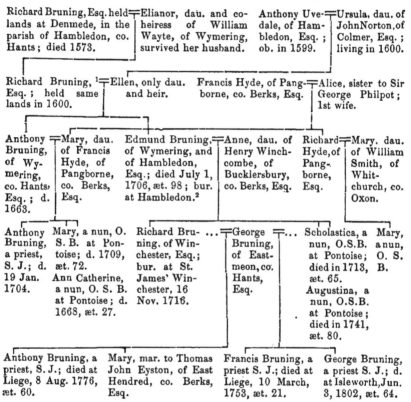

Richard Bruning, Esq. held lands at Denmede, in the parish of Hambledon, co. Hants; died 1573. ⊤ Elianor, dau. and co-heiress of William Wayte, of Wymering, survived her husband.

Anthony Uve-dale, of Hambledon, Esq.; ob. in 1599. ⊤ Ursula, dau. of John Norton, of Colmer, Esq.; living in 1600.

Richard Bruning, [1] Esq.; held same lands in 1600. ⊤ Ellen, only dau. and heir.

Francis Hyde, of Pangborne, co. Berks, Esq. ⊤ Alice, sister to Sir George Philpot; 1st wife.

Anthony Bruning, of Wymering, co. Hants, Esq.; d. 1663. ⊤ Mary, dau. of Francis Hyde, of Pangborne, co. Berks, Esq.

Edmund Bruning, of Wymering, and of Hambledon, Esq.; died July 1, 1706, æt. 98; bur. at Hambledon.[2] ⊤ Anne, dau. of Henry Winchcombe, of Bucklersbury, co. Berks, Esq.

Richard Hyde, of Pangborne, Esq. ⊤ Mary, dau. of William Smith, of Whitchurch, co. Oxon.

Anthony Bruning, a priest, S. J.; d. 19 Jan. 1704.

Mary, a nun, O. S. B. at Pontoise; d. 1709, æt. 72.
Ann Catherine, a nun, O. S. B. at Pontoise; d. 1668, æt. 27.

Richard Bruning, of Winchester, Esq.; bur. at St. James' Winchester, 16 Nov. 1716. ...⊤ George Bruning, of Eastmeon, co. Hants, Esq. ⊤ ...

Scholastica, a nun, O.S.B. at Pontoise; died in 1713, æt. 65.
Augustina, a nun, O.S.B. at Pontoise; died in 1741, æt. 80.

Mary, a nun, O. S. B.

Anthony Bruning, a priest, S. J.; died at Liege, 8 Aug. 1776, æt. 60.

Mary, mar. to Thomas John Eyston, of East Hendred, co. Berks, Esq.

Francis Bruning, a priest S. J.; died at Liege, 10 March, 1753, æt. 21.

George Bruning, a priest S. J.; d. at Isleworth, Jun. 3, 1802, æt. 64.

[1] Richard Bruning had an elder brother Francis, who died s. p. in 1596, and to whom he was heir. Their sister Mary was married to Henry Blanchard, J.P. of co. Berks, and was mother of Dame Alexia Blanchard, 4th Abbess of Brussels, O.S.B. who died 1651.

[2] On 13 April, 1671, Edmund Bruning, Esq. of Hambledon and Elizabeth his wife were excommunicated for not going to church. This lady must have been his second wife.

Frances Bruning was at school at Hammersmith in 1677.

[*A note upon this family has been inserted in p. 512.*]

LIST OF THE GRAVESTONES IN THE CEMETERY ATTACHED TO THE
CONVENT AT HAMMERSMITH.

Top Row, beginning from the corner nearest the great iron gate.

1. Dame M. Gertrude Sweeney + 10 Feby. 1859, aged 39, professed 15.

2. Sister M. Placida Kavanagh + 24 Sept. 1855, aged 59, prof. 37.

3. Dame M. Walburga Woollett + 19 May 1854, aged 37, prof. 11.

4. Dame M. Maura Carrington + 16 March 1854, aged 79, pr. 55.

5. Dame M. Agnes Philipe + 6 Novr. 1853, aged 57, pr. 25.

6. Charlotte Amalia Baroness da Torre de Moncorvo, born 15 Aug. 1806, died 7 Feby. 1840.

7. Dame M. Aloysia Westby + 22 July 1859, aged 39, prof. 19.

8. Dame M. Placida Shea + 24 Novr. 1861, aged 52, pr. 30.

9. Lady M. Placida Messenger, Abbess of the Benedictines late of Dunkirk, died 30 Aug. 1828, aged 77, prof. 56. (Professed at Pontoise.)

Second Row, beginning from the left, as before.

1. Dame M. Austin Le Dily + 10 Jany. 1849, aged 57, prof. 19.

2. Sister M. Maura Hough + 22 Aug. 1848, aged 49, pr. 24.

3. Sister M. Benedict Scholefield + 17 July 1853, aged 43, pr. 16.

4. Sister M. Winifred Tobin + 12 Decr. 1846, aged 90, pr. 65.

5. Dame M. Lucy Sturdy + 28 Decr. 1840, aged 64, pr. 35.

6. Dame M. Teresa Meade + 25 Decr. 1840, aged 71, pr. 31.

7. Dame M. Aloysia Sisson + 22 Decr. 1832, aged 40, pr. 19.

8. Sister M. Agnes Bend + 5 Sept. 1832, aged 82, pr. 54.

. Dame M. Victoria Whitehall + 12 June 1830, aged 69, pr. 47.

1 . Sister M. Magdalen Berry + 8 Jany. 1829, aged 69, prof. 38.

1&. Sister Ann Benedict Godwin + 24 Aug. 1828, aged 81, pr. 60.

1 . Dame M. Magdalen McMillan + 24 Oct. 1826, aged 42, pr. 17.

1&. Dame M. Catharine Smith + 20 May 1841, aged 43, pr. 21.

Third Row.

1. Sister M. Gertrude Marshall + 25 April 1855, aged 63, prof. 30.

2. Mrs. Marcella Dillon + 16 Aug. 1811, aged 77. (Religious of the former stablishment.)

3. Sister Agatha Thickness + 9 June 1811, aged 58, prof. 37. (Rel. of a French House of Benedictines at Ardres.)

4. Dame M. Winifred Clarke + 29 March 1809, aged 76, prof. 37. (Pr. at Pontoise.)

5. Miss Catherine Brown + 30 June 1808, aged 14.

6. Dame M. Agnes Parkes + 23 Feby. 1808, aged 45, prof. 21.

7. Dame M. Gertrude Wells + 3 Nov. 1807, aged 83, pr. 61.

8. Sister M. Elizabeth Charnley + 3 June 1807, aged 73, pr. 49.

9. Sister M. Austin Hurley + 30 March 1821, aged 39, pr. 3.

10. Mrs. Mary Joseph Woods + 19 April 1822, aged 80. (Rel. of the former establishment.)

11. Dame M. Frances Markham + 25 Feby. 1824, aged 70, prof. 47. (Pr. at Pontoise.)

12. Sister M. Catherine Riordan + 12 May 1852, aged 29, pr. 3.

Fourth Row.

1. Miss Mary McCarthy + 6 July, 1808, aged 3 years and 6 months.
2. Mrs. Arabella Kirwan + 21 July, 1800, aged 76. (Rel. of a convent of French Ursulines.)
3. Dame M. Placida Macclesfield + 29 Decr. 1799, aged 68, prof. 41.
4. Dame Joseph Teresa Kane + 26 Decr. 1799, aged 48, prof. 24.
5. Sister M. Margaret Evans + 8 Feby. 1799, aged 77, pr. 52. (Pr. at Pontoise.)
6. Dame M. Michael Prescott + 31 Decr. 1798, aged 67, pr. 43.
7. Dame M. Benedict Sheldon + 1 May, 1798, aged 78, pr.
8. Dame M. Joseph Mostyn + 21 Nov. 1806, aged 56, prof. 32.
9. Miss Maria Prujean + 14 Nov. 1826, aged 52.
10. Sister M. Scholastica Phesackelly + 13 Febr. 1823, aged 70, pr. 47.
11. Sister Monica Parry + 7 June, 1825, aged 76. (A poor Clare of Dunkirk.)
12. Rose Mary Josephine Dunn + 5 Feb. 1849, aged 57.

Fifth Row.

1. Dame M. Benedict Willoughby + 16 July, 1804, aged 62, prof. 42.
2. Dame M. Lucy Barkeley + 16 June, 1801, aged 77, pr. 59.
3. Dame M. Teresa Armstrong + 24 July, 1800, aged 73. (Prof. at Pontoise after 1751.)
4. Lady M. Magdalen Prujean + 15 May, 1812, aged 86, prof. 60 ; Abbess of the Benedictines, late of Dunkirk, 34.
5. Lady M. Ann Clavering + 8 Nov. 1795, aged 64, pr. 44. (Tenth and last Abbess of Pontoise.)
6. Mrs. Mary Trant + 11 Feb. 1798, aged 73. (An Ursuline in a French community, of which Mrs. Arabella Kirwan was many years superior.)
7. Rev. John Lee + 11 March, 1822, aged 82.
8. Rev. François Bellisent + 8 Aug. 1838, aged 72.
9. Rev. Mariano Gil de Tejada (no stone).
10. Mrs. Jane Dawes + 14 Sept. 1838, aged 84.
11. Mrs. Mary Jackson + 12 Oct. 1845, aged 71. (A faithful old servant of our community.)

Lowest Row.

1. Rev. Nicholas Clavering + 18 Oct. 1805, aged 77. (Brother to the abbess, and last chaplain of the Pontoise community.)
2. Mrs. Mary Bostock + 24 March, 1817, in her 80th year.
3. Rev. John Newsham + 11 June, 1825, aged 83.
4. Mrs. Jane Campbell + 9 March, 1832, in her 80th year.
5. Mrs. Frances Ann Carroll + 21 May, 1834, aged 79.
6. Miss Margaret Bosville + 18 Nov. 1834, aged 80.
7. Elizabeth Beck, &c., many years confidential servant of the Jerningham and Bedingfeld families, died 16 May, 1850, aged 70. (This stone is between the fifth and last row.)

A practice which formerly prevailed in Scotland, whereby Peers
were enabled, with the consent of the Crown, to alter the succession to
their dignities and designate their next heir, has been much misunderstood by recent writers, and even denied to have existed. There are,
however, many examples of it: as the Earldoms of Errol and Breadalbane, the old Barony of Dingwall, and the Peerages of Rutherford,
Cardross, &c. Respecting the last an amusing anecdote is given in a
dissertation upon Heirs Male, which was published by Mr. Alexander
Sinclair in 1837. It relates to the Earl of Buchan, who was also Lord
Cardross from 1767 to 1829 :—

" The second example is the creation of the Barony of Cardross,
granted to John twenty-third Earl of Mar, K.G., and his heirs male
and assignees. He settled it upon his third son Henry, the second
son of his second marriage, and the heirs male of his body, but reserving his own life-rent; and he dying before him, his son succeeded his
grandfather, and got a new patent to the heirs male of his body, under
certain conditions, and with similar powers, which, however, were
never exercised; and his descendant, who is also Earl of Buchan, has
the Peerage. The late Earl of Buchan, perhaps misled by Grose's
Antiquities, supposed that every Lord Cardross had the right of nominating any person to succeed ; and one day, after a jovial dinner,
taking a great liking to one of the company, he made known his
fancied privilege and intention accordingly to create his favourite a
peer. The party followed up the hint, got a paper signed on the
spot, and treated the new Lord Cardross with all the respect due to so
exalted a personage. Next day, still believing in his powers, his
lordship was so distressed at the loss he conceived himself and the
family to have sustained, that the patent was surrendered with less
unwillingness than he expected."

The treasurer Earl of Mar, by his first wife Anne Drummond, aunt
of the first and second Earls of Perth, had a son and heir to that
earldom. By his second wife Lady Mary Stuart, daughter of King
James's cousin, and great favourite, Esme Duke of Lennox, he had
several sons; and the object in bestowing upon him in 1606 this
Barony of Cardross so unrestricted evidently was to establish a

separate line, as might be best for that family. It was confirmed in 1610, but the power of designation was not exercised till 1617, when, Mary's eldest son having realised the acquisition of the Earldom of Buchan, Cardross was settled on Henry, her second son.

The earl died in 1634, but Henry died before him, in 1628, so that the title descended to Henry's son David, who became the second Lord Cardross. He obtained a grant in 1663-4, also with powers of nomination, like his grandfather, "to the heirs male of his body," with the express conditions, &c. to be contained in any writing by the said Lord at any time of life, even up to the moment of death, which the aforesaid heirs male are to be bound to observe as if expressed in the charter whereby they are to have right to the title; whom failing, to any person or any persons whom the said Lord may nominate at any time of life, &c. under these said limitations, &c.; whom all failing, to the said David Lord Cardross and his nearest legitimate heirs and assigns whatever. (Great Seal Book, LXII. 9.)

As this power was never exercised, the succession to the title remains vested in heirs male of his body so long as they last, and there are many of them, viz.: the heirs male of the Buchan family, Lord Erskine's family, the Erskines of Carnock, and now also of Cardross, Linlathen, Venlaw. All these must intercept the title from the present Mrs. Biber Erskine,[1] or any other heir female.

2. I shall now exemplify THE EARLDOM OF ERROL. In 1541 there was a doubt whether the direct heir female or the cousin and collateral heir male should get the title; but, after nearly a year's suspense, Sir George Hay, of Logiealmond, the heir male, was admitted to succeed, apparently on the condition that Andrew, his eldest son, should marry the heiress.

The family then continued for five generations, down to Gilbert eleventh earl, who had no children. He therefore applied for permission

---

[1] The Hon. John Berry Biber-Erskine, (such are her names,) the elder daughter of the late Henry Lord Cardross (who died in 1836), having married in 1856 the Rev. George Eden Biber, succeeded to the estate of Dryburgh on the death of her grandfather Henry David, 12th Earl of Buchan, in 1857. Her friends have supposed that she was also entitled to the Barony of Cardross, in pursuance of the terms of the remainder settled in a charter dated 10 Feb. 1663-4. It has recently, however, been acknowledged that such a supposition was groundless, having rested only on an inaccurate statement of the remainders given in Douglas's *Peerage of Scotland*. The discussion has been carried on in the *Edinburgh Courant* and the London *Morning Post*, and the particulars will be found fully related in the *Gentleman's Magazine* for April 1866.

to carry on the family, and obtained powers of nomination, by grant from the Crown, in 1666, to designate as his heirs, even up to the moment of death, any person or any persons whom he might appoint to succeed him. In 1674 he proceeded to exercise this right, by settling the earldom (after any family he might have) upon his nearest heir male, Sir John Hay, of Keillor, with a remainder to females. This was confirmed by charter under the great seal, and the present earl could not have succeeded to the title without this settlement, by which alone it was conveyed to his great-great-grandfather through two female descents. This is only one of many cases which antiquaries in England zealously strive to resist as beyond all legal powers, notwithstanding the proofs that numerous Peerages have been so conveyed, and still exist, upon this very authority. Down to the Union every Peer in Scotland could, with the consent of the Crown, alter the succession in every generation according to his own whim! even retaining the original precedency. In 1796 the right of succession was disputed but established.

The other cases may be briefly adverted to :—

3. THE EARLDOM OF BREADALBANE was a substitute for that of Caithness, which had been previously conferred in 1677. Sir John Campbell of Glenurchy, baronet, was then created Earl of Caithness, to him and the heirs male of his body, with power to select whichever son he might choose to succeed, even at the period of his death; whom failing, to his nearest heirs male whatever. But George Sinclair, the heir male of the old family, being supported by the Duke of York, and allowed to prove his right, got this cancelled, and the intruder was instead created Earl of Breadalbane and Holland in 1681, with remainder to which ever of his sons by his deceased wife Lady Mary Rich he might designate by writing at any time of his life; whom failing, to any other heirs male of his own body; whom failing, to his nearest legitimate heirs male; whom failing, to his legitimate heirs whatever. His object in acquiring this power was to set aside his eldest son Duncan, Lord Ormelie, as incompetent to represent the family. Accordingly he nominated his second son John his heir, and he became second Earl in 1716. His right was disputed by Lord Saltoun, who called him Mr. John Campbell, and referred to his elder brother Lord Ormelie, when his vote was objected to at the election in 1721; but the objections were not sustained, and his vote remained good, and he was afterwards twice elected to represent the Scotch Peerage in 1736 and 1741. Thus the power of nomination

was established.   The assumption of the supplementary earldom seems a dubious compliment to his brother-in-law the Earl of Warwick and Holland, whose title continued till 1756.

4. Andrew Rutherford, a general recommended by the King of France to King Charles II. was by him created LORD RUTHERFORD in 1661, with remainder to the heirs male of his body, whom failing, to any person or persons whom, while he lived, or even at his death, he might please to designate to succeed him ; and thereafter to his heirs of entail and provision according to his nomination to the said dignity, under the conditions and restrictions he might prescribe.   He was afterwards advanced to be Earl of Teviot in 1663, but only with limitation to the heirs male of his body.   He sailed about, and was said to have made a will at every port ; but by his last will at Portsmouth, 23rd Dec. 1663, he made a settlement of his title, with lands, debts, executry, all mixed up with the Peerage, appointing as his universal heir Sir Thomas Rutherford of Hunthill (from whose family he was considered to be derived) ; then to the eldest son of Sir Thomas ; and, failing them, to the nearest heirs male of Sir Thomas ; whom all failing, to the eldest daughter of Sir Thomas.   It is singular that he had a brother, Mr. William Rutherford, whose will is recorded with that of the Earl 8th June, 1688.   Being Governor of Tangier, the Earl of Teviot was killed in a sally against the Moors in 1664, when Sir Thomas became second Lord Rutherford, and was served heir of entail and provision in his title and lands.   He died without issue in 1668 ; and his brother Archibald succeeded as third Lord, and was served heir in 1670.   He sat in Parliament as Lord Rutherford, and died in 1685, also without issue.   His brother Robert now became fourth Lord, sat in Parliament in 1698, and voted at elections down to 1715.   He died without issue in 1724, being the fourth Lord in succession who had no family ; and the title opened to the heirs male collateral of Hunthill, and has long been disputed between alleged heirs male and the descendants of the Earl's sister Christian, who married Robert Duric of Grange.   Sometimes two Lords Rutherford have voted and protested together ; and the question is not decided.

5. Andrew Keith was created LORD DINGWALL to him and his heirs male and assigns in 1583-4.   The grant was ratified by Parliament in 1584.   A charter passed the great seal 3rd Aug. 1587, to him and the heirs male of his body ; who failing, to his nearest lawful heirs male whatever.   Having no heirs, he soon resigned his Peerage into the King's hands, and obtained a new charter 24th Nov. 1591, to himself

and his heirs male *and assigns whatever*, with the dignity, &c. of Lord of Parliament. This was confirmed by Parliament in 1592. He proceeded to assign it to Sir William Keith of Delny, with whom no relationship is stated; and Sir William had a charter accordingly 22nd Jan. 1592-3, to him and his heirs male whatever, to succeed to the Peerage on the grantor's death.

The title seems to have ceased in 1606, when it was not in the list of ranking, and both Delny and Dingwall were sold to the celebrated James first Lord Balmerinoch in 1608, and transferred by him to King James's favourite gentleman of the bedchamber, Sir Richard Preston, who was created Lord Dingwall 8th June, 1609, with remainder to his heirs and assigns whatever, confirmed by Act of Parliament 17th June, 1609. In 1614 the King procured for him an illustrious alliance with Lady Elizabeth Butler, only child of Thomas tenth Earl of Ormonde, widow of her cousin Theobald Viscount Tulleophillim, who left her a young widow without issue in 1613. Her father, who had been blind for many years, settled all his estates, except one manor, on his nephew Walter Bulter, his heir male and successor in the earldom, and soon after died in 1614, about the time of the above second marriage. Walter became eleventh Earl; but the King insisted on his surrendering the estates to his *protégé*, and, when Earl Walter refused to part with his property, James seized them, and imprisoned the Earl in the Fleet, while he constituted himself umpire after thus violently prejudging the case ! The Earl would not yield up his right, and he remained for eight years in cruel confinement with scanty supplies, till the King's death released him in 1625, and King Charles I. began to allow justice to be done. Meantime his rival flourished, and in 1622 was created Earl of Desmond in Ireland on pretence of his wife's grandmother being heir of that house. This was in pursuance of a scheme that his only daughter Lady Elizabeth Preston, then aged eight, should be married to George Fielding, second son of the Countess of Denbigh, niece of the absolute Duke of Buckingham, and he was appointed to succeed to the earldom; but this was the only part of the plot which came to pass. The King's death in 1625, the Duke of Buckingham's assassination on 28th August 1628, the Earl of Desmond her father being drowned in his voyage from Dublin to England 28th Oct. 1628, within a few days of the death of her mother in Wales, altered everything. Her wardship was granted to the Earl of Holland, who sold her for 15,000*l.* to be married to her cousin, James Butler, afterwards the great Duke of

Ormonde, grandson and heir of the imprisoned Earl (and son of Thomas Lord Thurles, who was drowned in 1619 in his passage from England to Ireland), when, to make assurance doubly sure and keep his son safe from interference, his wardship was given to Lord Desmond the usurper. The marriage took effect in 1629 while the heiress was still very young. Their grandson the second Duke and Lord Dingwall incurred forfeiture in 1715, otherwise Earl Cowper would be Lord Dingwall.

These examples would be sufficient to prove the exercise of this mode of inheritance in regard to peerages in Scotland: but I may take this opportunity to give in addition a brief account of what occurred in regard to the Earldom of Stair.

John Viscount Stair was in 1703 created EARL OF STAIR, with remainder to the heirs male of his body; whom failing, to the heirs male of his father. He died 8th Jan. 1707, and his son John succeeded as second Earl, and was afterwards the famous field marshal. He had no family, and, as his next brother William Dalrymple had married the Countess of Dumfries, (a much older title,) he negotiated for an alteration in the succession of his own earldom. In the same year that he succeeded to the peerage he surrendered it into the hands of the Queen, and obtained a new patent to himself and the heirs male of his body; whom failing, to such person or persons descended from the first Viscount of Stair as he should nominate and appoint by a writing in his lifetime; whom failing, to his immediate younger brother William, and then to James the second son of the said William by Penelope Countess of Dumfries, with many other complicated arrangements. This was confirmed by charter and ratified by Parliament.

Accordingly, 31st March, 1747, he made a nomination to John Dalrymple, eldest son of his brother George, to succeed him. He died two months after, when James and John both assumed to be Earls of Stair (William the father of James being then deceased); but a deed after the Union was not supported, and James succeeded. John was thus disappointed for twenty-one years; but then he became fifth Earl, instead of third, on the death without issue of William fourth Earl of Dumfries and Stair in 1768.

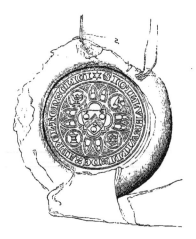

THE ARMS OF APPLETON.

This Seal presents on a shield of arms a chevron (shaded with the lines now used to designate gules) between three apples in a hanging position. It is not easy to make out the four emblems which occupy the circular panels of the seal; but the fourth is clearly a Katharine-wheel, and all were not improbably emblems of the saints to whom the clerk was devoted.

It may fairly be presumed that the Appletons scattered up and down on the Tees arose from Appleton Wiske in Allertonshire or East Appleton near Richmond. From the superior execution of the seal engraved we are inclined to think that William de Appelton, like Wycliffe, was not merely named after the place of his birth, that his surname and arms were settled in his family, and that he belonged to a race of the name which occurs in considerable social status in the early part of the thirteenth century in connection with the constables of Richmond.

The seal (to which my attention has been directed by my friend Mr. Longstaffe of Gateshead) has been found attached to a document (one of a large collection in private hands) in which there is no mention of its original owner. It is dated at Stokton [upon Tees] on Thursday after the Feast of the Purification of B. V. M. 1370, and is a quitclaim by Robert Lukline, chaplain, to William Chapman, of "Wlston," [hodie Wolviston] of the grantor's right in all the lands which the same Chapman and he had in "Wlliston" of the gift of Thomas de Gretham. It does not follow conclusively that Appleton was then dead; but as he is not a witness, and the instrument does not state that his seal was borrowed in consequence of the grantor's not being known, the probability is that he was so, and that it was appropriated by Robert Lukline to his own use.

I beg to place it on record in your pages as the earliest evidence hitherto discovered for the arms of Appleton.   J. R A.

THE FAMILY OF TEMPLE.

No. II.

In pursuance of our proposition, made in p. 396, we proceed to trace some of the junior branches of the wide-spreading family of Temple ; and we shall first follow the second line of Baronets, which enjoyed from the year 1749 to 1786 the dignity conferred on Sir Thomas Temple of Stowe in the year 1611.

TEMPLE, OF STANTON BARRY, CO. BUCKINGHAM.

On the death of Field-Marshal Lord Viscount Cobham, in 1749, the title of Baronet devolved on Sir William Temple, who was a great-grandson of Sir John Temple, of Stanton Barry, co. Buckingham, second son of the first Baronet.

SIR JOHN TEMPLE was born, it would seem, in the year 1593,[1] and, if so, he was knighted when only in his twentieth year. That honour was conferred upon him by King James I. at Royston, on the 21st of March, 1612-13.

His marriage must also have taken place at an early age, for at his death Sept. 23, 1632, his eldest son Peter was aged 19, and therefore born in 1613. The following entries of the baptisms of his children are from the register of Stowe:—

1614. Thomas, son of Sir John Temple, Knt., Jan. 10.
1616. Dorothy, daughter of Sir John Temple, Oct. 17.
1617. John, son of Sir John Temple, Nov. 14.[2]
1619. Hester, daughter of Sir John Temple, Sept. 5.
1620. John, son of Sir John Temple, Nov. 6.
1622. Edmund, son of Sir John Temple, June 6.
1623. Mary, daughter of Sir John Temple, Aug. 5.

---

[1] Peter (afterwards the second Baronet), son of Thomas Temple, esq., was baptised at Stowe, Oct. 10, 1592. John, his next son, Nov. 10, 1593. In the extracts from the register of Stowe (*misstated as being from* Sibbesdon), History of Leic. iv. 958, there is also " John, son of Thomas Temple, esq., bapt. Jan. 26, 1597," in which entry there is probably some mistake.

[2] 1617[-18] John, son of Sir Peter Temple, knt., *buried* Jan. 17. (In this burial the father's name is probably mistaken.)

From these entries occurring at Stowe, it is probable that Sir
John Temple was throughout those years continuing to reside in
his father's house. It is on record that his own mansion at
Stanton Barry[1] was let to the Lord Viscount Purbeck, as appears
by the following memorandum:—

A°. 1624. The Lord Viscount Purbeck rented the manor-house [of
Stanton Barry] of the Temples to be near Dr. Napïer, Rector of
Lynford, who undertook the cure of him, he being a lunatick. (Brownè
Willis's *History of the Hundred of Newport*, Addit. M.S. Brit. Mus.
5839, p. 352.)

This accounts for the name of Sir John Temple's fourth and
youngest son, Sir Purbeck Temple, who will be noticed hereafter.

Sir John lost his wife in 1625; and he afterwards married
Frances,[2] widow of Thomas Alston, gent.[3] of Gedding-hall, in
Polstead, Suffolk (fourth son of William Alston, esq. of Saham),
and daughter of Simon Blomfield, esq. of Coddenham, in the
same county.

His funeral certificate is as follows:—

[Coll. Arm. I. 23, fol. 75.]

The right worshipfull Sir John Temple of Stanton in y[e] county of
Buckingham Knight departed this mortall life at Bidlesden in y[e] county
aforesaid y[e] 23th of September 1632 and was interred in the parrish
church of Stanton aforesaid within 3 dayes after. He was y[e] 2[d] sonne
of Sir Thomas Temple of Stowe in the county of Buckingham Knight
and Baronett. He maried Dorothy one of y[e] daughters and co-heires
of Edmund Lee of Stanton aforesaid, by whom he hath yssue 4 sonnes
and 3 daughters: Peter Temple sonne and heir, Thomas 2[d], Edmund 3[d],
and Purbeck youngest sonne, all as yett unmaried. Dorothy eldest daughter, Hester 2d, and Mary youngest, all likewise unmarried. The Defunct
maried to his 2[d] wife Frances y[e] widow of (*blank*) Alston of Suff. and
da. of Blumfeild of Suffolk aforesaid, by whom he hath not any yssue;

---

[1] At the inquisition held on the death of Sir John Temple, it was found that he
died seized of the manor and rectory of Stanton Barry, held of the manor of East
Greenwich.

[2] Baptised at Coddenham, 8th Sept. 1612.

[3] Baptised at Newton, Suffolk, 23rd Feb. 1564 ; buried there 25th Jan. 1619. See
a pedigree of Alston in Davy's Suffolk Collections, vol. xxxviii. (Brit. Mus. Addit.
MS. 19,114.)

who, togeither with Thomas Tyrrill of the Inner Temple Esq. and John Moore of Moreborne in the county of Leicester, are his Executors nominated by his last will and testament. This Certificate was taken by Geo. Owen, Yorke Herauld, ye 28th of January 1633, to be recorded in the Office of Armes, and is testified to be true by ye subscription of the forenamed Mr. Tyrrill. (*Signed*) Thomas Tyrrell.

Arms, Sable, a chevron between three martlets argent, a crescent for difference; the impalement left blank.

Sir John Temple's three daughters were married,—Dorothy, to John Alston, esq. of the Inner Temple, and of Pavenham, co. Bedford, one of the younger sons of his second wife; Hester, to Edward Paschal, of co. Essex, esq.; and Mary, to Robert Nelson, esq. of Gray's Inn.

In his will, which is dated on the 18th of Sept. 1632, a few days before his death, Sir John Temple is styled of Biddlesden, co. Buckingham. He leaves the manor of Stanton after the death of Frances his wife to his son Peter, and his heirs for ever. The manor of Morebarne, and divers lands, &c. in Lutterworth, co. Leic. to be sold if necessary to pay his debts and raise portions for his children. Whereas there was due to him after the death of Sir Edmond Lenthall, Knt. 3,500*l.* or thereabouts, his executors were to compound with Sir Edmond if he and Sir John Lenthall, " my brother-in-law,[1]" shall so desire. Executors his wife, his friend Thomas Tirrell of the Inner Temple, esquire, and John Moore his faithful servant. Signed in presence of Frances Temple, John Lenthall, Edward Dawson, Richard Grenvill,[2] and Thomas Tirrell. Proved 26 Oct. 1632. (P. C. C., 98 *Audelay.*)

The will of his widow Dame Frances Temple, of Great Wodhull alias Odell, co. Bedford, is dated August 3, 1642. John Earl of Peterborough, by indenture dated 4 Nov. 11 Car. I. had leased to her the manor of Grafton alias Grafton Underwood, co. Northampton, excepting the advowson and parsonage, for 99 years, and the testatrix by deed dated 1 Aug. (two days before the date of her will) had for 4,320*l.* assigned the same to Frances Alston her daughter; and the Earl had assigned the reversion to Edward and John Alston two of her sons. She leaves her daughter also 2,700*l.* in money, for which she was to give a sufficient release to the estate of her late father Thomas Alston

---

[1] Sir John Lenthall had married Bridget Temple, one of the testator's sisters.

[2] Probably the future husband of his son's widow: see p. 519.

gentleman deceased, and to the estate of William Alston the testatrix's eldest son lately deceased.   To her son Sir Thomas Alston all the furniture in the chamber called the Matted Chamber where he now lodgeth.   To Edmond and Purbeck Temple sons of her late husband Sir John Temple, each 200*l.*   To her kinswomen and servants Anna Alston and Frances Parke, each 40*l.*   To her kinsman John Blomefield son of Symon B. of Codenham gent. deceased 20*l.*   For a monument to be erected to her son William in Woodhull church 100*l.* Sons Edward and John Alston executors.   Proved 9 Aug. 1647.   (183 *Fines.*)

In the church of Stanton Barry are the following inscriptions, placed upon three stones which comprehend the breadth of the pavement within the communion rails [1]:—

1. Here rest the Bodys of Sir JOHN TEMPLE, Knight, and of Dame DOROTHY his first wife, one of the two daughters and heirs of Edmund Lee, Esq. late Lord of this Mannor,[2] by whom he had issue living at the time of his death 4 sonnes and 3 daughters.   She dyed y^e . . . . . . day of . . . . . . 1625, and he dyed the 23 day of Sept. 1632, Dame Frances his 2^d Wife surviving, who placed heere this Marble.

ARMS. 1 and 4, an eagle displayed; 2 and 3, two bars charged with six martlets; impaling a fess between three crescents, a martlet for difference, *Lee.*

2. Here lyeth the Body of Dame ELINOR TEMPLE, relict of Sir Peter Temple, Knt.   She was eldest daughter of Sir Timothy Tyrrill of Okeley in this county Knt. by Elinor, daughter of Sir William Kingsmill of Hampshire, Knight.   She departed this life May ye 24th; 1671, in the 57 year of her age.

ARMS. *Temple* quarterly as above,[3] impaling two chevronels within a bordure engrailed, for *Tyrrill.*

3. Here lyeth the Body of CHARLES TYRRILL, 4th son of Sir Timothy Tyrrill of Okeley in the county of Bucks, who died the 19 of March 1694, in the 60 year of his Age.[4]

ARMS. *Tyrrill.*

[1] Willis's Hundred of Newport, as transcribed in Cole's Collections (Addit. MS. 5839), fol. 355, compared with Lipscomb, *History of Buckinghamshire*, iv. 350.

[2] Willis makes this note, "Edmund Lea's wife Dorothy was dau. of Browne Lord Montacute, as in Collins's Peerage, iv. 22.   But she seems to have been his second wife."   For "wife" read daughter: see note in p. 485 of the present volume, but there for "Edward" read Edmund.

[3] By Lipscombe described as, "Quarterly, *Cobham, Leofric,* and *Temple,*" as if there had been three quarterings instead of two.   [4] Printed 69th in Lipscombe.

SIR PETER TEMPLE, whose wife is commemorated by the
second of these inscriptions, succeeded his father at Stanton
Barry in 1632, and was sheriff of Buckinghamshire in 1635.[1]
He was knighted on the 6th June, 1641; but it is difficult to
trace any other particulars respecting him, as his uncle, the
second Baronet of Stowe, bore the same name, and was living
until the year 1653, being one of the members for the town of
Buckingham, and so zealous a partisan of the Parliament, that
he was nominated one of the commissioners for the trial of the
King, but either from prudential or other reasons abstained from
any attendance.

In the year 1649 " Sir Peter Temple's in Lincoln's Inn
Fields" is mentioned as a resort of Lieut.-Generall Cromwell ;[2]
but which Sir Peter there resided is uncertain.

Some years later the present Sir Peter gave to the world a
small religious volume, now exceedingly rare,[3] and bearing the
following title:—

MAN'S MASTER-PIECE, or the best Improvement of the worst Condition.
In the exercise of a Christian Duty. On six considerable actions: 1.
The Contempt of the World. 2. The judgment of God against the

[1] Sir Peter Temple, the second Baronet, succeeded his father in 1625. He could
not, therefore, be the Sheriff of 1635, who was an Esquire, but is designated by Lipscombe (in his List of Sheriffs, vol. i. p. xvii.) as " Peter Temple, Esq. of Stowe." In
his pedigree of Temple (under Stowe, vol. iii. p. 86) Lipscombe enters " Sir Peter
Temple, Knt. and Bart. of Stowe, Sheriff of Bucks 1635; ob. 12 Sept. eod. an.; bur.
at Stowe." But the Journals of the Commons show that Sir Peter the Baronet was
a member of the House throughout the Long Parliament, and for some years much
troubled by his debts, regarding which there are many particulars; and in Willis's
Hundred of Buckingham, p. 286, among Burials at Stowe, occurs "Sir Peter
Temple, Bart. Anno 1653."

[2] " A Most Learned, Conscientious, and Devout Exercise; held forth the last
Lord's day, at Sir Peter Temple's, in Lincoln's Inn Fields; by Lieut.-Generall Crum-
well. As it was faithfully taken in Characters by Aaron Guerdon. London:
printed in the yeare 1649." [Published June 25th.] 4to. pp. 16. This is the title
of a political squib, of which an original copy is in King George III.'s collection of
pamphlets at the British Museum, vol. 10, art. 427. Its contents have been thought
so curious that it was reprinted in 1743, 8vo. and again in the Harleian Miscellany,
8vo. 1808, vol. xi.

[3] A copy of that book, at the sale of the Stowe collection, produced 2l. 9s. The
portraits alone have sometimes brought as much or more. There are also copies of
them made by W. Richardson 1799. Granger, in his *Biographical History of
England*, was unable to identify the persons represented by these portraits. Con-

Wicked, &c. 3. Meditations on Repentance. 4. Meditations on the Holy Supper. 5. Meditations on Afflictions and Martyrdom. 6. With a Meditation for one that is Sick. By P. T. Knt. London, 1658. 12mo. pp. 252.

In this volume are portraits of Sir Peter and his wife Dame Elinor, engraved by R. Gaywood.

They are both represented as busts placed upon pedestals. In the background of Sir Peter are his arms: 1 and 4, a displayed eagle; 2 and 3, a fess between three crescents (Lee); impaling two chevronels within a bordure engrailed (Tyrrill); and for crest, an eagle rising from a ducal coronet. Behind the lady is a shield bearing on the dexter side a displayed eagle only; impaling her arms as on the other plate. Inscription:—

The Lady

ELI^{nor} TEMPLE.

Her Exact'st Port^rature *neerest the Life*

Is Vertues Patterne, Mother, Mayd & Wife,

Whose Name's, *her* Glorious *Character to bost,*

This Liveing TEMPLE *of the* Holy Ghost.

The death of Sir Peter Temple occurred somewhat mysteriously at Norwich shortly before the Restoration, according to the following entry in the registry of burials at St. Peter's Mancroft in that city:—

sulting the pedigrees of Earl Temple and Lord Palmerston, and finding " only one Sir Peter (the 2d Baronet of Stowe) in both families," neither of whose two wives was named Eleanor, he came to the conclusion that Gaywood's portrait represented Peter Temple the Regicide, (of Temple Hall, co. Leic. M.P. for the town of Leicester, and already noticed in p. 390,) of whom he proceeds to give some account. This misled other authors, particularly Mark Noble in his *Lives of the Regicides,* and Caulfield, the editor of a reprint of *The High Court of Justice,* in which, at p. 34, (after some ridiculous remarks on " Sir Peter Temple the Regicide Baronet,") he relates the following particulars of the fate of the original plates by Gaywood: " The late Marquis of Buckingham, who was a distinguished patron of Sherwin the engraver, put into his hands the two copper-plates of Sir Peter and his lady, for the purpose of taking off a few impressions; but by some mischance the plates were lost, and sold to a dealer in old metal for the weight of copper, from whom they were purchased by a man named Lemoine, who parted with them to the elder Graves the printseller for half a guinea; at whose death, at the sale of his stock of prints and copper-plates, these appearing among the rest, were claimed and given up to the Marquis; the impressions for years previous to this discovery of the plates mostly selling from two to three guineas each."

1659 (-60) Jan. 14. A Gent. stranger, called by the name of John Browne, otherwise afterwards his buryeall accounted by the name of Sir Peter Temple.

The epitaph of the Lady Elinor Temple, already given, contains no mention of her second husband; but she was remarried to Richard Grenville, esq. of Wootton, M.P. for Buckinghamshire during the Commonwealth,[1] and who died in 1665, leaving her still surviving. She had no issue by him; but her children by Sir Peter Temple were,—1, John; 2, Timothy; 3, Henry; 4, Thomas; 5, William; and Eleanor.[2] The last became the wife of Richard Grenville, esq. of Wootton, M.P. for Andover and for Buckingham, and by him the progenitrix of the present Temple-Grenvilles, as shown in the annexed pedigree.

The will of Dame Elianor Temple al's Grenville, of Wotton

[1] The Grenvilles for three generations persevered in marrying a Temple, thus strengthening their claims upon the family to the representation of which they ultimately succeeded. These marriages will be shown most clearly by the following table:

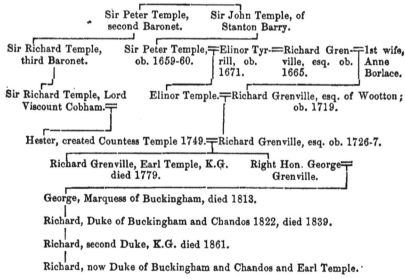

The latter descents are given to correct the table in p. 397, where, from the first and second Dukes being inadvertently confused, there is one generation less. The husband of the Countess Temple was there (also in error) named George Grenville instead of Richard.

[2] Visitation of Buckinghamshire.

Underwood in the county of Bucks, widow, was made on the
15th May 1671. She desired to be buried at Stanton Berry:
bequeathed to her daughter Elianor, wife of Richard Grenville
of Wotton Underwood, 500*l.*; to her son William Temple, 300*l.*,
on attaining the age of five-and-twenty; if her executors should
find him worthy and deserving of it; to her brother Sir Timothy
Tyrrill, 10*l.* She appoints her eldest son John Temple, marchant in Smyrna, and her daughter Elianor aforesaid executors.
Proved 30 May 1671. (70 *Duke.*)

The eldest son, John Temple (who was ætat. 6 in 1641), died
at Smyrna without issue in 1676.

Stanton Barry was sold to Sir John Wittewronge, Bart. about
1662 or 1663. (Willis's Newport Hundred.)

The next heir of this family, WILLIAM TEMPLE, Esq.,
youngest son of Sir Peter Temple, Knt. (his brothers Timothy,
Henry, and Thomas, being all dead before 1683, at which date
he is styled "now eldest son of Sir Peter Temple of Staunton-
bury,") was seated at Lillingston Dayrell, in the same county;
and was buried at Buckingham on the 27th of August, 1706.
He married Mary daughter of Mr. Green of Kent (she was living
17 Aug. 1716,) and had issue two sons, Sir William and Sir
Peter, afterwards the fifth and sixth Baronets; and two daughters,—Mary, born 1691, married to John Baldwin, of Buckinghamshire, gentleman, and died a widow without issue 1767; and
Anne, born 1696, married to Hugh Coffel of Buckinghamshire,
and went to America.

V. Sir WILLIAM TEMPLE, who became the fifth Baronet,
was born in April 1694, and was for some time resident in the
town of Buckingham.[1]　About the year 1738 he purchased Nash
House, an estate at Kempsey, in Worcestershire.[2]　On the death of
Field-Marshal Richard Lord Viscount Cobham, Sept. 15, 1749,
he succeeded to the dignity of Baronet. Dying on the 16th
April, 1760, he was buried at Kempsey.[3]　He had married first

[1] He is styled William Temple, of the town of Buckingham, Esq. in a deed of
bargain and sale, dated 17th April, 1716: quoted among the proofs of the pedigree in
Baronets, Coll. Arm. vol. i. p. 35.

[2] Nash, Hist. of Worc. vol. ii. p. 20.

[3] See the epitaphs of "the Hon. Sir William Temple, Bart." and his wives at
Kempsey, in Nash, *Hist. of Worcestershire*, Supplt. p. 45.

in May, 1718, Elizabeth daughter and sole heir of Peter Paxton, of Buckingham, M.D., and Elizabeth his wife; she died in 1729, and was buried in the church of Martin Hussentree, co. Worcester, having had issue (besides four children who died infants), a son Paxton Temple, Esq. born in April, 1720, and died in London unmarried 1745; and a daughter Henrietta, born Dec. 1723, and married to William Dicken of Shenton, co. Salop, gentleman (further mentioned hereafter). Sir William married, secondly, in Nov. 1731, Elizabeth, daughter of Hugh Ethersey, of Leckhamstead, co. Bucks, gentleman; she died Dec. 2, 1762, aged 67, and was buried at Kempsey. By that lady he had an only child, Anne-Sophia, born Jan. 2, 1734, the wife of her cousin Sir Richard Temple the seventh Baronet.

VI. Sir PETER TEMPLE (previously of the town of Buckingham,) became the sixth Baronet, but survived his brother for only ten months, dying on the 15th Nov. 1761, when he was buried at Drayton, co. Oxford. He had married twice; first, in 1719, Elizabeth Broughton, of Longdon, co. Stafford; she died 1726, having had issue Elizabeth, born 1720, died unmarried 1742, and buried at Buckingham; and Peter Temple, born in 1741, who, being in his Majesty's sea service, died unmarried at Portsmouth (of the small-pox) in 1748, and was there buried. Sir Peter married secondly, in 1729, Elizabeth, daughter of John Mold, of Charlton, co. Oxford, gentleman; and she dying June 1759 was buried at Drayton aforesaid, having had issue Sir Richard Temple, the seventh Baronet; and two daughters, Mary, who died young; and Anne, born Feb. 1733, died unmarried 10 Jan. 1782, and was buried at Drayton.

VII. Sir RICHARD TEMPLE, the only surviving son and heir, was born on the 1st June, 1731. He married at Kempsey, co. Worcester, June 24, 1758, Anna-Sophia, daughter of his uncle Sir William, and was subsequently seated at Nash House, in that parish, which came to him by his wife. Having succeeded his father in Feb. 1761, he was in the following month appointed a Commissioner of the Navy, and in March 1763 Comptroller of Cash of the Revenue of Excise. The latter office he held until his death, which occurred at Bath, Nov. 15, 1786.

He had several children, who all died young;[1] one of them we
find commemorated by the following inscription in the church of
St. Augustine at Hackney:—[2]

In Memory of Miss SOPHIA TEMPLE, only daughter of Sir Richard
Temple, Bart. by Dame Ann Sophia his wife, who departed this life
Sept. the 13th, 1775, aged 13 years.

Sir Richard Temple died without surviving issue on the 15th
of November, 1786.

On the 23rd Sept. 1796, the royal licence was granted to John
Dicken of Nash, co. Worcester, and Stonehouse, co. Devon,
esquire, eldest son and heir of William Dicken, late of Shenton,
co. Salop, gentleman, and Henrietta, daughter and coheir of Sir
William Temple, Bart. to take the name and arms of Temple ;
the license recognising the fact that Dame Anne Sophia Temple,
only sister of the Petitioner's mother, and relict of Sir Richard
Temple, Bart. one of the Commissioners of the Navy and Controller of Cash of the revenue of the Exchequer, was the second
daughter and coheir of the said Sir William Temple, and had no
(surviving) issue.[3]

SIR THOMAS TEMPLE.

Sir Thomas Temple, the second son of Sir John Temple of
Stanton Barry was appointed by Cromwell in 1656 to be
Governor of Acadie, otherwise called Nova Scotia, under the
designation of Colonel Thomas Temple esquire ; and he received
a renewal of that office from King Charles II. There is no
doubt that he was created one of the Nova Scotia Baronets, as he
is so designated in the will of his brother Sir Purbeck Temple.
He lived for several years at Boston in New England :[4] and made
a will there dated on the 14th Oct. 1671, which is still on record

[1] The particulars now given of the fifth, sixth, and seventh Baronets (for the most
part hitherto unpublished) have been chiefly derived from the pedigree attested by
the hand of Sir Richard Temple, June 29, 1784, in the record of Baronets' Pedigrees
in the College of Arms, vol. i. pp. 36, 37.

[2] Robinson's History of Hackney, p. 45.

[3] I. 35, in Coll. Arm. fol. 93.

[4] The Heraldic Journal, (Boston, June 1865,) vol. i. p. 92.

 at Boston, bearing the seal of which an engraving is annexed. In this will he is styled Knight and Baronet, and he names — my brother Edmond Temple's children,—my brother Robert Nelson,— cousin John Nelson, — cousin Temple Nelson, — cousin Adolphe Andrews which was in New England, — cousin Mrs. Katherine Wolverston daughter of Mrs. Adolphea Longfield [or Longueville],—"cozen Thomas Temple, *i.e.* Dr. Temple's son,"—and cousin John Temple.

Afterwards, having returned to England, Sir Thomas Temple made a second will, dated on the 27th March, 1674. It is a nuncupative one, as follows:

March the seven and twentyth 1674. This day my uncle Sir Thomas Temple, being very sick but in full and perfect sence and settled mind, before Mr. Rogers and his Lady Margarett Rogers- did declare this his last Will and Testament. Imprimis, he gave as followeth: To his maids Elleanor and Elizabeth Three pownds each. To his man Morgan in New England, to be paid by Captain Lake at his coming over, Tenn pownds to himself and Six pownds for his passage. To his Doctor Tenn pownds. To the Apothecary what is due. More to his man Morgan what is due for wages to be paid by Mr. Ticknall. He declared all in the house to be Mrs. Martin's owne proper goods excepting his wearing clothes and linnen and some few bookes which he gave to his nephew John Nelson. To Sr Robert Viner Six pownds ten shillings. To Elizabeth Martin the silver porringer and fyve spoones. To Mr. Bignall a Sadler at York house gate Twenty-two pownds. To Mr. Bagnall of the New Exchange Twelve pownds if not already paid All the remainder of the money in the Countesse of Angleseyes handes to his cosens Mris Wolverston, Mris Elenor Harvey and to Mris Temple, and the Bedd and all the furniture and trunck belonging to it to his said cosens. What is due to Doctor Willis and Sr John Coridon's apothecary to be paid. Of the debt due from the King he disposed of as followeth—if ever paid:—To the right honourable the Countesse of Anglesey One thousand pownds. To Mr. Rogers and his wife Five hundred pownds. To his cosen John Nelson One thousand pownds. When his debtes are paid the greatest part of the remainder to the Colledg at Cambridge in New England Two hundred pownds. To Mrs. Martin and her daughters each of them One hundred pownds. To Mr. Ticknall out of what is in his own hands Fyve hundred pownds. This being read, he did acknowledg it to be his last Will and Testa-

ment. In witnes hereof I have sett my hand and seale, THOMAS
TEMPLE.[1] Testes, George Wood, William Lishman, Mr. Rogers and
my nephew Executors. Proved 27 July 1674 by John Nelson one of
the executors. (93 *Bunce.*)

The interment of Sir Thomas Temple has been found at.
Ealing, co. Middlesex, where it is thus recorded in the register:
" Sir Thomas Temple buried March 28, 1674."
He appears not to have ever married.[2]

TEMPLE, OF SULBY AND SIBBERTOFT, CO. NORTHAMPTON.

The third son of Sir John Temple of Stanton Barry was
EDMUND TEMPLE, esquire, of Sulby in Northamptonshire.

He was a Colonel in the Parliament's service, and in Sept. 1648
his petition respecting his great losses and sufferings and the payment of his arrears, was recommended by the House of Lords to
the consideration of the Commons: who in May 1649 appointed
a committee to audit his accounts for his services in Ireland.

He married in 1647 Eleanor, daughter and coheir of Sir
Stephen Harvey, of Hardingstone, co. Northampton, K.B. She
died Nov. 23, 1660, aged 33, and was buried at Welford in the
same county, where she was commemorated as " Vxor, Mater,
Christiana, omnimodâ virtute clarissima."[3]

The will of Edmund Temple, of Sulby, co. Northampton,
esquire, is dated Aug. 20, 1664. He desires to be buried by
his deceased wife in his own aile of Welford church. He mentions his estates of Sulby abbey grounds or pasturage, of Welford,
the rectory of Raunce (*i. e.* Raunds), and lands at Moreton Mor-
rell, co. Warw. which he entails on the heirs male of his eldest
and other sons, and for want of such heirs to his heirs female, of
all and every of his daughters, to be equally divided; remainders
to Sir Purbeck Temple his brother, and his heirs male; and to
his dear sister Dorothea Alston, and the heirs of her body for
ever. He names his seven children Stephen, Mary, John, Elli-

---

[1] Sir Thomas Temple appears to have signed the will himself, though it was written
by the hand of his nephew and executor John Nelson.

[2] In the pedigree in the History of Leicestershire, iv. 960, he is made the father of
the children of his brother Edmund. This error was derived from Le Neve's MS.
Collections for the Baronets.

[3] See her epitaph printed in Bridges's Northamptonshire, i. 596.

nor, Dorothea, Edmond, and Stephanor, leaving to each of the six younger 500*l.* To his sister Alston and his sister Nelson 10*l.* a-piece to buy them mourning; and if my eldest brother Sir Thomas Temple shall be in England and living, 10*l.* to buy him mourning. His loving brother Sir Purbeck Temple of Edgcomb, co. Surrey, knt. to be his executor. In a memorandum annexed, Whereas my brother Sir Thomas Temple is indebted to me between 2 and 3,000*l.* my desire is that it be paid, and divided to and between all my younger children. Sir Purbeck Temple renouncing, administration was granted to John Fiennes, esq. guardian of the son and heir Stephen, March 30, 1668; and on the 10th Nov. following to Stephen himself, he being then of age. (36 *Hene.*)

STEPHEN TEMPLE did not long survive his father. His will is dated on the 12th Oct. 1672. To be buried in Welford church. Names his brother John the next heir-at-law, his brother and sisters Edmund, Elinor, and Stephanor. (Mary and Dorothea are not mentioned.) Proved Oct. 22, 1672, by his executor John Fiennes, esq. (117 *Earl.*)

In the same year (1672) a house at Boston in New England was sold by Sir Thomas Temple to Stephen, son and heir apparent of Colonel Edmund Temple; and in 1690 the same house was sold by John Temple of Sibbertoft in Northamptonshire and Edmund Temple of the borough of Leicester (apparently the surviving brothers of Stephen). The deed was " signed, sealed, and delivered by Ellen, widow of Edmund Temple:"[1] from which it appears that Edmund Temple of Leicester died about the same time. In a document dated 22 August, 1683, John and Edmund were both named, and Purbeck, a son of Edmund.[2] This last is also named in the will of his godfather Sir Purbeck Temple (given hereafter), and was therefore living in 1693.

JOHN TEMPLE esquire, of Sibbertoft, died there in Feb. 1701-2, aged 52, having married Martha ———, who died in 1727. They had issue six children: 1. Stephana, born in 1680, married 29 Dec. 1701 to Edward Gilbert; 2. Frances, born in 1682; 3. Richard, born in 1683; 4. Thomasine, born in 1685;

---

[1] The Heraldic Journal, 1865, p. 94, from papers in the possession of Mr. Winthrop.   [2] Baronets, vol. i. (MS. in Coll. Arm.)

5. Mary, born in 1687 (buried same year); and 6. Purbeck, born in 1689,[1] another godson of Sir Purbeck Temple, and mentioned in his will.

PURBECK TEMPLE, Esq. of Sibbertoft, died on the 16th of May 1763, aged 74; having married Mary —— who died 1771: and they had issue, 1. Mary, who died unmarried Dec. 5, 1753; 2. Martha, who died unmarried April 8, 1791; 3. Elizabeth, who died unmarried May 11, 1799; and 4. Edward, who died unmarried Sept. 15, 1796.

There appears every probability that the last-named Edward was actually the Baronet for the last ten years of his life, unless there was any issue in the male line existing from his uncle Richard. At any event, it is clear that until his decease the dignity could not have devolved on any younger branch of the family.

The following are extracts from the parish register of Welford:[2]

The Baptisms from 1622 to 1700 are so mutilated that few of them can be decyphered.

Burials.

1661-2, March 4.   Hester, dau. of Edmond Temple, Esq. of Sibbertoft.

1664, Dec. 19.   Mary, dau. of Edmond Temple, of Old Sulby, Esq.

1667-8, March 9.   Edmond Temple, of Old Sulby, Esq.

1671-2, March 13.   Dorothie, dau. of Edmond Temple, Esq. of Old Sulby, dec[d].

1672, Oct. 26.   Stephen Temple, of Old Sulby, Esq.

1687, Sept. 24.   Mary, dau. of John Temple, Esq. and Martha his wife.

1701-2, Feb. 22.   M[r]. Temple of Sibbertoft was interred in his own proper burying place in the parish church at Welford.

SIR PURBECK TEMPLE.

The fourth and youngest son of Sir John Temple of Stanton Barry was Sir Purbeck Temple, named after the Viscount his father's tenant, as already noticed in p. 514. His name occurs

---

[1] These dates are from an interleaved copy of Debrett's Baronetage, edit. 1840, in the possession of George W. Collen, esq. Portcullis, and were communicated to him as the Editor of that work.

[2] Communicated by George Edward Adams, esq. F.S.A. Rougedragon. The registers of Sibbertoft do not begin until 1680 for Baptisms and Marriages, and not until 1695 for Burials. We have not learned that they contain any Temples.

as Captain and Colonel Purbeck Temple during the civil war. On the 30th September, 1644, he was summoned to the House of Commons and personally thanked by the Speaker for the capture of eighteen packs of clothes at Islip, sent into the garrison of Newport Pagnel; and on the 9th August, 1645, he was nomiated Governor of Henley.[1] He was knighted by King Charles II. on the 3rd September, 1660. He is styled as of Edgcomb (or Addiscombe) in Surrey, and as "one of the Gentlemen of his Majesty's most honourable Privy Chamber in ordinary," in Bysshe's Visitation of Surrey 1662. By the same record, which is signed in his autograph, (D. 15 in Coll. Arm., fol. 63,) it appears that he had married Sarah daughter of Robert Draper, of Remenham in Berkshire, esquire, but had no children.

Sir Purbeck died in August 1695 and was buried at Islington, co. Middlesex.

The will of Sir Purbeck Temple of Adgcombe place near Croydon is dated July 14, 1693. "To be buried where my loving wife Sarah shall be pleased to be buried by me, desiring that our coffins may touch each other: and my funerall to be solempnized in the night with all privacy and without any pomp." To his godson Purbeck Temple[2] son of the Hon. Sir Richard Temple, Bart. and K.B. all his arms and furniture of warr, excepting such as his wife shall reserve for defence of her house: also that debt which Minheer dee Grave burgomaster of Amsterdam and all that Sir Thomas Temple Baronet of Nova Scotia owed him. To his godson Henry son of the right hon. the Earl of Londonderry 10l. To his godson Purbeck Temple son of Edmond Temple of Leicester 10l. To his goddaughters Elizabeth Narburrough and Sarah Hallett, each 5l. To his nephew William Temple esquire, son of Sir Peter Temple his eldest brother, one shilling. To his honorable kinsman Sir Richard Temple 10l. To his honoured niece Elianor Greenvile 10l. To his godson Purbeck Temple, son of John Temple of Sibbertoft, that 5l. that his father owed him. To his cousin Martha

---

[1] See the Journals of the House of Commons.

[2] This Purbeck Temple esq. was buried at Stowe, March 5, 1698. (Browne Willis, *Hundred of Buckingham.*) In the pedigree, *History of Leicestershire*, iv. 960, the year is misprinted 1678. From regard to Sir Purbeck Temple, Purbeck became a frequent baptismal name in the Temple family, and from that it was carried into others. Maria, a daughter of Sir Richard Temple, was married first to Richard West, D.D. Archdeacon of Berkshire, and secondly to Sir John Langham, Bart. By the latter she had issue a son, Purbeck Langham, and a daughter, Anne.

Temple daughter of John, 20l. to pay for a year's schooling and board‑ing. To his nephew John Temple 5l. To his kind friend Sir Thomas Culpepper all his Greek, Latin, and French books, and 5l. and to his son William Culpepper 5l. To his cousin Francis Naylor and his wife 5l. a piece. To his tenant Mrs Caverly of Rootham in Kent all the debt she owed. To George Hodges his waterman's son 5l. to buy him a mourning coat and his badge in silver. To his loving neighbour Thomas Beck of Croydon 5l. to buy a piece of plate. To his honoured brother Sir Thomas Draper, Bart. mourning. He forgives to his niece Wittney the debt her husband owed him. Recommends his nephew William Draper to his wife's kindness. " And it is my express wish and meaning that my said nephew William Temple (although he be my heir at law) shall have no part of or benefit by my said estate reall or personal whatever, except the legacy of one shilling aforesaid." Resi-due of personal estate and all real estate to his wife. Proved 27 Nov. 1695. (63 *Irby*.)

His widow survived to the year 1700, when we find the fol-lowing passage in the Diary of John Evelyn:

Feb. 13, 1700. I was at the funerall of my Lady Temple, who was buried at Islington, brought from Adscomb neere Croydon. She left my son-in-law Draper, her nephew, the mansion-house of Adscomb, very nobly and completely furnish'd, with the estate about it, with plate and jewels to the value in all of about 20,000l. She was a very prudent lady, gave many great legacies,[1] with 500l. to the poore of Islington, where her husband Sir Purbeck Temple was buried, both dying without issue.

Lady Temple's bequest to the poor of Islington was to be appropriated towards the maintenance and education of as many poor children of the parish as possible. The way in which it was expended in purchasing a freehold estate at Potter's Bar will be found in Lewis's History of that parish, 4to. 1842, p. 443.

---

[1] The will of Dame Sarah Temple is dated April 8, 1696. It mentions the five daughters of John Temple of Sibbertoft, and the three children of Edmond Temple late of Leicester; her nephew John Baber and Mary his wife: her nephew Purbeck Turner, and Elizabeth, Katharine, and Anne daughters of her niece Elizabeth Turner. (40 *Noel*.) This will is of considerable length; but the register that contains it is not yet opened for literary purposes.

(To be continued.)

MAXWELL OF POLLOK.

The Nova Scotia baronetcy of Maxwell of Pollok has, under very unusual and peculiar circumstances, devolved upon a new family. Sir John Maxwell, (late M.P. for Lanarkshire,) died on the 6th June, 1865 ; and, being the last descendant in the male line from the first Baronet, it has been supposed by the uninformed that the dignity had become extinct, and the Baronetages of Dodd and Debrett respectively for the present year have consequently omitted their articles on the family.

The name and title have, however, been assumed by Sir John Maxwell's nephew, William Stirling, esq. of Keir, M.P. for Perthshire, and, as we are informed, upon the best authority.

Sir John Maxwell, the thirteenth of Pollok, was created a Baronet of Nova Scotia, by King Charles I. in June 1633. The patent was, in the usual terms, to him and the heirs male of his body; and, as he died without male issue on the 1st Nov. 1647, the dignity then became extinct.

He left his estate to Sir George Maxwell, younger of Auldhouse, the heir-apparent of his then heir-male. Sir George was already a knight, and survived to the year 1677 ; but in 1672, by a royal charter, the estate of Pollok was disjoined from the barony of Mearns, of which it previously formed a part, and was erected into a separate barony, to be called the barony of Pollok, and to be held as one whole and free barony of the Princes and Stewards of Scotland. This was consequent upon the marriage settlement of John, son of Sir George, who was subsequently, during his father's lifetime, designated as the Laird of Pollok younger.

After Sir George Maxwell's death, his son became desirous to revive the dignity held by his predecessor in the reign of Charles the First. According to a memorandum made in 1682, or shortly before, it appears that the rank was deemed essential to the maintenance of his proper position, the memorandum stating that the family and house of Pollok-Maxwell had enjoyed for several ages the dignity of a barony, with the order of Knighthood, and had therefore been reckoned one of the first and most ancient of that degree in the West of Scotland. Sir George, having been knighted some years before Sir John's death (as stated in the memorial for a re-grant of the title,) had not thought of the renewal of the Baronetcy ; but his son John Maxwell, now of Pollok, "without the least undue affectation, but only to maintain the honor of his ancestores," petitioned the King " that the title might be revived, and a patent granted in his favour, bearing priviledge and precedence from the date of the former."

The main object of the memorial was granted. The title and dignity of a Knight Baronet (*Militis Baronetti*) was conferred by patent dated at Whitehall, April 12, 1682. Allusion is made therein to the dignity having been previously enjoyed by Sir John Maxwell of Neather Pollock ; but, as nothing is said in regard to precedence, that of course dated from 1682.

Sir John Maxwell, who assumed the title of Lord Pollok on being appointed an ordinary Lord of Session in 1699, had no children; and he in consequence obtained a second patent from Queen Anne, dated 27th March 1707, extending the limitation of heirs to succeed to the title of Knight Baronet to the heirs of entail succeeding to the estate of Pollok. The words of the patent are—titulum et dignitatem, gradum, et honorem Militis Baronetti dicto domino Joanni et hæredibus masculis ex suo corpore; quibus deficientibus, aliis suis hæredibus talziæ quibusque in ejus infeofamentis terrarum suarum et status contentis.[1]

It has been upon the authority of these words that the dignity has been assumed by Mr. Stirling of Keir. On the decease of the eighth Baronet in the male line, Sir John Maxwell of Pollok, on the 6th June 1865, there were no male heirs left of the body of Sir John the grantee. The seventh Baronet had issue three children; namely, the late Baronet, a daughter who died unmarried in 1841, and another daughter, Elizabeth, who was married in 1815 to Archibald Stirling, of Keir, Esq. Of that marriage the member for Perthshire is the heir. This gentleman has, since the death of his maternal uncle, adopted the name of Maxwell after his patronymic, and has further assumed the title of Baronet. This we are told has been done under the advice and with the approval of counsel learned in the law; it has been acknowledged in the House of Commons, in the proceedings of which his name now appears as Sir William Stirling Maxwell, Bart., and it has been sanctioned by her Majesty, in her receptions at Court on the 23d of March, when Sir William Stirling Maxwell was presented " on succeeding to his Baronetcy," by the Earl of Leven and Melville (his wife's uncle), and Lady Anna Stirling Maxwell (on her marriage, which also took place last year,) by the Countess of Leven and Melville.

THE FAMILIES OF BURNETT.

To the Editor of the HERALD AND GENEALOGIST.

Sir,—The remarks on the families and arms of Burnett introduced into your notice of the *History of Clerkenwell* interested me much. In the absence of direct evidence, there seems a strong probability that the Scottish Burnetts descend from the Burnards, who, from the date of Domesday, have been settled in Hampshire and Wiltshire. Burnetts or Burnards (the latter spelling is more frequent in old charters) first appear in the south of Scotland in the twelfth century, simultaneously with a number of settlers from the other side of the border, and the seals represented in p. 447 are

---

[1] Both the patents of Baronetage are printed in that magnificent private work, the *Memoirs of the Maxwells of Pollok,* by WILLIAM FRASER. 1863. 4to.

paralleled by that of Sir Richard Burnard, lord of Farningdoun in Roxburghshire in 1252, which bears for its device a leaf (Laing's *Scottish Seals*,
p. 30). The leaf afterwards became three leaves; and, though usually
blazoned holly leaves, they may have originally been, as Nisbet suggests,
Burnet leaves. The hunting-horn which appears along with the three
leaves in the coat of the Burnetts of Leys, is said to have been added in
reference to the office held by the family of Royal Forester. The mullet in
the Bishop's coat (p. 446) is the mark of cadency adopted by his father
Lord Crimond.

I can attach no weight to the story quoted (p. 447) from Seton's *Heraldry*,
regarding the family crest and motto, and as little to the statements regarding
the chieftancy. The Leys charters are older than those of Barns. The oldest
of the former bears date 1324, while the pedigree of the latter family
cannot, I believe, with any certainty, be traced higher than the beginning
of the sixteenth century. Barns's alleged descent from, or representation
of, "Robertus de Burnetvilla, miles," a subscribing witness to charters in
the reign of David I., is purely conjectural. The addition of a chief to the
arms in the Barns coat would rather raise a presumption of cadetcy.
There can be little doubt that the Burnetts of Burnetland, Farningdoun,
Barns, and Leys, were all kinsmen; but nothing whatever is known of their
precise relationship or respective seniority. The ancestors of the Leys
family doubtless migrated from the south to the north of Scotland, and the
first of them regarding whom there is any certain information is Alexander Burnard, who, in 1324, was rewarded for his adherence to the fortunes
of King Robert Bruce with considerable possessions in Aberdeenshire.

The Leys branch has all along been far more important than Barns terri-
torially, and has produced not a few persons of note besides the Bishop.

While both Leys and its cadets still own much of their lands, the estate
of Barns has, I am sorry to say, passed to other possessors in the present
generation. Crathes Castle, the seat of the Burnetts of Leys, may be numbered among the finest old baronial residences in Scotland.

On the establishment of the present Lyon Register in 1672, thirteen coats
were placed on record for Burnetts,—three for the Barns branch, and ten
for Leys and its cadets. They are not given very accurately in Burke's
Armory. The coat on Bishop Burnett's tomb is on record for the Bishop's
eldest brother, Dr. (afterwards Sir) Thomas Burnett, Physician to Charles
II. Their father, Lord Crimond, was third brother of Sir Thomas Burnett
of Leys, first Baronet.

This Sir Thomas, though he took part up to a certain point with the
Covenanters, was much trusted by Charles the First, and was a firm friend
and coadjutor of Montrose. In 1638 we find him, along with Montrose, a
subscribing witness to a document limiting and restricting the "solemn
League and Covenant" in a spirit of moderation unusual at that time. His
immediate younger brother James (older than Lord Crimond) acquired
Craigmyle and other extensive lands in Aberdeenshire by marriage with

Elizabeth, only daughter of Thomas Burnett of Craigmyle, and representative maternally of the Craigmyles of that ilk, an extinct family whose coat (Azure, two garbs in chief, and a crescent in base or) has ever since been quartered by the branches of the family descended of this marriage. This James Burnett of Craigmyle figures much in the local history of the time, having been, like his brother, identified with the Covenanting cause. We find him taken prisoner by the Earl of Aboyne and King's troops in 1639, but set at liberty almost immediately on taking the oaths of allegiance. He is described in Gordon's *History of Scots Affairs* (Spalding Club) as "a gentleman of great wisdome, and one who favoured the King, tho' he dwelt among the Covenanters ; and was loved and respected by all." The author of *Memorialls of the Trubles in Scotland*, usually vehement in his denunciation of all adherents of the Covenant, characterises him as a " peciabill weill-set gentilman."

The laird of Craigmyle had a large progeny. His eldest son's male issue became extinct in the second generation; three coheiresses, however, managing to carry off the Craigmyle estates, notwithstanding a settlement on heirs male.

His second son, Thomas, of Kemnay, was the father of another Thomas so designated, who was perhaps the most remarkable man of the family, though now less remembered than the Bishop. Some of his letters, and various particulars regarding him, not altogether to be relied on, will be found in the State Papers edited by Mr. J. M. Kemble. He was a voluminous correspondent of Leibnitz, the Electress Sophia, his cousin the Bishop, and many other eminent literary and political people of his time. He resided much at the Court of Hanover, and was employed by the Electress in a number of her more delicate negociations. In the course of one of his political missions he got imprisoned in the Bastille on some frivolous charge, but was eventually liberated by the Duchess of Orleans at the instance of the Electress and the Queen of Prussia. The Electress endeavoured to procure from the English Court some substantial acknowledgement of his services: but, notwithstanding a promise from George I., he received no such mark of royal favour, though he lived for several years after the accession of the House of Hanover. His son, George Burnett, was best known as one of the chief agricultural improvers of his day, and is celebrated by Lord Kames for having converted (at Kemnay) a peat-moss into the most beautiful gardens and pleasure-grounds in Scotland. He married the elder daughter of Sir Alexander Burnett, of Leys, and the succession to the Leys estates was last century the subject of a protracted lawsuit between Alexander Burnett of Kemnay, son of this marriage, the heir of line, and Sir Thomas, Sir Alexander's nephew, the heir male, the House of Lords eventually deciding in favour of the heir male. This Alexander Burnett of Kemnay was long British Secretary of Embassy at Berlin, and attended Frederick the Great in all the campaigns of the Seven Years' War, remaining at the Prussian court after Sir Andrew Mitchell's death, as Chargé d'Affaires. Mr. George Burnett, the Lyon Depute since 1863, and at present interim Lyon King of Arms, is one of his grandsons.

James, third son of James Burnett, of Craigmyle, the Covenanter, was great-grandfather of the eminent, accomplished, and eccentric Scottish judge, James Burnett, Lord Monboddo; who, in a treatise " On the Origin and Progress of Language," set forth, along with many learned and philosophical speculations, the identity of mankind with the monkey tribe, and maintained that the human race were originally furnished with tails. In allusion to this notion, it is said that Lord Kames, to whom he would on one occasion have yielded precedence, declined it, saying, " By no means, my Lord; you must walk first, that I may see your tail." One of Lord Monboddo's characteristic traits was his admiration of the ancients, in imitation of whom he gave classical suppers once a week. He visited London once a year, always performing the journey on horseback: and objected to enter a carriage, on the ground that it was derogatory to the dignity of human nature to be dragged at the tails of horses instead of being mounted on their backs. With all his peculiarities, he was a distinguished lawyer and upright judge, and his judicial opinions were often affirmed by the House of Lords when directly opposed to those of all his colleagues.

This branch of the family gave birth to another Scots lawyer of note, John Burnett, Judge-Admiral of Scotland, nephew of Lord Monboddo.

Among noteworthy scions of the Burnetts of Leys, was also the Bishop's grand-uncle, Dr. Gilbert Burnett, who enjoyed a considerable reputation in his day for certain philosophical writings. He was Professor of Philosophy soon after the Reformation, first at Basle, and afterwards at Montauban; and his works were ordered by a general synod of the French Protestants to be printed at the expense of the clergy. His "Book of Ethics" was published at Leyden in 1649.

The notices of the Bishop's branch of the family in *Playfair's Baronetage of Scotland* and elsewhere are very inaccurate. The following will be found more trustworthy.

Lord Crimond was born about 1592, and died in 1661, the same year in which he was elevated to the bench, leaving by his second wife Rachael Johnstone sister of the forfeited Lord Warrieston, three sons, Thomas, Robert, and Gilbert, and a daughter, Rachael, married to Sir Thomas Nicolson of Cockburnspath, Lord Advocate. He had been previously married to Bethia seventh and youngest daughter and coheir of William Maule of Glaster, son of Robert Maule of Panmure, by whom he had a daughter Bethia, who died soon after her mother in 1623. Lord Crimond's eldest son, Sir Thomas Burnett, physician successively to Charles II., James II., William III., and Anne, died in 1704. I do not know whom he married, but he had a son, Gilbert, Advocate, and one of the Commissioners of Excise for Scotland, whose only child Anna was wife to James Halyburton of Pitcur; and a daughter, Helen, married first to William Crawfurd of

Auchenames, and afterwards to Ralph Dundas, of Manour, Perthshire, of whom there are numerous descendants. Lord Crimond's son Robert was at the bar, and died unmarried in 1662, the year following his father.

Bishop Burnett was three times married, 1st to Lady Margaret Kennedy, daughter of John sixth Earl of Cassillis; 2ndly to Mary, daughter of James Scot of the Hague; and 3dly to the daughter of Sir Richard Blake and widow of Sir Robert Berkeley of Spetchley. All his family (except two daughters by the third marriage, who died in childhood,) were by his second wife, Miss Scott. The eldest son, William, was Governor of New York and New Jersey 1720, and of Massachusetts Bay 1728. He died 7th September, 1729, having been twice married, first, to Mary, daughter of Doctor John Stanhope, Dean of Canterbury, by whom he had a son, Gilbert, who, according to a letter of his kinsman the Rev. Mr. Williams, of Wellsbourn, was "a most accomplished gentleman and a most incorrigible rake, who died early in life, but not before he had absolutely exhausted a handsome fortune, leaving his son without a penny." (*Biographia Britannica*, vol. v. of 2nd edition, Additional Corrigenda.) The son here alluded to (born 1740) was Doctor Thomas Burnett, of Chigwell, whose widow (mentioned in your note p. 448) seems to have survived their only child, a daughter. By his second wife, Mary, daughter of the Hon. Abraham Vanhorne, New York, Governor Burnett had a son, William, and a daughter, Mary, who married the Hon. William Browne of Salem, and had issue. Governor Burnett had also a natural son, Captain Burnett, R.N., who died before 1789. I think he is probably to be identified with a Captain Thomas Burnett, R.N., whose son Major-General John Burnett died s. p., and whose daughter, Mrs. Biddulph, died in 1844. Bishop Burnett's second son, Gilbert, was, as you mention, chaplain to George I. and died unmarried. His third and youngest son, Sir Thomas Burnett, judge in the Court of Common Pleas, and author of the memoir of his father appended to the " History of his Own Time," also died unmarried. Dr. Burnett of Chigwell was, so far as I am aware, the last descendant in the male line of the Bishop. Of the two daughters of the Bishop who grew up, the elder, Mary, married David Mitchell, nephew of Admiral Mitchell, and her children were all dead without issue in 1788. The younger, Elizabeth, was the wife of Lord Chancellor West of Ireland, and had a son, Richard West, the poet, and friend of Gray and Horace Walpole, who died without issue; and a daughter, Mary, who married John Williams of Pembrokeshire, and had a son, who, in 1789, was vicar of Wellsbourn, Warwickshire, and the father of three children. If any of his descendants survive, they would seem to be the sole remaining legitimate descendants of Bishop Burnett.

The Barns as well as the Leys Burnetts produced a prelate—Alexander, Bishop of Aberdeen in 1663, Archbishop of Glasgow in 1664, and afterwards of St. Andrew's, in which last see he immediately succeeded Sharpe. He had a daughter Anne, married, first to Alexander 7th Lord Elphinstone, and afterwards to Patrick 3rd Lord Elibank. Another daughter,

Mary, was the first wife of Roderick Mackenzie of Prestonhall, third son of Sir John Mackenzie of Tarbat, Bart. a Member of the Scottish Parliament, and afterwards a judge of the Court of Session by the title of Lord Prestonhall, who was attainted in consequence of participation in the rebellion of 1715. This lady died in 1699, leaving a son Alexander, attainted on the same ground as his father, who married Amelia eldest daughter and heir of Hugh tenth Lord Lovat. Hugh Mackenzie or Fraser, the son of this marriage, claimed in right of his mother the title of Lord Lovat, which however was in 1730 adjudged by the Court of Session, then seemingly considered a competent judicatory in Peerage questions, to Simon Fraser the heir male.

I am, &c. Scotus.

From another Correspondent we have received the following catalogue of his requirements as to the several families of Burnet or Burnett:

I want all particulars of the family of Rev. Gilbert Burnet, Curate of St. James, Clerkenwell, 1743, and who is said to have had twenty brothers and sisters living at that period.

Also particulars of Alexander Burnet, Archbishop of St. Andrew's. He had some descendants who settled southwards, but I cannot trace them.

Who was Dr. Burnett, living 1698, a Doctor of Physic, that had two sons, Obadiah and Nathaniel?

Who was John Burnett, who died in London 1635, who had a brother Ralph, and had issue John and William Burnett, of Kent?

In 1642 there was a Robert Burnett, who had brothers John and William, and sons John and William.

Henry Burnett, who died 1665, was of St. Magdalene, Bermondsey; and had a brother Richard, who had a son John; and another brother Joseph, who had sons Walter and Joseph. A George Burnett died 1695; Thomas Burnett died 1691; Benjamin Burnett lived in Austin Friars, 1789; Noel Burnett, a Spanish merchant, was living 1736 in Gracechurch Street; Thomas Burnett, stockbroker, 1768; the Rev. Bristowe Burnett, of Exeter Street, Strand, died 1795 at South Lambeth. Any particulars or information concerning any of these would much oblige   H. G. B.

THE FAMILIES OF STODDARD, STODART, &c.

To the Editor of the Herald and Genealogist.

Edinburgh.

Dear Sir,—I observe that, in the review of Mr. Anderson's recent performance on Surnames (p. 354), you have devoted some attention to the name of Stodart. Will you allow me to offer you a few notes on the English form of the name, which may be traced for some centuries back.

The Visitation pedigrees generally make it "Stoddard." Near Chapel en le Frith, in Derbyshire there are lands of Stodard, from which the family may have taken its name. The most important family bearing the name was seated at Mottingham in Kent, and a very incomplete account of it is to be found in Hasted. Some of its members were knighted. They held the manor of Tickenhurst, reg. Hen. VI. till nearly the close of Elizabeth's reign. In 1575 Sir Nicholas Stoddard of Mottingham had a grant of the manor and rectory of Lewisham. Richard Stoddard sat in Parliament 6th Hen. VI. for New Romney. On the death issueless and intestate, 1765, of Nicholas Stoddard of Mottingham, a long Chancery suit arose, which ended in favour of William Bowreman, an heir through females; but I need not enlarge on the details.

On the establishment of the new Lyon Register, 1672, William Stoddert, of South House, in the county of Edinburgh, was one of the first to record his armorial bearings, Argent, a fess nebuly between three stars of six points sable. His estate passed by marriage into the families of Fullerton of Kinnaber and Carnegie of Pitarrow, and has been sold; but descendants in the male line of the same family exist, of whom one has recently matriculated these bearings with a bordure gules.

The earliest mention of the name I have met with in Scotland is in 1376, when David Stodhirde, John Studehird, and William Studhird are mentioned in the "Registrum Honoris de Morton" as tenants of Douglas, Lord of Dalkeith. From one of these probably derived the branch which possessed South House and Straiton, in the parish of Liberton, adjoining Dalkeith. Cadets of this family have held the estates of Kailzie, Peebleshire; Ormiston Hill, Mid-Lothian, Whitsomehill, Berwickshire, &c. George Tweedie Stodart, Esq. of Oliver, in Tweeddale, inherits that property from his maternal uncle Laurence Tweedie, the last of the elder branch of an ancient house long famous for its turbulence and local influence.

Several of its members sat in Parliament: Thomas Stodart, of Williamhope, in 16— for Selkirkshire; Thomas Stoddart, 1678, for the burgh of Lanark, &c. The estate of Williamhope, after being for several generations in the possession of his ancestors, was sold by the father of the late Admiral Pringle Stoddart, whose eldest son, a member of the Scottish bar, is now the representative.

Another branch has long held Ballendrick and other lands in Perthshire. In 1479 John Stoddart is accused of having, along with Moray of Abercairny and Alexander Rollok, made a forcible attack on the property of Patrick Cuninghame, deceased, and nine years later Robert and Andrew Stoddart are condemned to make amends for a similar outrage against James Earl of Buchan; male heirs exist, but the direct line is represented by co-heiresses, one of whom married Captain Savile, another a brother of Sir Thomas Erskine, Bart.

In the *New England Genealogical Magazine* is given a pedigree of the Stoddards of Boston, U.S., who have produced men of distinction in the church, army, law, diplomacy, and a living poet of some reputation. The founder went to New England 1639, and his wife was a sister of Sir George Downing, Bart., who was grandfather of the founder of Downing College, Cambridge.

Sir John Stoddart's family was from the North of England, and their pedigree is registered in the College of Arms.

The Stotherts of Cargen and Blaiket are nearly related to the Empress Eugénie, by the marriage of John Kirkpatrick of Culloch with Janet Stothert heiress of Tarscrechan, daughter of Thomas Stothert of Arkland, but their paternal descent is not traceable far back.

Faithfully yours,   S * *

TRADE-MARKS AND CRESTS.

If we may trust the report which has reached us of a recent case in the Court of Chancery, it would seem that some of our best Equity lawyers have not graduated in the laws of the Court of Chivalry.

In a judgment given by Vice-Chancellor Sir William Page Wood on the 9-th March in the cause of Standish *v.* Whitwell he is reported to have delivered the following very heterodox doctrine—"With respect to the use of the Crest by the Defendants, *the use and possession of a family seul were quite sufficient foundation for their use of this Crest, even though it was not registered in the Heralds' College*, and nineteen-twentieths of the people who used Crests had no better title for such use."

The "use and possession" which the judge in this case pronounced to be sufficient was, it appears, founded merely upon a seal, which had been used for a certain time, but without any pretension whatever better than an arbitrary choice or accidental acquisition.

The circumstances of the case were as follows : the plaintiffs, carrying on business under the title of *The Eagle Coal and Iron Company*, at West Bromwich, in Staffordshire, have for the last twenty years used for their mark an eagle with outspread wings, and their iron, which has acquired considerable reputation, has been commonly known as Eagle Iron. The defendants, Messrs. Whitwell and Co. being iron-manufacturers at the

Thornaby ironworks, Stockton-upon-Tees, about May 1865, adopted an eagle with outspread wings similar to that of the plaintiffs, accompanied with their initials " W. W. and Co." as a distinctive mark for the better qualities of iron which they then began to manufacture.

On discovering the sale of this Eagle Iron at a lower price than their own, the plaintiffs complained of the infringement of their trade mark ; when the defendants stated that the Eagle was their Family Crest, and that they had not been aware that there was any Company already using such a brand. In the correspondence that ensued, the plaintiffs stated that, " after searching the heraldry books, and the records of Heralds' College, they had failed to find any such Crest belonging to the family of Whitwell." The defendants replied that, " whether registered at the Heralds' College or not, the Crest of an Eagle had been used by their family for thirty years, and at least two generations previously ;" and they sent an impression of the seal that exhibited it.

Such were the heraldic arguments on either side: the plaintiffs believing, or affecting to believe, that the allegation of a " family crest " was a fraudulent pretence ; and the defendants, who adhered to more meek and pacific language, representing such a view of their conduct as a harsh and unjustifiable imputation.

The Vice-Chancellor appears to have coincided with the latter view, for, whilst he regarded a decree for an Injunction as of course, he reprobated the imputations of fraud which the legal advisers of the plaintiffs had in the first instance advanced, and on that account disallowed the plaintiffs the cost of their first affidavit, which asserted this charge of fraud as to the use of the Crest by the defendants.

The result from the Heraldic point of view seems to be, that a Trademark is a matter of much greater sanctity than a Family Crest. The former may confidently claim the protection of the Court of Chancery. The latter, even though a *timbria Aquilæ*, and almost of royal dignity, may be assumed *mero motu et arbitrio*, and a usurpation of thirty years or so is deemed "sufficient" to give a prescriptive right to it ! The Trader is protected and favoured : his mark may not be copied. The Gentleman is put out of court : his mark may be pilfered at will. An old Seal of Arms or of a Crest may be bought at a pawnbroker's, and its use for a certain period will give a " sufficient " title to it, even though it may not be registered at the Heralds' College to the name of its new possessor.

We find by the current edition of Debrett's Peerage that all the Judges really have coat-armour and crests of their own, and we hope that most of them entertain a more just view of the rights of property in such hereditary " marks " of distinction than has in this case been professed by Sir William Page Wood.

NOBLE AND GENTLE MEN OF ENGLAND.

The Noble and Gentle Men of England; or, Notes touching the Arms and Descents of the ancient Knightly and Gentle Houses of England, arranged in their respective Counties. Attempted by EVELYN PHILIP SHIRLEY, Esq. M.A., F.S.A., late one of the Knights of the Shire for the county of Warwick. Westminster: John Bowyer Nichols and Sons. Third Edition: Corrected 1866. Small 4to. pp. ix. 329.

The interest that has been taken in this work, and the estimate formed of its judicious and impartial execution, has been proved by the steady demand for it from the time of its first publication, and by the fact of a third edition being now required,—the first having appeared in 1859.

Most of our readers are probably acquainted with the plan upon which it is compiled. It is confined to those families still existing in the male line who were established as Knightly or Gentle houses before the commencement of the sixteenth century, and who still retain possession of their ancient estates, or at least some portion of them. The author does not profess to give an account of all those families whose descent may possibly be traced beyond the year 1500, but merely of those who were in the position of what we now call County Families before that period. The whole number who are found entitled to this distinction within the stipulated conditions are 331.

Since the book was first printed in the year 1859, the male lines of three families, whose names were originally comprehended in it, have become extinct, viz. Cotton, of Landwade in the county of Cambridge; Hornyold, of Blackmore Park; and Hanford, of Wollashill, both in Worcestershire. On the other hand, eight others have been ascertained to have a claim to admission; four of which were introduced into the second edition, and four others into the present. These are,—one of the county of Buckingham, Lovett of Liscombe; one of Cornwall, Bassett of Tehidy; one of Devonshire, Huyshe of Sand; four of Lincolnshire, Patten of Bank Hall, Bertie of Uffington, Anderson of Brocklesby, and Massingberd of Wrangle; and one of Somerset, Upton of Ashton Court. The two first named are families of very high antiquity; but, their landed property being until lately in female hands, they could not take place in the first edition according to the rules which the author had laid down.

In other respects this new edition has been carefully revised and corrected, and the author has given the results of further investigation, and of the information derived from many friends and correspondents, by interweaving various interesting particulars throughout.

The author by no means denies that there may still be other families possessing a fair claim to this distinction, but which has not hitherto been established by adequate proof. The removal of obscurities in such cases must be the task of the parties interested.

We hope, however, that Mr. Shirley will be induced to continue his work to a later period of our history. A series of the Families which arose in the 16th century, chiefly on the Dissolution of Religious Houses, would alone form a volume of interest, whilst it would present a curious practical contradiction to the fanciful notions broached in Spelman's *History of Sacrilege*. But he may in the first instance, perhaps, describe those families which still apparently exist under names of the highest antiquity, but are actually represented by heirs-general that have assumed those names.

Before we conclude, a few words may be said upon the three families above-mentioned as recently extinct.

COTTON, of Landwade, co. Cambridge. There are places named Cotton in the counties of Kent and Suffolk, as well as Cambridge, and it is doubtful from which of them this family was derived. Sir Thomas Cotton, the grandson of Sir Henry, acquired the manor of Landwade in the reign of Edward III. by marriage with Alice, daughter and heir of John de Hastings, whose family had held it from the year 1251. His descendant was raised to the rank of Baronet in 1640, and Sir St. Vincent Cotton, who died in 1863, was the sixth who had borne the title. The family had removed to Madingley in the same county, after marrying the heiress of Hinde in the reign of Charles I.

ARMS.—*Sable, a chevron between three gryphon's heads erased argent.*

HORNYOLD, of Blackmore Park, in Hanley, co. Worcester. The first recorded ancestor lived at the same place in the reign of Edward III. Thomas Charles Hornyold, esq. died in January 1859; but the name has been assumed by his nephew and successor, John Vincent Gandolfi, esq., so that this is a family that would reappear in the volume we have suggested to Mr. Shirley.

ARMS.—*Azure, a bend embattled counter-embattled argent.* (A greyhound courant sable was subsequently added to the bend, between two escallops argent on the field.)

HANFORD, of Wollashill, co. Worcester. This family was descended from one of ancient estate in Cheshire, deriving its name from Hanford or Honford in that county. Wollashill came to them from the heiress of Huggeford, in the year 1536. The last representative, John Compton Hanford, esq. died on the 19th June, 1860. The elder line of the family became extinct in 1513.

ARMS. *Sable, an estoile of eight points argent.*

An Index to the Pedigrees contained in the printed Heralds' Visitations, etc. etc. By GEORGE W. MARSHALL, LL.M. of the Middle Temple, Barrister-at-law. London : Robert Hardwicke, 192, Piccadilly. 1866. 8vo. pp. viii. 164. (Price 6*s.*)

COLEMAN'S General Index to Printed Pedigrees; which are to be found in all the principal County and Local Histories, and in many printed Genealogies : under Alphabetical arrangement. With an Appendix commencing at page 106. Published and sold by James Coleman, Heraldic and Genealogical Bookseller, 22, High Street, Bloomsbury, London, W.C. 1866. 8vo. pp. viii. 156. (Price 8*s.* 6*d.* Large paper, 10*s.*)

Index to Printed Pedigrees, contained in County and Local Histories, and in the more important Genealogical Collections. By CHARLES BRIDGER, Hon. Mem. Soc. Antiquaries of Newcastle-upon-Tyne. London : John Russell Smith, 36, Soho Square. 1866. 8vo. Parts I. II. III. each of 32 pages. 6*d.* each.

It is now some years since Mr. R. Sims supplied the genealogical inquirer with an exceedingly useful Index to the Pedigrees and Arms contained in the Heralds' Visitations and other Genealogical Manuscripts in the British Museum (8vo. 1849), and before that time and since it must have frequently occurred to those engaged in such researches that a general index to the pedigrees printed in our County Histories and other important works of topography and genealogy would be an acquisition of corresponding value and utility : for, though certain families have their sole *habitat* in a well-known locality, where they can be sought without uncertainty, there are many that have had properties in various districts, or have ramified into branches which have settled in distant counties, and have consequently been described by several historians.

It is strange that after this *desideratum* had remained so long unsupplied, three parties should have come forward at the same time with books which are certainly in some measure rival works.

Mr. MARSHALL's Index is confined to the printed Heralds' Visitations : books not much known, and some of them not easily met with, but of which we have already taken the pains to give a particular account.[1] The Index has been compiled with evident care. In order to render it as complete as possible, " each pedigree has been inspected, and the name, if spelt in different ways, doubly indexed, and, as far as possible, the name of the principal place at which the family resided is added." It includes the pedigrees printed in Berry's *County Genealogies*, the greater part of which were derived from the Visitations.

Mr. COLEMAN's compilation attempts still more. It offers references to " all the principal County and Local Histories ;" and in the Preface it is stated to be an attempt to place nearly 10,000 pedigrees under alphabeti-

[1] Contained in our Parts IX. X. XI. and XII. Mr. Marshall has added the pressmarks by which the copies at the British Museum may be found, a service by no means to be undervalued.

cal arrangement: but in this statement there is surely some miscalculation, as we do not find that the entries reach to 6,500. It is said that "every Pedigree of three or more generations has been noticed:" by which we understand every tabular pedigree, for the book does not seem to include any narrative pedigrees. We do not find Hasted's Kent or Morant's Essex among the works referred to, we presume because their accounts of families are not tabular. But there are other important omissions for which the same apology cannot be made. Among the first-rate county histories containing tabular pedigrees Hunter's South Yorkshire, Raine's North Durham, and Whitaker's Richmondshire, are unindexed; so also are Horsfield's Sussex, and Cartwright's Rape of Bramber: besides scores of minor topographical works not less important than those rehearsed in the catalogue. That the work has been compiled in haste is further shown by its being thrown into two alphabets, the second being nearly half the extent of the first.

In forming such indexes with a view to practical utility, it is desirable not only to notice various spellings of some names, but in certain instances to adopt in addition an accepted modern form where an old one would escape recognition. Both the editors are deficient in this respect. We allude more particularly to their entries referring to Tonge's Visitation of the Northern Counties. It will scarcely occur to an ordinary inquirer in search for the pedigrees of Fulthorpe, Haldenby, Slingsby, Thwaites, &c. that he has to look for them under the uncouth guise of Foltherop, Hawdonbe, Selyngesby, Thoattes, and so on.

So far as they go, both these manuals are of unquestionable utility; but a book of this kind, to be really complete, should include narrative as well as tabular pedigrees, and particularly the articles in the best Peerages and Baronetages.

We had written the foregoing remarks before we were aware that we had to add the title of a *third* book of the same kind to this review. In the Preface of the second there was this passage, which we did not immediately understand: "Mr. Coleman originally intended to have published the Index in Parts of 16 pp., and to have issued them with his Catalogues; but that plan has been ungraciously interfered with." Upon inquiry we found that this alluded to the work of Mr. Bridger. This is a portion of the manual that gentleman has long been preparing for *The Bibliography of Heraldry and Genealogy*, and which was announced by him (in May 1864) in our Tenth Part, when he stated (at p. 376 of Vol. II.) that he should add "an Index to the Line Pedigrees in the County Histories and other topographical works." He now explains that he has found it necessary to print this Index as a separate work, partly on account of the extent of his materials, and partly because of "the announcement of a rival Index."

Such are the conflicting statements of these competitors. We have only to add that there are certainly fewer marks of haste about Mr. Bridger's compilation, and that he has proceeded altogether upon a better plan.

The books are taken up in turn in an alphabetical arrangement of the Counties to which they relate : and the pedigrees in each book are alphabetically indexed. The books are numbered, and a General Index to be appended at the close will refer to each number.

In confirmation of the view we have already taken, we find Mr. Bridger indexing the *narrative* pedigrees (and they amount to very nearly 400 entries) published in the edition of Westcote's *View of Devonshire* produced by the late Dr. Oliver and Mr. Pitman Jones in 1845. These are *not* given by Mr. Coleman.

The Author announces his intention to include other pedigrees which are in the narrative form, a plan which, if carried out with judgment, is certainly most desirable. It will be remembered that even some of the heralds' visitations take that form, in the same manner as those in Westcote's Devonshire.

We still entertain our opinion that the Peerages and Baronetages should be similarly treated, either in this Index, or in a corresponding one. Of course the selection must be made of some of their leading Editions for this purpose[1]; and if the dates of the Creations and Extinctions of Titles were incorporated, those dates would form guides to tell whether certain families are likely to be found in such other volumes of this class as happen to stand on the shelves of our libraries.

Mr. Bridger's Third Part brings us well through the County of Northampton, which we presume is fairly half-way.

Dod's Peerage, Baronetage, and Knightage of Great Britain and Ireland, for 1866, including all the Titled Classes. Twenty-sixth Year. 12mo. pp. 770. (Price 10*s.* 6*d.*)

For minute and accurate biographical particulars, and the accumulation of a multiplicity of facts and dates, we know of no work that has ever rivalled this of the late Captain Dod : and it appears to be maintained with faithful care by the present editor. He remarks that the unceasing influence of births, deaths, and marriages occurring among seven or eight thousand individuals, at home and abroad, has produced during the past year its usual striking effects ; to all of which he has been duly alive, as well as to the various new creations, preferments, and promotions. The fresh articles, arising either from creations or successions during the year 1865, are more than seventy in number.

In a genealogical point of view, we have always lamented the suppression of the Christian names of the wives of the persons commemorated : their insertion, instead of the article *the*, would add a few letters only to each article, and therefore not increase materially the bulk of the whole.

[1] If Dugdale's Baronage is so indexed, it will be desirable also to add references to the addenda to that work printed in the Collectanea Topogr. et Genealogica, partly written by Dugdale himself, and partly by Francis Townsend, Windsor.

DEBRETT's Illustrated Peerage, of the United Kingdom of Great Britain and Ireland.
    1866. 12mo. pp. xxxvi. 612. (Price 7s.)

DEBRETT's Illustrated Baronetage, Knightage, and House of Commons, of the United
    Kingdom of Great Britain and Ireland. 1866. 12mo. pp. 612. (Price 7s.).

We gave so careful an account in p. 93 of our present volume of the plan
and arrangement of these two companion manuals, as they were published
for the year 1865, that it will only be necessary, in regard to those for the
present year, to describe the further improvements that are made in them.

In the Peerage, the chief addition is a brief biography of the immediate
predecessor of each existing Peer. This is a useful feature : but it has led
to continual repetitions, as, after the marriages of the deceased peers are
stated, each living dowager is again described in a paragraph by herself.
In other respects the book is confined to the living members of the peerage,
—the deceased children, even of the present peers, being excluded. The
Younger Sons and Married Daughters, either of present or deceased Peers,
are (if still living,) distinctly described in a second alphabet : in this
department the merit of a large accession of biographical particulars is
claimed for the present edition. It may be observed, however, that dates
are but partially sprinkled in this part of the book.

We must repeat our objection to the useless insertion, as articles in the
main alphabetical arrangement, of every inferior title of peerage held by
Peers, for they consist of names which are generally unknown to the world,
and will never be looked for. If these were reduced to the second titles
only (which are borne by heirs apparent) space might be found for more
useful particulars, such as the origin and rise of families, and their most
illustrious members.

In the Baronetage some brief ancestral account of the family is generally,
but not universally, given.

We still cannot see the advantage of inserting in a Peerage the names of
the advowsons of which each Peer is patron. Why not equally describe his
political influence, or his estates, or his country seats ?

The engravings of arms are very unequal: some good, some indifferent,
and some bad and nearly worn out. The blazon is full, and when compared
with the cuts, may serve for a lesson in the art of armory : but it is obscured
by excessive punctuation. Take as an example the arms of Earl Russell :—

Argent: a lion rampant, gules, on a chief, sable, three escallops, of the field, over
the centre escallop, a mullet.

which would be infinitely clearer thus—

Argent, a lion rampant gules, on a chief sable three escallops of the field, a mullet
for difference.

The Bishops form a very numerous supplement of the volume, including
not only those who are members of the House of Lords, but all who now
occupy that station whether in the three Kingdoms, in the Colonies, or elsewhere in connection with the Episcopal communion of the Church of England.

Counting 28 English Archbishops and Bishops, 12 Irish, 8 Scotish, 44 Colonial, 5 Missionary, and 6 Retired, the total of these prelates is 103. They are followed by all the members of Convocation, with their preferments, occupying fourteen pages. Then come the Judges, with biographical and genealogical particulars, and their armorial bearings: succeeded by several lists, such as are usually sought in the Court Kalendar; the whole terminating with a Grammar of Heraldry, and an account of the principal Orders of Knighthood. Altogether, there is a great deal for your money, and indeed more than appears directly in accordance with the object of the work.

To DEBRETT's *Baronetage* for 1866 is appended *The Knightage*, occupying fifty-eight pages; and after that the *House of Commons*, occupying ninety pages. The latter is arranged in the alphabet of places (to which of course there is an index of surnames), and biographical notices are given of all the members—except Baronets, for whom reference is made to the former pages of the book. Debrett thus incroaches upon the field of another useful manual of Captain Dod; confining, however, his political information to the initials C. for Conservative, and L. for Liberal.

The amount of labour involved in all this must be immense, and more particularly if the materials are fairly collected, and not derived in the main from other works of the kind. The *Peerage and Baronetage* of Sir BERNARD BURKE has, of late years, been very copious and complete in contemporary genealogy; whilst the works of the late Captain Dod have been distinguished beyond all precedent for the aggregation of multitudinous biographical facts, combined with minute accuracy. It is difficult, if not impossible, to rival either of those works within a less compass. However, a healthy and honest competition is always advantageous to the public, who will not fail eventually to distinguish the labourer who is most persevering and painstaking.

We have noticed elsewhere in our present Part two errors in the present Baronetage of Debrett, one of commission and the other of omission, as regards entire articles: the Baronetage of Dymoke, which is really extinct, is erroneously continued; and that of Maxwell, inherited by Sir William Stirling, is omitted, but must be reinstated in the next edition.

A brief Biographical Dictionary. Compiled and arranged by the Rev. CHARLES HOLE, B.A. Trinity College, Cambridge. Second Edition. London and Cambridge: Macmillan and Co. 1866. 12mo. pp. xvi. 485.

A dictionary which contains within so brief and portable a compass the dates and leading characteristics of about 18,000 of the most eminent and remarkable men and women that have flourished in all ages of the world, forms a manual that is continually useful, and we cannot be surprised that, after a few months' experience of the first edition, the public should require a second.

˙To show its plan we copy the entries under a great English name :— ˛

CROMWELL, Thomas, Earl of Essex   .   .   .   .   .   1490*—July 28, 1540.
CROMWELL, Oliver.   Protector.   L. by James Heath, 1663;
   Raguenet, 1691 ; Leti, 1692 ; Burton ; Isaac Kimber,
   1725; J. Banks, 1739; F. Peck, 1740 ; Dr. Wm. Harris,
   1762 ; Mark Noble, 1791; Bishop Russell ; Oliver Crom-
   well, 1822; Villemain, 1819; Southey; Philarète Chasles,
   1847; F. P. G. Guizot, 1854 ; Hazlitt, 1857 ; Sawford ;
   Wilson ; Thomas Carlyle; Merle D'Aubigné .   .   .   1599—Sept. 3, 1658.
CROMWELL, Richard, son.   [Protector 1658—59.]   .   .   1626—July 13, 1712.
CROMWELL, Henry, br. Lord Lieutenant of Ireland   .   .   1628—Mar. 25, 1675.

The dates are those of birth and death ; the (*) denoting uncertainty.
In recent cases, especially, it is a great assistance to have a ready reference
to dates of death, as they conduct at once to further information in contemporary obituaries.   In regard to authors, Mr. Hole names the productions by which they are best known.   In all cases he mentions "Lives" that
have appeared as distinct works: but it is seldom that he has occasion to
occupy so many lines with the names of their writers as he has done for
Oliver Cromwell.   Occasionally he requires two or three; but more usually
comprises in a single line of this excellent manual all that is necessary to
identify and characterize the individual.

HERALDIC CHRONICLE FOR 1865.

Jan. 5. Harry Ernest *Clay*, of Hanford, co. Dorset, esq. Second Secretary
of Embassy at Paris, in compliance with the will of Henry Ker Seymer of
Hanford esq. and of a direction in a certain deed of tailzie, to take the surnames of KER and SEYMER after Clay, and bear the arms of Ker and
Seymer quarterly with Clay.

Jan. 14. John *Hancock*, of Tilehurst, co. Berks. Capt. R.N. eldest son
and heir of late Rear-Adm. John Hiett Hancock, C.B. the brother of Lucy
Liebenrood of Tilehurst, widow of John Engleberts Liebenrood esq. in
compliance with the will of his said aunt to, take the name and arms of
LIEBENROOD in lieu of his own.

Jan. 17. Martin Leslie *Haworth*, of Shrubhill, Dorking, co. Surrey, esq.
eldest son of Martin Edw. Haworth, of Balham Wood co. Hertf. esq. by
Mary Elizabeth second dau. of Henrietta Anne Leslie, Countess of Rothes,
in compliance with the will of his great-aunt Lady Elizabeth Jane Watkin,
of Dorking, widow of Augustus Watkin, a Major 13th drag. younger dau.
and coh. of George Wm. Leslie, Earl of Rothes, to take the name of LESLIE
instead of Haworth, and bear the arms of Leslie only.

March 2. Roddam John *Falder* of Ballucushan, in the Isle of Man, and
of Roddam, in the parish of Ilderton, co. Northumberland, esq. eldest son of

Joseph Falder of Alnwick, surgeon, deceased, in compliance with the will of Adm. Robert Roddam, R.N. to take the name of RODDAM only, and bear the arms of Roddam.

March 8. James Frederick D'Arley *Street*, of Mottram hall in the parish of Prestbury, co. Chester, esq. late Captain R. Art. and Julia Catherine his wife, youngest of the three daughters and coheirs of Henry Wright clerk, M.A. late of Mottram hall deceased, in compliance with the will of the said H. W. to take the name of WRIGHT instead of Street; she to bear the arms of Wright, and he the arms of Wright quarterly with those of Street.

March 10. Le Marchant *Thomas* of Seaview, in the Isle of Wight, esq. eldest son and heir of John Thomas of London merchant, by Anne dau. of Josias Le Marchant of La Haye du Puits, in the Island of Guernsey, deceased, to bear the name of LE MARCHANT after Thomas, and bear the arms of Le Marchant quarterly with those of Thomas.

Charles William *Allen*, of Titley Court co. Heref. esq. in compliance with the will of Dame Elizabeth Coffin, wife of Sir Isaac Coffin, formerly Sir Isaac Greenly, Bart. to take the name and bear the arms of GREENLY only.

March 16. William Henry *Harrison* of Welton house in the parish of Welton cum Milton co. York esq. eldest son and heir of Wm. H. Harrison of Ripon M.D. by Mary his wife, sister of Sophia Broadley of Welton house spinster, in compliance with the will of said S. B. to take the name of BROADLEY after Harrison, and bear the arms of Broadley quarterly in the first quarter with those of Harrison.

March 17. Richard Walter Byrd Mirehouse (heretofore *Levett*) a minor of the age of fifteen years, eldest son of Richard Byrd Levett, of Milford hall co. Staff. esq. late Lieut.-Colonel Stafford Rifles, by Mary Elizabeth eldest dau. of John Mirehouse of Bangeston and Brownslade co. Pembroke and Upper Seymour-st. co. Middx. esq. to continue to use the name of MIREHOUSE.

Sir George *Strickland*, of Boynton, Bart. second but eldest surviving son of Sir Wm. S. late of Boynton by Henrietta 3d dau. and coh. of Nathaniel Cholmley, of Howsham co. York, in compliance with an indenture of settlement 24 June 1796 to take the name of CHOLMELEY only, and bear the arms of Cholmeley and Wentworth.

March 21. George Lawrence Ricketts *Wilkinson*, of Chesterfield, gentleman, eldest son of George Yeldham Wilkinson (formerly Ricketts) of Tapton house, Chesterfield, esq. to take the name of RICKETTS in lieu of Wilkinson.

March 23. Henry Andrew Grant *Cookson*, of Oaklands, in the island of Jersey, esq. Seigneur des Augrès et de Godeaulx, in the said island, late Lieut. 22nd Foot, to discontinue the name of Cookson and reassume the surnames of EVANS-GORDON.

March 28. John Dryden *Pigott*, of Sundorne castle, co. Salop, clerk, Rector of Edgmond, eldest son of John Dryden Pigott, of Edgmond, clerk, deceased, in compliance with the will of his cousin-german Andrew Wm.

Corbet, of Sundorne castle, esq. M.P. for Shrewsbury, to take the name of
Corbet instead of Pigott, and bear the arms of Corbet quarterly in the
first quarter with his own arms.

April 10. Claud Hamilton *Hamilton*, esq. (formerly Brown) of Calcutta,
having, in compliance with the will of his uncle Claud Hamilton, esq.
assumed the name of Hamilton instead of *Brown*, has received the licence
and authority of the Lord Lyon King of Arms to bear such arms as are
described in the letters patent issued by the Lyon Depute 29 March, 1865.

April 28. Died, aged 64, the Hon. Sir Henry Dymoke, of Scrivelsby
Court, co. Lincoln, Bart. Hereditary Champion of her Majesty: being the
17th who had held that office, including his ancestors the Marmyons. (See
the *History of the Family of Marmyon*, by T. S. Banks, 1817, 8vo.) It has
been remarked that two of Sir Henry's ancestors officiated at three corona-
tions, Sir Robert Dymoke at those of Richard III., Henry VII. and
Henry VIII., and his son Sir Edward at those of Edward VI., Mary, and
Elizabeth. Sir Henry Dymoke also might have officiated at three. At
that of George IV. he took the place of his father (who was then living),
the Rev. John Dymoke: at those of William IV. and her present Majesty
he was ready for the service, but this time-honoured ceremonial was dis-
pensed with. By her Majesty's favour he was, however, advanced to the
dignity of a Baronet, by patent dated September, 1841: the Champions
having heretofore usually received the honour of Knighthood. As the
remainder of the Baronetcy was merely in the usual terms to the issue
male of the body of the grantee, and he had no son, the title has become
Extinct with him. The family, however, continues, and is now represented
by Sir Henry's brother, the Hon. and Rev. John Dymoke, Rector of
Scrivelsby and Roughton, who has a son and heir apparent, Henry Lionel
Dymoke, esq. born in 1833.

The inheritance of the office of Champion, however, does not necessarily
descend in the male line, but is dependent on *the tenure of the manor of
Scrivelsby*, which is held in Grand Serjeantry by the performance of that
service. If that estate has actually passed to the Rev. John Dymoke—and
that such is the fact we find asserted in Burke's *Peerage and Baronetage*
for the present year, it may be concluded that the office of Champion has
accompanied it. The late Baronet has left an only daughter—Emma-Jane,
married in 1861 to Francis Houlton Hartwell, esq. eldest son of Sir Bro-
drick Hartwell, Bart., and she has three daughters.

May 6. Robert *Richardson*, of Sussex gardens and the Middle Temple,
barrister at law, and Maria Louisa his wife, only child and heir expectant
of Henry Gardner of Westbourne terrace and of Clerkenwell brewer, to
take the name of Gardner after Richardson.

May 9. George Benvenuto *Mathew*, esq. C.B. Minister plenipotentiary
to the Republics of Central America, in compliance with the desire
(repeatedly expressed in his lifetime) of his kinsman Abednego Mathew,
of the Lyth in the parish of Ellesmere, co. Salop, esq. deceased, from whom

he inherited the estates of Buckleys in the island of St. Christopher, W.I. and the Lyth aforesaid, to take the name of BUCKLEY before MATHEW.

May 19. Died at Easton Lodge, Essex, aged 79, the Right Hon. Henry Viscount MAYNARD, Baron Maynard, and a Baronet, Lord Lieutenant and Vice Admiral of Essex. The family of Maynard, formerly of Devonshire, settled in Essex towards the end of the reign of Elizabeth, Sir Henry Maynard, sometime secretary to Lord Burghley, having purchased the manor of Little Easton. His eldest son Henry was created a Baronet at the foundation of that order in 1611, created an Irish Baron in 1620, and Lord Maynard of Estaines ad Turrim alias Little Easton in Essex in 1627. His descendant Charles the sixth Lord was the last of the elder male line of the family, and on his death in 1775 the dignities above mentioned expired ; but he had been in 1766 created Baron Maynard of Much Easton and Viscount Maynard of Easton Lodge, with remainder to his collateral heir male, the descendant of Charles brother to the first Lord, and whose son Sir William Maynard had been created a Baronet in 1681. It was Sir Charles Maynard the fifth Baronet of the second creation who inherited the Viscounty in 1775 ; and, dying in 1824, was succeeded by his nephew Henry, now deceased, with whom the titles again become Extinct. (See a memoir of the late Viscount in the Gentleman's Magazine for August 1865.)

May 22. William Henley *Pearson*, of Rochetts, co. Essex, Bailbrook lodge, Batheaston, co. Som. and Norland-sq. co. Middx. clerk, M.A. Preb. of Heytesbury, and Martha his wife, only child and heir of late Osborne Markham of Rochetts, esq. and of Martha Honora Georgina his wife (afterwards Jervis[1]), eldest dau. and coh. of Wm. Henry Jervis (formerly Ricketts) Capt. R.N. who was the eldest son of Wm. Henry Ricketts, esq. and Mary his wife, sister to Adm. John Earl of St. Vincent, Viscount St. Vincent, and Baron Jervis of Meaford, co. Somerset, G.C.B., to take the name of JERVIS only, in lieu of Pearson ; the said Martha to bear the arms of Jervis, and the said William Henley Jervis to bear the arms of Jervis quarterly with those of Pearson.[2]

July 5. John *Soden*, of the Circus, Bath, esq. and Henrietta Corbet his wife, eldest dau. of Charles Decimus Williames late of Brithdir, co. Montg. esq. by Henrietta his wife, sister of Athelstan Corbet of Ynys y Maengwyn, co. Merion. esq. all deceased, in compliance with the will of the said Athelstan Corbet,—he (John Soden) to take the name of CORBET only, and

---

[1] Martha Honora Georgina (Lady) Jervis died at Batheaston, Feb. 26, 1865, aged 70. Her father Captain Ricketts, being nephew and heir presumptive to Admiral the Earl of St. Vincent, assumed the name of Jervis (by sign manual) in 1801. She was married first in 1821 to Osborne Markham, esq. youngest son of the Archbishop of York; and secondly, in 1834, to Lieut.-General Sir William Cockburn, Bart., who died in 1835. She took the name of Jervis on the death of the Earl in 1823. (See further in the Gentleman's Magazine for May 1865, p. 646.)

[2] Mr. Jervis is the second son of the late Very Rev. Hugh Nicholas Pearson, D.D. Dean of Salisbury.

quarter the arms of Corbet with Soden, and Henrietta Corbet Soden to
bear the arms of Corbet quarterly with Williames; and the arms of Corbet
quarterly with Soden to be taken by their issue.

July 18.   John Harris *Peter*, of Colquite in the parish of St. Mabyn in
Cornwall, esq. in compliance with the last will of his great-uncle Deeble
Peter, late of Colquite, esq. to take the name of HOBLYN after Peter, and
bear the arms of Hoblyn quarterly with Peter.

July 20.   Edward John *Stracey*, of Sprowston, co. Norfolk, and Boston
house in Brentford, co. Middx. late Lieut.-Col. Scots Fusilier Guards, in
compliance with the will of James Clitherow, of Boston house, esq. to take
the name of CLITHEROW after Stracey, and bear the arms of Clitherow
quarterly with his own.

Aug. 1.   Richard Napoleon *Lee*, of the Middle Temple, barrister-at-law,
in compliance with the will of Richard Thornton,[1] of Old Swan wharf near

---

[1] Mr. Thornton, who died on the 20th June 1865, at his residence, Cannon Hill,
near Merton, was an eminent merchant of London, and underwriter at Lloyd's, but
was not related to the family of Thornton of Clapham, which has long been distinguished in the city, and has supplied many members to parliament.   Mr. Richard
Thornton was born at Burton in Lonsdale in 1776, and received his education at
Christ's Hospital.   Probate of his will, which is dated March 24, 1865, passed the
seal in the Court of Probate on the 26th of July.   The executors and trustees
are Messrs. Thomas Thornton and Richard Thornton West (the testator's nephews);
Mr. Richard Napoleon Lee, of the Middle Temple, barrister-at-law; Mr. Alfred
Pulford, of St. James's street, army tailor; and the testator's sister, Mrs. Ellen
Simpson, widow.   The personal estate was sworn under 2,800,000*l.*   To his nephew
Mr. Thomas Thornton the testator has left all his freehold, copyhold, and leasehold
property for his absolute use.   To Mrs. Ellen Simpson 100,000*l.*; to his nephew
Mr. William (Richard ?) Thornton West 300,000*l.*; to his clerks Mr. John Browne
and Mr. Sugden Neele 20,000*l.* each; to the Leathersellers' Company 5,000*l.*; to
Christ's Hospital 5,000*l.*; and 10,000*l.* to Hetherington's Charity for the Blind.   To
St. Luke's Hospital, St. Mark's Hospital for Fistula, St. Thomas's Hospital, Guy's
Hospital, Bethlehem Hospital, Magdalen Hospital, Orthopœdic Hospital, London
Hospital, Hospital for Incurables, Sailors' Hospital on board the Dreadnought, Vic-
toria Park Hospital, City of London Truss Society, National Lifeboat Institution,
Merchant Seamen's Orphan Asylum, London Orphan Asylum, Infant Orphan Asylum,
British Orphan Asylum, Female Orphan Asylum, Deaf and Dumb Asylum, Indigent
Blind Asylum, Asylum for Idiots, Asylum for Fatherless Children, Ladies' Charity
School in Queen's-square, St. Ann's Society's Schools, and National Benevolent Insti-
tution, 2000*l.* each.   There is also a bequest of 10,000*l.* in trust for the support of
schools erected by the deceased at Burton in Lonsdale, and for educating and
apprenticing as many poor children as the fund will allow; 500*l.* for the
relief of the poor at Burton, 10,000*l.* in trust for schools at Merton and for educating and apprenticing poor children, and 1,000*l.* for the relief of the poor at
Merton.   (All these legacies to be paid free of duty.)   To Mr. Richard Napoleon
Lee the testator leaves 400,000*l.*, on condition of his obtaining a licence within
twelve months to take and use the surname of Thornton.   To Ellen wife of Mr. Alfred

London Bridge and of Cannon hill near Merton, co. Surrey, esq. to take the name of THORNTON instead of Lee.

Sept. 15. George Merrikin *Lowis,* of Grainthorpe, co. Linc. farmer, the reputed son of Edward Merrikin, late of Conisholme in the said co. farmer, to discontinue the name of Lowis, and use the surname of MERRIKIN.

Sept. 29. The Rev. Roger Dawson Dawson Duffield, of Coverham and of Cray, co. York, LL.D. and Rector of Sephton, co. Lanc. out of respect to the memory of his great-uncle Roger Dawson of Carlton, in the parish of Coverham, esq. to continue to use the name of DAWSON before DUFFIELD.

Oct. 10. Arthur Charles *Lowe,* of Court of Hill, co. Salop, esq. sometime Colonel in the army, second but only surviving son of Thomas Humphrey Lowe, late of Bromsgrove, esq. by Lucy, eldest dau. and coheir of Thomas Hill, late of Court of Hill, esq. M.P. for Leominster, to take the name of HILL in lieu of Lowe, and bear the arms of Hill.

Oct. 18. Died, at Brockett hall, Hertfordshire, aged 81, the Right Hon. Henry John Temple, third Viscount PALMERSTON, of Palmerston, co. Dublin, and Baron Temple, of Mount Temple, county Sligo, in the peerage of Ireland (1722), K.G. and First Lord of the Treasury. He was the third who had enjoyed the peerage, which was conferred upon his great-grandfather in 1722, and it has become Extinct upon his death. (See the fuller particulars previously given in p. 401.)

Oct. 23. John *Tucker,* now of Ashcote near Napier, in the province of Hawkes Bay, New Zealand, gentleman, and Mary Lydia his wife, only child of Robert Dean Bayly, formerly of Abbot's Legh, co. Som. and now of Bath, esq. in compliance with the will of Margaret A'Deane, of Alderley, co. Glouc. spinster, to take the name of A'DEANE instead of Tucker, and bear the arms of A'Deane.

Oct. 25. Rev. Robert *Cobb,* B.A. Rector of Thwaite St. Mary and Ellingham, Norf. eldest son and heir of Benj. Cobb, late of Lydd, co. Kent, esq. by Frances his wife, eldest dau. of John Cartwright, of Ixworth abbey, co. Suffolk, esq. in compliance with the will of his cousin and brother-in-law Richard Norton Cartwright, of Ixworth abbey, esq. to take the name

---

Pulford (another executor) a life interest is devised in the sum of 300,000*l.*, with like provision for Mr. Pulford if he should survive his wife; the capital to their children on their death. To the Misses Margaret and Eliza Lee, of Ventnor, Isle of Wight, a life interest in the sum of 200,000*l.*: to Ellen wife of the testator's nephew Thomas Thornton the interest of 30,000*l.* for the benefit of herself and children upon the trusts of her marriage settlement. There are also bequests to others of the testator's nephews, nieces, and other persons. The residue of the personalty is bequeathed equally between his two nephews and executors, Thomas Thornton and Richard Thornton West. The deceased had erected and endowed the schools at Burton (at the cost it is said of 40,000*l.*) during his lifetime. He had also built and endowed, nearly thirty years ago, almshouses at Barnet for thirteen members of his company, the Leathersellers. That company has commissioned Mr. Thomas Earle, sculptor, of Brompton, to execute a bust of the deceased.

of CARTWRIGHT instead of Cobb, and bear the arms of Cartwright quarterly with his own.

Nov. 6. Charles Barber *Banning*, postmaster of Liverpool, and Louisa Sophia his wife, dau. of Richard Meadowcroft Whitlow, of Southport, co. Lanc. esq. in compliance with the will of John Greaves, of Irlam hall, esq. to take the surname of GREAVES in addition to Banning; she to bear the arms of Greaves quarterly with Whitlow, and he to bear the arms of Greaves quarterly with Banning.

Nov. 11. George Watkin *Rice*, of Llwyn y Brain, co. Carmarth. esq. formerly Captain 23d R. W. Fusiliers, and late Major R. Carm. Mil., in compliance with the will of George Price Watkins, of Broadway, co. Carm. to take the name of WATKINS only and quarter the arms of Watkins with his own.

Nov. 22. Died, at Scawby hall, Lincolnshire, aged 51, Sir John NEL- THORPE, the eighth Baronet. Sir John Nelthorpe, of Gray's Inn, was created a Baronet in 1666, with remainder to his nephew Goddard Nel- thorpe, from whom the Baronet now deceased was the last descendant in the male line, and the dignity has consequently become Extinct. The family has been seated in Lincolnshire from the time of the first Baronet : his great-great-grandfather was of Staplehurst, in Kent.

Dec. 8. Died at Stonyhurst college, Lancashire, aged 71, Sir Charles Robert TEMPEST, Bart. of Broughton hall, Yorkshire. He was the eldest son of Stephen Tempest, esq. of Broughton hall, who died in 1824, by Elizabeth, daughter of Henry Blundell, esq. of Ince Blundell, co. Lanc. and was created a Baronet in 1841. In 1859 he claimed the BARONY OF SCALES, (or de Scailes as he was advised to term it,) as a descendant of Margaret eldest daughter and coheir of Robert third Lord Scales, wife of Sir Robert Howard, (ancestor, by his *second* wife, of the Dukes of Nor- folk,) the sister of which Margaret was the wife of Sir Roger Felbrigge, and left issue. (See the *Collectanea Topog. et Genealogica*, vol. iv. p. 260, and Courthope's *Historic Peerage of England*, 1857, p. 426.) The claim was heard in a Committee of Privileges in the House of Lords, August 11, 1859, but its further consideration adjourned *sine die*. Sir C. R. Tempest having died unmarried, the Baronetcy has become Extinct, but the repre- sentation of this family is continued by his nephew Charles Henry Tempest, esq.

Dec. 11. Died at Firgrove, near Weybridge, aged 81, Sir John EAST- HOPE, the first Baronet of that place. He was the second son of Thomas Easthope, esq. of Tewkesbury, by Elizabeth, dau. of John Leaver, esq. of Overbury, co. Worc. Sir John (who was formerly M.P. for St. Alban's, Banbury, and Leicester, and proprietor of *The Morning Chronicle*,) was created a Baronet in 1841. He was twice married; but, having only daughters, his dignity has become Extinct. (See memoir in the Gentle- man's Magazine for January, 1866.)

Dec. 19. Sir John Romilly, Master of the Rolls, created a Baron of the

United Kingdom by the title of BARON ROMILLY of Barry, co. Glamorgan.
The Rt. Hon. Sir Francis Thornhill Baring created a Baron of the United
Kingdom by the title of BARON NORTHBROOK, of Stratton, co. Southampton.

Dec. 20. Henry Mayhew (heretofore Courtney) of Leamington, co.
Warw. esq. late Captain Stafford Rifles, to discontinue the name of *Mayhew*
and use that of COURTNEY only.

Dec. 22 William West James *Bruce*, esq. brevet-Major in the army
and Capt. 94th regt., in compliance with the last will of his maternal uncle
Captain Richard Basset, of Beaupré, co. Glamorgan, takes the surname and
arms of BASSET only.

Dec. 24· Died, at Burntisland, Fifeshire, Sir John MALCOLM, of Balbedie, co. Fife: a Nova Scotia creation of 1665. He is noticed in Dod's
Peerage, &c. for 1865 as "son of Sir Michael Malcolm the previous Baronet, by the youngest daughter of John Forbes, esq. of Bridge End, Perthshire. Born at Balbedie 1828, succeeded on the death of his father." In
Debrett's Baronetage as "Born 1828; succeeded his father 1833;" but a
note is appended, "This baronetcy is questioned." Debrett for 1866 reports
it as Extinct.

ROYAL LICENCES FOR CHANGES OF NAMES AND ARMS, REGISTERED IN THE
OFFICE OF ARMS AT DUBLIN.

1864, *June* 21. William *Rowan*, of Carrickfergus, gentleman, to take the
surname and bear the arms of LEGG.

(*Same day,*) Stewart Durance Davis *Cartwright,* of the 15th Hussars,
and Constance Isabella Enery, only child and heiress of William Hamilton
Enery, late of Ballyconnell House, in the co. Cavan, esquire, a justice of
the peace, to take the surname of ENERY and bear the arms of Enery
quarterly, on the solemnization of their marriage.

Oct. 1. William *Arthurs*, M.A. vicar of the united parishes of Strad-
bally and Moyanna, Queen's co. reputed son of Sir John Rowland Eustace,
Knt. K.H. Lieut.-General in the Army, to take the surname of EUSTACE
only, and bear the arms of Eustace, with due distinctions.

Nov. 4. Edward William *Grainger*, esq. late of the co. Meath, and now
resident in Bavaria; that he and the other descendants of his grandfather
Edward Francis Grainger and Rose Parry his wife may take the surname
and arms of PARRY, in lieu of the surname and arms of Grainger.

1865, *Jan.* 28. Augusta Liviscount Richardson *Massy*, of Oaklands, co.
Tyrone, widow of Hugh Massy, of that place; that she and her issue may
take the surname and bear the arms of RICHARDSON.

April 21. William Clifford Bermingham *Trotter*, of Quansborough, co.
Galway, esq. a justice of the peace for that county, son of the late Thomas
Bermingham Trotter, and grandson and heir of the late Clifford Trotter,
esq. of Clough House, co. Down, to take the surname and bear the arms of
RUTHVEN.

Oct. 13. George Wilson *Day*, of Dublin, takes the surname of LEWIS, instead of Day.

Oct. 24. John Thomas *Stewart*, esq. of Ballyatwood house, co. Down, now resident at Fulwood Park, near Cheltenham, only son and heir of John Stewart, esq. of Dublin, by Harriet Louisa his late wife, dau. and co-heiress of the late Hans Mark Hamill, esq. of Ballyatwood house, takes the surname of HAMILL before that of STEWART, and the arms of Hamill quarterly with those of Stewart.

NAMES ASSUMED PRÓPRIO MOTU.

(Continued from vol. II. p. 552.)

Jan. 4, 1865. Isaac *Moses*, of Kensington park gardens, assumes the additional name of MARSDEN—by deed enrolled in Chancery.

Feb. 15. Mary Anne *Barton*, of St. George's terrace, Hyde park, widow, discontinues the name of Barton, assumes that of PERRINS, and adds Perrins to her Christian names, intending to be known as Mary Anne Perrins Perrins.

March 1. Charles Ottley *Groom*, of Southwell cottage, Kingsdown, Bristol, assumes the name of his late grandfather Archibald NAPIER, of Tobago ; and signs the announcement Charles Ottley Groom Napier, F.A.S.L.

March 17. John Aaron *Aarons*, late of St. Mark's college, Chelsea, now of Wiltshire place, Brixton, abandons the name of Aarons, and assumes that of MILLER, being the surname of his late grandfather Thomas Miller, of Thorpe Saxlingham, Norfolk.

March 18. William *Hart*, Quarter-master of H.M. 44th regt. stationed at Belgaum, E.I. takes the name of M'HARG, in addition to Hart.

March 21. John Anthony *Sparvel*, of Knockhold lodge, Swanscombe, Kent, assumes the additional name of BAYLY.

March 27. James Brown *Simpson*, of Dunse-bank, in the parish of Kirkby Ravensworth, co. York, esq. renounces the name of Simpson for that of LISTER.

April 10. L. A. *Durieu*, of Mornington-road, Middlesex, adopts the surname of DURRIEU.

April 21. George *Gammie*, of Shotover house, co. Oxford, and Stockbridge, co. Hants. esq. assumes in addition the name of MAITLAND.

April 25. The Rev. Richard King *Sampson*, of Pevensey, Sussex, relinquishes the surname of Sampson, and assumes that of KING only.

May 6. Paul Hyman *Sternschuss*, of Cagedale, in the parish of Clehongre, Herefordshire, and incumbent of Newton, in the same county, takes the additional name of STRONG.

May 8. John Harris *Badcock* and Charles Henry Badcock, of Gosport, Hants, adopt the additional name of HARRIS.

May 13. Charles John *Quarrill* and Thomas Arthur Quarrill, of Greville place, St. John's Wood, Middlesex, lamp and lustre manufacturers, renounce, discontinue, and abandon the surname of Quarrill, and assume, take, and adopt the surname of GREENE—enrolled in Chancery.

May 14. Betty *Walker*, widow, Anne *Walker*, spinster, and Mary *Pennington*, spinster, severally assume the surname of TETLOW only, pursuant to the will of Robert Tetlow, late of Skirden, in the parish of Bolton by Bowland, W. R. York, yeoman, proved at Wakefield June 21, 1865.

May 15. The Rev. George Deakin *Onley*, of Bransford, co. Worc. in pursuance of the last will of William Prattenton, of Clareland, in the parish of Hartlebury, esq. assumes the name of PRATTENTON after Onley,

June 6. John *Cox*, of Upper Clapton and Woburn place, esq. assumes, in addition, the surname of WENTWORTH.

June 13. The Rev. Forbes *Smith*, Rector of Aston Botterell, co. Salop, J.P., resumes the family name of DE HERIZ, the lineal descent of his family from William de Heriz, of Withcock, co. Leic. having been duly registered in the Office of Arms, Dublin.[1]

July 1. Henry *Gamman*, of Stoke Newington and Fenchurch buildings, shipbroker, assumes the name of GARIMAN, instead of Gamman.

July 26. John *Lloyd*, of Brighton, gent. assumes the additional name of ELSEGOOD.

Aug. 3. John Chichester *Burnard*, of Stoke house, co. Somerset, in pursuance of the will of John H. Chichester, of Stoke house, esq. assumes the surname of CHICHESTER, in addition to his other names.

Frederick Dundas *Faithfull*, esq. of H.M. Bombay Civil service, takes the name of CHAUNTRELL, in lieu of Faithfull—by deed enrolled in Chancery.

Aug. 10. Giles *Clarke*, of Hendon, co. Midd. esq. out of respect to the memory of his godfather Giles Earle, esq. deceased, takes in addition the name of EARLE.

Aug. 17. Isaac John *Penney*, of Enfield, Middlesex, assistant schoolmaster, adopts the surnames of COWDEN COLE, in lieu of Penney.

Aug. 24. George Richard *Griffith*, esq. in consequence of his accession to the estate of the late John WALDIE, esq.[2] of Hendersyde, Kelsoe, will henceforth call and subscribe himself George Waldie Griffith.

—— Henry Parker *Denton*, of Styrrup, co. Nottingham, farmer, assumes the name of PARKER, instead of Denton—by deed enrolled in Chancery.

Sept. 7. Annie Ada *Vaughan*, of Abergavenny, takes the additional name of LEAR.

Oct. 31. William *Bromwich*, of Manchester, gentleman (by deed poll to be enrolled in Chancery), assumes the additional name of RYDER.

Nov. 17. George John *Eastes*, late of Keppel street, Russell-sq. and now of Bradford, takes the name of D'ESTE, in lieu of Eastes.

---

[1] An article on the genealogical pretensions of Smith *alias* Heriz, will be found in *The Herald and Topographer*, vol. iii. p. 255.

[2] See some notice of this family in our vol. ii. p. 244.

Nov. 23. Thomas Arthur *Beard*, late of Surbiton, now, of Paris, takes in addition the surname of DE BEAUCHAMP.

Nov. 29. Howel Maddock Arthur Owen, formerly *Jones*, of Wepre hall, co. Flint, afterwards of Sidmouth, and now of Ryde, I.W. esq. resumes his original family name of OWEN.

Nov. 30. Charles Wm. Carter *Madden*, of West Horrington, Wells, co; Somerset, takes in addition the name of MEDLYCOTT.

Dec. 14. John Wheeler, of Southsea, Herts, assumes the surname of CORNELIUS before WHEELER.

Dec. 21. William *Tomkyns*, of Southern house, in Pittville, Cheltenham, assumes the additional name of GRAFTON.

ADDITIONS AND CORRECTIONS.

Vol. II. p. 448. Amy-Mary-Anne, wife of Capt Edward Talbot Thackeray, V.C., R. Engineers, died at Allahabad, Hindostan, July 9, 1865.

Vol. III. pp. 10, 216. THE ARMS OF MONTFORD.—In 1200 Amaury Earl of Gloucester, of his own free will, and by command of King John, quitclaimed to the King of France the city of Evreux and the Evrecin; to the deeds of the ratification of which acts two seals are appended, with the legends, SIGILLVM ALMARICI CÓMITIS GLOVERNIE, one representing him on horseback armed, and the other having an impression, both on the front and reverse, of his shield of arms *party per pale indented*, the latter being inscribed *Secretum Comitis Glovernie*. He married Milesendis daughter of Hugh de Gournay, and had with her in dower the vill of Sottevilla in the *pays de Caux*, and Mapledurham and Petersfield in England; but, the Earl dying without issue in 1214, she remarried William de Cantilupe junior, son of an English baron of the same name. (Stapleton's Observations on the Rolls of the Norman Exchequer, vol. i. p. cxliv.)

P. 82. Mr. George Gwilt, F.S.A. left *five* daughters: viz.—1. Mary-Anne-Milligan, married first in 1826 to William Lemon Dunlap, surgeon E.I. Co.'s service, secondly in 1830 to George Hutchings, of Wadham college, Oxford, and the 69th Bengal N. Inf.; 2. Sarah, married in 1824 to Mr. Thomas Catsworth; 3. Hannah, married in 1828 to William Jackson, esq. solicitor and prothonotary, of Southwark; 4. Georgiana Matilda, married in 1839 to Major Sarrazin of the French army; and 5. Adeline, married to the Rev. M. G. G. Jolley, M.A. of Clare hall, Cambridge.

P. 91. THOMAS CRANLEY, ARCHBISHOP OF DUBLIN, was never a friar. He was a secular priest, and born, I believe, at Cranley in Surrey. All his orders from acolythe to the priesthood were conferred upon him by William of Wykeham Bishop of Winchester, and he was ordained *ad titulum domus Sancti Johannis Oxon.*   F. J. B.

P. 95. BROWNE OF ELSING. Batts and Astleys should be Pratts and

Astleys. The Pratts are of Ryston Hall, co. Norfolk; the Astleys are now Barons Hastings.

P. 102. The Temple Effigies. "The upper lip is without any moustache,"—this is remarked as peculiar to the effigy formerly attributed to Geoffrey de Magnaville, and to one other only, among those at the Temple. In the woodcut (p. 103) the engraver has unfortunately misunderstood his drawing in this very particular, and has added a moustache! This accident was not observed before the engraving was printed, or it might have been readily removed. In other respects the cut is a faithful copy of Mr. Richardson's drawing.

P. 119, line 18, *instead of the words,* "and a copy of Sir Henry Lee's arms as set forth on his garter-plate, still existing at St. George's, Windsor —restored by Sir C. G. Young, Garter," *read as follows :* one of which is a fragment of the inscription to Sir Henry Lee, and the other the shield of arms of his father Sir Anthony, quarterly of eight, the quarterings being the same as those on Sir Henry's garter-plate still existing at Windsor, (and described in p. 120), but differently arranged.

P. 155, line 3, for Roche *read* Rooke.

P. 205 note. The creation of Sir Thomas Puckering as a Baronet was really on the 25th Nov. 1611, not 1612, as has been since shown in pp. 449, 450. The like remark applies to the creation of Sir Edward Devereux (mentioned in p. 352)

P. 216. We were deceived by Mr. Suckling's drawing into supposing that Waldegrave of Lawford in Essex charged his coat with an estoile. A friend who has recently examined the monument in Lawford church from which the shield was (inaccurately) copied by Mr. Suckling reports that it is only the ordinary difference for a third son—a mullet, viz. for "Edward Waldegrave, Esq. third son of George Waldegrave, of Smalbridge, in Suffolk, Esq." as he is described by Morant, i. 436.

P. 235. The Drinking-Horn of King Henry VII. is still preserved at Golden Grove, and the following description of it was given by Sir Samuel R. Meyrick, the Editor of Lewis Dwnn's *Heraldic Visitations of Wales,* printed for the Welsh MSS. Society, 4to. 1846.

"On the march of the Earl of Richmond from Milford to Shrewsbury, he was received and highly entertained at Llwyn-Davydd in the parish of Llandysilio Gogo, Cardiganshire, by its owner this Davydd ap Jeuan; and tradition says that his daughter yielded up her charms to add to the gratification of the noble guest. If that be true, it was probably a natural daughter, as Lewys Dwnn, in the above pedigree, does not assign any daughter by either of his wives. Be that as it may, after the hero of Bosworth had become King Henry VII. he made a present of a hêr las, or grey drinking-horn, tipped and mounted on silver in such exquisite taste, as to induce the belief that the stand must have been designed by an Italian artist. This is formed by the Royal Supporters, the Greyhound of the family, and the Dragon of Cadwaladr; and they might have had between them the Royal Arms, as a bit of silver projecting seems to point out a deficiency. The height is about eight or nine inches, and it is double that length. In the time of the civil wars it was given to Richard second Earl of Carbury, who commanded the district, and thus became deposited at Golden Grove in Carmarthenshire, where it is still preserved by the Earl of Cawdor, to whose liberality the Society is indebted for the Frontispiece to this Volume, which affords of it an admirable idea, though it does not do full justice to its merit. The following night, the Earl of Richmond was received by Einion ap Davydd Llwyd of Wern-newydd, in the parish of Llanarth, in the same county, who tried to out-do Davydd ap Jeuan in the splendour of his hospitality; and, as no horn was sent to him, the before-mentioned tradition tacitly receives a sort of corroboration. From the Poems of Lewys Glyn Cothi, we learn that at this time the houses of the Welsh gentry were amply supplied with foreign wines." (p. 80.)

P. 355. The Surname Cowherd or Coward.—That Cowherd was an hereditary surname in the North of England. is shown by various docu-ments cited by Surtees in his *History of Durham*, vol. ii. p. 374. One of them is a remarkable letter of Richard Earl of Salisbury (circ. 1450) to the Prior of Durham, beginning thus—" Reverent Fader in God, and our right trusty frende and goshepe, we grete you well, and have understood the passing of late to God's mercie of Richard Cowhird, which, as did diverse his auncestors, had and occupied the office of Forester of Bewrepark [Beaurepaire, or *de Bello Reditu*, but often called, as Surtees remarks, most corruptly Bear Park], as semblably (as we have bene informed) shuld occupie after hym his sone and heire Willyam Cowhird our servant," &c.

Roger Cowherd had been Forester under prior Fossour 1353.

Richard his son, by patent for life 1381. William, son of Richard, sub-custos 1383. See also the Index to *The Priory of Finchale* (Surtees Society, 1837.)

" The Billinghams of Crook Hall, in the suburbs of Durham, were de-scended from *John the Cowhird* of Billingham, who had the luck to marry a sister of Richard Kellaw, Bishop of Durham, in the reign of Edward II. From this period the family assumed the local name of Billingham, and settled at Crook Hall, where, until the year 1657, they resided, and ranked among the principal gentry of the county." (The late Rev. James Raine, in *Durham Wills and Inventories*, Surtees Society 1835, i. 417.)

P. 372. The Family of Markland. One of Mr. Markland's uncles was Edward Markland, esq. born 1748, and described in the pedigree as " of Leeds," where he served Mayor in 1790 and 1807. He was afterwards one of the Police Magistrates at Queen Square, Westminster; and died at Bath on the 17th March, 1832, when a memoir of him was given in the Gentleman's Magazine, vol. CII. i. 372. Whilst engaged in commerce in

Spain, he had married, in 1774, Elizabeth Sophia, daughter and coheiress of Josiah Hardy, esq. then British Consul at Cadiz, and granddaughter of Admiral Sir Charles Hardy, senior: and he left surviving issue three sons and two daughters. His second son was Rear-Adm. John Duff Markland, C.B. and Knt. of Leopold of Austria, of whom a memoir is given in the Gentleman's Magazine for Oct. 1848, p. 424. He died at Bath, Aug. 28, 1848, in his 68th year, having married on the 8th March, 1814, Helen. Ellery, eldest daughter of Lewis Dymoke Grosvenor Tregonwell, esq. of Cranbourne Lodge, co. Dorset, and Bourne House, Hants, by whom he left one surviving son and three daughters: see them described in the pedigree of Tregonwell, *History of Dorsetshire*, third edit. i. 161.

Both the biographical memoirs above mentioned were drawn up by the late James Heywood Markland, esq. F.R.S. and S.A.

P. 384. Dr. JAMES LIND, F.R.S. the genealogist of his family, died at the house of his son-in-law William Burnie, esq. in Russell Square, Oct. 17, 1812. A memoir of him has been contributed by the authors of the *Athenæ Cantabrigienses* to the *Gentleman's Magazine* for Nov. 1865.

NOTES AND QUERIES.

GREIG.—I am very anxious to obtain information respecting the family of Sir Samuel Greig, the celebrated Russian admiral, and give the following particulars in the hope that some of your readers may be able to add to them:—

Samuel Greig was born on the 30th Nov. 1735, at a small town in Fifeshire, his father being Mr. Charles Greig, a large shipowner, and his mother a daughter of . . . Charteris (qu. Christian name?) of Burntisland, Esq. Young Greig entered the royal navy, and attained the rank of lieutenant under Admiral Lord Hawke. In 1769, at the instance of Count Brown of the Russian navy, Governor-General of Riga, &c., Lieut. Greig applied to the Crown for leave to quit the English for the Russian navy, which being granted, he went to Cronstadt, and was soon after placed in command of one of the ships of Count Orloff's squadron. I will not occupy your space by detailing the career of Sir Samuel Greig: suffice it to say that he became Lord High Admiral of Russia, and received six orders of knighthood, three of which are registered in the Heralds' College, London. After a brilliant and eventful career he departed this life on the 15th October, 1788, and was buried in the Cathedral of Revel with great state.

Admiral Greig married a Russian lady, and by her had three sons and one daughter. Of the former the two elder, having been educated at the University of Edinburgh, entered the Russian navy, and it is probable that the youngest did the same, as their father directed that all his sons should finish their education in Edinburgh, and then be apprenticed in merchant vessels, that, on the expiration of their apprenticeship, they should enter the British navy, and finally the Russian service. The second son, Capt. Samuel Greig, married Mary daughter of Vice-Admiral Sir William George Fairfax, R.N., (afterwards the wife of Mr. William Somerville, a lady whose name is familiar for her learned writings,) and by her was father of Woronzow Greig, M.A. Trin. Coll. Camb., F.R.S., and barrister-at law, for many years clerk of the peace for Surrey. Mr. Woronzow Greig was born in 1805, and died unmarried on the 20th October, 1865.

Another grandson of the admiral (by which son I know not) was an officer of artillery to the Grand Duke Constantine of Russia, and served at Sevastopol during the war in 1854-6.

I shall be very glad of any information respecting either the ancestors or descendants of Admiral Greig, the name of his wife, armorial bearings, &c. What inscription is there at Revel to the memory of the admiral?

A Mr. John Greig, cousin to the admiral, was living in or near London at the end of the last century, and was twice married. By his first wife he had an only daughter born 1742, who was married at St. Botolph's, Bishopgate Street, on the 11th December, 1762, to Robert Norman, Esq., the witnesses being John and Patrick Greig, and died on the 20th August, 1790. By his second wife Mr. Greig left a son, the Rev. John Greig, M.A., Rector of St. Nicholas Worcester, who died unmarried in May 1819, and was buried at Claines, Worcestershire. In his will, dated 4th February, 1819, he mentions John Greig, of Islington, engraver, to whom he leaves a legacy. Is anything known of him?—J. A. PN.

SHAKSPEARE WILL FROM DOCTORS COMMONS.

(Fines 131.) On 28th Decr 1642, *John Shakspeare* of Budbrooke, co. Warwick, made and declared his will nuncupative in the manner following:—

To Nicholas Shakspeare his best suite of apparell.

To his father-in-law, Thomas Burbidge, his best bootes.

To Edward Bishop and Richard Bishop, minor, of Barkeswell, each of them 2s. 6d.

Item, to Mary Shakspeare 2s.

To Isabell Poole, late servant to Nicholas Shakspeare, 10s. To Thomas Wotton of Budbrooke, one paire of leathern breeches. To Richard Webb and Richd. Sharples of Hampton, to helpe to carry him to church, twelve pence a-piece. Lastly, he made Anne Burbidge, now the wife of William Shottesworth of Packwood, his executrix. These words, or the like in effect, were uttered and spoken in presence and hearing of Nicholas Shakspeare, Mary Shakspeare, and Thomas Wotton. (Signed by them.)

INDEX I.—HERALDIC AND GENERAL.

INDEX II.—ARMS, CRESTS, &c.

INDEX III.—PERSONS AND PLACES.

Lightning Source UK Ltd.
Milton Keynes UK
UKHW020329280219
338009UK00006B/595/P